For the
Glory OF God

For the
Glory OF God

RECOVERING A
BIBLICAL THEOLOGY *of* WORSHIP

DANIEL I. BLOCK

Ⓑ
Baker Academic
a division of Baker Publishing Group
Grand Rapids, Michigan

© 2014 by Daniel I. Block

Published by Baker Academic
a division of Baker Publishing Group
P.O. Box 6287, Grand Rapids, MI 49516-6287
www.bakeracademic.com

Printed in the United States of America

Library of Congress Cataloging-in-Publication Data
Block, Daniel Isaac, 1943–
    For the glory of God : recovering a biblical theology of worship / Daniel I. Block.
      pages cm
    Includes bibliographical references and index.
    ISBN 978-0-8010-2698-0 (cloth)
    1. Worship. I. Title.
  BV10.3.B56 2014
  248.3—dc23   2014003670

In keeping with biblical principles of creation stewardship, Baker Publishing Group advocates the responsible use of our natural resources. As a member of the Green Press Initiative, our company uses recycled paper when possible. The text paper of this book is composed in part of post-consumer waste.

14 15 16 17 18 19 20   7 6 5 4 3 2 1

To David and Elma Lepp,
my beloved father- and mother-in-law,
whose daily lives and service in the church
have brought great glory to God and inspiration to his people

Contents

Illustrations

Tables

Preface

A number of years ago I preached in a large church with three Sunday morning services. I shall never forget when, at a transitional moment in the service, the "pastor of music and worship" declared to the congregation, "Now, before we continue our worship, let me read a passage from Colossians 3"—as if reading and hearing the Scriptures are not exercises in worship.

This restricted notion of worship is common in our day and is reflected in the ubiquitous labeling of CDs as "praise and worship" music, the specification in church bulletins of the singing period as "worship time," and the identification of musicians on the pastoral staff as "worship ministers" or "ministers of worship arts." In fact, the worship industry tends to equate worship not only with music but also with a particular type of music: contemporary praise.

These practices raise all sorts of questions, not only about the significance of other aspects of the Sunday service (prayer, preaching, testimonials, etc.) but also about religious rituals in the Bible and the Scriptures' relatively minor emphasis on music in worship. Not only is music rarely associated with worship in the New Testament[1] but the Pentateuch is altogether silent on music associated with tabernacle worship. All of this highlights our skewed preoccupation with music in the current conflicts over worship.

But the worship issues faced by the evangelical church at the beginning of the twenty-first century are much deeper than differences in musical taste,

---

1. References to music in the context of corporate worship occur only in Eph. 5:19; Col. 3:16; Heb. 2:12; and Rev. 5:9; 14:3; 15:3. In the ESV (NT), the word "music" occurs only once (Luke 15:25); "song/songs" five times (Eph. 5:19; Col. 3:16; Rev. 5:9; 14:3; 15:3); "melody" once (Eph. 5:19); the verb "sing/sang/singing" thirteen times (Matt. 11:17; Luke 7:32; Acts 16:25; Rom. 15:9, a quotation of an OT text; 1 Cor. 14:15 [2×]; Eph. 5:19; Col. 3:16; Heb. 2:12; James 5:13; Rev. 5:9; 14:3; 15:3). However, the passages in the Gospels do not involve liturgical worship, and Acts 16:25; 1 Cor. 14:15; and James 5:13 involve informal personal worship.

which turns out to be only a symptom of a much more serious problem. In a recent book on worship, Edith Humphrey correctly identifies five maladies that plague worship in the North American church: (1) trivializing worship by a preoccupation with atmospherics/mood (it's all about how worship makes me feel); (2) misdirecting worship by having a human-centered rather than God-centered focus (it's all about me, the worshiper); (3) deadening worship by substituting stones for bread (the loss of the Word of God); (4) perverting worship with emotional, self-indulgent experiences at the expense of true liturgy; and (5) exploiting worship with market-driven values.[2] After observing trends in worship for a half century, I agree with Humphrey completely.

In the interest of fairness and full disclosure, I should share the experiences that have shaped me spiritually and that have been formative in the passion with which I write this book. I came to faith and was nurtured through the ministry of a small Mennonite Brethren church in rural Saskatchewan, Canada. Since my father was a pastor, devoted to the study and proclamation of the Word of God, and since my mother was an incredible woman of prayer, I was introduced to the practice of worship very early in my life. In our home, each day began with morning devotions. When the oldest boys had come in from milking the cows, we would all sit around the table, and my father would read from his big German Bible. We would then sing a song, picked by one of the children (we took turns from oldest to youngest), and then we would stand up to pray (a posture brought by my father from Russia in 1926). When I was young, my father's prayers seemed to go on forever. Meanwhile, the porridge was getting cold and stiff.

Evening devotions were conducted in our bedrooms. We children had three bedrooms upstairs: one for my sister and the other two—labeled "Kids' Ward" and "Men's Ward"—had to do for twelve brothers. (We grew up sleeping three in a bed. Those of us in the younger half would be happy when an older brother left home, because this allowed the next in line to graduate from the Kids' Ward to the room where the big boys slept.) The occupants of each ward would sit on the edges of their beds while one of the brothers read from the Bible. Then we would kneel and pray—always from oldest to youngest. On more than one occasion, by the time it was the youngest guy's turn to pray, he would be sound asleep on his knees. The rest of us would quietly crawl under our blankets, snickering, and taking bets on how long this kid would remain in this position.

This was family worship for us six decades ago. As I write, those scenes seem worlds away. But we still worship. To be sure, our patterns of worship

2. Edith M. Humphrey, *Grand Entrance: Worship on Earth as in Heaven* (Grand Rapids: Brazos, 2011), 155–87.

have changed. Since those early days our family's church affiliations have moved successively from Mennonite Brethren to Evangelical Free, the Brethren Assembly (in Great Britain), the Baptist General Conference, and Southern Baptist. Now my wife, Ellen, and I attend College Church, an independent church in Wheaton, Illinois, with roots in Congregationalism. Besides being a part of these varied congregations, I have served as interim pastor and preached in innumerable contexts, ranging from small, independent church plants to the Roman Catholic Cathedral of Saint Paul in Minnesota. I have also preached in Colombia, England, Denmark, Greece, Russia, Hong Kong, Singapore, and Kenya. Over the course of seven decades, I have had the supreme joy of witnessing God's people at worship in many forms and styles.

These experiences have forced me to ask a host of questions about the nature of true worship. What kinds of worship are appropriate? More specifically, what kinds of worship represent true worship of the one true and living God? And how do we determine this? In recent decades people have answered these questions in vastly different ways. On one end of the spectrum, we find churches like Willow Creek Community Church in South Barrington, Illinois, and Saddleback Church in Lake Forest, California, which take their cues from their surrounding cultures. On the other end, we find many making the move to Canterbury, Rome, or Byzantium, where centuries-old liturgical patterns of worship are used and contemporary culture is resisted. Indeed, these days if people ask what kind of church you attend, they are probably not inquiring about denomination, but about worship style: traditional, liturgical, or contemporary? Whereas past debates about worship revolved around the use of musical instruments, creeds, formal benedictions, confessions of sin, and prepared prayers, in many congregations today they revolve around musical style.

Readers of this volume will want to consult the works of others who have provided superb studies of worship in the Scriptures. I especially commend *Engaging with God: A Biblical Theology of Worship*, by David Peterson.[3] Although it lacks the balance we seek here, it offers a thorough New Testament theology of worship. Alongside this volume, Allen P. Ross offers an excellent study in *Recalling the Hope of Glory: Biblical Worship from the Garden to the New Creation*.[4] Ross traces the history of worship in the Scriptures, beginning with worship in the garden of Eden and concluding with worship in the book of Revelation. Along the way he offers invaluable counsel for establishing credible and authentic worship practices today.

---

3. David G. Peterson, *Engaging with God: A Biblical Theology of Worship* (Downers Grove, IL: InterVarsity, 1992).
4. Allen P. Ross, *Recalling the Hope of Glory: Biblical Worship from the Garden to the New Creation* (Grand Rapids: Kregel, 2006).

Although the perspectives I present in this volume generally agree with those of Ross, I have arranged my material topically rather than serially. Each chapter is a study of its own. I begin by asking three fundamental questions: What do the Scriptures have in mind when they speak of worship (chap. 1)? Who is the object of true worship (chap. 2)? Whose worship is acceptable to God (chap. 3)? Building on chapter 3, chapters 4 and 5 explore worship as expressed outside of corporate gatherings, in one's personal ethics, vocation, and home life. Chapters 6–10 turn to corporate worship, focusing on elements that have become vital to Christian worship: the ordinances (chap. 6), the ministry of the Word (chap. 7), prayer (chap. 8), music (chap. 9), and offerings and sacrifice (chap. 10). The final three chapters return to more general topics: the place of corporate worship within the drama of life (chap. 11), the importance of space set aside for worship (chap. 12), and the role of leaders in promoting genuine worship (chap. 13). Readers will notice that the bulk of the discussion involves exploration of specific biblical texts to establish patterns of worship and the underlying theological convictions that are rooted in Scripture. Many chapters end with practical suggestions for implementing biblical-theological principles in worship today.

This book is intended for the church—not only for pastors and church leaders but also for laypeople. I have selected, arranged, and presented these topics to orient readers to biblical perspectives and to encourage conversation among the people of God. Although each chapter is an independent unit, I hope that by organizing the book into thirteen chapters this volume might serve as a resource for quarterly Bible studies or adult classes as well as semester courses in colleges and seminaries. Since the analyses presented are grounded in the Scriptures and essential orthodox theological commitments, this volume should have broad if not universal appeal. Because a biblical theology of worship should underlie all worship, most of the principles espoused here apply across denominational, cultural, and geographic boundaries.

Finally, this volume presents *a* biblical theology of worship. This is neither the definitive nor the last word on the subject. On the contrary, what is written here is written in soft-lead pencil, subject to revision based on further study of the Scriptures and the counsel of the community of faith. I offer this work to the church as a resource, not so much to give answers to issues that congregations face, as to provoke and inspire discussion. For every opinion expressed, readers should adopt the attitude of the Bereans (or Beroeans) in Acts 17:11, who, upon hearing Paul and Silas, examined the Scriptures to see if their teaching was true. If it was necessary for the Bereans to check Paul's words, how much more needful is it for readers to subject my interpretations to the standard of the Scriptures? In the end, God is most glorified and his people most transformed when they worship him, not according to the whims of a fallen human interpreter, but in response to his revelation of himself and in accordance with his will.

I conclude the preface with an explanation for my rendering of the divine in the First Testament with the four consonants YHWH (the Tetragrammaton).[5] In the period between the Testaments, Jews stopped pronouncing the name and substituted it with the title *'ădônāy*, which means "Lord, Master." This practice is reflected in the Greek translation of the First Testament, the Septuagint, where YHWH is consistently rendered as *kyrios*, "Lord," which translates *'ădônāy* rather than transliterating the name represented by YHWH. This practice carries over into the New Testament, where quotations of texts from the First Testament also consistently render YHWH as *kyrios*, and into English translations as "LORD." In print the capitalization of all the letters helpfully distinguishes this epithet from *'ădônāy*, which is properly represented by "Lord," but in oral reading the two are indistinguishable. This creates significant interpretive problems, since most readers of Scripture pay no attention to the capitalized spelling, even though the connotations and implications of referring to someone by name or by title are quite different. Traditionally, when rendered as a name, English translations have vocalized YHWH as "Jehovah,"[6] which artificially combines the consonants of YHWH with the vowels of *'ădônāy*. Although the original pronunciation of the name is uncertain, today non-Jewish scholars generally reject the artificial construct "Jehovah" and prefer to render the name as "Yahweh," which is also a hypothetical form. I am grateful that God expressly revealed his name to his people and invited them to address him by name (e.g., Exod. 3:13–15). Because of the uncertainty of the name's original vocalization and in deference to Jewish sensibilities, in this volume I render the divine name simply with the English letters of the Tetragrammaton, YHWH. The only exceptions occur in direct quotations of English versions or secondary authors that use "LORD."

5. Unless otherwise indicated, all translations of biblical texts are my own. Where the English and Hebrew or Septuagint numbers differ, I have indicated the latter inside square brackets: e.g., Ps. 22:23 [24].

6. See Exod. 6:3; Ps. 83:18; Isa. 12:2; 26:4. The form is also reflected (cf. KJV) in the names Jehovah-jireh (Gen. 22:14), Jehovah-nissi (Exod. 17:15), and Jehovah-shalom (Judg. 6:24).

Acknowledgments

The present volume has a long history. My concern for the subject of worship practices was inspired in part by worship experiences with God's people in many parts of the world and in part by observing the frustrations many have expressed over the changes in worship happening in their churches. For some any change is unwelcome; for others no change is enough. How shall we address these conflicting perspectives? Some congregations unravel over tensions in "worship style" while others spring up overnight catering to the particular stylistic whims of specific demographic groups. And a full building is viewed as proof that what they are doing must be right.

The seed for this volume was planted by discussions with friends two decades ago when we began to ask, "What does God think of what we are doing?" Of course this led to several additional questions: "Does it matter what God thinks of what we are doing?" "How can we know what God thinks of what we are doing?" In reflecting on these questions I became increasingly convinced that the answers may only be determined by careful attention to the Scriptures, our only sure and authoritative guide for spiritual truth.

Along the way many have aided and inspired me with their responses to these questions, whether in writing or through their public addresses or through personal conversation. I am especially grateful to Daniel Akin (currently president of Southeastern Baptist Theological Seminary [Wake Forest] and formerly vice president and academic dean of the Southern Baptist Theological Seminary [Louisville]) and the music faculty of the latter institution for encouraging me to develop a course on "A Biblical Theology of Worship." The syllabus for that course has evolved into the present manuscript. It has been a special delight to share my discoveries with hundreds of students in academic institutions around the world. Whether at Wheaton College or in Hong Kong or in

Greece, it has been exciting to watch eyes light up as students grasp biblical insights and especially as those insights translate into changes in dispositions and practices of personal and corporate worship. I have also been inspired by God's people in the churches as I have had opportunity to test my theories within the contexts of specific congregations. Their responses keep reminding me that conversations about worship should not be restricted to "professional worshipers," that is, worship leaders. Worship that pleases God should be everyone's concern. I am especially grateful for the friendship of colleagues whose insights have prodded me to reassess my own views and inspired me to follow them in their thinking on these matters: Chip Stam, Tom Bolton, Donald Hustad, Chuck King, Gerard and Jane Sundberg, to name just a few.

More practically, I am grateful for a series of doctoral students who have assisted me in my thinking on these matters and who have aided me at various stages in the development of this volume: Kenneth Turner, Rebekah Josberger, Christopher Ansberry, Rahel Schafer, and Matt Newkirk. I am especially grateful to Heather Surls, for her invaluable assistance in editing and reducing a much larger manuscript to the present size. In the end my graduate assistants Daniel Lanz and Michelle Knight, as well as my wife Ellen, spent long hours on the tedious work of indexing. I am grateful to them all.

Of course this project would never have seen the light of day if I had not had the firm support of the people at Baker Publishing Group, who have worked patiently and diligently with me to produce the present volume. Jim Kinney, editorial director at Baker Academic, has overseen the process from the beginning, guiding me in crafting a manuscript that is accessible and usable for a broad readership. I owe a special debt of gratitude to Brian Bolger and the editorial crew at Baker, who with their careful reading have alerted me to many obscurities and infelicities of style and inadvertent misrepresentations of data. Rachel Klompmaker has skillfully supervised the preparation of the illustrative material.

I am grateful to the administrators and my faculty colleagues at Wheaton College for the unwavering institutional support and encouragement they offer, not only by creating a wonderful teaching environment but also for providing the resources for research. A semester in Wheaton College's Hawthorne House, a three-minute walk from the Tyndale House library in Cambridge, England, where my office overlooked a lovely garden, made the composition of several of these chapters even more delightful. I cannot adequately express how thankful I am to Bud and Betty Knoedler, who have given so generously to underwrite my professorial chair. It is a special grace to know them not only as supporters of Wheaton College but also as personal friends and as fellow worshipers at College Church. Ellen and I are grateful for their daily prayers on our behalf. I eagerly also acknowledge Ellen, the delight of my life, who has stood by me as a gracious friend and counselor for more than four decades. Without her love and wisdom the work represented here either would never have been finished or would have taken a different turn.

Words cannot express the debt of gratitude I owe to those who planted the seeds for my disposition toward worship, particularly toward life as worship over the years. My father, Isaac H. Block, an immigrant to Canada from Stalinist Russia in 1926 and a faithful Mennonite Brethren minister, inspired me with his love for the Scriptures and his extraordinary orthopraxy: for him life was worship. My siblings and I all remember our mother Ella Block as a woman of prayer. Indeed, when we heard of her sudden passing into glory fifteen years ago my first thought was, now who will pray for us? Specific praise must go to the two special people to whom this book is dedicated, my father- and mother-in-law, David and Elma Lepp. David was a dairy farmer in northern Saskatchewan, but his heart was in the church, where he taught an adult Sunday school class and directed the music for more than three decades. Elma's expressions of worship were different; she resisted standing before people but delighted in working behind the scenes to ensure that others were cared for and that worship in its variegated forms happened "in decency and order."

Finally, in reflecting on the production of a book like this, it would be hypocritical not to declare that ultimately all praise and glory must go to God. Unlike others who serve gods of wood and stone, that have eyes but don't see, ears but don't hear, and mouths but don't speak, we have a God who speaks. By his grace he revealed himself to Israel by name, deed, and word, but he has revealed himself to us climactically and superlatively in the person of Jesus Christ. To him be ultimate praise and glory.

The tasks to which the Lord has called us offer unlimited opportunities to express true worship. This book is offered to God as a reverential act of submission and homage in response to his gracious revelation of himself. We praise God for these opportunities and hope that our efforts will bring great glory to him. Adapting the words of the psalmist we pray,

> Let the favor of YHWH our God be upon us;
> Establish the work of our hands—
> Yes, establish the work of our minds and our hands!
> (Psalm 90:17)

1

Toward a Holistic, Biblical Understanding of Worship

The time is coming—indeed it has arrived—when true worshipers will worship the Father in spirit and in truth. The Father is looking for worshipers who will worship him this way. (John 4:23)[1]

To be human is to worship. This statement is supported in the Scriptures,[2] declared in our creeds,[3] and evident from history. While the impulse to worship someone higher than ourselves seems innate, the types of beings that people worship are diverse. These may be plotted along a continuum, from concrete objects identified with divinities (animism) to the abstraction of divinity and the separation of God from material reality.[4] Secular historians assume that this continuum reflects the evolutionary development of religion from primitive to sophisticated, and that modern, Western secularism—liberated from notions of divine realities—represents the zenith of history.

1. Unless otherwise indicated, all translations of biblical texts are my own.
2. Note the inclusive nature of Ps. 150:6: "Let all who have breath praise YHWH."
3. Note the first question posed by the Westminster Shorter Catechism (1647) and the answer proposed: "What is the chief end of man? Man's chief end is to glorify God, and to enjoy him forever."
4. For further discussion, see "Idolatry: The Problem of False Worship" in chap. 2, below.

We are concerned with Christian worship here, which in its orthodox forms is committedly monotheistic but also mysteriously trinitarian, acknowledging the one Triune God as Father, Son, and Holy Spirit. In recent decades the evangelical church in North America and Europe has struggled to establish broadly appealing patterns of worship, a struggle we have exported to other parts of the world. Frequently the tensions revolve around music and whether it should follow traditional or contemporary tastes. Increasingly we see congregations respond to these tensions in one of three ways: (1) they split into two or more churches, so each is free to pursue its preferences; (2) they establish multiple worship services, each gratifying one of these musical tastes; or (3) they adopt the philosophy of the contemporary music and worship industry, simply marginalizing those with traditional hymnic preferences and forcing them to leave or retreat into passive, resigned modes. While these responses have made worship attractive for younger people, their effects on the church's witness are disastrous. Instead of worship uniting God's people, conflicts over worship have divided them.

The Scriptural Basis of Worship That Glorifies God

In the hubbub over worship styles, I sometimes wonder if we have explored seriously enough what the Scriptures have to say about acceptable worship. In evangelicals' recent fascination with ancient practices and perspectives, we often observe a tendency to accept early worship forms as authoritative but a decreasing attention to the scriptural theology of worship. Sometimes enthusiasm for the worship traditions and practices of the early church pushes features of these as normative and threatens the Reformation principle of *sola scriptura*, even when these lack explicit biblical warrant.

But even if we agree that the Scriptures are our ultimate authority for faith and life, we are divided on how we should use the Scriptures in designing corporate Christian worship. On the one hand, some adhere to the *regulative principle*, which says that true worship involves only components expressly prescribed in Scripture and forbids anything not prescribed.[5] In extreme mani-

---

5. See, e.g., question 51 of the Westminster Shorter Catechism:

Q. What is forbidden in the second commandment?

A. The second commandment forbiddeth the worshiping of God by images, or any other way not appointed in his word.

Or the fuller commentary in question 109 and the answer of the Westminster Larger Catechism:

Q. What are the sins forbidden in the second commandment?

A. The sins forbidden in the second commandment are, all devising, counseling, commanding, using, and anywise approving, any religious worship not instituted by God himself; tolerating a

festations, churches that follow this principle reject musical instruments and the singing of songs not based on the Psalms. On the other hand, many prefer the *normative principle*, which allows Christians to incorporate in their worship forms and practices not forbidden by Scripture,[6] provided they promote order in worship and do not contradict scriptural principles. While the former is quite restrictive, the latter opens doors to creative and expressive worship. Our challenge, then, is ensuring that even when forms of worship are culturally determined, the principles underlying them are biblically rooted and theologically formed.

But even when we agree that the Scriptures alone should be our ultimate authority for Christian worship, we are divided on which Scriptures are determinative for Christian worship. Should our worship be governed by the whole Bible or only by the teachings and practices of the New Testament?[7] While rarely stated, the latter is implied by many scholars who write on this subject. In what I consider to be one of the most important books on worship, *Engaging with God: A Biblical Theology of Worship*, David Peterson sets out "to expose the discontinuity between the Testaments" on the subject of worship.[8] Although Peterson presents his book as a biblical theology of worship, and although the First Testament[9] is three times the length of the

---

false religion; the making any representation of God, of all or of any of the three persons, either inwardly in our mind, or outwardly in any kind of image or likeness of any creature: Whatsoever; all worshiping of it, or God in it or by it; the making of any representation of feigned deities, and all worship of them, or service belonging to them; all superstitious devices, corrupting the worship of God, adding to it, or taking from it, whether invented and taken up of ourselves, or received by tradition from others, though under the title of antiquity, custom, devotion, good intent, or any other pretense: Whatsoever; simony; sacrilege; all neglect, contempt, hindering, and opposing the worship and ordinances which God has appointed.

6. The principle is followed by Lutherans. Note article 15 of the Augsburg Confession: "Of Usages in the Church they teach that those ought to be observed which may be observed without sin, and which are profitable unto tranquility and good order in the Church, as particular holy-days, festivals, and the like. Nevertheless, concerning such things men are admonished that consciences are not to be burdened, as though such observance was necessary to salvation." However, it is more closely associated with the great sixteenth-century Anglican priest Richard Hooker and often referred to as "the Hooker Principle."

7. For a helpful introduction to this subject, see Michael A. Farley, "What Is 'Biblical' Worship? Biblical Hermeneutics and Evangelical Theologies of *Worship*," *Journal of the Evangelical Theological Society* 51 (2008): 591–613.

8. Peterson, *Engaging with God*, 24.

9. The dismissive disposition toward the Hebrew Bible is both reflected in and fostered by the continued designation of the prior Scriptures as the "Old Testament." This expression connotes unfortunate notions of antiquity and out-of-dateness, as if God's earlier revelation has been supplanted and rendered obsolete by later revelation. Observing that we have inherited the phrase from the patristic period, John Goldingay rightly questions it "because it . . . suggests something antiquated and inferior left behind by a dead person." See his *Old Testament Theology*, vol. 1, *Israel's Gospel* (Downers Grove, IL: InterVarsity, 2003), 15. Although the reference is not to the

New Testament and probably contains a hundred times more information on worship, Peterson disposes of its treatment of the subject in fifty-six pages, while devoting almost two hundred pages to the New Testament. For Peterson, the First Testament's focus on place, festivals, and priestly rituals provides a foil against which to interpret New Testament worship, which is centered on a person, involves all of life, and focuses on edification when it speaks of gathered Christians.[10]

This problem also appears in John Piper's work. In a sermon titled "Worship God!,"[11] Piper contrasts First Testament and New Testament worship, asserting that First Testament worship was external, involving form and ritual, while New Testament worship concerns internal spiritual experience.[12] Such generalizations are misleading on several counts. First, they underestimate the liturgical nature of worship in the New Testament. What can be more cultic and formal than the Lord's Supper, the worship experience par excellence prescribed by Jesus, or the ritual of baptism, called for in the Great Commission? Acts 2:41–42 describes the early church engaged in a series of external activities: baptism, instruction, fellowship, breaking bread, and prayer.

Second, generalizations like these misrepresent worship as it is actually presented in the First Testament. D. A. Carson is correct to interpret Jesus' statement in John 4:21–24 as a prediction of a day when the focus of worship will shift from place to manner, and to suggest that "in spirit and in truth" is "a way of saying that we must worship God *by means of Christ*. In him the reality has dawned and the shadows are being swept away."[13] And Peterson is also correct to suggest that the worship "in spirit and in truth" contrasts "with

Old Testament, when the book of Hebrews compares the previous covenant with the later one, he speaks of them as "first" (*prōtē diathēkē*) and "new" (*diathēkē kainē*) covenants, respectively (Heb. 9:15). Thus, throughout this book, I will use First Testament for the former Scriptures.

10. Similar perspectives are reflected in D. A. Carson's essay "Worship under the Word," in *Worship by the Book*, ed. D. A. Carson (Grand Rapids: Eerdmans, 2002), 11–63. Carson cautions against exaggerating the differences between the forms of worship under the Israelite and the new covenants. However, this is what he does when he uses Rom. 12:1–2 to illustrate the change in the language of worship, which under the old covenant was bound up with temple and priestly service, but under the new departs from the cultus (37). Also, in his presentation of Christian worship, he speaks of the New Testament as our guide (44). This comment implies that the practice of first-century Christians as described and commanded in the NT alone provides the norms for Christian worship, a point observed also by Farley, "What Is 'Biblical' Worship?," 595–96.

11. John Piper, "Worship God!" (November 9, 1997), http://www.desiringgod.org/Resource Library/Sermons/ByDate/1997/1016_Worship_God/.

12. Piper (ibid.) declares, "You can see what is happening in the NT. Worship is being significantly de-institutionalized, de-localized, de-ritualized. The whole thrust is being taken off of ceremony and seasons and places and forms; and is being shifted to what is happening in the heart—not just on Sunday, but every day and all the time in all of life."

13. Carson, "Worship under the Word," 37.

the symbolic and typical" represented by First Testament forms. However, his portrayal of worship "in truth" as "real and genuine worship" rendered by "true worshippers" is problematic.[14] In ancient Israel the worship of many folks was true; that is, it was both real and genuine. Peterson is also correct when he says that worship "in spirit" refers to the Holy Spirit, "who regenerates us, brings new life, and confirms us in the truth." However, if this represents a change, then we must admit that in ancient Israel worshipers were unregenerate, lacked new life, and were not confirmed in the truth. This does not seem to match the image of Caleb, who possessed a different spirit and "was full after God" (Num. 14:24; Deut. 1:36; Josh. 14:9), or of David, who authored so many of the psalms, or of Isaiah in Isaiah 6.

Piper's interpretation of Jesus' statement is even more problematic.

> I take "in spirit" to mean that this true worship is carried along by the Holy Spirit and is happening mainly as an inward, spiritual event, not mainly as an outward bodily event. And I take "in truth" to mean that this true worship is a response to true views of God and is shaped and guided by true views of God.[15]

If this is correct, and if Jesus intended to contrast First Testament and New Testament worship this way, then we must concede that in ancient Israel (1) true worship was never carried along by the Spirit, (2) worship was primarily a matter of external actions rather than inward spiritual events, and (3) the Israelites lacked true views of God that would have guided true worship. By driving these wedges between the Testaments, we dismiss the only Bible that Jesus and the New Testament authors had as irrelevant and lacking authority for us, and we sweep away significant continuities between the faith of ancient Israel and the early church. In so doing, we impose problems that may have existed within the Judaisms of Jesus' day onto ancient Israel, refuse to let the First Testament speak for itself, and deny the true worshipers in Israel the hope that YHWH offered them with his gracious revelation.[16] Furthermore, we rob the church of a rich resource for establishing permanent theological principles that could and probably should guide our worship.

But evangelicals are often inconsistent in the way they treat the First Testament. Most believers find the Psalms to be a rich resource for personal and corporate Christian worship, but they do so without realizing that the entire

14. Peterson, *Engaging with God*, 98–99.
15. Piper, "Worship God!"
16. For a fuller discussion of the issue, see Daniel I. Block, "'In Spirit and in Truth': The Mosaic Vision of Worship," in *The Gospel according to Moses: Theological and Ethical Reflections on the Book of Deuteronomy* (Eugene, OR: Wipf & Stock, 2012), 272–98.

Psalter is rooted in the Torah, especially the book of Deuteronomy.[17] To dismiss Deuteronomy and the rest of the constitutional revelation found in Exodus–Numbers as irrelevant for establishing the theology and practice of worship is to violate Paul's own declaration in 2 Timothy 3:16–17. However, this marginalization also violates the intentions of the psalmists, who would have been horrified to observe Christians' elevation of the authority of the Psalms above the Torah. Those who will not take seriously the authority and transformative power of the Pentateuch and the rest of the First Testament have no right to appeal, nor grounds for appealing, to the book of Psalms in worship.

In addition to a commitment to let all Scripture contribute to the recovery of a biblical theology of worship, this book is driven by two other foundational principles. First, true worship is essentially a vertical exercise, the human response to the divine Creator and Redeemer. For this reason the goal of authentic worship is the glory of God rather than the pleasure of human beings, which means that forms of worship should conform to the will of God rather than to the whims of fallen humanity. Second, knowledge of the nature and forms of worship that glorify God comes primarily from Scripture. We recognize that all truth is God's truth and that nature proclaims the powerful Creator, which drives us to worship. However, as the written revelation of God, the Scriptures serve as the primary source for developing a theology of worship and establishing forms of worship that please God. Accordingly, in the studies that follow, we will keep our fingers in the biblical text, seeking to find in it the principles and patterns of worship that should drive us today.

The New Testament's Contribution to Contemporary Christian Worship

Although many find their primary cues for planning Christian worship in popular culture, evangelicals generally recognize the authoritative role of the New Testament for establishing the principles and practices of Christian worship. And we do so despite the fact that the New Testament actually provides little instruction on formal corporate gatherings. In the Gospels we find a great deal of information on Jesus Christ, the object and focus of Christian worship, but neither he nor the apostles offer detailed counsel on how we

---

17. This is highlighted in the so-called Torah Psalms: Pss. 1; 19; and 119. The references to "the Torah of YHWH" (generally mistranslated as "the law of the LORD") refer not to the word of God in general but to the account of God's actions on Israel's behalf, the written body of revelation received at Sinai, and especially to Moses' exposition of the revelation in Deuteronomy. See further D. I. Block, *How I Love Your Torah, O LORD! Studies in the Book of Deuteronomy* (Eugene, OR: Cascade Books, 2011), xi–xv.

should practice it, except to emphasize the ordinances of the Lord's Supper (Matt. 26:17–30; Mark 14:22–26; Luke 22:14–20; cf. also 1 Cor. 11:23–34) and baptism (Matt. 28:18–20). In the book of Acts, Luke narrates many scenes of the church at worship (e.g., Acts 2:41–47) but provides little concrete instruction on normative practices for the future church.

In his Epistles, Paul often deals with abuses in the churches he founded (e.g., 1 Cor. 11–14; 1 Tim. 2:8–15), and while the principles underlying Ephesians 5:15–21 and Colossians 3:12–17 have obvious implications for corporate worship, Paul's concern here is the daily conduct of believers rather than the liturgy of the church. His instructions in the Pastoral Epistles speak more to the character and conduct of those who lead the church than to the practice of corporate worship. The Epistle to the Hebrews has more to say about worship than any of the preceding texts, showing the contrasts between Christian worship and the worship of ancient Israel, while also emphasizing the continuity of worship and the importance of reverence and awe in acceptable worship. The book of Revelation provides the most detailed information on Christian worship, but this worship is located in heaven rather than on earth.

The First Testament's Gift to Contemporary Christian Worship

But why should we not study the First Testament to understand what true worship—even for Christians—might look like? To be sure, in the light of Christ, the forms have changed—the sacrifices, the Levitical priesthood, and the temple have all been declared passé through the death and resurrection of Jesus—but does this mean that God's first instructions on worship have no bearing on contemporary worship? Hardly. If Jesus Christ is YHWH, the God of Israel in human flesh (Matt. 1:23; John 1:23; Rom. 10:13; Phil. 2:11), and if Jesus Christ is eternally changeless (Heb. 13:8), we should at least expect continuity of principle between the Testaments. When we explore the forms of ancient Israelite worship and their underlying theology, we discover a remarkable continuity of perspective between the Testaments. Jesus does not declare the old theology obsolete; rather, in him the theology underlying Israelite worship finds its fulfillment.

As we will see, because of Christ's sacrificial work, both the Israelite rituals were and our own corporate expressions of faith are effective in maintaining covenant relationship with God—assuming they are offered in accord with his revealed will. Although most assume that unless the New Testament reiterates notions found in the First Testament the latter are obsolete, we should probably assume the opposite: unless the New Testament expressly declares First Testament notions obsolete, they continue. This may account for the relative silence of the New Testament on many matters, including creation, certain ethical issues, and principles of worship. Since the same Holy Spirit inspired all of Scripture, we should not hesitate to go to the First Testament to seek the mind of God for us.

The Dimensions of Biblical Worship

A recovery of biblical worship must begin with definitions. What does the word "worship" mean? Even more important, what does the concept of worship mean? Discussion of these questions usually begins with the English word "worship," which consists of two elements, "worth" and "ship." As a verb, worship involves one person's recognition of another person's superior status or honor. Theologians often restrict the expression of this recognition toward the Deity, but this is not how worship has been traditionally understood. When I was a university student in Saskatoon, Saskatchewan, the mayor was the featured speaker at an event. When the time came for him to speak, he was introduced as "His worship, Mayor Buckwold." Calling the mayor this was not an act of idolatry; it simply reflected the normal meaning of the English word.

If, however, we are trying to develop a biblical understanding of worship or an understanding of biblical worship, both the etymology and the usage of the English word are irrelevant. What matters is the vocabulary the Scriptures use for worship in general and for corporate liturgical exercises that we call worship. Although both Testaments employ a wide range of expressions for concepts and actions associated with worship, they may be divided into three broad categories: dispositional expressions (worship as attitude), physical expressions (worship as gesture), and liturgical expressions (worship as ritual). Remarkably, if not ironically, the words that are usually translated as "worship" in English versions have little to do with either praise or music, as today's popular Christian culture suggests.

Worship as Attitude

Appealing to biblical texts like 1 Samuel 16:7 for support, many suggest that God's attitude toward us is determined by what is in our hearts rather than by our external, observable behavior. However, this idea tears such statements out of their contexts and assumes a faulty view of the relationship between one's actions and one's being—as if they can be divorced.[18]

18. This attitude is also reflected in the common adage "God hates the sin but loves the sinner." God does in fact hate sin (Deut. 12:31; 16:22), but the Scriptures do not hesitate to use

Several biblical texts highlight the importance of a proper disposition in worship. In Psalm 24:3 the psalmist asks, "Who may climb the mountain of YHWH, and who may rise in his holy place?" which is to say, whose worship is acceptable to God? Among the answers given we find "whoever has a pure heart."[19] In Deuteronomy 10:12–13, Moses gives the normative First Testament perspective in catechetical fashion.

Q. And now, O Israel, what does YHWH your God ask of you?

A. To fear [yārē'] YHWH your God; to walk in all his ways [hālak bĕkol-dĕrākāyw]; to love ['āhab] him, to serve ['ābad] YHWH your God with all your heart and with all your being, and to keep [šāmar] the commands and ordinances of YHWH that I am commanding you today for your own good.

Perhaps for ease of memory, Moses summarizes the evidence of true devotion to YHWH with five verbs, one for each finger. He sets the stage with the opening verb, "to fear," and represents the fulcrum with the middle verb, "to love."

The primary word for "fear" in the First Testament (yārē') is used in two senses, depending on the relationship between the people in question. In the face of the unknown, enemy armies, wild animals, death, and even YHWH (Jer. 5:22; Mic. 7:17; Job 9:35), it often denotes "terror, fright."[20] The same word was also used to express reverence for and trusting awe of a superior.[21] Like Deuteronomy 10:12, the Wisdom writings teach that the fear of God is the first principle of wisdom.[22]

---

the same verb (śānē') to speak of God's disposition toward people: Hosea 9:15; Mal. 1:3; Pss. 5:5; 11:5; Prov. 6:16–19.

19. The psalmist (24:4) uses a rare term, bar (from brr), which occurs elsewhere only in Pss. 19:8 [9]; 73:1; Job 11:4; Prov. 14:4; Song 6:9, 10. Here the "pure heart" (bar-lēbāb) substitutes for "perfection of heart" (tom-lēbāb, 1 Kings 9:4; Pss. 78:72; 101:2). Where the English and Hebrew or Septuagint numbers differ, I have indicated the latter inside square brackets.

20. The frequency of this word and the breadth of vocabulary in this semantic field reflect the fearful realities of life in the ancient Near East. Other expressions for terror include šāta', "to be dismayed" (Isa. 41:10, 23); hātat, "be dismayed" (Deut. 1:21; 31:8; Josh. 8:1); hāpaz, "to be alarmed" (Deut. 20:3); hārad, "to tremble" (Isa. 41:5; 1 Sam. 28:5); 'āraṣ, "to tremble" (Deut. 7:21; 20:3); hyl, "to writhe in anguish, pain" (Zech. 9:5); ṣārar, "to be distressed" (Gen. 32:7 [8]); pāhad, "to tremble" (Deut. 2:25; 11:25).

21. This could involve respect for other human beings or objects, such as children's respect of parents (Lev. 19:3), the people's awe before a leader (Josh. 4:14; 1 Kings 3:28) or an object (Lev. 19:30; 26:2), or creatures' awe before human beings as representatives of God (Gen. 9:2). Often yārē' functions as a variant for kibbēd, "to honor." Cf. Exod. 20:12 and Deut. 5:16 with Lev. 19:3.

22. Prov. 1:7, 29; 2:5; 9:10; 15:33; Job 28:28; Ps. 111:10; cf. Isa. 11:2; 33:6. Second Kings 17:35, 37, 38, prohibits "fearing" other gods (see KJV).

The prophet Malachi highlights the link between fear and acceptable worship by addressing a series of problems in the postexilic community, all rooted in the absence of the fear of YHWH.[23] Some involve social diseases, but the book is dominated by abuses related directly to worship: contempt for the sacrifices (1:6–12, 13b), boredom in worship (1:13a), a calloused disposition toward vows (1:14), ministerial irresponsibility and infidelity (2:1–9), ingratitude and stinginess in tithing (3:7–12), and arrogance toward YHWH (3:13–15). Remarkably, Malachi's prescription for this malaise is to return to the Torah of Moses and YHWH's revelation at Horeb (4:4). Through hearing the Torah "in the presence of YHWH" (*lipnê yhwh*), the awesome effect of God's original self-revelation will be repeated (Deut. 14:23). Thus, reading the Torah underlies hearing, which underlies learning, which underlies fearing YHWH, which underlies obedience, which underlies life.

Reading → Hearing → Learning → *Fearing* → Obeying → Living

This perspective is found throughout the Scriptures. Responding to the people's demand for a king, Samuel declared, "Only fear [*yārē'*] YHWH and serve [*'ābad*] him in truth [*be'ĕmet*] with all your heart. For consider what great things he has done for you" (1 Sam. 12:24–25).[24] In the Psalms, true worshipers are characterized as "YHWH-fearers" (*yir'ê*).[25] Such worshipers glorify God and stand in awe of him (22:23 [24]); they know his covenant (25:14); they are promised blessing (5:12 [13]; cf. v. 7 [8]; 112:1; 128:1); their cries for help are heard (145:19); they walk in the ways of God (128:1); they hope in salvation (85:9 [10]); they ponder and declare the works of God (64:9 [10]); they trust in YHWH as their help and shield (115:11); and they live righteously and are secure in him (25:11–15; 34:8–22 [9–23]; 86:11; 103:17–18). As we will see, these are dimensions of true and acceptable worship.

The idea that a proper disposition is fundamental to acceptable worship carries over into the New Testament.[26] Like Hebrew *yārē'*, Greek *phobeomai*

---

23. References to fear (derivatives of *yārē'*) and honor (*kibbēd*) toward God or his name occur in Mal. 1:6, 14; 2:2, 5; 3:5, 16a, 16b, 4:2 [3:20]. See also 4:5 [3:23], which speaks of the great and fearful (*nôrā'*) day of YHWH.

24. Jesus describes this kind of worship as worship "in spirit and in truth" (John 4:23–24). For the close association of "fear" with cultic activity in YHWH's honor, see Josh. 22:25; 2 Kings 17:32–34; Isa. 29:13.

25. Pss. 15:4; 22:23, 25 [24, 26]; 25:12, 14; 31:19 [20]; 33:18; 34:7, 9 [8, 10]; 60:4 [6]; 61:5 [6]; 85:9 [10]; 66:16; 103:11, 13, 17; 111:5; 118:4; 119:74, 79; 145:19; 147:11.

26. New Testament authors express dispositional aspects of worship with four word groups: *phobeomai*, *sebomai* (and other *seb-* words), *eusebeomai*, *eulabeomai*. The roots of all these may be traced to the LXX renderings of Hebrew *yārē'*.

may express fright, but it also expresses devotion, piety, and respect.[27] In Acts, Luke characterizes the pious as "god-fearers" (*phoboumenoi*).[28] Elsewhere, those with the appropriate disposition toward God are characterized as "pious/ devout,"[29] "serving God with fear,"[30] and reverent.[31] First Timothy 6:11 is typical: "But as for you, man of God, shun all this; pursue righteousness, godliness [*eusebeia*], faith, love, endurance, gentleness" (NRSV).[32]

First and New Testament perspectives on a proper disposition as a precondition for acceptable worship are indistinguishable. This is demonstrated by the repetition of the Supreme Command, which calls God's people to love him with all their hearts/minds (Deut. 6:5; cf. Matt. 22:37; Mark 12:30; Luke 10:27); by Jesus' citation of Isaiah 29:13 in Matthew 15:8; and by his declaration "Blessed are the pure in heart, for they will see God" (Matt. 5:8). Confronted with the glory of God, Paul fell to the ground in reverence and awe (Acts 9:4), as do the heavenly worshipers in Revelation 5:14. Echoing First Testament images and language, the author of Hebrews challenged his original readers and challenges us.

> Having received a kingdom that cannot be shaken, let us be thankful, offering worship [*latreuō*] to God that is acceptable [*euarestōs*] *with* reverence [*eulabeia*] and awe [*deos*],[33] for our God is a consuming fire. (Heb. 12:28–29)

27. Luke 1:50; cf. Pss. 23:4; 103:11, 13, 17.

28. Acts 10:2, 22, 35 (Cornelius); 13:16, 26 (Israelites in the synagogue at Pisidian Antioch). These seem to be practicing Jews, but in v. 43 Luke calls God-fearing converts to Judaism *sebomenoi prosēlytoi*, "proselyte fearers," which corresponds to *yir'ê*, "YHWH-fearers" in the Psalms (as in Ps. 15:4). Occasionally the word also functions as a substitute for faith and means "trusting awe": Rom. 11:20; 2 Cor. 5:11 (cf. the references to being of good courage in vv. 6, 8); 2 Cor. 7:11; perhaps Phil. 2:12.

29. Greek *eulabeia/eulabēs/eulabeomai*: thus, e.g., Simeon was "righteous and pious" (*dikaios kai eulabēs*, Luke 2:25). See also Acts 2:5; 8:2; 22:12; Heb. 5:7; 11:7.

30. The *sebomai* word group: note Jesus' quotation of Isa. 29:13 in Matt. 15:8–9 (= Mark 7:6–7). See also Acts 16:14; 18:7; 18:13. In Rom. 1:25 Paul charges the ungodly with exchanging the truth of God for a lie and misdirecting their "worship" (*sebazomai*) and cultic service (*latreuein*) away from the Creator to the creature. The expression *sebō* refers to expressions of devotion to a god through gestures, rites, and ceremonies. In New Testament times it referred to "former polytheists who accepted the ethical monotheism of Israel and attended the synagogue, but who did not obligate themselves to keep the whole Mosaic law; in particular, the males did not submit to circumcision." Thus W. Bauer, F. Danker, W. Arndt, and F. Gingrich, eds. [BDAG], *A Greek-English Lexicon of the New Testament and Other Early Christian Literature*, 3rd ed. (Chicago: University of Chicago Press, 2000), 918. Cf. Josephus, *Jewish Antiquities* 14.110. On the expression, see Michael Wilcox ("The 'God-Fearers' in Acts: A Reconsideration," *Journal for the Study of the New Testament* 13 [1981]: 102–22), who suggests the emphasis is on piety, not a group's distinctiveness.

31. The *eusebeō* word group: Acts 10:2, 7; 2 Pet. 2:9; 2 Tim. 3:12; Titus 2:12. The abstract noun *eusebeia*, "piety, godliness, loyalty, fear of God," is common.

32. See, e.g., Acts 3:12; 1 Tim. 2:2; 3:16; 4:7–8; 6:3, 5–6; 2 Tim. 3:5; Titus 1:1; 2 Pet. 1:3, 6.

33. The author adds to the awe by using a word, *deos*, that occurs nowhere else in the First or New Testaments. In extrabiblical Greek the word means "fear, alarm, reverence." See H. G.

This statement warns against treating worship casually; without a proper disposition, our worship of the living God is rejected.

Worship as Physical Gesture

Consideration of the gestures of worship in Scripture must begin with the Hebrew word *hištaḥāwâ* and its Greek counterpart, *proskyneō*. Although English translations commonly render both verbs as "worship," most people have no clue what these words communicate in the Bible. Both literally refer to subjects prostrated before a superior, a posture that states the equivalent of "Long live the king."[34] This interpretation is reinforced by adverbial modifiers that appear with the Hebrew word: "to the ground,"[35] "with nose/face to the ground,"[36] and "to/on his nose" (Num. 22:31), as well as a series of other verbs with which it is associated: "to bow one's head" in homage,[37] "to crouch" or "fall to one's knees" before God or a king,[38] "to prostrate oneself,"[39] or simply "to fall down."[40] Two texts illustrate dramatically the meaning of *hištaḥāwâ*:

> Kings will be your foster fathers,
> and their queens your nursing mothers.
> With their faces to the ground they will bow down [*hištaḥāwâ*] to you,
> and lick the dust of your feet.
> Then you will know that I am YHWH;
> those who wait for me shall not be put to shame. (Isa. 49:23)

Liddell, R. Scott, H. S. Jones, and R. McKenzie [LSJM], *A Greek-English Lexicon*, 9th ed. (Oxford: Oxford University Press, 1996), 379, s.v. δέος.

34. Contra Peterson (*Engaging with God*, 57–58, 75) and Andrew Hill (*Enter His Courts with Praise: Old Testament Worship for the New Testament Church* [Nashville: Star Song, 1993], 7), the Hebrew word is a Hishtaphel form of the root *ḥāyâ/ḥāwâ*, "to live." For full discussion see Siegfried Kreuzer, "Zur Bedeutung und Etymologie von *hištaḥăwâ/yštḥwy*," *Vetus Testamentum* 35 (1985): 39–60; cf. also T. Fretheim, in *New International Dictionary of Old Testament Theology and Exegesis* [*NIDOTTE*], ed. W. A. VanGemeren (Grand Rapids: Eerdmans, 1997), 2:42–44.

35. See, e.g., Gen. 18:2; 24:52; Ruth 2:10; 1 Sam. 25:23; 2 Kings 2:15; 4:37.

36. See, e.g., Gen. 19:1; 42:6; 48:12; 1 Sam. 25:41; 2 Sam. 14:33; Isa. 49:23; Neh. 8:6.

37. Hebrew *qādad* is related to *qodqōd*, "head, skull," and Akkadian *qadādu*, "to bow very low." Second Chron. 29:30 links the word with verbal praise. Hebrew *kāpap* occurs in a "worshipful" sense in Mic. 6:6. Elsewhere it reflects imposed humiliation (Isa. 58:5; Pss. 57:6 [7]; 145:14; 146:8).

38. Hebrew *kāra'* (Esther 3:2, 5; Pss. 22:29 [30]; 95:6; 2 Chron. 29:29). Cf. Judg. 7:5–6; 1 Kings 8:54; 19:18; 2 Kings 1:13; Ezra 9:5; Ps. 72:9; Isa. 45:23. Hebrew *bārak* in the sense of "kneel" is rare (Ps. 95:6; cf. Gen. 24:11 [of camels]; 2 Chron. 6:13).

39. Hebrew *sāgad* (Dan. 3:5–28; cf. also 2:46). The word occurs with *hištaḥāwâ* in Isa. 44:15, 19; 46:6.

40. Hebrew *nāpal* (Ruth 2:10; 1 Sam. 20:41; 2 Sam. 1:2; 14:4; 2 Kings 4:37; Job 1:20).

O come, let us prostrate [*ḥištaḥăwă*] and bow down [*kāraʿ*],
let us kneel [*bārak*] before YHWH, our Maker!
For he is our God, and we are the people of his pasture,
and the sheep of his hand. (Ps. 95:7)

The prostration expressed by *ḥištaḥăwâ* and other similar words was not limited to the worship of the Deity. In the ancient world and many cultures today, lower-class individuals would customarily prostrate before social, economic, and political superiors.[41]

Figure 1.1. A second-millennium-BC Egyptian image of homage on limestone from the necropolis at Thebes
(From Adolf Erman, *Ägypten und ägyptisches Leben im Altertum*, edited by H. Ranke [Tübingen: Mohr (Siebeck), 1923], 477, figure 188, attributed ultimately to Achille-Constant-Théodore-Émile Prisse D'Avennes, *Histoire de l'art Égyptien d'après les monuments depuis les temps les plus reculés jusqu'à la domination romaine* [Paris: A. Bertrand, 1878], Dessin #3.)

Although people in the Bible often responded spontaneously to divine favor or revelation with prostration,[42] the gesture is also common in formal ritual contexts. In Genesis 22:5 Abraham instructs his servants to wait at the bottom of Mount Moriah while he and Isaac go up the mountain to "worship" (*ḥištaḥăwâ*). When Solomon had finished building the temple and the divine glory took up residence there, the people bowed (*kāraʿ*) on the pavement with their noses to the ground, prostrated themselves (*ḥištaḥăwâ*), and gave thanks to YHWH (2 Chron. 7:3). Centuries later, at a communal gathering probably at this same place, all the people stood to their feet when Ezra rose and opened the Torah scroll. After he had blessed them, they responded with a verbal "Amen! Amen!" and raised their hands; they bowed their heads (*qādad*) and prostrated themselves (*ḥištaḥăwâ*) before YHWH (Neh. 8:6).

The motif of prostration before YHWH is especially common in the Psalms and Isaiah,[43] where descriptions of such gestures are not limited to Israel. Psalmists (22:27–29 [28–30]; 72:11; 86:9) and prophets (Isa. 49:7; Zeph. 2:11)

41. For a variety of First Testament examples, see Gen. 19:1; 23:7, 12; 33:3; 42:6; 43:26, 28; Ruth 2:10; 1 Sam. 20:41; 24:8 [9]; 28:14; 2 Kings 2:15. For examples in royal courts, see 2 Sam. 14:4, 22, 33; 15:5; 16:4; 2 Chron. 24:17. These verbs appear naturally in royal psalms: Pss. 22:29 [30]; 72:9, 11.

42. See Gen. 24:26, 48, 52; Exod. 4:31; 34:8; Num. 22:31; Josh. 5:14; Judg. 7:15; 2 Sam. 12:20; 1 Kings 1:47; Job 1:20.

43. See Pss. 22:27, 29 [28, 30]; 29:2; 86:9; 95:6; 96:9; 132:7; 138:2; Isa. 27:13; 45:14; 49:7; 60:14; 66:23.

Figure 1.2. A first-millennium-BC Neo-Assyrian image of homage (Photograph by Kim Walton, courtesy of the British Museum. Used with permission.)

envision a day when all kings and nations will prostrate themselves before YHWH. Indeed, poets even speak of heavenly creatures as worshiping before him (Pss. 29:1–2; 97:7). Note especially Nehemiah 9:6:

> You are YHWH, you alone; you have made heaven, the heaven of heavens, with all their host, the earth and all that is on it, the seas and all that is in them. To all of them you give life, and the host of heaven are prostrate [hištaḥăwâ] before you.

Following the lead of the Septuagint, the Greek translation of the Hebrew Scriptures (abbreviated LXX), the New Testament replaces Hebrew hištaḥăwâ with *proskyneō*, whose range of meaning is similar.[44] While the roots of the word are obscure, the verb expresses the widespread custom of kneeling before a superior and kissing his feet, the hem of his garment, or the ground, and in a derived sense means "to worship."[45] The word occurs many times in the Gospels and Acts—though as a general term for Christian worship only in Acts 24:11—and in Revelation. These physical expressions of homage always occur before superiors who are truly or supposedly divine.[46] The New Testament

44. Hebrew hištaḥăwâ and Aramaic sĕgid are rendered in the LXX almost exclusively with *proskyneō*, though this word is occasionally also used for nāšaq, "to kiss" (1 Kings 19:18); 'ābad, "to serve" (Ps. 97:7); and kāra', "to bow/bend the knee."

45. See H. Greeven, "*proskyneō, proskynētēs*," in *Theological Dictionary of the New Testament* [*TDNT*], ed. G. Kittel and G. Friedrich, trans. G. W. Bromiley (Grand Rapids: Eerdmans, 1964–76), 6:758–66. Scholars generally view *proskyneō* as a combination of *pros*, "toward," and *kyneō*, "to kiss."

46. God (Matt. 4:10; John 4:20, 21, 22, 23, 24; 1 Cor. 14:25; Rev. 7:11; 11:16; 14:7; 15:4; 19:4, 10; 22:9), God incarnate in Jesus (Matt. 2:2, 8, 11; 8:2; 9:18; 14:33; 15:25; 18:26; 20:20; 28:9, 17;

uses several additional words to speak of physical prostration as a gesture of worship. Sometimes, such homage is described simply as "falling down" (*piptō*)[47] or "kneeling down" (*gonypeteō*) before a person.[48] Such genuflection expresses self-abasement, submission, or worship.

Some argue that the infrequency of *proskyneō* in Paul's writings highlights the discontinuity between First and New Testament worship. Since in ancient Israel worship focused on place and external expressions, supposedly place and external forms are irrelevant in Christian worship because of the shift to worship "in spirit and in truth" (John 4:24). And since in the Gospels Jesus is physically present to receive worship, Paul's Letters assume that the day announced in John 4:20–21 has arrived.

This interpretation is doubtful on several counts. First, the argument is grounded on silence. Just because Paul uses *proskyneō* only in 1 Corinthians 14:25 does not mean he rejects the propriety of physical gestures of homage in Christian worship. On the contrary, in this context he speaks quite naturally of an unbeliever entering the assembly of God's people, being convicted of his sin, falling on his face and worshiping (*proskyneō*), and verbally acknowledging that God is among them. Indeed, the absence of the word elsewhere in Paul's writings could mean that he assumes that traditional understandings continue. Nowhere does he or anyone else declare that the work of Christ renders genuflection outmoded and obsolete.

Second, this emphasis on the contrast between the exteriority and cultic nature of First Testament worship and the interiority and spiritual nature of Christian worship reflects a misunderstanding of true Israelite worship. Beginning with Cain and Abel and running through the Torah and the Prophets, we see that the heart and life of a person provided the lens through which their

---

Mark 5:6; 15:19; Luke 24:52; John 9:38; Heb. 1:6; Rev. 4:10; 5:14; 7:11), Satan (Matt. 4:9; Luke 4:7, 8), demons (Rev. 9:20), the dragon (13:4), the beast and his image (13:4, 8, 12, 15; 14:9, 11; 16:2; 19:20; 20:4), images (Acts 7:43; cf. Amos 5:26), and angels (Rev. 19:10 and 22:8–9, where the interpreting angel rejects John's homage). Cf. Greeven, in *TDNT* 6:763.

47. Greek *piptō*: without a modifier, Matt. 18:29; Rev. 5:14; before a person, Rev. 4:10; 5:8; 7:11; on one's face, Matt. 17:6; 26:39; Luke 5:12; 17:16; 1 Cor. 14:25; Rev. 7:11; 11:16; on/to the ground, Mark 14:35; on/at/before someone's feet, Matt. 18:29; Luke 8:41; 17:16; Mark 5:22; John 11:32; Acts 10:25; Rev. 4:10; 5:8; 7:11; 19:10. This physical gesture accompanies verbal petitions (Mark 5:22 = Luke 8:41; Luke 5:12), expressions of gratitude (Luke 17:16), greetings (John 11:32), or prayers (Matt. 26:39 = Mark 14:35).

48. In Matt. 27:29 *gonypeteō* is used of the soldiers' mocking homage of Jesus the king (the parallel in Mark 15:19 uses the fuller expression *tithenai ta gonata*, "to place, give the knee"); cf. the explicit expression "to bend the knee" (*kamptō ta gonata*) in Rom. 11:4; Eph. 3:14; Phil. 2:10. This gesture precedes a verbal petition in Matt. 17:14; Mark 1:40 (the parallel in Matt. 8:2 reads *proskyneō*); 10:17. Indeed, prayer itself may be referred to periphrastically as "to give/set the knees" (*tithenai ta gonata*, Luke 22:41 [the parallels in Matt. 26:39 and Mark 14:35 read "he fell on his face" and "he fell to the ground," respectively]; Acts 7:60; 9:40; 20:36; 21:5).

worship was evaluated. While Deuteronomy has a great deal to say about worship, it says virtually nothing about the externals. The focus is entirely on worship "in spirit and in truth."[49]

Third, this view overlooks the hard evidence of Paul's own practice and writings. In Acts 24:11 he declares that he arrived in Jerusalem twelve days earlier for the purpose of worship (*proskyneō*). Before he leaves Ephesus, Paul kneels down (*tithenai ta gonata*) and prays with the elders (Acts 20:36), and later he does the same at Tyre (Acts 21:5). In Ephesians 3:14 Paul expresses his awe for having been chosen as the object and vehicle of God's amazing grace by "bending my knee" (*kamptō ta gonata mou*) before the Father. According to Romans 11:4 Paul found inspiration for the faithful in his day in the seven thousand who had not bowed the knee to Baal in Elijah's day.[50] Most important, in Philippians 2:10 he declares that God has exalted Jesus for the express purpose of gaining the obeisance (*pan gony kamptō*) of all.

Finally, this insistence on the contrast between First Testament and New Testament worship misunderstands John 4:20–21. Jesus does not announce the end of genuflection and the beginning of inner, spiritual worship in this passage. As if to highlight the continuity of prostration, in verses 21–24 he uses the word *proskyneō* eight times. Jesus' point was not that inner submission has replaced external gestures or that individualistic devotion has replaced corporate expressions of worship. The change is in the place of worship. Since Jesus is both the temple and the object of worship, future prostration before the Father will be disconnected from Jerusalem.[51]

Many evangelical churches resist physical prostration as an expression of homage and submission before God. This resistance represents both an unfortunate overreaction to Roman Catholic abuses and the arrogance of our culture. Although genuflection before a superior is universally recognized as a legitimate expression of respect, Western culture, impatient with expressions of deference, has discarded these millennia-old symbolic gestures.[52]

---

49. See further Block, "Mosaic Vision of Worship," 272–98.

50. In quoting 1 Kings 19:18 in Rom. 11:4, Paul substitutes *kamptō* for LXX *oklazō* (for Hebrew *kāraʿ*, "to bend [the knee]"). Greek *oklazō*, "to crouch down, squat," occurs elsewhere in LXX only in 1 Sam. 4:19 (crouching to give birth) and 1 Kings 8:54 (Solomon arose from his knees).

51. On which, see further Daniel I. Block, "Eden: A Temple? A Reassessment of the Biblical Evidence," in *From Creation to New Creation: Biblical Theology and Exegesis*, edited by D. M. Gurtner and B. L. Gladd (Peabody, MA: Hendrickson, 2013), 3–32.

52. Note the furor in politically conservative circles over President Obama's bowing before foreign dignitaries when greeting them. For representative images, see http://www.google.com/search?q=obama-bows-before-japan-emperor-hirohito&hl=en&tbm=isch&tbo=u&source=univ&sa=X&ei=o102UcesCoe70QG0qIDICg&ved=0CDwQsAQ&biw=800&bih=403; http://sharprightturn.wordpress.com/2009/04/02/obama-bows-to-saudi-king/.

Of course, prostration is not the only physical gesture by which to express homage before God. Worship often involves other physical postures (lying, sitting, standing), as well as actions performed with the hands (clapping, raising of hands) or feet (marching in procession, dancing, jumping). For the moment, we observe only that the dominant physical gesture of worship in the Scriptures is prostration. Our contemporary squabbles over worship rarely—if ever—include discussions of physically bending the knee before God, which may be a measure of how uninterested people are in truly biblical worship. Surely worship that pleases God involves bodily gestures of subordination and submission.

Worship as Cultic Ritual

In evangelical circles, the word "cult" is generally associated with religious groups that appear to resemble historic Christianity but replace cardinal Christian doctrines with heretical views.[53] In popular media the word identifies a small, often sinister religious group—usually led by a charismatic leader—that brainwashes its members and promotes the notion of the imminent end of the world. Here and throughout this book, I use the term "cult" according to its classical definition, relating not to fringe religious groups but to legitimate forms and systems of religious worship, especially external rites and ceremonies where homage is given to divine beings.[54] Such rituals may express the piety of individuals, families, or larger communities. Our exploration into how the Scriptures speak about cultic rituals will begin with general expressions and then move to specific vocabulary.

In the First Testament, Hebrew *ʿābad*, "to serve," is the most general expression associated with cultic service. By definition, one who "serves" advances the agenda of another person either by carrying out the superior's agenda or simply by living according to the superior's will. Many important Israelite figures, cultic and otherwise, bore the title "YHWH's servant" (*ʿebed yhwh*).[55] This epithet does not suggest menial roles but reflects an elevated status;

53. The popular book on the subject, Walter Martin's *Kingdom of the Cults*, ed. R. Zacharias, rev. ed. (Bloomington, MN: Bethany House: 2003), investigates Jehovah's Witnesses, Christian Science, Church of Jesus Christ of Latter-Day Saints (Mormon), Scientology, and the Unification Church, among others.

54. See the definition in the *Oxford English Dictionary* (Oxford: Oxford University Press, 1984), 1246.

55. Abraham (Ps. 105:6, 42); Abraham, Isaac, Jacob (Exod. 32:13); Caleb (Num. 14:24); Moses (e.g., Exod. 14:31; Josh. 1:1); Joshua (Josh. 24:29; Judg. 2:8); David (e.g., 2 Sam. 7; 1 Kings 8:66); Elijah (2 Kings 10:10); the prophets (2 Kings 17:13).

those so designated had access to YHWH's court and were sent out to represent him. At Sinai the Israelites ceased to be the slaves (*'ăbādîm*) of Pharaoh (Exod. 5:15–15) and were formally inducted into the office of "vassal" (*'ebed*) of YHWH, commissioned with his agenda.[56] According to Deuteronomy 10:12–11:1, Israelites would fulfill this role by fearing YHWH, walking in his ways, demonstrating covenant commitment to him, serving (*'ābad*) him wholeheartedly, and obeying all his commands. All of life was to be an expression of service to YHWH.

However, the verb "to serve" *may* involve cultic service to YHWH. In the Exodus narratives, Moses begs Pharaoh to release the Israelites so they may go on a three-day journey into the desert to "serve" YHWH.[57] Since Exodus 5:1 specifies the event as a "feast for YHWH," and since other texts speak of sacrificial rituals (*zebah, zĕbāhîm*)[58] and whole burnt offerings (10:25–26), some translations render the word as "worship." In the regulations concerning the tabernacle rituals, the root is often used of Levitical and priestly ministry,[59] and Numbers 16:9 refers to the ritual as "serving the service [*'ābad 'ăbōdâ*] of the tabernacle of YHWH." The word may also be used of cultic service for other gods;[60] however, this cultic usage is not the most common.

A second expression, *šērēt*, "to minister, serve," involves a narrower range of meaning. Like *'ābad*, this verb speaks fundamentally of service rendered to a superior by a person of lower rank, often as a personal attendant,[61] and may apply directly to the "ministry to God."[62] However, usually the verb refers to cultic service involving the sanctuary,[63] the altar (Exod. 30:20; Joel 1:9, 13) and cultic instruments and furniture,[64] or to service as temple guards (Ezek. 44:11). Elsewhere we learn this service also involved music (1 Chron. 6:32

---

56. Although the terms are not used, Exod 19:4–6 summarizes that mission. Here YHWH charges Israel with the same mission he had assigned earlier to Abraham (cf. Gen. 12:1–3; 17:1–8; 18:19).

57. See Exod. 3:12; 4:23; 7:16; 8:1 [7:26], 16 [20]; 9:1, 13; 10:3, 7, 8, 11, 24, 26; 12:31.

58. See Exod. 5:3, 8, 17; 8:8, 25–29 [21–25]; 10:25.

59. As in Num. 3:7–8; 4:23, 30, 47; 8:11, 19–26. Note also the noun *'ăbōdâ*, "service" (e.g., Exod. 12:25–26; Num. 4:4, 19, 47; 18:7, 21, 23; Josh. 22:27; 1 Chron. 6:32, 48; 2 Chron. 34:13; 35:16; Neh. 10:37 [38]).

60. See, e.g., Deut. 4:19; 8:19; 2 Kings 10:18–19, 21–23.

61. See, e.g., Gen. 39:4; 40:4; Exod. 24:13; Num. 3:6; Josh. 1:1; 1 Kings 19:21; 2 Kings 4:43; 6:15; 2 Chron. 8:14. In royal contexts it refers to courtly attendants (2 Sam. 13:17–18; 1 Kings 1:4; 10:5; 2 Chron. 22:8; Esther 1:10) or military officials (1 Chron. 27:1; 28:1).

62. See Deut. 10:8 ("to stand before YHWH and serve Him"); 17:12; 18:5, 7; 21:5; 1 Sam. 2:11, 18; 3:1; 1 Chron. 15:2; 23:13; 2 Chron. 13:10; 29:11. Isaiah 56:6 and 61:6 look forward to a day when foreigners and laypeople will serve YHWH; Pss. 103:21 and 104:4 speak of heavenly beings serving (*šērēt*) him.

63. As in Num. 1:50; Ezek. 44:27; 45:4–5; 46:24.

64. See Num. 3:31; 4:9, 12, 14; 2 Kings 25:14 = Jer. 52:18; 2 Chron. 24:14.

[17]), handling the ark of the covenant (16:4, 37), petitioning, giving thanks, and praising YHWH (1 Chron. 16:4; cf. 2 Chron. 5:13–14).

The noun *kōhēn*, "priest," occurs more than seven hundred times in the First Testament. However, the verb *kihēn*, "to serve, act as priest," is relatively rare.[65] While the root of both words involves mediation between divine and earthly realms, the usage of the verb is more restricted; and most references are associated with priestly office, including ordination to priestly service.[66]

Several additional expressions have liturgical implications. The phrases "to stand before" (*'āmad lipnê*) YHWH and "to walk before" (*hithallēk/hālak lipnê*) YHWH, derive from the royal court.[67] A person who stood or walked "before the king" or "in the palace of the king" was authorized by the king to enter his presence and serve as his courtier (Dan. 1:4). One who stood/walked before YHWH had access to the divine court and was commissioned for service on his behalf.[68] The idiom "to follow/walk after [a god]" may denote fidelity to YHWH (1 Kings 14:8), but usually the expression bears the negative sense of following illegitimate deities,[69] as in Jeremiah 8:2:

And they will spread them [the bones of the people of Jerusalem] out to the sun, the moon, and to all the host of heaven, which they have loved [*'āhab*], and which they have served [*'ābad*], and which they have gone after [*hālak 'aḥărê*], and which they have sought [*dāraš*], and to which they have prostrated themselves [*hištaḥăwâ*].

While texts that speak of "walking after YHWH" are rare, the expression may speak generally of devotion to YHWH rather than liturgical service in

65. See, e.g., Exod. 28:1, 3–4, 41; 29:1, 44; 30:30; Lev. 7:35; 16:32; Num. 3:3–4; Deut. 10:6.

66. J. A. Davies, *A Royal Priesthood: Literary and Intertextual Perspectives on the Image of Israel in Exodus 19.6*, Journal for the Study of the Old Testament: Supplement Series 395 (New York: T&T Clark, 2004), 86–100. Ezekiel 44:13 narrows the expression to the performance of cultic rituals by the sons of Zadok. Hosea 4:6 alludes to the priestly task of teaching the Torah of God, a function that Mal. 2:1–9 treats in greater detail.

67. Variations of the idiom are used of Moses (Ps. 106:23), subsequent prophets (Deut. 18:5, 7; 1 Kings 17:1; 18:15; 2 Kings 3:14; 5:16; Jer. 15:1; 23:18, 22; cf. 18:20), Rechabites (Jer. 35:19), and in legal contexts (Jer. 7:10), but it is also applied to priests and Levites (Zech. 3:1; cf. Deut. 10:8; 18:7; 1 Kings 8:11). Psalms 134:1 and 135:2 speak simply of standing in YHWH's house.

68. Persons so designated who served as agents of God include the patriarchs (Gen. 17:1; 24:40; 48:15), priests (1 Sam. 2:30), and kings: David (1 Kings 3:6; 8:25; 9:4; presumably also Pss. 56:13 [14]; 116:9), Solomon (1 Kings 9:4), and Hezekiah (2 Kings 20:3 = Isa. 38:3). The meaning of this expression differs significantly from "to walk with" (*hithallēk 'et*) YHWH, which expresses more general piety: Enoch, Gen. 5:22, 24; Noah, Gen. 6:9; Levitical priests, Mal. 2:6.

69. Often with *'ābad*, "to serve," and *hištaḥăwâ*, "to prostrate [before]": Deut. 8:19; Judg. 2:19; 2 Kings 23:3; 25:6; Jer. 13:10; 25:6. The idiom apparently derives from the practice of following statues of deities in religious procession.

particular.[70] Beyond these general expressions, the First Testament speaks of the full range of liturgical worship: prayer, singing, lamentation, fasting, and so forth.[71]

The New Testament is clear that Jesus' self-sacrificial ministry signaled the end of tabernacle and temple rituals. Nevertheless, it uses First Testament language of cultic service to speak of Christian worship. Corresponding to the Hebrew word *'ābad*, we encounter *douleuō*, "to serve." Matthew 6:24 illustrates this general expression of vassalage/service: "No one can serve two masters, for either he will reject the one and be committed to the other, or he will be devoted to the one and despise the other. You cannot serve God and money." Elsewhere Paul speaks of the Thessalonians who turned from idols to serve the living and true God.[72] As heir to the First Testament and in the train of the LXX, the related noun *doulos*, "servant," is often used of devotees and servants of God in the New Testament.[73] Paul freely alternates *doulos*, "servant," and *apostolos*, "messenger, envoy," suggesting that *doulos* does not mean primarily "slave" or "bondslave" but functions as an honorific designation referring to "a specially appointed and commissioned agent" of God.[74] Yet the verb was also used more generally for all believers, who serve (*douleuō*) Christ daily with righteous actions and are committed to peace and the building up of the saints. Since we serve the Lord Christ, we will receive a reward from him (Col. 3:24) and the approval of others

70. See, e.g., Deut. 13:3–4 [4–5]; 1 Kings 14:8; 18:21; Jer. 2:2; Hosea 11:10; 2 Chron. 34:31. This idiom is distinct from expressions like "walking in YHWH's ways" (Deut. 28:9; 1 Kings 11:33, 38; 2 Kings 21:22; Pss. 81:13; 119:3; 128:1; Jer. 7:23)—as opposed to "walking in the way not good" (Isa. 65:2)—or "walking in his command/statutes/Torah/truth," which bear a pronounced ethical sense (2 Chron. 17:4; Jer. 32:23; 44:10; Ezek. 5:6, 7; 18:9, 17; 20:13, 21, 16; Pss. 26:3; 86:11; 119:1).

71. From the prophets alone: prayer (*tepillâ*, see, e.g., Isa. 1:15; 37:4; 56:7; Jon. 2:7 [2:8]; Hab. 3:1), singing (*zimmēr*, Isa. 12:5; *šîr*, Isa. 26:1; 30:29; 42:10; Jer. 20:13; Amos 5:23; 8:10), lamentation (*qînâ*, Jer. 9:20; Ezek. 32:16; Amos 8:10), fasting (*ṣûm*, see, e.g., Isa. 58:3–5; Jer. 14:12; 36:6, 9; Jon. 3:5; Zech. 7:5; 8:19), sacrifices and offerings of all sorts (Isa. 1:11; 19:21), vows (*neder*, Isa. 19:21; Jon. 1:16; Mal. 1:14), festivals (*mô'ădîm*, Isa. 33:20; Ezek. 36:38; Hosea 2:11 [13]; Zech. 8:19), pilgrimages (*ḥag*, see, e.g., Isa. 30:29; Ezek. 45:17; 46:11; Hosea 2:11 [13]; 9:5), reading the word of YHWH (Jer. 36:6, 13–16), and teaching Torah (Mal. 2:6–8).

72. See 1 Thess. 1:9; cf. Acts 20:19; Rom. 7:6; 12:11. In Rom. 7:25 Paul says he serves the *nomos* (Torah) of God with his mind, while serving the *nomos* of sin with his flesh.

73. Moses the *doulos* of God (Rev. 15:3); prophets in general (10:7; 11:18; cf., e.g., 2 Kings 17:13, 23); apostles (Acts 4:29; 16:17); God-fearing people (cf. Luke 2:29; 1 Cor. 7:22; Eph. 6:6; 1 Pet. 2:16; Rev. 1:1; 2:20; 7:3; 19:2, 5; 22:3, 6).

74. "Servant" of Christ and "apostle" are Paul's favorite official self-designations. For *doulos*, see Rom. 1:1; Gal. 1:10; Phil. 1:1; cf. Col. 4:12; 2 Tim. 2:24; James 1:1; Jude 1; Rev. 22:3. For *apostolos*, see Rom. 1:1; 11:13; 1 Cor. 1:1; 9:1–2; 15:9; 2 Cor. 1:1 (cf. 12:12); Gal. 1:1; Eph. 1:1; Col. 1:1; 1 Tim. 1:1; 2:7; 2 Tim. 1:1, 11; Titus 1:1. See also 1 Pet. 1:1; 2 Pet. 1:1.

(Rom. 14:17–18).[75] Remarkably *doulos* is never used specifically of cultic service; servitude to Christ involves a lifestyle totally devoted to him and is a precondition for acceptable liturgical worship.

This conclusion is reinforced by another verb, *latreuō*, which also means "to serve" but is linked more closely to carrying out religious and cultic duties.[76] In the Exodus narratives Moses repeatedly demands, "Let my people go that they may serve [LXX *latreuō*] me in the desert,"[77] but references to a feast (8:26) and sacrifices (10:25–26) also suggest cultic activity.[78] Often *latreuō* refers to righteous conduct of the people generally (Deut. 10:12), but the verb usually involves service to God by priests or Levites in the sanctuary. In the New Testament this word occasionally functions as a general expression for worship (including lifestyle, ethical conduct),[79] but it also refers to prayer (Luke 2:37) or unspecified actions in the presence of God.[80] In Acts 7:7 *latreuō* refers to cultic service of the people (feasts and sacrifices) in the desert, and in Acts 7:42 and Romans 1:25 it speaks of sacrificial ministry offered to God rather than to other gods.

In Romans 12:1 Paul captures perfectly the Mosaic vision of wholehearted and full-bodied worship:

> I appeal to you therefore, brothers and sisters, by the mercies of God, to present your bodies [*sōmata*] as a living sacrifice, holy [*thysian zōsan hagian euareston*] and acceptable to God, which is your reasonable/logical service [*logikēn latreian*].

Translations that render *logikēn latreian* as "spiritual worship" (ESV, NRSV) or "your true and proper worship" (NIV) obscure the echo of Deuteronomy 10:12. Although this text has little to do with liturgical service, the LXX renders Hebrew *'ābad*, "to serve," as *latreuō*. The translators of the Authorized Version (KJV) got Romans 12:1 right when they rendered *logikēn latreian* as "reasonable service," provided that by "service" we mean full-bodied and wholehearted vassaldom: all of life devoted to God, having been transformed

---

75. Christians are also called to serve earthly superiors well (Eph. 6:7) and to serve one another within the church (Gal. 5:13; Phil. 2:22).

76. See H. Strathmann, in *TDNT* 4:58–65. Except for Num. 16:9 and Ezek. 20:32 (*šērēt*), Deut. 11:28 (*hālak 'aḥărê*), and the Aramaic of Daniel (*pĕlaḥ*)—of ninety occurrences in LXX, *latreuō* always translates *'ābad*, "to serve." However, when *'ābad* is used in the general sense of "serving," *douleuō* is preferred.

77. See Exod. 4:23; 7:16; 8:1 [7:26 LXX], 20 [16]; 9:1, 13; 10:3, 7, 8, 24, 26.

78. Remarkably, the LXX lends Deut. 10:12–13 and Josh. 24:19 a cultic nuance by using this term for *'ābad*.

79. See Matt. 4:10 = Luke 4:8, cf. Deut. 6:13; Luke 1:74; Acts 24:14; 27:23; Phil. 3:3; 2 Tim. 1:3; Heb. 9:14; 12:28.

80. As in Acts 26:7; Rev. 7:15; 22:3.

and renewed from the inside out, which is exactly what Paul develops in Romans 12–15. This is the logical and reasonable response to the redemption we have received through the cross (Rom. 1–11), even as Israel's wholehearted and full-bodied vassaldom was the logical and reasonable response to YHWH's magnificent acts of redemption (Deut. 4:32–40; 6:20–25).

The most explicit New Testament expression for cultic and ritual service rendered to God is *leitourgeō*, which underlies the English word "liturgy."[81] In the New Testament this word group sometimes refers to general service,[82] but cognate nouns are also used of Zechariah's priestly service in Luke 1:23 (*leitourgia*) and as a figure of speech in Romans 15:16 for a "minister" (*leitourgos*) of Christ Jesus who engages in the "priestly ministry" (*hierourgeō*) of the gospel. Steeped in the vocabulary of the First Testament cult, the author of Hebrews demonstrates that Jesus Christ's onetime sacrifice for sins has ended the priestly service (*leitourgein*) and committed the ultimate "liturgical" act by which we are sanctified (Heb. 10:10–12). Likewise, he is our high priest, seated at the right hand of the throne of God, a minister (*leitourgos*) in the sanctuary, in the true tent that the Lord has set up (Heb. 8:1–2).

The term *hierourgeō*, "to act as priest," appears in the New Testament only in Romans 15:16. A related form, *hierateuō*, "to minister as priest," occurs in Luke 1:8, while verse 9 refers to the custom of the priestly office as *hierateia*. First Corinthians 9:13 speaks of "performing holy services of the temple" (*hieros*), and Titus 2:3 calls for older women to be reverent in their behavior—that is, act in a way befitting a holy person (*hieroprepēs*). Revelation 20:6 (cf. 1:6; 5:10) speaks of Christians as "priests of God" (*hiereis tou theou*), and Peter considers Christians "a holy priesthood" (*hieratouma hagion*, 1 Pet. 2:5) and "a priesthood of royal rank" (*basileion hierateuma*, 2:9). Revelation 5:10 sings of people from every tribe and nation being made a kingdom and priests (*hiereis*).[83]

The New Testament freely uses cultic expressions for the ministry that Christians perform for Christ, but unlike the First Testament, it hesitates to

81. The verb *leitourgeō*, "to minister," occurs only three times in the New Testament (Acts 13:2; Rom. 15:27; Heb. 10:11); the noun *leitourgia*, "ministry, liturgy," six times (Luke 1:23; 2 Cor. 9:12; Phil. 2:17, 30; Heb. 8:6; 9:21); *leitourgos*, the one who conducts the ministry, five times (Rom. 13:6; 15:16; Phil. 2:25; Heb. 1:7; 8:2); and *leitourgikos*, "ordained for ministry," once (Heb. 1:14). For a full discussion, see Strathmann, in *TDNT* 4:215–31.

82. Acts 13:2; Rom. 13:6; Rom. 15:27; 2 Cor. 9:12; Phil. 2:25, 30; Heb. 1:7, 14. The term appears over a hundred times in the LXX, usually for Hebrew *šērēt*, but when this word is not concerned with cultic matters, other terms may be used.

83. Elsewhere references to the priesthood usually apply either to the priests in Jewish cultic service or to Christ as high priest, who institutes a better priesthood and offers superior priestly service.

speak of corporate worship in cultic terms.[84] Paul speaks of himself being poured out as a liquid offering over the sacrifice and service of his readers' faith (*leitourgia tēs pisteōs*, Phil. 2:17), but the gathering of God's people for worship is never explicitly called a liturgical event.

Synthesis: A Working Explanation of Worship for Our Time

How shall we synthesize this lexical material to formulate a biblical definition of worship for our time? A bewildering array of definitions has already been proposed in the ever-expanding literature on the topic.[85] The preceding discussion shows that neither the First nor the New Testament tried to capture the concept with a single word. We may characterize constituent parts of worship as mystery, celebration, life, dialogue, offering, or eschatological fulfillment, but to define biblical worship is to confine it. At best we may try to describe the phenomena.

Pagan worship focuses on corporate and individual cultic efforts seeking to mollify the gods[86] and secure their blessing. Today many Christians' understanding of worship differs little from that of pagans, except perhaps that God is singular and the forms of worship come from traditions more or less rooted in the Scriptures. Largely divorced from life, such worship represents a pattern of religious activities driven by a deep-seated sense of obligation to God and a concern to win his favor. But this understanding is unbiblical; it separates worship from daily life and compartmentalizes human existence into the sacred and the secular.

To account for the dimensions of worship reflected in the Scriptures, we need a much more comprehensive explanation. In simplest terms, worship is "the human response to God." However, to reflect the complexity of the biblical picture, I propose the following:

> True worship involves reverential human acts of submission and homage before the divine Sovereign in response to his gracious revelation of himself and in accord with his will.

84. K. L. Schmidt (in *TDNT* 3:158) may be right in suggesting that focusing on the cult could easily lead to synergism.

85. See the list from Ron Man, *Worship Notes* 3/7 (July, 2008). http://www.worr.org/images /File/3-7P&Wb.pdf. F. M. Segler, (*Understanding, Preparing for, and Practicing Christian Worship*, 2nd rev. ed. [Nashville: Broadman & Holman, 1996], 7–11) says "worship" defies definition.

86. Described idiomatically as "to smooth, sweeten the face" (*ḥillâ pānîm*) of the deity. For vestiges of this notion, see Exod. 32:11; 1 Sam. 13:12; 1 Kings 13:6; 2 Kings 13:4; 2 Chron. 33:12; Ps. 119:58; Jer. 26:19; Dan. 9:13; Zech. 7:2; 8:21–22; Mal. 1:9. The idiom is also used of mollifying humans: Job 11:19; Ps. 45:12 [13]; Prov. 19:6.

This is not so much a definition of worship as a description of the phenomena. While the following chapters will expound on this statement, I will lay the groundwork with some brief commentary.

First, the Scriptures call for worship that is true as opposed to false. Everyone worships. The problem is that not everyone worships truly. Those who direct their worship to gods other than the God revealed in Scripture or who worship the living God in ways contrary to his revealed will worship falsely. Whether we interpret obedience "before YHWH" in everyday conduct cultically or ethically (Deut. 6:25), to walk before him in truth/faithfulness (*be'ĕmet*) with our whole heart/mind (*bĕkol-lēbāb*) and being (*bĕkol-nepeš*, 1 Kings 2:4) demands integrity: consistency between confession and practice and consistency between what God seeks and what we present.

Second, true worship involves reverent awe. Evangelical worship today often lacks gravitas appropriate to the occasion and the divine Auditor who invites us to an audience with him. In Israelite worship, the concern for reverence was expressed through the design of the tabernacle and temple and by the priests' attire, which was intended to promote dignity (*kābôd*) and royal beauty (*tip'eret*, Exod. 28:2, 40). True worship need not be humorless, but neither will it be casual or flippant.

Third, true worship is a *human* response. The Scriptures inform us that angelic creatures worship God by their words and by their actions as messengers of God and agents of providence (Isa. 6), and that the entire universe is involved in worshipful activity (Pss. 19:1–6; 50:6; 148). However, although Scripture envisions the ultimate restoration of fallen creation, its words are intended for human beings and primarily concern their relationship with God. In this book the concern is not how the rest of the universe glorifies God but how *we* worship God—how we respond to the Westminster Catechism's declaration that "the chief end of *man* [humanity] is to glorify God, and to enjoy him forever."

Fourth, true worship involves action. It is not primarily interior, as if God is concerned only about what is in our hearts and disinterested in external ritual and ethical expressions. Although many aspects of God remain a mystery to us, biblical religion is not mystical, nor is it primarily cultic or formulaic. Some challenge us to treat "worship" as a verb,[87] which is fine, so long as we recognize that true worship involves actions that demonstrate covenant commitment to and love for God, and that our daily lives are characterized

---

87. See particularly Robert E. Webber, *Worship Is a Verb: Celebrating God's Mighty Deeds of Salvation* (Nashville: Star Song, 2006). Webber's concern is primarily the engagement of the congregation in liturgical gatherings.

by reverence and awe before him. As the prophets declare (1 Sam. 15:22; Mic. 6:8) and Jesus himself affirms (Matt. 23:23), obedience to the revealed ethical will of God must take priority over cultic ritual expression.

Fifth, true worship expresses the submission and homage of a person of lower rank before a superior. While the Scriptures speak of covenant arrangements between equals (Gen. 31:44–54), the relationship between God and his people is by definition asymmetrical. By grace, the Creator of the universe and the Redeemer of Israel invites us to covenant relationship, but this covenant is fundamentally monergistic (instituted by one party): God selects the covenant partner, establishes the terms, and determines the consequences of the vassals' response. True worship lets God be God on his terms, and we submit to him as Lord with reverent and trusting awe.

Sixth, while human subordinates may express their humility before human superiors by bowing and prostration, only the divine Sovereign is worthy of actual worship—assuming that we understand worship as veneration of the One who is the source and sustainer of all things and on whom we are absolutely dependent. This God has graciously revealed himself in the First Testament by name as YHWH and by actions as Creator and Redeemer. In the New Testament he has revealed himself primarily as the incarnate Son, but also as the Triune God: Father, Son, and Holy Spirit.

Seventh, true worship involves reactive communication. We could not worship God acceptably if he had not taken the initiative both to communicate with us and to open our eyes to his communication, whether in creation, history, or Scripture. The universe declares the transcendent qualities and glory of God in a general sense, but only through his specific revelation in deed and word do we learn of his specific character and attributes. True worship involves communication through action—demonstrating covenant commitment to God and our fellow human beings because he first loved us (Exod. 20:2; 1 John 4:19).

Eighth, for worshipers' acts of homage to be favorably received by God, they must align with his will rather than with the impulses of depraved human imagination. Forms of worship may vary from culture to culture, but true worship comes from hearts totally devoted to God and determined to please him. Scripture clearly reveals the forms of *ethical* worship acceptable to God, and since the New Testament gives minimal attention to corporate worship, true Christian worship should be grounded on theological principles established in the First Testament. Unless the New Testament expressly declares those principles to be obsolete, we should assume continuity.

In part, evangelical Christians quarrel over the nature of true worship, especially its cultic expression, because the New Testament hesitates to prescribe any liturgy when it describes the gatherings of Christians. In these assemblies, the emphasis seems to have been on edification and encouragement, serving one another, and challenging one another to faith and good works. While liturgical homage to God appears to be deemphasized, the First and New Testaments agree that all of life should be a service of worship. Adapting the second verse of the Shema (Deut. 6:5), we may represent true worship diagrammatically as in figure 1.3.

FIGURE 1.3
The Dimensions of Devotion

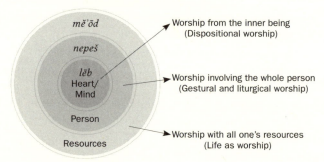

This understanding of worship as being wholehearted and full-bodied is not a novel New Testament idea. It runs like a thread from Genesis 4 (the

FIGURE 1.4
The Dimensions of Biblical Worship

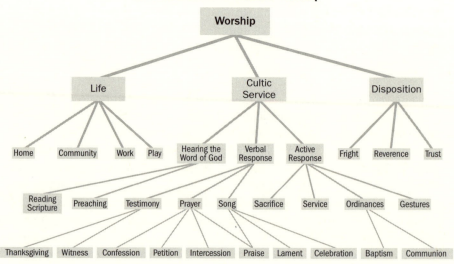

worship of Cain and Abel) through Revelation 19 (the worship of those invited to the marriage supper of the Lamb). Nor is cultic language absent from New Testament references to the gathering of God's people. Not only are Jesus' instructions for the Lord's Supper profoundly cultic but Hebrews 10:19–31 also calls on Christians to "draw near [to God] with a sincere heart" and admonishes them not to neglect participating in the assembly of God's people. Hebrews 12:28–29 reinforces the assumption of 10:26–31, that Christians' relationship to God closely resembles the Israelites' relationship to YHWH.

These summary talking points will all resurface in subsequent chapters; for now they declare our understanding of "true worship." Worship is indeed a complex matter, encompassing all of life. The relationships among the various facets of worship are illustrated in figure 1.4.

2

The Object of Worship

True worship involves reverential human acts of submission and hom-
age before the divine Sovereign in response to his gracious revelation of
himself and in accord with his will.

If our understanding of the nature and dimensions of worship is correct, we
first need to recognize the object of true worship. Here I do not mean, "What
is the objective, or goal, of our worship?" Rather, I am using the word "object" in its grammatical sense: in true worship, who is the object of the verb
"to worship"? To grasp the significance of this question, we need to examine
alternative worship systems.

Idolatry: The Problem of False Worship

What is idolatry? If we define an idol as "an illegitimate object of worship,"
then idolatry is "false worship, involving reverential human acts of submission
and homage before beings or objects in the place of the one true God." To
understand the exceptional nature of true, scriptural worship, we must place
biblical religion within its ancient Near Eastern context.

Scholars of religion have divided religious systems into four broad categories
reflected in the objects of worship: animism, polytheism, henotheism, and
monotheism. Within an evolutionary framework, monotheism is considered the

highest form of religion (fig. 2.1). While examples of animism are difficult to identify in the First Testament,[1] evidence for polytheism and henotheism is clear.[2]

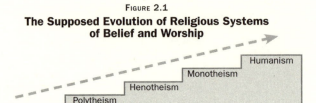

FIGURE 2.1
The Supposed Evolution of Religious Systems of Belief and Worship

Animism: Worshipers believe that objects are inhabited by personalized supernatural beings and that these spirits govern human existence: object and supernatural being are virtually equated.

Polytheism: Worshipers believe that many gods exist simultaneously, and that these gods govern human existence. These divinities may be closely associated with physical objects, but they exist apart from them, often being perceived as dwelling in a realm (heaven or otherwise) beyond the realm of human existence.

Henotheism: Worshipers believe that many gods exist simultaneously, and that many or all may govern human existence, but that an individual or community is governed in particular by a single member of the pantheon, perceived as the patron/matron of the community.

Monotheism: Worshipers believe that there is only one God, and the existence of all other deities is categorically rejected.

Humanism: Worshipers claim to believe in no deity at all, but in effect make Self or matter the measure of all things.

In ancient times, idolatry was problematic only in Yahwistic Israel and among peoples adhering to faiths derived from Israelite Yahwism (Judaism, Christianity, and Islam). The First Testament's prohibition of the worship of gods other than YHWH is unique in the ancient Near East. Most people assumed that if individuals or groups moved from one region to another, they would come under the jurisdiction of another territorial deity or group of deities. Although some gods were territorial (note expressions like "the gods of the lands," 2 Kings 18:33–35), others were functional (gods of war, the storm, love, etc.). Some divinities could be represented by manufactured images; others were identified with natural objects (sun, moon, stars, etc.).[3] In these idolatrous systems, the gods tended to be quite tolerant, not minding if their devotees worshiped deities other than themselves. Thus YHWH's command that Israel worship no other divinities—indeed, his very denial of their existence—was unprecedented.[4]

1. Pentateuchal events associated with trees (Gen. 12:6–8; 13:18; 18:1; 35:4; Exod. 3:2–5) or springs and wells (Gen. 14:7; Num. 21:17–18) are sometimes cited, but these interpretations are forced. There is no hint that either trees or springs are identified with deities.

2. The former is reflected in the frequent use of the plural "gods" (*'ĕlōhîm*), and the latter in references to Chemosh as "the god of Moab" and Milkom as "the god of the Ammonites" (1 Kings 11:33) on the one hand, and the Ammonites as "the people of Milkom" (Jer. 49:1, "his people") and Moabites as "the people of Chemosh" on the other (Num. 21:29; Jer. 48:46).

3. For a comprehensive list, see Deut. 4:15–19.

4. For further discussion, see Daniel I. Block, "Other Religions in Old Testament Theology," in *Biblical Faith and Other Religions: An Evangelical Assessment*, ed. D. W. Baker (Grand Rapids:

The Nature of an Idol: An Idolater's Perspective

Because the biblical perspective on idolatry is consistently negative and hostile, it is helpful to try to understand idolatry from the perspective of idolaters: people who viewed themselves as faithful devotees of legitimate divinities. Several ancient texts from Assyria explain how a physical object was thought to become a god.[5] From the idolaters' point of view, the production of a cult statue was a complex process involving both heavenly and earthly "hands." The process by which an ordinary piece of wood or stone was transformed into an idol animated by the spirit of the god it represented proceeded as follows:

  a. Artisans were carefully chosen and ritually consecrated, preparing them to enter the temple workshop, where statues of the gods and other sacred objects were made and animated.
  b. The artisans crafted the image, using the materials available (wood, stone, clay, metal, bone, etc.).
  c. Through special rites of divination, a propitious day in a favorable month was chosen for the "birth of the god."
  d. By special incantations and a ritual referred to as "the opening of the mouth" or "the washing of the mouth," the god was "born"; that is, a physical object was transformed into a living representative of the deity,[6] capable of smelling incense, drinking water, eating food, hearing prayers, and speaking words of reassurance or hope.
  e. Special rituals were performed to disassociate images from the human hands that made them, reinforcing the conviction that they were indeed divine creations. The artisans denied under oath that they had made the images, affirmed that they had been made by the craft deities, and had their hands cut off. The tools used to make the image were returned to the craft god by wrapping them in the carcass of a sheep and throwing them into the river.
  f. The gods were installed in the "holy of holies" of their temples, constructed as their official residences.

Kregel, 2004), 43–78; reprinted in Block, *The Gospel according to Moses: Theological and Ethical Reflections on the Book of Deuteronomy* (Eugene, OR: Wipf & Stock, 2012), 200–236.

5. See C. Walker and M. B. Dick, "The Induction of the Cult Image in Ancient Mesopotamia: The Mesopotamian *mīs pî* Ritual," in *Born in Heaven, Made on Earth: The Making of the Cult Image in the Ancient Near East*, ed. M. B. Dick (Winona Lake, IN: Eisenbrauns, 1999), 55–121.

6. In one attested instance, the statue was brought to an orchard next to a canal, where it was purified with holy water from a sacred basin, and its mouth was washed four times with honey, special soap, cedar, and cypress. The ritual, by which the spirit of the god whom it represented was to enter the statue and animate it, apparently imitated the actions of a midwife, who cleans and opens the breathing passage of an infant at birth.

g. To ensure the gods' favorable disposition toward worshipers, priests were appointed to care for the deities' material needs: animal and vegetarian sacrifices to satisfy their appetites and incense as a soothing aroma. The cult statues were regularly bathed, dressed in fine garments, put to bed, and treated to festivities and musical entertainment.

The Nature of an Idol: The Biblical Perspective

The attitude of faithful Israelites toward idolatry is reflected in the breadth of their vocabulary for idols. Idols are merely "the work of human hands,"[7] illusions,[8] and rubbish of the most abominable sort.[9] The biblical penchant for parodying idols and idolatrous practices is also embedded in narrative texts. For example, (1) Rachel's household gods (tĕrāpîm) could not protect themselves from her uncleanness (Gen. 31:33–35); (2) the golden calf could not protect itself from being ground into powder (Exod. 32:1–6, 20–24); (3) the images of Baal and Asherah could not defend themselves against Gideon (Judg. 6:25–32); (4) the images of Dagon fell in a heap of rubble before the ark of YHWH (1 Sam. 5:1–5); and (5) the prophets of Baal at

---

7. For variations of the Hebrew expression ma'ăśēh yĕdê 'ādām: Deut. 4:28; 27:15; 2 Kings 19:18 (= Isa. 37:19 = 2 Chron. 32:19); Pss. 115:4; 135:15; Isa. 2:8; Jer. 1:16; 10:3, 9; 25:6–7; 44:8; Hosea 14:3 [4]; Mic. 5:13 [12]; 2 Chron. 34:25. Specific expressions for images include "images" (ṣelem, Num. 33:52; Ezek. 7:20; Amos 5:26), "carvings" (pesel, Deut. 4:16, 23, 25), "sculptures" (sēmel, Ezek. 8:3, 5; 2 Chron. 33:7, 15), "likenesses" (tĕmûnâ, Deut. 4:16, 23, 25), "picture reliefs" (maśkît, Ezek. 8:12), "replicas" (tabnît, Ezek. 8:10), and "molds" ("molten images," nesek; created either by pouring liquid metal into a mold or plating an image with metal leaf; Isa. 41:29; 48:5; Jer. 10:14; 51:17).

8. "Effigies" ('āṣāb/'ōṣeb, 1 Sam. 31:9; 2 Sam. 5:21; 1 Chron. 10:9; Hosea 8:4; 13:2; 14:8 [9]; Isa. 10:11; 46:1; 48:5; Jer. 50:2; Mic. 1:7; Zech. 13:2; Pss. 106:36, 38; 115:4; 135:15; 139:24); "nothings" ('ĕlîlîm, Lev. 19:4; 26:1; Isa. 2:8, 18, 20; 10:10, 11; 19:1, 3; 31:7; Hab. 2:18; Pss. 96:5; 97:7; 1 Chron. 16:26); "nothingness" ('āwen, Isa. 66:3; cf. 41:29; 1 Sam. 15:23; cf. Hosea 4:15; 10:8, [Beth]-Awen); "worthless objects" (hablê-šāwĕ', Jon. 2:8 [9]; Ps. 31:6 [7]; cf. Ps. 24:4; Jer. 18:15); "vanity" (hebel, Deut. 32:21; 1 Kings 16:13, 26; 2 Kings 17:15; Jer. 2:5; 8:19; 10:8; 14:22; Jon. 2:8 [9]; Ps. 31:6 [7]); "illusions" (šeqer, Isa. 44:20; Jer. 10:14; 16:19; 51:17).

9. Ezekiel's favorite word for idols is gillûlîm, "dung pellets," probably derived from the peanut-like shape of sheep excrement (Ezek. 6:4 [+ 38×]; cf. Lev. 26:30; Deut. 29:17 [16]; 1 Kings 15:12; 21:26; 2 Kings 17:12; 21:11, 21), but he also calls them "detestable things" (šiqquṣîm, Ezek. 5:11; 7:20; 11:18, 21; 20:7–8, 30; 37:23; cf. Deut. 29:17 [16]; 2 Kings 23:24; 2 Chron. 15:8; Isa. 66:3; Jer. 4:1; 7:30; 13:27; 16:18; 32:34). Elsewhere they are characterized as "abominations" (tō'ēbôt, Deut. 32:16; Isa. 44:19; cf. Deut. 13:14 [15]; 17:4; the worship of foreign gods). To these expressions we might add "frightful images" ('êmîm, Jer. 50:38) and "teraphim (tĕrāpîm, Gen. 31:19, 34, 35; Judg. 17:5; 18:14, 17, 18, 20; 1 Sam. 15:23; 19:13, 16; 2 Kings 23:24; Ezek. 21:21 [26]; Hosea 3:4; Zech. 10:2). This word is related to Hittite tarpi, "a spirit that can on some occasions be regarded as protective and on others malevolent," sometimes identified with demons; cf. Dictionary of Deities and Demons in the Bible [DDD], ed. K. van der Toorn, B. Becking, and P. W. van der Horst (Leiden: Brill, 1995), 844–50.

Mount Carmel were impotent before Elijah (1 Kings 18:20–39). The psalmist highlights the contrast between idols and YHWH, who rules from heaven and does whatever he pleases.

> Their idols are silver and gold, the work of human hands.
> They have mouths, but do not speak; eyes, but do not see.
> They have ears, but do not hear; noses, but do not smell.
> They have hands, but do not feel; feet, but do not walk;
> they make no sound in their throats.
> Those who make them are like them;
> so are all who trust in them. (Ps. 115:4–8 NRSV)[10]

The most scathing parodies occur in the Prophets, and among these, the most direct are found in Isaiah. The prophet lays the foundation of his mockery in 40:19–20, expands on it in 41:5–7, and fully develops his taunt in 44:9–20.[11] The only appropriate way to handle idols was to demolish them, grind them to dust, and scatter the remains over flowing brooks or graves.[12]

The disposition of the First Testament toward idolatry continues in the New. In classical Greek the expression *eidōlon* was used of both physical images and phantoms, shadows of the reality. This usage carries over into the New Testament.[13] Romans 1:23 uses the concrete term "icon" (*eikōn*), but elsewhere Paul refers to idols as "so-called gods" (*legomenoi theoi*, 1 Cor. 8:5) or "beings that by nature are no gods at all" (Gal. 4:8). The New Testament links all kinds of moral and social evils with idolatry.[14] In Romans 1:18–23 Paul links idolatry to thankless hearts and foolish minds and views it as the height of folly; instead of gaining the favor of the Deity, idolatry results in rejection. In Acts 17:16–31 Paul presents the New Testament's most fully developed portrayal of idolatry. The altar he saw in Athens dedicated "To an unknown God" symbolized both the tragic ignorance of idolaters and the futility of their worship. By contrast, he introduced the Athenians to the true God, who needs no human care, gives life to all living things, is the source

10. See also Deut. 4:25–31; Ps. 135:15–18; cf. Job 31:24–28.

11. See also Hosea 8:4–6; 13:2–3; Mic. 5:12–13; Hab. 2:18–19; Jer. 10:1–6.

12. See 2 Kings 23:4–20 (cf. 2 Chron. 34:33); also cf. Exod. 32:15–20; Num. 25:1–9; Judg. 6:25–27; 2 Kings 10:18–28; 18:1–5 (cf. 2 Chron. 31:1). In Deut. 13 Moses prescribed the death penalty by stoning for any who would lead others to worship any god other than YHWH.

13. In designations for idols (Acts 15:20; cf. 15:29 and 21:25, *eidōlothytos*, "offered to idols," as also in 1 Cor. 8:4, 7; 10:19; cf. *eidōlon*, "idol," in 2 Cor. 6:16; 1 Thess. 1:9; 1 John 5:21), anyone who practices idolatry is an "idolater" (*eidōlatrēs*, 1 Cor. 5:10–11; 6:9; 10:7; Eph. 5:5; Rev. 21:8; 22:15), engaging in "idolatry" (*eidōlatria*, 1 Cor. 10:14; Gal. 5:20; Col. 3:5; 1 Pet. 4:3). Acts 17:16 describes Athens as full of idols (*kateidōlos*).

14. See 1 Cor. 5:9–13; Gal. 5:20; Col. 3:5; 1 Pet. 4:1–5.

and director of human history, lets himself be found by those who seek him, and will ultimately judge the world through Jesus Christ.[15]

The problem of idolatry and the plight of idolaters are illustrated dramatically in a prayer discovered in the ruins of Ashurbanipal's library in Nineveh, dating to 668–633 BC.

Prayer to Every God

May the fury of my lord's heart be quieted toward me.
May the god who is not known be quieted toward me;
May the goddess who is not known be quieted toward me.
May the god whom I know or do not know be quieted toward me;
May the goddess whom I know or do not know be quieted toward me.
May the heart of my god be quieted toward me;
May the heart of my goddess be quieted toward me;
May my god and goddess be quieted toward me.
May the god [who has become angry with me] be quieted toward me;
May the goddess [who has become angry with me] be quieted toward me.

(My) transgressions are many; great are (my) sins.
The transgression which I have committed, indeed I do not know;
The sin which I have done, indeed I do not know.
The forbidden thing which I have eaten, indeed I do not know;
The prohibited (place) on which I have set foot, indeed I do not know.
The lord in the anger of his heart looked at me;
The god in the rage of his heart confronted me;
When the goddess was angry with me, she made me become ill.
The god whom I know or do not know has oppressed me;
The goddess whom I know or do not know has placed suffering upon me.
Although I am constantly looking for help, no one takes me by the
    hand;
When I weep they do not come to my side.
I utter laments, but no one hears me;
I am troubled; I am overwhelmed; I cannot see.
O my god, merciful one, I address to you the prayer,
"Ever incline to me";
I kiss the feet of my goddess; I crawl before you.

How long, O my goddess, whom I know or do not know,
ere your hostile heart will be quieted?
Man is dumb; he knows nothing;

15. For additional polemical attacks on idolatry, see 1 Cor. 6:9–11; 8:1–13; 2 Cor. 6:14–18; Gal. 5:16–21; Col. 3:5–7; Rev. 21:6–8; 22:15.

Mankind, everyone that exists,—what does he know?
Whether he is committing sin or doing good, he does not even know.
O my lord, do not cast your servant down;
He is plunged into the waters of a swamp; take him by the hand.
The sin which I have done, turn into goodness;
The transgression which I have committed, let the wind carry away;
My many misdeeds strip off like a garment.
O my god, (my) transgressions are seven times seven;
remove my transgressions;

Remove my transgressions (and) I will sing your praise.
May your heart, like the heart of a real mother, be quieted toward me;
Like a real mother (and) a real father may it be quieted toward me.[16]

This piece gives the modern reader a remarkable window into the religious psyche of the ancients. The worshiper expresses certainty of three facts: the gods are angry with him, his sin has caused this anger, and he must do something to placate their wrath. But his ignorance is also threefold: he does not know which god is angry, he does not know what crime has provoked the god's fury, and he does not know what it will take to placate the god's wrath.

Into this dark world, the revelation of the true God shines like a beacon of glory and grace. Israel's God has introduced himself by name; Israel's God has revealed himself in word and deed; Israel's God has declared the boundaries of acceptable and unacceptable conduct; Israel's God has provided a way of forgiveness that actually solves the human problem. No wonder the psalmists could celebrate with such joy the life to be found in the Torah (Ps. 119).

YHWH: The Object of Israel's Worship

Who is this God we encounter in the Bible? We will address this question by looking first at the God who invites worship in the First Testament and then at the God who invites worship in the New Testament.

The Titles and Name of the God of Israel

Like the gods of other peoples, the God of Israel is identified by a series of epithets: (1) Elohim (ʾĕlōhîm), the generic designation for deity;[17] (2) El

16. Adapted from J. B. Pritchard, ed., *Ancient Near Eastern Texts Relating to the Old Testament*, 3rd ed. (Princeton: Princeton University Press, 1969), 391–92.
17. It occurs 2,570 times. Elohim is the plural of majesty for Eloah (57×, most frequently in Job and other poetic writings—e.g., Deut. 32:15, 17; Pss. 50:22; 139:19; Prov. 30:5; Isa. 44:8; Hab. 1:11; Neh. 9:17; cf. 2 Chron. 32:15; Dan. 11:37–39) and Aramaic Elah (100×).

(*'ēl*), the name of the high God in the Canaanite pantheon but also claimed by YHWH;[18] (3) Shadday (*šadday*), usually rendered "Almighty,"[19] but probably alluding to his role as the One who presides over the heavenly court on the mountain of God;[20] (4) "Most High" (*'elyôn*), from a root meaning "to be high";[21] (5) "Lord, Master" (*'ădōnāy*), emphasizing his power over all the earth;[22] (6) "Master, owner" (*ba'al*), as in the personal name Bealyah, "YHWH is Baal" (1 Chron. 12:5 [6]);[23] (7) "King" (*melek*), who reigns over the heavenly hosts,[24] Israel,[25] and the nations (Jer. 10:7);[26] (8) "Father" (*'āb*), as in the personal name Abijah, "YHWH is [my] Father" (1 Sam. 8:2); (9) "Mighty One" (*'ăbîr*);[27] and (10) "Fear" (*paḥad*) (Gen. 31:42, 53).

The God of Israel shares some of these epithets with other gods; others he usurps since he alone is worthy of the title. But what is most remarkable is that the God of Israel introduces himself by name, YHWH (Exod. 3:15).

18. See Gen. 33:20, "El the God of Israel"; 46:3, "El the God of your father." This name occurs alone most frequently in Job (55×) and other poetic texts (Isa. 14:4–20; Ezek. 28:2). But it also appears often in association with other expressions: El-Elyon, "God Most High" (Gen. 14:22); El-Olam, "God of Eternity" (Gen. 21:33); El-Shaddai, "God of the Heavenly Courtiers" (Gen. 17:1; 28:3; 35:11; 43:14; 48:3; Exod. 6:3; Ezek. 10:5); El-Roi, "God who sees me" (Gen. 16:13); El-Qannâ, "God of Passion" (Exod. 20:5; Deut. 4:24; 5:9; 6:15; cf. Exod. 34:14, YHWH Qannâ); cf. the pagan El-berith/Baal-berith in Judg. 9:46).

19. From Greek *pantocrator*, "All-powerful, Omnipotent One" (cf. 2 Cor. 6:18).

20. Appearing forty-eight times, alone forty-one times; see Gen. 49:25; Num. 24:4, 16; Ruth 1:20, 21; Pss. 68:14 [15]; 91:1; Isa. 13:6; Ezek. 1:24; thirty-one times in Job. The term has been associated with Hebrew *šādayim*, "breasts" (hence, "the God who nurtures, nourishes, blesses"), and Akkadian *šadu*, "mountain." The best clue comes from ninth- to eighth-century-BC Aramaic texts from Deir 'Allā in Jordan, where the plural *šdyn* (//'lhyn) refers to members of the heavenly court, divine beings who intercede before El on behalf of the people of Sukkoth.

21. The name *'elyôn* appears alone in Ps. 9:2 [3]; Isa. 14:14; in combination with other names in Pss. 7:17 [18]; 57:2 [3]; 73:11; cf. "Sons of Elyon" in Ps. 82:6; "saints of Elyon" in Dan. 7:18, 22, 25, 27. Abbreviated forms of the name appear in Hosea 11:7 and perhaps in 1 Sam. 2:10.

22. Used 450 times, of which about 350 apply to God. See Josh. 3:13; Pss. 97:5; 114:7; Isa. 10:33; Mic. 4:13; Zech. 4:14; 6:5; of his authority over all people, Exod. 34:23–24; Isa. 1:24; 3:1; 19:4. The title is often used of others; cf. Deut. 10:17: "YHWH your God is the God of gods and Lord of lords"; and Pss. 135:5; 136:2–3.

23. The name Eshbaal, "Man of Baal" (1 Chron. 8:33; 9:39) may identify YHWH with Baal, though the rendering of the name as Ishbosheth ("Man of Shame") by the earlier historian (2 Sam. 2–4) suggests it reflects Saul's religious syncretism: cf. Jer. 3:24; 11:13; Hosea 9:10. In the Prophets the designations YHWH and Baal are incompatible (1 Kings 18; Hosea 2:16 [18]).

24. See Isa. 6:5; Jer. 46:18; 48:15; 51:57.

25. See Num. 23:21; Deut. 33:5; 1 Sam. 8:7; 12:12; Isa. 33:22; 41:21; 43:15; 44:6; Zeph. 3:15; cf. Pss. 98:6; 145:1.

26. And related epithets: "Eternal King," Jer. 10:10; "Glorious King," Ps. 24:7–10; "Great King," Pss. 47:2 [3]; 95:3; Mal. 1:14; "King YHWH," Zech. 14:16–17. For other references to YHWH as "king," see Num. 23:21; Deut. 33:5; Jer. 8:19; Mic. 2:13; Zech. 14:9; Pss. 5:3; 29:10; 44:5; 47:7; 48:3; 68:24 [25]; 74:12; 84:3 [4]; 149:2.

27. See "Mighty One of Jacob" in Gen. 49:24; Ps. 132:2, 5; Isa. 49:26; 60:16. Elsewhere the word is used of extraordinary human or animal strength (Judg. 5:22; Ps. 76:5).

Rightly understood, this is the only name he bears; all the designations listed above are epithets and titles that people ascribe to God, but this is the name he claims for himself. Whatever its etymology and dictionary definition,[28] YHWH reveals the significance of his name in the exodus. The name YHWH identifies the God who declares by action, "I will be there—to deliver you," "I will be there—to reveal myself to you," "I will be there—to care for you," "I will be there—to fulfill my promises to the Fathers," and "I will be there—to take you as my covenant people" (Exod. 6:3; 19:4–6).

In English translations, the personal name of God is rendered as LORD, and the consistent rendering in the LXX is Greek *kyrios*.[29] Partly because the Decalogue prohibits bearing the name of God in vain,[30] by the time the Septuagint was being translated in the third century BC, Jews had developed such fear of mispronouncing God's name that they stopped saying it out loud.[31] To guard against this, in oral reading they substituted *YHWH* with euphemisms, like *ha-Shem* ("the Name") or *Adonai* ('*ădōnāy*, "lord"), which explains why the translators of the LXX consistently rendered it as *kyrios* (= "lord").[32] This practice carried over into New Testament citations of First Testament

28. The Tetragrammaton, YHWH, is a third-person imperfect form, perhaps meaning "He will be" or "He will cause to be" (if understood as a *pi'el*; Exod. 3:15), though he introduces himself in Exod. 3:14 with the first person, *'ehyeh*, "I will be." Presumably the third-person form became conventional because it was deemed inappropriate for a person to refer to God as Ehyeh, "I will be"—until Jesus claims the first-person name, as in John 18:4–8. The fact that the name is used especially in personal and covenantal contexts renders unlikely the interpretation "the self-existent one," which would be more at home in Greek metaphysical thought than in the real world of the First Testament, where YHWH is known through his interaction with his creation, whether human or more broadly.

29. Because the vocalization of the name is uncertain, I reproduce only the consonants as written in the Hebrew. The traditional pronunciation found in KJV, "Jehovah" (Gen. 22:14; Exod. 6:3; 17:15; Judg. 6:24; Ps. 83:18; Isa. 12:2; 26:4), and ironically common in contemporary music, is certainly wrong. This is an artificial construct created by combining the consonants of *yhwh* with the vowels of *'ădōnāy*.

30. To them, "You shall not take the name of YHWH in vain" supposedly meant "You shall not mispronounce it" or "You shall not pronounce it in a wrong context (outside the temple)." See the Mishnah, [*m.*] *Tamid* 7.2, "In the sanctuary one says the Name as it is written, but in the provinces, with a euphemism." See also Josephus, *Jewish Antiquities* 2.12.4; among the Dead Sea Scrolls, *Community Rule* [1QS] 6.27b–7.2a; *m. Soṭah* 7.6; *m. Tamid* 7.2; *m. Sanhedrin* 10.1; *m. Berakot* 9.5; in the Babylonian Talmud, [*b.*] *Pesaḥim* 50a; *b. Soṭah* 38b. Whoever violates this command would be cursed by God. Cf. L. F. Hartman and S. D. Sperling, "God, Names of," in *Encyclopaedia Judaica*, ed. F. Skolnik, 2nd ed. (Farmington Hills, MI: Thomson Gale, 2007), 7:675.

31. Cf. Lev. 24:16: Hebrew *wĕnōqēb šēm-yhwh môt yûmāt*, translated by *TANAKH* as "If he also pronounces the name LORD, he shall be put to death."

32. However, some early manuscripts of LXX render the name with the Tetragrammaton in archaic script or as Greek IAΩ (*IAŌ*). See Martin Rösel, "Names of God," in *Encyclopedia of the Dead Sea Scrolls*, ed. L. H. Schiffman and J. C. VanderKam (Oxford: Oxford University Press, 2000), 2:600–602.

texts involving the divine name[33] and into English translations of the name as "LORD." However, it is clear from theophoric names (names that include some portion of a divine name; e.g., Jerem*iah*, *Jeho*shaphat) in the Hebrew Bible and from the Lachish letters that the name was regularly pronounced with its vowels until after the fall of Jerusalem in 586 BC.[34]

While Christians debate whether the name should be pronounced in private or corporate worship,[35] it seems tragic that its pronunciation has been lost. In a remarkable act of condescension, YHWH introduced himself by name (Exod. 3:15; 34:6–7), thereby highlighting the personal nature of covenant relationship and inviting his people to address him not merely as a heavenly official but as their personal God.

The Nature of the God of Israel

The God of Israel was worthy of Israel's worship for many reasons. Since he is the Creator of all things, he alone deserves worship. This theme is celebrated in Genesis 1:1–2:4a, a catechetical composition written in praise of God (Elohim), Creator of the universe; also in narrative prose (2:4b–25); and in blessings (14:19). Melchizedek blessed Abraham in the name of El Elyon, Creator of Heaven and Earth, but this role was also a favorite theme of psalmists,[36] sages,[37] and prophets.[38] Isaiah's hymns of praise to God as Creator are driven by a pastoral passion to reassure Israel that the one who chose Israel is the Creator of all. Although Israel was in exile, God had not abdicated his throne or been deposed. He exercised sovereignty over the nations, proved

33. Though often unsignaled in English translations of New Testament citations of First Testament texts: e.g., Rom. 10:13, "Everyone who calls on the name of YHWH shall be saved" (cf. NRSV).

34. Note all the names ending in *-iah* (presumably from the first part of the name *Yahweh*) in Nehemiah 10–12. Scholars conventionally insert *e* as the vowel between *w* and *h*, hence *Yahweh*. To this day orthodox Jews refer to YHWH with *ha-Shem* (*ha-Šem*) or "the Ineffable Name." Joel M. Hoffman (*In the Beginning: A Short History of the Hebrew Language* [New York: New York University Press, 2004], 44–47) argues that the Tetragrammaton was never pronounced; the combination of magical letters had symbolic power.

35. Note the directive from the Vatican in the letter concerning divine worship and the sacraments, *Liturgiam Authenticam*, "On the Use of Vernacular Languages in the Publication of the Books of the Roman Liturgy," dated May 7, 2001: "In accordance with immemorial tradition, which indeed is already evident in the above-mentioned 'Septuagint' version, the name of almighty God expressed by the Hebrew Tetragrammaton (YHWH) and rendered in Latin by the word *Dominus*, is to be rendered into any given vernacular by a word equivalent in meaning."

36. See Pss. 8; 19:1–6; 29; 33; 104; 115; 135; 136:1–9; 139; 148.

37. See Job 6:24–41:34; Prov. 8:1–31; Eccles. 12:1–7.

38. See Isa. 40:12–31; 45:1–13; 48:1–19; 65:17–25; 66:1–2; cf. Jer. 10:12–16; 51:15–23; Amos 5:8–9.

the other gods to be nothing, remained true to his promises, and would bring Israel back to Zion.

The Scriptures open with a picture of cosmic covenant-like relationship, with humans assigned a special role to care for the world and ensure that the covenant relationship functions smoothly, that all creation might declare the glory of God.[39] Within this relationship human beings worship God most faithfully by caring for his world (fig. 2.2).

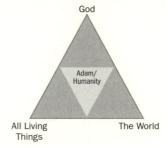

FIGURE 2.2
The Cosmic Administrative Order

Although humankind failed miserably, in his mercy God called Abraham to bring blessing to a world under the curse because of human rebellion. God formalized Abraham's role by establishing a covenant relationship with him, promising him and his descendants the land of Canaan (Gen. 15:18–21) and promising to be his God and the God of his descendants (17:1–8).[40] YHWH was especially worthy of worship because of the favor he showed his people: (1) as Israel's Savior, he redeemed them from bondage in Egypt;[41] (2) as Israel's divine Patron, he protected his people, cared for them, and provided them a secure homeland (Deut. 1:31; 8:2–4, 15–16; 26:1–15); (3) as Israel's Suzerain, he called them to covenant relationship with himself (Exod. 19:4–6); (4) as Israel's Friend, he revealed himself and his will to them (Deut. 4:5–8); and (5) as Israel's Judge, he threatened judgment for infidelity, but also promised ultimate restoration.[42]

But YHWH did not call Israel to himself primarily for Israel's sake. He redeemed the descendants of Abraham and established his covenant with

39. See Gen. 1:26–28; 2:15; Ps. 8.

40. "I will be your God" is the first part of the covenant formula "I will be your God, and you shall be my people." Echoes of God's promises to and covenant with Abraham punctuate the patriarchal narratives. See Gen. 12:1–3; 15:1–21; 17:1–8; 21:12; 22:14–19; 24:7, 27; 26:2–5, 24–25; 28:10–17; 35:9–13; 48:14–20; cf. Deut. 1:8; 4:36–37; 7:6–9; 30:20.

41. See, e.g., Exod. 2:22–24; 3:6–10, 13–17; 6:2–9. Note also Deut. 4:32–37. Hebrew 'āhab, usually rendered "to love," means "to be covenantally committed to someone so that one always acts in the interests of that person."

42. See, e.g., Lev. 26:40–45; Deut. 4:30–33; 30:1–7; cf. Ps. 105; Mic. 7:9–10.

them so that they might bear his name and that through them he might bless the world (Gen. 12:3). Deuteronomy 26:19 summarizes their mission as being his holy kingdom of priests: "He will set you high above all the nations he has made for [his] praise, fame, and honor, and so that you will be a people holy to YHWH your God, as he promised" (cf. Exod. 19:4–6). Surely for this grace he was worthy of worship.

However, YHWH was worthy of worship for another grace: his friendship with Israel demonstrated in the revelation of his will (cf. John 14–15). We must highlight this aspect because of the pervasively negative views of the First Testament in evangelical churches—views that raise serious doubts about whether the God of Israel deserved worship. To many Christians, the First and New Testaments paint drastically contrasting pictures of God. They delight in the God of grace and love they find in the New Testament, but like Marcion, a second-century heretic, they reject the wrathful and violent God of Israel (fig. 2.3).

FIGURE 2.3
Contrasting Biblical Images of God as Popularly Perceived

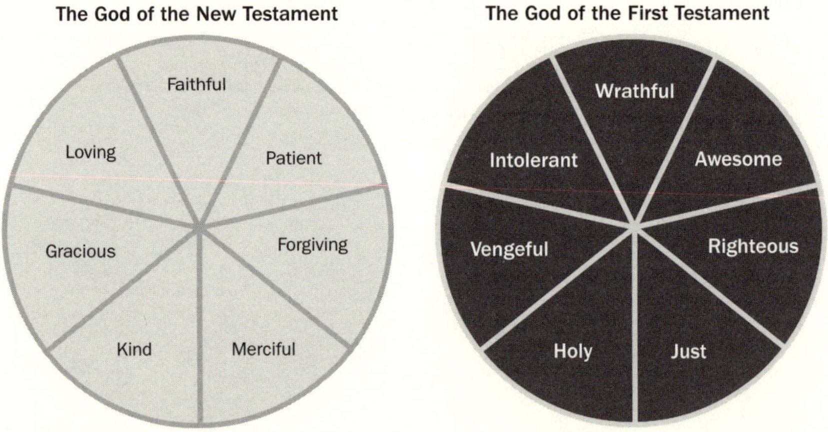

The God of the New Testament

The God of the First Testament

The God of the New Testament: Faithful, Loving, Patient, Gracious, Forgiving, Kind, Merciful

The God of the First Testament: Wrathful, Intolerant, Awesome, Vengeful, Righteous, Holy, Just

But is this the way the Hebrew Scriptures portray God? To answer this question, we should let God speak for himself. In response to Moses' request for a vision of his glory, YHWH appeared and declared,

> YHWH, YHWH, merciful [raḥûm] and gracious [ḥannûn] El, slow to anger ['erek 'appayim], and abounding in unfailing love [ḥesed] and faithfulness ['ĕmet], who keeps unfailing love [ḥesed] for thousands, forgiving iniquity and transgression and sin, but who will by no means clear the guilty, punishing children and children's children for the sins of the fathers to the third and the fourth generation. (Exod. 34:6–7)

This image (fig. 2.4) differs radically from the common stereotype. Indeed, of the seven characteristics listed, only one matches what many expect. The resemblance of YHWH as he defines himself to "the New Testament God" is striking, as is Moses' response: "Moses immediately bowed his head [*qādad*] toward the earth, and prostrated himself [*hištaḥăwâ*]" (Exod. 34:8). Echoes of this self-description reverberate throughout the First Testament, proving this to be the normative view of YHWH.[43]

FIGURE 2.4

The Image of God as Presented in Exodus 34:6–7

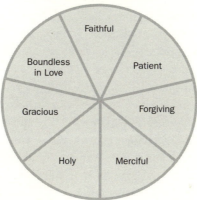

This understanding of YHWH spills over into the New Testament. Decades after Jesus' ascension, John reflected on the significance of the incarnation: "The Word became flesh and lived among us, and we have seen his glory, the glory as of a father's only son, *full of grace and truth*" (John 1:14). Here "glory" (*doxa*) recalls Moses' request in Exodus 33, and Greek *charis* and *alētheia*, "grace" and "truth," are shorthand for Exodus 34:6–7 as a whole. Jesus is YHWH, the God of Israel who had revealed himself to Moses.

Reflections on Two Worship Texts in the First Testament

Two profound worship texts from the First Testament concretize these observations on YHWH as the object of worship: Exodus 19–20 and Psalm 95.

Israel's Audience with God at Sinai (Exodus 19–24). Exodus 19–20 presents the most impressive corporate earthly worship event in all of Scripture.[44] For

---

43. We hear the most dramatic echo of Exod. 34:6–7 in Jon. 4:2, but see also Gen. 6:8; Num. 14:18; Neh. 9:17; Pss. 51:1; 86:5, 15; 103:8; 108:4; 145:8; Joel 2:13; Mic. 7:18–20.

44. The corporate worship scenes in Revelation are all located in heaven.

several months the Israelites had been on the march, headed for the promised land. But instead of traveling northeast, toward the land of Canaan, YHWH led them south, deep into the Sinai Peninsula. Finally they arrived in the desert of Sinai, where they camped before the mountain of God (18:5; 19:2). YHWH had predicted this event in 3:12, when he told Moses that his arrival back at this mountain would prove that God had sent him. But this moment would also mark the formal establishment of the Israelites as the vassals of YHWH.[45] This was Israel's appointment with the God who had revealed himself to Moses.

Chapters 19–24 describe a most remarkable event: YHWH not only revealed himself to his people in blazing glory, but he also graciously entered into covenant relationship with them. The event climaxes in chapter 24, when Moses, Aaron, Nadab, Abihu, and seventy representatives of the people celebrated the new relationship with a banquet in the presence of God (24:9–11). What a moment that was! Eating in the presence of God, yet he did not stretch out his hand against them. This narrative provides a remarkable picture of the God who would claim Israel's exclusive worship, and who now claims ours.

First of all, this narrative shows that the God who calls Israel to worship is YHWH, who faithfully keeps his covenant. Sinai represents the high point of the Pentateuchal plot (fig. 2.5) and the fulfillment of YHWH's promise to Abraham in Genesis 17:7: "I will establish [hēqîm] my covenant between me and you, and your descendants after you throughout their generations, as an everlasting covenant, to be your God and the God of your descendants after you."

Second, the God who calls Israel to worship him is their gracious redeemer. YHWH summarizes the brief history of Israel's relationship with himself in Exodus 19:4: "You saw what I did to the Egyptians, and how I carried you on eagles' wings and brought you to myself." If it were not for his saving and sustaining acts, the Israelites would have remained in Egypt, making bricks without straw.

Third, the God who calls Israel to worship him calls them primarily to a relationship with himself rather than to a code of conduct. YHWH's statement at the end of verse 4 is profound: "I brought you to myself." Herein lies the key to the significance of Sinai in the history of Israel and in biblical traditions: this was the mountain of God,[46] where the divine King invited his chosen people into his presence.

---

45. Note the frequent references to serving (‘ābad) God on this mountain in the preceding narratives: Exod. 3:12; 4:23; 7:16; 8:1 [7:26]; 8:20 [16]; 9:1, 13; 10:3, 7, 8, 11, 24, 26; 12:31.

46. As in Exod. 3:1; 4:27; 18:5; 24:13.

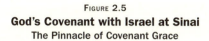

FIGURE 2.5
God's Covenant with Israel at Sinai
The Pinnacle of Covenant Grace

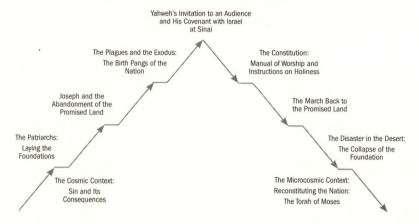

Fourth, the God who calls Israel to worship him also calls them to obedience. With privilege comes responsibility. In this unequal relationship, YHWH appeals to his vassals to listen to his voice and to keep his covenant (Exod. 19:5). We should interpret this not as the imposition of an impossible burden but as an announcement of the appropriate response to his grace. Such a covenant between a divinity and a human population was unprecedented in the ancient world. The God who had called Israel to himself also determined the boundaries of covenant righteousness and graciously revealed them to his people.

Fifth, the God who calls Israel to worship him assigns to them the mission of representing him to the world. Israel's privileged status is summarized in three expressions: they are YHWH's treasured people (*'am sĕgullâ*), his royal priesthood (*mamleket kōhănîm*), and his holy nation (*gôy qādôš*, 19:5–6). The ceremonies that followed in chapters 19–24 bound Israel to YHWH in covenant relationship and in so doing also inducted them into the priesthood.[47] YHWH chose the descendants of Abraham not for their own sakes but for the sake of all people. As Abraham was called to be a blessing to the world,[48] so they were to be bearers of the light of his grace to a world languishing under the curse of sin.

47. See J. A. Davies, *A Royal Priesthood: Literary and Intertextual Perspectives on an Image of Israel in Exodus 19.6*, Journal for the Study of the Old Testament: Supplement Series 395 (New York: Continuum, 2004). For a summary statement, see J. A. Davies, "A Royal Priesthood: Literary and Intertextual Perspectives on and Image of Israel in Exodus 19:6," *Tyndale Bulletin* 53, no. 1 (2002): 157–59.

48. See Gen. 12:3; 18:18; 22:18; 26:4; 28:14.

Sixth, the God who calls Israel to worship him reveals to them his indescribable glory and holiness. Following three days of purification rituals, Moses brings the people up to the foot of the mountain. As YHWH descends on the mountain, the entire earth seems to come alive: thunder roars, lightning flashes, a dense cloud settles over the mountain, a fire ascends heavenward from the mountain, and the ground beneath them quakes. At the climactic moment, the sound of a trumpet signals the arrival of the King and invites the people to move in closer for their meeting with God.[49] Standing in awe at the foot of the mountain, they await the emergence of the King from his heavenly throne room. When the Creator of the cosmos appears on terra firma, the site shakes and lights up.

Seventh, the God who calls Israel to worship him speaks to his people. YHWH is a communicating God! The narrator presents this encounter as Israel's audience with their divine Redeemer. Having witnessed the glory of the great King with their eyes, they also hear his voice with their ears (19:19). Unlike the gods of the nations, which have mouths but do not speak (Pss. 115:1–8; 135:15–18), Israel's God has no mouth and yet speaks audibly, in "the language of Canaan" (Isa. 19:18), the adopted language of an otherwise insignificant band of slaves whom he has freed. The experience is unprecedented (Deut. 4:32–36) and terrifying (Exod. 20:18–21; cf. Deut. 5:23–27), but Moses reassures the Israelites that, while those in covenant relationship with YHWH must be awed by his glory, they need not be afraid. As a sign and seal of his acceptance, YHWH invites the elders of the people to eat the fellowship covenant meal in his presence (Exod. 24:9–11).

A Hymnic Invitation to an Audience with God (Psalm 95). Scholars often refer to psalms like Psalm 95 as "Enthronement Psalms" or "Divine Kingship" psalms because they celebrate the kingship of YHWH.[50] The element common to all is an enthusiastic acclamation of YHWH as King over the nations and the earth. Unlike Psalms 96–99, which call on the nations to join in the celebration of YHWH's kingship, Psalm 95 represents an impassioned plea to Israel, the community of faith, for true and authentic worship. The psalm can be divided into three parts, each contributing directly to the development of this theme.

49. The purpose of the event is conveyed in the expression *liqrā't hā'ĕlōhîm*, "to meet God" (Exod. 19:17).

50. See also Pss. 47:2; 93:1; 95:3; 96:10; 97:1; 98:6; 99:1. Psalm 100 lacks the formal declaration "YHWH is king!" or "YHWH reigns!" yet clearly continues this theme of the nations shouting joyfully to YHWH as they enter his presence and echoes the language of Ps. 95.

I. The call to true and authentic worship (vv. 1–5)

II. The nature of true and authentic worship (vv. 6–7b)

III. The evidence of true and authentic worship (vv. 7c–11)

Striking shifts in mood mark the transitions from one section to another. In verses 1–5 the psalmist calls on devotees of YHWH to sing for joy, to approach him with thanksgiving, and to shout joyfully to him with psalms of praise.[51] However, in verses 6–7b the mood changes dramatically. The excitement and enthusiasm of verses 1–2 are replaced by a controlled and measured appeal to worship YHWH. In verses 7c–11 the tone becomes somber as the psalmist warns his people to heed the voice of God. Two vital questions face us in this context: Who is this God who invites Israel to worship? And why is he worthy of their worship? The psalmist answers the questions in three dimensions.

YHWH is worthy of worship because he is supreme among the gods. The psalmist's logic is striking. After calling his fellow Israelites to come and sing for joy to YHWH, in verses 3–5 he describes why this is such an awesome privilege. He declares YHWH's supremacy among the gods first by identifying him as *'ēl gādôl*, "the Great El." As noted earlier, "El" may function generically as an epithet meaning "God," but it is often used as a title for YHWH.[52] From hundreds of clay tablets discovered at Ras Shamra (Ugarit) in northern Syria, we know that El was the highest god of the Canaanite pantheon (fig. 2.6). He was known as the "Father of Years," creator of all things, Bull El, husband of Asherah, and father of all the other gods. However, here the psalmist declares, "YHWH is the great El." No other god is worthy of this title.[53] In fact, YHWH is worthy of worship because he is "a great King, above all gods."[54]

YHWH is worthy of worship because he is sovereign over the cosmos. In verses 4–5 the psalmist declares that YHWH owns the universe: he holds the world in his hand, he owns the mountaintops, and he is the Creator of everything that exists. That is why he is worthy of worship. This is what David celebrates in 1 Chronicles 29:11–13:

> Yours, O YHWH, is the greatness and the power and the glory and the victory and the majesty, for all that is in the heavens and in the earth is yours. Yours is the

51. Based on our study in the previous chapter, technically the worship does not begin until v. 6. In 95:1–5 the psalmist invites us to join in celebration in anticipation of worship—because YHWH has invited us to an audience with himself. In v. 6 we finally encounter words for worship: to prostrate oneself before God (*hištaḥăwâ*); to bend the knee (*kāraʿ*, cf. 1 Kings 19:18); to kneel down (*bārak*, cf. 2 Chron. 6:13, *bārak ʿal-birkāyw*).

52. Often in combination with another expression. See n. 18 above.

53. See Deut. 10:17; Neh. 9:32; Jer. 32:18; Dan. 9:4.

54. We hear echoes of this expression in several psalms that follow: Pss. 96:4–5; 97:9; 135:5–10.

kingdom, O YHWH, and you are exalted as head above all. Both riches and honor come from you, and you rule over all. In your hand are power and might, and you have the power to make great and to give strength to all. And now we thank you, our God, and praise your glorious name.

YHWH is worthy of worship because he has graciously established a special relationship with his people. For all the psalmist's enthusiasm over YHWH's cosmic right to worship, YHWH's special relationship with his people excites him most. Reflecting the experiences of the exodus from Egypt and the meeting at Sinai, the psalmist rejoices in YHWH, the rock of Israel's salvation (Ps. 95:1),[55] and in the fact that "He is our God" (v. 7).[56] Using a familiar pastoral metaphor, the psalmist describes YHWH's relationship with Israel as that of a shepherd and his sheep. The reference to "people of his pasture" in verse 7 and in Psalm 100:3 alludes to YHWH's provision of a homeland for Israel. Although YHWH gave them the land of Canaan as a special grant where they could prosper, this is YHWH's pasture: he owns the land. The characterization of Israel as the sheep of his hand shows the other side of a coin illustrated by Psalm 23:4: Israel's divine shepherd walks with his people through darkest valleys and ensures their security with his staff. This is the God whom the Israelites worshiped: a God who is supreme over all, but who delights in fellowship with his people.

Figure 2.6. An image of El in the Israel Museum (Photograph by J. Marr Miller. Used with permission.)

God the Father and God the Son: The Objects of Christian Worship

The doxologies, prayers, and hymns of the New Testament provide a window into how first-generation believers answered the question, who is the object of true Christian worship?[57] We should not be surprised if God (*ho theos*) is

55. This curious expression appears elsewhere only in Ps. 89:26 [27] (= 2 Sam. 22:47) but seems to have been inspired by Israel's national anthem (Deut. 32:3–4, 15). The "Maker" label describes YHWH's act of salvation (Ps. 95:6; cf. Ps. 100:1–3).

56. This combination of saving and covenantal acts accords perfectly with the goal of the exodus declared in Lev. 22:32b–33; 26:45; Num. 15:41.

57. English "doxology" derives from the Greek word *doxa*, "praise, honor, glory," + *logos*, "word, utterance," hence *doxologia*, "word of praise." Doxologies typically begin with "Blessed be . . ." (Hebrew *bārûk*; Greek *eulogētos*), followed by a title or name for God and then some

regularly the object of verbs of glorification and praise.[58] Zechariah was still in the world of the First Testament when at the birth of John the Baptist he declared, "Blessed be the Lord God of Israel [*kyrios ho theos tou Israel*], for he has visited and redeemed his people" (Luke 1:68). Here *kyrios* obviously represents YHWH. However, the New Testament increasingly identifies God as the Father of Jesus Christ. In 2 Corinthians 1:3 Paul declares, "Blessed be the God and Father of our Lord Jesus Christ, the Father of mercies and God of all comfort" (ESV). Here the object of worship is the First Person of the Trinity, the Father of "our Lord [*kyrios*] Jesus Messiah" (Greek *christos*). Ephesians 1:3 is similar: "Blessed be the God and Father of our Lord Jesus Christ, who has blessed us in Christ with every spiritual blessing in the heavenly places." Paul then explains how God's gracious work is accomplished entirely through Jesus Christ (vv. 4–13).[59]

In the doxologies we also observe a shift from praising God the Father to explicit praise of the Son, Jesus Christ. Whereas the people's acclamation at Jesus' triumphal entry into Jerusalem acknowledged him as the Davidic Messiah and King of Israel who comes in the name of the Lord (*kyrios* = YHWH; Matt. 21:9; John 12:13), several benedictory declarations recognize Jesus as worthy of worship, equal to the Father.

> Now may the God of peace who brought again from the dead our Lord Jesus, the great shepherd of the sheep, by the blood of the eternal covenant, equip you with everything good that you may do his will, working in us that which is pleasing in his sight, through Jesus Christ, to whom be glory forever and ever. Amen. (Heb. 13:20–21 ESV)

> Now to him who is able to keep you from stumbling and to present you blameless before the presence of his glory with great joy, to the only God, our Savior, through Jesus Christ our Lord, be glory, majesty, dominion, and authority, before all time and now and forever. Amen. (Jude 24–25 ESV)

> To him who loves us and has freed us from our sins by his blood and made us a kingdom, priests to his God and Father, to him be glory and dominion forever and ever. Amen. (Rev. 1:5–6 ESV)

---

attribute or demonstration of an attribute that inspired the utterance. For First Testament examples, see Gen. 24:27; Exod. 18:10; 1 Chron. 16:36; Ruth 4:14.

58. Greek *aineō/ainos*, "to praise": e.g., Luke 2:20; 18:43; 19:37; Acts 2:47; 3:8–9; Rom. 15:11; *eulogeō/eulogētos/eulogia*: e.g., Luke 1:64; 2:28; 24:53; Rom. 9:5; Rev. 7:12; *doxazō/doxa*: e.g., Matt. 9:8 (= Mark 2:12; Luke 5:26); 15:31 (the "God of Israel"); Luke 2:14, 20; 17:15; John 9:24; Acts 4:21; 12:23; Rom. 1:21; 15:9; 1 Cor. 6:20; Phil. 1:11; Rev. 14:7; *charis/charitos*, Rom. 6:17; 7:25; 1 Cor. 15:57; 2 Cor. 2:14; 8:16. For additional texts, see appendix A.

59. Cf. Rom. 15:6; 2 Cor. 11:31; Gal. 1:5; Phil. 2:11; 1 Pet. 1:3.

> I charge you in the presence of God, who gives life to all things, and of Christ
> Jesus, who in his testimony before Pontius Pilate made the good confession,
> to keep the commandment unstained and free from reproach until the appear-
> ing of our Lord Jesus Christ, which he will display at the proper time—he
> who is the blessed and only Sovereign, the King of kings and Lord of lords,
> who alone has immortality, who dwells in unapproachable light, whom no
> one has ever seen or can see. To him be honor and eternal dominion. Amen.
> (1 Tim. 6:13–16 ESV)

> . . . in order that in everything God may be glorified through Jesus Christ. To
> him belong glory and dominion forever and ever. Amen. (1 Pet. 4:11 ESV; cf.
> 2 Pet. 3:18)

Some of these may be ambiguous, but the book of Revelation unequivocally
attributes legitimate worship to Jesus Christ. The living creatures, elders,
angels, and myriads of others around the throne declare with a loud voice:

> "Worthy is the Lamb who was slain, to receive power [*dynamis*] and wealth
> [*ploutos*] and wisdom [*sophia*] and might [*ischys*] and honor [*timē*] and glory
> [*doxa*] and blessing [*eulogia*]!" [And all the creatures in the universe chime in],
> "To him who sits on the throne and to the Lamb be blessing [*eulogia*] and honor
> [*timē*] and glory [*doxa*] and might [*kratos*] forever and ever!" (Rev. 5:11–13 ESV)

Recognition of Jesus Christ as a legitimate object of worship is not limited
to doxologies. When those who attended the crucifixion of Jesus experienced
the earthquake, they were filled with awe (*phobeō*), declaring, "Surely this
was God's Son!" (Matt. 27:54). As for gestures of worship, Jesus accepted
the worship of a formerly leprous Samaritan, who "fell on his face at his feet,
giving him thanks" (Luke 17:16), and of Mary Magdalene and another Mary
(Matt. 28:9) and the eleven disciples (28:17), who prostrated themselves before
him after his resurrection.[60]

Worship may also be expressed in prayer. Jesus invited prayer to himself:
"If you ask anything of me in my name, I will do it" (John 14:14). Equating
Jesus with YHWH, in Romans 10:13 Paul cites Joel 2:32: "Everyone who calls
on the name of the LORD will be saved." Not only does this quotation identify
Jesus explicitly as YHWH (Paul's *kyrios* = Joel's *yhwh*), but it also offers
salvation to all who call on Jesus (cf. Acts 22:16).[61] Paul admits to praying to

---

60. Note also the prostration and confession from the lips of the man possessed by demons
in Luke 8:28.

61. On this text, see further Daniel I. Block, "Who Do Commentators Say 'the Lord' Is?
The Scandalous Rock of Romans 10:13," in *On the Writing of New Testament Commentaries:*

Jesus, declaring in 2 Corinthians 12:8 that three times he had entreated the Lord for relief from his thorn in the flesh. The Lord responded with promises that his grace would more than compensate for this malady. In 1 Corinthians 16:22 Paul prays in Aramaic: *Marana tha*, "Our Lord, come!"[62] Stephen provides the most dramatic illustration of praying to Jesus: "As they were stoning Stephen, he called out, 'Lord Jesus, receive my spirit.' And falling to his knees he cried out with a loud voice, 'Lord, do not hold this sin against them'" (Act 7:59–60 ESV).

The New Testament not only declares Jesus to be God—as in Thomas's confession, "My Lord and my God!" (John 20:28)—but more specifically it equates him with YHWH. John the Baptizer understood Jesus' status when he explained his own role by citing Isaiah 40:3: "I am the voice of one crying out in the desert, 'Make straight the way of the Lord [*kyrios*, from LXX, which represents Hebrew *yhwh*]'" (Matt. 3:3).[63] In his beautiful "Hymn to Christ" (*Carmen Christi*), Paul declares that one day all will worship Jesus.

> Let the same mind be in you that was in Christ Jesus,
>
> who, though he was in the form of God,
> > did not regard equality with God as something to be exploited,
> but emptied himself,
> > taking the form of a slave,
> > being born in human likeness.
> And being found in human form,
> > he humbled himself
> > and became obedient to the point of death—
> > even death on a cross.
>
> Therefore God also highly exalted him
> > and gave him the name that is above every name,
> so that at the name of Jesus every knee should bend,
> > in heaven and on earth and under the earth,
> and every tongue should confess that Jesus Christ is Lord [*kyrios* = *yhwh*],
> > to the glory of God the Father. (Phil. 2:5–11 NRSV)

Festschrift for Grant R. Osborne on the Occasion of his 70th Birthday, ed. S. E. Porter and E. Schnabel, Texts and Editions for New Testament Study 8 (Leiden: Brill, 2012), 173–92.

62. A Greek version of this prayer appears in Rev. 22:20: "Come, Lord Jesus" (*erchou, kyrie iēsou*).

63. For detailed development of the "Jesus is YHWH" theme in the book of Mark, see Rikki E. Watts, *Isaiah's New Exodus in Mark* (Grand Rapids: Baker Academic, 2001).

Where in the New Testament Is Worship of the Holy Spirit?

The worship that the New Testament ascribes to Jesus contrasts sharply with the inattention given to the Holy Spirit, the Third Person of the Trinity. While many doxologies glorify God generally, without specifying a person within the Trinity, the focus is usually on God the Father and in some cases on Jesus Christ. Remarkably, the doxologies never ascribe praise, honor, glory, dominion, or power to the Holy Spirit. This reserve is consistent with the portrayal of the Spirit generally in the New Testament. No one addresses the Holy Spirit in prayer, or bows down to the Holy Spirit, or serves him in a liturgical gesture. Put simply, in the Bible the Spirit is never the object of worship. This interpretation is reinforced by Philippians 3:3, in which Paul disavows the circumcision practiced by his own people as false. In contrast, people who are of the true circumcision[64] worship (*latreuō*, "cultic service") *in* the Spirit of God and glory in Christ Jesus. The Spirit drives the worship of believers yet does not receive worship.[65] The closest anyone in the New Testament comes to addressing the Spirit occurs in Paul's familiar benediction in 2 Corinthians 13:14 [13]: "May the grace of the Lord Jesus Christ, and the love of God, and the fellowship of the Holy Spirit be with you all" (NIV). While grace and love could conceivably have been interchanged and attributed either to the Father or to the Son, this is not the case with the Holy Spirit. Through the Spirit we experience *koinōnia* with one another and the Godhead.

In true worship, the persons of the Trinity may not be interchanged without changing the significance of their work. In general, the Holy Spirit functions as a Paraclete, "Helper," sent by the Father in the name of Christ (John 14:26). He is indeed the agent by which God's will is effected on earth, but the New Testament never suggests that the Holy Spirit seeks attention for himself or seeks the adoration of God's people.

These observations raise questions about the way Christians deal with the Spirit in worship. Under Pentecostal influence, recent movements in Protestant

64. That is, circumcision of the heart; cf. Rom. 2:25–29; Lev. 26:41; Deut. 10:16; 30:6; Jer. 4:4.

65. In the New Testament the Holy Spirit's role is to animate sinners who are dead in trespasses and sins and effect their adoption as sons and daughters of God (Rom. 8:1–25); intercede on behalf of the saints according to the will of God (Rom. 8:26–27); produce in worshipers the life of righteousness and godliness (Gal. 5:16–25); seal believers in Christ, guaranteeing their status as God's redeemed treasure to the praise of his glory (Eph. 1:13); focus attention on and glorify Jesus, and unite believers with him, guiding them into all God's truth, through which they are sanctified and unified (John 1:32–34; 16:7–16; 17:17–21); provide the unifying element for the church (Eph. 4:1–6); and bestow divine gifts and power upon believers for the edification of the church (1 Cor. 12:1–31). Father, Son, and Holy Spirit are indeed so united that when disciples are made, they are baptized in the name of the Father and the Son and the Holy Spirit (Matt. 28:19)—the only occurrence of this trinitarian formula in the New Testament.

worship have sought to thrust the Spirit into the foreground of worship. The impulse to address the Spirit or directly worship the Spirit is commonly reflected both in contemporary Christian music[66] and in prayers,[67] but this is not a new phenomenon. It is evident also in the familiar doxology known as the "Old 100th," arguably the most frequently sung lyrics in all English public worship.

> Praise God from whom all blessings flow;
> Praise him all creatures here below;
> Praise him above you heavenly host;
> Praise Father, Son, and Holy Ghost. Amen.[68]

However, the tradition is much older, being attested in the ancient *Gloria Patri*. Apparently the original wording of the first part of the doxology consisted only of *Gloria Patri per Filium in Spiritu Sancto* ("Glory to the Father, through the Son, in the Holy Spirit"). This version is modeled on the biblical formula for baptism (Matt. 28:19) and reflects the New Testament picture more closely than the version with which we are familiar (in Greek, Latin, English).

> Doxa Patri kai Huiō kai Hagiō Pneumati,
> kai nyn kai aei kai eis tous aiōnas tōn aiōnōn. Amēn.

> Gloria Patri, et Filio, et Spiritui Sancto.
> Sicut erat in principio, et nunc, et semper, et in sæcula sæculorum.
>   Amen.

> Glory be to the Father, and to the Son, and to the Holy Spirit;
> as it was in the beginning, is now, and ever shall be, world without end.
>   Amen.

66. See, e.g., the lyrics of Matt Brouwer, "Father/Jesus/Spirit I adore you, lay my life before you; how I love you"; Donna Adkins, "Father/Jesus/Spirit we love you, we worship and adore you"; and Graham Kendrick, "Father God/Jesus King/Spirit pure we worship you."

67. See the instructions on prayer by David Yonggi Cho, ostensibly based on the pattern of the Lord's Prayer.

> Then I turn to the Holy Spirit. "Dear Holy Spirit, You are with me and You are within me. You are my comforter. You have been sent to help me every day. I appreciate You. You are my lawyer. You are my revealer. You are my teacher who also disciplines me. You always guide me. You always strengthen me. I thank You for Your wisdom and knowledge. I appreciate You dear Holy Spirit. Oh, I welcome You, and appreciate You. I love You. I recognise You. I depend upon You. I will follow You. Oh, I praise You." Then I say, "Oh, dear triune God, I worship You. I praise You."

("Thy Name Is to Be Praised," http://www.cai.org/bible-studies/thy-name-be-praised.)

68. This doxology is actually the last verse of Thomas Ken's longer hymn, "Awake, My Soul, and with the Sun," published in 1674. The tune, attributed to Louis Bourgeios (1510–61), was published in Clément Marot and Théodore Beza's *Octante trois Pseaumes de David* [*Fourscore and Three Psalms of David*], 2nd ed. (Geneva: Jean Crespin, 1551).

The first line was modified in the fourth century in response to Arians, who claimed that since Jesus was begotten, he was neither eternal nor equal in divinity with the Father. By replacing the prepositions "through" and "in" with the conjunction "and," the post-Nicene church sought to ensure a proper stress on the coequality of each person of the Trinity. However, the urge to treat the Holy Spirit as an object of worship is extrabiblical; it derives not from Scripture but from philosophical and theological deduction. It assumes that since Father, Son, and Holy Spirit are equally divine, they are equally worthy of worship.

But does recognizing the equality of the three persons of the Trinity demand equal worship of each? On one extreme, we could argue that addressing the Holy Spirit in worship has no more biblical warrant than addressing prayers to Mary, saints, or angels. However, unlike these persons, the Holy Spirit is a part of the divine Trinity. The New Testament teaches that the Holy Spirit assists us in prayer (Rom. 8:26); convicts the world concerning "sin and righteousness and judgment" (John 16:8–11); and impels and inspires us to worship, by guiding us into truth, particularly in glorifying Jesus (John 16:13–15). By regenerating and animating us to new life in Christ, the Spirit qualifies and enables us to worship acceptably (Rom. 7:6).[69] While the New Testament is emphatic in characterizing true worship as "in Spirit" (John 4:24), "in/by the Spirit,"[70] and "through the Spirit" (Acts 4:25), it knows nothing of the worship of the Spirit.

Should Christian worship be trinitarian or binitarian—addressing only the Father and the Son?[71] If we agree that it should be trinitarian, how would this look in practice? The biblical pattern suggests that this does not call for the three persons of the Triune God to receive equal and identical attention in worship. The pattern established by Jesus in the Lord's Prayer (Matt. 6:9–13) appropriately addresses praise and prayer to the Father, though other texts demonstrate that these may also be directed to the Son. When we read Scripture, the focus will be on God the Father or Jesus Christ the Son. However, it seems that the Holy Spirit is most honored when we accept his conviction of sin, his transforming and sanctifying work within us, and his guidance in life and ministry, and when in response to his leading we prostrate ourselves before Jesus. The Spirit is also honored when we give thanks to the Father and the

69. E.g., John 6:63; Rom. 8:2, 9–10; 2 Cor. 3:6. On the analogy of Gen. 2:7; cf. Job 33:4.
70. *En* [*tō*] *pneumati*: e.g., Matt. 22:43–45 (= Mark 12:35–37); Luke 2:27; 10:21; Rom. 15:16; Jude 20.
71. For an excellent discussion of "The Binitarian Shape of Early Christian Worship," see Larry W. Hurtado, *At the Origins of Christian Worship: The Context and Character of Earliest Christian Devotion* (Grand Rapids: Eerdmans, 1999), 63–97.

Son for his presence and work within us, referring to him in the third person rather than addressing him directly. We are trinitarian when we acknowledge the presence and roles of all three persons of the Trinity, when we recite the trinitarian formulation of the rite of baptism (Matt. 28:19), and when we hear the benediction with which people are sent into the world at the end of corporate worship: "The grace of the Lord Jesus Christ, and the love of God, and the fellowship of the Holy Spirit be with you all" (2 Cor. 13:14 [13]).

But trinitarian worship need not be balanced, if by balanced we mean giving the three persons of the Godhead equal time and space. True Christian worship focuses particularly on Christ, through whose sacrificial death and justifying work sinners are qualified for worship, and through whose resurrection they hope in eternal life and worship in the presence of God.[72] This christocentric focus is most evident in Revelation 5:1–14. Having introduced the One who is worthy of worship as the Lion of Judah, the Root of David, and the Lamb, the passage offers three reasons why he is worthy of worship: (1) he was slain—the historical fact; (2) with his death he purchased for God a people from every tribe and nation—the missiological fact; and (3) through him the redeemed are made to be a kingdom and priests to God, and they shall reign on earth—the ecclesiological and eschatological fact. This worship begins with worshipers on their knees, is focused on the Son, and involves enthusiastic songs of praise and prayer.

72. See Heb. 10:1–31; also see the recent appeal by Bryan Chapell, *Christ-Centered Worship: Letting the Gospel Shape Our Practice* (Grand Rapids: Baker Academic, 2009).

3

The Subject of Worship

*True worship involves reverential human acts of submission and hom-
age before the divine Sovereign in response to his gracious revelation of
himself and in accord with his will.*

In this chapter we shift our focus from the object of true Christian worship
to the subject. I am using the word "subject" in its grammatical sense: who
is the subject of verbs expressing biblical worship? Here again we face two
questions: Whom does God invite into his presence? And whose worship will
God accept?

Before answering these questions from the Scriptures, we might consider
how they are answered in our day. Unfortunately, in some churches the answer
to "Who may worship here?" is still "Whoever has white skin" or "Whoever
has black skin." In some places, it is "Whoever has the right social status" or
"Whoever can contribute to the congregation's finances" or "Whoever will
dress right." Some churches answer the question simply with "Whoever."
Consider the invitation on the website of a church in Leeds, England:

Come as you are—to worship
    We welcome you to the community. Full stop. You do not need to be any-
thing. You don't need to be married with kids, or tee-total, or employed or in
good health and you certainly don't need to be holy. You can come from any

background—religious, social, cultural or racial. Jesus accepts everyone as they are and we aim to do the same.[1]

This attitude is also reflected in the words of a popular song: "Come, now is the time to worship. Come, now is the time to give your heart. Come, just as you are to worship. Come, just as you are before your God. Come."[2] Like congregations that design worship to attract as broad a range of people as possible, these lyrics seem to assume that anyone's worship is acceptable to God. Worship has become a come-as-you-are event, to which all are invited.

But is this the biblical view? We know that salvation is offered to sinners without preconditions—come as you are, and receive forgiveness as a free gift of grace (Eph. 2:8–9). Yet is the same true of worship, especially if we use the word as it is popularly understood, as liturgical and verbal expressions of piety—what Christians typically do together on Sundays? Is anyone and everyone's worship accepted by God? Here the issue is not the objective nature of true worship but the nature of the *worshiper* who appears before God "according to God's will." What are the preconditions to ritual worship toward which God responds favorably? This chapter will consider in order acceptable worship in the original sinless world, the postfall world, the world of ancient Israel, and the Christian world of the New Testament.

True Worship in a Sinless World

The possibility of true worship by human beings is rooted in the relationship that God established at creation. Genesis 1:1–2:4a shows that the arrival of human beings marked the climax of God's creative actions. The biblical account of creation emphasizes that human beings are earthlings, like all other living things,[3] and later declares that they participate in God's covenant with the cosmos (Gen. 9:1–17). However, Genesis 1–2 and Psalm 8 are also clear that our species has been assigned a special status and role within creation.[4]

1. "Come as You Are—to Worship," *Leeds Vineyard website*, http://www.wharfedale-vineyard .org/Articles/114920/Wharfedale_Vineyard/Resources/Teaching/Spirituality/Come_as_you.aspx.
2. Composed by Brian Doerksen. Full lyrics accessible at www.briandoerksen.com.
3. With land animals, (1) we were created on day six (Gen. 1:24–31); (2) we share the divine blessing and the mandate to multiply and fill the earth (1:22, 28); (3) we share vegetation as food (1:29–30); (4) we trace our origin to the earth itself (2:5–7; cf. 1:24); and (5) we share the generic classification "living creature" (*nepeš ḥayyâ*, 2:7; cf. 1:20, 21, 24).
4. (1) We humans were created last; (2) we alone are presented as the product of divine deliberation (Gen. 1:26); (3) the description of our creation is more intensive and extensive than that of any other element of creation (vv. 26–30); (4) our creation is described with *bārā'*, a word that always involves a special creative act of God (cf. vv. 1, 27 [3×]); (5) our status is

If the Westminster Shorter Catechism is correct in declaring that the chief end of humanity is to glorify God and enjoy him forever, we do well to ask how people were to glorify God in this new world.

While Genesis 1–2 presents the world in general and the garden of Eden in particular as sacred space, it is doubtful that God conceived and biblical authors perceived the cosmos as a temple. Whereas temples in the ancient world were designed as earthly residences for the gods, the Scriptures never suggest that God created the world so he might have a home. Furthermore, Genesis 1–2 lacks any hints of the liturgical actions we associate with worship.[5] However, if we understand worship more broadly as reverential human acts of submission and homage before the divine Sovereign, then true worship takes on a very mundane character.[6] God created humankind to be his representatives on earth, and he has authorized us to govern it on his behalf. Psalm 8 reflects our place in the administration of the cosmos; God has charged us to rule over all that he had made (v. 6 [7]). The psalmist expresses poetically what YHWH had said in Genesis 1:28: "Be fruitful and multiply and fill the earth; subdue it and govern all the creatures God has made." In keeping with this status, YHWH has crowned us with "glory" and "majesty," royal qualities that belong to God himself.[7] Accordingly, we glorify God and express our reverence and awe before him best when we fulfill this mandate and govern the world in keeping with his will.[8]

This role is fulfilled in Genesis 2:4b–25, which describes God's installing Adam as "king" in his royal garden. Again, liturgical expressions for worship are missing, but the entire picture involves life in the sacred world that God has made. On one hand, God grants humans the privilege of enjoying the beauty of his creation, eating the food he provides, and experiencing life symbolized

---

defined as "the image of God" (ṣelem ʾĕlōhîm, 1:26–28); (6) God blessed us and authorized us to govern the created world (v. 28); (7) after we were created, YHWH pronounced the world extremely good (ṭôb mĕʾōd, v. 31); and (8) God did not celebrate by sanctifying the seventh day until we were created.

5. For fuller exploration of this issue, see Daniel I. Block, "Eden: A Temple? A Reassessment of the Biblical Evidence," in *From Creation to New Creation: Biblical Theology and Exegesis*, edited by D. M. Gurtner and B. L. Gladd (Peabody, MA: Hendrickson, 2013), 10–11.

6. While in everyday speech "mundane" often means "ordinary, average, uninteresting," technically it means "of or pertaining to the world; worldly; earthly; terrestrial."

7. These two expressions are used together of God in Ps. 145:5, 12.

8. In Gen. 1:28 the words "to subdue" (kābaš) and "to exercise dominion" (rādâ) call for an aggressive though not exploitative style of royal leadership. For fuller discussion of this issue, see Daniel I. Block, "To Serve and to Keep: Toward a Biblical Understanding of Humanity's Responsibility in the Face of the Biodiversity Crisis," in *Keeping God's Earth: The Global Environment in Biblical Perspective*, ed. D. I. Block and N. J. Toly (Downers Grove, IL: InterVarsity, 2010), 116–42.

by the tree of life (2:9; cf. v. 16). On the other hand, God charged Adam to care for the garden by "serving" (*'ābad*)[9] and "guarding" (*šāmar*) it (2:15).[10] The choice of verbs is intentional, suggesting that the world was not created for humans, but humans were created to serve the interests of the world. Like conductors of orchestras and choirs, humans as images of God have been charged with the sacred task of aiding all creation in its symphony of praise to God. This is spiritual worship at its finest, and persons whose worship is pleasing to God are those who delight in his creation and take care of it in its own interests and for God's glory.

True Worship in a Postfall World

Genesis 3 recounts the saddest episode in human history. God had graciously given humans charge over all creation, provided them with every necessity for life and well-being, and revealed to them the nature of appropriate worship. In enjoying the privileges and exercising their responsibilities as images of God, the first humans demonstrated reverence toward him. But all that changed in Genesis 3. This chapter exposes the nature and consequences of false worship. In false worship God's subjects (1) listen to other voices rather than his; (2) submit to creatures lower than themselves, not to mention lower than God (cf. Ps. 8; Rom. 1:18–26); (3) exchange the truth for a lie (cf. Rom. 1:25), twisting the perception of a benevolent and gracious Creator into a mean-spirited and jealous God; (4) usurp status and prerogatives reserved for God alone; (5) allow appetites of physical existence to drown out spiritual appetites; and (6) replace fear and service of the Creator with self-service and self-interest.[11]

9. Although many translations render *'ābad* as "till" or "cultivate," when the word is used of cultivation, the object of the verb is usually *hā'ădāmâ*, "the ground" (Gen. 2:5; 3:23; 4:2, 12; 2 Sam. 9:10; Prov. 12:11; 28:19; Zech. 13:5). The closest analogue to this construction occurs in Deut. 28:39, where *kerem*, "vineyard," is the object of this verb. But a garden (*gan*) is more than soil. The present garden consists of vegetation of all kinds (Gen. 2:9), rivers (2:10–14), precious metals and gemstones (2:12), and all sorts of land and sky creatures (2:19–20). Strictly speaking, the verb "to serve" assumes the subordination of the subject of the verb to its object, reinforcing the notion that both verbs, "to serve" and "to keep, guard," demand that the subjects expend their efforts in the interests of and for the well-being of the objects.

10. That the verbs *'ābad*, "to serve," and *šāmar*, "to keep, guard," should later be used together when speaking of the service of the Levites in the tabernacle (Num. 3:7–8; 8:26; 18:5–6) does not mean that the garden is perceived as a temple. However, it does suggest that the tabernacle and the temple were portrayed as miniature Edens.

11. In an oracle against the king of Tyre (Ezek. 28:12–14), Ezekiel paints a colorful picture of false worship in the garden of God: because of self-interest, the king exploited the garden and his role in it.

Genesis 3 ends with a dramatic picture of two people whose worship has been rejected by God. The consequences are disastrous. False worship (1) destroys the innocence and beauty of human relationships (3:7); (2) exchanges fellowship with the Creator for hiding from him (3:8); (3) transforms "fear" (*yārē'*) from godly "reverence, awe, respect," into "terror, fright" (3:10); (4) yields alienation from God, alienation between worshipers (3:7, 12, 16),[12] and alienation between humankind and the world we were to govern (3:17–18); (5) results in pain in fundamental human enterprises such as childbirth and food production; and (6) leads to death (cf. 2:17; 3:16).

Remarkably, God does not give up on his creation; he continues to seek the worship of human beings and the praise of all he has made. The origins of formal ways of expressing communion with God are unclear, but it seems that when God expelled Adam and Eve from the garden, he revealed liturgical forms by which reverent awe could be acceptably expressed. Without explanation Genesis 4–11 presents people as worshiping God in many different ways: presenting him tribute offerings (4:1–5); relating to him by his name, YHWH (4:26); walking with him (5:22, 24; 6:9);[13] living righteously and blamelessly (6:9); obeying him, even when it seems ridiculous (6:14–22); trusting him for deliverance from the judgment (7:1–8:19); presenting sacrifices of thanksgiving (8:20–22); accepting God's covenant with the cosmos and the renewal of the mandate to govern the world for him (9:1–17); and being fruitful, multiplying and filling the earth (9:18–19). These all represent reverential acts of homage and submission in accord with the will of God.

Most of these expressions of worship were accepted by God,[14] but a key question remains: how did people know whether these rites would work? Genesis 4–11 is silent on the revelation of God's name, the boundaries of appropriate and inappropriate behavior, and the effective response to sinful behavior. Still, people invoked the name of YHWH (4:26); their offensive behavior was specifically identified as "sin" (*ḥaṭṭā't*, 4:7), "evil" (*rā'â/ra'*, 6:5; 8:21), "corrupting" (*nišḥat*, 6:11–13), "violent" (*ḥāmās*, 6:11, 13), and "leaving the presence of YHWH" (4:16); murderous acts were condemned (4:9–12; cf. 4:23–24). Meanwhile, acceptable people were characterized as "righteous"

---

12. The man and woman were embarrassed in each other's presence; instead of accepting responsibility for their own sin, they divert blame; instead of accepting her complementary role as helper, the woman resented male headship and sought to usurp it for herself; instead of exercising loving and responsible leadership, man perverted headship into a position of power and rule (*māšal*, 3:16).

13. This rare idiom is found elsewhere only in Mic. 6:8 and Rev. 3:4.

14. See especially Gen. 8:21, where the expression "YHWH smelled the soothing aroma" reflects a favorable response. Variations of "soothing aroma" (*rēaḥ nîḥōaḥ*) are common in contexts involving burnt offerings: see, e.g., Exod. 29:18, 25, 41; Lev. 1:9, 13, 17.

(ṣaddîq, 6:9; 7:1), "blameless" (tāmîm, 6:9), and "walking with God" (5:22, 24; 6:9). While evidence for God's revelation of the boundaries of acceptable and unacceptable behavior—whether ethical or cultic—is scant, he was obviously communicating with human beings, for Noah acted "according to all that God had commanded him" (6:22; cf. 7:5, 9, 16).

When Noah and his family emerged from the ark, they responded by building an altar to YHWH and presenting whole burnt offerings, which YHWH obviously accepted (8:20–21; see note 14 above). How did Noah know this was an appropriate response to their rescue from the flood? Remarkably, YHWH's earlier command to take on board the ark seven extra pairs of clean animals and birds (7:2–3) takes for granted that Noah knew the boundaries between clean and unclean (outlined later in Lev. 11 and Deut. 14). We may speculate that as Adam and Eve were leaving the garden of Eden, God revealed to them the basic structures of the ritual world: the name by which they could address him, the boundaries of sin and righteousness as well as of clean and unclean objects, and the appropriate responses to sin. We may also hypothesize that, although peoples outside the biblical tradition have corrupted that revelation, the universal sense of accountability to deity and the impulse to relate to deity through sacrifice, prayer, and other rituals are rooted in that revelation.

But why were the liturgical responses cited above acceptable to God? Is it only because the forms of worship were correct? Genesis 6:8–9 answers these questions in part, at least with respect to Noah: he found grace in the eyes of YHWH (v. 8), and he was a righteous and blameless man who walked with God (v. 9). Because he was righteous, Noah demonstrated trust in God through obedience and then celebrated YHWH's deliverance from the flood with liturgical expressions of gratitude.

The first account of ritual worship in the First Testament (4:1–8) provides a classic narrative answer to the issue that concerns us in this chapter: whose worship is acceptable to God? While some suggest that YHWH rejected Cain's offering because it did not involve a blood sacrifice, this answer is doubtful. First of all, the text says nothing about "sin-offerings" or "substitutionary atonement," or even about sacrifice. Second, the author intentionally identifies both Cain's and Abel's offerings by the same name, minḥâ, which refers simply to a gift or tribute presented to God.[15] Third, since grain and cereal tribute offerings feature prominently in Israel's sacrificial system, there is obviously

---

15. This word can apply to any offering, grain or animal, and may also be used in a general sense of "tribute," a gift brought by a subject to his overlord, whether that overlord be human (Judg. 3:15–18) or divine, or even a gift given to secure the goodwill of another person (Gen. 32:20).

nothing wrong with offering grain as a *minḥâ*.[16] This is what Cain's work produced, so this is what he brought.

Then what was Cain's problem? The reference to the quality of Abel's offering—he brought the firstlings of the flock, particularly their most desirable parts—and its silence on the quality of Cain's offering may be a clue. As a horticultural counterpart to Abel's "firstlings," Cain should probably have brought a *minḥat bikkûrîm*, "a grain offering of the firstfruits" (Lev. 2:14). However, the narrator provides firmer evidence through the sentence structure in Genesis 4:4b–5a: "Now YHWH looked with favor at Abel and his offering, but at Cain and his offering he did not look with favor."[17] By placing his name ahead of the offering, the sentence focuses on Cain the worshiper rather than on the offering or on God the respondent. This construction reinforces the signal sent by the awkward construction of verse 4a. Whereas the word order of verse 3 is natural, suggesting initially that Cain's act of worship was normal, the statement concerning Abel's action is emphatic: "Oh, and Abel brought, indeed he, from the firstborn of his flock and from their fatty portions." The construction is intentionally awkward in Hebrew, as is also my rendering in English to draw attention to the man. God accepted Abel's offering because he considered Abel to be righteous (cf. Heb. 11:4).

This narrator's characterization of Abel contrasts sharply with that of Cain. Although the form of Cain's worship seems to have been correct, the narrative suggests that Cain himself was the problem. The mundane description of his offering suggests that he was merely, perhaps dutifully, going through the motions. When Cain's offering was rejected, his face fell, not in humility and remorse, but in anger with YHWH for having rejected it and his failed sense of entitlement (v. 5b). In response to YHWH's gracious invitation to do well and find acceptance, he permitted sin to overpower him (v. 7). He consulted with his brother, not to learn from him the way of true worship, but to murder him (v. 8). When YHWH confronted him, he lied and claimed that he did not know what had happened to his brother (v. 9). When YHWH cursed him, he protested this unfairness and blamed YHWH for his fate (vv. 13–14). When YHWH graciously protected him from people like himself, he left the presence of God (v. 16). These proofs show that YHWH's assessment of Cain was correct and his rejection of his offering was justified (see fig. 3.1).

Figure 3.1 illustrates the difference between Cain's and Abel's understandings of the relationship between a worshiper's personal life and cultic ritual.

16. Distinguishing between Cain's offering and Abel's offering dates back to the translation of the Septuagint, which interprets Cain's offering as a *thysia*, "sacrifice," but Abel's as a *dōron*, "gift."

17. Hebrew *šāʿâ* means "to look upon [something] favorably" (Gen. 4:4–5).

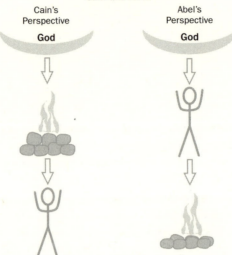

FIGURE 3.1
Two Perspectives on Worship:
Cain and Abel

Cain's Perspective   Abel's Perspective

Obviously God does not accept just anybody or everybody's worship. When peoples' hearts are pure and their lives exhibit righteousness, God responds favorably to their cultic worship. But God is not obligated to accept the worship of those whose hearts are hardened toward him and who live contrary to his will, even if the forms of their worship are correct. God looks upon the offering through the lens of the worshiper's heart and character rather than seeing the worshiper through the lens of the offering.

True Worship in Ancient Israel

While the world at large provides the context for the call and commission of Abraham, this event marks the beginning of the narratives of the patriarchs, which link the cosmic world of the descendants of Noah with the localized world of the Israelites, whom YHWH set high above the nations to proclaim his glory and grace. When we examine whose cultic worship was acceptable, two dimensions of the issue emerge: prerequisite ceremonial purity and prerequisite moral and spiritual integrity.

Ceremonial Prerequisites to Acceptable Worship

To understand ritual purity as a prerequisite to offering acceptable worship, we must consider the conceptual world of the First Testament. The ancients assumed a status continuum extending from abominable, which was to be destroyed, to absolutely holy, which was treasured and guarded (fig. 3.2). While the distinctions are not absolute, people, places, creatures, and inanimate objects fell into four basic categories: (1) that which is holy and may be in the presence of God; (2) that which is clean and may be used by the holy people of YHWH without further purification; (3) that which is unclean and may be used outside the holy community once purified (Gen. 9:3; Deut. 14:21); and (4) that which is abominable and banned from human use by utterly destroying it (*heḥĕrîm*, Deut. 7:26; 13:14–15 [15–16]).

FIGURE 3.2
The Sacred–Clean–Unclean–Abominable Continuum

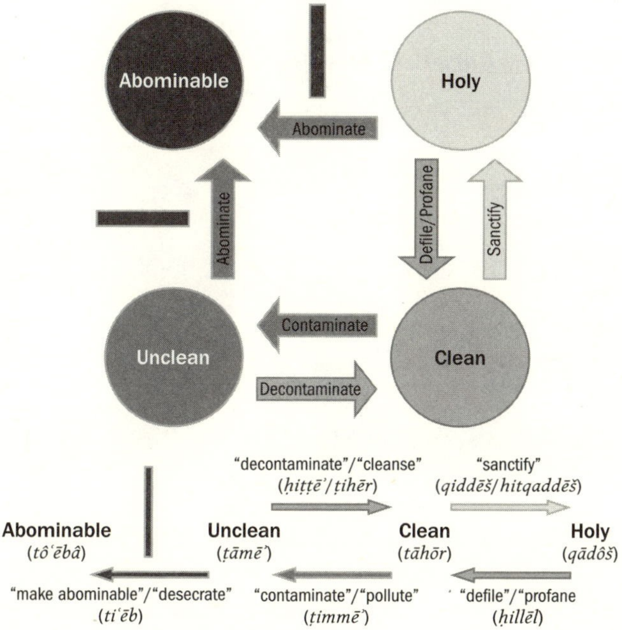

Holy objects became defiled through contact with what was unclean; they required sanctifying rituals to restore them to holy use. Clean objects could be rendered holy through consecration rituals, but they could also be contaminated through sin or contact with what was unclean. They had to be purified through rituals to restore them to use. Uncleanness could be removed only through ritual washings and sacrifice. Holy people, objects, and places could be rendered abominable through involvement in the most heinous crimes: idolatry, witchcraft and sorcery, murder, or sexual immorality. Within the conceptual universe of the First Testament, the world and its population were perceived as a series of concentric circles, with the intensity of holiness increasing as one moved from the outside to the center.

This conceptual world is reflected in scenes of the corporate worship at Mount Sinai described in Exodus 19 (fig. 3.3). Here YHWH, the king of the universe, invites this former band of slaves to an audience with himself. On the third day the ram's horn sounds, announcing the arrival of the King and signaling the people to rise and come to the foot of the mountain, which will serve as his earthly court. But their approach is anything but casual; since an audience with the great King on holy ground demands ritually holy worshipers, before they meet with YHWH, they spend three days preparing for the encounter.

Figure 3.3
The Gradations of Holiness at Mount Sinai

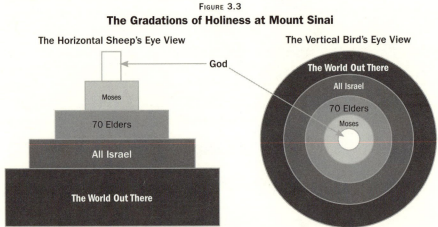

First, at YHWH's command, the Israelites consecrate the mountain itself (v. 23), marking it off by establishing a boundary around it (vv. 12–13a). YHWH declares encroachment upon the sacred space a capital offense;[18] anyone who touches the edge of the space is to be executed. Later YHWH adds that if out of curiosity the people break through the barrier to gaze at him, he will break out against them and many will die (vv. 21–24).

Second, the priests must consecrate themselves (v. 22). Since Aaron and the Levites have not yet been formally ordained as priests (cf. Exod. 28–29), it is unclear who these priests are or how they are installed. While the definition

---

18. Hebrew *môt yûmat*, "he shall surely be put to death," is a legal formulation derived from the court. See, e.g., Gen. 26:11; Exod. 19:12; 21:12, 15–17.

of priests as "those who approach YHWH" (19:22) identifies them as professional worshipers (cf. Deut. 10:8), even those who are by definition "holy" must consecrate themselves to prevent YHWH's anger.

Third, the people must be consecrated (Exod. 19:10, 14–15). The nature of these consecration rituals is unclear, though the narrator notes that Moses consecrates them and the people wash their clothes. Verse 15 suggests that Moses also tells the men not to approach women. While obviously a temporary prohibition on sexual activity, this odd prohibition may function as shorthand for abstinence from all kinds of activities that might otherwise be normal and right but in this circumstance would be a distraction.

Modern readers may not be familiar with this conceptual world where YHWH lives above the universe in glory and holiness. When he descends on Mount Sinai, the place was transformed into supremely sacred space. The boundary around the mountain served two purposes: to guard the sanctity of the place and to protect the people from the full dose of divine holiness, which would have been lethal. Accordingly, when the people heard the trumpet, they rose in anticipation of the divine King's appearance but climbed only as high as he permitted (vv. 16–17). Later, when the covenant was ratified, YHWH invited Moses, Aaron, Narab, Abihu, and the seventy representatives of the people to move to the next stage for an increasingly sacred phase of the ritual (24:1): eating in the presence of God (24:9–11). Only Moses, the divinely appointed mediator, was privileged to move higher up the mountain and have YHWH speak to him face-to-face (19:19; 24:2, 12–18; 33:11–34:9).

Whereas Exodus 19 recounts a singular event, the idea of ritual purity as a prerequisite to acceptable worship surfaces repeatedly in later texts. In Leviticus 11:44 YHWH declares, "I am YHWH your God. So consecrate yourselves, and be holy, for I am holy" (cf. Lev. 20:7). With this charge all Israelites—not only priests—were reminded that holiness was to characterize their lives. Morally defiling sin and amorally defiling experiences would compromise their access to God.

Moral defilement could occur through intentional or inadvertent violation of the will of God. Penitential rites to remove the guilt of sin often resembled mourning rites and could include tearing or removing one's garments and replacing them with sackcloth,[19] sitting on ashes and throwing dust on one's head,[20] pulling the hair and beating the breast,[21] weeping and loud wailing,[22]

19. See, e.g., 1 Kings 20:31–32; 21:27; Neh. 9:1; Isa. 15:3; 22:12; Dan. 9:3; Jon. 3:5–6, 8.
20. As in Job 2:8; 42:6; Ezek. 27:30.
21. See Isa. 32:12; Ezek. 23:34; cf. Luke 18:13.
22. As in Judg. 20:26; 2 Kings 22:19; Ezra 10:1; Neh. 8:9; Jer. 4:8; Mic. 1:8.

shaving the head,[23] fasting,[24] ritual washing,[25] verbal confession,[26] and sacrifices of atonement.[27]

Purification of amoral defilement highlights the significance of ceremonial washings. Leviticus 15 lists a series of natural bodily emissions that result in ritual impurity and disqualify one from worship: discharges in general (vv. 1–12), seminal discharge (vv. 16–17), sexual intercourse (vv. 15–18), menstruation (vv. 19–24), and vaginal hemorrhage (vv. 25–30). To these we should add childbirth, which obviously involves discharges (Lev. 12:1–8), and all kinds of skin diseases represented by ṣāraʿat, commonly understood as "leprosy."[28] All of these were presumably considered defiling because, unlike cuts and scrapes, they involved discharges thought to emerge spontaneously from within the body.[29] Assuming defilement to be contagious, any contact with unclean people or unclean food (Lev. 11:24–28) would render one unclean, as would contact with a dead body (Num. 19:11–22).[30] Rituals for purification could involve washing one's body and clothing, animal sacrifices (Lev. 12:8), quarantine (13:45–46), and intensive priestly intervention, including sin and guilt offerings.

Although many Christians feel sorry for the Israelites' needing to keep such detailed ordinances, this disposition misunderstands their significance. Notions of clean and unclean and the need for rituals to remove defilement pervaded the ancient world,[31] and true devotees of YHWH would not have

23. Job 1:20; Jer. 41:5; 48:37; Ezek. 27:31; Mic. 1:16.

24. See, e.g., Judg. 20:26; 1 Sam. 7:6; 2 Sam. 12:16, 21–22; 1 Kings 21:27.

25. As in Isa. 1:16; Jer. 2:22.

26. See Ps. 51; Neh. 9; Dan. 9.

27. On sin and guilt/reparation offerings, see Lev. 4:1–6:7. The most poignant expression of grief over sin in the First Testament, Ps. 51:1–7, alludes to several of these rituals.

28. See Lev. 13–14; Deut. 24:8; 2 Kings 5:3, 6–7, 27; 2 Chron. 26:19. In recent decades scholars have rejected the notion that this was Hansen's disease (*elephantiasis graecorum*), which is incurable. See L. Koehler, W. Baumgartner, and J. J. Stamm, *The Hebrew and Aramaic Lexicon of the Old Testament* [*HALOT*], trans. and ed. M. E. J. Richardson (Leiden: Brill, 1994–99), 1057; D. P. Wright and R. N. Jones, "Leprosy," in *Anchor Bible Dictionary* [*ABD*], ed. D. N. Freedman (New York: Doubleday, 1992), 4:278. However, textual evidence from ancient Mesopotamia has recently surfaced suggesting that leprosy should not be excluded from the diseases represented by Hebrew ṣāraʿat. See J. Scurlock and B. R. Andersen, *Diagnoses in Assyrian and Babylonian Medicine: Ancient Sources, Translations, and Modern Medical Analyses* (Urbana: University of Illinois Press, 2005), 70–73.

29. The same would be true of garments (Lev. 13:47–59) or houses (Lev. 14:33–53) thought to be "leprous," that is, plagued by mold that seems to emerge from within the fabric or the walls.

30. Responding to Pharisaic preoccupation with ritual cleansing, Jesus alludes to the principle underlying the notion of emissive defilement in Matt. 15:11. Spiritualizing what is otherwise a very physical conception, he lists evil intentions, murder, adultery, fornication, theft, false witness, and slander as truly defiling emissions from the heart.

31. This is reflected in the "Prayer to Every God," cited in the previous chapter (pp. 34–35). The supplicant is keenly aware that dietary and spatial boundaries exist between what is clean

viewed them as burdensome. Also, for YHWH to reveal these regulations in such detail is a supreme grace, reflecting YHWH's desire for fellowship with his covenant people. Indeed, the more detailed the regulations, the less was left to guesswork and hence the greater the grace. In the context of these divinely revealed rituals, worshipers welcomed the priest's atoning intervention and anticipated his declaration, "You are clean!" (e.g., Lev. 12:7–8; 13:6). Purification rituals served the positive purpose of restoring defiled Israelites' access to YHWH and welcoming them back to worship.

Moral and Spiritual Prerequisites to Acceptable Worship

There was more to preparing for acceptable worship than external ritual, as David recognized after his adulterous affair with Bathsheba:

> For you have no delight in sacrifice;
>> if I were to give a burnt offering, you would not be pleased.
> The sacrifice acceptable to God is a broken spirit;
>> a broken and contrite heart, O God, you will not despise.
>> (Ps. 51:16–17 NRSV)

The psalmists' views on spiritual and moral prerequisites to acceptable worship are described explicitly in Psalms 15 and 24. Framed by a verbal picture of a conquering king returning from battle (24:1–2, 7–10), the psalmist calls the gates of the city to open and welcome YHWH of Hosts. But in verse 3 the psalmist asks, "Who may climb the hill of YHWH? And who may rise in his holy place?" This is royal court language, concerning admission to an audience with the king. In the ancient world, people could be invited to the throne room to give account for some misdeed, receive a commission from the earthly king, bring a petition, or receive some honor. Having been ushered into the king's presence, they would fall at the king's feet in a gesture of submission and homage and wait for a signal of acceptance, hopefully the tap of the scepter on their shoulder or the verbal declaration, "Stand, that I may speak with you" (cf. Ezek. 2:1). Psalm 24 envisions such a scene.

In effect the psalmist asks, "Whose homage will YHWH accept?" The psalmist does not answer with, "Come one, come all! Come as you are!" Rather, he specifies four prerequisites to acceptance from God: clean hands, a pure

---

and unclean, but he does not know where the boundaries are. On Hittite purification rituals, see J. C. Moyer, "Hittite and Israelite Cultic Practices: A Selective Comparison," in *Scripture in Context II: More Essays in Comparative Method*, ed. W. W. Hallo et al. (Winona Lake, IN: Eisenbrauns, 1983), 29–33. Moyer describes the impurity of pigs and dogs in Hittite culture.

heart, no compromised affections, and no false oaths. These are four marks of authentic spirituality, four evidences of a life that pleases God.

Clean hands. Opening with similar questions, Psalm 15 lists eleven specific actions that may be interpreted as commentary on "clean hands." Those whose cultic worship is acceptable are blameless; their actions are righteous; their thoughts and speech are characterized by integrity; they refuse to slander; they do no harm to neighbors; they do not ridicule their friends; they have no respect for scoundrels; they honor those who fear YHWH; they keep their word even when it turns out to be against their own interests; they refuse to take advantage of those economically marginalized; and they reject bribes offered to convict an innocent person. The concluding line is critical: those who act this way will never be shaken, which is another way of saying that their expressions of homage before YHWH are accepted, and they are secure in his presence.

A pure heart. The closest analogue to this expression (*bar lēbāb*) occurs in Psalm 73:1: "God is good to Israel, to those who are pure of heart"[32]—which means clean and righteous on the inside.[33] This addition recognizes that we may perform righteous acts out of duty or hypocrisy and thus not from the heart.[34]

Uncompromised devotion to YHWH. Those whose worship is acceptable have not lifted up their "soul" (*nāśā' nepeš*) to falsehood (Ps. 24:4). The statement seems odd, but the psalmist has in mind turning one's affections to idols, here characterized as illusory, false, wrong, and twisted. This reference to undivided affections represents the psalmist's version of the Shema (Deut. 6:4–5).

Fidelity to one's word. Those whose worship is acceptable have not been treacherous in their oaths. By definition, oaths guarantee that people will keep their word.

Psalm 24:5 announces the reward of those who meet these conditions: they will receive a blessing from YHWH, and they will receive a divine verdict of "Righteous."[35] Such pronouncements confirm that God has favorably received the worshiper's cultic expressions of homage.

These psalms offer a biblical corrective to a common but unhealthy notion that God looks only at our hearts rather than at our external actions. Some ground this understanding in 1 Samuel 16:7: "For YHWH sees not as humans

---

32. Other texts speak of a "clean heart" (*lēb ṭāhôr*, Ps. 51:10 [12]) and "purifying the heart" (*zikkâ lēbāb*, Ps. 73:13; Prov. 20:9).

33. Purity and righteousness are linked in Job 15:14; 25:4.

34. According to Jesus in Matt. 5:20, 27–28, the scribes and Pharisees embodied this common problem.

35. "Blessing" (*bĕrākâ*, a verbal declaration) and "righteousness" (*ṣĕdāqâ*) function as a parallel pair of verbal expressions: "He will receive [a pronouncement of] blessing from YHWH / and [he will receive a pronouncement of] righteousness from the God of his salvation" (Ps. 24:5). The first line alludes to the Aaronic benediction in Num. 6:24–26; the second recalls Deut. 6:25, "And it will be righteousness for us, if . . . ," that is, "YHWH will pronounce us righteous, if . . ."

see; humans look on the outward appearance, but YHWH looks on the heart." Not only does this idea misrepresent the verse, but the notion also is as questionable as "God hates the sin but loves the sinner."[36] The Scriptures refuse to divorce persons from their actions or their hearts from their deeds. Verbal confessions do not prove genuine piety, nor are they the main evidence of what is in the heart. Rather, actions that seek the honor of God and the well-being of others are proof of a transformed heart (Matt. 7:15–23; John 15:1–17).

As the northern kingdom (Israel) and the southern kingdom (Judah) approached their respective ends, YHWH graciously sent the prophets to warn the people of the coming dangers and to call them back to covenant righteousness. Even though the people's moral vision was disintegrating, they had maintained their cultic fervor. They seemed to think that if they performed the prescribed rituals, YHWH would be obligated to bless and protect them. Detached from the states of their hearts or their moral conduct, ritual performance became a formula for security.

This was the situation the prophets faced in the last centuries of the kingdoms of Israel and Judah. Speaking for YHWH, Amos responded to the problem in the northern kingdom in the eighth century BC.

> I hate, I reject your festivals,
>> and I take no delight in your solemn assemblies.
> Even though you offer me your burnt offerings and grain offerings,
>> I will not accept them;
> and the offerings of well-being of your fatted animals
>> I will not look upon.
> Remove from me the noise of your songs;
>> I will not listen to the music of your harps.
> But let justice roll down like waters,
>> and righteousness like an ever-flowing stream. (Amos 5:21–24)

This agrees with Hosea's assessment regarding both Ephraim and Judah.

> Your loyalty [ḥesed] is like morning fog,
>> and like dew it quickly disappears.
> I desire loyalty [ḥesed], not sacrifice;
>> the knowledge of God, rather than burnt offerings. (Hosea 6:4b, 6)

Earlier Hosea had presented YHWH's charges against Israel: false swearing, dishonesty, murder, theft, and adultery had replaced fidelity, loyalty, and the

---

36. See n. 18 in chap. 1 above.

knowledge of God; indeed, crime followed upon crime (4:1b–2). For their infidelity, the northern kingdom was destroyed by the Assyrians in 722 BC.

But hypocritical worship continued in Judah. Isaiah summarized the problem in 29:13: "This people draw near with their mouth, and they honor me with their lips, but their worship of me is a human commandment learned by rote." Echoing Psalms 15 and 24, in Isaiah 33:14b–16 the prophet asks, "Who among us can live with the devouring fire? Who among us can live with everlasting flames?" Then he answers:

> Those who walk righteously and speak uprightly,
>> who despise the gain of oppression,
> who wave away a bribe instead of accepting it,
>> who stop their ears from hearing of bloodshed
>> and shut their eyes from looking on evil,
> they will live on the heights;
>> their refuge will be the fortresses of rocks;
>> their food will be supplied, their water assured. (NRSV)

This prospect contrasts sharply with the scathing indictment of worship with which Isaiah opens. There the prophet portrays Judah as weighed down with sin (*ḥaṭṭā't*), perversion (*'āwōn*), evil (*ra'*), and corruption (*mašḥît*); they have rebelled (*pāša'*) against YHWH, abandoned (*'āzab*) him, treated the Holy One of Israel with contempt (*ni'ēṣ*), and turned (*nāzōr*) from him (Isa. 1:2–4). Like Sodom and Gomorrah the nation has rotted at the core (1:5–9). Therefore YHWH rejects all their cultic charades (1:11–15). Reminiscent of Psalms 15 and 24, Isaiah summarizes the moral prerequisites to acceptable cultic worship:

> Wash yourselves; make yourselves clean;
>> remove the evil of your actions from before my eyes;
> cease to do evil, learn to do good;
> seek justice, rescue the oppressed,
> defend the orphan, plead for the widow. (Isa. 1:16–17 NRSV)

Cultic performance matched by ethical righteousness results in forgiveness and well-being, but the absence of the latter yields rejection and judgment (1:18–20). Isaiah's rural countryman Micah advocated the same approach.

> With what shall I come before YHWH,
>> and bow myself before God on high?
> Shall I come before him with burnt offerings,
>> with yearling calves?

> Will YHWH take pleasure in thousands of rams,
>   with ten thousands of rivers of oil?
> Shall I offer my firstborn for my rebellion,
>   the fruit of my body for the sin of my soul?
> He has declared to you, O human, what is good,
>   and what YHWH requires of you:
> Doing justice, and loving kindness,
>   and walking humbly with your God. (Mic. 6:6–8)

Although Judah survived another century after Isaiah, the religious situation in Jerusalem remained largely unchanged. If anything, hypocrisy intensified. In Jeremiah's renowned "Temple Gate Sermon," delivered at the entrance to the place of worship (Jer. 7:1–8:3), the prophet espoused a Mosaic theology of worship rooted in Israel's knowledge of God and the privilege of covenant relationship. Mincing no words, he addressed the people's hypocrisy with three points. First, he declared that trust in the temple as the physical symbol of divine presence was no substitute for ethical conduct that serves the interest of others and reflects undivided devotion to YHWH (7:3–7). Second, given their criminal conduct and spiritual infidelity, the presence of these worshipers in the temple transformed the sacred residence of YHWH into a den of robbers (vv. 8–11). Third, the ceremonial performance of rituals is no substitute for a life of worship, everyday acts of submission and homage to the divine Sovereign in response to his revelation of himself and in accord with his will (vv. 21–26). On the surface Jeremiah's focused statement on sacrifices is shocking:

> Go ahead, add your burnt offerings to your other sacrifices and eat the meat yourselves! For when I brought your ancestors out of Egypt and spoke to them, I did not just give them commands about burnt offerings and sacrifices, but I gave them this command: Obey me, and I will be your God and you will be my people. Walk in obedience to all I command you, that it may go well with you. (Jer. 7:21–23 NIV)

Many have used statements like this to drive a wedge between the perspectives of Exodus-Leviticus and the Prophets and to argue that the prophetic emphasis on religion expressed in ethical conduct represents a higher view of religion than cultic expressions. However, this is a false dichotomy. On the one hand, the prophetic statements represent hyperbolic rhetoric, attempting to restore balance to the people's views on worship rather than categorical rejections of cultic worship. On the other hand, prescriptive pentateuchal texts like the Book of the Covenant (Exod. 20:22–23:19) and the Instructions on Holiness (Lev. 17–26) integrate and alternate appeals for cultic service with ethical obedience. To express devotion to YHWH in the context of holy places, times, and rituals is useless and meaningless if people are not wholly devoted to God outside these contexts.

The problem of hypocritical worship resurfaced in the postexilic period. Whereas earlier prophets had repeatedly accused the people of camouflaging moral and spiritual evils with liturgical scrupulosity, the prophet Malachi charges them with contempt for and boredom in cultic worship (Mal. 1:6–9, 13a). The absence of reverent awe before God is evident in every aspect of life: the people are cynical about YHWH's love for them (1:2–5) and his justice (2:17); the offerings they present are defiled and defective (1:6–9, 12–13); the priests despise and abuse their office (2:1–9); the men are compromising and faithless in their marriages (2:10–16); people are heartless toward those who are socially and economically marginalized (3:5); they are stingy in their contributions to the temple (3:7–12); and they are perverse in their understanding of covenant relationship (3:13–15). Malachi illustrates the disconnection between their ethical conduct and liturgical expressions of piety in 2:13–14.

> Here's another thing you do. You cover YHWH's altar with tears, weeping and groaning because he pays no attention to your offerings and is not pleased with what you offer.

And so the people ask, "What's the problem?"

> Surely YHWH has witnessed what happens between you and your wife [whom you married] in your youth, but whom you have betrayed, though she is your companion and your wife by covenant.

So the doors to the temple should be locked (1:10). God is not obligated to accept the cultic worship of those who fail to keep their marriage vows (cf. 1 Pet. 3:7). Indeed, YHWH warns that he will come against those who do not fear him and purge their dross like a refiner's fire, yielding a community that will bring righteous offerings (Mal. 3:1–4).

Despite his denunciation of the impious in Jerusalem, Malachi recognizes the positive effect of worship for those who fear YHWH. Since YHWH has written their names in the book of remembrance, and since he treats them as his own special treasure and his children (3:16–18), their future is secure. These will not only survive the judgment but will also triumph over the wicked (4:1–3 [3:19–21]).

As the light of prophetic revelation among God's people was waning, Malachi reaffirmed YHWH's requirement of full-bodied and comprehensive worship. The key to divine favor was neither the sacrifices people brought nor the fervor with which they performed their cultic service but fidelity to YHWH, demonstrated in righteous living.

True Worship in the New Testament

The arrival of YHWH incarnate in Christ resulted in fundamental changes in the cultic expression of covenant relationship with God. As the heart of sacred space, the temple was rendered irrelevant: with Christ's death, sacrifices for the removal of sin were terminated (Heb. 10:1–18); with his entrance into the true and heavenly temple, the intermediary role of the priesthood ended; and with his institution of the new covenant, the old ethnic markers of clean and unclean evaporated. But did this mean that old expressions of holiness as prerequisites to acceptable worship were dissolved as well?

A cursory reading of the New Testament suggests that its characters and authors were as comfortable with the language of holiness as those of the First Testament. The New Testament frequently refers to First Testament realities as holy,[37] but it does not hesitate to apply the root *hagios*, "dedicated to God, sacred," to present and future realities as well.[38] This description is expected with reference to God, who is referred to as "Holy Father" (John 17:11), the holy Lord God Almighty (Rev. 4:8), the holy and true Sovereign Lord (6:10), the only holy One (15:4), the One who bears a holy name (Luke 1:49), and the One who dwells in heaven, his holy temple (Heb. 8:2; 9:12; 10:19). The epithet also applies to Jesus, who is the Holy One of God[39] or the Holy One,[40] God's holy Servant (Acts 4:27, 30), a holy high priest (Heb. 7:26), the holy One who calls us (1 Pet. 1:15), and the One we are to treat as holy (3:15). The expression is most commonly applied to the Third Person of the Trinity, the Holy Spirit (ninety times) or the Spirit of holiness (Rom. 1:4).

37. God's holy prophets (Luke 1:70; Acts 3:21; 2 Pet. 3:2); holy women (1 Pet. 3:5); God's holy covenant (Luke 1:72); holy blessings of David (Acts 13:34); the Holy Scriptures (Rom. 1:2; cf. sacred writings, *hiera grammata*, in 2 Tim. 3:15); the holy Torah (Rom. 7:12); God's holy commandment (2 Pet. 2:21); holy place (temple/tabernacle, Matt. 24:15; Heb. 9:1–3, 24–25; 13:11); holy ground (Acts 7:33); the firstborn, who is holy to the Lord (Luke 2:23); dough of firstfruit offerings (Rom. 11:16); sacred temple service (*hieros*, 1 Cor. 9:13).

38. God's holy apostles and prophets (Eph. 3:5); holy angels (Mark 8:38; Luke 9:26; Acts 10:22; Rev. 14:10); God's holy ones (Jude 14); a holy man (John the Baptist, Mark 6:20); Jerusalem as the Holy City (Matt. 4:5; 27:53; Rev. 11:2; 21:2, 10; 22:19); the temple in Jerusalem (Acts 6:13; 21:28); the gold of the temple (Matt. 23:17); the offering and the altar (23:19); holy mountain (of transfiguration, 2 Pet. 1:18); holy things kept from dogs (Matt. 7:6).

39. *Ho hagios tou theou*, Mark 1:24; Luke 4:34; John 6:69.

40. *Ho hagios*, 1 John 2:20; Rev. 3:7; 6:10; *ho hosios*, Acts 2:27; 13:35; Heb. 7:26; Rev. 16:5.

But our present concern is the significance of holiness in the life and worship of God's people. The status of believers as "holy ones" is expressed with epithets like "saints" (*hagioi*, over sixty times), "holy brothers [and sisters]" (*adelphoi hagioi*, Heb. 3:1), "those who are sanctified" (Acts 20:32), "a holy priesthood" (1 Pet. 2:5), "a holy nation" (2:9), and "priests of God and Christ" (*hiereis*, Rev. 20:6). Along with the status of holiness, we also find the command to be holy. In 1 Peter 1:16 the apostle reaffirms the First Testament ethical principle of *imitatio Dei* with, "You shall be holy, for I am holy" (cf. Lev. 11:44–45; 19:2; 20:7).

But what has this to do with our worship? Do the First Testament's preconditions to acceptable worship still stand? The question may be addressed by examining Jesus' and the apostles' attitudes toward the worship that was being practiced in Jerusalem, and then by exploring how the Epistles and Revelation speak about the worship of Christ's followers.

Jesus' Teaching on the Prerequisites to Acceptable Worship

The problems earlier prophets had addressed persisted in Jesus' day. His response to the cult as practiced in the temple and the form of religiosity advocated by religious leaders indicates that he targeted the scribes and Pharisees. Their scrupulous adherence to all kinds of regulations—many man-made rules,[41] some exploited for pompous show of devotion[42]—masked hearts that were defiled and foul.[43] Viewing themselves as piety police, they seemed especially obsessed with the Sabbath and railed on those who did not keep it according to their definitions. By contrast, true to the gracious spirit of the Sabbath ordinance and the Torah as a whole, Jesus called for covenant righteousness, citing Hosea 6:6: "I desire mercy and not sacrifice."[44] He demonstrated what this meant by eating with sinners and tax collectors,[45] pleading with the rich ruler to sell all that he had and give to the poor,[46] commending the prayer of the tax collector in contrast to the self-affirmation of the Pharisee (Luke 18:9–14), presenting a good Samaritan as an example (10:25–37), applauding the generosity and honor of a widow who gave two mites to the temple treasury,[47] and honoring the faith and generosity of Zacchaeus (19:1–10). Through a series

41. Tithing mint and dill and cumin (Matt. 23:23; Luke 11:42).
42. Sounding trumpets as they gave alms, standing and praying in synagogues and street corners, intentionally looking scruffy to show they were fasting (Matt. 6:1–18).
43. See Matt. 15:1–20; cf. Luke 16:14–18.
44. See Matt. 12:1–8; cf. Mark 2:23–28; Luke 6:1–5.
45. See Matt. 9:10–13 = Mark 2:15–17 = Luke 5:28–32.
46. See Matt. 19:16–22 = Mark 10:17–30 = Luke 18:18–30.
47. See Mark 12:41–44 = Luke 21:1–4.

of "oracles of doom,"[48] he exposed the scribes' and Pharisees' lack of spiritual integrity and showed that their worship was obviously not acceptable to God.

Then whose worship *will* God receive? Jesus answered this question in his response to two queries addressed to him: How does one enter the kingdom of heaven? How does one gain eternal life? In the Gospel of John his answers are profoundly spiritual and theological. Who enters the kingdom of heaven? All who are born from above of water and the Spirit (3:5). Who receives eternal life? All who believe in the Son (3:15–18, 36), drink the water that Jesus offers (4:14), hear Jesus and believe in the One who sent him (5:24), recognize the testimony of the Scriptures to Jesus (5:39), look to the Son and believe in him (6:40, 47), receive Jesus' words (6:68), listen to his voice and follow him (10:27–29), are willing to lose their lives by following Jesus (12:25), and know the Father, the only true God, and Jesus Christ whom he sent (17:2–3). To this list we could add Jesus' parable of the Vine and the Vinedresser (15:1–11). The branches that bear fruit—covenant righteousness demonstrated by obedience to the revealed will of God—are pruned by the Father, are purified by Jesus' word, and draw their life from him. These are secure in the love of the Father and the Son and experience full joy. The worship offered by branches that bear no fruit is rejected; they are cut off and tossed into the fire.[49]

In the Synoptic Gospels, Jesus' answers to these questions appear more practical. He sets the record straight on who may enter the kingdom of heaven: "Unless your righteousness exceeds that of the scribes and Pharisees, you will never enter" (Matt. 5:20). Who exhibits this superior righteousness? Not those who verbally declare their submission and homage with "Lord, Lord," but all who do the will of Jesus' Father in heaven (7:21). Such obedience is displayed when people humble themselves and become like little children;[50] take care of the poor;[51] submit to the Father and Messiah and accept the role of servant to all (Matt. 23:9–13); put the kingdom of God above all else;[52] and demonstrate true righteousness by feeding the hungry, giving drink to the thirsty, inviting in the stranger, clothing the naked, and standing by the sick and the prisoners (Matt. 25:31–46; Luke 10:25–37).

These acts are not simply variant expressions of the piety of the scribes and Pharisees. The ethic to which Jesus calls his followers is fundamentally self-sacrificing rather than self-serving. This ethic assumes the ethic of the Torah,

48. See Matt. 23:1–39; cf. Mark 12:1–12; Luke 20:45–46.
49. This parable represents the New Testament equivalent to the covenant blessings and curses in Lev. 26 and Deut. 28.
50. See Matt. 18:2–3; Mark 10:14–15; Luke 18:16–17.
51. See Matt. 19:16–24; Mark 10:17–25; Luke 18:18–25.
52. See Matt. 19:28–30; Mark 9:47; 10:28–31; Luke 18:28–30.

which Jesus summarizes in the Great Command: "You shall demonstrate love for YHWH your God with all your heart, and love for your neighbor as you do for yourself" (Matt. 22:37–39; Mark 12:30–31; Luke 10:27). As we shall see in the next chapter, the actions for which Jesus appealed are the natural fruit of those who are in the Vine, and represent the prerequisites to cultic service that is acceptable to God.

The Early Church's Teaching on Acceptable Worship

Jesus' denunciations of the scribes and Pharisees apparently went unheeded, for in Acts 6–7 we encounter Stephen's accusers, who charge him with blasphemy against all things Jewish. After reviewing Israel's history of rebellion before the council of Jewish leaders, Stephen observes that despite their privileged history as recipients and custodians of divine revelation, their betrayal and murder of Jesus were consistent with their history of rebellion against the Holy Spirit and their persecution of the agents of divine revelation (7:51–53). For all their concern to guard the sanctity of tradition and temple, they are truly criminals. With this sorry history and with their present treatment of Stephen as one who is accused of leading the people away from YHWH (cf. Deut. 13), their own expressions of piety are unacceptable to God; their only hope is the intercession of their victim and the grace of the Lord Jesus.

The problem of hypocritical worship was not limited to the Jewish leaders. Earlier, in Acts 5:1–11, Luke reported the case of Ananias and Sapphira: like Cain, they display cultic piety at the cost of their lives. Claiming to bring all the profits from the sale of their land, they deposit only a portion at the apostles' feet.[53] Their death on the spot demonstrates that integrity of heart continues to be a prerequisite for acceptable cultic service in the church.

Paul reinforces this principle repeatedly in his Epistles, especially in Romans and Galatians. Reminiscent of Jeremiah, in Romans 2 he argues that possession of the Torah is no substitute for living according to the Torah (vv. 12–24), and physical circumcision is no substitute for circumcision of the heart, demonstrated in keeping the law. Those physically circumcised may receive the praise of men, but those with circumcised hearts receive the praise of God (vv. 25–29; cf. Gal. 2). In Romans 9:14–33 Paul advances this argument, declaring that even though gentiles may not possess the Torah, when they by faith attain the righteousness called for by the Torah, they are accepted by God. By contrast, although Israel possesses the Torah, God has

---

53. As described in Acts 4:33–37, the practice seems to have emerged spontaneously to take care of the needs of the poor among them.

rejected them and their cultic expressions of piety because they have lacked faith. With considerable detail in chapters 12–15, Paul develops the practical outworking of the transforming gospel of faith. But he lays the foundation in 12:1–2: acceptable worship requires offering oneself as a living and holy sacrifice. As in Deuteronomy 6:5 and 10:12–11:1, this is full-bodied devotion, reasonable service acceptable to God, and true worship.

The church at Corinth was plagued by dissension over worship and worship styles. In 1 Corinthians 11:17–34 Paul warns the congregation that they may not take for granted God's approval of their participation in the Lord's Supper. If the believers tolerate injustices and divisions within the church, then partaking of the bread and wine expresses contempt for the church and brings shame on those who have been exploited (vv. 17–22). Furthermore, if people participate in the communion meal when spiritually and ethically unfit, they become accomplices in the death of Christ and subject to divine judgment (vv. 27–34). Paul's plea for integrity in worship continues in chapters 12–14. Prophetic utterances, speaking in tongues, and literally giving oneself up as a whole burnt offering (13:3) do not impress God if the members of the body do not show love by seeking the others' well-being.

Hebrews 12:14 provides the most direct declaration of the preconditions to acceptable worship in the New Testament: "Pursue peace with everyone, and the holiness without which no one will see the Lord" (NRSV). This appeal summarizes what the author has spelled out in greater detail in 10:19–31. In view of the access to God that the ministry of Christ has made available, we must stimulate one another to love and good deeds and encourage each other as we gather (vv. 19–25). This is pursuing peace. At the same time, we must refuse willful sin, for if, having learned of the truth, we persist in sin, we will surely experience the judgment of God (vv. 26–31). This is pursuing holiness.

These concerns underlie the later appeal for "reverence and awe" as the dispositional prerequisites to acceptable worship (12:28–29). The goal of pursuing peace and holiness is "seeing the Lord," which implies having been accepted by God (12:14). Thus the two preconditions bring our discussion full circle. Although most translations rightly suggest that peace involves the relationship between the addressee and others, the peace is best served when *all* seek others' well-being. As Paul had suggested in 1 Corinthians 11, without personal holiness, participation in the sacred rituals of worship will not open the door to the divine throne room.

In the book of Revelation, Jesus instructs John to write to the angel of the church in Sardis (Rev. 3:1–6). He declares that though this church thinks it is alive, their deeds prove that it is dead (3:1). However, Jesus observes that some in Sardis have not soiled their garments. As marks of their acceptance by God, they are invited to walk with him, they are clothed in white, their names are indelibly recorded in the book of life, and they are introduced by name before the Father and the heavenly court. There is no greater privilege or honor than this. Those with ears to hear, let them hear. If we keep our garments clean, we too will walk with the Lord in white.

Application to the Church Today

Our discussion has assumed that corporate worship involves an audience with God and that God establishes the grounds for participation in this audience. Right of access may not be taken for granted or claimed as an entitlement; the invitation to worship is neither universal nor unconditional. Hebrews 10:19–22 clearly spells out the basis of our access to God's presence:

> And so, dear brothers and sisters, we can boldly enter heaven's Most Holy Place because of the blood of Jesus. By his death, Jesus opened a new and life-giving way through the curtain into the Most Holy Place. And since we have a great High Priest who rules over God's house, let us go right into the presence of God with sincere hearts fully trusting him. For our guilty consciences have been sprinkled with Christ's blood to make us clean, and our bodies have been washed with pure water. (NLT)

However, having experienced the grace of Christ in salvation does not mean that we may be casual about worship or that our cultic expressions are automatically acceptable to God. By God's grace we have been declared holy; our robes have been made white by the blood of the Lamb (Rev. 7:14). But with this indicative declaration comes an imperative: "Be holy, for I [the Lord your God] am holy" (1 Pet. 1:16; cf. Lev. 19:2).

Although the scene of the marriage of the Lamb and his bride in Revelation 19:7–8 is set in the eschatological future, the description of the bride's preparation accords perfectly with the prerequisites to acceptable worship elsewhere in Scripture. The scene echoes what we observed in Exodus 19, the moment when YHWH, the divine husband, entered into a marriage covenant relationship with Israel (e.g., Ezek. 16:8–10).[54] Having rescued his people from bondage and brought them to himself (Exod. 19:4), he charged them to prepare for the "marriage event" by consecrating themselves and washing their garments (v. 10). Revelation 19:7–8 presupposes 7:14 and declares that the bride of the Lamb has prepared herself and clothed herself in "fine linen bright and pure."

---

54. In Jewish tradition, the event at Sinai was known as the "Day of Espousals" (*Song of Songs Rabbah* 3.11.2; Babylonian Talumd, *Ta'anit* 26b).

While the NIV interprets the garments to be the object of the previous verb, "it was given to her" (*edothē*), it is more natural to interpret this verb as divine authorization to prepare for and come to the event.[55] By adding that the fine linen represents "the righteous acts of the saints" (NIV),[56] John recognizes the delicate balance between grace and response, privilege and responsibility. The bride possesses both the objective (7:14) and subjective qualifications for admission to the wedding.[57] This is not a salvation by works (Titus 3:5), but a salvation that works, creating in us overwhelming gratitude for the grace we have received and transforming us to seek the goodwill and pleasure of God.

But how can we translate this into our own regular experience? Does this mean that we need to practice the purification rituals found in the First Testament and performed with such scrupulosity in early Judaism? Although we did not follow these procedures when I was young, I can remember the sort of ritual preparation for Sunday-morning worship that we observed. By about 3:00 PM on Saturday afternoon, the pace of life on the farm would slow down. We would milk the cows early and then observe what my mother called *Feierabend*, "celebration evening." After supper we would polish our shoes, prepare our Sunday-school lessons, and then read or play a game while Mother put the last-minute touches on the Sunday noon meal (generally a cold meal). We would go to bed relaxed and get up the next morning refreshed and ready for worship.

This seems worlds away from where we are today. Life is much more complicated. For many, Sunday morning is just as hectic as any other day. By the time we arrive at the church, we are out of breath, our tempers are short, and we have scarcely had worship on our minds. But, blissfully, we imagine that all we need to do is show up in church and God will be impressed. So we take pride in being in the service on Sunday morning, and if we are involved in youth activities, in campus charities, or in Bible studies, we are obviously exceptionally spiritual. However, this scarcely fits the picture painted in Hebrews 10 and 12.

---

55. In keeping with the reference to "those who are invited" (*hoi keklēmenoi*) to the marriage supper in Rev. 19:9. While the preconditioned salvation (7:14) and the authorization both represent divine provisions (*edothē* is a divine passive, 19:8), the object of "it was given to her" is not the garments but the donning of the garments (*hina peribalētai byssinon*, "to put on linen"). While G. K. Beale grants that this expression means "bestowal of authority, power" (*The Book of Revelation: A Commentary on the Greek Text*, New International Greek Testament Commentary [Grand Rapids: Eerdmans, 1999], 943), his rendering of the idiom in this context as "ability to clothe herself" (942) is unnecessary.

56. "Righteous acts" (*dikaiōmata*) is shorthand for covenant righteousness demonstrated in obedience to the revealed will of God, which Jesus refers to as "keeping my commands" (John 14:15, 21; 15:10).

57. Assuming that those who have experienced the imputed righteousness of Christ will demonstrate the righteousness of Christ in action.

How then can our worship be more glorifying to God? How can it be more transformative and transforming? How can we ensure integrity in our worship, so that when we approach the throne of grace, we will survive the encounter (Isa. 33:14; Heb. 12:29) and "see the Lord" (Heb. 12:14)? Will we be invited to stand (Pss. 15:1; 24:3)? Will we hear God's voice as he speaks to us (95:7), hear his pronouncement of acceptance and blessing (24:5), be invited to walk with God, be given garments of white, and hear our names presented to the Father by the Son (Rev. 3:4–5)?

The New Testament offers clear instruction on this point. Therefore let us examine ourselves to ensure that we do not presume upon a favorable response and participate in worship unworthily (1 Cor. 11:28–29). Let us hear and submit to God's Word, for in it we learn God's definition of acceptable worship and the boundaries of human behavior (2 Tim. 3:16–17). Let us cleanse out the old leaven (1 Cor. 5:7), confessing our sins and receiving God's assurance of forgiveness (1 John 1:9). Let us recognize that by his Holy Spirit, God dwells within our bodies as redeemed persons, and let us keep these temples pure by fleeing sin of every kind (1 Cor. 6:18–20). Let us recognize that as the covenant community of believers, we are the temple of God, and let us avoid all contamination from going after other gods and compromising ourselves with what is unclean (2 Cor. 6:14–18). Let us recognize that unless our lives are offered as sacrifices to God (Rom. 12:1–2), any cultic worship we offer will not be acceptable to him. Let us pray that through his Word and by his Holy Spirit, the Lord would fill us with reverence and awe, so that when we come before him, we might express our submission and homage in ways that please him. Finally, let us receive his blessing with joy, knowing that our worship, driven by the Holy Spirit and focused on Jesus Christ the Son, is pleasing to God the Father.

4

Daily Life as Worship

True worship involves reverential human acts of submission and homage before the divine Sovereign in response to his gracious revelation of himself and in accord with his will.

In the previous chapter we established that while the call to salvation is unconditional, the call to worship is conditional and subject to the spiritual and moral condition of the worshiper. In chapter 3 the concern was with worship in formal cultic contexts. However, if our description of true worship is correct, reverential human acts of submission and homage before God need not be restricted to communal gatherings or individual cultic rituals. Unless the worshiper walks with God in daily life, no cultic acts will impress God positively. Speaking biblically and theologically, the sacred and the secular may not be divorced. However, if one feels compelled to separate them, *life as worship* takes precedence over cultic and liturgical expressions of worship. True worship is expressed *primarily* in everyday conduct.

This idea deserves further investigation. We could approach this subject by revisiting texts that highlight the priority of ethical response over cultic performance.[1] Instead, I shall explore four texts from the First Testament

---

1. E.g., 1 Sam. 15:22–23; Pss. 15; 24; 40:4–8; Isa. 1:10–20; 29:13–14; 33:14–15; Jer. 7:1–11, 21–26; Ezek. 33:30–33; Hosea 6:6–11; Joel 2:12–17; Amos 5:18–27; Mic. 6:6–8; Hag. 2:10–19; Zech. 7:1–14; Mal. 1:1–14; 2:10–16.

that highlight the notion that all of life is to be viewed as worship, and then conclude with some reflections from the perspective of the New Testament.

The Ethical Expression of Worship

Some readers may resist the notion that the primary response to the revelation of God's will at Sinai was defined in ethical rather than ceremonial terms. But this idea should not surprise us, especially if we remember that covenants involve primarily relationships between people rather than commitment to a code of conduct or liturgical regulations. Unless we recognize this, we will not grasp the biblical vision of ethical behavior as worship.

Many Christians believe that approaches to ethics and morality in the First and New Testaments represent fundamentally different points of view; whereas Israelite ethics were based on law revealed by God on high, New Testament ethics arise from a personal relationship with God incarnate in Jesus Christ. Accordingly, we expect the culture of ancient Israel and the culture of the church to be quite different, if not actually opposed to each other.

The normative Israelite ethical vision rests on three pillars: (1) the principle of *imago dei*: as images of God, human beings govern the world on his behalf; (2) the principle of *imitatio dei*: the people of God imitate his character and actions; and (3) the principle of *conventio dei*:[2] God's covenant people serve him and others rather than themselves.[3] The significance of the first will become apparent when we explore work as worship in the next chapter. The second and third are fundamental to the discussion that follows here.

It may be helpful to begin our exploration of biblical ethics as worship by examining the differences between societies based on law and societies based on relationship. First Testament scholar George Mendenhall has contributed significantly to this discussion by identifying some of these differences (table 4.1).

Table 4.1. A Comparison of How Societies Are Founded

	Founded on Covenant	Founded on Law
Purpose	Creates a community where none existed before, by establishing a common relationship (covenant) with a common lord.	Presupposes a social order in which law serves as an instrument for maintaining an orderly freedom and security.

2. A new word (neologism) artificially created to match *imitatio* and *imago*.

3. To these three we might add a fourth pillar: a cosmological ethic, according to which we recognize/respect the order of the universe and discipline our conduct to conform to that order. This principle is important to the ethic of the Wisdom writings.

	Founded on Covenant	Founded on Law
Basis	Gratitude: response to benefits already received, usually by grace.	Social fear: by threat of force, attempts to protect society from disruption and attack.
Enactment	By voluntary act in which each individual willingly accepts the obligations presented.	By competent social authority, obligating all individuals by virtue of status as members of the social organization, usually by birth.
Validity	Binding on each person without regard to social context; as universally applicable as God himself, reflecting a vision of the "omnipresence of God."	Dependent on social boundary lines; irrelevant to those who cross the boundary of the social order.
Sanctions	Not controlled by social organizations, but connected with cause-and-effect concepts in human history; includes both positive and negative sanctions.	Enforced by social organization through its chosen authorities; sanctions are largely negative, though nonpolitical organizations use economic motivations and prestige to obtain conformity.
Norms	Typically presented as verbal abstractions, the definition of which is an obligation of persons in concrete circumstances and expressing the "fear of God"; conformity based on commitment to seeking the interest of the next person, whether God or fellow citizens.	Defined by social authority in advance, usually with specific sanctions defined for specific violations; arbitrary and formal in nature since only visible actions may be assessed in lawcourts; conformity based on self-interest.
Orientation	Toward the future: promotes reliable individual behavior, thereby providing a basis for both private and public security; predictions of consequences extend to four generations in case of violation (the definition of a household).	Toward the past: attempts to punish violations of the public order to make that public order more secure; it is oriented toward the future only in the sense that it gives advance warning of penalties the society has power to impose on violators; very short attention span (statute of limitations).
Social Aspect	Obligations are individual, but consequences (blessings and curses) are of necessity social since they are "acts of God"—drought, epidemic, defeat in war, and the like powerfully reinforce individual responsibility to society and social responsibility to refrain from protecting the guilty.	Obligations defined by society are binding on all members, but sanctions are imposed only on guilty individuals, involving adversarial procedures and rites; a form of warfare pitting society against the guilty.
Evolution	Forms basis for social custom especially in early stages. As social control takes over, it may degenerate into mere ritual reinforcement of a social solidarity.	Presupposes a customary morality that it attempts to protect but cannot create. Tends to become increasingly rigid in formal definition and devoid of real ethical content.

Continued

	Founded on Covenant	Founded on Law
Continuity	Since it is not produced by society, it cannot be guaranteed by society; essentially private, individual, independent of roles, encouraged through persons with no legislative authority: prophets, the Christ, apostles. Destruction of a particular social control system, therefore, does not mean the end of the value system.	Cannot exist apart from social institutions—king, priest, political officers, legislative, executive, judicial; ceases to exist when political structures fall.

Adapted from George Mendenhall, "The Conflict between Value Systems and Social Control," in *Unity and Diversity: Essays on the History, Literature, and Religion of the Ancient Near East*, ed. J. J. M. Roberts (Baltimore: Johns Hopkins University Press, 1975), 211. For his full discussion, see 169–80.

Here we ask, on which side of this ledger was ancient Israel? The New Testament suggests that the Jewish society encountered by Jesus and Paul was grounded in laws and obligations, but was this true of ancient Israel? And even if it was, is this the way God intended it to be? In answering these questions, we should be cautious about imposing the deontological ethical vision of Judaism in Jesus and Paul's day onto ancient Israel;[4] instead, we must explore the biblical evidence itself for the type of society God envisioned in his revelation at Sinai and through the Torah of Deuteronomy. We will examine four readily identifiable documents embedded in the Pentateuch. Whether or not we agree that these should be classified by genre as "law," they functioned as constitutional documents for Israel.

The Decalogue and Life as Worship

Exodus 20:2–17, along with its parallel in Deuteronomy 5:6–21, is a self-contained covenant document, identified by name in Scripture as "The Ten Words"[5] and inscribed in duplicate on two stone slabs called "the tablets of the covenant."[6] The "words" (*haddĕbārîm*) inscribed on these tablets represented a transcript of the speech YHWH gave directly to Israel when he invited them to an audience with him at Sinai. Although the Decalogue was the only part

4. Deontological ethics grounds the morality of action on conformity to rules and views ethical performance as a fulfillment of obligations. *Deontology* derives from Greek *deon*, "obligation, duty," and *logia*, "words [about]."

5. As in Exod. 34:28; Deut. 4:13; 10:4. Hebrew *'ăśeret haddĕbārîm*; Greek *ta deka hrēmata* or *hoi deka logoi*, from which we get "Decalogue." Identifying these as "The Ten Commandments" is misleading because it obscures the significance of the Hebrew (and Greek) designations and is ill-advised because it involves an archaic word, "commandment," that is rarely used in everyday speech.

6. Hebrew *lûḥōt habbĕrît*, Deut. 9:9, 11, 15.

of the Sinai revelation that the people heard directly from YHWH, it was only the beginning of his communication there and ultimately functioned as a summary statement of his will revealed in greater detail in subsequent addresses. We should interpret this document not as a law code but as a foundational covenant document, intended to create a picture of life within the community of faith governed by covenant principles.[7]

Contrary to popular visual reproductions of the Decalogue, this document does not begin with a command ("You shall have no other gods besides me"), but with the gospel. As in other ancient Near Eastern treaty documents, the preamble (Exod. 20:2; Deut. 5:6) serves two purposes. First, it identifies the divine Suzerain by name and by his relationship to Israel: "I am YHWH your God." This statement reinforces the idea that covenants are based on personal relationships. Second, the preamble summarizes the history of this relationship to this point: "who brought you out of the land of Egypt, out of the house of slavery." This statement reviews what YHWH has said at the outset of these proceedings: "You have seen what I did to the Egyptians, how I carried you on eagles' wings and brought you to myself" (Exod. 19:4).

This glorious gospel sets the stage for the stipulations that follow. Despite the complete absence of cultic or liturgical features, the Decalogue functions as a worship text, instructing the Israelites concerning reverential human acts of submission and homage before the divine Sovereign in response to his gracious revelation of himself and in accord with his will. Significantly, these principles are not addressed to the world at large, nor are they given to Israel in Egypt as prerequisites to their rescue. They are addressed to a people already redeemed, and summarize the appropriate response to the incredible grace they have received.[8] As a worship text, it reflects a remarkably comprehensive view of life, calling for vigilant commitment in at least four dimensions (table 4.2).

This document is a special kind of worship text, which we may interpret as Israel's Magna Carta, and perhaps the world's oldest bill of rights. But whose rights does it serve? To answer this question, we must identify the addressee. Although the Decalogue has binding authority for all Israelites, strictly speaking it is addressed to individual adult male heads of households—households including male and female slaves, livestock, and non-Israelite workers. Apparently

7. For a fuller discussion of the form and function of the Decalogue, see Daniel I. Block, "Reading the Decalogue Right to Left: The Ten Principles of Covenant Relationship in the Hebrew Bible," in *How I Love Your Torah, O Lord! Studies in the Book of Deuteronomy* (Eugene, OR: Cascade Books, 2011), 21–55.

8. Contrary to Martin Luther and many of his followers, these "words" are not presented as "natural law," or even distinctly moral law, in contrast to Israelite covenant law in the rest of the Pentateuch.

Table 4.2. Dimensions of Covenant Commitment
in the Decalogue (Deuteronomic Version)

God and Israel: I am YHWH your God, who brought you out of the land of Egypt, out of the house of slavery.

An Israelite and His* God	An Israelite and His Household	An Israelite and His Neighbors	An Israelite and His Heart
You shall have no other gods before me. You shall not make for yourself an idol, whether in the form of anything that is in heaven above, or that is on the earth beneath, or that is in the water under the earth. You shall not bow down to them or worship them; for I, YHWH your God, am an impassioned God, punishing children for the iniquity of parents to the third and the fourth generation of those who reject me, but showing steadfast love to the thousandth generation of those who love me and keep my commandments.	Observe the Sabbath day and keep it holy, as YHWH your God commanded you. Six days you shall labor and do all your work; but the seventh day is a Sabbath to YHWH your God; in it you shall not do any work—you, or your son, or your daughter, or your manservant, or your maidservant, or your ox, or your ass, or any of your cattle, or the sojourner who is within your gates—that your manservant and your maidservant may rest as well as you. You shall remember that you were a servant in the land of Egypt, and YHWH your God brought you out from there with a mighty hand and an outstretched arm; therefore YHWH your God commanded you to keep the Sabbath day.	You shall not kill. And you shall not commit adultery. And you shall not steal.	And you shall not covet your neighbor's wife.
You shall not bear the name of YHWH your God in vain, for YHWH will not acquit anyone who bears his name in vain.	Honor your father and your mother, as YHWH your God commanded you; that your days may be prolonged, and that it may go well with you, in the land which YHWH your God gives you.	And you shall not testify falsely against your neighbor.	And you shall not desire your neighbor's house, field, manservant, maidservant, ox, donkey, or anything else that belongs to your neighbor.

* I use the masculine because of the gendered nature of the Hebrew Decalogue.

an Israelite man's aged parents still live with him, and he is tempted to commit adultery, testify falsely against his neighbor in legal proceedings, and covet his neighbor's wife and property, including house and field.

Unlike modern bills of rights, the Decalogue is not interested in the addressee's rights but seeks to protect a man's household and neighbors by reining in his propensity to abuse them. The Decalogue envisions a community that has been freed from the tyranny of Egypt but would be under the constant threat of those with social and economic power behaving like little pharaohs.[9] Each principle seeks to protect the rights of someone else in the face of abusive heads of households. The first two commands protect YHWH's rights, and the remainder protects other people's rights (table 4.3).[10]

Table 4.3. The Decalogue: The World's Oldest Bill of Rights

	Command	Rights Involved
	I am YHWH your God, who brought you out of the land of Egypt, out of the house of slavery.	The gospel base of the bill of rights (cf. Deut. 6:20–25)
1	You shall have no other gods before me; you shall not make for yourself a carved image . . . to bow down to them or serve them.	YHWH has the right to his people's exclusive allegiance.
2	You shall not bear the name of YHWH your God in vain.	YHWH has the right to proper representation and loyal service.
3	Remember the Sabbath day, to keep it holy.	YHWH has the right to our time and our trust (Exod. 20:10–11). My household has the right to humane treatment from me (Deut. 5:14–15).
4	Honor your father and your mother.	My parents have the right to my respect and care.
5	You shall not murder.	Others have the right to life.
6	You shall not commit adultery.	Others have the right to sexual purity and secure marriages.
7	You shall not steal.	Others have the right to property.
8	You shall not bear false witness against your neighbor.	My neighbor has the right to an honest representation and reputation, especially in court.
9*	You shall not covet your neighbor's wife.	My neighbor has the right to freedom from fear that I desire his wife.
10	You shall not covet your neighbor's house, field, human resources, animal resources, or anything else.	My neighbor has the right to freedom from fear that I desire his household resources.

* Following the order in Deut. 5:21, which clarifies some of the ambiguity of Exod. 20:17.

9. Note the framing of the document with references to the "house of slaves" (*bêt 'ăbādîm*, Deut. 5:6) in the preamble and "your neighbor's house" (*bêt rē'ekā*, 5:21) in the last command—especially in the Deuteronomic version.

10. The discourse grammar of the text argues in favor of the Roman Catholic and Lutheran numbering of the commands over the Reformed numbering. See further Block, "Reading the Decalogue Right to Left," 56–60.

In short, the Decalogue charges heads of households to be covenantally committed to YHWH, their households, and their neighbors, so that they will resist seeking their own advantage at others' expenses and will always seek others' interests above their own. This is why Jesus can distill this document to two commands: "You shall demonstrate love for YHWH your God with all your heart and with all your being and with all your resources,"[11] and "You shall demonstrate love for your neighbor as yourself"[12] (see fig. 4:1).

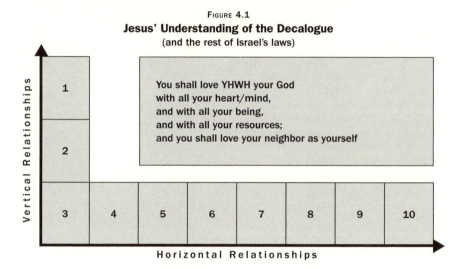

FIGURE 4.1
Jesus' Understanding of the Decalogue
(and the rest of Israel's laws)

Now we also begin to understand the biblical notion of "love." As used in the Bible, Hebrew *'āhab* and Greek *agapaō* mean "to demonstrate covenant commitment through actions that serve the other person's interest and well-being." This is what YHWH demonstrated when he chose Abraham and his descendants as his covenant people, rescued Israel from Egypt, gave them Canaan as their grant of land (Deut. 4:37–38; 7:6–8; 10:15), protected them from their enemies (Deut. 23:5), established the Davidic monarchy (1 Kings 10:9; 2 Chron. 2:11; 9:8), and restored Israel from exile (Isa. 43:4–7; 54:8–10; Jer. 31:3; Hosea 3:1). This is what YHWH demonstrates when he executes justice and cares for the righteous, for orphans, widows, and aliens (Deut. 10:18; Ps. 146:8–9), and disciplines his children (Prov. 3:12; Heb. 12:6). This is

11. On this interpretation of the Shema, see below.
12. For a convincing discussion of *'āhab*, "love," as active and concrete demonstration of commitment to the well-being of others rather than an abstract emotional expression, see A. Malamat, "'You Shall Love Your Neighbor as Yourself': A Case of Misinterpretation?" in *Die hebräische Bibel und ihre Nachgeschichte: Festschrift für Rolf Rendtorff zum 65. Geburtstag*, ed. E. Blum et al. (Neukirchen/Vluyn: Neukirchener Verlag, 1990), 111–15.

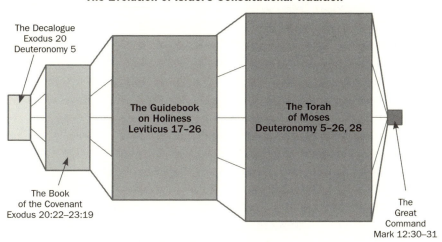

FIGURE 4.2
The Evolution of Israel's Constitutional Tradition

what God demonstrated for the world when he gave his only Son (John 3:16; Gal. 2:20; 1 John 4:10). This is what Jesus demonstrated when he offered his life for sinners (Eph. 5:2, 25–29; Rev. 1:5). And this is what we demonstrate when we are totally devoted to God, when we bear his name with honor and represent him well, when we walk in his ways and obey his will, when we care for the needy and are gracious to the undeserving (Deut. 10:12, 19; 11:1; Matt. 25:34–40), and when we love our enemies and pray for those who abuse us (Prov. 25:21–22; Matt. 5:43–48; Rom. 12:20). In this regard the Decalogue creates a covenantal worldview, concretizing and applying to life the great command summarized by Jesus, and laying the foundation for the rest of Israel's constitutional documents that follow Exodus 20. The relationship of the Decalogue to the rest of Israel's constitutional documents is illustrated above (fig. 4.2).

None of these documents was intended to be exhaustive, least of all the Decalogue, which functions as a paradigmatic catechetical text, consisting of ten principles probably for ease of memorization—one principle for each finger. After the Decalogue, the Book of the Covenant (Exod. 20:22–23:19),[13] the Guidebook on Holiness (Lev. 17–26),[14] and the Torah of Moses[15] build

13. The name translates *sēper habbĕrît*, literally, "document of the covenant," in Exod. 24:7. Books as we know them were not invented for another millennium.

14. Scholars generally refer to Lev. 17–26 as the Holiness Code, but this misleads the reader to anticipate a formal legal code. The term "holiness" reflects the pervasive emphasis of these chapters. See, e.g., Lev. 19:2.

15. The name derives from the book of Deuteronomy itself, which repeatedly refers to Moses' final pastoral addresses as "this Torah" or "this Torah document" (Deut. 1:5; 4:8; 17:18–19; 27:3,

on one another. These documents exhibit a consistent perspective, but they paint an increasingly focused picture of life lived in covenant commitment to God and the community. This is true worship: consistent reverential acts of submission and homage before the divine Sovereign in response to his gracious revelation of himself and in accord with his will.

Leviticus 17–26: Guidebook on Holiness and Life as Worship

An investigation into the First Testament's disposition toward daily life as worship may well begin with 1 Peter 1:13–2:12, which looks to Leviticus 19 as a paradigmatic text. This passage presents a focused picture of holiness as a way of life and worship. Leviticus 19 is a self-contained literary unit within the instructions on holiness, which in turn are embedded in a book whose central theme is *the grace of YHWH expressed in revelation of what it means to be his holy people.* The first sixteen chapters look like a manual for priests on how to maintain a holy community through sacrificial rituals (1:1–7:38), the institution of the priesthood (8:1–10:20), instructions on ritual purity (11:1–15:33), and observance of the holiest day in Israel's religious calendar, Yom Kippur, the Day of Atonement (16:1–34). These are followed by detailed instructions on holy living (17:1–25:55), which conclude with an appeal to covenant loyalty through promised blessings and threatened curses (26:1–45).[16] Leviticus 26:46 signals the end of the original constitutional document: "These are the ordinances and judgments and instructions that YHWH granted [as the terms of the covenant] between himself and the people of Israel on Mount Sinai through Moses."

This was not an agreement between equals,[17] but a suzerainty covenant between a divine Superior and his vassals. As Israel's Redeemer, Patron, and Lord, YHWH determined every detail of the covenant: he graciously chose Abraham and his descendants to be his covenant partner (Gen. 17:7); he fixed the context for ratifying with Abraham's descendants the covenant that he had originally made with the first patriarch (Exod. 2:23–25; 3:12; 19:1–6); he

8, 26; 28:58, 61; 29:20–21, 27, 29 [19–20, 26, 28]; 30:10; 31:9, 11–12, 24, 26; 32:46). The Hebrew word *tôrâ* does not mean "law" but "authoritative instruction," which may take the form of command, but may also involve story, song, genealogy, prayer, etc. The semantic range of the Hebrew word in Deuteronomy is reflected exactly in Greek as *didaskalia* and *didachē*, which are rightly rendered "teaching, doctrine" in the New Testament.

16. All these elements are integral to the covenant that YHWH made with Israel. Somewhat like the amendments to the United States Constitution, YHWH will add further stipulations that bear equal authority: Lev. 27:1–34; Num. 5:1–6:27; 8:1–26; 15:1–41; 18:1–19:22; 28:1–30:16; 35:1–34.

17. Like the covenant that Jacob and Laban negotiate in Gen. 31:43–55 [31:43–32:1].

determined the procedure for its ratification (19:7–24:11); he determined the terms of the covenant;[18] he provided the transcript and symbol of the covenant to function as a sign and guarantee of its validity;[19] and he determined the consequences of fidelity and infidelity.[20] Nothing about this covenant was negotiated. In its establishment the Israelites had only one decision to make: to commit themselves to the covenant Lord without reservation or qualification and to accept the mission for which YHWH had called Abraham—to be an agent of grace to the world.

As its title suggests, the Guidebook on Holiness emphasizes the notion of sanctity: YHWH identifies himself as the Holy One (Lev. 19:2; 20:26; 21:8) and the One who makes Israel holy;[21] he challenges Israel to "sanctify yourselves" (20:7) and "be holy";[22] and he characterizes many articles and persons discussed as holy.[23] The guidebook deals with wide-ranging subjects, including moral exhortations, cultic regulations, and legal prescriptions (table 4.4).

Table 4.4. A Call to Holiness: Structure of Leviticus 17–25

1.	Guarding the sanctity of life	17:1–18:30
	a. Regulations concerning blood	17:1–16
	b. Taboos involving sexual conduct	18:1–30
2.	Guarding the sanctity of the community	19:1–20:27
	a. The dimensions of holiness	19:1–37
	b. The seriousness of holiness	20:1–27
3.	Guarding the sanctity of cultic worship	21:1–24:23
	a. The sanctity of the priesthood	21:1–24
	b. The sanctity of gifts for God	22:1–33
	c. The sanctity of holy days	23:1–44
	d. The sanctity of the tabernacle	24:1–9
	e. The sanctity of the divine name	24:10–23
4.	Guarding the sanctity of the land	25:1–55
5.	The closing appeal to covenantal fidelity	26:1–46

How ancient Israelites used this Guidebook on Holiness is unclear. Some suggest that it served as a catechism for a sanctuary school or as a handbook for Levites and priests as they taught the people throughout the land. As in the

18. Exod. 20:1–17; 20:22–23:19; 25:1–31:17; Lev. 1:1–26:46.
19. Exod. 24:12–18; 31:18; 34:1, 27–28.
20. See Lev. 26; Deut. 28.
21. That is, "he sanctifies them"; Lev. 20:8, 24–26; 21:8, 15, 23; 22:9, 16, 32.
22. See Lev. 19:2; 20:7, 26 (to YHWH); 21:6a, 6b (cf. vv. 7, 8).
23. YHWH's name, Lev. 20:3; 22:2, 32; sacrificial food, 19:8; ordinary food, 19:24; sacred bread, 21:22; 24:9; food dedicated to YHWH, 22:2, 3, 4, 6, 10, 14, 15, 16; convocations, 23:2, 3, 4, 7, 8, 21, 24, 27, 35, 36, 37; a place (tabernacle), 24:9; a time (Year of Jubilee), 25:12.

Decalogue, these regulations are addressed primarily to heads of households, assuming that if those in charge of domestic units live according to the covenant, the health of the nation will be assured.

Two foundational statements frame Leviticus 19: YHWH begins by declaring, "You shall be holy, for I, YHWH your God, am holy" (v. 2a), and concludes with "I am YHWH your God, who brought you out of the land of Egypt; so you shall keep all my ordinances and judgments, and you shall do them: I am YHWH" (vv. 36b–37). This framework provides the lens for interpreting the intervening prescriptions. Rather than functioning as a legal or cultic code, this collection of commands creates a picture of worship that arises out of a particular vision of God and out of gratitude for his incredible grace.

The chapter alternates between explicit commands or prohibitions[24] and contextually qualified commands and prohibitions.[25] The list of injunctions exhibits five significant features.[26] First, it bears obvious links to the Decalogue.[27] Although some suggest that "this speech is an exposition of the Decalogue,"[28] we should rather read this chapter as an exposition of the conceptual world summarized by the Decalogue.[29]

Second, reminders of who is talking—"I am YHWH your God"—interrupt this series of injunctions fifteen times.[30] These insertions remind hearers of the name they bear and whom they represent, and that the Object of worship, rather than the worshipers themselves, ultimately defines true

24. Cast in the forms of "You shall . . ." and "You shall not . . ." These are often referred to as apodictic laws.

25. Beginning with "If . . ." or "When . . ." These are referred to as casuistic laws. By word count, apodictic commands exceed casuistic commands by about 25 percent.

26. For a helpful discussion of the literary and substantive features of this text, see Elmer A. Martens, "How Is the Christian to Construe Old Testament Law?," *Bulletin for Biblical Research* 12 (2002): 199–216.

27. John E. Hartley, *Leviticus*, Word Biblical Commentary (Dallas: Word, 1992), 310–11. Hartley identifies the following correlations (according to the traditional Reformed numbering): Command no. 2, Exod. 20:4–6 and Lev. 19:4a; no. 3, Exod. 20:7 and Lev. 19:12; no. 4, Exod. 20:8–12 and Lev. 19:3a, 30a; no. 5, Exod. 20:12 and Lev. 19:3a; no. 6, Exod. 20:13 and Lev. 19:16a; no. 7, Exod. 20:14 and Lev. 19:29 (20–22); no. 8, Exod. 20:15 and Lev. 19:11a, 13 (35–36); no. 9, Exod. 20:16 and Lev. 19:11b, 16a; no. 10, Exod. 20:17 and Lev. 19:17–18 (9–10).

28. Ibid., 311.

29. The focus on holiness, the inclusion of many elements not found or only hinted at in the Decalogue, the attention to socially marginalized groups, the changes in vocabulary where linkages seem the firmest, and the rearrangement of subjects—such features caution against Hartley's approach.

30. Three forms of the self-introduction formula occur: (1) the simple form, "I am YHWH" (Lev. 19:12, 14, 16, 18, 28, 39, 32, 37); (2) a middle form, "I am YHWH your God" (vv. 3, 4, 10, 25, 31, 34); and (3) the full form, "I am YHWH your God, who brought you out of the land of Egypt" (v. 36), which links this chapter directly with the Decalogue.

worship. Furthermore, the full form ("I am YHWH your God, who brought you out of the land of Egypt") in verse 36 reminds readers that this document was produced for the redeemed. These stipulations do not inaugurate relationship with God but define responses to a relationship God has already established.

Third, YHWH does not define holiness in interior, mystical, or spiritual terms, as if it were merely a matter of the heart or simply of communion with God (cf. Eph. 5:15–6:20). Rather, holiness is defined by observable actions: people are what they do.

Fourth, the commands are remarkably diverse, including instructions concerning vertical, horizontal, and even environmental dimensions of covenant fidelity. The apparently random order of the topics reinforces the idea that all of life is to be holy.[31] YHWH's people may not compartmentalize life into sacred, moral, and civil spheres. To grasp the multidimensional and practical nature of holiness and the practice of true worship, it may be helpful to regroup them according to logical categories.

Regulations Governing Vertical Relations

Vertical ordinances governing the relationship between God and his people may be classified according to four general categories.

General or foundational principles. In addition to the general vertical statements that frame Leviticus 19 (vv. 2, 37), "My ordinances you must keep" (v. 19a) functions like a fulcrum in keeping two roughly equal parts in balance. Twice YHWH appeals to the people to fear (*yārēʾ*) him (vv. 14, 32). Centuries later, Israel's sages would emphasize that "the fear of YHWH is the first principle of wisdom."[32] Here YHWH declares that fear is fundamental to the life of holiness and necessary in true worship. When awe before the divine King is lacking, the sense of accountability lapses, and motivation for self-discipline wanes.[33] Verse 12 highlights the problem of swearing falsely by YHWH's name, primarily because of its effect on his reputation. To bear the name of YHWH (see the second command of the Decalogue) and then misrepresent him or abuse his name in false oaths presents a fundamental contradiction.

---

31. See further below. For an attempt to establish an order in the topics, see Jonathan Magonet, "The Structure and Meaning of Leviticus 19," *Hebrew Annual Review* 7 (1983): 151–67.

32. As in Job 28:28; Ps. 111:10; Prov. 1:7; 9:10; 15:33; Eccles. 12:13.

33. Malachi highlights the link between reverence for God and personal conduct; cf. above, "Worship as Attitude," in chap. 1; "Moral and Spiritual Prerequisites to Acceptable Worship," in chap. 3.

Cultic practices. Twice YHWH calls for the proper observance of his Sabbaths (Lev. 19:3, 30). While the Sabbath principle derives from the Decalogue (Exod. 20:8–11), this injunction extends to all divinely appointed festival days when work was to cease. The charge concerning peace offerings in Leviticus 19:5–8 summarizes and simplifies the detailed regulations spelled out in chapter 7. While the real issue in the law concerning an adulterous affair with a slave girl (19:20–22) is ethical, the instructions for responding are cultic, applying the reparation offering as outlined in Leviticus 5. The plea for reverence (*yārē'*) toward YHWH's sanctuary in 19:30 recognizes the tabernacle complex as the sacred dwelling of the divine king and shows that the awe due him (vv. 14, 32) extends to his glorious residence.

Practices with theological undertones. Several commands are neither overtly cultic nor ethical but represent distinctly Israelite cultural practices based on theological principles. Leviticus 19:19 prohibits a triad of unholy mixtures: mating diverse animals, planting diverse seed, and wearing diverse clothing. YHWH's people were to respect the distinctions he had established; their lives and their property were to be characterized by order.[34] The prohibition on eating meat from an animal whose blood was not drained at the time of slaughter summarizes the fuller statement in 17:10–16. This law is grounded in the conviction that all life is sacred. Since the life of the flesh is in the blood, its sanctity must be protected by spilling the blood of the animal on the ground and prohibiting human consumption of it.

Taboos on pagan practices. Many of the religious practices of the Canaanites and surrounding peoples were forbidden in Israel. Leviticus 19 alludes to several of these. The prohibition of worshiping gods other than YHWH, disparagingly designated as *'ĕlîlîm*, "nothings/godlings" (v. 4), and the ban on making images of deity reinforce the first command of the Decalogue (Exod. 20:3–6). The ban on bodily disfigurement with tattoos and certain kinds of haircuts (Lev. 19:27–28) alludes to important aspects of pagan mourning rites. Deuteronomy 14:1–2 affirms that the external appearance of God's people should reflect their status as the children of YHWH and his treasured holy people. Although divination, necromancy,[35] and sorcery (Lev. 19:31) were common in the ancient world, they were emphatically repudiated

---

34. Mary Douglas has observed that "holiness requires that individuals shall conform to the class to which they belong. And holiness requires that different classes of things shall not be confused. . . . Holiness means keeping distinct the categories of creation. It therefore involves correct definition, discrimination and order." See her work *Purity and Danger: An Analysis of the Concepts of Pollution and Taboo* (London: Routledge, 2003), 54.

35. Here necromancy means turning to "spirits of the ancestors" (*'ōbōt*), who reside in the netherworld, and wizards (*yiddĕ'ōnîm*, literally, "knowing ones"; Lev. 20:27), i.e., those skilled in making contact with the dead, or the ghosts they call up.

in Israel as human attempts to manipulate deity (Deut. 18:10–12). YHWH speaks and acts in his own time, for his own reasons, and in response to his own prescribed conditions.

Regulations Governing Horizontal Relations

Two general concerns underlie the regulations governing human relations: maintaining order in society and protecting the weak and vulnerable. Regarding the former, Leviticus 19 seems particularly concerned to guard normal *family relations*. Perhaps recognizing that holiness and true worship begin at home, the prescriptions open with a call for respect/reverence (*yārē'*) toward one's mother and father (v. 3). Verse 32 links this idea with the fear of YHWH and extends the demand for respect to the aged. Children are to revere their seniors, brothers are to love one another (v. 17), and parents are not to exploit or degrade their children (v. 29). The prohibition on sending one's daughter out as a harlot guards her purity, her relationship with her father, and the sanctity of the land. No crimes are purely private.

Verses 11–18 involve basic principles governing neighborly relations within *the community*. First, neighbors are to treat one another with honesty and integrity (vv. 11–12). Stealing, duplicitous dealing, and false oaths in YHWH's name destroy communal health and defile God's sacred name. Second, neighbors are not to take advantage of one another. A common thread in the actions cited in verse 13 is the social superiority of one neighbor over another. A stronger neighbor may be tempted to oppress a weaker one, take his goods by force, or withhold the wages of the neighbor who has been contracted for day labor. Third, neighbors are to settle disputes fairly and without partiality (vv. 15–16). Justice is served neither by sentimental pity for the poor nor by deference to the powerful. Fairness precludes defamatory slander, threats on another's life, or false accusations of crimes that demand the death penalty. Fourth, neighbors are to be covenantally committed to one another (vv. 17–18). As noted earlier, Hebrew *'āhab* means *to demonstrate covenant commitment with action in the other person's interest*. The opposite expression, *śānē'*, does not mean simply "to hate" but also "to reject" (Deut. 5:9–10). Where there is annoyance, frank reproof is in order, but a person must guard against sin, bearing grudges, and personal vengeance. The addition of "as yourself" to "You shall love your neighbor" is not a call for self-love. Rather, it demands that YHWH's people act in the interests of their fellow Israelites as spontaneously and naturally as they do in their own interests.

Finally, these stipulations emphasize the importance of *protecting the weak and vulnerable*. This text identifies the poor (*'ānî*, Lev. 19:10; cf. *dal* in v. 15),

hired hands (*śākîr*, v. 13), and aliens (*gēr*, vv. 10, 33–34) as particularly vulnerable to exploitation and abuse. The poor included native Israelites (e.g.,
orphans, widows) who lacked economic support, usually because of the death
of the primary breadwinner. Hired hands depended on their employer for
support. "Aliens" refers to non-Israelites who resided temporarily within the
community but did not enjoy the rights of full citizenship. For their sake people
were to leave the edges of the fields unharvested and grapes that fell to the
ground ungathered (vv. 9–10). This remarkably humanitarian tone climaxes
in verses 32–36. Rather than taking advantage of aliens, Israelites were to
extend to them the same covenantal commitment they expressed toward their
countrymen. Recalling their own experience in Egypt, they should understand
the pain of alienation and exploitation and guard against it in their own land,
treating non-Israelites not as the Israelites have been treated by the Egyptians
but as YHWH has treated them.

Verse 14 guards the rights of the physically handicapped. This statement
intentionally links the prohibition of pranks on the blind and deaf with the
fear of YHWH. As recognized by Proverbs 14:31 and 17:5 (and Jesus in Matt.
25:31–36), all humans are created as images of God, regardless of physical
condition; the way we treat others reflects our attitude toward the One in
whose image they are made (cf. Matt. 25:31–46).

Reflections on the Abiding Significance of Leviticus 19

In the history of the church we have applied the notion of "holy" ("saints")
to three kinds of people: (1) specific persons whom the church beatifies;[36] (2) extraordinarily religious people, especially ascetics who renounce the world; and
(3) people whose holiness is essentially interior if not mystical, having to do
with private spiritual communion with God. Leviticus 19 will not allow this
restrictive understanding. Its call to holiness addresses all Israelites without
reference to cult activity or extraordinary spiritual endowments or internal
piety. To be sure, the notions of "fear" and "love" are rooted within the heart,
but both require demonstration in action.

To summarize, Leviticus 19 teaches several important lessons about holiness and life as worship in ancient Israel. First, life as worship was to be
motivated by knowledge of the character of God and by the experience of
his grace. Holiness was not a burdensome legal imposition but a privilege
involving a grateful response to a gracious God. Second, this sort of worship

36. In such cases the church declares a deceased person to have been uniquely blessed and
therefore worthy of religious veneration in a particular place or congregation.

was not displayed primarily by external liturgical actions or interior mystical qualities but in actions driven by love for God and love for one's fellow human being. Third, commitment to holiness affected every area of life. Those who viewed life as worship would not compartmentalize activities into sacred and profane. In everyday speech, personal morality, social relationships, and business conduct, Israelites were to do all for the glory of God and the benefit of others (cf. 1 Cor. 10:31).

But what has this text to teach Christians about holiness and life as worship?[37] In answering the question, we need to consider several significant factors. First, the God who speaks here is the Triune God, who is incarnate in Jesus Christ. The voice that Moses heard defining the dimensions of holiness in Leviticus 19 is the same voice that the disciples heard in the Sermon on the Mount (Matt. 5–7) and in the upper room, saying, "If you love me, you will keep my commands" (John 14:15; cf. vv. 21, 23; 15:10).

Second, as Peter affirms, the ethical principle of *imitatio Dei* still stands: "As the one who called you is holy, so be holy yourselves in all your behavior; because it is written, 'You shall be holy, for I am holy'" (1 Pet. 1:15–16). In similar vein, Hebrews 12:14 reminds us that unless we pursue holiness, we will not see God. To grasp how Peter and the author of Hebrews understood "holiness," we need to look to texts like Leviticus 19.

Third, true worship demonstrated by holy living arises out of a profound sense of gratitude for divine grace. The relationship between Israel's redemption and their ethical response is paradigmatic for our own approach to life as worship. Far from being a burdensome divinely imposed duty, the memory of our own salvation should inspire gratitude and yield awed trust before God, personal purity, and a commitment to others' well-being, especially those who are marginalized.

Fourth, while the spiritual disciplines of prayer, reading Scripture, meditation, and silence before God are indispensable for spiritual growth, authentic piety is demonstrated first and foremost in observable actions demonstrating love for God, fellow human beings, and even the environment. This is a full-bodied biblical understanding of holiness.

As with the Decalogue, the aim of Leviticus 19 and the instructions on holiness is not legislative but rhetorical and pastoral, seeking to create a moral vision and an ethical universe within which people apply their principles. In that sense, Leviticus 19 has paradigmatic authority for us,[38]

37. For a helpful discussion of this text and its relevance for Christians, see Martens, "How Is the Christian to Construe Old Testament Law?," 211–15.
38. On First Testament law as paradigmatic for Christians, see C. J. H. Wright, *Old Testament Ethics for the People of God* (Downers Grove, IL: InterVarsity, 2004), 65–75.

even though many Christians resist this notion and dismiss texts like this as irrelevant for the church. Assuming that life within the new covenant is governed by fundamentally different principles than life within the old,[39] they argue that Christians are obligated only to those First Testament laws that are explicitly reaffirmed in the New Testament.[40] Even if we grant the validity of this principle, it is striking, first, how few of the ordinances in this chapter are explicitly declared obsolete in Christ,[41] and second, how many are explicitly reiterated and reinforced in the New Testament. Indeed, the overwhelming majority of regulations presented here are affirmed in the New Testament:

Holiness (v. 2; cf. 1 Pet. 1:15–16)

Reverence for YHWH (vv. 14, 32; cf. 1 Pet. 2:17; Rev. 14:7)

Respect for parents (v. 3; Eph. 6:1; Col. 3:20)

Respect for the aged (v. 32; Rom. 13:7; 1 Tim. 5:1)

Obedience to YHWH's commandments (vv. 19, 37; cf., e.g., John 14:15)

Idolatry (v. 4a; cf. 1 Cor. 10:14; Gal. 5:20; Col. 3:5; 1 Pet. 4:3; Rev. 22:15)

Prohibition on images (v. 4b; cf. Rom. 1:23)

Lying, deceit, false oaths (vv. 11–12; cf. Matt. 5:33–37; Rom. 13:9; 1 Tim. 1:10; James 5:12)

Theft, robbery (v. 11; cf. Matt. 19:18; 23:25; John 10:8; Acts 19:37; Eph. 4:28)

Withholding wages (v. 13; cf. Rom. 13:8; James 5:4)

Cursing the deaf, tripping up the blind (v. 14; cf. James 3:9)

Judicial partiality (v. 15; cf. 1 Tim. 5:21; perhaps James 2:9)

Mistreatment of outsiders (vv. 10, 33–34; cf. Rom. 12:20)

Slander (v. 16; cf. 2 Cor. 12:20; Eph. 4:31; 2 Tim. 3:3)

Life-threatening actions (v. 16; cf. James 2:11)

Rejection of brothers/neighbors (v. 17; cf. Matt. 5:22; James 4:11)

---

39. Embodied in expressions like "the law of love" (Rom. 13:8, 10) or "the law of Christ" (1 Cor. 9:21; Gal. 6:2), which are supposedly distinct from, if not antithetical to, the law of the First Testament.

40. See Gordon Fee and Douglas Stuart, *How to Read the Bible for All Its Worth* (Grand Rapids: Zondervan, 1982), 139.

41. For example, the command concerning peace offerings (vv. 5–8), probably the prohibitions on cross-breeding animals, sowing two kinds of crops in the same field, and wearing clothing made of two kinds of materials, which may be more concerned with marking ethnic boundaries than ethical boundaries. However, a permanent principle of holiness may still underlie even these regulations; for the holy, all of life is to be ordered, even as the universe is ordered, rather than random or chaotic.

Seeking revenge (v. 18; cf. Heb. 10:30; Rom. 12:19)

Bearing a grudge (v. 18; cf. Matt. 6:14–15; 18:35; Eph. 4:32)

Loving one's neighbor/the alien (vv. 17, 34; cf. Matt. 5:44; Mark 12:31; Rom. 13:9; Gal. 5:14)

Consuming meat with blood (v. 26; cf. Acts 15:20)

Divination, sorcery, necromancy (v. 31; cf. Gal. 5:20; Rev. 9:21; 18:23; 21:8; 22:15)

Degradation of daughters by prostitution (v. 29; cf. 1 Cor. 6:9; Rev. 22:15)

Integrity in business (vv. 35–36; cf. 1 Tim. 3:3, 8; Titus 1:7; 1 Pet. 5:2)

Indeed, the New Testament contains similar catalogs of holy behavior.[42] Furthermore, many of the specific commands in Leviticus 19 are grounded in permanent theological principles, for which Christians should find appropriate expressions. Not reaping the edges of fields or picking up fallen grapes was an Israelite expression of normative Christian compassion toward the vulnerable (cf. Matt. 25:35–46). The prohibition on "Canaanite" haircuts and disfiguring the body applies to believers who view their bodies as instruments for glorifying God rather than self (1 Cor. 6:20). Reverence for the old sanctuary is replaced by reverence for the body in the individual (1 Cor. 6:19) and collective (2 Cor. 6:14–18) sense, but it still applies to any structure we designate as the house of God. The prohibition on eating fruit from newly planted trees should be reflected today in believers' stewardship of YHWH's resources.

True worshipers find their inspiration, nourishment, and instruction in the whole counsel of God. Those who have been redeemed recognize that all of life is to be an expression of worship and that God delights in wholehearted and full-bodied holiness. Those who have been raised with Christ (Col. 1) set their minds on things above rather than on earthly things. Those who have died with Christ consider themselves dead to immorality, impurity, passion, evil desire, and greed, which amounts to idolatry. They put aside anger, malice, slander, and abusive speech. They stop lying to one another. They lay aside the old Canaanite self with its abominable practices and put on hearts of compassion, kindness, humility, gentleness, and brotherly love to all, even our enemies. Those whose burdens have been lifted by Christ bear each other's burdens and forgive each other as the Lord has forgiven them. The time has come for the Word of God to transform them into holy images of Christ, worshiping him in spirit and in truth and in accordance with his will.

42. Rom. 12:1–15:13; 1 Cor. 5:9–13; 6:5–11; Gal. 5:13–26; Eph. 5:1–6:13; 1 Tim. 2:1–6:19; Titus 1:5–9; 2:1–3:14; the Letter of James; 1 Pet. 1:13–3:16.

Deuteronomy: The Torah of Moses and Life as Worship

The Torah of Moses in the book of Deuteronomy reinforces the vision of life as worship from beginning to end. Two texts are especially important for establishing the theological foundations for this concept. We touched on both in the first chapter, but they deserve further attention here.

The Shema (Deut. 6:4–5) represents one of the most important verbal symbols of Judaism. Indeed, this is as close as early Judaism came to the notion of a creed. To this day, orthodox Jews recite these verses in the morning when they wake up and at night before they fall asleep. Although interpretation of the Shema as a declaration of God's unity has a long history,[43] within the broader literary and historical context of Deuteronomy 6, this interpretation is unlikely.[44] The issue here is not "How many is God?" but "Who is the God of Israel?" To this question the Israelites were to respond in unison and without compromise, "Our God is YHWH, YHWH alone!" The remainder of chapter 6 confirms that the concern here is the first principle of covenant relationship in the Decalogue: "You shall have no other gods besides me." Israel was to cling to YHWH alone. The Shema is a cry of allegiance, an affirmation of covenant commitment. Whether or not people descended from Abraham, the true covenant community consisted of those for whom this declaration was a verbal badge of identity and who demonstrated this commitment with uncompromising covenant loyalty (cf. v. 5).

In verse 5 Moses clarifies what he means by exclusive allegiance to YHWH. As noted earlier, Hebrew *'āhab* speaks of a fundamental disposition of commitment within a covenant relationship that seeks the well-being and pleasure of one's covenant partner through concrete actions, often without regard for oneself. YHWH demonstrated his love for Abraham, Isaac, and Jacob by choosing their descendants and rescuing them from slavery in Egypt (4:37; 23:5). Now Moses asks his people to reciprocate and prove their verbal commitment in verse 4 with unreserved love.[45]

---

43. This interpretation is reflected in the Greek citations of the Shema in the New Testament: Matt. 22:37; Mark 12:30; Luke 10:27.

44. For a detailed discussion of the Shema and a defense of the interpretation represented here, see Daniel I. Block, "How Many Is God? An Investigation into the Meaning of Deuteronomy 6:4–5," in *How I Love Your Torah, O Lord!*, 73–97; previously published in *Journal of the Evangelical Theological Society* 47 (2004): 193–212; Block, *Deuteronomy*, NIV Application Commentary (Grand Rapids: Zondervan, 2010), 181–84.

45. In Deuteronomy *'āhab* is not primarily an emotional term but covenant commitment demonstrated in action: holding fast (*dābaq*) to YHWH (11:22; 30:20), listening to his voice (30:20), fearing him (10:12), walking in his ways (10:12; 11:22; 19:9; 30:16), and serving him (10:12; 11:13).

Moses highlights the intensity of such love for YHWH with three qualifiers: with one's whole *lēb*, *nepeš*, and *mě'ōd*. While commonly rendered "with all your heart, soul, and strength," this reading obscures the profundity of the statement. Some Christian interpreters have used this statement to argue that human beings consist essentially of mind/intellect, soul, and spiritual/moral power (fig. 4.3). However, 6:4 is not a Greek psychological (and partitive) statement, but an emphatic reinforcement of the call for absolute, singular, and total devotion to YHWH.[46] Proceeding from the inside out, these expressions represent three concentric circles, each of which represents a sphere of human existence (fig. 4.4).

FIGURE 4.3

Psychological Interpretation of Deuteronomy 6:5

Literally, *lēb* denotes "heart," but it is mostly used metaphorically for the seat of emotions or intellect or both. Since biblical Hebrew has no separate word for "mind," the *lēb* is both "feeler" and "thinker."[47] Although *nepeš* denotes "throat, gullet," the word is used in a variety of metaphorical senses.[48] Here it refers to one's entire person. Except in 2 Kings 23:25, which echoes this text, *mě'ōd* is always used adverbially, meaning "very, exceedingly." This obviously makes no sense in English, but in Semitic languages, words from the same root are used adjectivally for "much, numerous," and as a noun, meaning

46. Cf. S. Dean McBride, "The Yoke of the Kingdom: An Exposition of Deuteronomy 6:4–5," *Interpretation* 27, no. 3 (1973): 273–306.

47. For this reason, when Mark reports Jesus' quotation of this verse in 12:30, he actually cites four Greek words: *kardia* (= Hebrew *lēb*), *psychē* (= Hebrew *nepeš*), *dianoia* (= Hebrew *lēb*), and *ischys* (= Hebrew *mě'ōd*).

48. "Appetite/desire" (Prov. 23:2; Eccles. 6:7); "life" (Gen. 9:5; Deut. 12:23; 2 Sam. 23:17; Jon. 2:5 [6]); a person as a "living being" (e.g., Ezek. 4:14); the whole self (Lev. 26:11); even a corpse (21:11).

FIGURE 4.4
Literary Interpretation of Deuteronomy 6:5

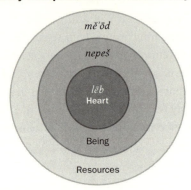

"large quantity."[49] This suits this context well, suggesting the broader sense of "resources," which would include physical, economic, and social strength, and even the physical resources one owns: house, fields, livestock, family, and servants. Everything is to be devoted to YHWH; nothing may be devoted to another god. The progression of Moses' vocabulary now becomes apparent. Beginning with the inner being, he moves to the whole person and then to all one owns. True worship involves covenant commitment rooted in the heart and extending to every aspect of one's being.[50]

But what does worship with this kind of commitment look like in practice? Deuteronomy 10:12–11:1 provides the answer.[51] The boundaries of this unit are marked by an opening question, "What does YHWH your God ask of you?" (10:12a),[52] and a summary answer in 11:1, "So you shall love YHWH your God." The opening question sets the agenda: what kind of worship does YHWH seek? Each of Moses' three responses begins with a concrete answer and then provides a rationale, focusing on the God whom the Israelites are privileged to serve (table

49. *The Assyrian Dictionary of the Oriental Institute of the University of Chicago* (Chicago: University of Chicago Press, 1956–), 10/1 (*M*): 19–20. In Ugaritic *mad/mid* means "great, strong, much"; *Kirta* 1.2.35 (S. B. Parker et al., *Ugaritic Narrative Poetry* [Atlanta: Scholars Press, 1997], 15); *Baal Cycle* 10.v.15 (Parker, *Ugaritic Narrative Poetry*, 130); cf. L. Koehler, W. Baumgartner, and J. J. Stamm, *The Hebrew and Aramaic Lexicon of the Old Testament* [*HALOT*], trans. and ed. M. E. J. Richardson (Leiden: Brill, 1994–99), 2:538.

50. The serial use of three words expresses the superlative degree. Just as "iniquity, rebellion, and sin" in Exod. 34:7 refers to "every conceivable sin," so "heart, life, and property" refers to every part of a person.

51. This new paragraph opens with the Hebrew word *wĕʿattâ*, which, like *oun*, "therefore," in Rom. 12:1, signals a discussion of the implications of what has preceded.

52. The opening question is reminiscent of Micah's statement in Mic. 6:8: "He has told you, O man, what is good; and what YHWH requires of you."

4.5). In each case the rationale begins doxologically, highlighting YHWH's transcendent greatness and describing his gracious condescension to human beings in general (see table 4.5, no. 2) and to Israel in particular (nos. 1, 3). The requirement at the head of each column represents their response of worship.

Today many think the answer to Moses' opening question was something like "To perform the rituals as specified and to be scrupulous in the presentation of your offerings," or "To keep all the commands of YHWH." However, Moses' answers go a very different direction. His first answer (Deut. 10:12b–15) uses five key verbs: (1) fear YHWH your God;[53] (2) walk in all his ways;[54] (3) love YHWH your God;[55] (4) serve YHWH your God with your whole being;[56] and (5) keep his commands and decrees.[57] Since Moses' five responses correspond to the five fingers on one's hand, they could be easily memorized and recited (fig. 4.5).[58] An imaginative reading of this text might even associate the five responses with specific digits.

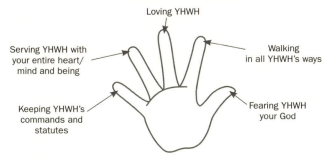

FIGURE 4.5
The Dimensions of True Worship

Loving YHWH

Serving YHWH with your entire heart/ mind and being

Walking in all YHWH's ways

Keeping YHWH's commands and statutes

Fearing YHWH your God

(1) *The thumb: fearing YHWH*. Moses gives pride of place to fear (*yārē'*), which in Deuteronomy means something like "trusting awe" or "awed trust." He hereby reinforces his own emphasis elsewhere and prepares the way for the fundamental tenet of biblical wisdom: "The fear of YHWH is the first principle of wisdom."[59]

53. Cf. 4:10; 5:29; 6:2, 13, 24; 8:6; 10:20; 13:4, 11 [5, 12]; 14:23; 17:13, 19; 19:20; 31:12–13.
54. Cf. 5:33; 8:6; 10:12; 11:22; 13:4–5 [5–6]; 19:9; 26:17; 28:9; 30:16.
55. Cf. 6:5; 11:1, 13, 22; 13:3 [4]; 19:9; 30:6, 16, 20.
56. Cf. 6:13; 10:20; 11:13; 13:4 [5]; also 28:47.
57. Cf. 4:2, 6, 40; 5:10, 29; 6:2, 17; 7:9, 12; 8:2, 6, 11; 10:13; 11:1, 8; 13:4, 18 [5, 19]; 17:19; 19:9; 26:17–18; 27:1; 28:9, 45; 29:9 [8]; 30:10, 16.
58. Which compares with the Decalogue, whose ten principles correspond to the digits on both hands. See Block, "Reading the Decalogue Right to Left," 24–25.
59. E.g., Job 28:28; Ps. 111:10; Prov. 1:7; 9:10; 15:33; Eccles. 12:13; cf. Prov. 15:16; 19:23; 22:4.

Table 4.5. Dimensions of True Worship in Deuteronomy 10:12–11:1

The central issue   So what does YHWH your God ask of you? (10:12a)

	The Requirements	The Basis of the Requirements	
		YHWH's Transcendent Status	YHWH's Gracious Presence
1 (10:12b–15)	You shall fear YHWH your God, walk in all his ways, love him, and serve YHWH your God with all your heart and with all your soul, and keep the commands and statutes of YHWH, which I am commanding you today for your good. (10:12b–13)	Look, to YHWH your God belong heaven and the heaven of heavens, the earth with all that is in it. (10:14)	Yet YHWH set his heart in love on your fathers and chose their offspring after them, you above all peoples, as you are this day. (10:15)
2 (10:16–19)	Circumcise therefore the foreskin of your heart, and be no longer stubborn. (10:16)	For YHWH your God is God of gods and Lord of lords, the great, the mighty, and the awesome God. . . . (10:17a)	. . . who is not partial and takes no bribe. He executes justice for the fatherless and the widow, and loves the sojourner, giving him food and clothing. Love the sojourner, therefore, for you were sojourners in the land of Egypt. (10:17b–19)
3 (10:20–22)	You shall fear YHWH your God. You shall serve him and hold fast to him, and by his name you shall swear. (10:20)	He is your praise. He is your God, who has done for you these great and terrifying things that your eyes have seen. (10:21)	Your fathers went down to Egypt seventy persons, and now YHWH your God has made you as numerous as the stars of heaven. (10:22)

The conclusion   You shall therefore love YHWH your God and keep his charge, his statutes, his rules, and his commands always. (11:1)

(2) *The index finger: "walking in all the ways of YHWH."* This phrase is delightfully ambiguous, meaning either "to live as YHWH has revealed we should live" or "to live as YHWH himself lives," that is, to emulate his character and actions.[60] Moses' index finger appropriately points people in the way to go.

(3) *The middle finger: loving YHWH.* Although the first principle of wisdom is "fearing YHWH," godly piety requires love (*'āhab*). By placing love at the center, Moses reinforces the place of the Supreme Command and echoes the Shema, which demands loving YHWH your God with all your heart and being and resources (6:5). Remarkably, when he resumes the theme of love in verse 15, he speaks first of God's love for his people and then calls on the people to emulate that love.

(4) *The ring finger: serving YHWH out of deep covenant commitment.* In our culture the ring on this finger symbolizes a married couple's commitment and submission to each other. "To serve YHWH" does not refer primarily to cultic service but to living as faithful vassals of YHWH.[61] The addition of "with all your heart/mind [*lēb*] and with all your being [*nepeš*]" reinforces the appeal for the vassal's total submission to his Suzerain.

(5) *The little finger: keeping the commands and statutes of YHWH.* Moses leaves for the last what many Christians view as the essence of Old Testament religion: obedience to the commands of God. However, obedience is preceded by the weightier matters of Torah (Matt. 23:23; Luke 11:42): fear, commitment to YHWH's ways, love, and willing servitude.

Moses' response captures the message of Deuteronomy, especially as it relates to the worshipful human response to divine grace. It is a comprehensive response, involving fundamental dispositions (fear, love) and active expressions (walk, serve, keep). In Moses' view, attitude and action are interrelated. Without fear and love, walking, serving, and keeping all the commands become legalistic efforts at gaining the favor of God. Conversely, without walking, serving, and keeping the commands, fear and love are useless and dead.[62]

60. This ethical principle is known as *imitatio Dei*, "the imitation of God." Here (Deut. 10:10–19) Moses calls for compassion and justice toward the vulnerable, just as YHWH exercises compassion and justice. See also Lev. 19:2.

61. The word *'ābad* occurs frequently in the exodus and plague narratives of Exod. 3–10, speaking of what the Israelites would do at Sinai (3:12; 4:23; 7:16; 8:1 [7:26], 20 [16]; 9:1, 13; 10:3, 7, 8, 11, 24, 26; 12:31). Perhaps because Exod. 5:1 and 8:25, 28 indicate that the Sinai event would include cultic service, many translations render *'ābad* as "worship." However, this is quite misleading. The focus of the events at Sinai is on the rituals by which the Israelites, who had been "slaves" (*'ăbādîm*) of Pharaoh, become "vassals" (*'ăbādîm*) of YHWH. Cf. 14:12, where the people declare their preference for slavery to Pharaoh over death in the desert as YHWH's duped servants.

62. "Fear and love" express covenant commitment, which may be viewed as the Mosaic counterpart to *pistis*, the New Testament word for "faith." James caught the spirit of this text

In his second answer (v. 16) Moses calls the Israelites to circumcise their hearts and stop stiffening their necks (cf. KJV). The first command is odd because circumcision involves a surgical act by one person on another, and hearts/minds (*lēb*) obviously do not have foreskins. Ezekiel's version of this metaphor is more natural: "Rid yourselves of all the offenses you have committed, and get a new heart and a new spirit" (Ezek. 18:31). Moses does not explain what he means by a circumcised heart except to juxtapose it with "stiffening the neck." This metaphor recalls Deuteronomy 9:6, where Moses had denounced the people as persistently "stiff-necked," a bovine metaphor he had learned from YHWH himself (9:13). The proximity of these metaphors[63] suggests that a circumcised heart represents a disposition that has ceased resisting the will of YHWH and is soft and sensitive toward him. Moses confirms this understanding in 30:6–8, where he declares that YHWH will circumcise the Israelites' hearts so they will love him with their whole heart and being, and that a circumcised heart is marked by obedience to the revealed will of YHWH. In 10:17b–19 this circumcised heart will be expressed by caring for the needs of the marginalized as God himself does. Jesus declares in Matthew 25:31–46 that this is worship of the highest order, and when done in the name of Christ, it guarantees acceptance with God.

In his third answer (v. 20), Moses returns to the nature and focus of allegiance. The grammar is emphatic, cast in the form of four parallel statements:

[Only] YHWH your God you shall fear.

[Only] him you shall serve.

[Only] to him you shall hold fast.

[Only] by his name you shall swear. (cf. 6:13)

Here and in verses 20–21 Moses shifts attention from the subject of the worshipful action (vv. 12b–13) to the object of worship (YHWH). He concludes (11:1) by synthesizing the three answers he has given to the question raised in 10:12a. True worship involves exclusive covenant commitment to YHWH, demonstrated in full obedience to the will of God revealed at Sinai and expounded in the addresses of Moses on the plains of Moab.

---

precisely in James 2:14–26. See R. Stein, "'Saved by Faith [Alone]' in Paul versus 'Not Saved by Faith Alone' in James," *Southern Baptist Journal of Theology* 4, no. 3 (2000): 4–19.

63. Although Moses identifies the stiffened object as the "neck," the statement conveys a subtle double entendre. Combining motifs of circumcision and stiffening invites hearers to think in terms of the penis as a sex organ, specifically its erection, referred to as "big of flesh" in Ezek. 16:26 (cf. 23:20).

Reflections on the Abiding Significance of the Torah of Moses

With this understanding of true worship in Deuteronomy, we discover that Paul's call for full-bodied sacrifice in Romans 12:1–2 was neither revolutionary nor new, but a perfect restatement of the Mosaic vision of worship.[64] But now we also understand Jesus' words to his disciples: "If you love me, you will keep my commandments" (John 14:15). Jesus hereby affirms that the fundamental principles governing worship in the First Testament carry over into the New. After all, the God incarnate in "Jesus Christ is the same yesterday and today and forever" (Heb. 13:8 NIV). This is also the perspective we hear in James, who stresses that followers of God must do his will, not just hear it.

> Those who look into the perfect law, the law of liberty, and persevere, being not hearers who forget but doers who act—they will be blessed in their doing. If any think they are religious, and do not bridle their tongues but deceive their hearts, their religion is worthless. Religion that is pure and undefiled before God, the Father, is this: to care for orphans and widows in their distress, and to keep oneself unstained by the world. (James 1:25–27 NRSV).

Here James is thoroughly Mosaic. It is not that the law itself liberates, but it is liberating to know "the perfect Torah, the Torah of liberty," which is the will of God graciously revealed to those who, like Israel, have been liberated.[65] Reverential homage and submission demonstrated by joyful conformity to the will of God in all of life brings glory to God and ensures that cultic expressions of worship will be received favorably by God. This is the imputed righteousness of Christ lived out, so that through the Spirit, by faith, we "await the hope of righteousness" (Gal. 5:5). Like the blessing and declaration of righteousness in Psalm 24:5, this is the true benefit of worship that pleases God. Those who fear YHWH, walk in his ways, demonstrate love for him, and serve him alone—such people show their vassalage in scrupulous but joyful obedience. Having done so, they will hear the most welcome words from God's lips: "Well done, good and faithful vassal. You have been faithful . . . ; enter into the joy of your Suzerain" (Matt. 25:21, 23).

---

64. For a brief discussion of Rom. 12:1–2, see near the end of the section "Worship as Cultic Ritual" in chap. 1, above.

65. On *eleutheria* meaning "the state of being free," see W. Bauer, F. Danker, W. Arndt, and F. Gingrich, eds. [BDAG], *A Greek-English Lexicon of the New Testament and Other Early Christian Literature*, 3rd ed. (Chicago: University of Chicago Press, 2000), 316; cf. 1 Pet. 2:16; 2 Pet. 2:19.

5

Family Life and Work as Worship

True worship involves reverential human acts of submission and homage before the divine Sovereign in response to his gracious revelation of himself and in accord with his will.

I applaud parents who place a high value on formal family worship, by which I mean daily reading the Scriptures and praying together. However, it may catch readers by surprise to learn that biblical support for this pattern is embarrassingly limited. Although the modern practice assumes literacy and the presence of a copy of the Scriptures in each household, theoretically it could have been the pattern in ancient Israel as well.[1] In that oral culture people's meditation on and recitation of the Scriptures would have relied minimally on those who led in family devotions having memorized the Torah.[2] Like any ritual, setting aside special times for spiritual exercises may compartmentalize

---

1. Though some recent studies of family religion in ancient Israel have focused on the role of women and the place of rituals as well as male and female figurines in domestic religion. See P. R. S. Moorey, *Idols of the People: Miniature Images of Clay in the Ancient Near East* (Oxford: Oxford University Press, 2003); Beth Alpert Nakhai, "Household Religion and Women's Religion in Iron Age Israel," lecture delivered at Wheaton College, September 19, 2013. For fuller discussions of family religion in ancient Israel, see Susan Ackerman, "Household Religion, Family Religion, and Women's Religion in Ancient Israel," in *Household and Family Religion in Antiquity*, edited by John Bodel and Saul M. Olyan (Oxford: Blackwell, 2008), 127–58.

2. See further below in chapter 7 under "The Torah in the Life and Worship of Each First Testament Believer."

life into sacred and profane spheres. Bible reading and prayer may become little more than a beautiful frame intended to impress God (and others) if the picture within the frame is ugly. Like the observances of the Israelites in the days of the prophets, daily rituals may create a false sense of security. If we start the day with God, we think, he owes us a good day; if we have a bad day, it is because we missed our devotions in the morning.

In the light of the previous chapter, family worship is best viewed holistically, which means that all domestic activities should involve *acts of submission and homage before the divine Sovereign in response to his gracious revelation of himself and in accord with his will.* This also means that God is most pleased with the worship of the household and its members when they fulfill the roles God intends for them within the home. Therefore, in addition to exploring formal worship at the family level, we will explore how individuals in Israelite households demonstrated their homage and submission to God through fulfilling their respective roles. We will conclude by examining a particular aspect of family life as worship, namely, work and vocation.

The Biblical Understanding of Family

The Western concept of a nuclear family, consisting of a father and mother and biological or adopted children, finds little support in the Scriptures. Indeed, peoples in other parts of the world understand many biblical perspectives on family much better than we do. We cannot understand the Israelite family without recognizing the broader sociological context within which families functioned in Israel.[3] Genesis 10 portrays the entire world as one large family, consisting of three primary branches of peoples descended from the three sons of Noah and his wife.[4] The First Testament perceives the Israelites as one branch of this large family, whose ethnic cohesion is grounded in descent from a common ancestor. This cohesion is reflected in references to the nation as ʿam, "people," from a root signifying "paternal uncle," and collective phrases like "sons of Israel" (*běnê-yiśrāʾēl*) and "house of Israel" (*bêt-yiśrāʾēl*). The

3. For a fuller discussion of the concepts discussed here, see Daniel I. Block, "Marriage and Family in Ancient Israel," in *Marriage and Family in the Biblical World*, ed. K. Campbell (Downers Grove, IL: InterVarsity, 2003), 33–102.

4. See Gen. 9:18–19. This view is unparalleled in ancient literature. On Gen. 10, see further Daniel I. Block, "Table of Nations," *International Standard Bible Encyclopedia* [*ISBE*], ed. G. W. Bromiley et al., rev. ed. (Grand Rapids: Eerdmans, 1979–88), 4:707–13; Kenneth A. Mathews, "The Table of Nations: The 'Also' Peoples," *Southern Baptist Journal of Theology* [*SBJT*] 5 (2001): 42–57.

nation consisted of twelve tribes (*šēbeṭ* or *maṭṭeh*), identified by the names of their ancestors, the twelve sons of Jacob.

The everyday life of individual Israelites was determined more by the next two levels in the genealogical hierarchy, the clan (*mišpāḥâ*) and the household (*bayit*).[5] The territory of a clan typically incorporated villages and towns where the members lived, along with the agricultural land between. The rosters of troops in Numbers 1 and 26 suggest that the nation's military forces were recruited and organized by clan. Within the territory of the clan, each household farmed its grant of patrimonial land (*naḥălâ*), but the clan was ultimately responsible for maintaining its integrity. In terms of cultic worship, guarding against cultic defection (Lev. 20:5), arranging for Passover celebrations (Exod. 12:21) and community sacrifices (1 Sam. 20:6, 29), observing mourning rituals (Zech. 12:10–14), and in later times celebrating the Festival of Purim (Esther 9:28)—all happened at the level of the clan.

Ancient Israelite clans consisted of smaller units, households, which were actually large extended families (fig. 5.1). The identification of these domestic units as "the house of the father" (*bêt 'āb*) reflects their social structure. They typically involved a male elder, his wife/wives, his sons and their wives, grandsons and their wives, and conceivably great-grandchildren, as well as unmarried descendants. The household also included unrelated dependents; male and female hired servants and slaves, along with their families; resident laborers; and on occasion resident Levites (Judg. 17:7–13). With an average life span of forty to fifty years, in monogamous situations, a household could

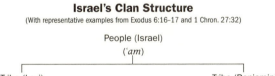

FIGURE 5.1
Israel's Clan Structure
(With representative examples from Exodus 6:16–17 and 1 Chron. 27:32)

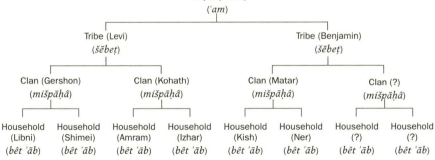

5. Anthropologists and sociologists often define a "clan" as an exogamous kinship group (marriage within the clan is forbidden), but this does not fit the Israelite picture. In the absence of a better term, we use the word to designate the subgroup smaller than a tribe but larger and more complex than a family.

have totaled twenty to twenty-five persons, though a smaller count of fifteen was probably more common. To accommodate these people, domestic compounds often contained multiple dwellings.

Family Religious Observances as Worship in the Scriptures

While the Scriptures present worship within Israel's national cultic system in great detail, information on formal family worship is limited. The reasons for this are clear. First, for the most part the Scriptures portray formal religious exercises either as personal/individual actions or as religious events involving the entire community. Instances of what we call "family worship" are rare. Second, while expressions of individual piety are evident throughout, the Scriptures were produced and preserved for public worship. Therefore, in attempting to reconstruct family worship in ancient Israel, we must strain the evidence for cultic exercises performed by and for individual families with a rather fine sieve.

Ritual Family Worship in Prepatriarchal Times

Genesis 8:20–9:17 provides the most striking illustration of ritual family worship in prepatriarchal times. In response to the salvation of himself, his family, and the animals in the ark, Noah built an altar and presented whole burnt offerings to YHWH. The narrator declares that the scent of the offerings was a "soothing aroma" in YHWH's nostrils (8:21a), and that he responded by promising never again to destroy the earth by flood (vv. 21b–22). Furthermore, as he had promised in Genesis 6:18, YHWH confirmed with Noah his covenants with Adam by blessing Noah (9:1); reaffirming humankind's status as his images, with full authority to govern the world (9:1–7); and explicitly declaring his covenant commitment to the cosmos (9:8–17). This was acceptable family worship, led by the head of the household.

Ritual Family Worship in Patriarchal Times

While the book of Job does not come from the patriarchal period, the picture of family worship in the prologue reflects patterns typical of this time. The scene opens with Job, the head of the household, sending for his children and performing cultic activities on their behalf (1:1–5). Both the narrator and God characterize Job as meeting the prerequisites for acceptable worship: he was "blameless and upright, he feared God, and turned from evil" (1:1, 8). Job performed these rituals early in the morning, consecrating his children and offering up whole burnt offerings for each one.

In Genesis Abraham's pilgrimage is punctuated by altars that he constructed at significant stopping places in gratitude for God's providential care (Gen. 12:7–8; 13:4, 18; 22:9). The narrative is silent on the involvement of his family, except concerning the rite of circumcision. Obeying God's command and as a sign that he had accepted the role of vassal, Abraham circumcised himself (at age ninety-nine), his son (at age thirteen), and all the males in his household (Gen. 17:22–27). Later Abraham also circumcised Isaac on the eighth day, according to the divine command (21:4). In Genesis 22 Isaac was a passive victim of his father's worship (cf. v. 5).

We could interpret Isaac's blessing of his sons in Genesis 27 as a family worship event, but this is not normal worship. In the opening conversation with Esau (27:1–5), the patriarch expressed no sensitivity to God's promises that he inherited from his father, Abraham, nor to the earlier oracle of God concerning his sons (25:21–26). Furthermore, Isaac intended to bless his first son in a private ceremony, deliberately excluding his wife and his son Jacob. The ritual appears to be spiritual, but the motivation is suspect; instead of uniting the family, it divided them and caused its ultimate disintegration.

Genesis 35:1–15 recounts the most impressive example of family worship in the patriarchal narratives. Reminding Jacob that he is the God who had appeared to him when he was fleeing from Esau, YHWH told him to go to Bethel and build an altar there. Jacob recognized the sanctity of this journey and its destination, and charged all in his household to prepare for the pilgrimage by discarding their foreign gods, purifying themselves, and changing their garments (v. 2). After Jacob had buried the foreign gods, the surrounding cities were struck by a divine terror, undoubtedly evidence that YHWH had accepted Jacob's worship. Arriving at his destination, Jacob built an altar and renamed Bethel "El-Bethel" ("The God of Bethel") to commemorate God's earlier self-revelation there. God reappeared to Jacob, renaming him, reintroducing himself as "El-Shadday," and reiterating the covenant promises he had made to Abraham and Isaac. Jacob responded to this signal that his worship had been accepted with further ritual acts: erecting a commemorative pillar, pouring a libation on it, and anointing it with oil. He thereby confirmed the sanctity of the place that would become a significant center of false worship in later times (1 Kings 12:25–33).

The Mosaic Vision for Ritual Family Worship

The narratives concerning the period from the death of Jacob to the death of Moses deal almost exclusively with the entire community of Israel, the

Passover being one significant domestic exception (Exod. 12–13). As originally prescribed and observed, this was a family festival celebrated in Israelite homes. Later the Passover was identified as one of three annual mandatory festivals before YHWH in which all males were to participate (Exod. 23:14–17; Deut. 16:1–17). Exodus 12–13 spells out the prescribed rituals in detail.

Since the Passover was prescribed by God himself, this festival obviously involved rituals of submission and homage before him. In Exodus 12:1–13 the Passover looks like a onetime, future-oriented event through which God tested the faith of his people and isolated those he would redeem from Egyptian bondage. However, verses 14–28 and 40–51 institutionalize it as an annual ritual commemorating YHWH's deliverance. Its purpose is to keep alive the memory of God's grace, thereby providing constant motivation for worship (cf. Deut. 6:20–25).

The Passover ceremonies involved all the members of the household—native and alien—who had identified with the community through circumcision. As an annual family celebration, the Passover assumed that the memory of God's redemption was best kept alive through household worship and placed responsibility for keeping that memory alive on the heads of households—not on professional cultic officials.[6] The fact that Jesus celebrated the festival in the upper room with his "family" of disciples (Matt. 26:17–25) confirms that the festival had not lost its domestic flavor. To this day the Passover is celebrated in homes rather than in synagogues.

In the first observance of the Passover, the key ritual act involved daubing the blood of a slaughtered lamb on the doorframes of the Israelites' houses. By this act they declared their trust in YHWH to rescue them from slavery. On that night, when the destroying angel passed through Egypt to slay the firstborn son in every household, he passed over the houses that had blood on their doorframes. Meanwhile, within Israelite houses the family members ate the Passover meal, which consisted of bitter herbs (Exod. 12:8), the roasted meat of the lamb (Exod. 12:21–28; 13:1–16), and unleavened bread (Deut. 16:3). By participating in this meal, later generations identified with the exodus generation and celebrated their participation in God's great act of deliverance. Although these texts never hint that this event prefigured a future greater deliverance from sin or that the lamb prefigured the Lamb of God, with this symbolic action YHWH established the ritual vocabulary with which Jesus' sacrifice would later be interpreted.

6. Though later texts note the involvement of priests and Levites, as in the days of Hezekiah (2 Chron. 30:13–22) and Josiah (35:1–19) and in postexilic Jerusalem after the temple had been rebuilt (Ezra 6:19–22).

The book of Deuteronomy contains additional hints of family worship. In 26:1–15 Moses prescribes a ritual linked to the harvest of firstfruits. Although it was to take place at the sanctuary in the presence of the priest, Levites and aliens from the worshiper's hometown were to be invited to the event (v. 11). Assuming that the children and servants of the principal worshiper were also included,[7] everyone would hear the head of the household recite the "little catechism," reviewing the history of YHWH's grace to his people, and declare that the gift he brought to YHWH was concrete evidence of God's continued grace (vv. 5–10).

In Deuteronomy 6 Moses provides instructions for two kinds of domestic religious exercises. First, in verses 4–9 (and 11:18–20) Moses appeals to heads of households to declare their covenant commitment to YHWH at three levels: (1) the personal level ("These words shall be on your heart"); (2) the domestic level ("You shall teach them to your children"); and (3) the community level ("You shall inscribe them on your hands, wear them on your foreheads, write them on the doorposts of your houses and gates"). Moses assumed that lessons of spiritual commitment and faith were best taught within the context of a life of commitment and through consistent repetition.[8] Rather than relegating instructional worship to the classroom, or compartmentalizing it to ten minutes of family devotions in the morning or evening, or assigning the task to professionals (like Levites), he emphasized that true family worship should happen spontaneously, as adults seize opportunities to teach the Torah, refresh the memories of God's grace, and inculcate sound theological convictions and commitments.[9] It takes a village[10] to teach and model faith before children. In a community of faith, worship and the spiritual nurture of children are everybody's duty.

Second, Moses provides an example of how this might happen. In Deuteronomy 6:20–25 he imagines a context—perhaps at the supper table—when children might voice their curiosity over Israel's distinctive lifestyle: "What is the meaning of the stipulations, statutes, and ordinances that YHWH our God has commanded you?" (v. 20). This is not a request for a detailed exposition of every one of the Torah's 613 commands, but for clarification of the significance of the entire package of regulations governing Israel's cult and

---

7. Cf. the emphasis on "sons and daughters" and "male and female servants" in other family celebrations at the central sanctuary: Deut. 12:12, 18; 16:11, 14.

8. The verb *šinnēn*, "to teach," derives from the same root as the number "two," *šěnayim*, and means to repeat over and over again; Deut. 11:19 uses the common word *limmēd*, "to teach."

9. When sitting or walking, lying down or standing up—these are merisms, figures of speech for "all the time, at every opportunity."

10. Adapted from the title of Hillary Rodham Clinton's book *It Takes a Village: And Other Lessons Children Teach Us* (New York: Simon & Schuster, 1996).

ethic. Moses' prescribed response is illuminating; instead of addressing the laws directly ("It is our duty to keep them!"), he seizes the opportunity to declare the gospel within which YHWH gave the revelation. He hereby advises heads of households not to speak of Israel's duties before YHWH without first declaring the privilege they enjoy as his chosen, redeemed, and commissioned people. After reminding the youthful inquirer of the history of God's grace and the life-giving function of the Torah, he challenges hearers to obedience. This is acceptable worship all around.

Ritual Family Worship in Post-Mosaic Israel

Unfortunately, most illustrations of family worship presented in the narratives of Joshua, Judges, and the early chapters of 1 Samuel are negative. Joshua 7:16–26 illustrates the consequences of the head of a household engaging in false worship. In keeping with the first command of the Decalogue, because of Achan's disobedience and wickedness, his entire family perished.

Judges 17 offers the fullest account of family worship in the biblical narratives. But this family is spiritually schizophrenic. On one hand, Micah has an orthodox Yahwistic name, meaning "Who is like YHWH?" And having stolen eleven hundred pieces of silver from his mother, he confesses his sin, to which she responds by blessing him in the name of YHWH (17:2) and dedicating the returned silver to YHWH. On the other hand, this masks a deeply flawed household, in which many actions—both ethical and cultic—are the antithesis of true worship. Micah's crime violates both the Decalogue's command to honor parents and the prohibition against stealing. However, the cultic crimes of this household are especially egregious. When Micah's mother later asks him to make an idolatrous image with the silver that has been dedicated to YHWH (v. 3b), Micah hires a silversmith, who creates an idol that Micah installs in his house (v. 4). Having constructed a temple (*bêt 'ĕlōhîm*, literally, "a house of God"; v. 5) for the image, he dresses it in divine royal finery (the ephod), adds other sacred images (teraphim), and installs one of his own sons as priest. This is a self-contained and privately designed family cult, which, according to Deuteronomy 13, demands the death penalty.

But the story does not end here. Micah hires a shiftless Levite, who lacks both a sense of calling and theological convictions. He agrees to be Micah's household priest, with the honorific title of "father" (Judg. 17:10). Once installed, instead of calling the household to repent and renew their covenant commitments, he tells clients exactly what they want to hear (18:3–6) and ultimately sells his services to the highest and most prestigious bidder (18:19).

In the end, he accepts the promotion from a mere family priest to priest of an entire tribe, officiating at the tribal shrine.[11] These were dark days; the Israelites as a nation and as individual households were doing what was right in their own eyes (17:6; 21:25).

Despite the vast body of narrative and prophetic literature on monarchic and postexilic Israel, windows on family worship are virtually nonexistent, and the hints we find are syncretistic.[12]

Ritual Family Worship in the New Testament

Information on family worship is equally scarce in the New Testament. In Matthew 18:1–6 Jesus warns against causing little ones to stumble, but this is scarcely a reference to formal cultic worship. Martha, Mary, and Lazarus represent a household devoted to Jesus and eager to host him (Luke 10:38–42; John 11). In John 4:46–53 we encounter a government official and his entire household who believe in Jesus after the official's son was healed.

Acts 10:2 calls Cornelius a pious man who, along with his household, fears God and expresses this fear in worshipful acts of generous giving and prayer. In response to his prayer, God gives him a vision of a man in bright clothing, who declares that God has heard his prayer and is pleased with his generosity (vv. 30–31). This man instructs Cornelius to call for Peter, who is in Joppa. When Peter comes and tells them of Jesus, Cornelius and all at his house believe and receive the same outpouring of the Holy Spirit as Jews in Jerusalem received at Pentecost. As an act of worship, they are all baptized (vv. 44–48). In Peter's report of this event (11:14), the reference to "you and your household" suggests that those assembled "in the presence of God" (10:33) are members of Cornelius's household, though they may include some in his official entourage.

Others whose households are said to have participated in their conversion include Lydia of Thyatira (Acts 16:14–15), Crispus of Corinth (18:8), and the Philippian jailer (16:31–34). However, these events are significant as the beginnings of new churches rather than illustrative of established family worship. Young Timothy was the product of conscientious instruction by his grandmother and mother (2 Tim. 3:14–15; cf. 1 Tim. 1:5). Otherwise, Paul's instructions on worship all relate to ministry in church contexts.

11. Perhaps most shocking of all, this Levite was a grandson of Moses (18:30). For further discussion of these issues, see Daniel I. Block, *Judges, Ruth*, New American Commentary (Nashville: Broadman & Holman, 1999), 273–515.
12. Thus we have Jeremiah's reference to women burning incense and offering libations and sweet cakes to the Queen of Heaven (Jer. 44:3, 9, 15–19).

Family Life as Worship in the Scriptures

Though the Scriptures offer limited help on ritual family worship, they offer a great deal of insight into biblical notions of everyday family life as worship. Although the constitutional documents in the Pentateuch present an idealized picture of how family units should have functioned, the real picture is painted in the narratives. Given Israel's history of rebellion, it is not surprising that the ideals were rarely reached. The idolatry at the heart of the nation's infidelity was also a problem at the domestic level.[13] With spiritual infidelity came a host of social and moral ills.[14] Our attempt to recover a normative biblical view of family life as worship will look beyond the narratives to the constitutional documents, exploring the roles that members of the household should have played.

Marriage and Fatherhood as Worship

The Hebrew expression for family, *bêt 'āb*, "father's house," reflects the patricentricity of Israelite families. As elsewhere in the ancient Near East, Israelite families were patrilineal (official lines of descent were traced through the father's line), patrilocal (married women joined the households of their husbands), and patriarchal (the father governed the household). Although the word "patriarchal" suits this sentence, I prefer to speak of the biblical ideal as "patricentric."[15] The term "patriarchy," literally, "the rule of the father," places inordinate emphasis on the authority of a father over his household. In spiritually compromised situations, such authority rapidly degenerates into self-centered and exploitative exercise of "fatherly power." Furthermore, in contrast to modern egalitarian arrangements, the word "patricentrism" reflects the biblical ideal of domestic headship.[16] Although the father was responsible for governing the household, the First Testament pays little attention to the

13. The story of Micah, the Levite, and the Danites in Judges 17–18 illustrates the problem at the domestic and tribal levels, but also within the Levitical priesthood, which was charged with guarding the faith.

14. For a study of the problem in the period of the Judges, see Daniel I. Block, "Unspeakable Crimes: The Abuse of Women in the Book of Judges," *SBJT* 2 (1998): 46–55.

15. For a defense of this stance, see Block, "Marriage and Family in Ancient Israel," 40–45.

16. This patricentrism is evident not only in the word for family ("father's house") but also in a host of other features: (1) genealogies traced descent through the male line; (2) married couples joined the household of the groom; (3) references to a man and his wife or children generally name the man first (Gen. 7:7); (4) children were born to the father (21:1–7); (5) fathers negotiated family disputes (13:1–13; 31:1–55); (6) God generally addressed male heads of households (3:9; 12:1; 35:1); (7) the male head of the household initiated family worship (Gen. 8:13–22; 12:7–8; 35:2–15; cf. Job 1:4–5); and (8) when men died without descendants, their "name" died (Deut. 25:5–6; Ruth 4:5, 10; 1 Sam. 24:18–22).

power of the husband and father.[17] In functional households the male head was neither despot nor dictator, and rather than evoking images of "ruler" or "boss," the term *'āb* expressed confidence, trust, and security. Like all leadership roles, fatherhood and headship were privileges granted to the leader to serve the interests of those in his charge.

But how did godly fathers perform acts of submission and homage before the divine Sovereign within the context of the family? In healthy domestic contexts, the man served his family by modeling strict personal fidelity to YHWH; leading the family in the national festivals; instructing the family in the traditions of the exodus and the Torah; managing the land and other resources according to Torah regulations to ensure the family's security with God; providing basic needs of food, shelter, clothing, and rest; defending against outside threats; representing the household in the assembly of citizens; maintaining the well-being of the individuals in the household and the harmonious operation of the family unit; and implementing decisions made at the level of the clan. But husbands and fathers had additional responsibilities related to specific members of the household.

Husbands' responsibilities toward wives. Husbands expressed fear for YHWH and honor for their wives by treating marriage as a divinely ordained covenant relationship (Prov. 2:17; Mal. 2:14).[18] Although Genesis 1–2 suggests that in an ideal world men treat their wives as their ontological equals, and though the Song of Songs celebrates love and lovemaking as an egalitarian affair, Hebrew expressions for marriage and sexual intercourse reflect male initiative.[19] The ultimate goal was to build a family (see Ruth 4:11), which begins with conception and pregnancy.

Generally husbands were to guarantee peace and security for their wives, a notion covered by the term *měnûḥâ*, "rest," in Ruth 1:9. They would do so not only by providing for their practical needs[20] but especially by their

17. Genesis 3:16 contains the only reference to a man's status as ruler over his wife. However, this text highlights the negative effects of the fall on marital relations: responsible headship degenerates to an inappropriate exercise of power over the woman.

18. While monogamous marriage represents the biblical norm (Gen. 2:21–24) and seems to have prevailed among the common folk, polygyny (more than one wife) apparently was not uncommon.

19. The latter is described as a man's "knowing" (*yādaʿ*) a woman (e.g., Gen. 4:1; 19:8), "entering" (*bôʾ 'el*) a woman (e.g., Gen. 6:4; 16:2, 4), "lying" (*šākab*) with a woman (e.g., Gen. 26:10; 30:15, 16), or giving a woman his penis (*nātan šěkobtô*; Lev. 18:20, 23; 20:15; Num. 5:20). In unwelcome contexts a man "humiliates" (*ʿinnâ*) a woman (e.g., Gen. 34:2; Judg. 19:24).

20. Exodus 21:7–11 prescribes providing her with food, clothing, and ointment/oil. This text concerns a concubine, but according to the rabbinic principle of *qal wa-homer* ("light to heavy": what applies in a minor case will also apply in a major case), this prescription surely applied to wives as well.

fidelity to their marriage commitments. The significance of this obligation is highlighted by the prohibition on adultery in the Decalogue, the primary covenant document.

In ancient Israel as today, marriages were not always happy, and some would end in divorce.[21] For a man to divorce his wife was ethically problematic at several levels. Unless a woman's father or brothers would take her in, a divorced woman would be without male provision and protection and in many instances forced into prostitution to earn a living. Malachi 2:10–16 speaks clearly about the spiritual and theological implications of divorce. First, along with other symptoms, the prevalence of divorce attests to a fundamental lack of reverence and fear toward YHWH. Second, divorce is an act of treachery against one's companion and a fundamental breach of covenant commitment to one's wife (v. 14). Third, divorce is like marriage to pagans, in being an act of treachery against the community ("brothers") and profaning God's covenant with Israel (v. 10). Fourth, intact marriages are the prerequisite to producing "godly offspring" (v. 15). People may perform the animal functions of procreation apart from marriage, but a stable home is indispensable for a people of faith to survive. Fifth, God rejects the offerings of men who commit treachery against their wives: no matter how frantically they plead for his attention, his obligation to the unfaithful is suspended (vv. 13b–16). Sixth, treachery is committed in the spirit (*rûaḥ*) before it is committed in action. God is not fooled by a man's external acts of devotion when the spirit is fundamentally treacherous. Consistent with the overall tenor of the First Testament, Malachi views divorce not as men's moral right but as their moral offense.

Remarkably, Deuteronomy 24:1–4 contains the only sustained instruction on divorce in the constitutional literature.[22] However, this text deals with a specific case, initiated by a heartless husband who has discovered something about his wife that he does not like.[23] Moses' purpose here is neither to autho-

21. Although Sarah orders Abraham to drive out (*yāpēš*) her handmaid Hagar (Gen. 21:10), Abraham's distress and the care he takes in sending her and Ishmael off suggest this is not presented as a divorce. Indeed, First Testament narratives do not report a single divorce case, and although the covenant stipulations include passing references to divorce (Lev. 21:7, 14; 22:13; Num. 30:9), the paucity of instructions on divorce (Deut. 21:14; 22:19, 29; 24:1–4) suggests that the situation envisioned in Israel was vastly different from the modern Western "culture of divorce." Judges 19:1–2 reports that a concubine (*pîlegeš*) left her husband and returned to her father's house.

22. By "constitutional literature" I mean the Pentateuchal material usually referred to as the "laws," including the Decalogue (Exod. 20:1–17; Deut. 5:6–21), the Covenant Document (Exod. 22:22–23:19), the Instructions on Holiness (Lev. 17–26); and the Mosaic Torah (Deut. 5–26, 28).

23. Deut. 22:14 [15] suggests that the expression *'erwat dābār*, literally, "nakedness of a matter" (Deut. 24:1), is not a moral issue but a physical problem, perhaps menstrual irregularity, that

rize divorce nor to regulate it, but to prevent further victimization of a woman who has been rejected by her first husband and publicly exposed, and who then lost a second husband. As Malachi reiterates (2:16),[24] godly husbands do not abuse their wives.[25]

Fathers' responsibilities toward children. A father's primary responsibility was to secure the well-being of his children and ensure that they would be able to carry on the family line and legacy. Paternal functions included naming children;[26] loving them, delighting in them, and treating them with compassion;[27] modeling deep personal commitment to YHWH and his Torah (Deut. 6:5–9); diligently instructing children in the Torah and the traditions of salvation and covenant (Exod. 12:24; 13:8; Deut. 6:7, 20–25); giving public witness to his spiritual commitment (Deut. 6:8–9); protecting children from God's fury through his own fidelity to YHWH (Exod. 20:5; Deut. 5:9); wise and just management of the household (e.g., Deut. 21:15–17); and arranging for the marriage of his children (Gen. 24; Judg. 14). Also, as in preparation for their death or other long-term separation, fathers pronounced blessings upon their children (Gen. 27; 48–49).[28]

Some paternal duties were gender specific. To prepare sons for leadership in this patricentric world, fathers circumcised them on the eighth day (Gen. 17:12; 21:4; Lev. 12:3); instructed them in the way of wisdom, specifically developing their character and skills for life and vocation (Prov. 1–9); and disciplined them when they erred. If sons refused to be corrected, fathers (and mothers) presented them to the communal leaders for discipline (Deut. 21:18–21).

Since marriages were patrilocal, the treatment of sons and daughters differed significantly, but this did not mean that daughters were treasured less

---

would keep the woman in a state of ritual uncleanness and prohibit her husband from having intercourse with her (Lev. 15:19–30). See further Daniel I. Block, *Deuteronomy*, NIV Application Commentary (Grand Rapids: Zondervan, 2010), 557–58.

24. Whether one follows the traditional interpretation, "I [God] hate divorce," or the alternative interpretation, "If he hates and divorces [his wife]" (HCSB), for a husband to divorce his wife is a wrongful act of violence (*ḥāmās*, Mal. 2:16).

25. For fuller commentary on Deut. 24:1–6, see Block, *Deuteronomy*, 556–65.

26. Yet we recognize that mothers often named their children as well. In naming a child, responsible parents gave expression to their faith and their aspirations for the child. Thus Jonathan means "YHWH has given [this child]"; Jochebed means "YHWH is glory."

27. Regarding children with "love" (*'āhab*, Prov. 13:24; Hosea 11:1–4); treasuring/taking delight in them (Ps. 128; Prov. 3:12; Ezek. 24:25); treating them with "compassion" (*riḥam*, Ps. 103:13).

28. In Gen. 24:60 Rebekah's brother and mother are also involved in her blessing before she leaves Aram to become the wife of Isaac.

(Ezek. 24:25).[29] Godly fathers protected their daughters from male predators so they would marry as virgins, thereby bringing honor to the family and purity to her husband (see Exod. 22:16–17; Deut. 22:13–21). Fathers sought to ensure a measure of economic security for their daughters by providing a "marriage present" from the patrimonial estate when they married (Gen. 24:59, 61; 29:24, 29; Judg. 1:11–12), and they protected their daughters from their own rash vows (Num. 30:2–15). But men never ceased to be fathers to their daughters. If a daughter's marriage soured, a father stood up for her in court, especially if her husband accused her of not having been a virgin at the time of marriage (Deut. 22:13–21). In case of divorce or the death of a husband, a daughter could return to her father's home.

While these are noble ideals, illustrations of paternal abuse of daughters abound. The book of Judges recounts episodes in which fathers sacrifice their daughters to serve the interests and honor of male guests (19:22–24), their own military honor (11:29–40), and sentimental loyalty to distant male relatives (21:19–24). Although commentators often assume such behavior was acceptable in patriarchal society, these are evidences of patricentrism run amok, in direct violation of normative values and legislation outlawing such exploitation.

Household heads' responsibilities toward servants/slaves. As already noted, Israelite households often included nonrelatives who had joined them by choice or economic necessity. These included non-Israelite aliens who left their home village and sought employment and shelter in an Israelite community; hired hands who contracted themselves to a household for daily wages; and slaves, who occupied the lowest rung on the social ladder.

Because these classes were all vulnerable to abuse and marginalization, regulations to protect their well-being figure prominently in the Pentateuch. The Sabbath command in the Decalogue sought to guarantee humane treatment for all members of the household (Exod. 20:10; Deut. 5:14). Other texts sought to ensure the well-being of indentured "Hebrew slaves," who out of economic necessity had sold their services to Israelite landholders (Exod. 21:1–23:33; Deut. 15:12–18). The Jubilee (Lev. 25) was instituted to maintain the integrity of all Israelite households by requiring Israelite landholders periodically to release countrymen who had fallen into economic slavery. Because both Israelite creditors and debtors stood before God as equals—they were all YHWH's purchased slaves—they were forbidden to enslave each other.

---

29. For examples of men responding warmly to daughters when they bring exceptional requests, see Num. 27:1–11 and Judg. 1:15.

Although slaves were viewed as household property, prohibitions against the oppression/exploitation of slaves appear repeatedly in Mosaic legislation. Indeed, Leviticus 19:34 and Deuteronomy 10:19 charge all Israelites to love aliens residing in their midst and to treat these outsiders with the same respect they show their countrymen. The Israelites' memory of their own experience as slaves in Egypt motivated compassion toward their own slaves (Exod. 22:21 [20]). But Deuteronomy 10:18 adds the dimension of *imitatio Dei*: YHWH's treatment of those who are economically and socially vulnerable is paradigmatic for Israel.[30]

It is difficult to determine the extent to which ancient Israelites adhered to these ideals. As the histories of Israel and Judah approached their ends, prophets repeatedly condemned those with political and social power for abusing and exploiting the weak and vulnerable. However, the prophets did not view themselves as social engineers, charged to reorder social structures. If householders oppressed their servants, the problem was personal and not necessarily systemic. The prophets called for repentance from the sin of exploitation and the replacement of stony hearts with hearts of flesh that were sensitive not only to YHWH (Deut. 4:8) but also to the plight of the weak among them.

Marriage and Motherhood as Worship

As already noted, the world of the Bible is andro- and patricentric. While the First Testament recognizes women as prophets, equal in authority to their male counterparts,[31] the offices of king, governor, priest, elder, judge, and general[32] were reserved for men only.[33] This exclusion from power positions in the community does not mean that women were second-class citizens. If

30. Cf. also Exod. 21:7–11, which safeguards Israelite females who were sold by their fathers as slaves, presumably because of debt.

31. Miriam (Exod. 15:20), Deborah (Judg. 4:4), Hannah (1 Sam. 2:1–10, Targum), Huldah (2 Kings 22:14).

32. Deborah was not an exception. Not only does the narrator explicitly classify her as a "prophetess" (*nĕbîʾâ*, Judg. 4:4), but all her functions in the narrative are prophetic: her "judgment" for which the Israelites came to her (4:4–5) was not to settle disputes but to declare YHWH's response to the national crisis created by Jabin and the Canaanites. As prophet, she called Barak (4:6–7), accompanied him (4:8–9), and declared the moment of attack (4:14). Otherwise she plays no military role at all and is absent from the actual battle account. Note also that she is missing from later lists of judges (1 Sam. 12:11; Heb. 11:32). See further Block, *Judges, Ruth*, 191–200.

33. The admission of women to the prophetic institution may relate to the ad hoc nature of the institution. Prophets had no enduring governmental authority over the people; they had no subjects who were obliged to follow their directives, and no territory over which they ruled.

the male head of the household was "king" in this domain, then his wife was "queen."[34] Though the narratives often paint a different picture, the oppressive "rule" (*māšal*, Gen. 3:16) of many self-interested males was a perversion of compassionate and responsible biblical ideals.

Many texts reflect wives' honorific status within the household: (1) in courtship and lovemaking husbands and wives related to one another as equals (Song of Songs); (2) in at least half the cases, wives/mothers, rather than husbands/fathers, named their children; (3) the Decalogue calls for equal honor for fathers *and mothers* (Exod. 20:12; Deut. 5:16; cf. Lev. 19:3); (4) both father and mother were to be involved in defense of their daughter if her virginity at the time of marriage was questioned (Deut. 22:13–15); (5) biblical wisdom placed instruction of a mother on par with that of a father (Prov. 1:8; 6:20); (6) the alphabetic portrait of wifely nobility in Proverbs 31:10–31 highlights her initiative, creativity, and energy; and (7) women participated freely in cultic gatherings (Deut. 12:12; 31:12; Neh. 8:3).[35] When young women married, they moved from being under the authority of their fathers to that of their husbands. In normal circumstances this authority was not oppressive; a strong husband offered security and well-being for one who otherwise would have been vulnerable to economic and physical ruin.

Wives' responsibilities toward husbands. The ideal represented in Genesis 1–2 suggests that wives played three significant roles in marriage. First, they aided their husbands in fulfilling the mandate pronounced in 1:28: "Be fruitful and multiply and fill the earth." Regardless of what Westerners think about the issue, in ancient Israel a wife's most important and honorific role was to provide her husband with children. These would provide security for aging parents, and in them parents were perceived to live on. For this

34. Genesis 1–2 lays the grounds for this status: (1) as image of God, *'ādām* was created male and female; (2) the plural pronouns and verbs in Gen. 1:28 assign the privilege and responsibility of governing the world to both men and women; (3) God solved Adam's "aloneness" by creating "a helper corresponding/as a complement to him" (*'ēzer kĕnegdô*), rather than a "servant," "maidservant" (*'āmâ*), or "female slave" (*šiphâ*, 2:18); (4) God created "woman" from the man's rib (near his heart!) rather than from his head or his feet (2:22); (5) the man identified the woman as *'iššâ* ("woman"), which by sound is linked with *'îš* ("man"); and (6) Gen. 2:24–25 highlights the mutuality of the marital relationship—together, married man and woman constitute one body, and they stand naked before one another with perfectly mutual confidence and trust.

35. In contrast to Herod's temple, which had separate courts for the women and gentiles, no First Testament sanctuaries (tabernacle, Davidic temple, Ezekiel's temple) excluded women or segregated them from men. Absent from the First Testament is the misogyny of Ben Sirach (Sir. 25:13–26:12) or the daily prayer recommended in the Babylonian Talmud: "A Jewish man is obligated to say the following prayer every day: 'Thank you God for not making me a gentile, a woman or a slave.'"

reason, failure to conceive was deemed a curse and a shameful disgrace (Gen. 30:1–2).

Second, wives aided husbands in serving and keeping the garden (Gen. 2:15)—which beyond Eden translated to the management of the household. Depending on the family's economic status, basic tasks included tending the garden, harvesting grain, cooking food, and clothing the family, and in households involving servants, supervising them in domestic chores. According to the picture of a middle-class wife in Proverbs 31:10–31, an honorable woman ('ēšet-ḥayil, v. 10) delighted in seeing to the well-being of her household. She was tireless in service to her husband and children, creative in endeavors, self-effacing in disposition, and compassionate in action. Though performed in the interests of the household, her mercantile activities also took her beyond the domestic compound. She confidently shopped abroad for the resources needed to maintain the household and marketed surplus goods produced by the household. Like Deborah and Huldah, some women were active outside the family.

Third, wives provided companionship for their husbands. Although functionally subordinate, women played important roles as husbands' confidants and trusted friends. In the Song of Songs, the Shulammite repeatedly celebrates the mutuality and equality, sympathy and love, commitment and compassion experienced in a healthy marriage.

> My beloved is mine, and I am his. (2:16)

> I am my beloved's, and my beloved is mine. (6:3)

> I am my beloved's, and his claim is on me. (7:10 [11])

This is not the lament of an oppressed woman in a patriarchal world but the celebration of security in a relationship of mutual love and commitment.

Mothers' responsibilities toward children. While Ezekiel 16:3–5 offers the First Testament's clearest picture of care for newborn infants,[36] Proverbs 31:10–31 summarizes mothers' basic responsibilities in the care of children: providing food, clothing, and shelter. Although fathers were also involved, during the child's first decade or so, its nurture was the special concern of the mother. In laying foundations for civilized behavior, excellent performance, and responsible decision making, the mother's role was as important as the father's. Once children reached adolescence, sons

---

36. The cord was carefully cut; the child was bathed in clean water, massaged with a saline solution, and wrapped tightly in bands of cloth.

would naturally spend more time with their fathers, developing skills and character required for responsible adulthood, though Proverbs 1:8 and 6:20 suggest that mothers continued to teach them. Meanwhile, mothers would prepare their daughters for their future roles as wives and mothers in their own households. Since marriages were patrilocal, teaching daughters how to adjust to new circumstances and family dynamics required sensitive guidance.

In Israel the mothers' interest in their children continued after they were married. Witnessing the birth of grandchildren, and in some cases great-grandchildren, was deemed a special blessing (Ruth 4:14–16). In households consisting of two or three generations, everyone bore responsibility for rearing the youngsters. Of course, daughters who had left home were always welcomed back for a visit, and those who had lost their husbands through death or divorce could return to the "mother's house" for refuge (Ruth 1:8).[37]

Wives' responsibilities toward servants. As expected in a patricentric culture, most Pentateuchal instructions concerning slaves are addressed to male heads of households. However, since wives were authority figures in the home, appeals for humane treatment of slaves would have applied to them as well. Pictures of mistresses' relationships with their servants in biblical narratives reflect the tension that often existed in these complex households.

Genesis 29:21–30:13 illustrates the relationship between a wife and a female servant in an Israelite household. When a rich man gave his daughter in marriage, the "marriage present" could include slave-girls (29:24, 29), who would serve the bride in her new home. The case of Sarah and Hagar in Genesis 16:1–16 and 21:8–21 demonstrates that wives could authorize their husbands to have intercourse with the slave-girls for the sake of procuring progeny. Once the husband had intercourse with a slave-girl, she was considered his wife (30:4, 9), though 35:22 explicitly recognizes Bilhah's secondary status by referring to her as Jacob's "concubine." As concubines, slave-girls' legal personality was divided: although they provided procreative favors for the male head of the household, they remained the property of their mistresses, who could order, discipline, and sell them. However, once a concubine had borne a child for the man, the mistress's rights were restricted. She could reduce her status within the household, but she was prohibited from selling her. When a slave-girl bore a child, the mistress could adopt the child as her own and exercise parental rights by naming the infant (30:6, 8, 11, 13).

37. Only here and in Song 3:4 is a domestic unit identified as a "mother's houses." Both instances concern the woman's relationship with her household of origin.

Childhood and Youth as Worship

Ancient Israelites placed a high value on children, acknowledging them as a mark of divine blessing (Ruth 4:13), special treasures given by YHWH (Pss. 127; 128), and the crowning glory of grandparents (Prov. 17:6). Indeed, to beget and bear children meant more than mere procreation; it signified cocreation—God's involving father and mother in creating images of himself. In a world languishing under the curse of death because of human sin, children of both genders represented the keys to humanity's survival (Gen. 5) and the fulfillment of the divine mandate to populate the entire earth (Gen. 1:28; 9:18–19). Conversely, whether due to barrenness or misfortune, childlessness was viewed as a curse. Within the household, children were not only considered an important economic asset, but parents also viewed themselves as living on in their children. Therefore the worst fate a man could experience was to have his "seed" cut off and his "name" eliminated.[38]

In Israelite households the firstborn played a special role. Although usually translated "firstborn," *běkôr* was a designation for rank, reflecting sociological rather than chronological priority.[39] With this status came the responsibility of taking care of the household and the parents as they aged, which explains why the inheritance of the designated "firstborn" was double the amount that the other siblings received. Usually the *běkôr* would be the eldest son,[40] though some might not qualify. In polygamous marriages this normally fell to the father's oldest son and would not be distributed among the oldest sons of each mother (Deut. 21:15–17). In addition to being favored by his father, in Israel the *běkôr* was also claimed by YHWH.[41]

All Hebrew males were to be circumcised on their eighth day (Gen. 17:9–14). Although the Israelites were only one of the Semitic peoples who practiced circumcision, for them the rite had special covenantal significance. Other than circumcision, the First Testament is silent on Israelites' celebrating children's passages from childhood to adolescence or adolescence to adulthood with special ceremonies. However, the registration of troops twenty years of age and older in Numbers 1 and 26 suggests that full adulthood was reached at the age of twenty.

38. See 1 Sam. 24:21 [22]; 2 Sam. 14:7. On this subject, see further Block, "Marriage and Family in Ancient Israel," 81.
39. Israel's status as YHWH's *běkôr* (Exod. 4:22) obviously derives not from the people's antiquity but from the status that YHWH assigned them (cf. Deut. 26:18–19).
40. Hence the closer definition of the *běkôr* as *peṭer-reḥem*, "that which opens the womb" (Exod. 13:11–15), or *rēʾšît ʾôn*, "the first of [procreative] strength" (Deut. 21:17).
41. "Firstborn" sons were consecrated and ritually transferred to YHWH through a special ceremony. See Exod. 13:2, 11–16.

Cast as a manual for instruction of a young man preparing for adulthood, the book of Proverbs offers a clear window into the ancient Israelite disposition toward youth. The vocabulary used to identify and describe the young is telling, suggesting that Israelites believed young people were fundamentally flawed intellectually, morally, and spiritually.[42] The thesis statement in Proverbs 1:2–7 suggests that preparing for responsible adulthood required gaining "wisdom," "understanding," "knowledge," "cleverness, smarts," "discretion, prudence," "perception," and skill through "discipline" (cf. 5:13; 30:3). The goal of instruction was wisdom (ḥokmâ), which covers practical and pragmatic subjects: personal etiquette, discipline and self-control in the face of inevitable sexual temptation, the importance of hard work and right speech, social skills needed to get along with the rest of the household (6:16–19), and general acceptance of the responsibilities of adulthood in the community. Achieving these goals required breaking stubborn wills, giving gullible minds a framework for evaluating ideas, softening hard hearts, and replacing self-centeredness with a sense of membership in and obligation to the community. Underlying this enterprise is a profound theological conviction that "the fear of YHWH is the first principle of wisdom" (Prov. 1:7). A young person who did not learn this remained a fool, and since a society of fools cannot prosper, the task of training children was the responsibility of the entire community.

Apart from overcoming the natural flaws of youthfulness, young people expressed homage and submission before the divine Sovereign by honoring their parents.[43] Not only did individual Israelites' futures depend on their respect for their pasts, but also Deuteronomy 21:18–21 declares persistent contempt for parents to be a capital offense. Ezekiel 22:7 lists dishonoring parents among

---

42. (1) Pĕtî, from a root pātâ, "to be open," hence a gullible person, easily seduced, whose mind is untrained to discern truth from falsehood and is therefore in need of guidance: e.g., Prov. 1:4, 32; 7:7; 8:5. (2) Lēṣ, from lûṣ, a fundamentally flawed scoffer or mocker, who displays his corruption by holding wisdom and instruction in derision and who is in need of humbling. The verb occurs in Prov. 3:34; 9:12; 14:9; 19:28; the noun in 1:22; 3:34; 9:7, 8. (3) Kĕsîl, a shameless, stupid, and insolent person, disinterested in wisdom and incorrigible in his ways: Prov. 3:35; 10:1; 13:20; 14:7, 33. (4) Ḥăsēr lēb, a mindless and heartless person, lacking in sense and needing discipline: Prov. 6:32; 7:7; 9:4, 16. (5) ʾĔwîl, an idiot, a morally stupid and thick-brained person, virtually indistinguishable from the kĕsîl. Both are characterized by ʾiwwelet, "moral corruption, folly," and both respond to discipline and correction with contempt. Various forms occur in Prov. 10:8, 10, 13–14, 21. (6) Siklût/śiklût, from sākāl, stupidity/an obtuse and stupid person, without any necessary moral connotations: siklût, Eccles. 1:17; 2:3, 12, 13; 7:25; 10:1, 13; sākāl, Eccles. 2:19; 7:17; 10:3, 14.

43. The vocabulary of respect involves verbs used elsewhere of worshipers' disposition toward YHWH: kabbēd, "to honor, ascribe glory to" (Exod. 20:12; Deut. 5:16); yārēʾ, "to fear, revere" (Lev. 19:3). Cast in apodictic form, the command allows no qualification, limitation, or termination.

the crimes that characterized his generation and ultimately led to the fall of Jerusalem in 586 BC. If people's fear of YHWH was measured by the degree to which they "walked in the ways of YHWH" (Deut. 10:12; 17:19; 31:12), then children's respect for parents was measured by the extent to which they walked in the ways of their parents (Prov. 1:8). Ancient Israelite children also honored their parents by providing a safety net in their old age, but their obligations extended beyond the elderly in their own houses. In Leviticus 19:32 YHWH calls on the younger generation to rise up before the gray-headed folks (cf. Job 29:8) and honor the face of the aged in the same breath that he calls upon them to revere (*yārē'*) their God.[44]

In Israelite households children and youth were expected to contribute to the household economy. Younger children could pick vegetables, gather fuel, and clean up after a meal. By the time they reached adolescence, tasks would be organized according to gender, training males for work that required greater strength and involved greater danger (hunting, handling livestock, butchering cattle and sheep, etc.), and females in the skills needed to run a household (harvesting vegetables, preparing food, spinning yarn, weaving garments, caring for babies; see Prov. 31:10–31). However, these divisions were not absolute; especially in harvesttime, men and women worked side by side (Ruth 2).

Youths nearing adulthood began to think about their roles in guarding the genealogical integrity of the family, which sometimes required implementing the *levirate* marriage. This institution involved a legally sanctioned union between a widow whose husband died without offspring and the brother of the deceased.[45] To maintain the name and family of the deceased, the first child born to this union assumed the name of the deceased. If the eligible male relative refused to fulfill his responsibility, in the presence of the elders the widow would remove the man's sandal and humiliate him by spitting in his face (Deut. 25:5–10; Ruth 4:7–8).

Senior Citizenship as Worship

The First Testament is not consistent in its definition of old age. Prior to the great flood, people lived for hundreds of years (Gen. 5; 11), but by the time of

44. See also Elihu's apologetic and respectful opening in Job 32:4 and the punishment of young lads for mocking the aged Elisha in 2 Kings 2:23–25.
45. For variations of this type of marriage in second-millennium-BC Ugaritic, Hittite, and Middle Assyrian sources, see Block, *Judges, Ruth*, 675–76; Raymond Westbrook, *Property and the Family in Biblical Law*, Journal for the Study of the Old Testament: Supplement Series 113 (Sheffield: JSOT Press, 1991), 87–89.

the patriarchs, Abraham and Sarah were considered old before they reached
the century mark (Gen. 17:1, 17).[46] From a later time, Psalm 90:10 reflects the
sober reality that "the days of our years are seventy years, and if by exceptional
strength, eighty years." David was "very old" at seventy (2 Sam. 5:4; 1 Kings
1:15; 2:11), and the books of Chronicles suggest that during the monarchy,
the life spans of the kings of Judah averaged forty-four years. Since common
citizens probably died even younger, a thirty-five-year-old person would have
been viewed as a mature if not senior citizen.[47]

While soberly recognizing the debilitating effects of age,[48] the Israelites could
also view growing old positively. In contrast to the longing for the "fountain
of youth," maturity was the Israelite ideal. People believed that the wicked
died young, and that to attain the "fullness of days," "a ripe old age," or
"satiation of days" was a sign of divine favor and a reward for faithfulness
to YHWH's covenant.[49]

But how would senior citizens express homage and submission before the
divine Sovereign within the household? Waning health obviously limited the
contributions they could make to a family economy, but so long as they were
able, aging women would assist in food preparation, making and mending
clothes, and tending infants. As the energy of men diminished, they would
stay closer to the house and provide assistance with its physical maintenance.
However, it seems the primary contribution of the aged involved their wisdom.
Younger women would drink deeply from the wisdom of the matriarchs in
housekeeping, child rearing, and preparing for marriage, while younger men
would learn from their elders how to manage the household, discipline unruly

46. Abraham lived 175 years; Isaac, 180; Jacob, 147; Moses, 120.

47. The rabbis considered the critical turning points of life as follows: 5 years, to begin
the study of Scripture; 10 years, for the study of the Mishnah; 13 years, for becoming subject
to the commandments; 15 years, for the study of the Talmud; 18 years, for the bridal canopy;
20 years, for pursuing military service; 30 years, for full strength; 40 years, for understanding;
50 years, for ability to give counsel; 60 years, for mature age (ziqnâ); 70 years, for a hoary
head (śêbâ); 80 years, a sign of superadded strength; 90 years, the age of bending figure; 100
years, to be as dead, having passed and ceased from the world; see Mishnah, 'Abot 5.21. This
compares with the ancient Mesopotamian Babylonian view that "60 is maturity; 70, length
of days; 80, old age; 90, extreme old age." For the seventh century BC text, see O. R. Gurney
and P. Hulin, The Sultantepe Tablets II (London: British Institute of Archaeology at Ankara,
1964), 400, 45–49.

48. Poignantly expressed by octogenarian Barzillai in 2 Sam. 19:34–35 [35–36]. For a variety
of physical maladies associated with aging, see Gen. 18:11–12; 1 Sam. 4:18; 1 Kings 1:1–4; 15:23;
Ps. 71:9; Eccles. 12:2–7. On the emotional stress of facing death, see Gen. 42:38; 44:29, 31.

49. See Exod. 20:12; Deut. 6:2, 22:7; 25:15; cf. Prov. 16:31: "A gray head is a crown of glory,
it is found in the conduct of righteousness." See also Prov. 17:6; Ps. 92:12–14 [13–15]; Sir. 25:6.
Isaiah 65:20 poses a puzzle to moderns: in the ideal world of the new heaven and the new earth,
everyone will grow old, and those who fail to reach a hundred will be considered accursed.

children, and relate to neighbors. The experience of the elderly was a special asset in the gate, where the "elders" (village council) would discuss issues that affected the community and adjudicate disputes among citizens.

As long as he was able, the senior male would be the spiritual head of the family. Apart from embodying mature piety and inspiring the household in daily expressions of devotion, he would play a leading role in the observance of the seventh-day Sabbath, annual religious rituals of the clan, and family festivals. His obligations probably also extended to observances related to the national religion: instructing the household in the Torah and the significance of Israel's national cult observances (Deut. 6:4–9, 20–25; 11:18–25); officiating at the Passover celebrations (Exod. 12:1–28, 43–51); leading the family, particularly the men, to the central shrine for annual pilgrimage festivals (Deut. 16:1–17); and keeping alive the national faith traditions (Deut. 26:1–15).[50]

Ancient Israelites responded to death in the family with emphatic verbal and nonverbal gestures of mourning: tearing garments, donning sackcloth, going barefoot, removing headgear, covering the beard, veiling the face, putting dust on the head, rolling in the dust, sitting on ash heaps, fasting, and loud laments.[51] For those with modest means, a proper interment involved burying the body in a shallow hole in the ground in a specially designated plot of land. For those in higher socioeconomic strata, this could involve tombs cut in the rock and large enough for multiple burials. By being "gathered to one's people" in a family tomb, the unity of the family was maintained even after death (cf., e.g., Gen. 25:8, 17; Deut. 32:50). The commands to honor parents applied even after they had died, but worship of the dead or attempts to communicate with them were prohibited.

Family Worship for Today

What can we learn about family worship from the First Testament? Ancient Israelite perceptions of family were grounded in the conviction that all human beings are created as images of God and that our humanity is expressed first and foremost in the context of community. For each member of the household,

---

50. Traditions of YHWH's election of the ancestors, his deliverance of the nation from the bondage of Egypt, his establishment of the covenant and the revelation of the covenant stipulations at Sinai, his providential care for Israel in the desert, and fulfillment of his promise to the ancestors by giving them the land they occupied.

51. For references, see R. de Vaux, *Ancient Israel: Its Life and Institutions* (New York: McGraw-Hill, 1961), 58–61. Mutilation of the body and shaving of heads and beards was condemned because of their association with pagan rites (Lev. 19:27–28; Deut. 14:1).

spiritual worship involved serving others and fulfilling one's obligations to the economic unit. In godly homes, spiritual nurture was a high priority so that all within the household loved and feared YHWH, treasured the memory of his saving and covenant-making acts, and demonstrated personal covenant commitment by walking in his ways and serving him only (Deut. 10:12–22). If we remember that the identity of an individual is tied to membership in a larger community, invest personal energies for the well-being of all, and keep faith as the basis of family cohesion, then we will be following First Testament ideals.

Work and Vocation as Worship

While the classical world of Greece and Rome held manual labor in disdain,[52] the Scriptures view work positively, as a fundamental dimension of our humanity.[53] To be human is to work, and to work is worship. In laying theological foundations for work as worship, we should note that the Scriptures portray God as the divine Worker. The Bible opens with a picture of God at work—speaking, creating, forming, building. Elsewhere not only does God appear as the subject of many "work" verbs,[54] but also people often refer to God metaphorically as a worker.[55] In the Decalogue the Sabbath command bases the six-plus-one-day pattern of work in Israel on the divine pattern (Exod. 20:9–11).

Work is the principal act of worship to which human beings are called. Like other creatures, humans work to secure their well-being and to preserve the species. However, the distinctive nature of human work is grounded in our status as God's images. God created the first humans specifically to govern the world on his behalf (Gen. 1:28), which meant "serving" and "guarding" his

---

52. Society was organized so that few could realize the high potential of a life free from manual labor—which explains why in the Greek city-states 80 percent of the people were slaves, whom Aristotle defined as tools endowed with life. *Politics* 1.4.2–3.31.

53. On this subject see Paul Stevens, *The Other Six Days: Vocation, Work, and Ministry in Biblical Perspective* (Grand Rapids: Eerdmans; Vancouver: Regent College, 1999), 106–30.

54. He "creates" (*bārā'*, Gen. 1:1); he "builds" (*bānâ*, 1 Sam. 2:35; 2 Sam. 7:27); he "makes" (*'āśâ*, Gen. 2:4); he "forms" (*yāṣar*, Gen. 2:7, 8). The products of divine work are called "the works of your/his hands" (*ma'ăśê yādêkā*, Ps. 8:6 [7]). See L. Koehler, W. Baumgartner, and J. J. Stamm, *The Hebrew and Aramaic Lexicon of the Old Testament* [*HALOT*], trans. and ed. M. E. J. Richardson (Leiden: Brill, 1994–99), 617.

55. Creator (Gen. 1–2; Job 10:3–12; Ps. 139:13–16), builder/architect (Prov. 8:27–31), musician/composer (Deut. 31:19), metalworker (Isa. 1:24–26), tailor (Job 29:14; Isa. 40:22), potter (Isa. 31:9), farmer (Hosea 10:11), shepherd (Ps. 23; Ezek. 34), tentmaker/camper (Job 9:8), temple designer and builder (Exod. 25; 35; 1 Chron. 28:11–19), scribe/writer (e.g., Exod. 24:12; 31:18; 34:28).

creation.[56] Indeed, God crowned humans with a measure of his own majesty and glory and put the entire universe under their feet (Ps. 8). Although in a fallen world work is often difficult and painful,[57] requiring us regularly to rest and be refreshed and renewed,[58] Genesis 1–2 reminds us that it is neither a consequence of the fall nor a condition from which we need redemption.

Despite human rebellion against God and our refusal to govern the world responsibly for him, God graciously withholds the full force of the curse so that we are actually able to accomplish tasks. Because of sin, every human effort is futile, empty, and vain, and God is just in making it so. However, by common grace he lifts the curse and replaces it with blessing, enabling humans to succeed in their efforts. Successes are marked by advances in culture (Gen. 4:16–22), prosperity (24:35; 26:12; 31:3–10; 33:10), fulfillment of commissions (24:12–14, 27, 48), and delight in work itself (Eccles. 2:24–26; 3:13; 5:18–20).[59] YHWH also grants the power to make wealth (Deut. 8:18). By grace he confirms the work of human hands (Ps. 90:17; cf. Isa. 26:12) and blesses it (Ps. 128; Prov. 10:22; Isa. 62:8–9; 65:23), and he actually gives joy in it (Num. 21:17–18; Isa. 9:3).

These facts help us understand the sin of idleness. Effects of the fall include human propensity to shirk responsibility, to view work as less than noble, to fail to grasp the honor of functioning as an image of God, and to refuse to work. Idleness is a prominent theme in Proverbs,[60] which portrays the sluggard as a tragicomic figure characterized by the laziness of an animal, preposterous excuses, and helplessness.[61] Sluggards will not begin tasks (6:9, 10) or finish them (12:27; 19:24; 26:15), will not face work (20:4; 22:13), and are persistently restless (10:26; 13:4; 15:19; 18:9; 21:25–26) rather

56. For discussion of this interpretation of the verbs *'ābad* and *šāmar* in Gen. 2:15, see Daniel I. Block, "To Serve and to Keep: Toward a Biblical Understanding of Humanity's Responsibility in the Face of the Biodiversity Crisis," in *Keeping God's Earth: The Global Environment in Biblical Perspective*, ed. Daniel I. Block and Noah J. Toly (Downers Grove, IL: InterVarsity, 2010), 116–42.

57. A hardship (*'iṣṣābôn*, Gen. 3:16, 17; 5:29; cf. *'eṣeb*, Gen. 3:16; Ps. 127:2; Prov. 5:10; 10:22), futile/transitory (*hebel*, Eccles. 1:14; 2:11, 17), trouble/troublesome (*'āmāl*, Ps. 90:10; Eccles. 1:3; 5:15; 6:7; 9:9), wearisome (*yĕgîa'*, Gen. 31:42; Job 3:17; Isa. 55:2).

58. The Hebrew verbs are respectively *nûaḥ* and *yinnāpēš* (Exod. 23:12; 31:17; 2 Sam. 16:14), and *yaḥălîp* (Isa. 40:31); see also Prov. 16:26; 22:4.

59. Indeed, in specific instances YHWH endows people with his Spirit in wisdom, understanding, knowledge, and every skill/ability in a craft, to perform the work of engravers, designers, tailors, and every kind of work (Exod. 35:31–35; cf. 4:11).

60. See Prov. 6:6–11; 10:26; 13:4; 15:19; 19:24; 20:4; 21:25; 22:13; 24:30–34; 26:13–16; cf. *'aṣlâ* and *'aṣlût*, "sluggishness," in 19:15; 31:27. For other texts on the problem of idleness, see 10:4–5; 12:24, 27; 18:9; 19:15; 20:13.

61. Similarly, Derek Kidner, *Proverbs*, Tyndale Old Testament Commentaries (Downers Grove, IL: InterVarsity, 1964), 42–43.

than focused. The sage's solution is to encourage them to learn from experience—though they tend to learn too late (6:11; 12:24; 24:30–31)—and from creatures as insignificant as ants, which teach that diligent workers do not need supervisors and take advantage of the opportunities that greet them (6:6–11; cf. 30:30–33).

The alternative to sloth is hard work—for the glory of God. Instructions on male diligence are scattered throughout Proverbs, which functions as a handbook to prepare youths for responsible citizenship and leadership within the community.[62] The wise young man receives instruction (24:32) and views work as fundamentally dignified and noble.[63] At the same time, Proverbs warns that work for the sake of getting rich is futile.[64]

Although the book of Proverbs is addressed to "my son," it concludes with a word for "my son" concerning "my daughter" (Prov. 31:10–31). This artfully composed alphabetic acrostic may have served as a kind of home-maker's catechism, taught by mothers to their daughters in preparation for adulthood and marriage, or by fathers who prepared their sons to marry well. Whereas Western popular culture views femininity in terms of beauty and charm, or even chiefly physical sexuality, this passage explicitly rejects such ephemeral definitions. This woman is characterized by responsibility, diligence, and commitment to her children, husband, and neighbors ahead of self. A noble woman does not praise herself or beg for people to notice her. She demonstrates fear in God by selfless hard work and letting the achievements of her hands speak for her. This is the worship of God at its most basic level.

In the Ben Asher tradition of the Hebrew canon, the book of Ruth follows immediately after Proverbs, suggesting that the editors viewed this Moabite woman as the embodiment of the virtues presented here.[65] But they seem also to have viewed other characters as models of the ideals in Proverbs. In that vein, I will conclude this subject with reflections on work as illustrated in the book of Ruth.[66] In contrast to Israel's leaders, whom the book of Judges portrays as moral and spiritual failures, this book involves ordinary people who work hard and play by the rules. The main characters express their piety

62. See Christopher B. Ansberry, *Be Wise, My Son, and Make My Heart Glad: An Exploration of the Courtly Nature of the Book of Proverbs*, Beihefte zur Zeitschrift für die alttestamentliche Wissenschaft 422 (Berlin: de Gruyter, 2011).

63. See Prov. 12:11, 14, 27; 13:11; 14:23; 16:26; 24:27; 28:19.

64. See Prov. 8:10, 19; 10:15–16; 11:4, 28; 13:7; 16:16; 22:1; 23:5; 28:20, 22.

65. In all of Scripture, only Ruth is called "a noble woman" (*'ēšet-ḥayil*), the expression that opens the poem (Prov. 31:10; cf. Ruth 3:10–11).

66. For fuller discussion, see "Ruth and Work," *The Theology of Work Project*, with contribution by Daniel I. Block, http://wiki.theologyofwork.org/old-testament/ruth-and-work.

with verbal declarations of faith and blessing[67] and demonstrate authentic righteousness in selfless "covenant loyalty" (ḥesed) to one another.[68] They are also people who treat work as worship and teach us important lessons on work.

a. Although human efforts to wrest bread from the ground are frustrated because of sin, by God's grace, work produces food (Ruth 1:1, 6).

b. Ruth demonstrates fear for God and honor to her mother-in-law by voluntarily putting herself at risk and going to work in a stranger's field (2:2).

c. Boaz demonstrates fear for God and respect for his workers by greeting them in the field with a blessing. The workers responded in kind (2:4).

d. Boaz demonstrates fear for God and respect for his workers by eating with them, sharing his food with the lowest among them (2:14), working with them at the winnowing, and sleeping with them out in the field (3:2–4, 14).

e. Boaz demonstrates fear for God and respect for his workers by establishing the world's earliest recorded anti-sexual-harassment policy, prohibiting the men in his workforce from troubling Ruth and requiring the women to let her work with them. Not only are they to permit her access to the water he provides for the workers, but they are also to go out of their way to assist her (2:8–9, 15–16).

f. Boaz demonstrates fear for God by viewing himself as the wings of God and providing shelter to the needy (2:12–13; cf. Prov. 14:31; 17:5).

g. Ruth expresses fear for God and respect for her employer by recognizing the grace she has received in being permitted to work since employment by another person is not a right but a privilege (2:2, 10).

h. YHWH blesses Ruth with fruit for her labors, so that when she beat the grain out of one day's gleanings, it measured one ephah—about five gallons (2:17)!

i. Naomi demonstrates fear for God and respect for an employer by blessing him for his kindness and generosity (2:19–20).

j. The workers express fear for God and respect for their employer and accept Ruth, a Moabite, as a coworker for the duration of the harvest (2:21–23).

---

67. Ruth 1:8–9; 2:4a–b; 2:12; 2:19 (without naming YHWH); 2:20; 3:10; 4:11–12; 4:14a, 14b–15. These benedictions are grounded in the assumption that YHWH is a gracious, covenant-keeping God.

68. For discussion, see Daniel I. Block, "Ruth 1: Book of," in *Dictionary of the Old Testament: Wisdom, Poetry and Writings*, ed. Tremper Longman III and Peter Enns (Downers Grove, IL: InterVarsity, 2008), 672–87.

  k. Because of Ruth's determination to provide for her mother-in-law, Boaz
     and the people of Bethlehem recognize in her the embodiment of *hesed*
     and the mark of female nobility (3:10–11).
  l. Boaz expresses fear for God and respect for his female worker by mar-
     rying her, although she is considered racially, economically, and socially
     inferior (4:1–13).
  m. The villagers of Bethlehem recognize that a person's well-being and
     the health of the family are dependent on the blessing of God, and they
     express fear for God and respect for Ruth by pronouncing this blessing
     on her (4:11–12).
  n. All human effort, even sexual intercourse, is dependent on God for the
     achievement of its desired goals (4:13–15).[69]

The New Testament provides no systematic or comprehensive treatment
of work as worship.[70] Jesus affirmed the dignity and nobility of work through
frequent reference to people at work in his teachings. As the son of a "carpen-
ter, craftsman" (*tektōn*, Matt. 13:55) and a craftsman himself in his early life
(Mark 6:3), he identified with workers and fulfilled the human role of "image
of God" through creative efforts. In the end his mission was to do the will of
God, who had sent him, and to finish God's work (John 4:34; 5:17; 6:28; 9:3).
    Apart from Paul's favorite self-designation as "servant of Christ Jesus,"[71]
his disposition toward work is reflected only in occasional comments. From
his most comprehensive statement in 2 Thessalonians 3:6–15 and elsewhere,
we learn that despite his learning and social status, Paul did not hesitate to
engage in physical work (Acts 20:34–35; 1 Cor. 4:12; 1 Thess. 2:9; 2 Thess.
3:8).[72] Beyond this we may summarize Paul's and the other apostles' teaching
on work as follows:

  a. Christians are to have the mind of Jesus Christ, who in the incarnation
     took on the form of a servant (Phil. 2:7).
  b. Slaves/servants must obey their earthly masters in all things as an act of
     worship to Christ. They work not merely to please humans, but with

    69. Ruth 1:4 suggests that Ruth had been married to Mahlon for ten years but that she had
not conceived.
    70. Curiously, few of the recent major dictionaries of the Bible (e.g., *Anchor Bible Diction-
ary*, InterVarsity's eight-volume set on the Old and New Testaments) include an article on
"Labor" or "Work."
    71. *Doulos Christou Iēsou*, Rom. 1:1; Gal. 1:10; Phil. 1:1; Col. 4:12; Titus 1:1; cf. his role
as "apostle of Jesus Christ by the will of God" (e.g., 1 Cor. 1:1.).
    72. Some have suggested that tent making was central to his personal life and the sustenance
of his ministry. P. W. Barnett, "Tentmaking," in Hawthorne, Martin, and Reid, *Dictionary of
Paul and His Letters*, 926.

sincerity of heart, fearing the Lord, which is their acceptable act of worship (Eph. 6:5–8; Col. 3:22–25).

c. Paul remonstrates sluggards who refuse to work, declaring that people are responsible for their own welfare; whoever does not work shall not eat (2 Thess. 3:10–11).

d. Recognizing that Christians can experience difficulties in the workplace, Paul encourages them to be steadfast, knowing that at the resurrection their labor will be rewarded by Christ (1 Cor. 15:58).

e. Paul recognizes that in Christ, slave and master are one, and they should treat each other accordingly (Philemon).

f. Christians must abandon a materialistic disposition toward life. Godliness with contentment and the treasures stored up in heaven through diligent work and generosity are supreme goals of labor (1 Tim. 6:6–10, 17–19).

g. James denounces the rich for exploiting their laborers and warns them that the wealth they gain at the expense of the poor is ephemeral (James 5:1–6).

h. Peter admonishes servants to serve respectfully and submissively, regardless of the character of their masters, for those who suffer unjustly will be rewarded by God (1 Pet. 2:18–20).

Today's Worship in Family Life and in Work

Having examined the teaching of Scripture on work and family life as worship, we may now reflect on its implications for today. Obviously we cannot roll back the clock; our present social circumstances and the nature of family relationships have changed drastically from those in the Bible. In the absence of texts that might serve as manuals for family worship, we are left to observe the principles at work in Scripture and apply them to our contexts.

First, according to the biblical picture, family worship is primarily a matter of life rather than formal religious rituals. The Scriptures refuse to compartmentalize life into spiritual and secular activities. At the same time, we cannot expect the next generation to adopt our spiritual values and beliefs if we do not deliberately and carefully train them (Prov. 22:6). While setting aside specific times in the morning or evening for religious exercises is commendable, this practice lacks biblical precedent. Furthermore, the training of children must extend beyond morning and/or evening devotions. Adults must seize every opportunity to instruct and guide the family in righteousness. For example, seeing a small child mesmerized by ants on the sidewalk opens a door for conversation on diligence, enthusiasm, and cooperation, not to mention the great and glorious God who created these amazing creatures.

Second, while mothers spend more time with small children than fathers, heads of households bear the primary responsibility for their children's instruction (e.g., Prov. 1:8). I do not intend to minimize the critical role of mothers in training children. But in our society many fathers are absent physically or emotionally, and, if they are present, they have retained adolescent values. Malachi reminds us that as a matter of principle, faithful husbands and healthy marriages are prerequisites to godly children (Mal. 2:15).

Third, just as the Israelites used the Passover for annual family celebrations of God's grace, so Christians should capitalize on the liturgical year to develop a sense of spiritual community with their forebears and to keep alive the memory of divine grace. Families would also do well to develop traditions that memorialize the grace of God in the life of their family. For second- or third-generation believers, such celebrations might commemorate turning points in the lives of parents or grandparents when the grace of God intervened. Otherwise, families could celebrate spiritual birthdays, significant answers to prayer, and even moments of intense grief that draw us to God.

Fourth, against the grain of modern culture, families need to develop a sense of identification with and accountability to the extended family. No one is an island. Births, marriages, and deaths involve families, not just individuals, and a crime against one is a crime against all. Furthermore, we should remember that our identity does not rest in our first names but in our surnames. Recovering family histories provides genealogical context and opportunities for worship.

With respect to work and vocation, Christians must recognize the dignity and value of work: it brings glory to God, it benefits others, it serves the world in which we live, and it is fundamental to our humanity. This explains why unemployment and underemployment are so dehumanizing. Since God has created us to do his work on earth, every legitimate occupation is God's work. Through us he makes, designs, organizes, beautifies, helps, leads, cultivates, cares, heals, empowers, informs, decorates, teaches, and loves. Furthermore, every talent is a gift on loan from God, given to us to be used for his glory and the benefit of his world.

Christians need to develop a sense of awe and gratitude before God, who blesses their work. In a fallen world, every accomplishment is a gift from God. Apart from divine grace, we would never achieve our goals. Papers we sit down to write would not get written; a meal so carefully planned would never turn out; the bridge we tried to build would never carry traffic; the chemical formula we tried to learn would never be mastered; and the cow we value for her high milk production would never bear a calf. Every project we tackle offers an opportunity not only to worship God in the work itself but also to declare our dependence on the Lord for his blessing, and in the end, to give thanks for the fruit of our labor. Although the line between consuming ourselves with work and working to our full capacity as stewards of God is fine, we need to work like an ox and relax like a lily. That is the challenge of work as worship (Luke 12:22–34).

6

The Ordinances as Worship

True worship involves reverential human acts of submission and homage before the divine Sovereign in response to his gracious revelation of himself and in accord with his will.

Having dealt at length with life as worship, we turn now to a series of topics more naturally associated with worship: liturgical exercises practiced by the assembled community of faith. Because baptism and the Lord's Supper are the only rituals mandated by Jesus, these provide a good place to begin. Baptism is a onetime rite of initiation into the body of Christ and the community of faith, while the Lord's Supper is a repeated rite through which believers celebrate the work of Christ and their membership in the community of faith.

While believers in baptistic and free churches tend to call these rites "ordinances," meaning "prescribed practices," and understand them as primarily commemorative, other traditions refer to them as "sacraments" and understand them as "means of grace," liturgical actions through which God mediates grace. A "sacrament" is commonly understood as "a means of consecrating, dedicating, or securing by a religious sanction."[1] To Catholics, sacraments are "means of salvation" by which persons become more fit to be justified by God. Grace is imparted whenever the sacrament is administered, regardless of the recipient's spiritual state.

1. *Oxford English Dictionary*, 2nd ed. (Oxford: Oxford University Press, 1989), 2616.

Although Roman Catholics recognize seven "sacraments,"[2] most evangelical Protestants recognize two required ordinances: baptism and the Lord's Supper.[3] They view the "means of grace" simply as provisions by which God's blessing comes to his people, and participating in them contributes nothing to fitness for justification; they are "media that transmit the grace of God."[4] While affirming that justification comes by faith alone through the work of Christ alone, Protestants recognize that the Holy Spirit uses many "means of grace" to bless the church: ministry of the Word, baptism, the Lord's Supper, prayer, worship, giving, fellowship, the exercise of spiritual gifts, evangelism, and so forth. Other "means of grace" relate to the seasons of life (child dedication, matrimony, funerals, etc.) or to the life of the Christian community (ordination and commissioning, church discipline and reconciliation, etc.). These are indeed sacred events, but because specific biblical prescription for them is lacking, most churches do not consider them to be "ordinances." Since ordinances are "sacred means of grace," we may call them "sacraments."[5] If they are properly performed for persons in right spiritual relationship with God, a divine work of grace occurs.

Baptism: The Christian Rite of Initiation[6]

Since many pedobaptists (those who practice infant baptism) in Reformed and Lutheran traditions link this ritual closely to circumcision, we must review the latter's significance in ancient Israel.

2. Baptism, confirmation, the Eucharist, penance, extreme unction (the last rites), holy orders (the priesthood and the diaconate), and matrimony.

3. Based on John 13, some, especially in Anabaptist traditions, also recognize footwashing as an ordinance. See H. S. Bender, "Footwashing," in *The Mennonite Encyclopedia* (Scottdale, PA: Mennonite Publishing House, 1956), 2:347–51. For discussion of the practice in the early church, see J. H. Neyrey, SJ, "The Foot Washing in John 13:6–11: Transformation Ritual or Ceremony?," in *The Social World of the First Christians: Essays in Honor of Wayne A. Meeks*, ed. L. M. White and O. L. Yarbrough (Minneapolis: Fortress, 1995), 198–213.

4. Clark H. Pinnock, *Flame of Love: A Theology of the Holy Spirit* (Downers Grove, IL: InterVarsity, 1996), 122. According to John Colwell, "Baptism is a means of . . . grace; it does not effect . . . grace; but it is the ordained means through which this grace is effected." See his *Promise and Presence: An Exploration of Sacramental Theology* (Milton Keynes: Paternoster, 2005), 113–14. Later (133) he writes, "Baptism is a sacrament; it is a means of grace; it is a human event through which a divine event is promised to occur."

5. See Anthony R. Cross, "The Evangelical Sacrament: *baptisma semper reformandum*," *Evangelical Quarterly* 80 (2008): 195–217.

6. It is impossible to write on a subject as important as this without betraying my personal convictions and occasionally expressing idiosyncratic opinions. While I have usually hesitated to be prescriptive in the application of the theology developed here, my background and broadly Anabaptistic convictions are most evident in this chapter. In this discussion, especially with

The Israelite Ordinance of Circumcision

Circumcision in the First Testament. The ritual of circumcision was so widely practiced in the ancient Near East[7] that Israelites considered uncircumcised persons to be barbarians.[8] While the origins of the rite are unclear, circumcision seems to have been generally performed at puberty, signifying a boy's passage to manhood and qualifying him to marry or assume full civic privileges and responsibilities.[9] Although it functioned as a rite of initiation in Israel, since it was performed on a son's eighth day of life, it scarcely served as a rite of passage.

Figure 6.1. This eleventh-century-BC ivory from Megiddo portrays a ruler seated on his throne between cherubim. Among those in the approaching procession is a soldier leading two circumcised nude captives. Were these Israelites appearing before Jabin, king of Hazor (Judg. 4:2)? (Photograph by J. Marr Miller. Used with permission.)

Genesis 17 offers a clear account of the significance of circumcision in Israel. The narrator presents Abraham's circumcision as the second of a two-part

respect to baptism as an act of worship, my interpretation of the biblical evidence reflects the stance of those who hold to "believers baptism." I have not given equal time to pedobaptistic views. Although Presbyterians and others in Reformed, Lutheran, and Anglican traditions are amply served by resources that defend and explicate the pedobaptistic perspective, the absence of a biblical theology of baptism is particularly evident in independent churches and free-church denominations, which tend to be baptistic in orientation. Hopefully this chapter will be a catalyst for reexamining what we are doing.

7. E.g., the non-Asiatic Philistines (Judg. 14:3; 1 Sam. 17:26, 36); Jer. 9:25–26 [24–25] suggests that Edomites, Ammonites, and Moabites observed some form of circumcision. See Jason S. DeRouchie, "Circumcision in the Hebrew Bible and Targums: Theology, Rhetoric, and the Handling of Metaphor," *Bulletin for Biblical Research* 14 (2004): 182–89.

8. According to Ezekiel the uncircumcised are consigned to the farthest and most undesirable recesses of Sheol, along with those who have been slain by the sword and presumably left unburied (Ezek. 32:17–21; cf. vv. 24–32; 31:18).

9. In Egypt circumcision was a rite of consecration to divine service and thus was required of all priests and of Pharaoh, the king-priest, also recognized as the son of God. See further Peter J. Gentry and Stephen J. Wellum, *Kingdom through Covenant: A Biblical-Theological Understanding of the Covenants*, (Wheaton: Crossway, 2012), 204–5. For further discussion of the rite in the ancient world and in Israel, see R. G. Hall, "Circumcision," *Anchor Bible Dictionary* [*ABD*], ed. D. N. Freedman (New York: Doubleday, 1992), 1:1025–31; T. Lewis and C. E. Armerding, "Circumcision," *International Standard Bible Encyclopedia* [*ISBE*], ed. G. W. Bromiley et al., rev. ed. (Grand Rapids: Eerdmans, 1979–88), 1:700–702.

covenant-ratification ritual, separated from the first phase by at least thirteen years.[10] In Genesis 15 YHWH had covenantally bound himself to Abraham by having a torch—the symbol of his presence—pass between the halves of animals sacrificed as part of this ratification ritual. In Genesis 17 YHWH prescribes circumcision as a permanent ordinance whereby Abraham and his descendants would bind themselves to this covenant.[11] Through circumcision male members of the covenant community were physically marked as the people of God and consecrated for their priestly mission of bringing divine blessing to the nations (cf. Gen. 12:3). Like a brand, circumcision was the mark of YHWH's claim on and ownership of a person. When Abraham was ninety-nine years old and his son Ishmael was thirteen, the patriarch declared his acceptance of the covenant relationship by circumcising himself and all males in his household (17:23–27).

It is difficult to assess how scrupulously the descendants of the patriarchs adhered to this ordinance. Genesis 34 suggests that three generations later circumcision had become a tool by which Jacob's sons manipulated outsiders.[12] Four hundred years later, not even the Levite Moses had kept the ordinance (Exod. 4:24–26). Nevertheless, Exodus 12:43–51 suggests that the Israelites who left Egypt were probably circumcised before they departed. Rather than functioning as a mark of exclusion, YHWH allowed non-Israelites to join the faith community (v. 48): all who identified with Israel and their Redeemer and who submitted to circumcision could partake in the first Passover and leave Egypt as members of the covenant community.

While this text illustrates the breadth of divine grace, it also opens the door to abuse. Within weeks of declaring their exclusive devotion to YHWH, the Israelites worshiped the golden calf (Exod. 32; Deut. 9), and months later, when they reached Kadesh-Barnea, masses of people refused to trust God and enter the land (Num. 14). Through circumcision those who left Egypt identified themselves as Israelites, but we discover quickly that there were two Israels from the outset: the majority claiming physical descent from Abraham, and the minority who were his spiritual descendants. Of the few who made up the latter, Caleb, the son of Jephunneh the Kenizzite, receives special

10. The flow of the narrative suggests that the events of Gen. 15 transpired before Ishmael was born; Gen. 17:25 notes that he was thirteen years old when Abraham circumcised him.

11. These two phases of the covenant ratification ritual (Gen. 15; 17) correspond to the sprinkling of the blood first on the altar (representing God) and then on the people in the covenant ratification ceremony at Sinai (Exod. 24:1–8).

12. Genesis 34 offers no hint that Jacob's sons put any spiritual stock in their circumcised status; they view it primarily as an ethnic marker. And in his response to his sons' actions, Jacob himself seems oblivious to the shame they have brought to the name of YHWH. He is concerned only about his personal well-being (v. 30).

commendation. Although Caleb was not even an ethnic Israelite, he is characterized by YHWH as having a different spirit and being full after YHWH (Num. 14:24; Deut. 1:36; Josh. 14:6–15).

It appears that through much of Israel's history many understood circumcision as a "sacrament," akin to the Roman Catholic view of baptism; it was not only a means of grace but also a "means of salvation." The rite itself was thought to secure one's place among YHWH's people, whether or not the person demonstrated personal faith through covenant righteousness, which led to the notion of circumcision of the heart. While the idea originated with YHWH (Lev. 26:41), in his closing pastoral addresses Moses appeals to his hearers to circumcise their hearts and cease being stubborn (Deut. 10:16). The marks of a circumcised heart included fearing, serving, and clinging to YHWH (v. 20). In 30:6 Moses treats circumcision of the heart as a divine surgical act that will result in true covenant commitment (*'āhab*, "love"). Centuries later, Jeremiah repeated Moses' call, pleading with the people of Judah to circumcise themselves to YHWH, which he clarified as "removing the foreskins of your hearts" (4:4). Later the prophet described Israel as "circumcised with a foreskin"—that is, "circumcised yet really *un*circumcised" (Jer. 9:25–26). Physical circumcision counted for nothing if unaccompanied by spiritual circumcision.

Circumcision in the New Testament. Although Jesus himself was circumcised on his eighth day, tensions within the early church revolved around this rite. Breaking definitively with Judaism, the Jerusalem Council determined that gentile believers did not need to be circumcised to become members of the new covenant community (Acts 15:1–29). Rather, the gift of the Holy Spirit signaled acceptance by God (v. 8).

Paul himself was inconsistent in applying this decision; to enhance his acceptance among the Jews of Asia Minor, in the very next chapter he had his spiritual son Timothy circumcised (Acts 16:3). However, the issue of circumcision was a lightning rod in his letters to the Romans and Galatians. To Judaizers he declared that physical circumcision was worthless even for Jews unless they were circumcised in their hearts (Rom. 2:25–29), and he cited Abraham as evidence for the priority of faith over the rite (4:1–25). In this respect Paul was fully in step with Moses and Jeremiah. But he went a step further: since Israel's significance as an ethnic entity changed dramatically with the coming of Christ, the ordinance was now passé. In Galatians 2:1–10 he emphatically rejected the notion of gentile circumcision as a prerequisite to acceptance with God. In Christ the ethnic marker separating Jews and gentiles was suspended; the new covenant community of faith was established through the work of the Spirit.

The Christian Ordinance of Baptism

The roots of the ordinance. Purification rituals involving water were common in the First Testament,[13] but their importance is also evident in "washing" metaphors used to speak of moral and spiritual cleansing (Pss. 24:4; 51:2, 7; Ezek. 36:25; Zech. 13:1). In the intertestamental period, the Pharisees extended the concern for priestly purity to the general population (Matt. 15:2; Mark 7:3).[14] The Qumran document *Community Rule* 3.4–9 expresses the theory behind ritual washing: "When his [an initiate's] flesh is sprinkled with purifying water and sanctified by cleansing water, it shall be made clean by the humble submission of his soul to all the precepts of God."[15]

The baptism of John the Baptist represented a transitional stage between Jewish purification rituals and Christian baptism.[16] His baptism differed from the ritual baths of Judaism in several aspects. (1) While ritual baths were self-administered, John baptized others. (2) While the ceremonial washings of Judaism had to be repeated with every defilement, John's baptism was a onetime event. (3) While the rituals of Judaism were preoccupied with ceremonial defilement, John's baptism was associated with repentance—turning from sin to a life of godliness. (4) While the rituals of Judaism were performed in man-made cisterns, John baptized in the Jordan River, a natural body of water. John's baptism was an initiatory rite, publicly marking the remnant who represented the kingdom of God.

When Jesus came to the Jordan, John recognized that he needed no baptism (Matt. 3:14). But Jesus insisted on baptism to fulfill all righteousness, which apparently signified his identification with the renewed people of God. This event coincided with the public announcement of Jesus as the messianic Son of God. Since Jesus was baptized by John (Mark 1:9) and some of John's disciples later joined Jesus (John 1:35–42), there seems to have been a link between John's baptism and the later Christian rite. However, Christian baptism involved baptism "in Jesus' name." The Great Commission (Matt.

13. On the Day of Atonement the high priest bathed before donning ritual vestments (Lev. 16:4); water was used for purification after contact with unclean objects (Lev. 11:24–40; 14:1–8; 15:1–13; Num. 19:1–22).

14. The intensity of the concern at the time of Christ is reflected in the number of ritual baths unearthed at Masada, Herodium, Jerusalem, and Qumran.

15. *Community Rule* [1QS] 3.4–9; in Géza Vermès, *The Complete Dead Sea Scrolls in English*, rev., exp. ed. (New York: Penguin, 1997), 100–101. Rabbinic literature speaks of "proselyte ritual ablutions" as a rite of initiation. See the Babylonian Talmud, [*b.*] *Yebamot* 46–47. However, the relationship between these texts and Christian baptism is dubious.

16. The ritual was so characteristic of John that both Josephus (*Jewish Antiquities* 18.116–19) and the Gospel writers (Matt. 3:1–12; Mark 1:2–11; Luke 3:1–20) characterize him as "John the Baptist/Baptizer."

28:18–20) suggests the Christian rite commenced after Jesus' ascension and the outpouring of the Holy Spirit in Jerusalem (Acts 2:37–41; cf. 19:1–7).

The nature and significance of Christian baptism. The English word "baptism" comes from the Greek verb *baptō*, meaning "to dip in, to dip under, to immerse," and its variant *baptizō*, "to immerse, sink down, drown, go under, bathe." The word was used occasionally of Jewish ablutions.[17] The fact that John baptized in the Jordan (Matt. 3:6, *en*, "in"; Mark 1:9, *eis*, "into") and that he and Jesus came up out of (*ek*) the water (Mark 1:10; cf. Acts 8:38–39) suggests support for the immersionist interpretation.[18] However, it is also possible that the baptizer used a pitcher or cupped his hands and dipped them into the water and released the water over the person's head.

Matthew's version of the Great Commission (28:18–20) contains the only reference to Christian baptism in the Gospels.[19] Claiming full authority, Jesus sends his disciples out to make disciples of all nations, baptizing them and teaching them to obey everything he had commanded.[20] Through baptism, believers in Christ become/are declared disciples; through teaching, their discipleship is nurtured. It is striking that the New Testament presents the trinitarian view of God most explicitly in the context of the rite of initiation; baptisms are to be performed "into [*eis*] the name of the Father and the Son and the Holy Spirit." Baptism grounds the relationship between those baptized and the Triune God, and the Triune God is the one they confess from this point onward.[21]

The practice of baptism in the book of Acts. As expected, Acts provides the most detailed information on the practice of baptism in the first-century church. Associated with repentance, faith, confession, and regeneration, baptism is presented as the rite of initiation whereby believers are stamped with the name of Christ and enter the covenant community (cf. 1 Cor. 12:13).

1. Baptism in Jerusalem (Acts 2:37–41). Addressing the large crowd at Pentecost, Peter exhorted the people to "repent, and let each of you be baptized

17. In Luke 11:38 the Pharisees are amazed that Jesus did not first wash (*baptizō*) before dinner. Cognate nouns include *baptisma* and *baptismos*. John is called *ho baptizōn*, "the baptizer" (Mark 1:4; 6:14), and *ho baptistēs*, "the baptist" (Matt. 3:1; 14:2; Luke 7:20, 33). The act of sprinkling is represented by the verb *rhantizō*.

18. For a full defense of the immersionist interpretations, see A. T. Robinson, "Baptism: Baptist View," in *ISBE*, rev. ed., 1:415–17; Everett Ferguson, *Baptism in the Early Church: History, Theology, and Liturgy in the First Five Centuries* (Grand Rapids: Eerdmans, 2009), 25–59.

19. A second reference is found in the longer ending of Mark (16:16), which is omitted in some of the oldest manuscripts.

20. On this text, see Andreas Köstenberger, "Baptism in the Gospels," in *Believer's Baptism: Sign of the New Covenant in Christ*, ed. T. R. Schreiner and S. D. Wright (Nashville: Broadman & Holman, 2006), 18–27.

21. See G. R. Beasley-Murray, "Baptism," in *Dictionary of Paul and His Letters*, ed. G. F. Hawthorne, R. P. Martin, and D. G. Reid (Downers Grove, IL: InterVarsity, 1993), 61.

for the forgiveness of your sins, and you will receive the gift of the Holy Spirit" (2:37–38). That day about three thousand people were baptized and added to the church. Peter presupposed baptism as a fundamental element of conversion: faith, repentance, confession, baptism, the gift of the Spirit.[22] "Repent and be baptized" was shorthand for the entire package.

2. Baptism in Samaria (Acts 8:9–17). In response to Philip's preaching of the good news of Jesus Christ, some Samaritans—men and women—received the word and were baptized "into [*eis*] the name of the Lord Jesus" (v. 16). Unlike the event in Jerusalem, the Holy Spirit did not "fall on" the new believers when they were baptized; this happened later, when the apostles laid hands on them (v. 17).

3. Baptism on the road to Gaza (Acts 8:26–40). Here baptism seems to be a natural part of the conversion experience. While the impulse behind the Ethiopian eunuch's insistence on being baptized is unclear, in response to hearing the good news of Jesus, the Ethiopian knew to request it. Philip, a recognized church leader (cf. Acts 6:5), administered the ordinance in a natural body of water.

4. Baptism in Damascus (Acts 9:10–18; 22:16). When the newly converted Saul/Paul arrived in Damascus, his host Ananias laid hands on him and baptized him. In Paul's later recollection of the event (22:16), he quoted Ananias's words: "Arise, and be baptized, and wash away your sins, calling on his name." This baptism followed conversion; it was associated with washing away sins (cf. Ps. 51) and was linked with calling on the name of Jesus.

5. Baptism in Caesarea (Acts 10:44–48). When the Holy Spirit came upon Cornelius and those in his house, Peter reasoned that baptism should not be refused them. In this instance the converts were baptized in the name of Jesus, clearly distinguishing this rite from Jewish ritual baptism.

6. Baptism in Philippi (Acts 16). Luke recounts two baptismal events here. According to verses 11–15, the first European convert to faith in Jesus Christ was a woman, a merchant who dealt in luxury fabrics and was already a worshiper of God, and whose heart had been prepared to receive the gospel. Though the text speaks only of Lydia's faith, Luke reports that she and her household were baptized. Does the "household" involve children, or are these her employees who also believe in Jesus? Since Luke identified Lydia by profession, the latter seems more likely.

The second baptism involved an unnamed jailer (vv. 19–34). After Paul and Silas's supernatural release from prison (v. 25), the jailer obviously believed in

22. See Robert H. Stein, "Baptism and Becoming a Christian in the New Testament," *Southern Baptist Journal of Theology* [*SBJT*] 2 (1998): 5–17; Stein, "Baptism in Luke-Acts," in Schreiner and Wright, *Believer's Baptism*, 35–66.

Jesus. He and his household were baptized, and he brought Paul and Silas to his house to celebrate. Again, it is unclear who was involved in the baptism. Although the concluding statement (v. 34) speaks only of the jailer's faith, the fact that "his entire household rejoiced that he had become a believer in God" suggests that they all became believers.[23]

7. Baptism in Corinth (Acts 18:8). Many Corinthians heard the gospel from Paul, believed, and were baptized. Hearing led to faith, which led naturally to baptism.

8. Baptism at Ephesus (Acts 19:1–7). Building on the work of John the Baptist, Paul baptized the believers "into [eis] the name of the Lord Jesus" and then laid his hands on them. Reminiscent of the earlier Pentecost experience, the Holy Spirit came upon them, inspiring them to speak in tongues and divine utterances. This event signaled the last of four stages in the redefinition of the covenant community in the book of Acts.[24] No longer were the people of God defined ethnically or geographically; the covenant community was found wherever people believed in Jesus and were baptized.

The teaching on baptism in the Epistles. Paul rarely speaks of water baptism in his epistles.[25] In Romans 6:1–11 he portrays water baptism as the physical act whereby believers identify with Christ in his death and resurrection. Those who have been justified by faith (Rom. 5:1) and have been baptized consider themselves dead to sin and alive to Christ. Even so, it is not the water of baptism that frees us from sin, but the blood of Christ.

In 1 Corinthians 1:14–17 Paul laments that baptism, which should be a symbol of unity in Christ, often brings division. In Corinth the problem revolved around who did the baptizing: Apollos, Cephas, or Paul. Paul stressed that baptism is not into the name of the baptizer, but into the name of Christ. His later declaration that Christians are washed, sanctified, and justified in the name of the Lord Jesus Christ and in the Spirit of our God (1 Cor. 6:11) alludes to baptism. In 1 Corinthians 10 Paul uses the Israelites' crossing of the Red Sea as a metaphor for baptism, warning those who have been baptized not to be like the Israelites and experience the judgment of God for their sin.

23. The accounts of both these events are too vague to support either pedobaptism or believers baptism.

24. Stage 1: The Holy Spirit was poured out on Jews from all over the world who believed in Jesus (Acts 2:1–47). Stage 2: The Holy Spirit was poured out on Samaritans (who were half-Jewish ethnically and spiritually—the Torah of Moses was their Scripture; 8:14–17). Stage 3: The Holy Spirit was poured out on Cornelius and his household (gentiles who feared the God of Israel) in the land of Palestine (10:44–48). Stage 4: The Holy Spirit was poured out on believers in Ephesus, far from the Holy Land (19:1–7).

25. On baptism in the Epistles, see Thomas R. Schreiner, "Baptism in the Epistles: An Initiation Rite for Believers," in Schreiner and Wright, *Believer's Baptism*, 67–96.

In 1 Corinthians 12:12–13 he asserts that physical baptism is an expression of the work of the Spirit in the believer's life. Since there is only one Spirit who baptizes believers into the body of Christ, baptism should unify believers.[26]

Paul had discussed this matter in his earlier Letter to the Galatians. Since all believers are sons of God through faith in Christ Jesus, and since all who have been baptized into Christ have clothed themselves with Christ (Gal. 3:27), baptism is a symbol of unity; in Christ, walls that separate Jews and Greeks, males and females, slaves and free are demolished. He reiterates this theme in Ephesians 4:3–6 by declaring the unity of the body in Spirit, faith, baptism, and devotion to the one God and Father of all. Colossians 2:11–12 is the only New Testament passage that links circumcision and baptism. Through the work of Christ, believers have been circumcised spiritually. Moreover, they have been buried with him in baptism and raised up through faith in the power of God, who raised Jesus from the dead.[27]

References to baptism are also rare in the General Epistles.[28] Hebrews 10:22 calls believers to "draw near to God with a sincere heart and with the full assurance that faith brings, having our hearts sprinkled to cleanse us from a guilty conscience and having our bodies washed with pure water" (NIV). This language recalls First Testament rituals but refers to Christian experience. First Peter 3:20–21 compares Christian baptism to the ark through which Noah and his family were saved by water when the rest of the population was destroyed by water. Parenthetically, Peter adds that it is not the water itself that removes the defilement, but the appeal for a good conscience; salvation is effected through the resurrection of Christ. The reference to the Spirit, water, and blood as witnesses to the work of Christ in 1 John 5:6–9 may also allude to baptism.[29]

Summary Reflections on Baptism in the Bible

Having surveyed the biblical evidence for the practice of baptism, several theological principles emerge. First, along with faith, repentance, confession, and the receipt of the Spirit, the New Testament presents baptism as a core element of conversion. Since the Great Commission presents baptism and

---

26. Apparently alluding to a problem in Corinth, in 1 Cor. 15:29 Paul repudiates the notion of baptism for the dead.

27. Paul never refers explicitly to baptism in the Pastoral Epistles, though his reference to "the washing of rebirth and renewal by the Holy Spirit" in Titus 3:5 conceptually recalls Jesus' conversation with Nicodemus in John 3.

28. The "washings" (*baptismois*) in Heb. 9:10 refer not to Christian baptism but to lustrations prescribed in First Testament cultic worship. This seems also to be the case in 6:2.

29. References to washing and water in Revelation (7:13–14; 22:1–15) refer not to baptism but to the cleansing and life-giving work of the Lamb and the Spirit of God.

teaching as the means whereby disciples are made, evangelism should include both the appeal to receive the grace that God offers in Jesus and a call to be baptized. In Acts, to be a Christian is to be baptized; the book knows nothing of an unbaptized Christian. In the New Testament, unbaptized persons had either refused to repent and believe in Jesus or had repented and believed but were physically unable to experience the rite (like the thief on the cross, Luke 23:39–43). This does not mean that baptism saves; on the contrary, apart from faith it has no value at all.

Second, water baptism is effective as an ordinance/sacrament only if accompanied by personal faith and repentance. This rite signifies that those being baptized have turned from sin to God, placed their faith in Christ, and been regenerated by the Holy Spirit. However, baptism is more than a ritual symbolic of an inner spiritual reality and more than a memorial of a past event; in the New Testament it is the act whereby believers identify with Christ and give public witness to their faith. This identification is reflected in three baptismal idioms involving the name of God/Christ: believers are baptized "in the name of Jesus Christ" (*en tō onomati Iēsou Christou*; Acts 10:48), or "on the name of Jesus Christ" (*epi tō onomati Iēsou Christou*; 2:38), or "into the name of the Lord Jesus" (*eis to onoma tou kyriou Iēsou*; 8:16; 19:5). In the last idiom the shift from "Jesus Christ" to "Lord Jesus" seems insignificant until we realize that the divine name YHWH underlies the epithet *kyrios*. The idiom of being baptized "into the name of Jesus" may relate to the ancient custom of branding slaves with the names of their owners.[30] From the time of their baptism, believers belong to the Lord Jesus; they represent him wherever they go, but they also trust only him for their own well-being (cf. 1 Pet. 4:12–19). This notion seems to underlie 1 Corinthians 1:13–15; Paul's converts did not bear the brand of his name: they bore the name of Christ. The Great Commission expands the divine claim to believers from the Second Person of the Trinity to include the Triune God; converts are to be baptized "into the name of the Father and the Son and the Holy Spirit" (Matt. 28:19).[31] Through baptism, people's passports change: their citizenship is transferred from the kingdom of darkness into the kingdom of God.

Third, while the mode of baptism is less consequential than the timing, baptism by immersion accords most closely with the meaning of the Greek word *baptizō*. The biblical narratives describe people as baptizing and being

---

30. See Daniel I. Block, "Bearing the Name of the LORD with Honor," in *How I Love Your Torah, O LORD! Studies in the Book of Deuteronomy* (Eugene, OR: Cascade Books, 2011), 61–72; originally published in *Bibliotheca Sacra* 168 (2011): 20–31.

31. See Charles A. Geischen, "The Divine Name in Ante-Nicene Christology," *Vigilae christianae* 57 (2007): 143–46.

baptized; they go into the water and come up out of the water. Immersion also accords most closely with the imagery of baptism as dying with Christ and rising to new life (Rom. 6:1–11).[32]

Fourth, New Testament baptism links the rite to commitment to the body of believers. Believers in Jesus were baptized not only into Christ but also "into one body" (1 Cor. 12:13). Since the church is the body of Christ, individual believers relate to Christ in the context of community. Through baptism they are initiated into the life of the church and born into the household of faith (Gal. 6:10).

Fifth, while the New Testament does not prescribe the location of baptism, performing the ordinance outdoors in a natural body of water accords most closely with narrative descriptions in Acts and with its function as an initiatory rite witnessed by the community of faith and the outside world, to whose way of life the candidate has died (Rom. 6:1–11). While differing in significance, the open and public nature of John's baptism of Jesus seems paradigmatic for Christian baptism.

Sixth, the fact that baptism is the only explicitly prescribed trinitarian liturgical act of worship in the New Testament highlights the importance of repeating the trinitarian formula whenever the rite is administered. It is also noteworthy that baptism is the only liturgical rite that is to be performed in the name of the Holy Spirit.

The Practice of Baptism in Worship Today

The ways ordinances are administered vary from church to church and from one part of the world to another. However practiced, the rite of baptism should be driven by scriptural ideals. In my consideration of the biblical evidence, I

---

32. Many who prefer pouring or sprinkling water over immersion link physical baptism with the bestowal of the Holy Spirit. The late first- to early second-century-AD *Didache* (*Teaching of the Lord to the Gentiles through the Twelve Apostles*) offers the earliest clear witness to affusion as the mode of baptism.

> Now concerning baptism, baptize as follows: after you have reviewed all these things, baptize in the name of the Father and of the Son and of the Holy Spirit in running water. But if you have no running water, then baptize in some other water; and if you are not able to baptize in cold water, then do so in warm. But if you have neither, then pour water on the head three times in the name of the Father and Son and Holy Spirit. And before the baptism, let the one baptizing and the one who is to be baptized fast, as well as any others who are able. Also, you must instruct the one who is to be baptized to fast for one or two days beforehand.

Didache 7.1–4, as translated by M. W. Holmes, *The Apostolic Fathers: Greek Texts and English Translations*, 3rd, rev. ed. (Grand Rapids: Baker Academic, 2007), 355. This document assumes baptism on confession of faith; its concession to affusion seems pragmatic.

obviously read the texts through baptistic and Anabaptistic lenses. Since this perspective continues in the following discussion, not all will find my proposals convincing. My goal here is not to challenge pedobaptistic perspectives but to invite readers in baptistic and free-church congregations to reflect more deeply on the biblical and theological principles that underlie the ordinances. The following considerations spring from the theological principles discussed above.

1. Evangelistic preaching should provide instruction on the nature and significance of baptism, presenting the latter as a fundamental part of the conversion experience. We are not saved by or through being baptized (baptismal regeneration), but unbaptized Christians are abnormal Christians.

2. As a corollary, only regenerate persons qualify for baptism. People who request baptism must give clear evidence that they are walking in newness of life. Where the personal costs of conversion are high (as in many missionary contexts), abusing this ordinance will rarely happen, but in "culturally Christian" communities, baptism may be easily used as a ticket to acceptance in the local church. This creates a situation resembling that of the Israelites, many of whom claimed membership in the community of faith because they were circumcised but gave little evidence of devotion to YHWH. The inclusion of such people blurs the ethical and spiritual boundaries between the church and the world, just as it blurred the boundaries between Israel and the surrounding nations for much of their history (fig. 6.2). Moses and Jeremiah envisioned the day when the ideal described in Deuteronomy 30 would be realized, the problem of two Israels would be resolved, and the boundaries of physical and spiritual Israel would be the same. Jesus Christ established the church as the new Israel of God (Gal. 6:16), made up exclusively of those who have repented, confessed him as Savior and Lord, bear the stamp of his name, are circumcised of heart and indwelt by the Spirit, and have been baptized into the body of Christ.

FIGURE 6.2

**The Relationship between Physical Israel and Spiritual Israel
As Perceived by Moses and Jeremiah**

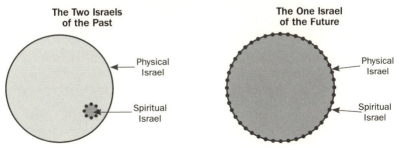

The Two Israels
of the Past

Physical
Israel

Spiritual
Israel

The One Israel
of the Future

Physical
Israel

Spiritual
Israel

3. We should deemphasize mere obedience to Christ as a motivation for baptism. As the act whereby we are buried with Christ and raised with him, this is not merely duty, which may easily degenerate to legalism, but the highest privilege imaginable.

4. Congregations should celebrate baptisms as highlights in the lives of individual believers and in the life of the church. Since baptism involves identification with the body of Christ as well as with its Head (Christ), decisions regarding baptism should be congregational affairs—not simply to empower the congregation, but to give the community opportunity to identify with candidates and declare their support for them in their walk with Christ.

5. Whether baptisms should be performed indoors or outdoors remains an open question. If the primary purpose of baptism is to declare publicly one's passage from the kingdom of darkness to the kingdom of light as a testimony to the world, an outdoor context is preferable. If the primary purpose is to declare one's union with the body of Christ, then baptism inside (or at) the church's meeting place may be justified. In the end, resources and weather may determine the context.[33]

Excursus: Infant Baptism

Despite the Anabaptist protest in the sixteenth and seventeenth centuries,[34] Lutherans, Calvinists, and Anglicans continued the pedobaptistic practice of Roman Catholics. Defenders of the practice acknowledge that the New Testament neither commands nor forbids infant baptism (perhaps because second-generation Christians were unknown in the earliest church), but they justify the practice with several weighty arguments, summarized below.[35]

First, emphasizing the continuity between old and new covenants, baptism is to the church what circumcision was to ancient Israelites. In Colossians 2:11–12 Paul seems to link the Jewish practice of circumcision with

33. My maternal grandfather was converted during the Christmas season in Russia. When he requested baptism, they chopped a hole in the ice and baptized him by immersion. For a graphic description of early Baptist practice in the United States, see Gregory A. Wills, *Democratic Religion: Freedom, Authority, and Church Discipline in the Baptist South, 1785–1900* (New York: Oxford University Press, 1997), 15–16.

34. Article 1 of the Schleitheim Confession refers to infant baptism as "the greatest and first abomination of the pope." See http://www.anabaptistwiki.org/mediawiki/index.php /SchleitheimConfession.

35. For fuller discussions, see T. M. Lindsay, "Baptism: Reformed View," *ISBE*, rev. ed., 1:418–23; and Hughes Oliphant Old, *Worship: Reformed according to Scripture*, rev. ed. (Louisville: Westminster John Knox, 2002), 7–22.

Christian baptism. Since children were included in First Testament promises to parents, New Testament promises to parents also extend to the children. Just as circumcision placed Israelite children within the sphere of the covenant and its blessings, so infant baptism places children within the sphere of the (new) covenant and its blessings.

Second, in Acts 2:38–39, which includes an invitation to baptism, Peter declares that the gospel promise is "to you and your children." On the principle of corporate solidarity, actions taken by heads of households implicate all members of the household. In Acts, furthermore, narratives describing the baptisms of individual converts include the baptisms of their households without explicit exemption (16:15, 33; cf. 1 Cor. 1:16).

Third, the church fathers attest to the early practice of infant baptism. Irenaeus, a convert of Polycarp, who was a disciple of John, suggested that the baptism of infants had been practiced for a long time (*Against Heresies* 2.22.4; cf. Fragment 34). Toward the end of the second century or the beginning of the third, Tertullian expressed his preference for adult baptism, but the mere mention of the infant rite confirms its antiquity. In the third century, Origen argued that because the church baptizes children, original sin must belong to them.[36]

The Lord's Supper

Apart from Jesus' command to baptize new believers (Matt. 28:19), the New Testament lacks explicit prescriptions on how to administer the ordinance of baptism. The situation is different with the Lord's Supper, which is prescribed in four contexts and is theologically interpreted in a fifth (John 6:47–51, 53–58). Table 6.1 presents a view of the prescriptive texts (all ESV).

Names for the Ordinance

Protestants refer to the ordinance instituted by Jesus with four primary designations.

The Lord's Supper (kyriakon deipnon). This designation, derived from 1 Corinthians 11:20, tends to be the preferred expression in evangelical circles. Like other expressions,[37] "Lord's Supper" highlights the monergistic nature of

36. For a detailed discussion of the practice of baptism in the early church, see Ferguson, *Baptism in the Early Church*. See also S. A. McKinion, "Baptism in the Patristic Writings," in Schreiner and Wright, *Believer's Baptism*, 163–88.

37. "Lord's Day" (*kyriakē hēmera*, Rev. 1:10), "Lord's Table" (*trapezēs kyriou*, 1 Cor. 10:21); "Lord's Cup" (*potērion kyriou*, 1 Cor. 10:21).

Table 6.1. Synoptic Texts on the Institution of the Lord's Supper

1 Corinthians 11:23–26	Mark 14:22–26	Matthew 26:26–30	Luke 22:14–20
For I received from the Lord what I also delivered to you,			And when the hour came, he reclined at table, and the apostles with him. And he said to them, "I have earnestly desired to eat *this Passover* with you before I suffer. For I tell you I will not eat it until it is fulfilled in the kingdom of God."
that the Lord Jesus on the night when he was betrayed took bread, and *when he had given thanks*, he broke it, and said,	And as they were eating, he took bread, and after blessing it broke it and gave it to them, and said,	Now as they were eating, Jesus took bread, and after blessing it broke it and gave it to the disciples, and said,	
"This is my body which is for you. Do this in remembrance of me."	"Take; this is my body."	"Take, eat; this is my body."	
In the same way also he took the cup, after supper,	And he took a cup, and *when he had given thanks* he gave it to them, and they all drank of it.	And he took a cup, and *when he had given thanks* he gave it to them,	And he took a cup, and *when he had given thanks,*
saying,	And he said to them,	saying,	he said,
"This cup is the *new covenant in my blood.*"	"This is *my blood of the covenant,* which is poured out for many."	"Drink of it, all of you, for this is *my blood of the covenant,* which is poured out for many *for the forgiveness of sins.* I tell you I will not drink again of this fruit of the vine until that day when I drink it new with you in my Father's kingdom."	"Take this, and divide it among yourselves. For I tell you that from now on I will not drink of the fruit of the vine until the kingdom of God comes."
Do this, as often as you drink it, in remembrance of me." For as often as you eat this bread and drink the cup, you proclaim the Lord's death until he comes.	Truly, I say to you, I will not drink again of the fruit of the vine until that day when I drink it new in the kingdom of God."		And he took bread, and *when he had given thanks,* he broke it and gave it to them, saying, "This is my body, which is given for you. Do this in remembrance of me."
	And when they had sung a hymn, they went out to the Mount of Olives.	And when they had sung a hymn, they went out to the Mount of Olives.	And likewise the cup after they had eaten, saying, "This cup that is poured out for you is *the new covenant in my blood.*"

Note: All texts are from the ESV. The highlighted elements are significant in the discussion below.

the meal: it is instituted by the Lord; its nature, meaning, and participants are defined by the Lord; and the participants eat as his privileged vassals. If the Tetragrammaton, YHWH, rather than *'ădōnāy*, "Master," underlies *kyrios*, we may link this meal to the meals at the central sanctuary hosted by YHWH in Israelite worship (e.g., Deut. 12:11–12).

Communion (koinōnia). In 1 Corinthians 10:16 Paul speaks of "the cup of blessing that we bless" as "fellowship in the blood of Christ" and "the bread that we break" as "fellowship in the body of Christ." The participants in this fellowship are united by covenant to each other and to Christ. In higher church circles this is also called "Holy Communion," in contrast to the common communion of regular worship.

The Eucharist. This designation, from *eucharistia*, "thanksgiving" (Hebrew *tôdâ*), is preferred by Roman Catholics and Anglicans. The word occurs in all four accounts of the institution of the meal. The motif of thanksgiving links it to the Jewish Passover, which involved thanksgiving prayers climaxing in the recitation of the Hallel Psalms (Pss. 113–18), which praise YHWH for his grace in rescuing Israel from Egypt. Jesus' use of this word expresses the proper disposition toward the event commemorated in the meal: thanksgiving for God's mission of salvation accomplished through his death.

The Breaking of Bread. In Brethren circles the weekly communion is called the "Breaking of Bread." This expression refers to a practice at gatherings of early Christians to break bread together (Acts 2:42, 46; 20:7; 27:35–36), though scholars debate whether these passages designate the Lord's Supper or simply fellowship over the dinner table.

The First Testament Background to the Lord's Supper

When Jesus instituted the Lord's Supper, he created a glorious helix blending at least three First Testament liturgical traditions: the Passover meal, the covenant ratification ceremony, and the sin offering (fig. 6.3).

The link between the Lord's Supper and the Israelite Passover is firmly established in the New Testament texts. Not only does Paul speak of Christ as "our Passover [lamb]" (1 Cor. 5:7),[38] but each of the Synoptic Gospels also notes that the institution of the Lord's Supper coincided with the Jewish Passover and Festival of Unleavened Bread.[39] Jesus timed this last meal with the disciples prior to his crucifixion to signal the shift in eras: the foundational Jewish festival celebrating Israel's release from slavery in Egypt would

---

38. In the LXX *pascha* identifies the Passover lamb in Exod. 12:21 and Deut. 16:2, 6 (cf. *phasek* in 2 Chron. 30:18).

39. See Matt. 26:2, 17; Mark 14:1, 12, 14; Luke 22:1, 7, 11, 15; cf. John 18:28.

FIGURE 6.3
The Eucharistic Helix

be transformed into a new Passover meal, the church's foundational festival celebrating Christians' release from slavery to sin and death. The association of the Lord's Supper with the Passover also highlighted Jesus' substitutionary role; because of his death, we need not die.

While the link between the Lord's Supper and Passover is universally recognized, the significance of the phrase "my blood of the covenant" is generally overlooked.[40] In the New Testament the phrase is found only in Matthew 26:28 and Mark 14:24, while the corresponding Hebrew expression (*dam-habbĕrît*) occurs in the First Testament only in the context of the covenant ratification ceremony at Sinai (Exod. 24:8). After symbolically binding YHWH to Israel by sprinkling the altar with blood from the whole burnt and peace offerings, Moses sprinkled the blood on the people, declaring, "See, the blood of the covenant that YHWH has made with you in accordance with all these words" (24:8). Through this symbolic act the Israelites were bound by covenant to YHWH. By using the expression "my blood of the covenant," Jesus declared that through his own sacrificial blood God binds himself to his new covenant people, and by drinking of it his people bind themselves to him. Thus, as a covenant ritual, participating in the Lord's Supper means not only claiming the privilege of covenant relationship but also committing oneself to fidelity to God's will.[41] In addition to the annual Passover, the Israelites celebrated

40. Luke 22:20 and 1 Cor. 11:25 read, "This cup is the new covenant in my blood."
41. In the original context, after reading the Decalogue and the Book of the Covenant, for the third time the people declared, "All that YHWH has spoken we will do" (Exod. 24:7; cf. 24:3 and 19:8).

their covenant relationship as a community whenever they came to the central sanctuary to eat in God's presence.[42] However, in the Lord's Supper we witness a remarkable transformation. Whereas Israelites would bring their offerings to YHWH, the divine Host, and eat them in his presence, in the Lord's Supper the divine Host offers himself for our spiritual nourishment (John 6:54–58).

Only Matthew links the Lord's Supper with First Testament sin offerings, which he does by adding one small phrase: "This is my blood of the covenant, which is poured out for many *for the forgiveness of sins*" (26:28).[43] Like John the Baptist's declaration, "See the Lamb of God, who takes away the sin of the world" (John 1:29, 36), this addition presents Jesus as a sin offering and links the Lord's Supper with Isaiah 53. By drinking the cup, worshipers celebrate the gracious forgiveness of the Lamb of God, who bears the iniquities of many (Isa. 53:11).

The Significance of the Lord's Supper in the New Testament

Having briefly examined First Testament antecedents for the Lord's Supper, we may now reflect on the significance of these links and on the theological significance of this ordinance in Christian worship.

First, in the ordinance of the Lord's Supper, believers celebrate the founding of the church as the new Israel of God. The New Testament is clear that Christ's sacrifice terminates the Levitical system of rituals associated with tabernacle and temple (Heb. 10:1–18). However, similar to the transformation of circumcision into baptism, with the death of Christ the Passover is transformed into the Eucharist. Whereas Israelites commemorated their deliverance from slavery in Egypt with the annual Passover festival, Christians celebrate their deliverance from the bondage of sin and their constitution as the new Israel of God repeatedly, whenever they eat at the Lord's Table.

Second, if true worship involves reverential human acts of submission and homage before the divine Sovereign in response to his gracious revelation of himself and in accord with his will, then the Lord's Supper affords believers the supreme opportunity for regular Christian worship in his presence. When Jesus sent Peter and John to find a furnished room for the Passover (Luke 22:8), he did so not only as the head of a human household but also as the divine Rabbi and Host of the meal. In so doing, he heightened the significance of the Israelites' experience "in the presence of YHWH,"[44] for YHWH was

42. See Deut. 12:7, 18; 14:23, 26; 15:20; 27:7.
43. This expression occurs in the other Gospels, but only in the context of "repentance for the forgiveness of sins" (cf. Mark 1:4; Luke 3:3; 24:47).
44. See Deut. 12:7, 12, 18; 14:23, 26; 15:20; 16:11, 16; 18:7, 13; 19:17; 26:5, 10, 13; 27:7.

now physically present and serving his guests. In the institution of the Lord's Supper, Jesus also heightened the significance of the meal itself. When he broke the bread, saying, "Take, eat; this is my body" (Matt. 26:26), and "Drink of it, all of you" (26:27), he did not do so as a mere Jewish rabbi; this was God in the flesh, inviting the disciples to eat in his presence and also to eat of him. Whenever Christians gather at the Lord's Table, they feast in his presence, are served by him, and eat of him.

The comments regarding eating "in the presence of the Lord" raise the question of the nature of the divine presence at the table. In what sense is Jesus Christ present in the Lord's Supper? Here we do well to avoid two extreme interpretations. The maximalist extreme is represented by Roman Catholics, whose doctrine of *transubstantiation* maintains that when the priest blesses the bread and wine, the elements are transformed into Christ's body and blood, and that with every Mass, Jesus Christ is sacrificed anew. The minimalist extreme, common in evangelical circles, reduces the Lord's Supper to mere memorial; it simply reminds worshipers of the past work of Christ and of a future meal to be eaten in his presence.

Here the Reformed doctrine of *dynamic* or *spiritual* presence is helpful.[45] According to John Calvin, Christ is present in the Lord's Supper, though neither bodily nor physically. Contrary to the Roman Catholic view, when we partake of the elements, we do not actually eat the body and drink the blood of Christ; but contrary to the strict memorialist view, when we eat and drink with hearts that are pure and lives that are clean, we do indeed experience anew the life-giving grace of Christ, who is personally present through his Spirit. But this grace is not experienced automatically; faith and openness to the work of the Spirit are prerequisites to the spiritually energizing work of Christ.[46]

Third, because the Lord's Supper has its roots in the Passover, in the covenant-ratification ceremony, and in the sin offering, participation in the

45. On the notion of Christ's presence in the sacrament as developed in the Reformed tradition, see Old, *Worship: Reformed according to Scripture*, 126–46. The Lutheran doctrine of *consubstantiation* declares that while the bread and wine are not transformed into the body and blood of Christ, the body and blood of Christ are present "in, with, and under" the bread and wine; the elements remain bread and wine, but Christ is present in body and blood concurrently. The Zwinglian doctrine of *commemoration* declares that the sacrament brings the death of Christ and the efficacy of his work to the mind of the believer, though Christ is present spiritually with the believers when they participate in the Lord's Supper. Through faith believers experience the spiritual presence of Christ.

46. For a Baptist theologian's fuller defense of the view that the Lord's Supper is more than a memorial, see Millard J. Erickson, *Christian Theology*, 2nd ed. (Grand Rapids: Baker, 1998), 5–27.

observance is reserved for believers. In the ordinance believers commemorate the substitutionary death of Jesus Christ on their behalf. They celebrate the forgiveness of their sins through the blood of Christ (Matt. 26:28), the establishment of God's new covenant with *them*, and their hope of one day eating this meal in the presence of God (Matt. 26:29; Mark 14:25; Rev. 19:7–10). As a Christian ritual the Lord's Supper is as discriminatory as the Passover was in Israel. The invitation to Jesus' table is not extended to all; uninvited guests who eat of the bread and drink of the cup render themselves guilty of the body and blood of Christ (1 Cor. 11:27) and expose themselves to divine judgment (11:29).[47] This is a family meal, an occasion for communion, and a place to declare our equality before God and delight in fellowship with God's people.

Fourth, in the ordinance of the Lord's Supper, believers celebrate the covenant of peace that God has made through the blood of the cross of Jesus (Col. 1:20) and anticipate the peace they will celebrate at the marriage supper of the Lamb. John describes this scene in Revelation 19:5–10 in terms that echo the "marriage" covenant with YHWH that Israel celebrated at Sinai (table 6.2).

Table 6.2. A Synopsis of Two Marriage Scenes

Feature	The Sinai Event (Exod. 19–24)	The Eschatological Event (Rev. 19:1–24)
The context	After the defeat of forces hostile to God and his people (19:4)	After the defeat of forces hostile to God and his people (19:2)
The Host	YHWH, the divine King and God of Israel (19:5–6, 18–20)	The Lord (= YHWH) our God, the Almighty, enthroned (19:1, 4–6)

Continued

47. The Anabaptists had it right:
Concerning the breaking of bread, we have become one and agree thus: all those who desire to break the one bread in remembrance of the broken body of Christ and all those who wish to drink of one drink in remembrance of the shed blood of Christ, they must beforehand be united in the one body of Christ, that is the congregation of God, whose head is Christ, and that by baptism. For as Paul indicates, we cannot be partakers at the same time of the table of the Lord and the table of devils. Nor can we at the same time partake and drink of the cup of the Lord and the cup of devils. That is: all those who have fellowship with the dead works of darkness have no part in the light. Thus all those who follow the devil and the world, have no part with those who have been called out of the world unto God. All those who lie in evil have no part in the good.
Article 3 in "Schleitheim Confession" accessible at http://www.anabaptistwiki.org/mediawiki /index.php/SchleitheimConfession. That this was the view of the early church is evident from *Didache* 9.5, "But let no one eat or drink of your Eucharist except those who have been baptized into the name of the Lord, for the Lord has spoken concerning this: Do not give what is holy to dogs." As translated by Holmes, *Apostolic Fathers*, 359.

Feature	The Sinai Event (Exod. 19–24)	The Eschatological Event (Rev. 19:1–24)
The status of the guests	(1) Servants/vassals of YHWH (*'ăbādîm*, Lev. 25:42; cf. the verb *'ābad*, "to serve," in Exod. 3:12) (2) Those who feared him (19:16; 20:18–20) (3) "A holy people" (*gôy qādōš* = *ethnos hagion*, 19:6; cf. "a holy people for YHWH," Deut. 14:2)	(1) Servants/vassals of God (*douloi*, 19:5; cf. *douloi kyriou* for *'abdê yhwh* in Pss. 134:1; 135:1, echoes of which are heard in Rev. 19:5) (2) Those who fear him, great and small (19:5), borrowed from Ps. 115:13, one of the Hallel Psalms sung at the Passover Seder. (3) The saints (*hagioi*, 19:8)
The representatives of the people	Elders (*zĕqēnîm*, Exod. 24:1, 9; Greek, *presbyteroi*)	Elders (*presbyteroi*, 19:4)
The attendant aural phenomena	The sound of thunder and a trumpet (19:16–19)	The sound of waters and mighty peals of thunder (19:6)
The preparation for the event	The people prepare by consecrating themselves and washing their garments (19:10–11, 14–15).	The bride prepares by clothing herself in fine linen, bright and clean (19:7–8).
The significance of the event*	A marriage covenant between YHWH and his people (19:4; cf. Isa. 54:5; Ezek. 16:8; Hosea 2:16, 19)	A marriage of the Lamb and his bride, the church (19:7)
The climactic moment	A meal in the presence of God (Exod. 24:10–11)	The marriage supper of the Lamb (19:9)

*The formula "I will take you to be my people, and I will be your God" (Exod. 6:7) is adapted from the ancient marriage formula, "I take you to be my wife, and I will be your husband" (cf. Lev. 26:12; Deut. 26:17–19). Thus Rev. 21:2–3 applies the covenant formula to the church, the bride adorned for her divine husband.

Just as Israel ate and drank in the presence of God to celebrate the *shalom* that God had provided through the marriage covenant at Sinai, so we look forward to eating and drinking in the presence of God at the marriage supper of the Lamb.

Fifth, although 1 Corinthians 11:27–34 highlights the gravity of participation in the Lord's Supper, calling worshipers to examine themselves, this meal is a "Eucharist," an occasion for thanksgiving. This tone is clearly reflected in *Didache* 9–10, which begins with a call for thanksgiving for the elements.

Now concerning the Eucharist, give thanks as follows:

First, concerning the cup:

We give thanks, our Father, for the holy vine of David your servant,
Which you have made known to us through Jesus, your servant;
to you be the glory forever.

Now concerning the broken bread:

> We give thanks, our Father, for the life and knowledge
> That you have made known to us through Jesus, your servant;
>> to you be glory forever.

After cautioning against participation by unbelievers, the author follows a healthy paradigm, calling for more general praise.

> And after you have had enough, give thanks as follows:

> We give you thanks, Holy Father, for your holy name,
>> which you have caused to dwell in our hearts,
> and for the knowledge and faith and immortality
>> that you have made known to us through Jesus your servant;
>> to you be the glory forever.
> You, almighty Master, created all things for your name's sake,
>> and gave food and drink to humans to enjoy,
> so that they might give you thanks;
>> but to us you have graciously given spiritual food and drink,
> and eternal life through your servant.
> Above all we give thanks to you because you are mighty;
>> to you be the glory forever.
> Remember your church, Lord, to deliver it from all evil
>> and to make it perfect in your love;
> and from the four winds gather the sanctified church
>>> into your kingdom, which you have prepared for it;
>>> for yours is the power and the glory forever.
> May grace come, and may this world pass away.

> Hosanna to the God of David.
> If anyone is holy, let him come; if anyone is not, let him repent.
> Maranatha! Amen.[48]

Finally, the Lord's Supper offers God's people an opportunity to express authentic piety with acts of compassion to other members of the community, especially to the poor. This is a particular concern for Paul in 1 Corinthians 11. In the church at Corinth the Lord's Table had apparently come to symbolize class distinctions within the church; some brought sumptuous fare to the meal and then hoarded it, while others went hungry (vv. 17–22, 33–34). But at the Lord's Table all are equal: social distinctions of life outside the church must be left behind. In his response Paul borrowed one more leaf from Moses' notebook.

---

48. Adapted from Holmes, *Apostolic Fathers*, 358–60.

Figure 6.4. Floor mosaic of the third-century-AD Megiddo prayer hall. The inscription reads, "The God-loving Akeptous has donated the table to God Jesus Christ as a memorial." (Photograph by Zev Radovan. Used with permission.)

In Deuteronomy, Moses had repeatedly called on heads of households to invite the marginalized—specifically widows, the fatherless, aliens, and Levites—to accompany the family to the central sanctuary (Deut. 14:29; 16:11, 14; 26:12–13). Membership in the covenant community is marked by love for God and for one's fellow believers, demonstrated in actions that serve their well-being.

I conclude this discussion with a reference to the remains of the earliest church in Israel yet discovered by archaeologists. The Megiddo "prison" prayer hall,[49] which dates to the first half of the third century AD, was used as a worship center by Christians in the Roman military camp nearby. The most spectacular feature of the site is a beautiful mosaic floor that includes the following inscription: "The God-loving Akeptous has donated the table to God Jesus Christ as a memorial" (fig. 6.4). It has been suggested that the table was located at the center of the room and was used for the Eucharist meal.[50]

Celebrating the Lord's Supper Today

Having explored the institution of the Lord's Supper, its origins and its significance, how might this theology affect the way we celebrate the ordinance?

49. So named because it was accidentally discovered on the grounds of the prison near Megiddo. For discussion, see Vassilios Tzaferis, "Inscribed 'To God Jesus Christ': Early Christian Prayer Hall Found in Megiddo Prison," *Biblical Archaeology Review* 33, no. 2 (March–April 2007): 38–49.

50. The mosaic contains not only the earliest inscriptional reference to Jesus Christ but also the earliest extrabiblical reference to Jesus Christ as God.

Above all, we recognize that no act of corporate worship is more important than communion at the Lord's Table, eating of the bread and drinking of the cup in commemoration of God's grace in Jesus Christ. The New Testament offers few prescriptions for corporate Christian worship; it does not tell us to meet on Sunday mornings, begin our services with song, listen to thirty-minute sermons, or pass around the offering plate. However, it does prescribe believers' regular participation in the Lord's Supper. Because Jesus invites us to eat at his table until he comes, we do well to highlight participation at the table as the most important expression of Christian worship. When people are converted and baptized into the name of Christ and into the church, their greatest delight should be fellowshipping at the Table of the Lord.

In keeping with the function of the Eucharist as both a commemoration of the death of Christ and an anticipation of his return, the Lord's Table should be treated as an occasion for solemn remembrance and exuberant celebration. Because the Lord's Supper is a supremely holy meal, all who participate should examine themselves and confess their sins before God and one another before participating.[51] To be invited to the Table of the Lord is an incredible grace, but the cost is sobering. Only through the sacrifice of Christ are deliverance from the kingdom of darkness, forgiveness of sin, and covenant relationship made possible. But they are possible, and this is cause for great joy! Having encountered Jesus anew in the meal, we depart with a song of praise on our lips.

The Lord's Supper is the defining ritual of the Christian community. In keeping with its function as a family meal, every effort should be made to make this an intimate affair. Although we should preserve a dignity appropriate to an event that bears the title "the Lord's Supper," dignity and intimacy need not be contradictory. Since our formal sanctuaries tend to inhibit the atmosphere of the original gathering in a borrowed room, churches might consider occasionally retiring to the fellowship hall for the ordinance. This could encourage sharing of Scripture, corporate prayer, and singing—all of it focused on Christ and his work.

While we always welcome outsiders to observe us at worship, since participating in Communion is the mark of a Christian community, we have missed the point of the meal if unbelievers do not understand that they are on the outside looking in. Given Paul's warning that persons who eat of the bread and drink of the cup unworthily bring on themselves the wrath of God, worship leaders who encourage them to do so are accomplices in the offense. Therefore we must "fence the Table," but we do so with grace and

51. Jesus' instructions regarding offerings in Matt. 5:23–24 apply here as well.

longing for the day when those who have not yet experienced salvation will participate freely with us.[52]

In keeping with the profoundly theological character of the Lord's Supper, we should capitalize on the ordinance as an occasion for instruction. Not only does it provide an excellent opportunity to highlight the links between First Testament worship and the meal, but regular participation also keeps alive the memory of our sinful past and the marvelous grace of God in Christ Jesus. In the First Testament, YHWH repeatedly introduces himself with "I am YHWH who brought you out of the land of Egypt, out of the house of slavery" (e.g., Exod. 20:2; Deut. 5:6). In the Eucharist, God introduces himself with "I am Jesus, the Christ, who redeemed you from the bondage of sin." This is the essence of the gospel.

Finally, since the Lord's Supper is a family meal, and since baptism is the rite by which believers are initiated into the family, participation in the Lord's Supper should be linked with baptism. For this reason, baptismal candidates should look forward with anticipation and excitement to their first Communion, and the church should provide instruction on these issues. While this conclusion is natural for congregations that practice believers baptism, in pedobaptist circles formal confirmation in the faith may serve as the equivalent.[53]

One important question remains: How often should we schedule Communion? While the New Testament does not answer the question directly, Acts 2:42 suggests that the early church's worship typically involved the apostles' teaching, fellowship, breaking bread, and prayer. "Breaking bread" may refer more generally to shared meals, but it seems best to understand this as a form of the Lord's Supper. The association of the Lord's Supper with the Lord's Table, the Lord's Cup, and the Lord's Day suggests that by the time Sunday was established as the day for Christians to gather for worship, the Eucharist was celebrated weekly. This remains the norm in Roman Catholic, Anglican, and Brethren congregations. Although the Reformers and Puritans were not agreed on how often the Lord's Supper should be observed, by scheduling it on a monthly or quarterly basis, they may have overreacted to abuses in the Catholic Mass. It seems the New Testament ideal of a weekly observance is

52. Congregations that plan Sunday morning services with primarily evangelistic goals in mind should consider scheduling the observance at other times.

53. These comments apply within the congregation. We recognize the right and the responsibility of every congregation to establish the theological parameters by which it will be governed. However, when it comes to fellowshipping with believers holding convictions on these matters that differ from our own, charity must be the watchword. Agreement on all doctrinal matters should not be a precondition to fellowship.

the most honoring to the Lord and the most spiritually rejuvenating for his people.[54]

I conclude with an anecdote from personal experience. While I was engaged in doctoral studies in 1978–80, the Bethany Prenton Brethren Assembly in a suburb of Liverpool blessed my family with the most satisfying church experience we have ever had. Among many delightful features of this congregation, the weekly Breaking of Bread service was new to us. Every Sunday morning, before the public family service, the members gathered for Communion. These were rich experiences, involving an intermingling of profound hymns, intense prayers of thanksgiving, and commentary from wise and mature members on Scriptures relating to the death of Christ and the salvation this achieved for us. This weekly rhythm not only determined my Sunday schedule but also had a profound effect on my entire week. Monday through Wednesday I basked in the afterglow of the previous Sunday, and from Thursday to Saturday I lived in anticipation of the coming Sunday. All of life was framed by reminders of God's grace embodied in the passion of Christ. There is no more precious or spiritually nourishing form of worship than eating with brothers and sisters in Christ at the table hosted by the Savior.

54. Some have argued that since First Testament roots of the Lord's Supper are found in the annual Passover, the Eucharist should be celebrated only once a year, perhaps on Maundy Thursday. But the Lord's Supper is more than a Christian Passover: it also incorporates traditions of covenant ratification and sacrifice for sin.

7

Hearing and Proclaiming the Scriptures in Worship

True worship involves reverential human acts of submission and homage before the divine Sovereign in response to his gracious revelation of himself and in accord with his will.

If true worship involves reverential human acts of submission and homage before the divine Sovereign in response to his gracious revelation of himself, then how does he reveal himself? We do not exclude the possibility that God can and does reveal himself through providential experiences, dreams, visions, or oracular inspiration; yet as a norm, knowledge of God comes through the written record of past revelation. If corporate worship involves an audience with God, and true worship is the engaged response to God's revelation, then ensuring that divine communication occurs is a high priority. In Roman Catholic, Anglican, and Lutheran traditions, revelation is focused on baptism and the Eucharist. In Reformed and free-church Protestantism, the revelation comes primarily through hearing the Word. This perspective used to be reflected in the architecture of churches, which featured two pulpits: a larger one, often raised above the people, from which the Word was read and proclaimed; and a smaller one, from which other aspects of the service were performed.[1] The diminished place of the Scriptures in many evangelical churches today is reflected in (1) replacing pulpits that highlight preachers' roles as spokespersons for God with nondescript or transparent stands, to make them more visible; (2) drastically reducing or eliminating the reading of Scripture in worship; (3) replacing sustained exposition of the Scriptures with short, topical homilies; and (4) substituting hymns steeped in the language and theology of Scripture with jingles that may borrow biblical phrases but are little more than sound bites empty of biblical meaning to many who sing them.

In this chapter we will explore the use of authoritative sacred writings in worship as presented in the Scriptures themselves, and then reflect on the implications that our conclusions have for worship today.

The First Testament's Use of Torah Texts in Worship

The Decalogue: Israel's First Scripture

According to Exodus 19–24 and Deuteronomy 5, the Decalogue was part of the speech that YHWH presented at Sinai when Israel came to the mountain for an audience with him. Although the revelation of the covenant would extend far beyond the Decalogue, this was the only part of Israel's constitutional literature that the people heard directly from God and that God himself transcribed. All subsequent revelation is preserved as divine speech to Moses, the covenant mediator, who transmitted it to the people (e.g., Exod. 20:22; 25:1–2). This makes the Decalogue a very special document.[2]

But the Decalogue is significant in other respects as well. As Israel's summary covenant document (Exod. 34:28),[3] it was cast in a form of ten principles, one for each finger, which meant it could be easily memorized ("treasured in one's heart," Ps. 119:11) and recited. In keeping with ancient Near Eastern

1. For a dramatic description of an event involving the former in Puritan New England, see Herman Melville's *Moby Dick*, Oxford World's Classics (Oxford: Oxford University Press, 2008), 33–35, "The Pulpit," in chap. 8.

2. For a fuller discussion of the nature and function of the Decalogue and the issues summarized below, see Daniel I. Block, "Reading the Decalogue Right to Left: The Ten Principles of Covenant Relationship in the Hebrew Bible," in *How I Love Your Torah, O LORD! Studies in the Book of Deuteronomy* (Eugene, OR: Cascade Books, 2011), 21–55.

3. Elsewhere this document is called "his [YHWH's] covenant" (Deut. 4:13) or "the tablets of the covenant" (Deut. 9:9–15), which were stored in "the ark of the covenant of YHWH/God" (Num. 10:33; 14:44; Deut. 10:8; 31:9, 25; Josh. 3:6, 8, 14; Judg. 20:27; 1 Sam. 4:4; 2 Sam. 15:24; 1 Chron. 16:6). Its covenantal (rather than legislative) nature is also reflected by the expression "the tablets of the Pact" (*luḥōt hā'ēdut*, often misleadingly translated as "the tablets of the testimony"; Exod. 31:18; 32:15; 34:29).

custom, duplicate copies of the Decalogue were produced and stored in the holy of holies (Deut. 10:1–5),[4] one copy to remind God of his commitment to Israel,[5] and the other to remind Israel of their commitment to him.[6] Also in keeping with ancient custom, the Decalogue was cast as a complete and self-contained entity, with its own formal introduction (the preamble), discreet number of terms (ten), narrative framework (Exod. 20:1, 18–21), and its own technical title, "The Ten Words" (Exod. 34:28; Deut. 4:13; 10:4).[7] Obviously the document was not intended to be exhaustive, nor was it cast as legislation to provide specific guidelines for judges in trying legal cases. Rather, it creates a spiritual worldview within which covenant people make ethical decisions, a worldview that Jesus summarized with the Supreme Command.[8]

The Decalogue is crafted as a worship document for the redeemed people of God, calling for a specific response to YHWH's revelation of himself through the exodus. The preamble, "I am YHWH your God who brought you out of the land of Egypt, out of the house of slavery," is fundamental to its interpretation. This document is neither addressed to humankind in general nor to be viewed as a summary of natural or moral law, in contrast to the rest of Israel's legislation. The obedience called for in the commands that follow represents the worshipful response to salvation received as a gift from YHWH (see Exod. 19:4–6). Without the preamble the "ten words" become legalistic and moralistic demands of people who lack both the motivation and the heart to fulfill them.

It is difficult to determine precisely what role the Decalogue played in Israel's worship. Moses used it in the last service over which he presided, reciting it at the beginning of his second address in Deuteronomy (5:6–21) and then spelling out how the worldview established by this document was to be played out

4. See Exod. 31:18; 32:15; 34:1, 4a, 4b, 29; Deut. 4:13; 5:22; 9:10, 11, 15, 17; 10:1, 3; 1 Kings 8:9; 2 Chron. 5:10; also plural references to the tablets without the number: Exod. 24:12; 32:16, 19; Deut. 9:9; 10:2, 4, 5.

5. Like the rainbow in Gen. 9:12–17.

6. The tradition that one tablet contained the vertical commands dealing with Israel's relationship to God and the other dealt with horizontal relationships is ancient, dating as far back as Philo (*On the Decalogue* 7.12, as in the Loeb Classical Library [LCL] [Cambridge, MA: Harvard University Press, 1984], 31) and Josephus (*Jewish Antiquities* 3.5.4, 8, in LCL [Cambridge, MA: Harvard University Press, 1978], 361, 365), then picked up by John Calvin (*Institutes of the Christian Religion*, ed. J. T. McNeill, Library of Christian Classics [London: SCM, 1961], 2.8.11, pp. 376–77) and many modern interpreters. While devotionally and homiletically interesting, the tradition is exegetically and contextually groundless.

7. Hence the Greek *deka-logos*. The Scriptures never refer to this text as "The Ten Commandments" but always classify its contents as "words" (*dĕbārîm*). See especially Exod. 34:27–28: "In accordance with these *words* I have made a covenant with you and with Israel. . . . And he wrote on the tablets the *words* of the covenant, the ten *words*."

8. See above, chaps. 1 and 4.

in life (5:22–26:19; 28:1–68). Although the spiritual commitment and social ethic called for by the Decalogue are clearly reflected in the preaching of the prophets (Hosea 4:2; Jer. 7:9), neither prophets nor psalmists provide any hints of the Decalogue's use in formal worship.[9] Some suggest that the Decalogue was regularly read at Shavuoth (*šābuʿôt*, the Festival of Weeks, Pentecost), which commemorated the moment of its original revelation. The ritual of that "day of the Assembly" (Deut. 9:10; 10:4; 18:16; cf. 4:10–14) supposedly featured the people's dramatic act: taking obligations of the Decalogue upon themselves by covenant and oath. However, clear evidence for this liturgical use is lacking in the First Testament.

Although the New Testament never formally cites the Decalogue as a cultic document, its spiritual and moral vision provides the basis for both Jesus' and Paul's ethical teaching. Jesus alludes to the Decalogue in the Sermon on the Mount (Matt. 5:21–37), and elsewhere he reduces the principles of the covenant to two commands: "You shall love the Lord your God with all your heart, and being, and mind, and resources, and you shall love your neighbor as yourself" (Matt. 22:34–40; Mark 12:29–31; Luke 10:25–27), but this is also a distillation of all the ordinances and instructions given at Sinai and Moses' exposition of the same in Deuteronomy.[10] However, Jesus does not make this statement within a liturgical context. Paul's (Rom. 8:7–13; 13:8–10; Eph. 6:1–4) and James's (2:8–13) citations of the Decalogue reflect long-standing Jewish catechetical tradition and the importance of the document in early Christian preaching, but they say little about it as a liturgical worship document.

Jewish tradition provides some evidence for the liturgical use of the Decalogue. *Tamid* 5.1 in the Mishnah suggests that in the Second Temple period, the morning ritual included the priestly recitation of the Decalogue as well as the Shema, plus Deuteronomy 11:13–21 and Numbers 15:37–41. The Nash

9. Although the references to theft, adultery, and falsehood in Ps. 50:16–19 may ultimately derive from the Decalogue, the differences between the divine self-introduction in 50:7 and the preamble to the Decalogue suggest influence from other constitutional documents. Psalm 81:9–10 [10–11] obviously remembers the revelation at Sinai and may allude to the preamble and the first principle of the Decalogue, though the resemblances to Lev. 11:45 and Deut. 20:1 are stronger than to Exod. 20:2. Indeed, the echo of the Shema in Psalm 81:8 [9] and the vocabulary around this verse sound more like the Deuteronomic Torah than the Decalogue. The text provides no clues on how the Decalogue was used in Israel's cult. For defense of the link to the Decalogue, see Moshe Weinfeld, "The Decalogue: Its Significance, Uniqueness, and Place in Israel's Tradition," in *Religion and Law: Biblical-Judaic and Islamic Perspectives*, ed. E. B. Firmage, B. G. Weiss, and J. W. Welch (Winona Lake, IN: Eisenbrauns, 1990), 12–15.

10. In Jesus' response to the young man's inquiry, he supplements commands in the Decalogue with "Do not defraud" (Greek *mē aposterēsēs*, Mark 10:19), which borrows LXX vocabulary from Exod. 21:10 and Mal. 3:5.

Papyrus[11] and phylacteries discovered in the caves of Qumran suggest that even while away from the temple, Jews would recite the Decalogue as a daily private ritual.[12] However, both the Babylonian and Palestinian Talmuds report that reciting the Decalogue in daily prayers was later forbidden by the rabbis because sectarians claimed it was the only part of the Bible revealed directly by God to Moses.[13] Eventually the rabbis forbade the inclusion of the Decalogue in phylacteries,[14] presumably in reaction to Christians' elevation of it over Israel's other constitutional documents.

Although the origins and the form of the Decalogue are unique, neither the First nor the New Testament elevates its authority above the rest of the constitutional documents. This contrasts sharply with common views among Christians. Whereas Christians generally ignore or reject the rest of the Sinai revelation and the Torah of Moses in Deuteronomy as irrelevant, they interpret the Decalogue as a distinctive statement of moral truth, universally applicable and permanently relevant.[15] This special treatment is unwarranted. The Decalogue's authority and universality are indistinguishable from the authority and universality of the other constitutional documents in the Pentateuch.[16]

The Covenant Document as Early Scripture (Exodus 20:22–23:19)

The expression "Book of the Covenant" refers to Exodus 20:22–23:19 and comes from Exodus 24:7, which describes Moses as reading the *sēper habbĕrît* before the people at Mount Sinai. Even though YHWH had declared the Decalogue directly to the people and provided them with a written copy, Moses

11. Ernst Würthwein, *The Text of the Old Testament*, trans. E. F. Rhodes, 2nd ed. (Grand Rapids: Eerdmans, 1995), 144.

12. In the Dead Sea Scrolls, fragments of the Decalogue occur on 4QPhyl[a] and 4QPhyl[b]. For a discussion of the phylacteries from Qumran and their liturgical significance, see Géza Vermès, "Pre-Mishnaic Jewish Worship and the Phylacteries from the Dead Sea," *Vetus Testamentum* 9 (1959): 65–72.

13. Palestinian Talmud, *Berakot 3c; and Berakot 12a*. See Vermès, "Pre-Mishnaic Jewish Worship," 69; L. H. Schiffmann, "Phylacteries and Mezuzot," in *Encyclopedia of the Dead Sea Scrolls*, ed. L. H. Schiffmann and J. C. VanderKam (Oxford: Oxford University Press, 2000), 2:676. The phylactery readings are based on the Deuteronomic version of the Decalogue. Although the Nash Papyrus follows Exod. 20:8–11 in grounding the Sabbath in creation, it exhibits heavy influence from Deuteronomy.

14. Cf. Mishnah, *Menahot 3.7; Kelim 18.8; Sanhedrin 11.3*. The decision is reflected in the early second-century-AD phylacteries found in the Wadi Muraba'at.

15. Martin Luther mistakenly elevated it to the status of natural law. See further Werner H. Schmidt, *Die Zehn Gebote im Rahmen alttestamentlicher Ethik*, Erträge der Forschung 281 (Darmstadt: Wissenschaftliche Buchgesellschaft, 1993), 20–21.

16. So also F. Crüsemann, *The Torah: Theology and Social History of Old Testament Law*, trans. A. W. Mahnke (Minneapolis: Fortress, 1996), 352–53.

recounted all the words and regulations that YHWH spoke to him on the mountain, and then he wrote them down in the Covenant Document, which he read aloud before the people.

Although the Covenant Document was used liturgically in this original covenant-ratification ceremony, we do not know if or how it was used in later worship. However, like the Decalogue, this too is obviously a worship text, as its chiastic arrangement highlights.

A   Introduction (20:22): Placing Israel's response to covenant in the present context of divine revelation
   B   Principles of worship (20:23–26): Highlighting Israel's cultic expression of devotion to YHWH
      C   Casuistic laws (21:1–22:20): Highlighting Israel's ethical expression of devotion to YHWH
      C′   Apodictic laws (22:21–23:9): Highlighting Israel's ethical expression of devotion to YHWH
   B′   Principles of worship (23:10–19): Highlighting Israel's cultic expression of devotion to YHWH
A′   Conclusion (23:20–33): Placing Israel's response to covenant in the future context of divine action

By framing prescriptions for daily life with prescriptions for cultic worship, YHWH reinforces the notion that worship is to inspire devotion to YHWH and create an ethical community of faith.

The Instructions on Holiness (Leviticus 17–26)

In Exodus 25 through Leviticus 16, instructions and regulations alternate with narrative accounts of the people's response.[17] The prescriptive material may be interpreted as a handbook for worship, dealing with onetime instructions on building a residence for YHWH (Exod. 25–31) and the consecration of Aaron and his line for the high priesthood (Lev. 8:1–35), as well as regulations for ongoing, regular worship: sacrifices presented by the priests on behalf of the people (Lev. 1–7), clean and unclean foods (Lev. 11), regulations regarding purification (Lev. 12–15), and the Day of Atonement (Lev. 16). These texts were especially important for priests, who prepared the people for worship and carried out the rituals at the central sanctuary.

---

17. The golden calf incident and its sequel, Exod. 32–34; the construction of the tabernacle and its furniture, Exod. 35–40 (response to Exod. 25–31); the consecration of Aaron, Lev. 8:36–9:24 (response to 8:1–35); crises regarding the sanctity of the cult (10:1–20).

Although these liturgical regulations do not explicitly build on the Decalogue, the Guidebook on Holiness (Lev. 17–26) expands and extends its worldview.[18] This section is cast as a series of divine speeches, each introduced with the divine speech formula "And YHWH spoke to Moses, saying."[19] It is punctuated by divine exhortations to keep all the statutes and judgments as preconditions for well-being,[20] declarations of the timeless nature of these statutes,[21] and YHWH's self-identification, "I am YHWH [your God]," reminding the people whose voice is behind Moses' voice.[22] These instructions conclude with blessings and curses that describe Israel's future, depending on whether they are faithful to YHWH's revealed will (Lev. 26). Although these instructions exhibit a strong oral rhetorical flavor and are obviously addressed to worshipers, they offer no clues on how the people are to use them in worship. Since most Israelites were illiterate, the instructions were probably intended for regular reading in cultic contexts.

The Torah of Deuteronomy as Scripture

The internal testimony of Deuteronomy. The bulk of Deuteronomy consists of Moses' farewell pastoral sermons delivered before the Israelites crossed the Jordan to the promised land. Moses is explicit, not only in asserting this Torah's divine authority and canonical status,[23] but also in prescribing its use in worship. Moses' speeches in Deuteronomy complete the revelatory process that gave the Israelites their core Scriptures. In the covenant-renewal ceremony that underlies the book, the Israelites commit themselves to the entire package: text and interpretation. It appears that all of Moses' formal utterances—the first (1:6–4:40), second (5:1–26:19; 28:1–68), and third (29:1–30:20) addresses,

18. On this document, see above, chap. 4.
19. As in Lev. 17:1; 18:1; 19:1; 20:1; 21:16; 22:1, 17, 26; 23:1, 9, 23, 26, 33; 24:1, 13; cf. also 25:1.
20. See Lev. 18:4–5, 26; 19:19, 37; 20:8, 22, 25:18; 26:3.
21. See Lev. 17:7; 23:14, 21, 31, 41; 24:3; cf. also Lev. 24:8, 9; Num. 15:15; 18:23; 19:10, 21.
22. As in Lev. 18:2, 4, 5, 6, 21, 30; 19:3, 4, 10, 12, 14, 16, 18, 25, 28, 30, 31, 32, 34, 36, 37; 20:7, 8, 24; 21:12, 15, 23; 22:2, 3, 8, 9, 16, 30, 31, 32, 33; 23:22, 43; 24:22; 25:17, 55; 26:1, 2, 13, 44, 45.
23. (1) Moses charged the people not to add to or delete any words from his instructions (Deut. 4:2). (2) The narrator declares the total coherence between Moses' instructions and YHWH's command to him (1:3; 34:9). (3) Notices of their timeless relevance punctuate the instructions (5:29; 6:24; 11:1; 12:1, 28; 14:23; 18:5; 19:9; 23:3, 6). (4) Moses declared that the people's well-being and their very life depend upon fidelity to this Torah (6:24–25; 32:44–47); indeed, he set before them the choice of blessing or curse (11:26–28; 30:15–20). (5) By prefacing his exposition of the Sinai revelation with the Decalogue (Deut. 5), Moses asserted the fundamental unity of his present utterances with the original covenant document. Indeed, the narrator concludes Moses' lengthy second address with a striking statement: "These are the words of the covenant that YHWH commanded Moses to make with the people of Israel in the land of Moab, in addition to [the words of] the covenant that he had made with them at Horeb" (29:1 [28:69]).

the Song (32:1–43), and the concluding blessing (33:1–29)—were transcribed immediately, and that when Joshua and his people crossed the river, the Levitical priests carried this collection of texts (cf. Deut. 33:10).[24] Eventually these were grouped together to form what we now know as the Pentateuch.

Although Jewish tradition later extended the scope of the word "Torah" to the entire Pentateuch, when used in Deuteronomy, the word applies only to material in this book. Moses knew that he spoke with divine authority and that the written copy of his Torah was to be treated as Sacred Scripture. Future kings were to copy it for themselves in the presence of the Levitical priests and read it constantly as a guide for personal conduct (Deut. 17:14–20).[25] In 31:9–13 Moses explicitly charges the Levites to read his Torah before all Israel—men, women, children, aliens—every seventh year at the Festival of Booths. Hearing the Torah should inspire reverent awe toward YHWH, which would yield obedience to his will and result in long life in the land (vv. 12–13).

The Torah in First Testament narratives. The book of Joshua refers to the Torah in five contexts.[26] Although the issue is not the public reading of the Torah but Israel's leader reading it for himself (cf. Deut. 17:14–20), in Joshua 1:7–8 YHWH promises Joshua that if he will keep the Torah in his mouth (i.e., memorize and recite it), meditate on it day and night, and live by it, then he will succeed in all his ventures. Joshua 8:30–35 recounts a public event on Mount Ebal: in compliance with Moses' prescriptions in Deuteronomy 27:1–8, he read every word of the Torah of Moses and copied it on stones. Later, after completing his military assignment and dividing the land among the tribes, Joshua exhorted the people to observe the Torah that Moses had commanded—to love YHWH their God with all their hearts, to walk in all his ways, to keep his commands, to hold fast to him, and to serve him with all their hearts and souls (Josh. 22:1–5). And following the pattern of Moses, prior to his own departure Joshua assembled Israel for his own final address, to challenge them once more to order their lives according to everything written in the Torah of Moses (chap. 23, esp. v. 6). The book concludes with a final

24. This collection would also have included the rest of the ordinances and regulations revealed by YHWH to Moses at Sinai (Exod. 20–31; Leviticus; large sections of Numbers), as well as a journal of the Israelites' travels (Num. 33:1–49) and perhaps the narratives of Genesis and the exodus out of Egypt (Exod. 1–18).

25. Note also Deut. 27:1–8, which calls for the ritual transcription of the Torah on stone pillars at Mount Ebal. On the significance of Deut. 27, see Daniel I. Block, "What Do These Stones Mean? The Riddle of Deuteronomy 27," *Journal of the Evangelical Theological Society* 56 (2013): 17–41; Block, *Deuteronomy*, NIV Application Commentary (Grand Rapids: Zondervan, 2010), 623–29.

26. In each instance the "Torah" in question involves Moses' addresses on the plains of Moab preserved in the book of Deuteronomy.

assembly of tribal leaders at Shechem for a covenant-renewal ceremony (Josh. 24). After appealing for scrupulous obedience to YHWH, Joshua recorded the event in writing, apparently including his speech, in the book of the Torah of God (v. 26).

After Joshua's death the Torah seems to have been forgotten. Within one generation the people lost the memory of YHWH's will and saving action (Judg. 2:6–3:6, esp. 2:10–12). First Samuel 3:1–3 observes that while Eli was priest, "the word of YHWH" was rare and visions were infrequent; the "lamp of God" was in danger of going out. The "word of YHWH" may refer to direct prophetic revelation (cf. vv. 19–21) or to the Torah, which was neglected in the worship of Israel. The books of Samuel never mention the Torah of Moses or of YHWH.

However, since psalms associated with David are laced with Deuteronomic language, it was not completely forgotten. David's song to YHWH in 2 Samuel 22 exhibits strong influence from Deuteronomy 32, and the language of verses 21–27 is quite Deuteronomic. When David claims that YHWH's judgments are before him and that he has not strayed from his ordinances, he confesses that he has been reading the Torah as Deuteronomy 17:14–20 instructs kings to do. He also alludes to Moses' speeches in Deuteronomy when he exhorts Solomon to keep the charge of YHWH as written in the Torah of Moses, so that he would succeed in all his ventures and YHWH would fulfill his promise of keeping one of his sons on the throne (1 Kings 2:2–4; 1 Chron. 22:12).

Chronicles links the word *tôrâ* with David only two additional times. The fact that David organized temple worship according to all that was written in the "Torah of YHWH" (1 Chron. 16:40) shows he treated it as authoritative Scripture. However, since the context involves the priesthood, here "Torah of YHWH" refers to the priestly regulations in Leviticus rather than to Deuteronomy (cf. 2 Chron. 23:18). By the time the books of Chronicles were written, the expression had apparently come to represent the Pentateuch more broadly. However, when Solomon acknowledged that David walked in the Torah of YHWH, and that his own success depended on adherence to the Torah (2 Chron. 6:16), the Chronicler used the expression in the more limited sense of Deuteronomy.

In 931 BC Jeroboam instituted a new religion for the northern kingdom (Israel), separate from the centralized worship of YHWH in Jerusalem. However, biblical authors assumed that the northern tribes remained accountable to the Torah. Second Kings 10:28–31 reports that although Jehu eradicated the worship of Baal from Israel, he continued to worship the golden calves at Bethel and Dan and did not walk in the Torah of YHWH with all his heart. Linking the fall of Israel to the Assyrians to their disposition toward the

Torah, the narrator of 2 Kings writes that the people refused YHWH's appeals through the prophets to return to the covenant and the Torah (2 Kings 17:13–17). Instead they committed the most egregious crimes against YHWH, rejecting the clear revelation of his will and the written documentation of that revelation in the Torah (17:34–41).

Second Chronicles 15:3 refers explicitly to the neglect of the Torah in worship. Here the prophet Azariah recalls a time when Israel was without the true God, without a teaching priest, and without Torah. Fulfilling the warnings in Deuteronomy, distress of all kinds pervaded the land, but when the people sought YHWH, he mercifully heard their prayers and restored their fortunes. Inspired by Azariah, King Asa instituted wide-ranging anti-idolatry reforms in accordance with Deuteronomy, which resulted in peace during his reign. Asa's son Jehoshaphat continued the reforms, sending his officials and twelve Levites and priests throughout Judah to teach the Torah of YHWH (2 Chron. 17:7–9).

According to 2 Chronicles 30, Hezekiah invited the people to Jerusalem for the Festival of Unleavened Bread and the Passover, which they celebrated according to the Torah of Moses (v. 16). This celebration precipitated a spiritual renewal, inspiring the people to go throughout the land—including Ephraim and Manasseh—and purge the countryside of idolatrous installations, in accordance with what they had heard in the Torah (31:1). Not satisfied with a singular festival, Hezekiah instituted wholesale reforms, reorganizing the priestly orders and rituals as prescribed in the Torah of YHWH (31:2–21). However, these reforms did not last long. With great vigor his son Manasseh pursued an idolatrous course, in flagrant violation of the Torah of Moses (2 Kings 21:8–9; 2 Chron. 33:8–9).

Decades later, in the 620s BC, while King Josiah's men were cleaning out the temple, they discovered the Torah scroll—presumably the book of Deuteronomy (2 Kings 22–23; 1 Chron. 34–35). Not knowing what to do with it, Hilkiah the high priest handed it to Shaphan the scribe, who took it to the king and read it in his hearing. Accepting the scroll's authority, Josiah called on Huldah the prophetess to explain the significance of the scroll. She commended the king for his genuine piety but announced the imminent demise of the nation, fulfilling the curses of the book (2 Kings 22:14–20; cf. Deut. 28:15–68). This event is of utmost significance, not only because Josiah illustrates the disposition all should have toward the Word of God, but also because it highlights the consequences of neglecting the voice of God, which is heard whenever the Torah is read.

The Torah in the Prophets. References to the Torah are common in the Prophets, usually in accusations for having forgotten it or living in violation of the covenant it represents. According to Hosea, in the eighth century BC the people of Israel (northern kingdom) were destroyed because they lacked knowledge of God, a lack attributed to the priests' forgetting the Torah (4:6). Later Hosea announced that because Israel had transgressed YHWH's covenant and rebelled against his Torah, he would pour out his fury on them and send them back to Egypt (8:1–14). In a similar vein, Amos declared that YHWH would send fire on Judah because the people had rejected his Torah and refused to obey his laws (2:4–5). Isaiah observed the same problem. He foresaw the end of Judah because "they rejected the Torah of YHWH of Hosts and despised the word of the Holy One of Israel" (5:24). The former probably refers to the Torah of Moses, while the latter may refer to utterances by prophets. In 8:16 the prophet calls on his disciples to bind up the testimony and seal the Torah, presumably to preserve it for a future day when people seek the divine will everywhere but in the written revelation of Moses.[27] Speaking of the exile as if it has already occurred, Isaiah 42:18–24 (esp. vv. 21, 24) shows YHWH's giving Israel as spoil to the nations, because the people refused to walk in his ways. A century later, Habakkuk complained that the land was full of violence, the Torah ignored, and justice miscarried at every turn; the priests had obviously failed their charge (1:1–4). Within a lengthy catalog of misdeeds in Jerusalem, Zephaniah accused the priests of profaning the sanctuary and doing violence to the Torah (3:1–7, esp. v. 4).

Jeremiah seemed especially concerned about the neglect of the Torah by the priests, and by implication, in the worship of the people. In 2:8 he suggests that the priests were not just unconcerned about the presence of YHWH; these professional handlers of the Torah did not even know God themselves. In 6:19 Jeremiah predicts disaster for his people because they have not listened to YHWH's words and have rejected his Torah. He suggests that it is possible to perform cultic duties scrupulously but still reject the Torah of YHWH. In his Temple Gate Sermon (Jer. 8:4–12), the prophet judges the people to be stupider than birds. Birds know the laws of nature and migrate on cue, but God's people do not know his ordinances. They claim to be wise because they possess the Torah (cf. Deut. 4:5–8), but the scribes have twisted it into a lie, and the sages have rejected YHWH's words. Jeremiah declares that possession of the Word of God is no substitute for living by it (see 7:1–11, 21–34). Later he adds that if people will not live by the Torah, then YHWH will judge them by the Torah.[28] Lamentations 2:9 mourns a threefold spiritual tragedy associated

27. The expression *tĕ'ûdâ*, usually rendered "testimony," is a variant of *'ēdut* in Deut. 4:45; 6:17; and 6:20, referring to the stipulations of the covenant as declared by Moses. According to Deut. 31:26 the Torah was to function as an *'ēd*, "witness," testifying against the people when they sinned.

28. See Jer. 9:12–16; 16:10–13; 26:1–6; 32:16–25; 44:1–14, esp. v. 10; 44:20–30, esp. v. 23.

with the destruction of the temple: instruction in the Torah has vanished, prophetic visions have ceased, and the elders sit in the dust, paralyzed by grief. However, Jeremiah insisted this would not be the last word; he anticipated the day when formal instruction in the Torah would be unnecessary, for God's people would have it written in their hearts (31:31–34).

The Torah in the postexilic community. When the Jews began to return from exile in Babylon in 538 BC, YHWH's eternal promises were fulfilled only in limited measure. Instead of a massive wave of returnees from all twelve tribes, only 42,360 (largely representing the tribes of Levi and Judah) came back (Ezra 2:64). Instead of occupying the entire promised land, they lived in Jerusalem and a small area around the city. Instead of being ruled by a sovereign Davidic king, his descendant Zerubbabel was a mere governor (Hag. 1:1). Instead of worshiping in a glorious temple like the original, the people worshiped in an unimpressive structure, to which the divine glory never returned (Hag. 2:1–9; cf. Mal. 3:1). Looking back on the causes of the exile, Zechariah declared that the people had hardened their hearts like flint so they could not hear the Torah or the words of YHWH sent by his Spirit through the prophets. Zechariah did not describe the context in which the people had heard the Torah, but this should have happened at the annual festivals (cf. Deut. 31:9–13) or in the daily temple services.

Although the completion of the second temple inspired a measure of spiritual renewal (Ezra 6:16–22), by the mid-fourth century BC many old problems had returned. The exile seemed to have weaned the people away from idolatry, but Torah godliness was still absent. Malachi placed the blame squarely on the shoulders of the priests (2:7–9), who had corrupted the covenant and their office. Instead of modeling the fear of YHWH by walking in his ways and embodying righteousness, the Levites had turned from the way. Instead of giving true instruction, they showed partiality in teaching the Torah, telling the people what they wanted to hear and causing many to stumble. Because of the professional ministers' failure, the people lacked the fear of God. Malachi's solution to the problem is striking: "Remember the Torah of my servant Moses, the statutes and ordinances that I commanded him at Horeb for all Israel" (Mal. 4:4). As Moses had emphasized repeatedly, the key to life is obedience; the key to obedience is reverent awe before YHWH; and the key to reverent awe is hearing the Torah (cf. Deut. 31:11–13).

Whereas Malachi exposed the problems with the priesthood, Ezra represented the solution. This priest determined to study the Torah of YHWH, apply its teaching to himself, and teach it precisely and comprehensively in Israel (Ezra 7:10). Nehemiah 8 illustrates his public performance by recounting one communal event where this happened. Responding to the people's hunger for the Torah,[29] from dawn to midday before men, women, and children Ezra read while his colleagues translated it and helped the people understand what was being read. The interpretation was necessary because the people returned from exile speaking Aramaic rather than Hebrew, the language of the Torah. Although the people initially responded to the Torah by weeping, encouraged by Nehemiah, they began to celebrate because they understood the words they had heard (Neh. 8:9–13). Because the people were so eager to hear the Torah, Ezra read from it every day for seven days during the Festival of Booths (Neh. 8:13–18).

The chain of events that began on the first day of the seventh month (Tishri 1; Neh. 8:2) climaxed on the twenty-fourth day with a penitential liturgy (Neh. 9:1–10:39) involving intense lamentation (fasting, sackcloth, dirt on their heads; 9:1), separation from all non-Israelites (9:2a), verbal confession of sin (9:2b), hearing the Torah for three hours (9:3a), prostration before YHWH (9:3b), crying out to YHWH by leaders (9:4), an extended blessing of YHWH by eight Levites (9:5–37), renewing the covenant, and recommitting to worshiping YHWH properly (9:38 [10:1]). The image of this worship event creates hope that YHWH may finally have established for himself a community of people covenantally committed to him and gladly living according to his will as spelled out in the Torah. But again the people of God disappoint. Not only does the book of Nehemiah end with more problems in this community, but also, when the curtain rises four hundred years later, the people we encounter are indeed committed to Torah, but they seem to have lost its heart; commitment to the Torah has trumped commitment to YHWH.[30]

The Torah in the Life and Worship of Each First Testament Believer

This survey of the use of the Torah has not exhausted First Testament references about reading the Scriptures. The Psalms are filled with such references, beginning with Psalm 1 and concentrated in the Torah psalms, 19:7–14 [8–15] and 119, both of which represent "meditations" (hegyôn) as called for by Psalm 1:2. The singular pronouns in the Torah psalms (1; 19; 119) assume individual

29. The length of time it took to read the Torah and its association with the Festival of Booths (Neh. 8:13–18) suggest the ritual involved primarily the book of Deuteronomy.

30. This is reflected in the rabbis, who asserted that if one were to choose between the two, abandoning God is preferable to abandoning the Torah. For discussion and references, see Jeffrey H. Tigay, "Parashat Terumah," in *Learn Torah With . . .*, ed. S. Kelman and J. L. Grishaver (Los Angeles: Alef Design Group, 1996), 141–47. See also Jacob Neusner, *The Treasury of Judaism: A New Collection and Translation of Essential Texts*, vol. 2, *The Life Cycle* (New York: Lanham, 2008), 77–78.

readers of the Torah rather than communal liturgical events.[31] Obviously this does not exclude their use in corporate worship, for what is true for the individual is also true for the group, and private meditation on the Torah prepares one for hearing it in worship.

On the surface Psalm 1 seems to address everyone. Strictly interpreted, however, the psalm associates the blessed person with counselors and seats of authority, suggesting that the real addressee is the king or a prince who aspires to the throne, and that the purpose of this psalm is to orient a royal reader on reading the Torah.[32] While verbal and conceptual links between this psalm and Joshua 1:7–8 reinforce this interpretation, the inspiration for Psalm 1 comes ultimately from Deuteronomy 17:14–20, where Moses emphasizes that the king is to concern himself with the Torah, copying it in the presence of the Levitical priests, taking it with him, and reading it every day of his life. By this interpretation Psalm 1 instructs royal readers on how to read the Torah for themselves to nourish their souls, offer guidance for life, and secure success in their reigns. However, since the king was to embody covenant righteousness for God's people, his example also offers lay readers insight into how they should meditate on the Torah.[33]

Most psalms reflect the perspective of private poets. However, the Psalter is a collection of prayers, laments, and hymns to be used in corporate worship. Whereas the communal Psalm 95 notes that those who worship in spirit and truth do not resist the word of God when he speaks (vv. 7c–11), Psalm 1 speaks of delighting in and meditating on the Torah of YHWH day and night, which means constantly living in the presence of God. In the Torah, God's people hear his voice, instructing, inspiring, challenging, and directing them. As in Deuteronomy, here *tôrâ* does means not "law" but "instruction," which may involve law, but it also includes story, song, instruction, and genealogy. Whether *tôrâ* here refers to the speeches of Moses in Deuteronomy (which seems most likely) or to the five books of the Pentateuch, the Torah is grounded in gospel. If *tôrâ* involves only or even primarily law, reading it brings no delight; but if

31. So also Pss. 37:31; 40:8 [9]; 89:30 [31]; 94:12. A similar individualistic emphasis is evident in references to the Torah in Proverbs (28:4, 7, 9; 29:18) and the allusion to the Torah in the charge to the reader to "fear God and keep his commands" in the postscript to Ecclesiastes (12:13–14).

32. Which accords with the royal nature of Ps. 2. On the entire Psalter as a royal/Davidic document, see Bruce K. Waltke, "Canonical Process Approach to the Psalms," in *Tradition and Testament: Essays in Honor of Charles Lee Feinberg*, ed. J. S. Feinberg and P. D. Feinberg (Chicago: Moody, 1981), 3–19; Waltke, *An Old Testament Theology: An Exegetical, Canonical, and Thematic Approach* (Grand Rapids: Zondervan, 2007), 873–74.

33. Since laypeople would not have owned copies of the Torah, and few would have been able to read, the basis of their meditation would be the Torah they had memorized and heard the Levitical priests read in worship.

it includes stories of God's grace, then God's people will find delight in it and want to meditate on it day and night. And God's grace is evident throughout: the promise of a seed through whom the head of the serpent will be crushed; the rescue of Noah and his family from the deluge; the call of Abraham; the preservation of Israel in Egypt while Canaan languished under a famine; the rescue of the nation from bondage in Egypt; the establishment of the covenant with Israel at Sinai; the revelation of God's will; the gift of the land of Canaan to the Israelites—to mention only a few.

The disposition of the psalmists toward the Torah is remarkable. Whereas not a single person in the First Testament declares their love for God,[34] in Psalm 119 the psalmist repeatedly declares his love for the Torah and the commands of YHWH with unembarrassed enthusiasm.[35] The Torah psalms remind Israelite worshipers that hearing the Torah should be their highest delight, but they also suggest to Christians that if they will not treasure the Torah, they have no right to claim the Psalms as Christian Scripture. The psalmists would not have approved of the weight Christians typically give to the Psalms at the expense of the Torah.

The Liturgical Use of Other Scriptures in the First Testament

Texts like the prayer of the prophet in Jonah 2 suggest that true believers in Israel were steeped, not only in the Torah, but also in many of the psalms, particularly those composed by David and the men he commissioned as musicians in temple worship—Asaph, Heman, and Ethan. Nevertheless, it is difficult to establish how these psalms were used in the cult. Royal psalms (2; 45; 72; 89; 110; 132) may have been used in liturgies celebrating the founding of the dynasty or in festivities inaugurating a new king in Jerusalem. Divine royal psalms (47; 93; 95–99) celebrate the kingship of YHWH.[36] Individual laments (3–7; 22; 51) probably arose out of personal experiences and were adapted for cultic use. Communal laments (44; 80), individual and communal hymns that call the assembly to praise YHWH (33; 66; 100; 105; 146–150), and songs of thanksgiving that praise God for specific acts of deliverance (67; 75; 107; 136) were probably written for corporate worship. The "songs of Zion" celebrate

34. The verb *'āhab*, "to love," never appears in first person with a speaker as subject and God as object. Psalms 18:1 [2] and 116:1 involve different constructions.

35. Psalm 119:97, 113, 119, 127, 159, 163, 165.

36. Based on Mesopotamian analogues, critical scholars often associate these with New Year celebrations. However, evidence for a New Year festival in the First Testament is lacking. See further, Daniel I. Block, "New Year," in *International Standard Bible Encyclopedia*, rev. ed. (Grand Rapids: Eerdmans, 1986), 3:529–32.

YHWH's choice of Zion as the place for his name to be established (46; 48; 76; 84; 87; 122). The forms of some psalms hint at their liturgical use. Some suggest an antiphonal dialogue (15; 24; 50; 81; 95; 115; 121; 132); others are associated with processions (48), covenant-renewal rituals (50), or festivals (81).

Intertextual connections within the Prophets suggest they were aware of each others' works.[37] However, the First Testament provides no evidence for the use of prophetic writings in cultic liturgy. For this we must look to the intertestamental period, specifically the rise of synagogue worship.

The Use of the Scriptures in Synagogue Worship

While the origins of the synagogue remain a mystery, Jewish worship in the synagogues away from the temple was driven by two primary concerns: to praise God and to educate the people. The latter was achieved by reading the Scriptures and hearing a sermon, but the Torah reading was the focus of these gatherings.[38] Indeed, the Torah scroll was treated like monarchs, icons, or idols in other cultures. Jeffrey Tigay writes,

> Like all of these, the Torah is carried in procession when it is taken out of the Ark to be read and when it is returned there after the reading. Like a king, an Ashkenazi Torah is dressed up in a mantle, belt, and crown, and even has a hand (the Torah pointer). The Torah is housed in an Ark which, in traditional Jewish sources, is called the *heikhal*, the "palace," and we pray facing this Ark. Ashkenazi . . . Torahs . . . indicate what the Biblical Ark indicates: access to God is not gained by means of idols but through the Torah and its commandments. In other words: the Torah and its commandments are more than a book and a series of rules and customs, they are a way of establishing a relationship with God and coming to know Him.[39]

Since Yahwism forbade images of the Deity, the ark of the covenant contained not an idol but the two tablets of the covenant. The declarations of love for the Torah in Psalm 119—where we might have expected declarations of love for YHWH—may have inspired the Jewish idea that first the Decalogue and

---

37. Jeremiah quotes Micah as a true prophet of YHWH (Jer. 26:18); Daniel (9:1–2) reads the prophecies of Jeremiah; Isaiah and Micah cite the same poem (Isa. 2:1–4 = Mic. 4:1–3); Ezek. 34 expands on Jer. 23:1–8. Also, 2 Kings 17:13–14 notes that the word of YHWH came repeatedly to the people of Israel through the prophets, but they refused to hear.

38. For a helpful study of the use of the Scriptures in early Jewish worship, see Michael Graves, "The Public Reading of Scripture in Early Judaism," *Journal of the Evangelical Theological Society* 50 (2007): 467–87.

39. Jeffrey H. Tigay, "Parashat Terumah," http://www.sas.upenn.edu/~jtigay/ark.htm.

later the entire Torah took the place of idols as symbols of God's presence. This conviction led to the custom of reading the Torah through in one year in Babylonia; according to Palestinian custom, this was done every three years (Babylonian Talmud, *Megillah* 29b). Worshipers celebrated the completion of the reading of the Torah with great joy. At least from the second century BC, after the reading of the assigned portion of the Torah, the scroll would be returned to the ark and a portion of the Prophets (*haftarah*) would be read. Since the Prophets were not revered as highly as the Torah, it was permissible to skip verses when reading.[40] The homily based on the reading would be delivered by a previously chosen person. In addition to these readings in regular worship, on festival days certain books would be read: the Song of Songs at Passover; Ruth at Pentecost/Shavuoth; Lamentations at the commemoration of the temple's destruction; Ecclesiastes at the Festival of Booths/Sukkoth; Esther at Purim. The Qumran evidence suggests that toward the close of the Second Temple period, the Psalms were also used widely in worship.[41]

Synagogue sermons consisted of homilies on specific subjects or expositions of portions of Scripture. The exposition of Scripture consisted of halakah, the study of the requirements of the law, and haggadah, illustrations of the teachings through stories, ethical sayings, and parables, with the goal of making the Scriptures relevant and interesting. Jesus' reading and exposition in Luke 4:21–27 and Paul's custom of commencing his work in new areas in the synagogues (Acts 13:15–41) suggest that ordination at local synagogues was not necessary.[42]

The Use of the Scriptures in New Testament Worship

The New Testament shows that the Jewish Scriptures continued to be treasured by the early church. However, we also witness the production of additional texts that were deemed authoritative—that is, the narrative Gospels and Acts, and the epistolary writings of the apostles.[43]

---

40. Larry Hurtado adds, "In Diaspora synagogues it is likely that the Scriptures were read in Greek . . . to meet the desire of Greek-speaking Jews to read and study their scriptures," which "would also have enabled Gentile visitors to Diaspora synagogues to follow things and to learn about Jewish religion." *At the Origins of Christian Worship: The Context and Character of Earliest Christian Devotion* (Grand Rapids: Eerdmans, 1999), 33–34.

41. In the morning and evening service, the Shema was recited antiphonally, beginning with Deut. 6:4–9, then adding Deut. 11:13–21 and Num. 15:37–41. On working days there were to be three readers, and on Sabbath or feast days at least five readers (Babylonian Talmud, *Berakot* 6a; Mishnah, *Megillah* 4.1–2, 3, 6).

42. For another early window into synagogue worship, see Philo, *Apology for the Jews* 7.12–14.

43. For an introductory discussion, see especially Ralph P. Martin, *Worship in the Early Church* (Grand Rapids: Eerdmans, 1975), 66–77; and Hughes Oliphant Old, *The Reading and*

The Scriptures in Worship in the Gospels

Since the Gospels describe a pre-Christian world, they provide little information on how the early church used the Scriptures in worship. Jesus used the Scriptures in a liturgical context only once, in the synagogue of Nazareth, his hometown (Luke 4:14–29). Having recently been baptized and publicly affirmed as the beloved Son of God (3:21–22), he returned to Galilee, where, like a young rabbi, he went from synagogue to synagogue, instructing the people. We do not know if the synagogue rabbis in Nazareth assigned him Isaiah 61:1–2 to read or if he chose it himself, but at the appropriate time he received the Isaiah scroll and stood to read. He opened the scroll, read the passage, handed the scroll back to the attendant, and sat down. With all eyes on him, he offered his interpretation of the text: "Today this Scripture is fulfilled in your hearing." The crowd was amazed that Joseph's son could speak so eloquently—until he claimed for himself the role of anointed liberator. This infuriated the rabbis, who were not interested in his instruction. Aware of the danger he was in, Jesus escaped the threats of his own townsfolk and headed northwest to Capernaum (4:31–37), where the authority with which he taught and healed continued to astound the people.

During his stays in Jerusalem, Jesus regularly went to the temple, where he taught, proclaimed the gospel, and engaged the people in conversation on issues related to the Scriptures—to the great consternation of the Jewish authorities.[44] But Jesus' teaching occurred primarily in noncultic contexts. He was a traveling rabbi, gathering followers as he shared the good news of the kingdom of God. The nature of his teaching is reflected in the Sermon on the Mount (Matt. 5–7) and the Olivet Discourse (Matt. 24; Mark 13). His words were laced with First Testament Scriptures as he declared his mission to fulfill the Torah and the prophets (Matt. 5:17–19). However, his authority came not only from his knowledge of the Hebrew Scriptures; his voice was also the voice of God himself. Jesus continued to teach after his death and resurrection. Apparently he delivered his most comprehensive exposition of the Scriptures to two unnamed disciples traveling from Emmaus to Jerusalem (Luke 24:27). These men interpreted Jesus' conversation as the "opening of the Scriptures" to an audience (v. 32). In so doing, Jesus provided a paradigm for later Christian preaching.

Preaching of the Scriptures in the Worship of the Early Church, vol. 1, *The Biblical Period* (Grand Rapids: Eerdmans, 1998), 111–250.

44. See Matt. 21:23; 26:55; Mark 12:35; 14:49; Luke 19:47; 20:1; 21:37; John 7:14, 28; 8:2, 20.

The Scriptures in Worship in Acts

In the book of Acts the apostles use the Scriptures in two different ways: *preaching*, proclaiming the messiahship of Jesus, usually to unbelievers; and *teaching*, instructing believers in the faith. In their preaching, the message (*kērygma*) tended to involve several characteristic motifs:[45] (1) this is the age of fulfillment; in Christ the First Testament prophecies and the hope of Israel have been and are being realized;[46] (2) this fulfillment is demonstrated in the life, death, and resurrection of Jesus the Messiah;[47] (3) through his resurrection Jesus is exalted as Lord;[48] (4) God's favor toward the church as the new covenant community is demonstrated in the pouring out of the Spirit;[49] and (5) if people repent, they receive forgiveness and the gift of the Holy Spirit.[50] Early evangelistic preaching apparently did not involve analytical arguments but instead made impassioned appeals to the Scriptures, demonstrating that Christ is the fulfillment of all Israel's hopes and that in the face of his death, resurrection, and exaltation, all must repent and submit to him. Although such preaching represents the preacher's worship, technically these sermons were appeals to the unconverted to join true worshipers by acknowledging Jesus as Lord and Savior.

The book of Acts is less clear on the use of the Scriptures when believers gathered. Acts 2:42 notes that believers in Jerusalem were devoted to fellowship, breaking bread, prayer, and the apostles' teaching. The last element probably involved systematic reading and interpretation of the Scriptures by the apostles, particularly how they should be understood in the light of Christ (cf. 5:28; 13:12). The Bereans of Acts 17:10–15 eagerly received the word of Paul and Silas, yet they studied the Scriptures carefully to see if their message accorded with the written revelation. Acts 18:24–26 characterizes Apollos as an eloquent Jew with a strong grasp of the Scriptures who was energized by the Spirit and taught accurately concerning Jesus. However, the apostles did not only teach the Scriptures; they also studied them for guidance on critical questions in the life of the church, as in the case of the debate about gentile converts and circumcision (15:1–21). Converts from Jewish Pharisaism appealed to Moses to demand that all be circumcised, but James quoted the prophets to argue that gentiles were to be included in the new covenant community.

45. Cf. Martin, *Worship in the Early Church*, 73–74.
46. Acts 2:16; 3:18, 24; 10:43; 13:17–41; 18:27–28.
47. Acts 2:24, 30, 32, 33; 3:15; 5:30; 10:37–39; 17:2–3, 31–32.
48. Acts 2:33–36; 3:13; 4:10–11; 5:30.
49. Acts 2:17–21; 5:32; cf. 8:14–24; 10:44–48; 19:1–7.
50. Acts 2:38; 3:19; 10:43; 15:8.

The Scriptures in Worship in the Epistles

Paul defines the basic apostolic stance regarding the Scriptures in 2 Timothy 3:15–17.

> From infancy you have known the sacred Scriptures, which are able to make you wise for salvation through faith in Christ Jesus. All Scripture [that is, the entire First Testament] is God-breathed and is effective for teaching, rebuking, correcting, and training in righteousness, so those who belong to God may be thoroughly equipped for every good work.

Timothy had learned this through the instruction he received from Paul (vv. 10, 14) and earlier through his mother Eunice and grandmother Lois (1:5; 3:15). But this represents private instruction at home; for information on how the Scriptures were used when Christians gathered, we must turn elsewhere.

Reading Scripture. Since the public recitation and reading of Scripture was part of temple and synagogue worship (see Luke 4:16; Acts 13:27; 15:21; 2 Cor. 3:15), it naturally became an important part of Christian worship. Paul explicitly exhorted Timothy to give attention to the public reading of Scripture, to exhortation, and to teaching (1 Tim. 4:13). By "Scripture" he meant the sacred writings of the First Testament, and as a student of the Pharisee Gamaliel (Acts 22:3), he presumably emphasized the Torah. However, a growing corpus of New Testament writings was soon being used in public worship as well. In Colossians 4:16 Paul assumed that his addressees would read his letter at their gatherings, and he charged them to have it read in the church of the Laodiceans as well. Meanwhile, he encouraged the Colossians to read a letter he wrote to the Laodiceans, which the Laodiceans were forwarding to the Colossians. Elsewhere Paul instructs the Thessalonians to have his letter "read to all the brothers [and sisters]" (1 Thess. 5:27).

Although allusions to the public reading of the Scriptures appear in several texts,[51] in New Testament times few would have had their own copies; as in ancient Israel, most people's only access was through oral reading by a lector. Reading the First Testament was apparently a high priority wherever churches were planted. The book of Galatians, written to gentile believers in Asia Minor, is steeped with allusions to First Testament texts that could only

---

51. The note "Let the reader understand," inserted in Matt. 24:15 and Mark 13:14, instructs the person charged with reading the Gospel (as Scripture) to the congregation to read with understanding. Revelation 1:3 promises a blessing to "the one who reads and those who hear the words of this prophecy," that is, who reads the book of Revelation to the seven churches addressed in the following chapters.

make sense to an audience familiar with them. In describing worship near the middle of the second century, Justin Martyr wrote,

> The memoirs of the Apostles and the writings of the prophets are read as long as time permits. Then, when the reader has ceased, the president gives verbal instruction and invitation to the imitation of these good things. Then we all rise together and pray. (*1 Apology* 67.3)

Justin's disposition toward the prophets (i.e., the First Testament) was rooted in the apostolic teaching of the first century.

Singing Scripture. In addition to hearing the Scriptures read, Paul encouraged Christians to sing or recite the Psalms to each other (1 Cor. 14:26; Eph. 5:18–19; Col. 3:16). These were probably the Psalms of the First Testament put to new melodies by Christians, Christian odes inspired by the Psalter, and other songs/poems embedded in First Testament narratives and the Prophets. James's call for the cheerful to sing praises in 5:13 may also refer to odes from the Psalter.

Instructing with the Scriptures. Although the New Testament distinguishes between preaching and teaching (Matt. 4:23; 11:1; Eph. 4:11; 1 Tim. 2:7; 2 Tim. 1:11; 4:2–4), the difference seemed to depend on the nature of the audience rather than the passion or energy with which the message was delivered. In the assembly of God's people, giving and receiving instruction was obviously a worship activity (cf. Mary in Luke 10:38–42). Paul defines the aim of such instruction as "equipping the saints for the work of service to the building up of the body of Christ" (Eph. 4:12). Those who offered such instruction were called "shepherds and teachers." Stressing the weight of a teacher's role, James 3:1 recognizes that teachers are accountable to God for every word they speak. However, Paul suggests in Romans 12:7 that responsibility for teaching is not restricted to professionals; it is a gift distributed by the Holy Spirit to certain members of the congregation (cf. 1 Cor. 14:26).

Even so, the New Testament distinction between preaching and teaching is not absolute. Jesus went about Galilee "teaching and preaching" (Matt. 4:23), expressions that Mark appears to use interchangeably.[52] Similarly, the apostolic witness to Christ in Acts is described as both "preaching" and "teaching" (Acts 5:42; 28:31; cf. Col. 1:28). New Testament teaching, which seems to have been an extension of preaching, may be defined as a rhetorically charged method of communicating the truth of God revealed in Christ and the Scriptures so that believers might come to a more perfect understanding and respond to God's

---

52. Cf. the references to teaching in Mark 1:21, 22, 27 with references to preaching in 1:14–15, 38–39.

revelation with acts of righteousness and compassion. By this definition the sermon could be both "preaching [*kērygma*] and teaching [*didachē*]."

Implications for Using the Scriptures in Worship Today

If our understanding of true worship is correct, then the integrity of worship depends upon the clarity of the divine revelation and the level of our understanding of God's will. Since the Scriptures represent the normative means by which God reveals himself, and since they are the only sure foundation of belief and practice acceptable to him, the reading and instruction of the Scriptures must be given the highest place in worship. But how should we do this in our modern context?

First, evangelicals must rediscover that the Scriptures were written to be heard; they were not written primarily to be preached.[53] Whether we are reading the book of Judges, the prophecies of Ezekiel, the Gospel of Mark, or the Epistle of James, the texts come to us as preaching. Despite creedal statements to the contrary, the relative absence of the Scriptures marks contemporary evangelical worship and reflects a very low view of Scripture. At best, the Scriptures are read piecemeal and impatiently, that we might get to the sermon—for our voice and our interpretation have become more important than the sacred Word of God. At worst, determined to be contemporary and relevant, we do not open the Scriptures at all, dismissing the practice as a fossil without vitality and usefulness. In so doing we displace the voice of God with the foolish babbling of mortals, foreclose the possibility of true worship, and intensify the famine for the Word of God in the land (Amos 8:11–14).

If true worship involves an audience with God, then the health of the church depends upon hearing the voice of God in the Scriptures (cf. Deut. 31:9–13). To ensure that God's voice is heard, we might consider the following suggestions:

1. *Devote more time to reading the Scriptures*—not just a verse or two from the Psalms as a quick call to worship, or a short text from Paul as a preface to the sermon.

2. *Read large blocks of Scripture at a time*. While chapter and verse divisions help us navigate the Scriptures, they are a supreme hindrance to reading holistically and comprehensively. Chapter and verse divisions encourage treatment of the Scriptures as fragments loosely strung together. For practical reasons we may want to break up larger books into

53. For a fuller discussion on the importance of the oral reading of Scripture in worship, see Daniel I. Block, "'That They May Hear': Biblical Foundations for the Oral Reading of Scripture in Worship," *Journal of Spiritual Formation and Soul Care* 5 (2012): 5–34.

smaller parts, but this should not blind us to the fact that Deuteronomy 5:1b–26:19 and 28:1–68, for example, were preached as a single, coherent whole. Paul wrote his Epistles so believers might hear the entire letter in one reading; the same is true of the Gospels and the book of Revelation. The Psalms and Lamentations, and perhaps some prophetic books, may be read piecemeal, because they are collections of independently delivered and composed utterances, but even then we should be sensitive to the coherence exhibited by the canonical forms of these books.[54]

3. *Promote an atmosphere of reverence when reading the Scriptures.* In the First Testament the Israelites stood in awe when God spoke (Exod. 19:17). It is appropriate to prostrate ourselves in homage before God when we enter his presence, but when he speaks, he calls us to rise (Ezek. 1:28–2:1). The people's response to Ezra's reading the Torah in Nehemiah 8:5 may be paradigmatic for our worship.

4. *Promote the expository reading of Scripture.* Expository reading means reading the Scriptures so that their literary qualities are appreciated, their message understood, and their transformative power experienced.[55]

5. *Prepare spiritually for the ministry of reading.* Reading Scripture in public worship is a sacred task, for the reader serves as the mouthpiece of God. Ezra exhibited the qualities of a model reader: "He had determined to study the Torah of YHWH, to apply it, and to teach his statutes and rules in Israel" (Ezra 7:10).

6. *Subordinate the sermon to the Scripture.* Let the voice of God be clear, and let the voice of the human mouthpiece be suppressed.

Second, evangelicals must rediscover the joy of reading and hearing Scripture together with other believers.[56] Hearing Scripture in worship is a communal

54. On the Monday of Holy Week, April 12, 2009, in the Wheaton College Chapel, we participated in a moving service involving an opening song, "To God Be the Glory"; oral reading of John 12:1–19; a congregational hymn, "Hosanna, Loud Hosanna"; a prayer by a student chaplain; the hymn "Our Great Savior"; an expository reading without comment of John 12:20–36a; 13:1–38; and 18:1–19:30 (from the New Living Translation); a hymn, "Lift High the Cross"; and then the benediction. The center of gravity of the service was the reading of Scripture, which took twenty-two minutes, but by the time it was finished, eighteen hundred college students sat in awed silence. Any commentary would have profaned this sacred moment.

55. For guidance in expository reading, see Thomas McComiskey, *Reading Scripture in Public: A Guide for Preachers and Lay Leaders* (Grand Rapids: Baker, 1991), 19, and Block, "'That They May Hear,'" 21–22. This could also involve developing creative ways of communicating Scripture, such as antiphonal and dramatic readings. For an illustration, see the dramatic reading of the book of Ruth, in Block, "'That They May Hear,'" appendix A, 24–34.

56. Oliver O'Donovan writes,

All serious reading of the canonical text has in view the catholic horizon. It is not because the church of the past bequeathed us a *different* text from that which it inherited, but because it shares a text with us, that we can read in hopeful anticipation that the insights

enterprise, involving full participation of those gathered, communion with the saints who have preceded us, and fellowship with those in far-off corners of the globe—wherever God's people gather for worship.

Third, evangelicals must rediscover that in singing and praying the Scriptures, they express themselves in forms pleasing to God and identify with God's people from ages past and from around the world. The prayer that the Lord taught his disciples (Matt. 6:9–13) and the Aaronic benediction of Numbers 6:24–26 are divinely ordained and paradigmatic. As reflected in Jonah's prayer (Jon. 2), the Scriptures should be so deeply ingrained in us that when we face the severest crises or most thrilling joys, we find strength and inspiration through fellowship with God's people everywhere who read, pray, and sing these same Scriptures.

Fourth, evangelicals should rediscover the fellowship and joy of spontaneous and planned sharing of Scripture. The New Testament does not restrict instruction in the Scriptures to church leaders. First Corinthians 14:26 calls believers to edify and encourage one another with a psalm or teaching or a revelation (new insights into a Scripture passage).

Fifth, evangelicals must rediscover the importance and nature of expository preaching. When the Scriptures are read, worshipers hear the voice of God. Where gaps exist between the world of the biblical author and modern readers, sound exposition is essential. Sound exposition requires preachers and teachers who are disciplined in study, scrupulous in application, and forthright in proclamation of the message of the Scriptures—not merely citing favorite passages that bolster a predetermined theology, but exploring the whole counsel of God. Through expository preaching God's people are nourished, transformed, equipped, and energized for divine service.

Sixth, evangelicals need to rediscover the transforming power of Scripture. When people hear the Word of God, they will learn to fear him. When they fear him, they will live in obedience to his will. And when they live in obedience to his will, they will be blessed (cf. Deut. 31:11–13).

---

of one generation and another will complement each other. Good interpretation catches the echo of the text as it bounces off different surfaces. So the readings of the past are a proper test of our readings, challenging us to demonstrate our care, good faith, and self-abnegating attention. And that, too, the Reformers knew very well.

"The Reading Church: Scriptural Authority in Practice," *Fulcrum: Renewing the Evangelical Centre*, April 29, 2009, http://www.fulcrum-anglican.org.uk/page.cfm?ID=422; emphasis original.

8

Prayer as Worship

True worship involves reverential human acts of submission and homage before the divine Sovereign in response to his gracious revelation of himself and in accord with his will.

Significant relationships always involve two-way communication. This is true in relations between two or more human beings, between human beings and their pets, and between human beings and God. But relationships with God are not like relationships with spouses or colleagues, whom we recognize as equals. God is our Sovereign, and we are his subjects. While God does not need us, we are in desperate need of him. The impulse of people everywhere to communicate with their gods, especially in times of distress, is reflected in many ancient Near Eastern texts.

In the prayer cited in chapter 2 ("Prayer to Every God"), the petitioner seeks relief from personal suffering, which he has experienced apparently because he has violated some divine law. He claims that his offenses have been committed unknowingly and complains that he does not even know which god he has offended. Indeed, he reasons that because the entire human race is ignorant of the will of the gods, he should not be singled out as an object of divine wrath.[1] In contrast, the Israelites were an extremely privileged

---

1. For another example, see the plea of the Hittite king Mursilis II (1321–1295 BC) for divine rescue from a plague that had struck his people. James B. Pritchard, ed., *Ancient Near*

people. Their God had introduced himself by name, he had clearly revealed his will to his people, and he heard his people when they prayed. Moses gave excited expression to YHWH's delight in two-way communication in Deuteronomy 4:6–8.

> Observe [these laws and regulations] faithfully, for that will be proof of your wisdom and discernment to other peoples, who on hearing of all these laws will say, "Surely, that great nation is a wise and discerning people." For what great nation is there that has a god so close at hand as is YHWH our God whenever we call upon him? Or what great nation has laws and rules as perfect as this whole Torah that I am setting before you this day?

Although the gods of other peoples are the work of human hands, made of wood and stone, and cannot see, hear, eat, or smell,[2] Israel's God has spoken to them—revealing to them a Torah that was the envy of the nations—and although he has no literal ears, he hears his people when they pray.[3] As *a reverential act of submission and homage before the divine Sovereign*, prayer is the supreme expression of verbal worship.

Biblical Expressions for Prayer

The English verb "to pray" means to ask a person for something as a favor or an act of grace. However, in common usage the word is used more narrowly for addressing God rather than a human superior; it is also used more broadly of confession, intercession, adoration, praise, and thanksgiving. Prayer is essentially a verbal act of faith; the one praying expects God to hear and to respond favorably.

The varied vocabulary for prayer in the Hebrew Bible reflects its importance in daily life and corporate worship. In the First Testament we find four specific words for prayer: *'ātar*, "to plead, supplicate";[4] *hitpallēl*, "to intercede for";[5]

Eastern Texts Relating to the Old Testament, 3rd ed. (Princeton: Princeton University Press, 1969), 391–92.

2. See Deut. 4:28; Pss. 115:3–8; 135:13–18; Isa. 44:12–20.

3. This privilege is reflected in the personal name Jaazaniah (*ya'ăzanyāhû*, "May YHWH hear'"), which was especially common at the end of Judah's history: 2 Kings 25:23; Jer. 35:3; 40:8; 42:1; Ezek. 8:11; 11:1.

4. See Gen. 25:21; Exod. 8:8, 28 [4, 24] (Hiphil), 30 [26] (Qal).

5. Usually intercession for someone else (e.g., Gen. 20:7; Num. 21:7; 1 Sam. 7:5; Job 42:8), though with some exceptions (1 Sam. 1:10; 2 Sam. 7:27; 1 Kings 8:30, 35, 42, 44, 48; 2 Chron. 7:14; Dan. 9:4). It always occurs in the reflexive Hitpael stem. Its relationship to the Piel, *pillēl*, "to pronounce judgment," is not clear, though the Hitpael is used in 1 Sam. 2:25 in the sense of "to be the arbiter, intercessor" (cf. Ezek. 16:52).

hithannēn, "to implore the mercy/grace of";[6] and *hitwaddâ*, from the root *yādâ*, "to praise"—though as an expression for prayer the word means "to confess one's own unworthiness," or "to confess sin."[7] In addition to these specific words for prayer, we find a variety of expressions that reflect the nature of the verbal utterance: "to call out to,"[8] "to cry out for help/deliverance,"[9] "to scream for help,"[10] "a ringing cry" (*rinnâ*) of jubilation[11] or lament,[12] or "to ask, request."[13] God's favorable response to all of these is expressed with *'ānâ*, "he answered" (Isa. 65:24), or *šāmaʿ*, "he heard." The First Testament also uses several metaphorical expressions for prayer. Sometimes people are described as "seeking the face of YHWH."[14] Where an oracle is desired (1 Sam. 9:9), people could "inquire" of God through a prophet or approach him directly (Gen. 25:22). God responds by letting himself be found (*māṣāʾ*, Deut. 4:29; 2 Chron. 15:2, 4, 15; Jer. 29:13) or answering (*'ānâ*) the search (Ps. 34:4 [5]).[15] Sometimes prayer involves "humbling oneself" (*niknaʿ*) before YHWH. Although this usage originates in the royal court, it usually speaks of inner humiliation before God.[16]

6. Psalm 142:2. At the human level this is what Joseph had sought from his brothers (Gen. 42:21). In Deut. 3:23 Moses implores YHWH to let him enter the promised land (cf. 1 Kings 8:33, 47, 59; 9:3).

7. See Lev. 5:5; 16:21; 26:40; Num. 5:7; Dan. 9:4, 20 (in parallel with *hitpallēl*); Ezra 10:1; Neh. 1:6; 9:2–3; 2 Chron. 30:22.

8. Hebrew *qārāʾ*: Pss. 30:8 [9]; 89:26 [27]; 130:1; 141:1.

9. Hebrew *ṣāʿaq/zāʿaq*: Exod. 17:4; Ps. 107:6, 28; Judg. 6:6, 7.

10. Hebrew *šāwaʿ*, Piel; Ps. 72:12; Lam. 3:8; Hab. 1:2.

11. See e.g., Pss. 17:1; 30:5 [6]; Isa. 14:7.

12. See 1 Kings 8:28 (*rinnâ ûtĕpillâ*); Pss. 17:1; 88:2 [3]; 119:169; 142:6 [7].

13. Hebrew *šāʾal*. When God is the object, the expression usually refers to a specific kind of prayer, requesting information, as in an oracular consultation. The sense of "prayer" is clearest in Zech. 10:1: "Ask YHWH for rain in the springtime." The word is also used of consulting intermediaries (1 Chron. 10:13; Ezek. 21:21 [26]), usually with a specific request (e.g., 1 Sam. 8:10; 12:13, 17, 19).

14. Expressed either with *dāraš* or *biqqēš*, both of which mean "to seek, inquire, investigate." While these two words often appear together (e.g., Judg. 6:29; 1 Chron. 16:11; Ps. 24:6) and are readily interchanged, with *dāraš* the seeking tends to reflect a positive relationship between "seeker" and "sought" (2 Chron. 7:14), while *biqqēš* suggests actions of one estranged from God (Hosea 3:4–5).

15. In Deut. 12:5, seeking YHWH involves a pilgrimage to the place he has chosen to establish his name.

16. As represented by Hezekiah (2 Chron. 32:26), Manasseh (33:12, 19), and Josiah (2 Kings 22:19; 2 Chron. 34:27). Refusal to humble oneself before the divine King has dire consequences, as Amon (2 Chron. 33:23) and Zedekiah (36:12) learned. This disposition is also expressed with the verb *'ānâ*, in the passive and reflexive stems, "to afflict oneself, be humbled." Ezra 9:5 uses the cognate noun, *taʿănît*, to describe Ezra's shocked/grieved reaction to the people's marrying foreign wives, demonstrated by tearing his clothes, pulling the hair from his head and beard, sitting in an appalled state, and fasting. On fasting as an expression of self-humiliation, see Ps.

Prayer is often associated with physical gestures, particularly prostrating oneself (*hištaḥăwâ*) before God (Neh. 9:3) or "kneeling before YHWH" (1 Kings 8:54; 2 Chron. 6:13; Ezra 9:5). While hands were raised in swearing oaths (HCSB mg.: Exod. 6:8; Ezek. 20:5, 15) or pronouncing blessings (Lev. 9:22; Ps. 134:2), this was usually a gesture of entreaty by worshipers, who would spread out their palms to YHWH,[17] to the temple,[18] or to the sky/heavens (1 Kings 8:22, 54; 2 Chron. 6:12–13).[19] Contrary to pervasive practice today, the First Testament rarely associates "raising the hands" with praise.[20] Less frequently, people would stand before YHWH.[21]

Second Samuel 7:18 (cf. 1 Chron. 17:16) presents an exceptional case of the supplicant sitting before YHWH. David's posture in response to the promise of an eternal dynasty recalls a series of sculptures of Gudea, king of Lagash (2150–2100 BC; fig. 8.1). Like Gudea, David was involved in temple building;

35:13; Isa. 58:5. This disposition before YHWH was required of all on the Day of Atonement (Lev. 16:31; 23:27).

17. Hebrew *pāraś yād/kap 'el yhwh*: Exod. 9:29, 33; Ezra 9:5; Job 11:13; Ps. 44:20 [21].

18. As in 1 Kings 8:38; 2 Chron. 6:29.

19. The related expression "to raise the hand" (*nāśā' yād*) is also used in the sense of "to appeal": Pss. 28:2; 119:48 (cf. v. 45); 141:2 (//*tĕpillâ*); Lam. 2:19. While 2 Kings 19:8–19 does not explicitly mention hands, Hezekiah illustrated the gesture by taking the written copy of an oral ultimatum from Sennacherib to the temple and spreading it out before YHWH. In Akkadian the idiom "to open the hands" means in effect "to pray." In a specific instance a worshiper laments, "My hands are full of suffering, curse, sin, etc." See further Wolfram von Soden, "*yād*," in *Theological Dictionary of the Old Testament*, ed. G. J. Botterweck and H. Ringgren, trans. J. T. Willis, G. W. Bromiley, and D. E. Green (Grand Rapids: Eerdmans, 1974–2006), 5:397.

20. In Ps. 63:4–5 [5–6] the psalmist declares his response to a desperate situation in which he had implored God for help. When he raised his hands in prayer/entreaty to God, God answered by filling them. The praise expressed in vv. 1–5 is his response to that help. Verses 4–5 are cast in chiastic parallelism, with the outer lines matching each other and the inner lines doing the same.

A So I will bless [*brk*] you as long as I live;   Vow of praise
B   in your name I lift up my hands;   Gesture of entreaty
B' my soul will be satisfied as with fat and rich food,   Declaration of trust
A' and my mouth will praise [*rinnâ*] you with joyful lips.   Vow of praise

"Lifting the hands" is not a synonym for "blessing" YHWH, but the gesture that led to his "soul's" being satisfied.

The context and structure of Ps. 134:1–3 suggest a similar situation: raising the hands toward the holy place is equivalent to pleading for a blessing. The pattern of clauses shifts from A B B' A' to A B A' B'. If we remove the subordinate clauses, "who stand by night in the house of YHWH" in v. 1b, and "who made heaven and earth" in v. 3b, we are left with four principal statements.

A Look! Praise [*brk*] YHWH, all servants of YHWH   Call to praise
B Raise your hands toward the holy place;   Call to prayer
A' And praise [*brk*] YHWH.   Call to praise
B' May YHWH bless you from Zion.   Expression of prayer

21. Thus Hannah stationed herself in the presence of the priest (*niṣṣebet 'immĕkem*) and prayed to YHWH (1 Sam. 1:26); Solomon stood (*'āmad*) before the altar and spread out his palms to heaven (1 Kings 8:22).

Figure 8.1. Gudea, temple builder of Lagash (Photograph by Kim Walton. Used with permission.)

like Gudea, David received a detailed plan of the temple, though David received it "in writing from the hand of YHWH" (1 Chron. 28:11–19). The posture may reflect his special status as the chosen founder of an eternal dynasty, from whom the Messiah would come.

The New Testament also has a variety of expressions for prayer. The verb *proseuchomai*, "to pray" (eighty times), and the noun *proseuchē*, "prayer" (thirty-six times), are found in the most familiar prayer passages.[22] The pattern of the LXX to render Hebrew *šā'al* as *aiteō*, "to ask, request," and the related noun *aitēma*, "request, prayer," continues in the New Testament.[23] Matthew 21:22 uses both expressions, "Whatever you ask for [*aiteō*] in prayer [*proseuchē*] with faith, you will receive." However, Hebrew *šā'al*, "to ask," was also represented by *erōtaō* or *eperōtaō*, and the corresponding noun, "prayer," with *eperōtēma*.[24] A final expression, *deomai*, "to beseech, to plead," and its cognate noun *deēsis*, "entreaty, plea," speaks of urgent prayer. This seems to have been a favorite word for Luke,[25] though it was used by others as well.[26]

The First Testament Practice of Prayer

Although the biblical vocabulary of prayer may teach us a lot, this spiritual discipline is best explored by looking at concrete examples of prayer. Because most readers are familiar with the Psalms, we will focus on prayers embedded

22. Matt. 6:5–6, 9; Luke 18:1; Acts 2:42; Eph. 6:18; James 5:17. In the LXX this word usually translates Hebrew *hitpallēl/těpillâ*. Underlying this word is the simpler form *euchomai/euchē*, "to pray/prayer," absent from the Gospels but occurring in James 5:15–16 as well as Rom. 9:3 and 3 John 2.

23. See, e.g., Matt. 7:7–11 (= Luke 11:9–13); John 14:13–14; Phil. 4:6; James 1:5–6; 1 John 3:22; 5:14–16.

24. The noun appears only in 1 Pet. 3:21, while the verb occurs in Mark 7:26; Luke 4:38; John 4:47; 16:26.

25. Luke 1:13; 2:37; 5:12; 9:38, 40; 10:2; 21:36; 22:32; Acts 8:22, 24; 10:2.

26. As in Rom. 1:10; Phil. 1:19; 1 Thess. 3:10; 2 Tim. 1:3; 1 Pet. 3:12.

in First Testament narratives.[27] These divide into three categories: (1) prayers that are purely personal and concern the interests of the one praying; (2) prayers that concern the well-being of the group but are presented individually, if not in private; and (3) prayers presented publicly, as the one who is praying speaks for the assembly. Although our primary concern in this book is corporate worship, individual expressions of homage through prayer provide a foil for examining public prayers at the end of this chapter.

Personal Prose Prayer

Although the narratives of Genesis 1–11 do not report any prayers, the observation that Enoch and Noah "walked with God" (5:21–24; 6:9) invites us to consider prayer not simply as an occasional conversation with God but also as a matter of continuous communion. The lives of these men were, in effect, "prayers" without speech and may illustrate what Paul meant when he encouraged us to "pray without ceasing" (1 Thess. 5:17; cf. Rom. 1:9). The narrator explicitly links Noah's communion with God with his righteous and blameless life (cf. Mic. 6:8; James 5:16).

First Testament narratives contain many prayers involving personal requests. Several features of these prayers deserve notice. First, prayers may be offered by anyone, anywhere, anytime: God's ears are not only open to priests or at official cultic events. Second, the form of private prayers is simple, reflecting responses specific to the present situation. Third, these prayers play a vital role in the narrative: the narrator's ultimate concern often involves YHWH's personal integrity, the fate of the covenant promise to the ancestors, and the weaknesses of the human characters on whose shoulders the plan of salvation rests. Fourth, the specificity and spontaneity of these prayers distinguish them from public prayers offered as part of corporate worship. The latter tend to be highly stylized, cast in conventional forms and offering few clues about the original context, which renders them universally reusable and repeatable.

Biblical narrators have recorded several exemplary personal prayers by major characters in the story.[28] For closer examination, however, I have selected a striking prayer of Abraham's trusted but unnamed servant (Gen. 24:12–14). He was sent to Mesopotamia by his master to find a wife for Isaac. In the

---

27. For a helpful study of many of these prayers, see Moshe Greenberg, *Biblical Prose Prayer: As a Window to the Popular Religion of Ancient Israel* (Berkeley: University of California Press, 1983).

28. Jacob, as he returns from Haran, before meeting Esau (Gen. 32:9–12 [10–13]); Samson (Judg. 16:28); Hannah (1 Sam. 1:11; 2:1–10). See also Moses' prayer, requesting permission to enter Canaan, embedded in the narrative recital of his first address (Deut. 3:23–28).

vicinity of Nahor, he paused beside a well to commit the mission to God. We may view his prayer as intercessory, since it concerns the well-being of his master's house and ultimately God's program of salvation for the world. However, because he requests assistance for himself (v. 12), this is a personal prayer. The prayer itself is a literary masterpiece, exhibiting several standard features of prose prayers.

(1) The invocative address: *"O YHWH, God of my master Abraham"* (v. 12a). Addressing YHWH by name, this man has direct access to God and obviously shares the faith of his master. Yet as a dutiful servant, he identifies YHWH as the God of his master Abraham, on whose mission he has been sent.

(2) The petition: *"Please grant me good fortune today, and demonstrate* hesed *to my master Abraham"* (v. 12b). Prayers often follow up the invocation with a description of the situation or an expression of unworthiness, but this man immediately declares his concern: he asks that YHWH grant him success and, in so doing, show covenant faithfulness to his master. His use of the word *hesed* (cf. 19:19; 20:13; 21:23) reflects his awareness of the stakes in this adventure. Fundamentally, *hesed* signifies fidelity to an established relationship, but applied to God, it embodies all his positive attributes: mercy, grace, compassion, love, kindness, loyalty, and faithfulness. This prayer is not only about personal success or the well-being of his master's family; it is also a test of YHWH's faithfulness.

(3) A description of the situation: *"Look. I am standing by the spring of water, and the daughters of the men of the city are coming out to draw water"* (v. 13). The opening "Look [*hinnēh*]" draws YHWH's attention to key elements in the scene: Abraham's envoy, the spring, and the candidates for a bride for Isaac.

(4) The specific request: *"Let the young woman to whom I shall say, 'Please let down your jar that I may drink,' and who shall say, 'Drink, and I will water your camels'—let her be the one whom you have appointed for your servant Isaac"* (v. 14a–b). Boldly, the servant presents his plan to YHWH. Although the conditions he sets seem arbitrary, he may intend his proposal as a test of the potential bride's character. Assuming that she will be friendly toward a total stranger, he calls for extraordinary effort by the girl.

(5) The motivation: *"This is how I will know that you have shown* hesed *to my master"* (v. 14c). The servant delivers a virtual ultimatum to YHWH, which is possible because his concern is not personal but the fortune of his master and ultimately the reputation of God.

The events that follow catch the man by surprise. Before he has finished his request, a beautiful girl of marriageable age appears and plays her role precisely as scripted (vv. 15–20). The man stares in awe, speechless, wondering whether YHWH is really fulfilling his mission. Obviously he does not know who this young woman is or whether she meets the criteria set by his master (v. 4). However, when she identifies herself and invites him to her home, he knows his prayer has been answered. Spontaneously, he prostrates himself before YHWH in submission and awe (v. 26) and acknowledges that all three issues in his opening petition have been answered: YHWH has proved himself faithful, his master's agenda has been met, and his personal mission has succeeded (v. 27).

Although God responds positively to this man's prayer, this is not always the case. In Deuteronomy 3:23–28 Moses recounts a personally frustrating—if not embarrassing—moment when YHWH refused to grant his demand for permission to enter the promised land.[29] God obviously heard Moses. However, sometimes prayer is not about bringing God's will into line with ours; it may also be about bringing our wills into conformity with his.

Intercessory Prayer for the Well-Being of Others

First Testament narratives contain many intercessory prayers. Abraham, "the friend"[30] and "prophet" of God, interceded for Sodom (Gen. 18:16–33) and for Abimelech (Gen. 20:7). Hezekiah (2 Kings 19:15–19) and Daniel (Dan. 9:1–19) prayed on behalf of their people. However, Moses offers the most dramatic examples of intercession on behalf of others.

The narratives recounting Israel's exodus from Egypt, their stay at Sinai, and their travels in the desert portray Moses as intercessor par excellence. He fulfilled this role with exceptional effectiveness on two occasions: when the Israelites worshiped the golden calf at Sinai, and when they refused to enter the promised land from Kadesh-Barnea. The Pentateuch preserves two accounts of the first event (Exod. 32:11–14; Deut. 9:26–29) and two of the second (Num. 14:13–19; Deut. 1:19–45). In both instances Moses' prayer was triggered by YHWH's fury and his determination to destroy his people because of their sin and faithlessness. According to YHWH's own analysis, in the first instance the Israelites manufactured a golden calf, prostrated themselves before it in submission and homage, sacrificed to it, and gave it credit for their salvation (Exod. 32:7–9). Furious over their ingratitude for his deliverance and their violation of the covenant they had just ratified, YHWH announced to Moses that he had rejected the nation and intended to start over with him. In the

29. YHWH explains his reasons for refusing Moses' request in Deut. 32:48–52.
30. Isa. 41:8 ('ōheb, "beloved"; LXX ēgapēsa; 2 Chron. 20:7, 'ōheb; LXX ēgapēmenō); James 2:23 (philos). On the biblical understanding of "friend" as "self-sacrificing confidant," see John 15:13–15.

Table 8.1. Moses' Argumentation in His Intercessory Prayers

Exodus 32:11–14 (at Sinai)	Deuteronomy 9:26–29 (at Sinai)	Numbers 14:13–19 (at Kadesh-Barnea)
1	Israel is YHWH's people, not his (v. 11a; cf. v. 7).	Israel is YHWH's people, not his (v. 26a; cf. 12).	
2	YHWH has invested great effort in saving the Israelites from the bondage of Egypt; by implication, to destroy them would mean this effort was wasted (v. 11b).	YHWH has invested great effort in saving the Israelites from the bondage of Egypt; by implication, to destroy them would mean this effort was wasted (v. 26b).	YHWH has invested great effort in saving the Israelites from the bondage of Egypt; by implication, to destroy them would mean this effort was wasted (v. 13).
3	YHWH's reputation among the nations will be damaged if he destroys Israel; they will think his intent was malicious from the beginning—to destroy them in the desert (v. 12).	YHWH must hold back for the sake of the patriarchs and overlook the sin of their descendants (v. 27).	YHWH has been uniquely close to his people: he is in their midst and has been personally leading them; by implication, it makes no sense to destroy them (v. 14).
4	YHWH must hold back for the sake of the patriarchs; he promised to multiply their seed and give them the land of Canaan as their possession forever (v. 13).	YHWH's reputation among the nations will be damaged if he destroys Israel; they will think that he brought them out to destroy them in the desert because he was unable to carry through on his promise to give them the land and because he hated them (v. 28).	YHWH's reputation among the nations will be damaged if he destroys Israel; they will think that he slaughtered them in the desert because he was unable to carry through on his promise to give them the land (vv. 15–16).
5		Israel is YHWH's people, not his (v. 29a; cf. v. 12).	YHWH's gracious character is in question; he has proved himself merciful in the past—may he be gracious again and forgive his people (vv. 17–19).
6		YHWH has invested great effort in saving the Israelites from the bondage of Egypt; by implication, to destroy them would mean this effort was wasted (v. 29b).	

second instance, YHWH interpreted Israel's refusal to enter the promised land from Kadesh-Barnea as a rejection of himself and blatant unbelief (Num. 14:11–12). Despite his demonstrations of power, compassion, and care on their behalf, they refused to trust him,[31] so he threatened to destroy them and transfer chosen-people status to Moses, making of him a nation stronger and greater than Israel would have become.

The nature of Moses' responses to these heady offers may be highlighted by viewing his argumentation with YHWH synoptically (table 8.1). In both instances Moses treated YHWH's threat to destroy the people as deadly serious. However, Moses rejected YHWH's demand to leave him alone so he could destroy them (Exod. 32:10; Deut. 9:14). By refusing YHWH's offer to make of him a nation (Exod. 32:11–14), and by asking YHWH to blot out his name from the book of life (if YHWH would not forgive them) but spare his people (Exod. 32:30–35), Moses comes close to the Suffering Servant of Isaiah 53. Neither in Exodus 32 nor in Deuteronomy 9 does Moses excuse his people or try to soften the seriousness of their sin. He can only appeal for mercy, YHWH's reputation, and his fidelity to his promise.

YHWH heard both prayers of Moses. In the first instance the change in divine disposition is expressed as *niham 'al*, "to regret, to change one's mind" (Exod. 32:14). In the second instance, YHWH responded by declaring that he had pardoned (*sālah*) the people's guilt in keeping with Moses' words (Num. 14:20). Israel would survive. However, the present generation, which had witnessed his signs and wonders in Egypt and in the wilderness, would not enter the promised land. YHWH would start over with their children.

The expression *niham*, used in the first case, is critical for establishing a biblical theology of prayer. Within the First Testament this verb occurs with God as its subject in three kinds of contexts to express (1) God's changing his mind from positive to negative,[32] (2) God's changing his mind from negative to positive,[33] and (3) God's response when his compassion wins over his wrath, despite the objects' unworthiness.[34]

But what does it mean for God to change his mind? This issue is extremely complex,[35] and a full response is beyond the scope of this discussion. However,

31. In his recollection of these events thirty-eight years later, Moses characterizes the Israelite response as stubbornness and rebellion (Deut. 1:26) and lack of trust in YHWH (v. 32).

32. YHWH "regretted" and grieved in his heart that he had made humankind on the earth (Gen. 6:6); YHWH "regretted" that he had made Saul king (1 Sam. 15:11, 35)—though Samuel declares that "the Glory of Israel does not lie or change his mind [*niham*], for he is not a man, that he should change his mind" (v. 29).

33. As in Exod. 32:14; cf. Joel 2:13; Jon. 4:2.

34. In Judg. 21:6, 15 *niham* describes the Israelites' "compassion" toward Benjamin after they had almost wiped out this tribe. With reference to God, see Judg. 2:18; Ps. 90:13; Jer. 15:6.

35. For a helpful survey of the issues, see M. Butterworth, "נחם," in *New International Dictionary of Old Testament Theology and Exegesis* [*NIDOTTE*], ed. W. A. VanGemeren (Grand Rapids: Eerdmans, 1997), 3:82.

in answering this question, we should avoid two extremes. First, contrary to the view of some open theists, the expression does not mean that events occur out of God's control or that outcomes catch him by surprise. Second, contrary to the view of extreme Calvinists, the expression is not merely an anthropomorphic or anthropopathic way of portraying God (metaphorically portraying him as if he were human). Nor may we dismiss the cases cited above as purely hypothetical: Moses certainly did not.

Indeed, the expression itself challenges the idea expressed in the Westminster Confession of Faith (2.1), that "God . . . is without body, parts, or passions." The first two elements are obviously correct, for God is spirit. But does he lack "passion"? On the contrary, YHWH's passion separates him from other so-called deities. He is not an idol of stone or wood, without feeling or heart, and therefore insensitive to the cries of his people or the intercession of a righteous man (James 5:16). While God is indeed sovereign over all, and while he is indeed immutable and changeless in his character, he is also a dynamic, living person who treasures his relationship with people. He responds to human sin with anger, but he reacts to repentant sinners with grace and mercy. God sees their deeds, knows their hearts, and responds accordingly. Herein lies our hope whenever we pray. In the mystery of divine providence, the free actions of human beings are significant. Because he is immutable in his character, changes in external circumstances move God to change his response.[36] According to the Scriptures, God relents when people threatened with judgment turn from their wickedness to righteousness or change their own minds about their status and actions.[37] As these texts demonstrate, God relents when a righteous person intercedes on behalf of those threatened with judgment (cf. also Amos 7:1–6).

Public Prayers of Celebration

In addition to personal prayers and prayers of intercession, First Testament narratives incorporate public prayers offered on behalf of or in the interest of the community. I shall examine two types of prayers: prayers at celebratory events and prayers recognizing communal grief.

The narratives of Samuel and 1 Chronicles incorporate several inspiring exemplars of David's prayers.[38] First Chronicles 29:10–20 may serve

36. See further Wayne Grudem, *Systematic Theology: An Introduction to Biblical Doctrine* (Grand Rapids: Zondervan, 1994), 165–66.

37. This was the case with the Ninevites (Jon. 3:5–10), and this is the basis of many of Jeremiah's appeals to his people (Jer. 8:6; 18:8, 10; 20:16; 26:3, 13, 19; 31:19; cf. 42:10).

38. Few match David's awed reaction to YHWH's promise of eternal title to the throne of Israel (2 Sam. 7:18–29), which he interprets as a "revelation for humanity" (*tôrat hā'ādām*). Identifying himself ten times as "your servant," he ends with a plea for YHWH to bless him

as a paradigmatic example of public prayer before the assembly of God's people. After announcing to the leaders of Israel that Solomon will fulfill his dream of building a temple for YHWH (28:1–8), David charges Solomon to serve YHWH with all his heart and as God's chosen instrument to build the temple (28:9–10, 20–21). After challenging the assembly to complete the project so dear to his heart (29:1–5), David ends by blessing YHWH with a most remarkable prayer (vv. 10–20). According to the narrative, this prayer represents David's final public words before he hands the reins of government to his son.

The introduction and opening invocation classify this prayer as a blessing (*bērēk*, v. 10), though David himself characterizes his utterance as thanksgiving (*hôdâ*) to God and praise (*hillēl*) to his glorious name (v. 13). Although consisting largely of praise to God (vv. 10b–17), David concludes with a petition on behalf of Solomon his son (vv. 18–19). The structure is clear:

1. *The opening blessing and praise (vv. 10b–13)*. David's corporate concern is apparent from the outset. By virtue of YHWH's covenant with him, David enjoys a special relationship with God (cf. Ps. 89), but David's use of the first-person plural (v. 13) reflects his corporate concern. In the opening blessing, David (a) identifies the addressee as YHWH, Israel's ancestral God; (b) doxologically ascribes to YHWH the transcendent attributes of greatness, power, glory, victory, and majesty; (c) recognizes YHWH as Lord and King of the universe; (d) acknowledges him as the source of riches and honor; government, power, and might; and greatness and strength for all; and (e) declares thanksgiving and praise to God.

2. *The central reflection on Israel's contributions to YHWH's house (vv. 14–17)*. An opening rhetorical question announces the critical issue: Israel is nothing apart from the grace that YHWH has lavished upon the people. With flourish and emphatic repetition, David acknowledges that the gifts the people have brought to YHWH to construct the temple are not theirs in the first place; they are returning to God what is his. Furthermore, David and his people have not presented these gifts under compulsion but with genuine integrity and delight.

3. *The concluding petition (vv. 18–19)*. The reference to YHWH, the God of the ancestors (now identified as Abraham, Isaac, and Israel), creates an inclusio with the opening blessing. David's petition consists of two requests: (a) that God will guard the people's present enthusiasm and keep their hearts directed toward himself, and (b) that God will give Solomon a perfect heart/

---

and fulfill the good word he has promised him. Although this prayer had national and universal implications, it was essentially a private prayer.

mind to keep the covenant through scrupulous obedience to all its terms, and to complete the construction project for which David has prepared.

Then David turns to the people, encouraging them to join him in blessing YHWH. They respond by blessing YHWH, bowing their heads to the ground, and thus prostrating themselves before YHWH and the king. Accompanied by thousands of sacrifices and celebrative feasting before YHWH, this is corporate prayer and worship at its best.

Solomon's blessing and prayer at the dedication of the temple is one of the longest in the Bible, and also one of the most instructive theologically (1 Kings 8:12–61). Technically, this is not a petition to God to solve a problem, an expression of praise, thanksgiving for deliverance, or a plea for forgiveness, but "a prayer *about* prayer," that is, "a prayer about the temple as the preeminent *place* of prayer."[39] After the glory of YHWH had moved from the holy of holies in the tabernacle to the holy of holies in the temple, establishing it as YHWH's dwelling place and marking it as supremely sacred space, Solomon speaks. His prayer consists of four utterances, whose lengths display a climactic progression.

The first address (1 Kings 8:12–13). Cast in poetic form, this speech acknowledges that the construction of the temple marks a turning point in the way YHWH dwells among his people. Whereas he has previously resided in the thick cloud, now he will dwell in this house. The language suggests that the temple represents a permanent replacement of Sinai (Exod. 20:21; Deut. 4:11; 5:22).

The second address (1 Kings 8:15–21). This speech is introduced as a blessing of the whole assembly of Israel, but the opening lines suggest that it is actually a blessing directed to God, consisting of five parts: (a) identification of the addressee as YHWH, the God of Israel; (b) a doxology, praising YHWH because his hands have fulfilled the promise his mouth made to David; (c) a quotation of YHWH's declaration to David that he has chosen him to rule his people;[40] (d) reflection on David's role in the temple project; and (e) recognition of the faithfulness of God in the completion of the temple (cf. 2 Sam. 7:8–16). Although Solomon describes his own action with four verbs ("I have risen," "I sit," "I have built," "I have provided"), he insists that these accomplishments are evidence of YHWH's faithfulness.

The third address (1 Kings 8:23–53). This speech can be classified as both a prayer (*tĕpillâ*, vv. 28, 29, 30) and a plea for grace (*tĕhinnâ*, vv. 28, 30, 59) on

---

39. Samuel E. Balentine, *Prayer in the Hebrew Bible: The Drama of Divine-Human Dialogue* (Minneapolis: Fortress, 1993), 80–81.

40. In obvious fulfillment of Deut. 17:14–20. The quotation highlights the primacy of the election of David over the election of a city among the tribal territories as a place to build a house for his name to be established.

behalf of the people. Solomon's posture—standing before the altar of YHWH in the presence of the people, with hands spread out toward heaven—symbolizes his role here. After the opening doxology—acknowledging YHWH's incomparability, his faithfulness to his covenant people, and his faithfulness to the covenant made with David (vv. 23–24)—Solomon pleads with YHWH to remain faithful to the promises he has made to David (vv. 25–26), to hear his present prayer (v. 28), and to hear the prayers of the king and the people in the future (vv. 29–30). However, verse 27 raises the key issue in the prayer as a whole: the relationship between this temple and a God who defies localization. God cannot be boxed in; yet for Israel, the temple functions as the primary link between heaven and earth (v. 30) and symbolizes YHWH's willingness to forgive the sins of all who call upon him.

The remainder of the address (vv. 31–53) develops these ideas with a series of scenarios in which people might direct their prayers toward the temple. Each focuses on "this house" but recognizes that YHWH must graciously hear in heaven and act from there (a) when an individual Israelite sins against another Israelite (vv. 31–32), (b) when YHWH's people are defeated before an enemy because they have sinned (vv. 33–34), (c) when drought ravages the land because Israel has sinned (vv. 35–36), (d) when famine strikes the land because Israel has sinned (vv. 37–40), (e) when foreigners address YHWH (vv. 41–43), (f) when the army goes to war at the command of YHWH (vv. 44–45), and (g) when Israel is taken into exile because of their sin (vv. 46–53).

The fourth address (1 Kings 8:54–61). Like the second address, this one is introduced as a blessing of the whole assembly of Israel, though again the opening lines suggest that it is actually a blessing directed to God. After addressing YHWH, Solomon offers a doxology of praise because YHWH has fulfilled his promises to Moses and given rest to his people. His petitions consist of a plea to YHWH to remain with his people and incline the Israelites' hearts to walk in all his ways, and a plea that the words of this prayer would remain before YHWH so that he might maintain the cause of his servant and his people, and so that all the peoples of the earth might know that YHWH is the only God. He concludes with an appeal to the people to be wholly devoted to YHWH and to demonstrate that devotion with obedience.

This prayer is extremely helpful in trying to understand prayer as worship. First, whereas in the narratives discussed above, prayer was at the periphery of the cult, here it is at the center of worship. Second, when Solomon prays, he addresses YHWH as a representative of the people. Third, Solomon addresses the only God, the faithful covenant-keeping God, and the guarantor of Israel's future security. Fourth, although prayers may be addressed toward the temple, this is not really where God lives. He hears the cries of the people from heaven, his true dwelling. Fifth, transcending ancient Near Eastern perspectives, YHWH is bound neither to the land nor to the physical descendants of Israel. By his grace he hears the cries of Israelites, but he will also hear the cries of foreigners. Sixth, the key to being heard by God is a penitent heart and a humble recognition that God is not obligated to hear anyone's prayers. However, through his promises and covenants, God has graciously and condescendingly obligated himself to his covenant people who walk in his ways.

Public Prayers Associated with Grief

The Scriptures offer a realistic portrait of life in a fallen world and often portray the causes of grief in brutally realistic terms. In response to Israel's defeat at Ai, Joshua and the elders address God urgently (Josh. 7:6–9) in a prayer that exhibits a clear structure: (1) the invocative address, "Ah, Lord YHWH" (v. 7a); (2) the lament (v. 7b); (3) the confession (v. 8); and (4) the concern (v. 9). Remarkably, this prayer contains no request; Joshua and the elders simply place their case before YHWH, presenting it as a theological crisis that he must resolve. Instead of answering the questions Joshua actually asks, God addresses the implied question: "Why have we been defeated by the enemy?" The enemy has defeated Israel, and YHWH will ultimately abandon them because Achan has taken from Jericho some things that God said should be devoted to destruction (cf. Deut. 7:25–26). The episode ends with a divine revelation of the solution for the defilement and the people's obedient response.

As in the preceding case, negative prayers often arise out of acts of rebellion against YHWH and usually involve confession of sin.[41] Nehemiah 9:5–38 contains a remarkable national prayer of confession. The shift in mood from Nehemiah 8 to chapter 9 is extreme, as exuberant celebration associated with the Festival of Booths (Sukkoth, Neh. 8:13–18) gives way to intense mourning (9:1–5a).[42] The text does not explain what has occasioned this dramatic change in tone,[43] but this silence may be intentional. Not every cultic observance in

41. See Dan. 9 and Ezra 9. On the theology of penitential prayers in the First Testament, see Mark J. Boda, "Confession as Theological Expressions: Ideological Origins of Penitential Prayer," in *Seeking the Favor of God*, vol. 1, *The Origins of Penitential Prayer in Second Temple Judaism*, ed. M. J. Boda, D. K. Falk, and R. A. Werline, SBL Early Judaism and Its Literature 21 (Atlanta: Society of Biblical Literature, 2006), 21–50.

42. The narrator does not specify the dates of the celebration, but if they were following the priestly calendar, the dates would have been Tishri 15–22, seven days of living in booths followed by a climactic eighth-day observance (Lev. 23:34–38).

43. The first impulse is to associate it with the Day of Atonement, the most solemn day of the year, also observed in the seventh month—except that it was scheduled for Tishri 10.

Israel was scheduled: some were spontaneous (cf. 2 Sam. 6). If this is a spontaneous observance arising from sustained reflection on the Torah they have been hearing for a week, then the gravity of Israel's sin that has caused the exile and the loss of the temple and its worship may finally be sinking in. The people recognize that they cannot move forward as a covenant community without corporate confession of their past sins, which are intricately linked to the present sins.

Nehemiah 9:5b–38 is cast as truly corporate prayer, recited by a chorus of Levites before the assembly. Unlike previous prayers, this one is cast entirely in poetic speech, appropriate for liturgical reading or recitation. The people's nonverbal actions highlight their disposition: they fast, don sackcloth, cover themselves with dirt, stand and confess, read from the Torah, prostrate themselves, and cry out with a loud voice (9:1–4). Although much of their prayer reviews the history of God's grace toward Israel, verse 3 classifies it as "confession" (*hitwaddâ*) and "[verbal] prostration" (*hištaḥăwâ*). However, the opening call to bless YHWH (v. 5b) reveals another dimension of the prayer. Throughout, it juxtaposes descriptions of the character and actions of the holy and gracious God with the rebellious character and actions of his people. This prayer is also impressive for its lofty theology. The opening blessing is followed by seven uneven strophes recalling YHWH's past actions on Israel's behalf and celebrating his character in the present.[44] This poem approaches pure confession—confessing the goodness and grace of God and also the sinfulness of humans. Although explicit petitions are kept to a minimum, throughout it breathes hope based on God's past and present goodness. In so doing it teaches that confession is a vital step toward restoration and *shalom* with God.

This prayer of confession involves a kind of prayer that is common in the Scriptures but rarely observed or even permitted in worship today. Seduced by a health-and-wealth gospel, we have developed the notion that the primary purpose of worship is to give us a spiritual high and that negative feelings and expressions of grief should be suppressed. However, the Scriptures portray worship, especially prayer, in brutally frank terms. Prayers may express submission, supplication, intercession, praise, thanksgiving, or adoration, but God's ears are also open to our laments and even our complaints. In the Psalter, psalms of lament actually outnumber psalms of praise two to one. Still, this kind of prayer is rare in Western evangelical worship.

By definition a lament is an expression of grief, pain, or anger, usually arising from personal or corporate calamity. As elsewhere in the ancient Near East,

---

44. Invocative blessing, Neh. 9:5; strophe 1, vv. 6–8; strophe 2, vv. 9–15; strophe 3, vv. 16–18; strophe 4, vv. 19–25; strophe 5, vv. 26–31; strophe 6, v. 32; strophe 7, vv. 33–38.

Israel's laments were prayed, sung, or wailed in response to death, devastation in war, crop failure, sickness, infertility, or consciousness of sin. Prayers of confession were often accompanied by nonverbal expressions of grief or anger, such as wearing sackcloth, going barefoot, covering the head, not washing or applying perfumes, throwing dirt in the air and on the head, rolling in the dust, sitting on the ash heap, shaving facial and head hair, lacerating the body, fasting, beating the breasts, weeping and wailing, and crying "Alas! Alas!" (*hô-hô*, Amos 5:16).[45]

Biblical Hebrew actually includes several paralinguistic expressions for woe.[46] Most of these are onomatopoeic utterances, equivalent to the Yiddish "*Oy vey!*" and the German "*Au weh!*" and the English "Ouch!" or "Woe!" or "Oh no!" Following these outbursts we often find the lamenter describing the problem to God. Often beginning with "Why?" or "How long?," the tone of laments may be harsh and hard, as worshipers speak their minds before God, frequently accusing him of injustice.

The goal of biblical laments was to engage God at all costs. With our sanitized views of propriety before God, modern readers sometimes find the frankness of biblical laments embarrassing, if not offensive. Outbursts like Job's (Job 3:1–26; 10:1–22) or the prophet Jeremiah's (Jer. 20:7–18) seem ill-becoming of virtuous people and prophets. However, as in human relationships, sometimes frank conversation with God is necessary. As in excited conversations between persons, Jeremiah's emotions oscillate between outbursts of frustration with God (Jer. 20:7–10, 14–18) and declarations of hope and confidence in him (vv. 11–13). Similar patterns occur in the Psalms. Psalm 13 expresses anguish over personal misfortune; Psalm 79 laments a national calamity, the destruction of Jerusalem; and Psalm 89 expresses grief over the demise of the Davidic monarchy (see esp. vv. 46–51).[47] The responses to questions of theodicy presented in the First Testament are illustrated in table 8.2.

Fundamentally, laments involve theodicy: Where is the justice of God? Where is the God of justice in human suffering? North American Christians find it difficult to accept that expressions of protest or puzzlement in the face of tragic experiences are legitimate acts of worship. But people in the two-thirds world, who are culturally much closer to ancient Israelites than Western urbanites, understand these prayers. Protestations need not be dismissed as faithless:

45. See also 2 Sam. 14:2; Jer. 14:2; Ezek. 20–24:15 ; 27:30; Mic. 1:8–10.

46. Hebrew *'ānnâ* (Exod. 32:31), *'ôy* (Num. 24:23), *'ăhâ* (Josh. 7:7), *hôy* (1 Kings 13:30), *'āḥ* (Ezek. 6:11), *hāh* (Ezek. 30:2), and *'ăbāl* (2 Sam. 14:5). Where these interjections are preserved in Greek, they are rendered as *ō* (2 Kings 3:10), *ō ō* (Num. 24:23); *a a* (Judg. 6:22; 11:35), *ouai* (1 Kings 13:30), or *oimmoi oimmoi oimmoi* (Joel 1:15).

47. On First Testament laments, see Balentine, *Prayer in the Hebrew Bible*, 146–98.

Table 8.2. The Responses of Faith to Suffering

Suffering Perceived As . . .	Response by the Sufferer	Answer of the Sufferer	Examples
Justified, warranted, deserved, punishment	Acceptance, repentance	God is just.	Deut. 28; Dan. 9; Ezra 9; Neh. 9
Not justified, unwarranted, undeserved punishment	Lament, protest	God is unjust, capricious, and unresponsive.	Job 3:1–26; 10:1–22; Jer. 11:18–12:6; 15:10–21; 20:7–18; Hab. 1:2–4
Redemptive/vicarious, God-ordained, positive	Obedience, acceptance as the calling of the faithful	God is sovereign and mysterious.	Isa. 50:4–11; 52:13–53:12

Adapted from Balentine, *Prayer in the Hebrew Bible*, 190–91.

they may actually be the opposite—expressions of trust in a God who cares, and pleas for his intervention. The sheer number of laments in Scripture demonstrates that God invites us to relate to him with transparency and honesty.

The New Testament Practice of Prayer

Compared to the wealth of information on prayer in the First Testament, the New Testament has relatively little to say, and the information it provides is heavily influenced by early Judaism. Money changers may have transformed the temple from being the place of sacrifices, Torah reading, and music into a robbers' den (Jer. 7:11), but Jesus viewed it as "a house of prayer."[48] Synagogue worship excluded sacrifices, but praise, Scripture reading, homilies, and prayer were important in worship.[49] Chanted psalms, closely tied to prayer, were considered sacrifices of the heart,[50] so that by the third century BC synagogues could also be called houses of prayer.[51] Indeed, synagogues were often oriented architecturally so that worshipers faced Jerusalem as they prayed.[52]

---

48. See Matt. 21:12–17; Mark 11:15–19; Luke 19:45–46; cf. Isa. 56:7. On temple worship in the first century AD, see S. Safrai, "The Temple," in *The Jewish People in the First Century*, ed. S. Safrai and M. Stern (Philadelphia: Fortress, 1987), 2:876–77, 885–86.

49. See Asher Finkel, "Prayer in Jewish Life of the First Century as Background to Early Christianity," in *Into God's Presence: Prayer in the New Testament*, ed. R. N. Longenecker, McMaster New Testament Studies (Grand Rapids: Eerdmans, 2001), 57.

50. S. Safrai, "The Synagogue," in Safrai and Stern, *The Jewish People in the First Century*, 2:917.

51. Eric M. Meyers, "Synagogue," in *Anchor Bible Dictionary* [*ABD*], ed. David Noel Freedman (New York: Doubleday, 1992), 6:252.

52. Larry W. Hurtado, *At the Origins of Christian Worship: The Context and Character of Earliest Christian Devotion* (Grand Rapids: Eerdmans, 1999), 36.

The types of prayers recited included blessings (praising God for creation and redemption, his covenant love for Israel, the Torah, and his providential care),[53] the Kaddish (blessing God's holy name), and the Eighteen Benedictions (blessing God for a wide range of benefactions). With this as background, we may now address the subject of prayer in the New Testament.

Prayer in the Life of Jesus

Jesus frequently expressed homage and submission to the Father through prayer. Whereas First Testament prayers addressed God by name, "YHWH," or by title, "Lord" or "God," Jesus addressed him as *Pater*[54] or *Abba* (Mark 14:36), both of which mean "Father."[55] He seems to have avoided "YHWH" because this was *his* name,[56] and "Lord" because, though submissive to the Father, he was not a slave but a son pursuing his Father's will.[57] We should not construe the epithet *Abba* as casual or informal, like English "Dada" or "Daddy."[58] "Father" expresses respect, trust, and security in a confident relationship.

Since Jesus often visited the temple and synagogues, he probably also participated in liturgical prayers.[59] But his prayers were not limited to corporate worship; he often withdrew from the crowds to pray before critical events (Mark 1:35; Luke 5:16).[60] Because these tended to be private moments of communion

53. See Allen P. Ross, *Recalling the Hope of Glory: Biblical Worship from the Garden to the New Creation* (Grand Rapids: Kregel, 2006), 361–62.

54. Matthew 6:9; 11:25; Luke 22:42; 23:34, 46; John 12:27–28; 17:1, 5, 11, 21, 24–25. The only exception to this paternal address occurs in Jesus' cry of dereliction in Matt. 27:46: "My God, My God, why have you abandoned me." However, this utterance is determined by Ps. 22:1 [2], which he quotes.

55. Correspondingly, at Jesus' baptism (Matt. 3:17) and transfiguration (17:5) the Father identifies him as "my beloved Son."

56. That he was YHWH incarnate is an overriding theme of the New Testament. See Charles A. Gieschen, "The Divine Name in Ante-Nicene Christology," *Vigilae christianae* 57 (2003): 115–58; Richard Bauckham, *Jesus and the God of Israel: God Crucified and Other Studies on the New Testament's Christology of Divine Identity* (Grand Rapids: Eerdmans, 2008), 127–51.

57. Luke 22:42; cf. Jesus' emphasis on having been sent by the Father: John 5:36–37; 6:44, 57; 8:16, 18, 42; 12:49; 17:21, 25; 20:21. In the parable of the rejected son sent by the father, Jesus distinguishes between himself and servants (Matt. 21:33–46; Mark 12:1–12; Luke 20:9–19).

58. James Barr, "'*ABBA*' Isn't 'Daddy,'" *Journal of Theological Studies* 39 (1988): 28–47.

59. See Grant Osborne, "Prayer in Corporate Worship in the New Testament," paper delivered to the Evangelical Theological Society in New Orleans, November 20, 2009.

60. His baptism (Luke 3:21), choosing the twelve apostles (Luke 6:12), after the beheading of John the Baptist (Matt. 14:23; Mark 6:46), when people brought children to him (Matt. 19:13), before the transfiguration (Luke 9:18, 28–29), before his crucifixion (Matt. 26:36–46; Mark 14:32–42; Luke 22:41–42).

with the Father, the preserved prayers of Jesus are few and fragmentary.[61] His intercessory prayer in John 17:1–26 is an exception and illustrates his approach to prayer most clearly. He opens with the invocative address "Father" and moves immediately to reflecting on the significance of this moment: he has been true to his commission; now it is time for the Father to glorify him (vv. 1–8). In the words that follow, he reveals his passion for his immediate followers (vv. 9–19) and for the generations to come (vv. 20–26). Though John is silent on the reaction of the disciples who heard these words in the upper room, they should have been greatly comforted.

In addition to practicing the presence of God through prayer, Jesus also taught his followers to pray. While discussing church discipline, he told his disciples, "Again, I tell you that if two of you on earth agree about anything you ask for, it will be done for you by my Father in heaven; for where two or three come together in my name, there am I with them" (Matt. 18:19–20). In the Sermon on the Mount, Jesus contrasts gentile prayers with how his followers should pray. The contexts in which they pray should differ (his disciples should pray in secret), but so should the way they pray: his followers should avoid endless repetitions, as if they need to convince God to listen to them. Prayer is not about informing God of our needs as if he is ignorant; instead, it is "a vehicle of humility, an expression of un-self-sufficiency, which in biblical thought, is the proper stance of humans before God."[62] In prayer we express our confidence in God to meet those needs. The prayer Jesus taught his disciples—commonly called "The Lord's Prayer"—is short, formal, formulaic, and poetic, and its structure is clear (Matt. 6:9–13).[63]

1. *The invocative address "Our Father."*[64] Jesus invites his disciples to address God as he does, since they are God's children. The notion of the fatherhood of God is not new to the New Testament but borrowed from the language of YHWH's covenant with Israel (cf. Deut. 14:1–2; 32:6, 18; Isa. 64:8[7]). The followers of Jesus represent the new covenant community.

2. *The description "in heaven."* This expression both distinguishes the addressee from earthly fathers and confesses what Solomon had acknowledged long ago in the dedication of the temple (1 Kings 8). God is not an earthling: his residence is in heaven.

61. Matthew 11:25–27; 26:39, 42 (cf. Mark 14:36; Luke 22:42); 27:46 (cf. Mark 15:34); Luke 23:46; John 11:41–42.

62. Thus Moshe Greenberg, "On the Refinement of the Conception of Prayer in Hebrew Scriptures," in *Studies in the Bible and Jewish Thought* (Philadelphia: Jewish Publication Society, 1995), 104.

63. In Luke 11:2–4 the prayer is taught in response to the disciples' specific request. Jesus may have repeated these instructions in more than one context.

64. Luke's version is more formal, omitting "Our" (Luke 11:2).

3. The Petition

> Hallowed be your name.
> Your kingdom come.
> Your will be done, on earth as it is in heaven.
> Give us this day our daily bread.
> And forgive us our debts,
>   as we also have forgiven our debtors.
> And do not bring us to the time of trial,
>   but rescue us from the evil one.[65]

The petition divides into two parts. First, it expresses the same concern for the glory of God and the sanctity of his reputation ("name") that we observed in the prayers of Moses, David, and Daniel. Second, it locates private concerns within the context of the broader and more significant concern for God's kingdom. Believers recognize that God's reputation depends upon the well-being of his people and that God's forgiveness of them is linked to their willingness to forgive others.

4. The motivation. "For yours is the kingdom, and the power, and the glory, forever. Amen." Whether original or not, the longer ending of Matthew 6:13 in some manuscripts reinforces the prayer's primary concern: the reputation of God.

Jesus expected and indeed commanded his followers to pray. If he needed this form of communion with the Father, how much more do we? To have this prayer ringing in our ears will inhibit preoccupation with gentile (i.e., self-centered, v. 7) concerns—personal well-being, health, happiness, and success—and keep us focused on the highest priority, the glory and reign of God.

Prayer in Acts

The book of Acts highlights the importance of prayer in the early church.[66] The earliest followers of Jesus met regularly to pray: in the upper room after

---

65. Greek *tou ponērou* (Matt. 6:13) is capable of several interpretations: (1) evil in general (ESV); (2) the evil one (NIV, NLT, NRSV); or (3) a particular kind of evil, equivalent to Hebrew *hārā'*, which LXX renders as *ta ponēra/ton ponēron* in Deuteronomy (e.g., 4:25; 9:18; 13:5, 11 [6, 12]). By this latter (preferred) interpretation, it is a prayer for deliverance from idolatry and the temptation to go after other gods.

66. As does the archaeological record. The earliest attested building built for worship in Palestine has been identified as a "prayer hall," though the table and the inscription highlight the role of the Eucharist in this place. In addition to the article cited above (in note 49 of chap. 6), see Yotam Tepper and Leah di Segni, *A Christian Prayer Hall of the Third Century CE at Kefar 'Óthnay (Legio)* (Jerusalem: IAA Publications, 2006); cf. Edward Adams, "The Ancient

Jesus' ascension (1:14), before selecting a successor to Judas (1:24–25), in the temple at "the time of prayer" (3:1), to ask for boldness (4:23–31), while dying as martyrs (7:59–60), when Samaritans were to receive the Holy Spirit (8:14–18), in response to a meeting with God (9:11), when they were persecuted and imprisoned (12:5–16), at special places of prayer (16:13, 16), and to pray for one another (20:32–36). Acts 2:42 identifies prayer as one of the four pillars on which the church was built, along with teaching, fellowship, and the breaking of bread. Describing the response to the first great persecution, the arrest and release of Peter and John, and a warning by the Sanhedrin to stop proclaiming Christ (4:1–22), Acts 4:23–31 preserves the most complete prayer in the book. This corporate prayer bears remarkable structural similarity to First Testament prayers.

1. *The invocative address "Sovereign Lord . . ." (v. 24).* Remarkably, here the disciples do not address God as "Father," as practiced and taught by Jesus.

2. *The description (vv. 24–28).* The bulk of the prayer acknowledges God as Creator of all and quotes God's declaration through David that the gentiles have raged against YHWH and his Anointed. In a shocking inversion of the image of raging gentiles, Peter and John speak of the Jewish leaders as enemies of God and his Messiah.

3. *The petition (vv. 29–30).* Identifying themselves with God and his Anointed, the disciples pray for boldness to speak God's message and for God to perform miracles, signs, and wonders through the name of his holy servant Jesus.

The effect of this prayer is striking: the house shakes; the believers are filled with the Holy Spirit and boldly declare the word of God; and they are united in their charity and testify to the resurrection of Jesus (vv. 31–35). Luke viewed prayer not only as the natural response of believers to their experiences but also as an opportunity to proclaim profound theology. The present rage against Jesus Christ was part and parcel of the rage of the gentiles against God and his Anointed. Prayer was the key to a new and dramatic work of God.

Prayer in the Epistles

In his Letters, Paul never offers a coherent treatise on prayer or an extended quotation of his prayers. This does not mean that prayer was not important to Paul. On the contrary, he laced the Epistles with incidental comments, allusions to, and reports about his own prayers, and he repeatedly asked people to pray for him.[67] In 1 Timothy 2:1–8 he urges intercession for everyone, including himself. As far as we can tell, like First Testament prayers, Paul's usually consisted of adoration, thanksgiving, and petition.[68]

Doxological outbursts of adoration, rooted in his religious heritage, punctuate Paul's writings. Following the *běrākâ*-formula prayer, he often began by blessing God and then praising him for action on behalf of his people: "Blessed be the God and Father of our Lord Jesus Christ, . . . who comforts us in all our troubles" (2 Cor. 1:3–4a), and "Blessed be the God and Father of our Lord Jesus Christ, who has blessed us in the heavenly realms with every spiritual blessing" (Eph. 1:3). At the end of these declarations he extolled God: "To him be the glory forever" (Rom. 11:36). "To the only wise God be glory forever through Jesus Christ" (16:27). "To whom be glory forever and ever" (Gal. 1:5). "To him be glory in the church and in Christ Jesus throughout all generations, forever and ever" (Eph. 3:21). "To our God and Father be glory forever and ever" (Phil. 4:20).[69]

Paul's thanksgiving is embodied in the word *eucharistein*, "to praise," which expresses thanksgiving for God's creative and saving work. He regularly opened his Letters with thanksgiving to God[70] and punctuated his Epistles with this word of praise.[71] In so doing, he modeled thanksgiving and praise as flowing naturally from the experience of God's grace and love.[72]

Paul often incorporated prayers of petition into expressions of thanksgiving. Sometimes he begins with "I remember you in my prayers at all times," and then presents his request on his addressees' behalf.[73] But he also inserted intercessory petitions (Rom. 10:1; 2 Cor. 13:9; Eph. 3:16–19) and "wish prayers"[74] into his Epistles. Aware of specific needs in the churches, he prayed that God would meet those needs and encouraged his readers to do the same.[75]

67. As in Rom. 15:30; 2 Cor. 1:8–11; Eph. 6:19, 20; Phil. 1:19; 1 Thess. 5:25; Philem. 22.

68. Richard N. Longenecker, "Prayer in the Pauline Letters," in Longenecker, *Into God's Presence*, 213.

69. See ibid., 215–17.

70. See Rom. 1:8; 1 Cor. 1:4; 2 Cor. 1:11; Eph. 1:16; Phil. 1:3; Col. 1:3, 12; 1 Thess. 1:2; 2 Thess. 1:3; Philem. 4.

71. According to Peter T. O'Brien ("Benediction, Blessing, Doxology, Thanksgiving," in *Dictionary of Jesus and the Gospels*, ed. J. B. Green and S. McKnight [Downers Grove, IL: InterVarsity, 1992], 69), Paul deals with the notion of *eucharistein* more than any other writer, pagan or Christian. This word and its derivatives occur forty-six times in his writings.

72. See ibid., 70; and more fully, Peter T. O'Brien, *Introductory Thanksgivings in the Letters of Paul*, Novum Testamentum Supplements 49 (Leiden: Brill, 1977); David Pao, *Thanksgiving: An Investigation of a Pauline Theme* (Downers Grove, IL: InterVarsity, 2002).

73. As in Rom. 1:9–10; Eph. 1:16; Phil. 1:4; Col. 1:9; 1 Thess. 1:3; 2 Thess. 1:11; 2 Tim. 1:3; Philem. 4.

74. See Rom. 15:5–6; 15:13; 2 Cor. 13:14; 1 Thess. 3:11–13; 5:23; 2 Thess. 2:16–17; 3:5, 16; 2 Tim. 4:16.

75. Longenecker, "Prayer in the Pauline Letters," 219–23.

For Paul, prayer was not primarily about getting God to do for him what he could not do for himself; instead, through prayer he expressed submission and homage to God and relinquished control of his affairs to God. Furthermore, Paul viewed prayer as a vehicle for expressing both faith and theology.[76]

Moving beyond the Pauline writings, Hebrews 12:22–29 presents a beautiful picture of corporate worship, highlighting the importance of thanksgiving.[77] On first sight the author appears to contrast the fright of the Israelites at Mount Sinai at the sight and voice of God (vv. 18–21; cf. Exod. 20:18–19; Deut. 5:23–27) with the confidence that new-covenant people have as they approach Mount Zion. However, the concluding appeal for reverence and awe and the reminder that "God is [still] a consuming fire" force us to reconsider this interpretation. Apparently employing the rabbinic method of arguing from the lesser to the greater, the author suggests that if the encounter with God at Sinai evoked awe, how much more should our entrance into the heavenly Jerusalem, where God is attended by his heavenly host, and where Jesus, the mediator of the new covenant, greets us. Our admission to this audience with the living God confirms our citizenship in a kingdom that cannot be shaken and should evoke unrestrained gratitude, which is our acceptable sacrifice of reverence and awe (v. 28). Worship with an eschatological vision involves sacrifices of praise because we have been invited to participate in this kingdom (Heb. 13:15–16).

James offers a two-sided picture of prayer. First, the privilege may be abused through wrong motives, expressing our hedonism and egocentrism, rather than concern for others or for the glory of God's name (4:2–3). Second, prayer is a gracious provision of God; when prayer is offered in faith by righteous intercessors in the contexts of confession, the healing resources of heaven become available to God's people (5:13–18).

In 1 Peter the apostle calls the church to a sober and clear vision of its place within God's saving work. Since the revelation of Jesus Christ is at hand (1:13), God's people must be disciplined, clearheaded, focused in their prayers (4:7), and vigilant in their personal ethical conduct, for the way we treat one another determines whether our prayers will be answered (3:7). However, true prayer is not merely an individual matter: it must also be a communal commitment. As Grant Osborne says, "The minds of the believers must be clear of all encumbrances, focused, and under the control of the Spirit as they move the church forward on its knees."[78]

76. For a helpful summary of Paul's theology of prayer, see W. B. Hunter, "Prayer," in *Dictionary of Paul and His Letters*, ed. G. F. Hawthorne, R. P. Martin, and D. G. Reid (Downers Grove: InterVarsity, 1993), 730–34.

77. So also Osborne, "Prayer in Corporate Worship in the New Testament," 11.

78. Ibid., 12.

The doxology ending the book of Jude (vv. 24–25) is often used as a benediction to end worship services. This short text is rightfully treasured by many as a favorite corporate prayer in the New Testament. Profound in its theology, it celebrates the status and character of God: he is sovereignly able to keep us from falling, but he also invites us to stand in his presence with great joy. Only this God is worthy of eternal praise and honor and glory, which he receives through the work of Jesus Christ. This prayer shows that one of the purposes of corporate prayer is to encourage God's people by reminding them of the infinite spiritual resources available through Christ.

The images of worship in the book of Revelation inspire God's people to persevere in faith when under stress and to participate in earthly worship in anticipation of eternal worship. We may divide the prayers involved in these worship scenes into two categories. First, some are hymns addressed to God, focusing on the vertical relationship between worshipers and the One worshiped.[79] While the boundaries between prayers and songs of adoration often blur, these hymns celebrate the power, glory, and wisdom of God with honor, praise, and thanksgiving. Appearing at critical junctures in the plot of the book, these worship scenes offer theological commentary on its events.[80] The second type of prayer involves horizontal petitions.[81] Together, these two types illustrate the kinds of prayers that should characterize our own worship.

Prayer in Christian Worship Today

From Genesis to Revelation we observe how God graciously speaks to human beings and graciously allows himself to be addressed by them. What distinguished YHWH, the God of Israel, from the gods of the peoples also distinguishes the God of the New Testament, YHWH incarnate in Jesus Christ, from the gods of Romans and Greeks: he is a communicating Deity. Thankfully, he continues to delight in hearing the prayers of his saints. But how can we apply the above observations on prayer to our worship so that our conversation pleases God and our prayers are answered? Here is a summary of biblical teaching on prayer to guide us in our theory and practice.

First, prayer is the supreme reverential verbal act of submission and homage before the divine Sovereign. Like all worship, true prayer is concerned primarily with the glory of God: human desires and wishes are subordinated

79. As in Rev. 4:8, 11; 5:9–10, 12, 13; 7:10, 12; 11:17–18; 15:3–4; 16:5–7; 19:1–8.
80. David G. Peterson, "Worship in the Revelation to John," *Reformed Theological Review* 47 (1988): 68–69, 75–76.
81. See Grant R. Osborne, *Revelation*, Baker Exegetical Commentary on the New Testament (Grand Rapids: Baker Academic, 2002), 46–49.

to his ultimate will and purposes. However, as a primary means of worship, by inviting us to pray, the living God offers a unique privilege: two-way communication with him.

Second, prayer is a privilege that serves many functions—praise, thanksgiving, adoration, communion, confession, complaint, supplication, intercession—and is open to all. While we are all encouraged to pray for one another, we are not dependent on the mediation of priests or deceased saints. Through Jesus, all believers have direct access to the Father.

Third, through public prayer, believers express, reinforce, and develop the theology of the church, and they express their oneness with each other and with Christ. At the same time, the medium of prayer offers instructional and inspirational opportunities to be reminded of the grace and glory of God.

Fourth, prayer is a powerful grace. When received, it has the potential to effect change in one of three ways: (1) Through prayer, circumstances change (Acts 12:1–17). (2) Through prayer, the pray-er changes. Prayer is not necessarily about getting God to do what we want him to do; it may also be the process whereby he gets us to do what he wants and to understand reality as he sees it (Deut. 3:23–28; Amos 7:1–9). (3) Through prayer, God's disposition and actions change (Exod. 32; Jon. 3). His immutable grace causes him to withdraw threats and grant forgiveness when people repent of sin or a righteous intercessor appeals on their behalf.

Finally, while the privilege of prayer is open to all, the Scriptures reveal that the forms and shapes of prayer vary depending on context. Prayers that arise out of personal experience are spontaneous, often conversational, and informal—though never casual. However, in the Scriptures prayers offered publicly on behalf of the congregation exhibit a significant rise in the literary register, so that many are cast in extremely sophisticated poetry. Of the prayers embedded in the narratives, this is most evident in Nehemiah 9 and David's prayer in 1 Chronicles 29:10–19, but it is reflected especially in the prayers in the Psalter. If corporate worship involves a corporate audience with the great King, surely the language of communication should adapt to the situation. Furthermore, since those who lead the community in prayer speak not for themselves but for all, such prayer must be disciplined, subordinating idiosyncratic interests and preferences to common concerns: the glory of God, the corporate celebration of his grace, and joint pleas for forgiveness. Public prayers in Scripture tend to follow a particular structure: a formal address to God, a recitation/celebration of his character and status, a description of present realities, and a petition for aid. They also tend to be cast in traditional form and language. Having our minds filled with the Scriptures, public prayers offer magnificent opportunities to identify with the saints of the past and with saints around the world whose minds are also filled with these same Scriptures.[82]

> God of hope, God of mercy,
> faithful God, forgiving God, holy God,
> We have your Word, your promise—and we trust in the fact that
>> the Lord is near to all who call upon him,
>> to all who call upon him in truth.
> We have been invited to ask, to seek, to knock, with promise of answer,
>> for we believe you rule over all,
>> and in your hand is power and might.
> So we address our petitions to
>> the King eternal, immortal, invisible, the only God,
>>> worthy to receive honor and glory for ever and ever.
> Father God, would that our moments of trust were with us always.
>> But events come into our lives and we are filled with questions.
> We need the reinforcement that you have the answers.
> We stand mute before inexplicable circumstances,
>> but there are no mysteries for you.
>> There are no facts you do not know;
>> no problems you cannot solve;
>> no events you cannot explain;
>> no hypocrisy through which you do not see;
>> no secrets of ours unknown to you.
> We are truly unmasked before you, and you see us as we really are—
>> filled with our pride,
>> our selfishness,
>> our shallowness,
>> our blatant carnality.
> We would despair were it not that
>> you, O Lord, are compassionate and gracious,
>> slow to anger and abounding in loving-kindness. . . .
> You have not dealt with us according to our sins,
>> for as high as the heavens are above the earth,
>> so great is your loving-kindness toward those who fear you.
> So we crave today
>> a clean life,
>> a quiet spirit,

82. When asked to pray in public on behalf of the assembly, we do well to write out our prayers, to borrow the language of biblical prayers, and to consult resources like the Anglican Book of Common Prayer, or *Valley of Vision: A Collection of Puritan Prayers and Devotions*, ed. A. G. Bennett (Carlisle, PA: Banner of Truth, 1975), or hymnbooks with theologically rich songs.

an honest tongue,
a believing heart,
a redeemed soul.
Thank you, God, that the blood of Jesus Christ
cleanses us from all unrighteousness.
Now, may we enjoy you forever!
Amen.[83]

83. Wendell C. Hawley, "Prayer Number Thirteen," in *A Pastor Prays for His People: A Collection of Wise and Loving Prayers to Help You through Life's Journey* (Carol Stream, IL: Tyndale, 2010), 33–34. With citations from Pss. 103:8, 10–11; 145:18; Matt. 7:7; 1 Tim. 1:17; Heb. 4:13; 1 John 1:9.

9

Music as Worship

True worship involves reverential human acts of submission and hom-
age before the divine Sovereign in response to his gracious revelation of
himself and in accord with his will.

It seems that nothing defines a people like its music. The music may be as plain
as rubbing a stick rhythmically across a corrugated surface or as complex as
a ballet by Pyotr Ilich Tchaikovsky. People are what they sing. If we would
understand a culture other than our own, we should start not by reading essays about it by so-called objective observers, but by listening to the music,
feeling its rhythm, and hearing the story of its poetry. This is as true of the
church as it is of the cultures of the people who make up the church. Luther
said, "If any would not sing and talk of what Christ has wrought for us, he
shows thereby that he does not really believe."

Although the songs we sing should bind us together, in our day music is
destroying the church. Whereas previous generations fought and divided over
doctrine, today we battle over worship style, which in most places means
the music. The tensions over these issues are intense.[1] Perhaps it is time to
ask what role the Scriptures expect music to play in worship and then reflect

1. Note the headline in the July 22, 1999, issue of *Christianity Today*, "Triumph of the Praise
Songs: How Guitars Beat Out the Organ in the Worship Wars."

221

theologically on the matter, rather than grounding our decisions on tradition, pragmatics, or personal taste.

The Place of Song in First Testament Worship

Musical invention and performance are fundamental to our humanity. To be human is to create. And if we define "artistic endeavor" as *the search for order in the universe and the representation of that order in appropriate aesthetic forms*, then the development and enjoyment of music is one of the facets of this work. Indeed, the first recorded human words in the Bible come in the form of a love song (Gen. 2:23), and Genesis 4:21 suggests that inventing musical instruments was as significant for the advancement of culture as constructing city walls, domesticating livestock, and discovering uses for metals.

The Place of Music in Daily Life

According to the Scriptures, from the dawn of history music was important in everyday life. Whether treading grapes (Jer. 25:30; 48:33), harvesting crops (Isa. 9:3), cooking meals (Ezek. 24:3–5),[2] or digging irrigation ditches or wells (Num. 21:17–18), people lifted the burden of hard work by singing or chanting. Music and dance were regular features of celebrations any time in life (Eccles. 3:4). People also celebrated in the vineyards (Judg. 21:19–21), after sheep were shorn (2 Sam. 13:28), at weddings (Judg. 14:14; cf. Matt. 22:1–13; John 2:1–11), at coronations (2 Sam. 15:10; 1 Kings 1:39–40), and on pilgrimages (2 Sam. 6:5). Song provided a powerful medium for celebrating love, as witnessed by the first ode in the Bible (Gen. 2:23) and "the most beautiful song of all" (*šîr haššîrîm*, Song of Songs). Isaiah taunted drunkards with a song (Isa. 24:9), and Job recognized the incongruence of innocent people suffering while children of the wicked sang, danced, and made music (Job 21:11–12). Among the affluent, certain kinds of music reflected decadence (Amos 6:4–5) or futility (Eccles. 2:8; 7:5; Isa. 5:12; 2 Sam. 19:35). Military leaders rallied troops with musical instruments (Josh. 6:3–16; Judg. 3:27; 6:34; 7:15–24), and victory was celebrated with song and dance.[3] Some early victory hymns were collected in "The Book of the Wars of YHWH" (Num. 21:14) and "The Book of Jashar" (Josh. 10:13).

Music was also important in times of tragedy; formal laments were composed at the death of significant persons (2 Sam. 1:17–27; 2 Chron. 35:25).

2. On the song in this text, see Daniel I. Block, *The Book of Ezekiel, Chapters 1–24*, New International Commentary on the Old Testament (Grand Rapids: Eerdmans, 1997), 770, 775–76.
3. As in Exod. 15:1–8; Judg. 5; 11:34; 1 Sam. 18:7.

Regarding the power of song, the wise man of Israel said, "Like one who takes off a garment on a cold day, or like vinegar on soda, is one who sings songs to a troubled heart" (Prov. 25:20).

First Testament Vocabulary of Music

The rich vocabulary of song, praise, and lamentation found in the First Testament reflects the importance of music in Israelite life generally and worship in particular. The latter is evident in the wide range of musical terms in the Psalter.

"Song, to sing" (šîr). This noun and its cognate verb most often refer to "songs of praise," as is illustrated dramatically in Exodus 15 and Judges 5. The imperative "Sing!" introduces several psalms or sections of psalms: hymnic songs of praise (Ps. 68:4 [5], 32 [33]), thanksgiving for God's works on Israel's behalf (Ps. 105:2 = 1 Chron. 16:9), and eschatological hymns (Ps. 96:1, 2; Isa. 42:10).[4] Psalmists often called for singing "a new song," especially in response to the experience of God's action,[5] but also in hymns declaring confidence in God's final act (Pss. 96:1; 98:1; 149:1; Isa. 42:10; cf. Rev. 5:9).[6]

"To praise, [song of] praise, hymn" (hallēl). While Hebrew *hallēl* expresses rightful praise for someone's good qualities, like that of a man for his wife (Prov. 31:28, 31), self-praise is to be avoided (27:2). In the First Testament praise is usually directed to God; indeed, Israel was chosen for God's glory and praise (Jer. 13:11), to reflect his praiseworthiness by the nation's well-being (Deut. 26:19). Headings like that of Psalm 145 suggest that a hymn (*tĕhillâ*) represents the primary vehicle of praise. Typically such hymns consist of a communal call to praise, followed by a statement of the reasons for praise: YHWH's greatness and grace (Ps. 113), his goodness in electing Israel (Ps. 135), his blessings (Ps. 147:12–20), his covenant love (Ps. 145), and his kingship (Ps. 146). The root *hll* also occurs in some psalms of "thanksgiving" that express gratitude for

---

4. See also the plural in Jer. 20:13 (*///hallēl*). The cohortative, "Let me sing," introduces the Song of Moses (Exod. 15:1) and the Song of Deborah (Judg. 5:3) and hymnic prologues to royal laments (Pss. 89:1 [2]; 101:1). It also concludes Ps. 104:33, a solo hymn. Elsewhere the form introduces vows of praise in individual laments (13:6; 27:6; 57:7 [8]; cf. 108:1 [2]), and the plural counterpart concludes 21:13 [14]. The first-person indicative occurs in 59:16 [17].

5. See esp. Pss. 33:1–3, in the light of vv. 20–22; 40:3 [4]; 144:9.

6. The noun "songs" is used of religious songs in general (Amos 8:3), but also specifically of songs of thanksgiving (2 Sam. 22:1 = the heading of Ps. 18:1; Pss. 28:7; 69:30 [31]), victory (Exod. 15:1), and an eschatological hymn in Isa. 26:1. Psalm 137:3–4 speaks of a special category of "songs of Zion" and "songs of YHWH." Included in this class would be Pss. 48; 76; 84; 87; and 122. Psalms 120–34, the Songs of Ascent, were sung by pilgrims as they climbed the hill to Zion for festival celebrations. See further L. C. Allen, "שִׁיר," in *New International Dictionary of Old Testament Theology and Exegesis* [*NIDOTTE*], ed. W. A. VanGemeren (Grand Rapids: Eerdmans, 1997), 4:99–100.

God's help (Ps. 18:3 [4] = 2 Sam. 22:4; Pss. 34:1 [2]; 40:3 [4]). Lament songs, typically pleading for God to intervene in crises, often conclude on notes of praise.[7] In 69:30–36 [31–37] a vow of thanksgiving turns into an expression of cosmic praise, and in 102:18–22 [19–23] the psalmist anticipates gentiles' joining Israel in praising God in Jerusalem.[8]

"Thanksgiving, to give thanks" (hôdâ/tôdâ). Whereas *hillēl* refers primarily to praise because of God's character and attributes, but also for his kind deeds toward humans, "thanksgiving" songs tend to praise God for specific aid in resolving a crisis.[9] Many individual and communal laments conclude with a declaration or vow of thanksgiving.[10] Occasionally psalmists offer thanks in anticipation of the resolution of a crisis (Ps. 28:7).[11] After opening with a call for thanksgiving, Psalm 118, a royal liturgy, describes the reasons for thanksgiving. Verses 19–21 reiterate the psalmist's determination to give thanks as the royal procession passes through the gate. While Psalm 30:4 [5] calls on the congregation to give thanks, the psalm ends with the psalmist's own resolve to do so. Psalm 138 extends the call to thanksgiving to all the kings of the earth.[12]

The distinctions between psalms of thanksgiving and hymns of praise are not absolute, and the verbs *hillēl* and *tôdâ* often appear together. Psalms 107; 118; and 136 all express thanksgiving for God's attributes, especially his immanent qualities of grace and *hesed*. Hymnic calls for praise often end with thanksgiving.[13] These psalms offer many reasons for praise and thanksgiving: YHWH's creation (33:2–9; 95:2), his kingship (99:4), his faithfulness in giving Israel the promised land (105:1 = 1 Chron. 16:8), his majesty and grace (Ps. 145), his relation to nature and to Israel (Ps. 147), his salvation and judgment of enemies (Pss. 75; 111), and his sovereignty (Ps. 92).[14]

7. As in Pss. 35:18, 28; 63:5 [6]; 71:14; 79:13; 106:47 = 1 Chron. 16:35; Ps. 109:30.

8. See further Allen, "הלל," 1:1035–38.

9. Thanksgiving sacrifices (*tôdâ*) represented a subgroup of "fellowship offering" (*šĕlāmîm*). Manasseh presented thank offerings in response to answered prayer (2 Chron. 33:13, 16). In 2 Chron. 29:31 the thank offering is a response to God for accepting a sin offering. Songs of thanksgiving are mentioned alongside thank offerings in Pss. 107:22; 116:17; and Jon. 2:9 [10].

10. For an individual, see Pss. 7:17 [18]; 35:18; 43:4; 54:6 [8]; 56:12 [13]; 57:9 [10]; 71:22; 109:30; 140:13 [14]; 142:7 [8]. For the group, see 79:13; 106:47 = 1 Chron. 16:35.

11. Thus Ps. 9, e.g., opens with a series of singular cohortative verbs: "Let me give thanks" (*'ôdâ*), "Let me recount" (*'ăsappĕrâ*), "Let me rejoice" (*'eśmĕḥâ*), "Let me exult" (*'e'elṣâ*), and "Let me sing praise" (*'ăzammĕrâ*).

12. Similar endings are found in Ps. 18:49 [50] = 2 Sam. 22:50; Ps. 116:17; Jon. 2:9 [10]. Psalm 107, one of the most impressive thanksgiving psalms, seems to preserve a thanksgiving liturgy. Psalm 100 may have served as a hymnic introduction to a thanksgiving service. Cf. Ps. 118:1, with antiphonal response in vv. 2–4; Jer. 33:10–11.

13. See 1 Chron. 16:41; 2 Chron. 7:3, 6; 20:21; Ezra 3:11; Ps. 106:1 = 1 Chron. 16:34.

14. Laments often conclude with, or are interrupted by, notes of praise (Pss. 42:5 [6], 11 [12]; 43:5; 44:8 [9]; 89:5 [6]). See further Allen, "ידה," 2:405–8.

"To make music/sing praise, song, music/singing, psalm" (zāmar, zāmîr, zimrâ, mizmôr). The root *zāmar* means "to play a musical instrument," usually stringed (Pss. 33:2; 98:5; 144:9; 147:7), but also percussion (149:3), and often involves singing with musical accompaniment (71:22–23). The noun *zimrâ* may mean simply "music" (Amos 5:23) or a song accompanied by instruments (Isa. 51:3). Both noun and verb are often associated with opening calls to praise in communal hymns[15] or renewed calls to praise.[16] In individual hymns, references to making music occur at the beginning (Ps. 146:2) or the end (Ps. 104:33).[17] Some laments call for music, though they may close with promises to give thanks if God answers prayer.[18]

Music as Worship in First Testament Narratives

The Song of the Sea (Exod. 15:1–18). The first reference to music as a part of worship occurs in Exodus 15, which celebrates YHWH's victory over Pharaoh and Israel's liberation from slavery. With exuberant and colorful words, the song focuses entirely on praise to God for his salvation.[19] At first the narrator identifies the singers as "Moses and the sons of Israel" (v. 1), but later he reports that Miriam led all the women in dance to the rhythm of small hand drums while the congregation sang. As elsewhere in the ancient world, women

15. Psalms 33:2; 66:2, 4; 68:4 [5]; 81:2 [3]; 95:2; 105:2; 135:3; 147:1.

16. Psalms 47:6–7 [7–8]; 68:32 [33]; 98:4–5; 147:7; 149:3.

17. Musical accompaniment may highlight calls for universal (Pss. 66:4; 68:32 [33]; 98:4) or permanent praise (104:33; 146:2), though this music may be precipitated by deliverance from enemies (9:1–2 [2–3]; 138:1). In Ps. 18:49 [50] = 2 Sam. 22:50 music ends a thanksgiving psalm; cf. Ps. 30:12 [13].

18. Psalms 7:17 [18]; 57:7–9 [8–10] = 108:1, 3 [2, 4]; 59:17 [18]; 61:8 [9]; 71:22–23; 144:9. In Ps. 21:13 [14] the psalmist promises to give thanks after God gives victory to the king, and in Ps. 75:2–9 [3–10] in response to a divine oracle and its explanation. Prophetic oracles of salvation speak of *zimrâ* (Isa. 51:3), but they also critique worship (Amos 5:23); cf. 2 Sam. 23:1; Job 35:10; Isa. 24:16; 25:5. The noun *mizmôr*, "psalm," is found in the headings of fifty-seven psalms, suggesting that they were to be sung to musical accompaniment. The English word "psalms" is a transliteration of Greek *psalmos*, which derives from *psallō*, "to pluck a stringed instrument." See further Allen, "זמר," 1:1116.

To this list we may add several rarer musical expressions. "To exalt, lift high" (*rômēm*, from the verb *rûm*, "to be high") introduces one thanksgiving psalm (30:1 [2]) and ends another (118:28; cf. 107:32). In Dan. 4:37 [34] the word ends a prayer of thanksgiving; cf. also Pss. 34:3 [4], for deliverance; 66:17, in the context of a lament. The noun *rômaēm* appears only in Ps. 149:6, an eschatological hymn involving praise in the midst of battle against the nations. "To burst into joyful song" (*pāṣaḥ*) expresses joy over redemption from oppression (Ps. 98:4; Isa. 14:7; 44:23; 49:13; 52:9; 54:1). "To praise" (*nāwâ*) appears only in Exod. 15:2. "Cult song" (*maśkîl*) appears in headings of thirteen psalms (Pss. 32; 42; 44; 45; 52–55; 74; 78; 88; 89; 89; 142). "Lament" (*qînâ*) is used in songs of mourning and woe. For discussion of laments as a genre, see R. W. Moberly, "Lament," *NIDOTTE* 4:866–84.

19. Compare also the Song of Deborah and Barak in Judg. 5.

played significant roles as singers and dancers in Israelite worship (see fig. 9.1).

The Song of the Calf (Exod. 32:1–20). Anxious over the disappearance of their leader, Moses, at Sinai the Israelites constructed a golden calf and worshiped it as the god who had brought them out of Egypt. Their celebration was marked by revelry (v. 6), loud singing (v. 18), and dancing (v. 19). By characterizing their worship as boisterous and loud, the narrator mocks idolatry—which is often associated with ecstatic and energetic exercises—because the gods do not hear (cf. 1 Kings 18).

The Anthem of the People of God (Deut. 31:14–32:47). Even though Deuteronomy 32 was dictated by YHWH to Moses (Deut. 32:19–22),

Figure 9.1. Women with tambourines (Photograph by J. Marr Miller. Used with permission.)

it is often identified as the Song of Moses (cf. Rev. 15:3). This remarkable composition, which testifies to the power of song to inspire, motivate, and energize faith, was intended to serve as Israel's national anthem.[20] YHWH explains the need for the song in 31:14–18. As had happened at Sinai, with Moses' imminent death, his restraining influence would be removed from the people, who would break the covenant and abandon YHWH for the gods of the land. Infuriated by their infidelity and ingratitude, YHWH would abandon them, hide his face, and bring on them the disasters spelled out in the covenant curses of Deuteronomy 28:15–68.

Remarkably, to replace Moses and keep the people on the right spiritual course, YHWH provided a song. This lyrical reminder of YHWH's past grace (32:1–14), his warnings against infidelity (vv. 15–25), and his promise of ultimate restoration (vv. 36–43) could go with them to the far corners of the land, testifying to YHWH's faithfulness in spite of the people's infidelity (v. 19). Moses exhorted his congregation to memorize the song because their lives depended upon it (32:44–47). This was not merely an entertaining piece of music; this poetic summary of Moses' sermons in Deuteronomy also contained the keys to life. The Israelites' status as the people of YHWH depended on these lyrics ringing in their ears and taking root in their hearts.

---

20. On which see Daniel I. Block, "The Power of Song: Reflections on Ancient Israel's National Anthem (Deuteronomy 32)," in *How I Love Your Torah, O LORD! Studies in the Book of Deuteronomy* (Eugene, OR: Cascade Books, 2011), 162–88.

This song is remarkable not only for its testimony to the power of music to govern lives but also for the profundity of its theological message. The song teaches that past experience of God's favor is no guarantee of present or future faithfulness, and that prosperity may be more perilous to the spiritual health of God's people than poverty. And it testifies to the power of song. While anthems are generally composed to embody the national spirit and inspire national pride, Israel's anthem was designed to keep alive the memory of YHWH's grace. This was indeed a new song, radically different from the song they had sung in Egypt and the songs of other peoples.

The Sound of Tabernacle Worship

For the modern worship industry, which defines worship primarily in terms of praise music, the biblical picture of tabernacle worship is embarrassing. Although Exodus 15:1–18 says that the Israelites responded to their rescue from slavery with song, the manual that YHWH provided for tabernacle worship (Exod. 25:1–Lev. 16:34) is silent about music, either instrumental or vocal. The nearest we come to it is the charge to blow the shofar to call people for worship on the Day of Atonement (Lev. 25:9),[21] and the ringing of the bells on the priest's robe inside the sanctuary (Exod. 28:33–35).

Some have argued that tabernacle worship was conducted in total silence, but this seems unlikely on several counts. First, vocal and instrumental music was common in worship throughout the ancient world.[22] Second, YHWH prescribed that silver trumpets be blown over whole burnt and peace offerings (Num. 10:1–10). Third, in the context of instructions on worship at the permanent sanctuary, Moses invited the Israelites to come and celebrate (śāmaḥ, "rejoice") in the presence of YHWH.[23] Not only is song a natural expression of joy, but this verb is also often associated with singing and instruments.[24] Fourth, later narratives do not suggest that David's use of vocal and instrumental music before the ark of the covenant in Jerusalem (1 Chron.

---

21. The shofar was also blown to summon the people and marshal the troops on other occasions (Lev. 25:9; Josh. 6:1–21; Ps. 81:3 [4]), perhaps even to commemorate YHWH's appearance on Sinai (Exod. 19:16, 19; 20:18; Pss. 47:5 [6]; 98:6; Joel 2:1). While its usefulness for melodic purposes was limited, Ps. 150:3 suggests that the shofar was used along with other instruments to praise YHWH.

22. See the poetic celebration of the Philistines in Judg. 16:23–24. On the decipherment and reconstruction of a Hurrian musical scale and a Hurrian hymn to Nikkal, the consort of the moon-god in fourteenth- to thirteenth-century-BC Ugarit, see Anne Draffkorn Kilmer, Richard L. Crocker, and Robert R. Brown, *Sounds from Silence: Recent Discoveries in Ancient Near Eastern Music* (Berkeley: Bit Enki Publications, 1976).

23. See Deut. 12:7, 12, 18; 14:26; 16:11, 14; 26:11; cf. also at Gerizim and Ebal, 27:7.

24. Job 21:12; Ps. 5:11; Zeph. 3:14; Zech. 2:10.

16:1–38) and the original tabernacle in Gibeon (16:39–42) was revolutionary.[25] To claim that tabernacle worship involved no music is to argue from silence.[26] Nonetheless, since we hear nothing about planning for music in worship until the time of David,[27] the silence of Exodus and Leviticus renders untenable the contemporary common equation of praise music with worship. Music may indeed be "both worship and an aid to worship,"[28] but it is neither indispensable for nor the primary element in biblical worship.

The Sound of First Temple Worship

David's personal interest in temple music was undoubtedly linked with his personal gifts and accomplishments as a musician. Saul recognized these gifts and hired David as court musician (1 Sam. 16:14–23; 18:10). In the end, David characterized himself as "the pleasant one of the songs of Israel" ("the sweet psalmist of Israel," 2 Sam. 23:1 NASB) and confessed that he was inspired by the Spirit of God in his poetic expression and performance (vv. 1–3). In David we witness the rare combination of deep spirituality, extraordinary musical giftedness, and exceptional organizational acumen.

The Chronicler provides detailed reports of David's involvement in organizing music for the worship of YHWH (1 Chron. 6:16–48 [Heb. 6:1–33]; 16:1–43; 23:1–32; 25:1–31). These texts portray David as the royal patron of the national religion with full authority to organize the temple cult (6:31). Since YHWH revealed to David the blueprint for the temple (28:11–19), we may surmise that he also authorized him to organize the temple cult. Since the Levites who had previously dismantled, transported, and reassembled the tabernacle (Num. 4:1–41) would no longer perform this service, it seems natural that David would assign them special duties associated with the permanent site (1 Chron. 23:1–27:34; esp. David's comment in 23:25–26). David assigned the Levites the task of "serving in song"[29] and appointed

---

25. Contra Peter Leithart, *From Silence to Song: The Davidic Liturgical Revolution* (Moscow, ID: Canon Press, 2003).

26. The repertoire of songs/poems might have included Jacob's blessing of his sons (Gen. 49), the Song of the Sea (Exod. 15:1–18), Balaam's oracles (Num. 22–24), Israel's national anthem (Deut. 32), Moses' blessing of the tribes (Deut. 33), Deborah's Song (Judg. 5), and Hannah's oracle (1 Sam. 2:1–10).

27. For a full discussion of music in ancient Israel, see Joachim Braun, *Music in Ancient Israel/Palestine* (Grand Rapids: Eerdmans, 2002).

28. Andrew Hill, *Enter His Courts with Praise: Old Testament Worship for the New Testament Church* (Nashville: Star Song, 1993), 114.

29. The Psalter suggests that the repertoire of the Levites included pleas for YHWH to have mercy and care for the people (Ps. 46), curses invoked on the wicked (Ps. 58), and recitation of the acts of God on Israel's behalf and on behalf of the king (Pss. 78; 81; 89; 105).

Kohathites to supervise and manage the musicians (6:31–48 [16–33]).[30] The Korahites, whose contributions are reflected in superscriptions of psalms bearing the name of Korah (Pss. 42; 44–49; 84–85; 87–88), formed another group (1 Chron. 6:22 [7]).

In preparation for bringing the ark to Jerusalem, David charged the leaders of the Levites to appoint men from their ranks as singers who should play loudly on musical instruments—harps, lyres, cymbals—to raise sounds of joy (1 Chron. 15:16).[31] He clearly demarked the orders of musicians: Heman, Asaph, and Ethan were appointed to sing with loud cymbals of bronze (15:17–19);[32] their relatives to play harps and lyres (15:20–21; 16:5); Chenaniah to lead the choir (15:22, 27); and priests to blow the trumpets (16:6). David appointed a specific group of Levites "to minister" before the ark, "to commemorate," "to give thanks," and "to praise" YHWH (16:4).[33]

Later David divided the Levitical musicians into twenty-four groups, each consisting of twelve men and yielding a total of 288 musicians (25:7–31). By casting lots for the order of service (25:8), he sought to ensure that the Levites submitted to the will of God, groups would not compete with each other, and everything in temple worship exuded order, glory, and praise—like the overall physical design of the place.[34]

The Sound of Second Temple Worship

Among those who returned from Babylon with Zerubbabel in 538 BC to rebuild the temple were 128 singers, descendants of Asaph (Ezra 2:41), and 200 additional singers, male and female (v. 65). The sons of Asaph played a special

30. The Chronicler's expression is strange: *he'ĕmîd 'al-yĕdê-šîr bêt yhwh*, literally, "David caused them to stand over the hands of song of the house of YHWH" (1 Chron. 6:16).

31. The music to be played and sung in the procession is characterized as "lifting high with sound for joy/celebration" (*hērîm-bĕqôl lĕśimḥâ*, 15:16).

32. Their names are attached to psalms: Asaph: Pss. 50; 73–83; Ethan: 89; Heman: 88. In 1 Chron. 25:1–8 the chief musicians' service is characterized as prophetic ministry, these three being identified as "prophets" (*nābî'*). Since Heman is also referred to as "the king's seer" (*ḥōzēh hammelek*, v. 5), these men obviously enjoyed special status in the court.

33. "To commemorate" often signifies mentioning God or the gods by name (Exod. 23:13; Josh. 23:7; Isa. 62:6; Amos 6:10), and may refer to invoking God in worship (Isa. 26:13; 48:1). When associated with thanksgiving and praise, it refers to commemorative songs of YHWH's past actions. However, since it is also applied to several lament psalms (38; 70), *hizkîr* may be used of reminders before God of one's dire situation. Elsewhere it involves causing a person's name to be celebrated (Ps. 45:17 [18]).

34. In the eighth century BC, Amos condemned empty worship that was not backed up by ethical living, in which case the music was nothing but noise in YHWH's ears (Amos 5:21–24). Later kings apparently tried to revive Davidic musical arrangements and Davidic compositions in worship (Hezekiah, in 2 Chron. 29:25–36; Josiah, in 35:15).

musical role at the dedication of the second temple's foundation (3:10–11). A generation or two later, when Nehemiah dedicated the rebuilt walls of Jerusalem, Levitical musicians from all over the region led the thanksgiving celebrations. The survival of these musical guilds attests to their importance in Israelite life even while in exile.

The contours of the Psalter may have been established by the time the books of Chronicles were written, but variations among the Masoretic text, the LXX, and the Dead Sea Scrolls suggest that the shape and contents of the Psalter were not settled until the time of Christ.[35] In the postexilic period many psalms written over the centuries were gathered into five collections, corresponding to the five books of the Torah. Doxologies at the ends of Psalms 41; 72; 89; and 106 mark the boundaries of these collections, with Psalm 150 serving as a final exclamation of praise to YHWH. The Psalter contains a vast collection of liturgies, meditations, prayers, and hymns, not only to be used in corporate worship but also to inspire and guide believers in every circumstance: when in need of rescue from enemies, healing from illness, vindication in the face of false accusations, and forgiveness for sin; when celebrating personal or communal experiences of divine grace; when bringing sacrifices to the temple; and when the nation was gathered in Jerusalem for the annual pilgrim festivals (Passover, Weeks, Booths).

The Place of Song in New Testament Worship

As in other areas of worship, the early church was influenced by the music of the synagogue as it evolved in the intertestamental period.[36] Borrowing heavily from temple worship, in synagogue liturgies the Psalter was used like a hymnbook. Specific psalms were read on holy days and special occasions, and within the service psalms or portions thereof were read or sung in response to Scripture readings. Liturgical prayers involved quotations of entire psalms or borrowing expressions and excerpts extensively from the Psalter.[37] Instruments played a minimal role, if any at all.[38]

35. On the growth of the Psalter and its use in Jewish worship, see Allen P. Ross, *Recalling the Hope of Glory: Biblical Worship from the Garden to the New Creation* (Grand Rapids: Kregel, 2006), 262–68.

36. For a fuller discussion, see John A. Lamb, *The Psalms in Christian Worship* (London: Faith Press, 1962), 12–17.

37. Jonah's prayer in Jon. 2 looks like a collage of Israel's worship literature.

38. Unlike the segment of Judaism represented by the Qumran scrolls. One scribe wrote,
I will sing with knowledge, and all my music shall be for the glory of God. (My) lyre and (my) harp shall sound for his holy order, and I will tune the pipes of my lips to His right measure. (*Community Rule* [1QS] 10.9)

Music in the Gospels and Acts

It is scarcely coincidental that the four-hundred-year silence of God between the Testaments was finally broken by glorious song. Remarkably, the Gospel most deeply colored by First Testament style of poetry was written by a gentile. Luke's account of Jesus' nativity includes five utterances cast in an elevated Hebrew poetic or semipoetic style: (1) Gabriel's announcement to Mary (1:30–33, 35–38), (2) Mary's response to Elizabeth's blessing (1:46–55), (3) Zechariah's blessing at the birth of John the Baptist (1:67–79), (4) the song of the angels (2:13–14), and (5) Simeon's blessing God at the sight of Jesus (2:28–32). These magnificent utterances were obviously inspired by God, but echoes of Israel's poetic and hymnic tradition suggest that those who spoke them were steeped in texts that had become an important part of Israel's liturgical tradition.

Apart from these poems at the beginning of Luke, references to music in the Gospels are rare. After Jesus instituted the Lord's Supper, those gathered in the room sang a hymn (Matt. 26:30; Mark 14:26). This "singing recitation" probably consisted of the second part of the Hallel Psalms (113–118), which were sung at every Passover.

In Acts 16:25 Luke describes a singular but most unusual worship scene: at midnight Paul and Silas prayed and "made hymns" to God in a prison cell. We do not know what kind of song this was, but in the LXX the word *hymnos* often translates Hebrew *tĕhillâ,* "praise."[39] Remarkably, this is the only reference to music in the book of Acts.

Music in the Pauline Epistles

References to music and song are also rare in the Pauline Epistles, and musical vocabulary is limited.[40] The word *psallō,* "to make music, make melody," occurs three times in Paul's Letters.[41] While the verb *hymneō,* "to sing a hymn," never occurs in his writings, the noun *hymnos* is found in Ephesians 5:19 and Colossians 3:16, alongside *ōdē,* "ode, song."[42]

---

39. Pss. 40:4 [39:4 LXX]; 65:2 [64:2]; 100:4 [99:4]; 119:171 [118:171]. The word also translates *tĕhillâ,* "prayer" (72:20 [71:20]), and *šîr,* "song" (Isa. 42:10). Generally *hymneō* translates *hillēl* (2 Chron. 29:30), though it is occasionally used for *šîr,* "to sing" (Ps. 65:14 [64:14]; Isa. 42:10), and *hôdâ,* "to give thanks" (Isa. 12:4; 25:1).

40. The only New Testament references to the use of the Psalms in corporate worship occur in 1 Cor. 14:26; Eph. 5:18–19; and Col. 3:16.

41. Rom. 15:9 (a quotation of Ps. 18:49 [50]; Hebrew *zimmēr*); 1 Cor. 14:15, "I shall make melody with the spirit and the mind"; and Eph. 5:19. The verb also appears in James 5:13.

42. In the LXX *ōdē* translates *šîr,* "song," as in "a new song" (Ps. 144:9 [143:9 LXX]; cf. Exod. 15:1). The noun appears five times in Revelation (5:9; 14:3 [2×]; 15:3 [2×]) and the cognate verb, *adō* appears an additional three times (5:9; 14:3; 15:3).

Table 9.1. A Synopsis of Ephesians 5:18–20 and Colossians 3:15–17

Ephesians 5:18–20	Colossians 3:15–17
	And let the peace of Christ rule in your hearts,
	to which indeed you were called in one body.
And do not get drunk with wine,	And be thankful (*eucharistoi ginesthe*).
for that is debauchery,	Let the word of Christ dwell in you richly,
but be filled with the Spirit,	in all wisdom teaching
addressing one another (*heautois*) ————————	and admonishing one another (*heautous*),
in psalms (*psalmos*) ———————	with thankfulness (*en chariti*)
and hymns (*hymnos*) ———————	in your hearts (*en tais kardiais*)
and spiritual songs (*pneumatikos*),	to God,
singing (*adō*) ———————	singing (*adō*)
and making melody (*psallō*) to the Lord	psalms (*psalmos*)
with your heart (*tē kardia*),	and hymns (*hymnos*)
	and spiritual songs (*pneumatikos*).
giving thanks (*eucharisteō*)	And whatever you do, do in word or deed,
always and for everything	do everything giving thanks (*eucharisteō*)
in the name of our Lord Jesus Christ, ———————	in the name of the Lord Jesus,
to God the Father. ———————	to God the Father through him.

These two texts are critical for understanding Paul's disposition toward music. They exhibit a common purpose and many common features, as table 9.1 illustrates. What conclusions concerning the relationship between music and worship may we draw from these texts? Although our observations will be based primarily on the Colossians passage, we may summarize the lessons from Ephesians first: (1) Music provides an outlet for demonstrating that one is filled with the Spirit. (2) Music is a means of promoting community in the body of Christ: we sing to one another. (3) Music is an expression of thanksgiving to God; believers need to be thankful in all circumstances. (4) Whether sung or played, music arising from a thankful heart brings great glory to God.

Colossians 3 reinforces these notions. Paul's instructions here should be interpreted within context, where the concern is much greater and deeper than music alone. First, if true worship involves reverential human acts of submission and homage before the divine Sovereign in response to his gracious revelation of himself and in accord with his will, then *true worship* will be expressed primarily by (1) clothing oneself with compassion, kindness, humility, gentleness, and patience; (2) bearing one another's burdens; (3) forgiving one another as Christ has forgiven us; (4) clothing ourselves with love; (5) letting the peace of Christ rule in us; (6) being thankful; (7) letting the word of Christ dwell in us richly; and (8) conducting our lives in the name of Jesus, giving thanks to God through him. In the tradition of Moses and the Prophets, Paul reminds

Colossian believers that truly worshipful music is preconditioned by truly worshipful living.

Second, truly worshipful music binds believers to Christ and to one another. In verse 11 Paul declares that in Christ the barriers have been eradicated between Greek and Jew, uncircumcised and circumcised, barbarian and Scythian, slave and free. Although many ethnic and social barriers remain in American evangelicalism, tragically these have been supplemented by concrete walls of divisive musical taste.

Third, truly worshipful music is an expression not only of Christ's reign of peace but also of the richly indwelling word of Christ. The word *plousiōs*, "richly," speaks of generous abundance and the deep substance of music that honors God. In contrast to the vacuous, repetitious, and mindless music of the world, truly worshipful music is filled with Scripture, the story of redemption, sound doctrine, and the glory of Christ. As an expression of the indwelling word of Christ, truly worshipful song revolves around the Word, rather than song, which is neither the primary focus nor form of worship. Music that glorifies the Father and the Son is driven by the Spirit and the Word. It is not merely emotive (driven by atmospherics), but instructive, didactic, informative, and transformative. Truly worshipful music admonishes the carnal, corrects the sinner, challenges the lazy, reproves the indulgent, encourages the depressed, comforts the sorrowful, and inspires the lethargic. As we saw in Deuteronomy 32, song offers a powerful medium for keeping alive the memory of God's gracious actions and our unworthiness, declaring the nature of holy and godly living, and offering hope in the midst of grief and stress.

Fourth, truly worshipful music is trinitarian. This does not mean that verbal expressions of worship may be addressed indiscriminately to the Father, the Son, and the Holy Spirit. Rather, energized by the Holy Spirit, true worship is directed to the Father, in the name of Jesus Christ.

Fifth, truly worshipful music arises from grateful hearts. That words for thanksgiving occur three times in this text (Col. 3:15, 16, 17) does not mean that lamentation has no place in Christian worship. Even as God's people confess their sin, pour out their grief, and vent their frustrations before him, they do so with deep gratitude, knowing that God hears whenever they call upon him, that his resources are adequate for every trial, and that the sacrifice of Christ is sufficient to cover every sin. Though we may enter the Lord's house with heavy hearts, hearing his words of presence ("I am with you!") comforts and strengthens us to leave with songs of hope and thanksgiving.

Fifth, truly worshipful music is rich in variety and comprehensive in scope. Paul uses three words for music in these two texts. Many understand "psalms" (*psalmoi*) to refer to the Psalter of the First Testament. This is a good place to start, but since the word derives from a root meaning "to pluck," and since the LXX tends to render Hebrew *zimmēr*, "to make melody," with this word, Paul may also have intended a narrower sense of instrumental music. The LXX tends to translate Hebrew *hillēl* as *hymnos*, suggesting that Paul may have used the word here in a narrow sense, referring to songs that glorify God for his attributes and his character. The adjective *pneumatikai*, "spiritual [songs, odes]," does not mean simply spirited music, but songs inspired by the Holy Spirit of God that direct people to Christ and inspire godly living. Spiritual songs have their origin in the Spirit rather than in the idols of novelty, creativity, popularity, fame, or money. Although it is unclear whether "psalms, hymns, and spiritual songs" function as synonyms or reflect three kinds of music, it is clear that together these terms signify all kinds of music.[43]

But how does Paul himself use hymnic material? Recent New Testament scholarship has recognized many poetic fragments embedded in his letters (see appendix B).[44] These texts inspire two observations. First, Paul's hymnic passages tend to focus on Christ. In Romans 11:33–36 he expresses awe at the mystery of God's ways, but when he speaks of Christ, his literary register rises. Second, except for Ephesians 4:4, the Holy Spirit is never mentioned in these passages. This does not mean he is absent. Rather, these all represent the genre of "spiritual odes" spoken of in Colossians 3:16 and Ephesians 5:19: they are songs inspired by the Spirit, who directs people to Jesus (cf. John 16:13–15).

Music in the Book of Revelation

Revelation is punctuated by outbursts of music and singing by a heavenly choir engaged in worship (4:8–11; 5:9–14; 11:16–18; 14:6–7; 15:2–4). These scenes of heavenly worship are significant for several reasons. First, the songs all have a pronounced Jewish flavor, suggesting heavy borrowing from the First Testament and synagogues of Greek-speaking Jews.[45] Second, in each case the singing occurs in the presence of the One seated on the throne and the presence of the Lamb, the only one worthy to open the seals (5:2–5). Third, sing-

---

43. In Hebrew the superlative degree is often expressed by using three semantically related terms. Thus, e.g., when YHWH says in Exod. 34:7 that he forgives "iniquity, rebellion, and sin," this means every kind of offense.

44. Texts that may be classified as hymnic: Phil. 2:5–11; Col. 1:15–20; 1 Tim. 1:17; 2:5–6; 3:16; 6:15–16; 2 Tim. 1:9–10; Titus 3:4–7. Texts that are more confessional than hymnic: Rom. 11:33–36 (incorporating Isa. 40:13–14); 1 Cor. 15:3–8; Eph. 4:4–6; 5:14; 2 Tim. 2:11–13. See also the non-Pauline hymnic fragment found in Heb. 1:3.

45. Thus Ralph P. Martin, *Worship in the Early Church* (Grand Rapids: Eerdmans, 1975), 45.

ing is one element of worship that also includes instrumental music, prayers, and prostration. Fourth, the singing is congregational. In Revelation 5:8–14 everyone in the courtroom sings: the four living creatures, the twenty-four elders, the angels around the throne, myriads of singers, every created thing in heaven, on earth, under the earth, and in the sea. Fifth, the worshipers sing a new song. The concern here is neither creativity nor novelty; the idioms and phrasing are entirely conventional and traditional, as is the expression "new song" itself.[46] This song is new because it celebrates the singer's deliverance from bondage (cf. Ps. 40:1–3 [2–4]), the appearance of Israel's King (Ps. 149:1–9), and the triumph of YHWH over the enemy (Ps. 98:1–3; Isa. 42:10). And it is new because it differs from the songs the world sings and the songs the redeemed used to sing. Sixth, it is a song reserved for the redeemed. Note especially Revelation 14:1–5:

> Then I looked, and there was the Lamb, standing on Mount Zion! And with him were one hundred forty-four thousand who had his name and his Father's name written on their foreheads. And I heard a voice from heaven like the sound of many waters and like the sound of loud thunder; the voice I heard was like the sound of harpists playing on their harps, and they sing a new song before the throne and before the four living creatures and before the elders. No one could learn that song except the one hundred forty-four thousand who have been redeemed from the earth. It is these who have not defiled themselves with women, for they are virgins; these follow the Lamb wherever he goes. They have been redeemed from humankind as first fruits for God and the Lamb, and in their mouth no lie was found; they are blameless. (NRSV)

These 144,000 have obviously met the prerequisites for acceptable worship.

Finally, these songs focus on the person of the Lamb and his saving work. This is evident especially in Revelation 5, which speaks of four dimensions of Jesus Christ's saving actions:[47] (a) the historical fact: he was slain (5:6, 9, 12; cf. Isa. 53:10); (b) the redemptive purpose: to purchase for God people from every tribe, tongue, people, and nation; (c) the ecclesiological accomplishment: they have been made a kingdom and priests for God; and (d) the cosmic goal: they will reign on the earth. Significantly, this song does not obscure the offense of the gospel: the slaughter of the Lamb. This event is the key, explaining why it is such a glorious song. The One seated on the throne and the Lamb have graciously carried out a plan of salvation conceived before the foundation of

---

46. Cf. Pss. 33:3; 40:3 [4]; 98:1; 149:1; Isa. 42:10; Rev. 5:9; 14:3.
47. Cf. Robert H. Mounce's identification of the threefold reason that the Lamb is worthy to open the book, in *The Book of Revelation*, New International Commentary on the New Testament (Grand Rapids: Eerdmans, 1977), 148.

the world[48] by which rebellious sinners, justifiably the objects of divine wrath, are redeemed and transformed into agents of his glory and holiness. This is a glorious song indeed!

The Importance of Song in Worship Today

Having explored the nature and place of music in the Scriptures, we may now reflect on the implications of these biblical perspectives for the role of music in worship today. I devote more space to application here than in preceding chapters because music has become arguably the most divisive factor in North American evangelicalism. Too often in worship wars, pragmatism ("What do people want?") and personal taste ("What do people like?"), rather than biblical perspectives or theology, drive the discussion, and music in worship is often designed to satisfy those whose worship is unacceptable to God. To achieve the highest administrative goal, that people will return next Sunday, the music must create a certain mood,[49] and the service must engage attendees like a theatrical performance or concert.

Delighted—if not intoxicated—by the crowds, we may be oblivious to the reality that a packed house may be proof of disingenuous (calculated) worship rather than worship acceptable to God. Ezekiel exposed the problem in his context in 33:30–33. The prophet was obviously an impressive communicator, and the fact that hardened people came in droves to watch and hear him did not mean that he softened his rhetoric or adopted a more casual and entertaining style. But the excitement of the worshipers could not mask their distorted dispositions toward God and his messenger. In our day the same distortions extend to the way we recruit staff. Ministers of music are hired for their musical skill, achievements, creativity, or enthusiasm on stage, without sufficient concern for their knowledge of Scripture, their orthodoxy, or their theology of worship.

In establishing the appropriate place and style of music in contemporary worship, we need to let the Scriptures inform our thinking about these matters. Some of the reflections that follow represent obvious conclusions from the biblical data already discussed; others are less obvious and may be more colored by my personal convictions. As elsewhere in this volume, my concern here is not to prescribe how individual congregations resolve these issues but to encourage discussion and suggest trajectories for designing worship that is acceptable to God and in accord with his will.

48. John 17:24; Eph. 1:4; 1 Pet. 1:20; Rev. 13:8.
49. Edith Humphrey speaks of preoccupation with atmospherics. See *Grand Entrance: Worship on Earth as in Heaven* (Grand Rapids: Baker Academic, 2011), 157–61.

First, evangelicals must recover music and song as expressions of submission and homage before the divine Sovereign in response to his gracious revelation of himself and in accord with his will. Christians must sing, not out of a sense of duty, but as a natural and spontaneous response to the exhibitions of divine glory in creation (cf. Rom. 1:19–21) and their own experience of salvation. A full citation of Luther's comment alluded to at the beginning of this chapter reflects the attitude we need.

> The worship in the New Testament Church is on a higher plane than that of the Old; the Psalmist refers to this fact when he says: "Sing unto the Lord a new song, sing unto the Lord all the earth." For God has made our hearts and spirits happy through His dear Son, whom He has delivered up that we might be redeemed from sin, death, and the devil. He who believes this sincerely and earnestly cannot help but be happy; he must cheerfully sing and talk about this, that others might hear it and come to Christ. If any would not sing and talk of what Christ has wrought for us, he shows thereby that he does not really believe and that he belongs not into the New Testament, which is an era of joy, but into the Old, which produces not the spirit of joy, but of unhappiness and discontent.[50]

Second, evangelicals must recover the centrality of Christ and the cross in their music. We have observed the christocentric focus of song in the New Testament, both in Paul's poetic fragments and Revelation's doxologies. It is excellent to celebrate God's glory, greatness, and majesty in our music. However, if this is all we sing about, worship may inspire excitement but be little more than a pep rally, with us gloating that we are on the winning side in the great cosmic battle. The Eucharist reminds us that our song must highlight the grace of God in Jesus Christ. Some contemporary songwriters seem hesitant on this point; notions of sacrifice impose upon the lyrics the pain of the incarnation and the cross (Phil. 2:5–11) and force us to confront the cause: our sin (Isaiah 53 put to music does not leave us feeling better about ourselves). However, unless we learn to sing this song first, songs of praise to the glorious heavenly King will not find acceptance with God (cf. Isa. 1). Furthermore, we sing this song because gratitude for divine grace in the cross of Christ grows in direct proportion to our sense of being undeserving and destitute without it.

Third, evangelicals must rediscover that the goal of congregational worship and of all ministry is the glory of God, and that God the Father and God the Son are most glorified when we sing of them and not of ourselves. This reminds us that our songs must be about God's love for us, not about our

---

50. From the foreword to the Valentin Babst *Gesangbuch* (*Geistliche Lieder*) of 1545, as translated by Walter E. Buszin, "Luther on Music," *Musical Quarterly* 32 (1946): 83.

love for him. This will caution us against using many songs that have become popular in our time. The melody of a song lyric like "I love you, Lord, and I lift my voice to worship you, O my soul, rejoice,"[51] is beautiful and easily grasped, but while ostensibly based on Psalm 18:1, the lyrics are questionable on several counts: (a) They are self-laudatory: I am singing about my love for God rather than his love for me.[52] (b) They virtually demand that God must accept my verbal expressions of love. However, as Cain learned, acceptability to God is determined not by cultic expressions of devotion but by one's life. Paul reminds us that whether we speak with human or angelic tongues, if covenant love in keeping with God's will is lacking in our actions, the sounds we produce are merely the din of gongs and clanging cymbals (1 Cor. 13:1). This song implores God to overlook our ethical failures and accept the syrupy and romantic utterances of our lips. (c) Verbal expressions of one's own love for God have no biblical warrant.[53] No one in the First Testament ever tells God, "I love you." Appeals to love God are common (Deut. 6:5), but no authors or characters have the audacity to claim that they measure up to the standard demanded by the word.[54] In any case, love is demonstrated in actions, and only God may judge whether these actions demonstrate true covenant love. The picture does not change in the New Testament.[55] While I would not for-

51. Lyrics by Laurie Klein, 1978. The song is reproduced in many hymnbooks. See, e.g., *The Worshiping Church*, ed. D. P. Hustad (Carol Stream, IL: Hope Publishing, 1990), no. 124, http://www.lyricstime.com/acappella-i-love-you-lord-lyrics.html.

52. The song is dominated by first-person-singular pronouns, including as subject of most of the main clauses, thus by definition making my own love the focus.

53. Compare also the traditional folk hymn "I love Thee, I love Thee." However, the potential offensiveness of the self-laudatory first three lines is ameliorated somewhat by the fourth line, which acknowledges that one's actions—not words—represent the test of love: "But how much I love Thee my actions will show."

54. The verb *'āhab*, "to love," never occurs with a first-person subject (singular or plural) and with God as the object. Psalm 18:1 [2] and 116:1 are not exceptions. In the former, rather than claiming that he loves God, the psalmist creates an awkward sentence. The psalmist wishes to express his positive disposition toward God, but to avoid the impression that God needs pity or mercy, he uses the *qal* form of *rḥm* (which occurs nowhere else) instead of the conventional *pi'el*. He cannot bring himself to tell God he loves him (*'āhab*). The issues are different in Ps. 116:1. Translated literally, the psalmist says, "I love . . . because YHWH hears my voice, my pleas for mercy." The object is missing, presumably because it would be presumptuous to declare explicitly his love for God.

55. In John 21:15–18 Peter refuses to confess verbally his "love" (Greek *agapaō* is equivalent to Hebrew *'āhab*) for Jesus; his threefold denial has proved that he does not. While scholars tend to dismiss his preference for *phileō*, "to love [as a member of the family]," as a stylistic variation, attention to how these notions are expressed in the First Testament suggests an intentional shift, which in the end Jesus is willing to grant (v. 16). For recent defense of this interpretation, see David Shepherd, "'Do You Love Me?' A Narrative-Critical Reappraisal of ἀγαπάω and φιλέω in John 21:15–17," *Journal of Biblical Literature* 129 (2010): 777–92. If 1 John 4:19 ("We love . . . because he first loved us") is thinking about love for God, the apostle expresses the same

bid others from telling God, "I love you," I myself cannot. Mouthing words is easy, but actions represent the real test. If we feel compelled to verbalize our love for God, the lyrics of the classic gospel song, "My Jesus, I love thee, I know thou art mine," by William R. Featherston (1864), are healthier than the words cited above. With these lyrics I acknowledge my sinfulness (v. 1), commemorate Jesus Christ's substitutionary suffering (v. 2), vow a life of devotion and praise (v. 3), and anticipate the eternal glory that is my hope. The lyrics of Henry Twells's "Not for Our Sins Alone" (1889) are even more modest and certainly more in accord with biblical patterns.[56]

1 Not for our sins alone
　Thy mercy, Lord, we sue;
　Let fall Thy pitying glance
　On our devotions, too,
　What we have done for Thee,
　And what we think to do.
2 The holiest hours we spend
　In prayer upon our knees,
　The times when most we deem
　The songs of praise will please,
　Thou Searcher of all hearts,
　Forgiveness pour on these.
3 And all the gifts we bring,
　And all the vows we make,
　And all the acts of love
　We plan for Thy dear sake,
　Into Thy pardoning thought,
　O God of mercy, take.
4 And most, when we, Thy flock,
　Before Thine altar bend,
　And strange, bewildering thoughts
　With those sweet moments blend,
　By Him Whose death we plead,
　Good Lord, Thy help extend.
5 Bow down Thine ear and hear!
　Open Thine eyes and see!
　Our very love is shame,

reserve as the psalmist in Ps. 116:1. He would not be so presumptuous as to declare explicitly that he loves God. On the other hand, in the context of the book, the statement probably means "We love one another because he first loved us," or "We love others because he first loved us."

56. See "Not for Our Sins Alone," *NetHymnal*, http://www.cyberhymnal.org/htm/n/f/n4osalon.htm.

And we must come to Thee
To make it of Thy grace
What Thou wouldst have it be.

Ultimately, we do not praise God by telling him we will praise him any more than we prove we love God by telling him that we do love him. Apart from actually recounting his glorious acts of creation and providence and his gracious acts of salvation, these are empty promises.

Fourth, evangelicals must rediscover that God approves of music rich in content and varied in style. As suggested above, with "psalms, hymns, and spiritual songs" Paul certainly had in mind a wide array of musical forms, richly embodying the Word of God and focused on Christ. And musical form matters. If wise persons recognize the order in the universe and let that order govern their lives, then the symmetry and harmony of their music will celebrate that order and praise the Creator responsible for it. Resisting the chaotic, the disjunctive, and the creative merely for the sake of creativity, robust hymns of praise and thanksgiving inspire and energize by reflecting the perfections of God and the design of his creation.

This does not mean that truly worshipful music is always in a major key, upbeat, and bright. We delude ourselves if through our music we create the impression that believers are always happy. Every assembly of worshipers includes a significant number who have had a distressing week and are scarred by intense grief and pain. It is not helpful pastorally to call these people to "praise God anyhow." Since expressions of frustration and anger with God have been canonized in the lament psalms, Jeremiah, and Job, our music must include opportunities for the troubled to unload their burdens. Communal song offers significant opportunity to lament with those who have fallen into sin and seek restoration with God (Ps. 51), who have experienced disaster and seek relief from the Lord, and who grieve and seek comfort in his presence (Ps. 23). Inspired music may indeed begin in a minor key, confessing the brokenness of the fallen world in general and our lives in particular, but like many psalms, it should end in a major key, celebrating the hope that Christ offers and the peace and joy that he gives.

If we accept that truly worshipful music may be varied in style and substance, who determines the appropriate idiom for worship? If the sacred spaces where we worship are microcosms of Eden and an ideally ordered world, then expressions of that order will also be countercultural. This means that the primary cues for appropriate music will be taken not from the world, which gives full vent to chaos and dysfunction and intentionally resists order, but from heaven, the place of our primary citizenship. When unbelievers witness the beauty and order of Christian worship, hopefully they will be moved to fall on their faces before God, declaring that he is certainly in the midst of his people (1 Cor. 14:25).

Concretely, congregations would do well to begin with psalms (or other biblical texts) set to music. Lyrics drawn directly from the Scriptures should respect their style and tone and involve entire passages, not simply slogans and sound bites to be repeated mindlessly. In addition to music grounded in specific biblical texts, we should also sing hymns that develop the profound theological themes of Scripture. Accordingly, we recognize that for the un-regenerate to sing "Amazing Grace" is fundamentally incongruous, if not outrightly blasphemous. This is the new song of the redeemed.

Fifth, evangelicals must realize that although music is an important element of biblical worship, music should not be equated with worship. The praise-and-worship industry has hijacked the word "worship" and redefined it as "praise music." We took a wrong turn when we accepted this redefinition and separated "proclamation" from worship. Evangelical worship must be rescued from the tyranny of the industry and the idolatry of popular culture. Not only does the Psalter remind us that worship involves every human emotion, but also the silence of Scripture on music in tabernacle worship and the worship of the early church remind us that music is only one (minor) element of worship. Acts 2:42 identifies the "weightier matters" of worship—instruction, fellowship, breaking of bread, and prayer—but says nothing about music. Furthermore, the pattern reflected in Psalm 95 suggests that we respond to the invitation to an audience with God with songs of joy (vv. 1–5), but once we have entered his presence, our mouths are silenced and our ears are opened to receive the life-giving words from his mouth (Pss. 24:5; 95:7c–11). This is the heart of worship. And having heard God speak, we do well to respond with corporate songs of praise and commitment to his will.

We took a second wrong turn when we isolated musicians as "ministers of worship." This is both unfair to those ministers and a violation of the pattern of Colossians 3. If we must use this title at all, it should be reserved for the one through whom the voice of God is heard most forthrightly, the one who reads and preaches the Word. Christ-centered worship is *Word* driven. The songs we sing and the music we play must be subservient to the Word that is read and preached.

Sixth, evangelicals must rediscover the biblical link between music that pleases God and lives that are in tune with his will. Unless we live in daily communion with God, and unless we are clothed with the righteousness of Christ and with garments of righteous living (Rev. 19:8)—governed by the peace of Christ and demonstrating thankfulness to God (Col. 3:12–17; Gal.

5:22–23)—any music we offer is mere "noise, tumult" in God's ears.[57] Regardless of the style of music chosen for worship, if performed with prideful hearts, the harmony of orchestral strains and the rhythm of guitars and drums are reduced to the noise of gongs and clanging cymbals (1 Cor. 13:1).

Seventh, evangelicals must rediscover that truly worshipful music is primarily congregational and unites the body of Christ. The New Testament pattern has everyone engaged, as worshipers sing to one another in psalms, hymns, and spiritual songs. A half century ago it was widely commented that in the United States, eleven to twelve o'clock on Sunday mornings was the most segregated hour of the week, because people of different races could not worship together. While we have made modest progress on these fronts, we could argue that for evangelicals this is becoming the most segregated hour of the week once more, though for completely different reasons. Separating congregations and worship services on the basis of different tastes in music and worship can scarcely be of God. Not only should our songs bring us together, but also older people need to witness the vibrancy and enthusiasm of youth, and young people need to learn from the maturity and experience of their seniors. Because true worship involves worshipers singing to one another, we need to rethink both the structure of our services and the design of our sanctuaries. The more congregations rely on musical professionals, the less the people will sing. And sanctuaries designed like theaters and concert halls are inimical to the growth of the body of Christ.

But how might congregations design the worship service to ensure that its music unites the body of Christ? Here are five considerations.

1. If true worship involves reverential acts of homage and submission, then music should be selected and presented to glorify God and promote reverence and awe. This commitment will naturally result in excluding certain kinds of music (narcissistic and subjective lyrics, jarring and raucous tunes).

2. The music of worship should be subordinate to the Word of worship, and planning should involve all the staff, particularly persons responsible for reading and proclaiming the Word.

3. Songs chosen for congregational singing should be singable, with tunes and lyrics that are readily grasped by worshipers. Worship is not enhanced by improvisation or unexpected rhythms that confuse and inhibit participation.

---

57. Hebrew *hāmôn*, Ezek. 26:13; Amos 5:23. Elsewhere the root used by Ezekiel and Amos applies to the sound of waves (Ps. 46:3 [4]; Isa. 51:15; Jer. 5:22; 31:35) and the noise of a crowd in turmoil and revolt (1 Sam. 4:14; 14:19; 2 Sam. 18:29; 1 Kings 18:41).

4. Assuming commitment to music that has theological and melodic integrity, corporate worship should regularly have something for everyone. Some speak of "blended worship," which connotes a centripetal approach, the emphasis being on satisfying various tastes. Perhaps we should rather speak of "distributed worship," which suggests a healthier centrifugal picture of reaching out and ministering to each other. Instead of asking, "What kind of music will you sing for me?" we might ask, "What kind of music may I sing for you?" In a healthy local manifestation of the body of Christ, people are not preoccupied with self-serving satisfaction of their own tastes. Following the adage "It is more blessed to give than to receive" (Acts 20:35), they minister to each other (fig. 9.2). While it may be helpful for the younger generation sometimes to recast the lyrics of traditional tunes in contemporary melodic forms, for the sake of older worshipers, songs should be sung in ways that minister to them also.

FIGURE 9.2

A Comparison of Blended and Distributive Approaches to Music in Worship

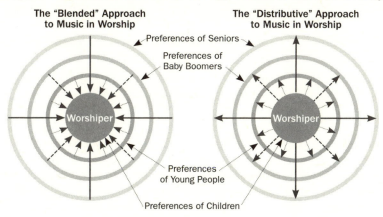

5. Over time, worshipers' musical tastes should mature. While mature Christians celebrate the faith and enthusiasm of younger believers, something is wrong if people who have been believers for ten or twenty years still crave the elementary lyrics and simple tunes they sang when they first came to faith. Just as we need to progress from milk to meat in our understanding of the Scriptures (Heb. 5:12–13; 1 Pet. 2:2), so in musical appreciation and taste the goal should be growth and maturation—the development of appetites for songs that are weightier theologically and more sophisticated musically (fig. 9.3).

While the music of worship should minister to all believers, definitions and standards of true worship arise out of mature reflection based upon intense

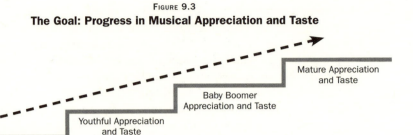

FIGURE 9.3
The Goal: Progress in Musical Appreciation and Taste

study of the Scriptures, a deep passion for God, and a genuine commitment to the community of faith. By definition, letting youthful values and tastes govern worship is hostile to spiritual growth. While the prevailing North American cultural environment idolizes youthfulness and suppresses maturity, the Scriptures call believers to abandon the folly, irresponsibility, and self-centeredness of youth in favor of responsible and self-sacrificing maturity in Christ.[58] We must make every effort to incorporate young people into the community of faith, but contempt for that which the mature treasure insults and marginalizes them and silences the steadying voice of elders.

Eighth, evangelicals must distinguish between worship and entertainment. Charles Spurgeon's distinction between music as entertainment and music as worship is as relevant today as it was in the nineteenth century.

> We would do well if we added to our godly service more singing. The world sings—the millions have their songs. And I must say the taste of the populace is a very remarkable taste just now as to its favorite songs. They are, many of them, so absurd and meaningless as to be unworthy of an idiot. I should insult an idiot if I could suppose that such songs as people sing nowadays would really be agreeable to him. Yet these things will be heard from men, and places will be thronged to listen to hear the stuff.
>
> Now, why should we, with the grand Psalms we have of David, with the noble hymns of Cowper, of Milton, of Watts—why should not we sing as well as they? Let us sing the songs of Zion—they are as cheerful as the songs of Sodom any day. Let us drown the howling nonsense of Gomorrah with the melodies of the New Jerusalem.[59]

---

58. For a telling analysis of the "juvenilization" of the American church and its consequences, see Thomas E. Bergler, *The Juvenilization of American Christianity* (Grand Rapids: Eerdmans, 2012).

59. From a sermon titled "More and More" (Sermon no. 998), delivered at the Metropolitan Tabernacle in Newington, UK, on July 2, 1871. See Charles Haddon Spurgeon, *Spurgeon's Sermons*, vol. 1, http://www.spurgeongems.org/sermons.htm.

There are places and times for God's people to gather for special music pro-grams and professional concerts, and these events may indeed be worship-ful experiences. However, they do not substitute for the regular assembly of believers for an audience with God, and the parameters that govern concert performances should not be allowed to compromise true worship. Ministers of every type may thirst for accolades, and audiences may indulge them with applause, but ultimately, the only person whose approval matters is the Lord. Worship is not about performers on the stage and an audience in the pews; it is about humble submission to the Lord as demonstrated in transformed hearts and lives. The primary purpose of music in worship is neither to create a certain mood nor to attract the unsaved to the service; it is to give voice to the praises and laments of God's people.

Ninth, evangelical leaders must rediscover the primary purpose of wor-ship—an audience with God—and lead in ways that support that agenda. If true worship involves reverential acts of homage and submission, then the goal of all who lead worship is to promote awe before God. Churches must hold ministers responsible for music to the same moral and spiritual standards as they do for those who proclaim the Word. Their function is pastoral. Like the priests of Israel, everything about their daily conduct, as well as their demeanor and appearance before God's people, should inspire respect for the ministry and especially reverence for God. The deportment, dress, diction, and stage manners of all must reflect the gravitas and privilege of representing God before the people. Although definitions of propriety vary from place to place and time to time, casualness in appearance, flippancy of style, and lighthearted and offhanded banter inhibit true worship. Worship leaders are not "masters of ceremony," and worshipful music is not about the musicians, any more than preaching is about the preacher. The primary identification of those who lead in worship is with the God whom they represent before the people.[60]

May the Lord have mercy on us and grant us all patience, both with those who are more mature and with those who are less mature than we. And in the sound and fury of the worship wars, may he make us all instruments of grace and peace for his own glory.

---

60. For this reason we might reconsider from where musicians minister. Among my most memorable worship experiences was the Sunday morning service at the Central Baptist Church in Moscow in 1993. After the reading of Scripture, a holy hush settled on the congregation. Then out of the heavens came the most glorious sound of singing. But there was no choir on the stage. I turned around and looked up at the rear balcony. There they were, fifty messengers of grace, blessing us in Russian, a foreign language for us, but it was indeed the melody of heaven.

10

Sacrifice and Offerings as Worship

True worship involves reverential human acts of submission and hom-
age before the divine Sovereign in response to his gracious revelation of
himself and in accord with his will.

From the dawn of history, human beings have sensed the need to present gifts
to a deity. In the context of worship, these gifts are commonly referred to as
"sacrifices" and "offerings." "Offering" may refer to any gift, irrespective of
kind, motivation, or recipient. However, "sacrifice" is a religious expression,
highlighting the gift as a holy offering to a deity.[1] Furthermore, "sacrifice" is
usually thought to involve immolation, that is, the destruction of the substance
offered: an animal is killed, liquids are poured out, grains and fruits are burned.
For the purposes of this discussion, offerings and sacrifices refer to those gifts
a human being presents to a deity as acts of submission and homage.

The origin of sacrifice is shrouded in mystery. From a sociological and anthropological standpoint, William Robertson Smith argued that sacrifice began
with the slaughter of an animal as a representative of both tribe and deity.[2]
When the people ate the flesh of the sacrifice, the tribe experienced communion
with their deity and ensured their well-being. This interpretation understands

1. The word is composed of two elements: *sacrum*, "dedicated, sacred," plus *facere*, *-fice*,
"to make."
2. William Robertson Smith, *Lectures on the Religion of the Semites: The Fundamental
Institutions*, 3rd ed. (London: Adam & Charles Black, 1927), 225–26.

the primary goals of sacrifice as communal and mystical: to promote spiritual unity within the tribe and communion between tribe and god.

The notion of sacrifice as a gift to a god developed much later, when tribes came under the influence of governments. Henri Hubert and Marcel Mauss agree that sacrifices were gifts, but the purpose of sacrifice was to create a link between the sacred and profane worlds.[3] Since an animal's body belonged to the physical world and its life to the spiritual, it may have served as a mediator. As mediator, the victim was identified with the sacrificer in the moment of consecration. No longer was the gift a mere commodity: "it [was] the subject in objective form."[4]

This gift theory fails to explain the asymmetry of sacrificial events.[5] How can a human give so little (a single animal) and expect so much from a deity (blessing, prosperity, long life, etc.)? Recent anthropological studies propose that by giving so much more than they receive, the gods establish their authority over the person presenting the sacrifice. Even so, there is a degree of equality in the exchange: for a human being to give little is much, and for a god to give much is little.

In ancient Mesopotamia sacrifices were viewed primarily as a means of caring for the gods and feeding them. This care involved providing deities with a temple in which to reside, keeping the faces of the images polished and their bodies regally clothed, and providing the gods with ample food, drink, and incense. These were necessary to keep deities happy and positively disposed toward their subjects and to pacify angry gods.[6]

The First Testament occasionally uses this kind of language in the context of sacrifices. The scent of acceptable sacrifices is often characterized as "a soothing aroma, a pleasing odor" (*rêaḥ nîḥōaḥ*, as in Gen. 8:21). The Scriptures also speak of sacrifices as "offerings of food due me" (Num. 28:2),[7] and the altar as "the table of YHWH" (Ezek. 39:20; 44:16; Mal. 1:7, 12). These formulations were borrowed from surrounding cultures, where it was actually believed that gods ate and drank what people offered them (see Deut. 32:38; Judg. 9:13). However, the psalmist ridicules the literal interpretation of such expressions in Psalm 50:7–15:

---

3. Henri Hubert and Marcel Mauss, "Essai sur la nature et la fonction du sacrifice," *L'Année sociologique* 2 (1897–98): 29–138.

4. Gary A. Anderson, "Sacrifice and Sacrificial Offerings," in *Anchor Bible Dictionary* [*ABD*], ed. D. N. Freedman (New York: Doubleday, 1992), 5:871.

5. So also ibid., 5:872.

6. Thus Mal. 1:9 speaks of "softening/smoothing [*ḥillâ*] God's face"—that is, removing his scowl.

7. Literally, "my offering, my food" (*qorbānî laḥmî*), and "my gifts, my pleasing aroma" (*'iššay rêaḥ nîḥōḥî*); cf. Lev. 3:11, 16; 21:6, 8, 17, 21–22; 22:25; Num. 28:24.

"Listen, my people, and I will speak;
    I will testify against you, Israel:
    I am God, your God.
I bring no charges against you concerning your sacrifices
    or concerning your burnt offerings, which are ever before me.
I have no need of a bull from your stall
    or of goats from your pens,
for every animal of the forest is mine,
    and the cattle on a thousand hills.
I know every bird in the mountains,
    and the insects in the fields are mine.
If I were hungry I would not tell you,
    for the world is mine, and all that is in it.
Do I eat the flesh of bulls
    or drink the blood of goats?

"Sacrifice thank offerings to God,
    fulfill your vows to the Most High,
and call on me in the day of trouble;
    I will deliver you, and you will honor me." (NIV)

The First Testament is clear about the origin and nature of sacrifices in Israel's cult, but it is silent on the absolute origins of sacrifice. The account of Cain and Abel in Genesis 4:3–5 takes this ritual for granted, offering no clues on how they got the idea of communing with God in this way. Did God reveal to Adam and Eve a system of fellowship sacrifices as he expelled them from the garden? Such revelation at the beginning of human history might explain why peoples all over the world sense the need to present offerings to the gods.

Sacrifice and Offerings in Ancient Israel

The breadth of vocabulary for sacrifices in the First Testament reflects the importance of the ritual in Israelite worship.[8] Many of the expressions related to sacrifice were shared with other Semitic peoples, which may explain in part why the Israelites were often tempted to adopt pagan views of sacrifice. However, the Scriptures insist that acceptable offerings and sacrifices are possible only because God has graciously revealed a system of cultic behavior that pleases him. When God's people depart from prescribed patterns, their worship is false.

8. For a fuller discussion of the material offered here, see Anderson, "Sacrifice and Sacrificial Offering," 870–86.

Biblical Evidence for the Origins of Sacrifice

As already noted, Genesis portrays the presentation of offerings to God as spontaneous reverential acts of homage and submission in response to God's revelation of himself through gifts of harvest (Gen. 4), deliverance (8:20–21), providential guidance (12:7–8; 13:4), theophanic revelation (28:18–22), or simply his presence (35:1–15). Abraham's near sacrifice of his son Isaac in Genesis 22:1–10 appears exceptional because YHWH demanded the sacrifice of a human being, but this is the first reported offering in response to an explicit command of God.

While in Genesis sacrifices usually are spontaneous if not instinctive responses to divine grace, almost one-third of the Sinai revelation involved instruction regarding sacrifices.[9] We should not interpret these instructions as burdensome demands but as supreme expressions of divine grace. The "Prayer to Every God," quoted above (in chap. 2), reflects ancient Near Easterners' deep awareness of sin, divine fury, and the need to placate the gods through ritual, whether prayer or sacrifice. However, the cultic systems of the Hittites, Assyrians, Babylonians, Aramaeans, Canaanites, and Egyptians seem to have been developed through trial and error, and worshipers often left cultic events with nagging doubts about their effectiveness. The psalmist was keenly aware of this problem, observing that even though images of the gods were carefully designed with mouths, ears, and eyes, they did not address, hear, or see their devotees (Ps. 135:15–18).

By contrast, the Israelites served the living God, who had introduced himself by name (Exod. 3:13–15; 6:2–8), rescued them from bondage, and called them to covenant relationship with himself. The detail with which YHWH instructed his people on matters of ritual and sacrifice represents an extraordinary gift (Deut. 4:6–8; 6:20–25); in fact, the greater the detail in the prescriptions, the less was left to guesswork and the greater the grace.[10] If God's people would express genuine reverence for him through obedience to the divine will, then their good, their survival, and their righteous standing before him were guaranteed (6:24–25).

The Kaleidoscope of First Testament Sacrifices

General expressions for sacrifice. The most common expression for "sacrifice," *zebah*, derives from the verb *zābah*, "to slaughter, butcher."[11] In a

---

9. Exodus 20:22–26; 23:14–19; 27:1–8; 29:1–30:10; Lev. 1:1–10:20; 14:1–17:16; 20:1–5; 22:1–23:44; 27:1–24; Num. 7:1–9:14.

10. For further discussion of these texts and the privilege of knowing the will of God, see Daniel I. Block, "The Grace of Torah: The Mosaic Prescription for Life (Deut. 4:1–8; 6:20–25)," *Bibliotheca sacra* 162 (2005): 3–22.

11. See Deut. 12:15, 21; 1 Sam. 28:24; 1 Kings 1:9, 19, 25; 19:21; 2 Chron. 18:2; Ezek. 34:3. In Phoenician it had the even broader meaning of "to cook, to prepare food."

sense every slaughter is a sacrifice: an animal gives its life for someone else. However, the verb is often used of specific kinds of sacrifices: whole burnt offerings (Exod. 20:24), peace/fellowship offerings (Exod. 20:24; Deut. 27:7), the Passover offering (Deut. 16:2, 5, 6), and thanksgiving offerings (Ps. 50:14, 23). Although not all altars involved sacrifice, the Hebrew word for "altar," *mizbēaḥ* ("place of sacrifice/slaughter"), comes from the same root.[12] Inside the tabernacle and temple complexes, the altar could be thought of as the hearth on which God's food was prepared.

The noun *zebaḥ* refers to sheep, goats, or cattle slaughtered "to create communion between the god to whom the sacrifice is made and the partners of the sacrifice, and communion between the partners themselves."[13] While offerings could be burned entirely on the altar (1 Kings 3:4), they were often eaten by worshipers as an act of communion with their god (Ps. 106:28) or with associates (Gen. 31:54; 1 Sam. 9:12–14, 22–24). The word was also used of the Passover lamb, eaten in the context of a family celebration (Deut. 16:2, 5, 6).

The word *minḥâ*, "gift, present, tribute," was used of a variety of gifts,[14] especially of tribute given by a vassal to an overlord[15] and as an expression of homage by a worshiper to God. Although the word could apply to animal offerings,[16] Leviticus tends to use it specifically for cereal/grain offerings (e.g., Lev. 2:1–16; 6:14–23 [7–16]).[17] The term *'iššeh* is often translated as "offering made by fire," as if it derives from *'ēš*, "fire," but this cannot be right.[18] Such offerings could be combined with offerings that were burned (Num. 15:25), but the word also refers to items that were not burned.[19] The last word, *nesek*,

12. Altars also functioned as memorials (e.g., Gen. 12:7; Exod. 17:15–16; Josh. 22:21–34; Judg. 6:23–24) or as places of oracular inquiry (2 Kings 16:15).

13. L. Koehler, W. Baumgartner, and J. J. Stamm, *The Hebrew and Aramaic Lexicon of the Old Testament* [*HALOT*], trans. and ed. M. E. J. Richardson (Leiden: Brill, 1994–99), 262. The word applies to both legitimate offerings to YHWH/God (Gen. 46:1; Exod. 3:18) and illegitimate offerings to other gods (generally, Exod. 22:20 [19]; Judg. 16:23), specifically to Asherah (2 Chron. 34:4), Dagon (Judg. 16:23), and their images (Exod. 32:8; 2 Chron. 34:4; Ezek. 16:20).

14. To express political alliance (2 Kings 20:12; 2 Chron. 9:24; Ps. 45:12 [13]; Isa. 39:1), to pacify a person in the face of strained relations (Gen. 32:13–14, 19, 20–21 [21–22]; 33:10; 43:11, 15, 23–24), by an inferior to a superior (Judg. 6:18; 1 Sam. 10:27; 2 Kings 8:8–9).

15. See Judg. 3:15, 17, 18; 2 Sam. 8:2, 6 = 1 Chron. 18:2, 6; 1 Kings 4:21 [5:1]; 2 Kings 17:3–4; 2 Chron. 17:11; 26:8; Ps. 72:10; Hosea 10:6.

16. Cain and Abel's offerings are both *minḥâ*'s, though one involved grain and the other a lamb (Gen. 4:3–5). The offering of Manoah and his wife consisted of a kid and grain (Judg. 13:19, 23).

17. Greek *korban*, "corban," in Mark 7:11 is a transliteration of Hebrew *qorbān*, "gift, offering," which is related to the verb *qārab*, "to be near," and *hiqrîb*, "to bring near, present."

18. The LXX translates the word as *karpōma*, "offering of fruit," as if cognate to *karpos*, "fruit."

19. Wine (Num. 15:10), the priestly allowance from the *šĕlāmîm* (Lev. 7:30–36), the bread of the Presence (Lev. 24:9). The word is linked etymologically to Ugaritic *iṯt*, "gift," and Arabic

"liquid offering" (from *nāsak*, "to pour"), refers to libations poured out il-
legitimately for idols[20] or legitimately for YHWH.[21] The liquid offered could
be olive oil (Gen. 35:14), wine (Exod. 29:40; Lev. 23:13), beer (Num. 28:7), and
even blood (Ps. 16:4). Ritual libations were often associated with grain offerings
(*minhâ*, e.g., Exod. 29:41) and whole burnt offerings (*'ôlâ*, e.g., Num. 28:10).

Whole burnt offerings ('ôlâ, Lev. 1:1–17). These offerings were burned up
completely on the altar, with their smoke/scent rising to God as a "pleasant
aroma," an idiom for an acceptable sacrifice.[22] The daily sacrifices to YHWH,
offered in the morning and evening (Exod. 29:38–42), consisted of a lamb and
cereal and liquid offerings. This offering celebrated YHWH's presence among
his people, so that the later loss of the sacrifice symbolized the severing of
their relationship (Dan. 8:11–12).

Fellowship offering (šĕlāmîm). Usually rendered "peace offerings," the
Hebrew expression comes from the same root as *šālôm*, though the actual
usage is both broader and narrower than this (Lev. 3:1–17; 7:11–18). This offering symbolized "a sacred gift of greeting," a cultic way of saying "*Šālôm!*"[23]
Where First Testament texts do not specify the type of "sacrifice" (*zebah*), they
probably refer to the *šĕlāmîm*, though this word is applied to several specific
types: "thanksgiving offerings" for blessings received (*tôdâ*, Lev. 7:12); "vo-
tive offerings" when deliverance has been received after a vow to God (*nēder*,
7:16); and "freewill offering" as an expression of general thanksgiving (*nĕdābâ*,
7:16). The "Passover sacrifice" (*pesah*, Exod. 12:1–28, 43–51) and "ordination
offering" (*millû'îm*, Lev. 7:37; 8:33) functioned much like *šĕlāmîm*. Unlike the
"whole burnt offering," only the fat and certain organs were burned on the
altar as part of these offerings.

To the broad category of fellowship offerings we should probably add the
consecration (*qiddēš*) of the firstborn of the herd and flock. As a symbolic

---

'*atātu*, "possessions." See further Jacob Milgrom, *Leviticus 1–16: A New Translation with
Introduction and Commentary*, Anchor Bible 3 (New York: Doubleday, 1991), 161–62.

20. As in Isa. 57:6; Jer. 7:18; 19:13; 32:29; 44:17, 19, 25; Ezek. 20:28.

21. See, e.g., Gen. 35:14; Exod. 29:40; Lev. 23:13.

22. Hebrew *rêah hannîhōah* (e.g., Gen. 8:20–21; Exod. 29:41). While never used of sacrifices,
the opposite of a "soothing aroma" is a "stench" (*bĕ'ōš*; e.g., Isa. 34:3; Amos 4:10; Joel 2:20). In
pagan and syncretistic contexts, burning one's child as a "whole burnt offering" was perceived
as the supreme act of devotion to deity (Judg. 11:29–40; 2 Kings 3:26–27).

23. Thus Baruch Levine, *Leviticus: The Traditional Hebrew Text with the New JPS Translation*, NJPS Torah Commentary (Philadelphia: Jewish Publication Society, 1994), 15. Animals
presented as *šĕlāmîm* offerings were ritually slaughtered and eaten by worshipers in the presence
of God as celebrative events (Deut. 27:7), the opposite of the mourning for which Isa. 22:12–14
calls. Since *šĕlāmîm* were presented and consumed in the context of fellowship with YHWH
and other members of the community, scholars often render the word "fellowship offering" or
"offering of well-being" (NJPS, NRSV).

gesture acknowledging that everything belonged to God, Israelites were to con-secrate the firstborn of their flocks and herds. But this sacrifice also provided the Israelites with reminders of their own special standing before YHWH.[24] The animals represented the Israelites themselves; although all the people of the earth belong to YHWH (Exod. 19:5; Ps. 50:12), he had claimed them as his own firstborn son (Exod. 4:22), specially consecrated for priestly service on his behalf. Deuteronomy 15:19–23 specifies that unblemished firstborn males of herd and flock were not to be raised either as draft animals or for their wool, but should provide food for fellowship meals attended by the entire family in YHWH's presence. In addition, this offering reminded the Israelites of YHWH's delight in fellowship with them. Every first birth by a ewe or cow signaled YHWH's invitation to come to the sanctuary, not merely to celebrate the animal's fertility, but also to dine at the table hosted by YHWH himself.

Purification offering (ḥaṭṭā't). Unlike the *šĕlāmîm*, this offering addressed the problem of defilement and impurity (Lev. 4:1–5:13). Because the Hebrew word is identical in form to the word for "sin," this sacrifice is usually called the "sin offering." However, since the word is also used in contexts of ritual defilement where no sin is involved,[25] it should probably be understood more generally as a "purification" or "decontamination" offering. While this sacrifice involved flesh (the fat portions for God, the rest for the priests) to atone for inadvertent sin, much of the ritual activity featured the blood of the animal. The blood was never applied to a person but always to some part of the sanctuary, apparently depending on the worshiper's social class.[26] For a common person it was applied to the altar of the burnt offering *outside the sanctuary* (Lev. 4:30); for the sin of the priest or the community as a whole, it was sprinkled on the incense altar and the veil separating the holy of holies from the outer room *within the sanctuary.*

On the Day of Atonement the blood that atoned for inadvertent sins was sprinkled "in front of the mercy seat," within the holy of holies (Lev. 16:14). Leviticus 4:20, 26, and 31 suggest that when purification offerings were presented for worshipers, atonement for them was actually achieved and sinners were actually forgiven. However, apparently the decontamina-tion did not leave the sanctuary, which necessitated a special annual obser-vance, the holiest day of all, the Day of Atonement (Lev. 16). On that day

24. As in Exod. 13:2, 11–16; 22:29b–30 [28b–29]; Num. 18:15–18.
25. Thus see Lev. 12; cf. v. 7: "The priest shall perform purgation for her [*kippēr*], and she [the unclean woman] shall be clean." See also cases involving Nazirites (Num. 6) and the instal-lation of a new altar (Lev. 8).
26. So also Milgrom, *Leviticus 1–16*, 255.

all the sin and impurity that had accumulated in the sanctuary over the year would be flushed and sent off into the desert, never to be held against the people again.

Leviticus 4:1–35 provides detailed instructions for the presentation of the "purification/decontamination" offering. Again, the ritual could vary, depending on the individual's status—priest, congregation, ruler, or commoner—but the basic procedure involved the following elements: (1) the sacrificial animal was brought to the tabernacle; (2) the worshiper laid his hands on the animal's head; (3) the animal was slain; (4) the blood rites were performed; (5) the animal's remains were disposed of by burning or being eaten; and (6) the priest formally pronounced forgiveness for the worshiper. This was the gospel at work.

Reparation offering ('āšām). Usually translated "guilt offering," this sacrifice sought to make right a wrong previously committed. Unlike most offerings, the *'āšām* could be paid or converted into a monetary equivalent. This offering is not well understood, in part because it applied to so many different situations. A key distinction between it and the purification offering seems to have been the worshiper's awareness of and remorse over guilt. Whereas the purification offering involved inadvertent (unintentional) sins later recognized by the sinner (Lev. 4), with the reparation offering a person felt guilty. The reparation offering sought to restore a broken relationship by the offender's paying full damages for a crime against a person, plus an additional amount. Presumably this was compensation for the emotional and social damage resulting from his crime, even before he brought the offering to the Lord.

Elevation offerings (tĕnûpâ)[27] and *contribution offerings (tĕrûmâ)*. The former involve the breast of the *šĕlāmîm*, the right hind thigh and fat of the ordination offering, and metals used in building the tabernacle,[28] but the nature of the offering is obscure (Lev. 7:28–34). The latter (commonly "heave offering") is equally obscure (e.g., Lev. 7:14, 32; Num. 18:28).[29] These words seem to represent two ways of dedicating something to YHWH. The former ritual occurred in the sanctuary, and the latter outside the sanctuary, either by oral declaration or physical manipulation.[30]

27. The common rendering "wave offering" assumes that *tĕnûpâ* derives from *nûp*, "to move back and forth," in front of the altar or before YHWH. Presumably the gift was placed on the palms and held up to YHWH as a rite of dedication. See further ibid., 430–31, 461–72; R. E. Averbeck, "נוף," in *New International Dictionary of Old Testament Theology and Exegesis* [*NIDOTTE*], ed. W. A. VanGemeren (Grand Rapids: Eerdmans, 1997), 3:63–67.

28. See Jacob Milgrom, *Numbers*, 425–26.

29. The word *tĕrûma* refers to an offering that is set apart as a consecrated gift, with the ritual transferring the object from the owner to God.

30. See further Averbeck, *NIDOTTE*, 4:335–37.

The Effectiveness of Sacrifices for First Testament Believers

Beyond the physical dimension, how did Israel's sacrificial system work? Leviticus 4–5 makes it clear that the sacrifices, particularly the purification and reparation offerings, worked when practiced according to the revealed will of YHWH: "The priest shall make atonement for the sin that he has committed, and he shall be forgiven."[31] This is also evident in David's exclamation in Psalm 32:1–2.

> Oh the privilege/joy of those whose transgression is forgiven,
>   whose sin is covered!
> Oh the privilege/joy of those to whom YHWH imputes no iniquity,
>   and in whose spirit there is no deceit.

But on what grounds did Israelites experience forgiveness of sins when they performed these rituals? And how are we to reconcile these texts with Hebrews 10:1–4, which declares that it is impossible for the blood of bulls and goats to take away sins?

Some answer these questions by arguing that when godly Israelites brought their sacrifices, they looked forward to Christ (Messiah), whose death would ultimately atone for their sins. However, the Pentateuch provides no evidence that First Testament believers expected a future Messiah to take the punishment for their sins and die in their place. Indeed, the revelation given at Sinai and associated with God's covenant with Israel is completely silent on a future Messiah.[32] The association of a messianic figure with sacrifice and substitutionary death occurs for the first time in Isaiah 52:13–53:12.[33] Here the rich tradition of atonement found in Israel's sacrificial theology and the tradition of the royal Messiah are conjoined in a glorious symphony of grace. However, by Isaiah's time Israel had been performing sacrifices at the tabernacle and temple for centuries—without a trace of messianic hope in the ritual itself.

If the Israelites did not see the Messiah in the priesthood or the sacrificial system until Isaiah 53, then how did they experience forgiveness? It is clear that when Israelites worshiped God, expressing their homage and submission

---

31. As in Lev. 4:20, 26, 31, 35; 5:10, 13, 16, 18; 6:7; also 19:22.

32. This is not to deny Messianic anticipation in the Pentateuch (cf. Gen. 3:15; 22:17 [singular "seed" of Abraham]; 49:10; Num. 24:17), but none of these are associated with Sinai or Moses, or the sacrificial system.

33. The First Testament portrays the Messiah ("Anointed One") as a fundamentally royal character who is a Davidic figure (1 Sam. 2:10; 2 Sam. 7). For a discussion of ancient Israel's view of the Messiah, see Daniel I. Block, "My Servant David: Ancient Israel's Vision of the Messiah," in *Israel's Messiah in the Bible and the Dead Sea Scrolls*, ed. R. S. Hess and M. D. Carroll R. (Grand Rapids: Baker Academic, 2003), 17–56.

with sacrifices in response to God's revelation and in accord with his will, they knew they were forgiven; God accepted their worship. But on what grounds? How can we reconcile the author of Hebrews, who writes that only the sacrifice of Christ can take away sin, and the repeated declarations of the priest that worshipers actually experienced forgiveness when they performed these rituals (see n. 31 above)?

The question may be answered from two perspectives. First, when First Testament saints presented sacrifices in faith, they based their hope of forgiveness on the word of God. Although the story of Cain (Gen. 4) and many other texts[34] demonstrate that mere performance of rituals does not guarantee divine favor or forgiveness of sin, YHWH had graciously revealed to the Israelites a way this could happen. The desired effect depended on worshipers' trust in the word of God and their covenant commitment to him. If they came to the ritual with clean hands and a pure heart (Pss. 15; 24), God would forgive them.

Second, when God observed faith demonstrated in a pure life and rituals performed as he instructed, he applied to that person the forgiveness made possible through the blood of Christ, whose redemptive work was "foreknown" (*proginōskō*)[35] and who was slain "before the foundation of the world." First Peter 1:18–21 summarizes the divine plan.

> You were ransomed from the futile ways inherited from your forefathers, not with perishable things such as silver or gold, but with the precious blood of Christ, like that of a lamb without blemish or spot. He was foreknown before the foundation of the world but was made manifest in the last times for the sake of you who through him are believers in God, who raised him from the dead and gave him glory, so that your faith and hope are in God. (ESV)

Within the broader context, 1 Peter 1:12–21 declares that the plan of salvation based on the sacrificial work of Christ was designed before the world was created, and that the provision of redemption through the shedding of the blood of the unblemished Lamb was the time-space manifestation of this divine plan. We find additional hints of God's redemptive work prior to creation elsewhere in the New Testament. Matthew 13:35 announces the revelation of a mystery—the inauguration of the kingdom of heaven—concealed since the day when God laid the foundations of the earth. Elsewhere Jesus himself declares that those who are blessed by his Father inherit the kingdom prepared for them "from the foundation of the world" (Matt. 25:34). In John 17:24 Jesus expresses his longing that those whom the Father has given him would

---

34. See Ps. 51; Isa. 1; Mic. 6:6–8.
35. For similar use of the verb, see Rom. 8:29; 11:2.

see the glory the Father gave him because he loved him "before the foundation of the world." However, Paul provides the most remarkable statement in Ephesians 1:3–10.

> Blessed be the God and Father of our Lord Jesus Christ, who has blessed us in Christ with every spiritual blessing in the heavenly places, even as he chose [*eklegomai*] us in him *before the foundation of the world*, that we should be holy and blameless before him. In love he predestined us for adoption as sons through Jesus Christ, according to the purpose of his will, to the praise of his glorious grace, with which he has blessed us in the Beloved. In him we have redemption through his blood, the forgiveness of our trespasses, according to the riches of his grace, which he lavished upon us, in all wisdom and insight making known to us the mystery of his will, according to his purpose, which he set forth in Christ as a plan for the fullness of time, to unite all things in him, things in heaven and things on earth. (ESV)[36]

The basis of forgiveness is the same for all: the sacrificial work of Christ—though we on this side of the cross have full revelation of the objective reality.

While the Sinai revelation seems to be silent on the person and work of the Messiah, we may still recognize hints of this in the divine provision of forgiveness to Israel. In Exodus 25:8–9, 40, YHWH instructed the Israelites to construct a residence for him, according to the "structure of the dwelling place" (*tabnît miškān*) that he would show him. Although *tabnît* is usually translated "pattern," it seems that Moses saw more than a blueprint or model.[37] Elsewhere *tabnît* usually refers to the object itself, rather than a copy or a plan of the object.[38] This raises questions concerning what YHWH showed Moses on the mountain. It seems he opened the windows of heaven, enabling Moses to see the heavenly reality, of which the tabernacle would be a replica. The LXX supports this interpretation by translating *tabnît* as "paradigm" (*paradeigma*) in Exodus 25:9 and as "type" (*typos*) in 25:40. This interpretation

---

36. Revelation 13:8 declares that the names of God's people are written "in the book of life belonging to the Lamb that was slain from the creation of the world" (cf. 17:8).

37. According to 1 Chron. 28:19, YHWH used his own handwriting in revealing to David all the structural details for the temple.

38. See Deut. 4:16–18 (the forms of idolatrous images); Josh. 22:28 (the structure of an altar); Pss. 106:20 (the form of an ox); 144:12 (the structure of a palace); Isa. 44:13 (the form of a man); Ezek. 8:3; 10:8 (the form of a hand); Ezek. 8:10 (the forms of all kinds of creatures). None of these texts involves a copy or plan; at issue is the object itself. Thus 2 Kings 16:10 may be an exception that proves the rule: "King Ahaz sent to Uriah the priest a model [*děmût*] of the altar, that is, its form/structure [*tabnît*] according to its entire construction." Obviously he did not send him the altar itself, but here the depiction is represented by *děmût*, "likeness," not *tabnît*, "structure, form."

accords perfectly with the book of Hebrews, which juxtaposes a series of expressions to describe the relationship between the tabernacle and the heavenly residence of God (table 10.1). On the mountain, Moses apparently saw the true heavenly dwelling of YHWH and then received instructions to have the Israelites construct a replica in which the sacrifices and rituals would represent the singular heavenly sacrifice of the true Lamb of God.

Table 10.1. The Relationship between the Heavenly Temple and the Earthly Tabernacle

Designations for the Heavenly Dwelling of God	Designations for the Earthly Dwelling of God
"type" (*typos*) Exod. 25:40; Acts 7:44; Heb. 8:5	"replica" (*hypodeigma*) Heb. 8:5; 9:23 "antitype" (*antitypos*) Heb. 9:24
"true" (*alēthinos*) Heb. 8:2; 9:24	"shadow" (*skia*) Heb. 9:24
"heavenly" (*epouranion*) Heb. 8:5; 9:23	"earthly" (*kosmikon*) Heb. 9:1 "of this creation" (*ktiseōs*) Heb. 9:11 "handmade" (*cheiropoiētos*) Heb. 9:11, 24

To clarify this concept an analogy from the sporting world might be helpful. The oldest trophy in North American professional sport is the Stanley Cup. Only one Stanley Cup exists; it is stored in the Hockey Hall of Fame in Toronto. Every year, each member of the winning team receives a replica of the trophy to display at home. Although the replica is not the real object, players display it proudly as a symbol of the reality located elsewhere. Similarly, the replica tabernacle and its rituals pointed to YHWH's heavenly temple and the sacrifice of Jesus Christ to which the triune God had committed himself before the foundation of the world. Whether or not Moses saw the sacrificed Son of God in the heavenly sanctuary, this sacrifice alone provides the grounds for our forgiveness and the forgiveness of the Israelites.

To explain how this worked, we might use another analogy from the world of electrical engineering. When we flick a light switch, neither we nor the switch creates light. Light is produced by energy constantly flowing through the circuits. In the sacrificial system, God graciously provided the Israelites with a "light switch": the ritual actions in the tabernacle triggered the application of divine power—the power to forgive made possible by the sacrifice of Christ.

The author of Hebrews was right: the blood of bulls and goats could not remove the Israelites' sins (Heb. 10:4). However, when faithful and godly Israelites trusted in the promise of God and presented their sacrifices as instructed by him, their sins were atoned for by Christ's sacrificial death. It is doubtful that many, if any, in ancient Israel understood the relationship between their replica actions and the real sacrifice of Christ. However, the efficacy of the rituals did not depend upon full and perfect knowledge; it depended on YHWH's word. Having presented their offerings in faith, faithful Israelites could rejoice in his forgiving grace.

The Tithe in the First Testament

"Tithe" is an old English rendering of Hebrew *'ăśîrît*, "tenths," a special class of offerings given by an inferior to a superior. Although the New Testament has little to say about the tithe (see Matt. 23:23), the First Testament presents this concept as a way to meet the economic needs of the worship center and of marginalized Israelites.

Precursors to the Israelite Tithe

Although we generally associate the tithe with Israel's cultic system, the concept did not originate with Moses. Upon Abraham's return from rescuing his nephew Lot, Melchizedek, the king of Salem and priest of El Elyon, invited him to a communion meal of bread and wine. Having received the Canaanite king's blessing in the name of El Elyon, the patriarch spontaneously offered him a tenth of the spoils of war (Gen. 14:17–20). Later Jacob responded to YHWH's appearance at Bethel by vowing to return one-tenth of all that God would give if he would return to this place (28:22). In both instances the narrator assumes familiarity with the custom, offering no clues about the origin or purpose of tithes.

Official Regulations concerning the Tithe

The conclusion of Leviticus suggests the Sinai revelation ended with regulations concerning the tithe (Lev. 27:30–34). Anticipating settled life in the promised land, YHWH challenged the Israelites to treat the tithe of all produce, whether from the field or herds, as holy and belonging to YHWH. However, the generosity and flexibility of the tithe regulations are striking. If people wished, they could redeem their tithe of the crop—presumably with silver shekel weights (cf. Num. 18:16; Deut. 14:24–26)—instead of in kind, provided they added one-fifth of its commercial value, apparently as compensation for the convenience. Also, the laws of purity applying to sacrificial offerings did not apply to tithes. Animals to be presented to YHWH were to be selected randomly as they passed under the rod—that is, as they were entering or leaving the fold. Whether the lot fell on a desirable or a weak specimen, it was not to be exchanged.

Numbers 18:21–32 supplements these regulations, providing a partial answer to the function of the tithe in Israel. People were to pay it to the Levites in return for their divine service. However, the Levites in turn were to offer to the high priest a tithe of the tithe that they received from the people. Unlike the animals randomly selected by the people, the Levites were to be selective, giving the priest only the best part. Since the Levites had no land, these tithes were the food supply for their households. Although they could consume it wherever they lived, they were to treat all the gifts brought to them as sacred and dedicated to YHWH. Failure to do so was a capital offense (Num. 18:32).

The Tithe in Deuteronomy

In Moses' second address to the Israelites on the plains of Moab, he offered pastoral instructions on tithing in three contexts. Far from being an economic or psychological burden, he presented the tithe as an extraordinary privilege and a remarkably humanitarian institution.[39] First, each call for the tithe was associated with an invitation to worship, specifically to eat and celebrate in the presence of YHWH.[40] Moses invited them to do so as entire households, including sons and daughters and male and female servants, but they were also to bring along the Levites in their towns, since the Levites had no land from which to draw their sustenance (Deut. 12:12, 18–19).

Second, Moses' instructions regarding tithes were remarkably generous. If the distance to the central sanctuary placed unrealistic or unreasonable burdens on worshipers, they could bring the equivalent amount in silver, with which they could purchase the necessities for the sacred meal (14:24–26).

Third, the tithe represented both an offering of thanksgiving for YHWH's gracious provision and an opportunity to reach out to marginalized members of the community. In addition to the Levites (Deut. 12:12, 18–19; 14:27, 29; 26:11–13), Moses specified the tithe as a means of caring for aliens, the fatherless, and widows (14:27–29; 26:12–14). He reinforced this notion with a call for a triennial tithe to be deposited in the gates of Israelite towns for the benefit of these vulnerable people. Inviting the poor to join in pilgrimages to the central sanctuary would meet their spiritual needs as they participated in corporate worship. But the benefits of these tithes would not extend beyond

39. Like the sabbatical years and the year of release for indentured servants (Deut. 15).
40. The verbs in Deut. 12:5–6 and 14:24–26 should be understood modally: "There you *may* go, and there you *may* bring your burnt offerings, . . . and there you *may* eat before YHWH your God, and you *may* celebrate, you and your households, in all that you undertake, in which YHWH your God has blessed you" (emphasis added).

the festive occasions. This tested the Israelites' commitment to their neighbors, reminding them that true worship involves more than correct liturgy: it also involves everyday compassion toward those in need.

Fourth, the tithe offered an occasion to highlight the difference between Israelite religion and Canaanite fertility religion. The ritual of the triennial tithe provided an occasion for worshipers to acknowledge not only that this produce was evidence of YHWH's blessing on the land but also that the land itself was a gift (Deut. 26:15). Furthermore, it offered an occasion to confess before YHWH that they had been faithful to the covenant in all respects (vv. 13–14). While caring for the poor was but one element of conduct according to the covenant, the deposition of the triennial tithe offered the Israelites an opportunity to declare their dependence on YHWH and to invoke his continued blessing on their labors and their land (14:29; 26:15).

The Tithe in the Prophets

Although the prophets often condemn the Israelites for oppressing the poor rather than caring for them, prophetic references to the tithe are rare. In Amos 4:4–5 the eighth-century prophet refers sarcastically to Israel's observance of cultic regulations even while they are guilty of all sorts of humanitarian crimes. In Malachi 3:7–12 the postexilic prophet begins his discussion of tithing with a pointed question: "Will a man rob God?"[41] In keeping with the disputational style of the book, the prophet quotes the people's plea of innocence: "Who, we? How have we robbed God?" Malachi's answer is cryptic: "In the tithe and the offering [těrûmâ]."[42] Having forgotten Nehemiah's appeal to deliver their tithes to maintain the temple ministry (Neh. 13:10–13), apparently the entire nation was languishing under a curse, presumably some form of crop failure (Mal. 3:9–11; cf. Deut. 26:12–14; 28:15–24).

Malachi's answer for this tightfistedness involves a requirement and a challenge. God demands that those who have withheld their offerings bring all that is due, so there may be food in YHWH's house. Fidelity to the covenant expressed in generosity at YHWH's house is a prerequisite for divine blessing. Then God invites the people to "test" him (Mal. 3:10b).[43] This is remarkable: YHWH invites the people to challenge him to prove that he is the faithful, covenant-keeping God. Under normal circumstances, to test YHWH is a sign

41. The word for "defraud" or "rob" (qāba') is common in later Jewish writings but rare in the First Testament. Outside this context (Mal. 3:8–9 [4×]), it appears only in Prov. 22:23.

42. See the brief discussion above, p. 72. In Exod. 29:27–28; Lev. 7:32; and Num. 5:9, the word applies to special contributions for priests.

43. Elsewhere this word bāḥan is used of testing the purity of gold (Job 23:10; Zech. 13:9).

of faithlessness.[44] But God reserves the right to suspend his own principles and is free to invite his people to test him.[45] In this exceptional instance he invites the people to test him, to see if he will not respond positively to generous giving. To those who accept the invitation, YHWH offers three promises (vv. 10–12): abundant rain, so that the fields will produce more than the people need; removal of the causes of the present failures in fields and vineyards;[46] and the blessing of the people around, when they see their prosperity.

Although Malachi's appeal for generosity in offerings for YHWH's work obviously applies to Christians (2 Cor. 9:7), we must be careful how we apply the prophet's specific message in our day. Not only must we be cautious about equating our material well-being with the well-being of the kingdom of God, but we must also be clear about the relationship between giving and getting. To give—even to worthy causes—in order that we may get reduces Christianity to a fertility religion. Although generosity is indeed a precondition to blessing, Deuteronomy portrays it as the supreme expression of gratitude for grace already received. Furthermore, giving should always be driven by concern for the honor of God. In keeping with Malachi's central thesis, the people's tightfistedness was on par with irreverence in worship (1:6–14), indifference to God's instruction (2:1–9), infidelity to marital covenants (2:10–16), and cynicism about God's justice (2:17). By offering incentives for generosity, charities often appeal to the lowest motivation. Passion for the glory of God and gratitude for his favor should be sufficient. People concerned about God's honor will support his work, his servants, and his place of worship generously, irrespective of return. Without fear of God, there is no gratitude for his grace; and without fear of God, contributions become self-interested investments.

Summary Observations on the Tithe

The First Testament presents four basic purposes for the tithe in Israel: (1) Practically, it provided a means to support priests and other cultic personnel. (2) Socially, it was a means of securing the well-being of the poor. (3) Nationally, it provided a precondition for God's blessing. And (4) spiritually, it provided a means for expressing a worshiper's fear of God. The First Testament

---

44. As Moses declared (Deut. 6:16) and Jesus affirmed (Matt. 4:7; Luke 4:12). Such testing calls for punishment: Exod. 17:2, 7; Num. 14:22; Pss. 78:18, 41, 56; 95:9; 106:14.

45. See his invitation to Ahaz in Isa. 7:11. The exceptional nature of YHWH's invitation in Malachi here is reflected in the addition of *bāzō't*, "in this" (Mal. 3:10), that is, "in this [exceptional] context."

46. The "devourer" (*'ōkēl*, Mal. 3:11) may refer to locusts (cf. Joel 1:4) or to a disease that causes vines to lose their grapes.

does not portray the tithe as prepayment for personal material gain. Within the context of Israel's entire cultic system, the tithe offered a concrete way of demonstrating gratitude, pure faith, and reverence toward God.

The historical accounts provide little information on how faithfully the Israelites observed the tithe ordinances. Perhaps exceptionally, 2 Chronicles 31:5–6 and 12 notes that in the context of Hezekiah's reforms the people enthusiastically brought their tithes to the temple. During the governorship of Nehemiah, the people living in and around Jerusalem for a time at least seem to have observed these regulations (Neh. 10:37–38; 12:44; 13:4–14). Beyond these notes our information on Israel's performance is limited.

Second Temple authorities added a host of minute regulations to the comparatively simple principles of the First Testament tithe, so that in Jesus' day a beautiful principle had been transformed into a grievous burden. Scrupulous tithing even of mint, dill, and cumin was demanded to earn acceptance with God (Matt. 23:23; cf. Luke 11:42). However, Jesus insisted such scrupulosity was no substitute for the weightier matters of Torah (Matt. 23:23–24): fearing God, walking in his ways, loving God, serving with one's whole self, and obeying wholeheartedly (Deut. 10:12–13).

Sacrifice and Offering in the New Testament

The Kaleidoscope of New Testament Sacrifices

Although the role of sacrifices shifts radically as we move to the New Testament, the breadth of vocabulary for "sacrifice" and "offering" is retained. The primary word for sacrifice in the New Testament is *thyō, thysia*, "to sacrifice, sacrifice, offering." Since in the LXX this root generally translates Hebrew *zābaḥ* and its cognates, it is not surprising that in the New Testament the word is used both in the common sense, "to slaughter, butcher,"[47] and in the sacred sense, "to kill a sacrificial victim."[48] The New Testament reiterates the First Testament principle that obedience is better than sacrifice (Matt. 9:13; 12:7; Mark 12:33; Heb. 10:8). The author of Hebrews emphasizes that while sacrifices at the tabernacle and temple were legitimate and effective means of maintaining covenant relationship in the old order, they have been superseded by the work of Christ. Paul also speaks of Jesus Christ as the supreme sacrifice. In Ephesians 5:2 he celebrates the amazing love of Christ, demonstrated in Christ's giving himself up as an offering and sacrifice to God, which God

47. See Matt. 22:4; Luke 15:23, 27, 30; Acts 10:13; 11:7, "Kill and eat."
48. Of the Passover Lamb: Mark 14:12; Luke 22:7; 1 Cor. 5:7.

received as a fragrant aroma.[49] In 1 Corinthians 10:18 he speaks of the Eucharist as a sacrificial meal; all who eat at the Lord's Table share in the body of Christ, just as in Israel those who ate sacrifices shared in the altar.

The word group involving *thysia* is also used for other offerings. Paul characterized the gift that the Philippians sent to Jerusalem through Epaphroditus as a fragrant aroma, an acceptable sacrifice, well-pleasing to God (Phil. 4:18). Picking up a First Testament theme, Hebrews 13:12 calls on believers to offer up a sacrifice of praise to God: the fruit of lips that give thanks to his name.[50] According to 1 Peter 2:5, Christians are being built up into a spiritual house for a holy priesthood to offer spiritual sacrifices (*pneumatikas thysias*) acceptable to God through Jesus Christ. Peter does not explain the phrase, but the rest of the chapter suggests that he means righteous living and bearing the name of the Lord in ways that honor him. This accords with Hebrews 13:16, which speaks of sacrifices involving good deeds and sharing. Paul took this notion a step further, saying that he himself was being poured out as a libation over the sacrificial offering of the Philippians' faith (Phil. 2:17).

However, as noted earlier,[51] we find the most comprehensive statement of Christian self-sacrifice in Romans 12:1, where Paul precisely recaptures the Mosaic vision of worship involving all of life.

> I appeal to you, therefore, brothers and sisters, by the mercies of God, to present your bodies [*sōmata*] as a living sacrifice, holy [*thysian zōsan hagian euareston*] and acceptable to God, which is your reasonable/logical service [*logikēn latreian*].

While Paul's statement here is striking, the concept is not new: Paul has recast some of the Shema (Deut. 6:5) in sacrificial language.

Another expression frequently linked with sacrifices and offerings is *prospherō*/*prosphora*, "to present/an offering." This verb often occurs with *dōron*, which may refer to a "gift" of tribute (Matt. 2:11; cf. Ps. 72:10) or to sacrifices presented in the temple or on the altar.[52] The verb is also used with *thysias*, "sacrifice,"[53] and the noun as "offering" for sin (Heb. 10:18). In a striking statement, Paul speaks of himself as a minister of Christ Jesus to the gentiles, as a priest ministering the gospel of God, so that his offer-

---

49. Greek *eis osmēn euōdias*, "as a soothing aroma" (Eph. 5:2), answers to *rēaḥ hannîḥōaḥ* in the First Testament (e.g., Gen. 8:21).

50. Cf. Pss. 27:6; 50:14, 23; 69:30–31 [31–32]; 107:22; 116:17. These texts do not view verbal expressions as substitutes for sacrifices, but as Moses instructs the people in Deut. 26:1–15, many of the sacrifices were accompanied by verbal expressions of thanksgiving.

51. For a fuller discussion of Rom. 12:1, see pp. 21–22 above.

52. See Matt. 5:23–24; 8:4; Heb. 5:1; cf. 8:3–4; 9:9.

53. As in Acts 7:42; Heb. 10:11; 11:4.

ing consisting of the gentiles might be acceptable, sanctified by the Holy Spirit (Rom. 15:16). Hebrews uses the expression repeatedly of the sacrifice of Christ: (a) Because he offered himself, Christ does not need to offer up daily sacrifices (7:27). (b) Christ offered himself without spot or blemish to cleanse the believers' conscience from dead works to serve the living and true God (9:14). And (c) Christ was offered once for all, to bear the sins of many (9:28; 10:10–14).

While James describes Abraham's sacrifice of Isaac as "offering up" (*anapherō*, James 2:21), elsewhere this word is applied to Christ in several different ways. First Peter 2:24 declares that Christ himself "offered up" our sins in his body on the cross that we might die to sin. In addition to speaking of Christ "offering up" himself (Heb. 7:27), Hebrews uses the word of offerings that Christians bring: sacrifices of praise to God (Heb. 13:15) and spiritual sacrifices acceptable to God through Jesus Christ (1 Pet. 2:5).[54]

The vocabulary of sacrifice is missing in Philippians 2:5–11. However, this beautiful ode to Christ offers a most impressive picture of Jesus' substitutionary sacrifice, while calling believers to follow him, being ready to give up their lives for the sake of others.

> In your relationships with one another, have the same mindset as Christ Jesus:
>
> Who, being in very nature God,
>> did not consider equality with God something to be used to his own advantage;
> rather, he made himself nothing by taking the very nature of a servant,
>> being made in human likeness.
> And being found in appearance as a man,
>> he humbled himself by becoming obedient to death—
>> even death on a cross! (Phil. 2:5–8 NIV)

The Lamb as an Image of Sacrifice in the Scriptures

It is appropriate that I should be reflecting on this subject on the Saturday between Good Friday and Easter Sunday. This is indeed the most blessed season of the year, as believers all over the world unite in their celebration of the sacrifice of Jesus Christ, the Son and the Lamb of God, who was

---

54. In addition to these general expressions for sacrifice, Mark 12:33 and Heb. 10:6, 8 refer to whole burnt offerings (*holokautōma*), and as already noted, Paul speaks of his own life as a libation poured out on behalf of those to whom he is called (Phil. 2:17; 2 Tim. 4:6).

slain in our place that we might live. The metaphor of Christ as the Lamb sacrificed for sins represents one of the most powerful images in the New Testament.

The First Testament provides background to the metaphor from several perspectives. First, although the sacrifice had nothing to do with atonement, in Genesis 22:13 God provided a ram that Abraham offered up as a whole burnt offering in place of his beloved son Isaac. In verse 7 Isaac had innocently asked his father, "Where is the sheep?" to which Abraham replied, "God will provide" (v. 8). Neither father nor son knew that the provision would be a ram caught in the thicket.

Second, the instructions for the Passover sacrifice in Exodus 12:1–5 call for the slaughter of a sheep and the daubing of its blood over the doorways of Israelites' houses to prevent the death of the firstborn in the family. The sacrificial animal was to be a perfect specimen, less than one year old, slaughtered as a substitute for the firstborn.

Third, lambs were commonly sacrificed as purification, or "de-sin" offerings. Although Leviticus 4:1–31 suggests that bulls and male goats are the default sacrificial animals, verses 32–35 allow female lambs as well.[55] Unlike the ram that substituted for Isaac, and unlike the Passover lambs, this creature was sacrificed to atone for sin.

Fourth, Isaiah 53 portrays the Servant of YHWH as a lamb led to the slaughter (v. 7), who offers himself as a reparation offering (ʾāšām, v. 10) and bears the sins of many (v. 12). This Lamb, a Davidic figure, is the Messiah, who dies for the sins of the people. In a gloriously ironic inversion, the shepherd of the sheep takes on the form of a sheep and gives his life for them.[56]

A consideration of Christ as the "Lamb of God" must begin with the portrayal of the Passover in the New Testament. Only four of thirty-one references to Christ as the Lamb occur outside the book of Revelation. Although 1 Peter 1:19 does not refer explicitly to the Passover, the language obviously derives from the original Passover and exodus narratives (e.g., Exod. 6:6; 13:13, 15), with references to the precious blood and the unblemished lamb. In the Greek text, 1 Corinthians 5:7 does not mention the lamb, but Paul declares that since "Christ our Passover has been sacrificed," we should celebrate the feast of deliverance "with the unleavened bread of sincerity and truth" (v. 8).

Luke links Jesus with the Passover when describing his first encounter with the public: on the Passover he was doing his Father's business in the temple,

55. See also Lev. 5:6–7; 9:3; 12:6–8; 14:13; Num. 6:14.
56. See further Block, "My Servant David," 49–55.

listening to the teachers of Torah and quizzing them (Luke 2:41–46). Thereafter in the Synoptic Gospels, the Passover surfaces only in the context of the Passion Narratives. They all note that the Jewish authorities plotted to kill Jesus and that he had his Last Supper with the disciples at Passover.[57] In each account Jesus presents himself as the head of a household of faith: he arranges for the Passover meal, which he transforms from a memorial of the exodus to a memorial of his own substitutionary death and ratification of the new covenant.

The Passover is more prominent in the Gospel of John, which associates the cleansing of the temple with the Passover (2:13, 23) and notes that as Jesus headed for Jerusalem, he signaled the ominous significance of the Passover for himself (6:4). Like the other evangelists, John links the Jewish authorities' plot to seize Jesus with the Passover (11:55–57). With obvious conceptual echoes of Exodus 12–13, Caiaphas remarked on the expedience of one man's dying for the people rather than an entire nation's perishing (John 11:50–51). Six days before the festival, Jesus announced his imminent burial (12:1–8). Later, John highlights the irony that those responsible for Jesus' death were scrupulous about Passover purity and custom (18:28, 39; cf. 19:31) but did not realize that they were committing the supremely defiling act by killing the true Passover Lamb.

While John's overall vision of the life and work of Christ perceives Christ as the new Passover victim, his grasp of Jesus Christ as "the Lamb of God" goes beyond this image. At his first appearance in the Gospel, John the Baptist formally introduces Jesus twice with "Behold the Lamb of God who takes away the sin of the world!" (John 1:29, 36). The expression "the Lamb of God" (*ho amnos tou theou*) is not found in the First Testament. On the surface, the genitive phrase suggests this is "the lamb that God would provide," as he had for Abraham, except that John adds, "who takes away the sin of the world." Since neither Genesis 22 nor the Passover lamb had anything to do with sin,[58] the expression "Lamb of God" alludes specifically to Isaiah 53:6–7, which presents the Lamb as the sacrifice for the sins of humankind. Like the Lamb of Isaiah 53, Jesus went to his death willingly; but unlike the Passover lamb, not a bone of his body was broken (John 19:36; cf. Exod. 12:46). Philip's conversation with the Ethiopian eunuch in Acts 8:32 reinforces the idea that Jesus' earliest followers perceived him as the Suffering Servant and Lamb of Isaiah 53.

---

57. See Matt. 26:1–5, 17–19; Mark 14:1–2, 12–16; Luke 22:1–2, 7–16; so also John 11:55–57.

58. The use of *amnos* rather than *probaton* for "lamb" also distances this statement from the Passover lamb. In Exod. 12 the LXX consistently renders Hebrew *śeh*, "sheep," as *probaton*; but *amnos* is common with reference to lambs sacrificed at the tabernacle (e.g., Lev. 12:6, 8).

The Lamb in the Book of Revelation

In the book of Revelation John mentions the Lamb more than two dozen times.[59] Whereas First Testament theophanies involved YHWH seated on his throne, the last theophany in Scripture features the Lamb. The logic of the Christo-theological portrayal proceeds as follows: Jesus is the Lamb; Jesus is God; therefore, the Lamb is God.[60] This means that worship of him is practically inseparable from the worship of God (see Rev. 5:11–14). In a sense Revelation as a whole is an exposition of John the Baptist's introduction: "Behold the Lamb of God who takes away the sin of the world." By this interpretation "Lamb of God" means "the Lamb who is God." Jesus Christ is indeed the Lamb that God provides and the Lamb who leads us to God, but he is more than this: Christ is God himself.

The image of the Lamb is ironic. On the one hand, he is slain and sacrificed (Rev. 5:6), but on the other, he is conquering and triumphant, the one to whom the entire cosmos is entrusted. The Lamb is a messianic figure: the lion of the tribe of Judah, the root and offspring of David, and the bright morning star (5:5–6; 22:16).

The Lamb's relationship to his redeemed people is established through the marriage supper (Rev. 19:1–10). The ancient covenant formula that had governed YHWH's relationship with Israel was "You shall be my people, and I will be your God" (e.g., Lev. 26:12; Jer. 30:22). In Revelation 21:3 this ancient covenant formula is implemented in the context of the new heaven and new earth, encompassing not only Jerusalem or Israel but also people from every tribe and nation, all whose names are written in the Lamb's book of life.

Revelation emphasizes that the Lamb's worthiness to receive worship is based on his sacrificial accomplishment: he was slain, and thereby he has purchased saints from every tribe and nation, a kingdom and priests to serve God and reign on earth (5:9–14). Jesus' self-sacrifice is the means whereby God's eternal plan for his people and the cosmos is fulfilled.

Reflections on Sacrifice and Offerings for Christians Today

If true worship involves reverential acts of submission and homage before the divine Sovereign in response to his gracious revelation of himself and in accord with his will, how should Christians respond sacrificially? This question may be answered from several angles.

59. In Rev. 5:6, 8, 12, 13; 6:1, 16; 7:9, 10, 14, 17; 12:11; 13:8; 14:4a, 4b, 10; 15:3; 17:14a, 14b; 19:7, 9; 21:9, 14, 22, 23; 22:1, 3.
60. See J. R. Miles, "Lamb," *ABD* 4:133.

First, rather than feeling sorry for First Testament saints obligated to express their faith with complex and seemingly endless sacrificial rituals, we should rejoice with them that YHWH revealed to them a way of fellowship and forgiveness that actually worked and solved their deepest spiritual problem. When they brought their offerings with pure hearts and righteous lives, they knew they were forgiven!

Second, fully aware of Jesus' role in the redemptive plan of God, we should offer humble homage and praise to Christ, the supreme sacrifice. Although Jewish believers observed the temple rituals as long as the temple stood, the message became increasingly clear: the sacrifice of Christ terminates the practice of literal sacrifice. New Testament writers regularly used First Testament language to describe Christ's sacrifice (cf. Eph. 5:1–2), but since he offered himself once for all, no more sacrificial offerings for the forgiveness of sins are needed. Jesus is indeed the perfect high priest, who needs no sacrifice for himself and has direct access to the heavenly tabernacle (Heb. 4:14–5:10; 7:26–8:6; 9:1–10:18). He is also the perfect and true sacrifice whose death alone makes divine forgiveness available to any human being in history.

Third, the First Testament principle "to obey is better than sacrifice" still stands (Matt. 9:13; 12:7; Mark 12:33; Heb. 10:8). The case of Ananias and Sapphira in Acts 5:1–6 reminds us that any ritual act of worship or sacrifice is repugnant to God if not matched by humility and righteousness in everyday life. Although New Testament believers are not obligated to keep First Testament sacrificial laws, the sacrifice required of Christians equals or exceeds that demanded of First Testament saints. The Lord calls us to offer ourselves as living sacrifices, and Jesus provides the model of self-sacrificing devotion to others (Phil. 2:5–11). Like Jesus, we are to take up our crosses and follow him (Matt. 10:34–39; Luke 9:23–24). For many this will involve more than daily self-denial; some will be called to give up their lives for the sake of the gospel, the well-being of the church, and the glory of God (cf. 2 Cor. 12:12; Phil. 2:17; 2 Tim. 4:6). This is true worship in response to the mercies of God (Rom. 12:1).

Fourth, evangelicals must be cured of their schizophrenic disposition toward biblical regulations concerning sacrifices and offerings. On the one hand, our leaders constantly declare that First Testament cultic laws no longer apply, but on the other, they cajole and pressure God's people to tithe. Their hypocritical appeals to an Israelite institution are apparently necessitated by two factors: (1) The New Testament makes no provision for a Christian equivalent to the Israelite tithe.[61] Churches and Christian charities need money and are

---

61. Matt. 23:23 comes the closest; Jesus rebukes the Jewish authorities for neglecting the weightier matters of Torah (justice, mercy, and faithfulness) while scrupulously tithing mint and dill and cumin. They should have done both.

dependent on the goodwill of God's people for it, but the New Testament does not prescribe a means for achieving this. (2) When the New Testament speaks of giving, the images are unrealistic and excessive and cannot be taken literally. This applies to the widow who embodied authentic piety by donating to the temple treasury all she owned (Mark 12:41–44), and to the rich young ruler whom Jesus challenged to sell all and give to the poor (Matt. 19:16–22). The only instructions focused on giving occur in 2 Corinthians 8:1–9:15, where Paul commends the Macedonian Christians for their generosity. However, here Paul presents an exemplary rather than prescribed model. These references exhaust New Testament teaching on what could remotely be considered Christian counterparts to tithes and offerings.

And so, even as they reject the application of Israel's other religious ordinances, ministers resort to First Testament proof texts to prick their peoples' consciences. Even then, they rarely take their cues from the constitutional literature but quickly appeal to Malachi 3, which is turned into a trump card for an evangelical version of an ancient fertility religion. Although rarely expressed so crassly, appeals for donations based on this text tend to proceed something like this:

> God expects his people to prosper, to be healthy, happy, and rich. After all, is he not a loving Father who delights in giving to his children? Furthermore, does his reputation not depend upon how well he provides for his own? Perhaps the reason you are not prospering or your business is failing is that you have not been giving your tithe to God. Take up Malachi's challenge. Test God. Start giving and see what he will do. God will take the little that you give him and multiply it many times over.

Indeed, some in effect reread Jesus' statement in Matthew 6:33 as "seek first the kingdom of God *so that* all these things may be added to you."[62] This not only inverts Jesus' intention but also flies in the face of consistent biblical calls for self-sacrifice rather than self-interest. True worship is expressed not by giving so we may get, but by giving because we have already freely received above and beyond what we deserve. Paul declares the New Testament principle in 2 Corinthians 9:7: "God loves the person who gives with enthusiasm." A generous spirit—which imitates Christ, who loved the church and gave himself for her (Eph. 5:25)—is the mark of deep reverence for God and of love for his people and his work. Deep-seated gratitude will be expressed by openhearted and openhanded generosity.

---

62. Compare Oral Roberts's second principle of "seed-faith": Give that it may be given to you. *The Miracle of Seed-Faith* (Grand Rapids: Fleming H. Revell, 1970), 17–20.

11

The Drama of Worship

True worship involves reverential human acts of submission and homage before the divine Sovereign in response to his gracious revelation of himself and in accord with his will.

Inspired by Willow Creek Community Church in South Barrington, Illinois, many churches now feature dramatic performances in Sunday morning services. Drama can be a powerful tool to seize attention, lower defenses so people are ready to receive the Word of God, illustrate biblical truth, and show how that truth may apply to life.

But this chapter is not about the use of drama *in* worship: our concern is the drama *of* worship. In the former, drama is used for rhetorical purposes, integrated with other aspects of the service to achieve a desired effect in the audience. Such dramatic performances may involve simple gestures, symbolic actions, responsive readings, or short skits. Their goal is rhetorical—to enhance communication to worshipers. This differs from the drama of worship, which perceives participation in worship as participating in God's great drama of redemption. God's people are not merely actors playing roles but actants in God's plan of redemption, which moves toward the eschatological triumph of his kingdom. What is more dramatic than Abraham's nearly sacrificing his son, the Israelites approaching Mount Sinai for an audience with God, Elijah's encounter with God at Horeb, or Jesus' washing his disciples' feet? And for worshipers today, what is more dramatic than partaking of the body and blood of Christ in the Lord's Supper?

Christians today would do well to reconsider their fascination with drama *in* worship and replace it with delight in the drama *of* worship. At its best, all worship is drama—entering the presence of God and celebrating, reliving, and actualizing his grace in life. If the weekly audience with God is perceived in dramatic terms, its goal is neither to entertain God nor to entertain spectators. Rather, it is to draw God's people into the cosmic drama of redemption, calling them to celebrate his grace and sending them out as redemptive agents of that grace.

The Drama of Worship in the First Testament

The First Testament is replete with appeals to Israel to keep alive the memory of God's creation and salvation. Three primary institutions helped to achieve this goal: the heptadic (seven-day and seven-year) rhythm of life; national festivals reenacting Israel's experience;[1] and ad hoc memorials and remembrances.[2] We will explore how the first two sought to keep alive the memory of YHWH's gracious acts of salvation, his covenant, revelation, and daily providential care.

Texts like the Shema suggest that faithful Israelites viewed all of life as sacred and that every deed was an act of worship. Those who love YHWH with all their heart/mind (*lēb*), being (*nepeš*), and resources (*mĕ'ōd*, Deut. 6:4–5) will also devote all time to him. In effect, every day is holy. However, just as some places and persons are exceptionally holy, so are certain times (fig. 11.1). Since Israel's sacred calendar involved both weekly and annual holidays, the issues in the chronological scheme are more complex than in either the spatial or the human scheme. Distributed throughout the year and concentrated at critical points in the calendar, particularly sacred "holidays" ("holy days," *qōdeš*) provided constant reminders that all of life was holy (fig. 11.2).

---

1. To national festivals we should add private and family observances: consecration of the firstborn (Exod. 13:1–16; Deut. 15:19–23), presentation of firstfruits of the harvest (Deut. 26:1–11), and the tithe (Deut. 14:22–27; 26:12–15).

2. Including written (e.g., the Book of YHWH's Victories, Exod. 17:14) and monumental memorials (crossing the Jordan, Josh. 4:6–8, 21–24); memorials to the spiritual unity of Israel (Josh. 22:26–29); covenant renewal (Josh. 24:25–27); and victories over enemies (e.g., the Philistines, 1 Sam. 7:12).

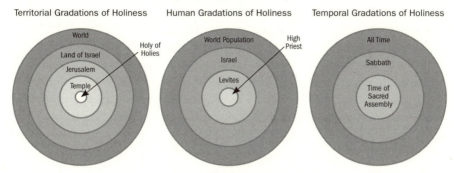

FIGURE **11.1**
Gradations of Sanctity

FIGURE **11.2**
Asymmetrical Temporal Gradations of Holiness

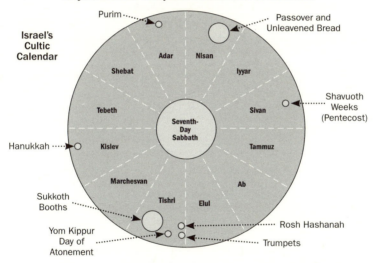

These holidays were "sabbaths." This word may designate any day that one abstains from normal work. However, Israel's economic and religious rhythm distinguished between two kinds of sabbaths: the weekly seventh-day "Sabbath," and "sabbaths" (plural) scattered throughout the year, including festivals at the beginning of a new month (new moon festivals)[3] and the annual festivals of Passover and Unleavened Bread, Weeks/Harvest (Shavuoth, Pentecost), Trumpets (Lev. 23:23–25), the Day of Atonement (Lev. 16:1–31), and Booths/Tabernacles (Sukkoth).

3. See Num. 29:6; 1 Sam. 20:5, 18, 24, 27; 2 Kings 4:23; Ezra 3:5; Ps. 81:3; Isa. 1:13; 66:23; Ezek. 46:1; 46:6; Amos 8:5.

The Seventh-Day Drama of Life

As elsewhere in the ancient Near Eastern world,[4] the number seven is the most significant number in the Bible, both in the First Testament[5] and in the New.[6] Although the search for the origins of a seven-day week outside the Bible has been fruitless, anthropologists speculate that it derives from the lunar month: twenty-eight days divided into four parts. While this could explain the seven-day week, it scarcely accounts for seven-year cycles, which are also common.[7] Furthermore, it overlooks the biblical data that root Israel's heptadic week in the pattern of God's actions in Genesis 1–2.

The Purpose of Israel's Seventh-Day Sabbath

While the narratives of Genesis give no evidence of the patriarchs' observing a seventh-day Sabbath, Exodus 12:15–20 and 16:22–30 suggest that their descendants observed a six-plus-one rhythm of time long before the ordinance on Sabbath-keeping was embedded in the Decalogue. The Scriptures do not trace the origins of this Sabbath, but they offer several explanations of its purpose. First, the Sabbath offered rest to people weary of workaday efforts to sustain life. By itself the word *šabbāt* carries no theological freight. It does not mean "to rest," but means simply "to stop, to desist." However, structured

4. See J. Friberg, "Numbers and Counting," in *Anchor Bible Dictionary* [*ABD*], ed. D. N. Freedman (New York: Doubleday, 1992), 4:1143–45. The number seven figures prominently in the ancient Mesopotamian epic of Gilgamesh. A group of seven gods, the Anunnaku, play an important role in the Babylonian story of Atrahasis and the Flood. The ziggurat at Uruk was seven stories high. In the Canaanite mythological texts from Ugarit (Ras Shamra), El and Asherah are the parents of seventy gods and goddesses. These texts describe the cycle of lean years as seven years in which Baal fails, eight in which the Rider of the Clouds provides no dew or rain.

5. God threatened sevenfold vengeance on anyone who would harm Cain (Gen. 4:15); seven lambs confirmed an oath (21:29–30); Balak built seven altars for Balaam on which he sacrificed seven bulls and seven rams (Num. 23:1,14, 29); the menorah had seven wicks (Exod. 25:31–37; Zech. 4:2); on the Day of Atonement blood was sprinkled on the cover of the ark seven times (Lev. 16:14, 19); lepers were washed seven times (Lev. 14:7, 16, 27; cf. 2 Kings 5:10). Note also the Table of Nations, which lists seventy nations descended from Noah (Gen. 10). Jeremiah predicted that the exile would last seventy years (Jer. 25:11).

6. This fascination with seven is especially prominent in Revelation: seven churches (1:4), seven candlesticks (1:12), seven stars (1:16), seven angels (1:20), seven fire lamps (4:5), seven spirits of God (1:4; 3:1; 4:5), a book with seven seals (5:1), a lamb with seven horns and seven eyes (5:6), seven angels with seven trumpets (8:2), a dragon and a beast with seven heads (12:3), seven last plagues (15:1), seven golden bowls (15:7).

7. Jacob worked seven years for each of his wives (Gen. 29:20); Egypt experienced seven years of good crops and seven years of famine (41:53–54); the Israelites picked manna for six days, but on the seventh there was none (Exod. 16); the Israelites marched around Jericho every day for seven days (Josh. 6:8–10); Samson's wedding festival lasted seven days (Judg. 14:12); Nebuchadnezzar was mad for seven years (Dan. 4:16, 23, 25, 32).

after the divine paradigm, the Sabbath was intended primarily as a day of rest and refreshment. Although Genesis 2:1–4a does not speak of God as "resting" (*nûaḥ*), this word appears in Exodus 20:11 with God as the subject. Exodus 31:17 is even more explicit: "On the seventh day he "ceased" working [*šābat*] and was refreshed." The last verb in this verse, *wayyinnāpaš*, means in effect "to catch one's breath" and is obviously an anthropomorphism—God never wearies (Isa. 40:28)—but it reflects the practical function of the Sabbath: this was YHWH's gracious gift to Israel, an invitation to leave the work of the week and rest.

Second, the Sabbath provided a means by which Israelites could declare their fundamentally theological perspective on the cosmos and on life. The Exodus version of the Decalogue (Exod. 20:8–11) grounds the human pattern of work and rest on God's calendar at creation. After working six days, God "stopped from all his work" and "blessed" and "sanctified" the seventh day. By using the same vocabulary, the third command draws Israelites into the drama of God's own creative activity and declares the conviction that God created all things.

Third, the Deuteronomic version of the Decalogue grounds the Sabbath ordinance on humanitarian considerations (Deut. 5:12–15). Remembering what it was like to work without rest in Egypt, heads of households were to ensure that everyone in their domestic unit enjoyed a day off: sons and daughters, male and female servants, even draft animals and foreigners in their midst (cf. Exod. 23:12). By granting Sabbath rest to all, heads of households were to participate in God's deliverance instead of ruling their households like miniature pharaohs. Furthermore, by welcoming the Sabbath, they celebrated their transfer of status from being slaves of the heartless Pharaoh of the exodus to being the privileged vassals of a Redeemer, who called them to covenant relationship, set them high above the nations (Deut. 26:16–19), and granted them one day of rest in seven.

Fourth, the weekly Sabbath functioned as a sign of YHWH's irrevocable covenant with his people (Exod. 31:12–17). Like the divine words of creation in Genesis 1, YHWH's speeches in Exodus 25–31 climax in the seventh speech, which is in effect an exposition of the Sabbath ordinance. Echoing Genesis 9:12–17, the key word *'ôt*, "attesting sign, mark" (Exod. 31:13, 17), suggests that the Sabbath was related to the covenant that YHWH made with Israel in the same way that the rainbow was related to the cosmic (Noachian) covenant: both were signs of God's eternal commitment. By sanctifying the seventh day, Israelites acknowledged that YHWH had set them apart as his holy people (v. 13). Failure to observe the Sabbath was a capital crime (v. 15), presumably because it signified rejection of YHWH, who sanctified them, and repudiation of his covenant; the Sabbath is an irrevocable sign (*'ôt hû' lĕ'ōlām*, v. 17) of an eternal covenant (*bĕrît 'ôlām*, v. 16).

Finally, the seventh-day Sabbath served as a constant test of Israel's fidelity to and trust in YHWH. By adhering to the six-plus-one rhythm of life, they declared their dependence on YHWH to provide for them in six days what they would need in seven. Thus the seventh day was both an invitation to delight in YHWH's rest and a challenge to submit to him with reverence and awe.

The Nature of Israel's Seventh-Day Sabbath

Despite the Sabbath's importance, the First Testament provides little information on how Israelites actually observed it. Verbs associated with the seventh day include "remember, take note of" (*zākar*, Exod. 20:8), "keep" (*šāmar*, Exod. 31:14; Deut. 5:12), and "do, execute" (*'āśâ*, Exod. 31:16). According to the pattern set by YHWH, the Israelites were to rest (*nûaḥ*) on the Sabbath and to bless (*bērēk*) and sanctify it (*qiddēš*, Exod. 20:11; cf. Gen. 2:3). To sanctify this day did not mean that only the seventh day was holy, any more than sanctifying the priests meant that only they were holy. Not only had Yahweh sanctified all the people of Israel but also for laypeople every day was sacred.[8]

Whereas physical objects were consecrated by anointing with oil, the First Testament never describes how the seventh day was consecrated. The enigmatic expression *miqrā'-qōdeš* in Leviticus 23:3 provides the best clue. Since *miqrā'* derives from the root *qārā'*, "to proclaim, to call out," *miqrā'-qōdeš* probably refers to a day set aside by a "holy proclamation," perhaps like calls to prayer from the minarets of mosques.[9] Numbers 10:2 prescribes the manufacture of two silver trumpets to be blown to summon the Israelites to move on during their trek from Sinai to the promised land. It is doubtful that each village or town would have had a silver trumpet, but shofars made of ibex or rams' horns would have been plentiful. Blown at sundown on the sixth day, the sound of the shofar would not summon people to assemble for worship, but

8. See Exod. 31:13; Lev. 20:8, 26; 21:8; 22:32; Deut. 7:6; 14:2, 21; 26:19; 28:9. Similarly, consecrating the altar (Exod. 29:36) does not mean it alone was holy; the term applies to the entire tabernacle and later the temple complex, which is called a *miqdāš*, "sanctuary, holy place" (Exod. 25:8).

9. With reference to the Sabbath, the rendering of *miqrā'-qōdeš* in Lev. 23:3 as "sacred assembly" (NIV) or "holy convocation" (ESV, NRSV) is misleading, suggesting a liturgical significance—people gathered for worship—that is otherwise lacking. Some occasions involved assemblies and cultic ritual (cf. Lev. 213:2–4, 37–38), but this is determined by the context rather than this phrase. The expression *miqrā'-qōdeš* is also used of other observances: the Festival of Unleavened Bread (Exod. 12:16; Num. 28:18, 25–26), the Festival of Trumpets (Num. 29:1), the Day of Atonement (Num. 29:7; cf. Lev. 16:29), and the Festival of Booths (Num. 29:12). Isa. 1:13 uses the expression *qĕrō' miqrā'* for the proclamation of all kinds of holy days, not limited to new moon and Sabbath observances.

simply signal that all work should cease. Numbers 28:9–10 calls for a special seventh-day Sabbath ritual at the central sanctuary—in addition to the daily offerings (cf. Ezek. 46:1, 9). However, the text does not say that this ritual was to be performed before a gathered assembly.

The superscription of Psalm 92 identifies this text as a hymn for Sabbath worship. The references to musical instruments (v. 3 [4]) and the house and courts of YHWH (v. 13 [14]) suggest worship at the central sanctuary. However, the psalmist may have been thinking of the national celebrations as he sang this song at home, since he used first-person-singular forms throughout. In any case, it would have been unreasonable and impossible for all Israelites to gather every week for worship at the central sanctuary once they had settled in the land.

Leviticus 23:3 explicitly declares that the seventh-day Sabbath was to be observed wherever the people lived. Whether the expression *môšĕbôt* refers to homes or villages, the First Testament is silent about weekly cultic worship in either context. We may speculate that Levitical priests provided leadership in weekly community-wide worship, but the Scriptures offer no information that aids in reconstructing their worship rituals. With the rise of synagogues, communal worship became a regular feature of the Sabbath worship, but this was a later development.

The First Testament specifies only one way of "remembering," "keeping," or "sanctifying" the seventh-day Sabbath: banning daily work performed to sustain life. Violating the sanctity of the Sabbath with work was a crime demanding death.[10] Obviously, this did not preclude eating, walking, demonstrating compassion to those in need, or taking care of livestock, as Jesus would teach and demonstrate.[11] This proscription did not curb all activity, but it offered people an opportunity to refresh themselves, a gift to which all were entitled (Deut. 5:14).

During the intertestamental period Jewish leaders imposed all sorts of Sabbath laws on the people, but this is not the vision of the Sabbath found in the First Testament. To the faithful in ancient Israel, the seventh-day Sabbath was not a burden but a gift to be celebrated, a part of the revelation of God's will that made Israel the envy of the nations (Deut. 4:6–8).

The Seventh-Day Sabbath in the New Testament

Jesus and the Sabbath. The Sabbath figures prominently in Jesus' ministry, especially in his altercations with Jewish leaders. Although he observed the

---

10. See Exod. 31:14–15; cf. 35:2; Num. 15:32–36.
11. As in Matt. 12:1–14; Mark 2:23–28; Luke 13:10–17; 14:1–5. Exodus 16:23 suggests meals were to be prepared the day before. The prohibition on lighting fires in Exod. 35:1–3 addresses the issue of cooking.

Sabbath by participating in synagogue worship,[12] he rejected the rabbinic understanding of the day as sovereign over human beings and recaptured its true meaning with his aphorism "The Sabbath was made for man, not man for the Sabbath" (Mark 2:27).[13] Defending the disciples' plucking of grain on the Sabbath, he challenged the casuistry of "the tradition of the elders" (Mark 7:3), as preserved in the Mishnah (*Šabbat* 7.2), which forbids reaping, threshing, winnowing, and grinding on the Sabbath. With the declaration "The Son of Man is sovereign [*kyrios*] even of the Sabbath" (Matt. 12:8; Mark 2:28; Luke 6:5), Jesus not only claimed ownership of the Sabbath institution but also identified himself as YHWH and declared that the Sabbath was not governed by man-made rules but by the will of the Creator.[14]

Jesus also challenged rabbinic casuistry with his Sabbath miracles and by announcing the breaking in of the kingdom of God. With his seven Sabbath healings, he both demonstrated that it was lawful to do good on this day (Matt. 12:12) and recaptured the notion that the Sabbath is a benefit to humankind rather than a burden.[15] His comment after healing the woman with the crooked back is striking: "Should not this woman, . . . whom Satan has kept bound for eighteen long years, be set free on the Sabbath day from what bound her?" (Luke 13:16 NIV). He thereby pointed to a deliverance greater than Israel's deliverance from Egypt.

Finally, in urging his followers to pray that their flight might not occur in winter or on the Sabbath, Jesus assumed that the institution would last into the eschaton. Gerhard Hasel rightly observes that Jesus "consistently rejected man-made sabbath *halakhah*. He freed the sabbath from human restrictions and encumbrances and restored it by showing its universal import for all men so that every person can be the beneficiary of the divine intentions and true purposes of sabbath rest and joy."[16]

The Sabbath in Acts. In Acts the apostles never suggest that the seventh-day Sabbath does not apply to Christians or that it is to be replaced by an alternate day.[17] Apart from incidental references to the Sabbath in Acts 1:12 and 15:21,

12. Luke 4:16; cf., e.g., Mark 1:21, 29; 3:1; Luke 4:44; 13:10.

13. His reference to "man" (*anthrōpos*) rather than to "Israel" assumes the creational basis for the observance and its universal validity. To him this was not a distinctly Israelite custom, as claimed by Judaism (*Jubilees* 2.18–20).

14. See further Gerhard F. Hasel, "Sabbath," *ABD* 5:855.

15. See, e.g., the healing of the man with a withered hand (Mark 3:1–6 = Matt. 12:9–14 = Luke 6:6–11); also Mark 1:21–28 = Luke 4:31–37; Mark 1:29–31; Luke 13:10–17; 14:1–6; John 5:1–18; 9:1–41.

16. Hasel, "Sabbath," 5:855.

17. Remarkably, neither the Jerusalem Council (Acts 15:1–29) nor anyone with apostolic authority spoke about the matter.

the narratives of Acts suggest that both Christians and Jews continued to worship on the seventh day.[18] Indeed the Sabbath figures prominently in Paul's ministry in Pisidian Antioch (13:13–52), Philippi (16:11–15), Thessalonica (17:1–9), and Corinth (18:1–4).[19] Like Jesus, the apostle worshiped in the synagogue on the Sabbath (17:2; cf. 24:14; 28:17) and took advantage of the opportunity to engage the worshipers and testify that Jesus was the Messiah.

The Sabbath in Paul's Letters. Paul's comments regarding the Sabbath are both scarce and vague. References to festivals and the new moon alongside "sabbaths" in Colossians 2:16 suggest that he did not have in mind the seventh-day Sabbath. Rather, as in Hebrew *šabbātôt*, the plural denotes "holy days" other than the seventh-day Sabbath. In 1 Corinthians 16:2 Paul challenges his readers to take up collections for the Lord's work on "the first day of each week." In this, his only reference to this day, he says nothing about Sabbath-keeping, Sabbath transformation, or the regular gathering of the congregation. At best Paul presupposed a weekly pattern of giving and assumed that the first day was convenient for people to deposit their gifts.

The Sabbath in Hebrews. With impressive metaphorical language, Hebrews 4:1–11 seizes on the notion of "Sabbath" rest to describe the "rest" that God grants to believers. In so doing, the author mixes two motifs. The predominant image in chapters 3–4 comes from Israel's desert wanderings and the failure of God's people to enter their "rest" (3:11; 4:5)—that is, to claim, occupy, and settle down in the promised land. This image of "rest" derives from Deuteronomy 12:9, where Hebrew *menûḥâ* and Greek *katapausis*, "rest," occur in parallel with "special grant" (*naḥālâ*) and "possession, property" (*klēronomia*), referring to Israel's secure occupation of the land, free from external threats. However, because of unbelief and rebellion, the exodus generation failed to enter the "[place of] rest" (*měnûḥâ*).

In Hebrews 4:3–4 the citation of Psalm 95:11, specifically the word "today" and the reference to "my rest," triggers a new train of thought involving God's own seventh-day Sabbath rest, after six days of creative work: "There remains therefore a Sabbath[20] for the people of God" (v. 9). The author hereby

18. We should not press the reference to "breaking bread on the first day of the week" in Acts 20:7 to mean the seventh-day Sabbath had been canceled. Perhaps the Ephesians found the first day an appropriate time to celebrate the common meal, or perhaps this was an occasional farewell meeting lasting until midnight and involving a meal (not necessarily the Lord's Supper).

19. Compare also the Western Text with reference to Ephesus in Acts 18:19: "When *he* came to Ephesus, and *on the next Sabbath* he left them there, but he himself went into the synagogue and had a discussion with the Jews" (italics indicates changes/additions). For discussion, see Philip W. Comfort, *New Testament Text and Translation Commentary* (Carol Stream, IL: Tyndale, 2008), 407.

20. The New Testament uses the noun *sabbatismos* only here, at Heb. 4:9.

declares that through Christ's work this Sabbath rest is made available to God's people, though he also warns his readers not to follow the exodus generation in forfeiting this rest through unbelief demonstrated in disobedience (v. 11). This Sabbath rest is not the post-eschaton Sabbath celebrated in heaven, nor the rest that believers experience in death, but a present rest enjoyed by those who believe (4:3), anticipating a greater future "rest" (4:11). Human Sabbath-keeping is a metaphor for cessation from works (4:10) in commemoration of God's rest at creation (4:4 = Gen. 2:2) and of salvation provided by Christ. The physical Sabbath rest that God's people enjoy reflects the inner spiritual rest, which is a deposit of the final eschatological rest proleptically experienced "today" (4:7).

To interpret Hebrews 4:1–11 as annulling the seventh-day Sabbath is unwarranted. Simply because a concept (Sabbath rest) is used metaphorically does not mean the original notion is irrelevant or terminated. Rather, Hebrews declares that by participating in the Sabbath rest by faith, Christians commemorate creation, celebrate salvation, and anticipate final consummation, restoration, and rest.[21]

The Seventh-Day Sabbath in the Early Church

As ties to Judaism loosened, Christians began to worship on Sunday.[22] Despite the absence of any mandate to terminate or replace the seventh-day Sabbath,[23] seeds for this shift are found in the New Testament. On this day Jesus rose from the grave (Luke 24:1) and appeared to his disciples to revitalize their faith and instruct them on the significance of the passion week (Luke 24:13–53). At Pentecost, fifty days after Passover, the Holy Spirit came upon the assembly of Jews who believed in Jesus, affirming and sealing them as his covenant community (Acts 2). Paul met with the Ephesian believers (Acts 20:7) on the first day of the week, and Corinthian believers gathered their gifts of charity on this day (1 Cor. 16:2). Furthermore, Revelation 1:10 calls the first day of the week "the Lord's day."[24]

21. See Hasel, "Sabbath," 5:856.

22. Hughes Oliphant Old (*Worship, Reformed according to Scripture*, rev. ed. [Louisville: Westminster John Knox, 2002], 25) overstates the case when he asserts that by coming to the disciples and breaking bread with them on the first day of the week, "Jesus took the initiative of making this the Christian day of worship."

23. See D. A. Carson, *From Sabbath to Lord's Day* (Grand Rapids: Zondervan, 1982), 85.

24. The Greek expression *hē kyriakē hēmera*, "the Lord's day" (Rev. 1:10), may be the equivalent of the Hebrew references to the seventh day (*yôm*) as *šabbat layhwh 'ĕlōhêkā*, "a Sabbath for/belonging to YHWH your God" (Exod. 20:10; Deut. 5:14). Likewise Lev. 25:2, 4 characterizes the seventh agricultural year (*šānâ*) as a *šabbat layhwh*.

This evidence is all circumstantial, and it falls short of prescribing a shift from a six-plus-one to a one-plus-six rhythm of life. Nevertheless, according to early Christian writers the custom of worshiping on the first day of the week was well established by the beginning of the second century AD.[25] The significance of the sanctified day also seemed to change. In contrast to Constantine's fourth-century-AD edict officially recognizing Sunday as a day of rest,[26] these early texts do not speak of "the Lord's day" as a day of rest but as a day of assembly to celebrate the saving work of Christ.[27] This completely transformed the First Testament perspective, which deemphasized the Sabbath assembly while celebrating God's original creative work (Exod. 20:11) and his salvation through resting (Deut. 5:15).

The way the day was sanctified also changed. Emphasizing the morality of the worshiper, the *Epistle of Barnabas* called for the sanctification of the person rather than the day. Justin Martyr viewed keeping the Sabbath primarily as a duty imposed on Jews by God because of their unrighteousness. In his *Dialogue with Trypho*, a Jew, he dismissed the seventh-day Sabbath as part of Israel's cultic obligations, along with circumcision, sacrifices, and the festival sabbaths.[28] Obviously this was a response to a problem within Judaism rather than the First Testament itself, which clearly distinguishes the seventh-day Sabbath from Israel's liturgical calendar and treats it as a gracious gift rather

25. For early textual evidence, see appendix C.

26. Sunday did not become the official day of rest until Emperor Constantine decreed the Sabbath replaced by the "Day of the Sun" in the fourth century.

> On the venerable Day of the Sun let the magistrates and people residing in cities rest, and let all workshops be closed. In the country, however, persons engaged in agriculture may freely and lawfully continue their pursuits; because it often happens that another day is not so suitable for grain-sowing or for vine-planting; lest by neglecting the proper moment for such operations the bounty of heaven should be lost. (Given the 7th day of March, Crispus and Constantine being consuls each of them for the second time [AD 321].)

Codex Justinianus 3.12.3; as translated in Philip Schaff, *History of the Christian Church*, 5th ed. (New York: Scribner, 1902), 3:380, note 1. If Constantine had intended hereby to decree Sunday to be the day of Christian worship, he probably would have replaced the pagan name with an overtly Christian designation.

27. While it is unclear whether Pliny the Younger was referring to Saturday or Sunday in his complaint in a letter to Emperor Trajan that Christians have a habit "of meeting on a certain fixed day before it was light," the reference clearly involves a distinctively Christian gathering. See Pliny, *Letters* 10.96–97, trans. W. Melmoth, Loeb Classical Library (New York: G. P. Putnam's Sons, 1924), 2:403. Regarding the origins of the Lord's day, Richard J. Bauckham concludes that "for the earliest Christians it was not a substitute for the Sabbath nor a day of rest nor related in any way to the fourth commandment." See Bauckham, "The Lord's Day," in Carson, *From Sabbath to Lord's Day*, 240.

28. Justin Martyr, *Dialogue with Trypho* 21–24, in Philip Schaff, ed., *Ante-Nicene Fathers*, vol. 1, *The Apostolic Fathers with Justin Martyr and Irenaeus* (1884; reprint, Peabody, MA: Hendrickson, 1995), 204–7.

than a legalistic duty. Justin Martyr's negative disposition toward Israel's cultic system rests on specious proof-texting of prophetic responses to Israel's abuses[29] rather than the normative instructions concerning the Sabbath and cultic observances in Israel's constitutional literature.

The Question of the Sabbath for Today

This discussion raises a host of questions for Christians regarding the place of a six-plus-one rhythm of life in general and the seventh-day Sabbath observance in particular. Many continue to view the weekly Sabbath as a part of Israel's cultic system terminated by the work of Christ. However, as we have seen, this reflects a fundamental misunderstanding of the function and nature of the seventh-day Sabbath in ancient Israel and is to be rejected for many reasons. First, the earliest references to the seventh-day Sabbath predate tabernacle worship and are disconnected from it (Exod. 16:22–30; cf. 12:14–20). Second, the Sabbath ordinance is embedded in the Decalogue, which is unconcerned with cultic matters; its agenda is theological and ethical. Third, the original Sabbath ordinance is rooted in creation and the cosmic order, not in Israel's unique and microcosmic role. Fourth, the revelation of the Sabbath ordinance is separated from the revelation of the worship system associated with the sanctuary. Fifth, although by keeping the Sabbath, Israelites commemorated their rescue from Egypt (Deut. 5:15), this noncultic observance also served as the sign par excellence of YHWH's gracious covenant relationship with his people (Exod. 31:12–17). Sixth, the First Testament witnesses are unanimous in portraying the seventh-day Sabbath primarily as a day of rest rather than a day for liturgical worship.

The sacrifice of Christ has indeed put an end to the rituals associated with tabernacle and temple. However, like the initiation rite of circumcision, which was replaced by baptism, and the Passover meal, which was replaced by the Lord's Supper, the seventh-day Sabbath seems to have morphed into a first-day celebration of the resurrection of Christ and the onset of the new age. The three observances listed all predated cultic rituals linked with tabernacle and temple, lacked involvement by priests, and were household rather than national observances. These features distinguish these customs from Israel's liturgical calendar and open the door to transformation rather than termination in the era of the new covenant. However, unlike the rites of baptism and the Lord's Supper, the New Testament never mandates the transformation of the seventh-day Sabbath into a first-day Lord's day, let alone making it a day of assembly.

29. See, e.g., Jer. 7:21–22; Ezek. 20:19–26; Amos 5:18–6:7.

What implications do these facts have for modern Christians' disposition toward the Sabbath? Obviously we cannot roll back the clock or return to the basically agrarian economy of ancient Israel or the New Testament. Life in modern urban and suburban contexts is much more complex than life two thousand years ago. Here are several principles to consider before we explore how we might observe the day in our context.

First, since the seventh-day Sabbath ordinance was grounded in cosmic rather than ethnocentric divine action, and since it was disconnected from Israel's cultic calendar, we may not dismiss it as passé like other cultic elements of the old covenant that find their perfection and fulfillment in Christ. Second, since the Sabbath ordinance is embedded in the Decalogue, which most Christians deem authoritative—even if they reject the rest of the constitutional literature—to delete only the Sabbath ordinance in light of the work of Christ is unwarranted and hypocritical. Third, although the Sabbath has come to be associated with liturgical worship, in the First Testament this was primarily a theological and humanitarian ordinance. Fourth, since the New Testament never abolishes the Sabbath, since Jesus and his disciples observed it without embarrassment, and since Jesus highlighted its true intent as a gift from God for the benefit of humankind, we should welcome it as an invitation to celebrate the creative and salvific acts of God through rest. Fifth, from a purely pragmatic point of view, working bodies need rest. For many, Sunday has become as frantic as every other day, a frenzy often compounded by the sense of obligation to attend church. This has become catch-up day, and communal worship interferes with that agenda.[30] Much of the dysfunction in our world derives from greed, impatience, and workaholism, which keep us on edge. Give us a break!

Instead of asking, "Do Christians need to observe the Sabbath?" we should be asking, "How should Christians keep the Sabbath so that the intent of this gift is honored and God is glorified?" Here are some practical suggestions for discussion.

First, Christians need to rediscover the Sabbath as a gift from God. If we observe this day primarily as a duty rather than a privilege, we have lost the heart of the gospel—just as the Jewish leaders of Jesus' day had lost it. God

30. For further and more detailed appeals to recover the Sabbath from various perspectives, see Mark Buchanan, *The Rest of God: Restoring Your Soul by Restoring the Sabbath* (Nashville: Nelson, 2006); Marva Dawn, *Keeping the Sabbath Wholly: Ceasing, Resting, Embracing, Feasting* (Grand Rapids: Eerdmans, 1989); Dawn, *The Sense of Call: A Sabbath Way of Life for Those Who Serve God, the Church, and the World* (Grand Rapids: Eerdmans, 2006); Norman Wirzba, *Living the Sabbath: Discovering the Rhythms of Rest and Delight* (Grand Rapids: Brazos, 2006). For a delightful book from a Jewish perspective on the sanctity of time, see Abraham Joshua Heschel, *The Sabbath: Its Meaning for Modern Man* (New York: Noonday Press, 1951).

does not impose the Sabbath on us; he invites us to receive it and celebrate his grace through rest.

Second, Christians should continue to view the Sabbath as a sign, a distinctive mark of God's covenant commitment to us—demonstrated with marvelous grace in Jesus Christ—and an opportunity to declare our commitment to him. The Sabbath serves as a barometer of our faith and the extent to which divine-kingdom values govern our lives. Each week I am faced with this question: "Can I trust God to take care of me on the seventh day, or am I faithless like the gentiles around me?"

Third, above all, Christians need to let the Sabbath be a day of rest. Unfortunately, for many, Sunday is the most frantic day of the week. The recovery of a six-plus-one (or one-plus-six) rhythm of life would not only help us catch our breath but also help us model for the world the peace they too may find in Jesus Christ. For employers and managers, the Sabbath offers a constant reminder that we are to embody the ethic of God himself, who rescued his people from the burdens of slave labor and granted his vassals one day in seven for rest and delight in life itself. As we are physically renewed, the Sabbath offers opportunity for spiritual renewal as well. While Sabbath assembly is not mandated in Scripture, this is an ideal day to gather in formal worship and experience renewal in our souls through an audience with God and fellowship with the saints.

Fourth, Christians should welcome the Sabbath as an opportunity for participation in the great drama of redemption. Once we were slaves to sin, bound in the kingdom of darkness, but we have been ushered into the eternal rest that God provides through Christ's saving work. In the Sabbath we are invited to enjoy in microcosm the final consummation, restoration, and rest.[31]

Fifth, in the absence of clear biblical warrant for the shift of the Lord's day from the last to the first day of the week, we need to be charitable toward Christians who worship on Saturday rather than Sunday as a matter of conviction,[32] necessity, or convenience. It seems more important *that a Sabbath day be observed* than *which Sabbath day is observed.*

Whether we worship corporately on Saturday or Sunday, we all need a Sabbath to rest. Those whose employment requires work on the first day of the week can honor God and refresh themselves by setting aside another day of worship in the form of rest and relaxation. At the same time, we must recognize that the form of rest and relaxation may legitimately vary from person to person. It may be restful and regenerative for a construction

31. See Hasel, "Sabbath," 5:856.
32. Seventh-day Adventists, Seventh-day Baptists, and other Sabbatarians.

worker to devote the Sabbath to reading, but this may not be the case for someone whose workaday life is spent in the books. I, for one, find nothing more rejuvenating than gardening, and if I thought only of myself, I would do all my yard work on Sunday. But I live in a community. I may plant flowers or dig weeds on Sunday, but in deference to my neighbors who may be trying to take a nap, I will not mow my lawn, even if it is relaxing and therapeutic for me.

Other Heptadic Dramas in Israel

In ancient Israel the pattern of dividing time into six-plus-one units extended beyond the week to years in three specific institutions: the seventh-year sabbatical, the seventh-year release, and the Year of Jubilee. Each institution involved worship and intensified the drama of creation/redemption in the six-plus-one principle.

The Sabbatical Year

The concept of "sabbatical year" is first introduced in the Book of the Covenant (Exod. 23:10–11) and then developed more fully in the "Instructions on Holiness" (Lev. 25:1–7). The sabbatical year called for cessation of all agricultural activity—no planting of crops or pruning of vineyards and olive groves. It gave the land a chance to rest and be rejuvenated by lying fallow for a year; thus it completed the covenantal triangle of sabbaticals: YHWH rested at the end of creation week (Exod. 20:11), Israel rested every seventh day (Exod. 20:9–10; 23:12), and the land rested every seventh year. The sabbatical year also reminded Israelites that the land was not theirs. On the one hand, the land was a grant (naḥălâ) held in trust and managed for the divine Landowner (Lev. 23:25). But the land belonged to all, including the creatures of the field. By observing the sabbatical year, Israelites relinquished their monopoly on its produce; they shared it with needy human beings and offered wild animals free access to whatever it produced naturally.

The sabbatical year posed an even more serious test of Israel's faith than the seventh-day Sabbath. Could they trust YHWH to provide for them if they left their tools and plows at home for a year? While we have little evidence that the Israelites ever observed this institution, YHWH's seriousness about it is reflected in the covenant curses, which linked the duration of Israel's exile as punishment for not keeping the sabbatical year.[33]

---

33. See Lev. 26:34–35, 43; 2 Chron. 36:21; cf. Jer. 25:12; 29:10; Dan. 9:2.

The Seventh-Year Release of Indentured Servants

The use of the word for "release" (šěmiṭṭâ, Deut. 15:1) links this institution to the sabbatical year,[34] though this policy involved humans rather than land, requiring creditors to remit all debts and release indentured servants in the seventh year (Exod. 21:2–22; Deut. 15:1–18). It is unclear whether the seventh year referred to a standardized year applying to all Israelites, or if it could vary, depending on the year a household was established.[35] In the interests of the marginalized, Moses instructed landowners to demonstrate soft hearts and open hands (Deut. 7–11; 18) toward the poor, forgiving debts without a grudge and releasing indentured servants with generous gifts and without regret (Exod. 21:2–6; Deut. 15:12–18). Whether male or female, if indentured servants enjoyed a confident and trusting relationship with their masters, they could remain with their households and signify their decision with a ritual piercing of the ear (Exod. 21:5–6; Deut. 15:17). While the First Testament provides no clear evidence that the Israelites kept this ordinance, such economic arrangements reinforce the notion that worship involves all of life and that those with means and the marginalized participate in the drama of redemption through practical acts of charity toward the poor (Deut. 15:15; cf. 10:17–19).

The Year of Jubilee

In the longer-range calendar, the year after the seventh sabbatical year (i.e., the fiftieth year) also bore special significance (Lev. 25:8–24). According to Leviticus 25:23, the Jubilee[36] reminded Israel of their status as resident aliens and guests in the territory owned by YHWH. Because they were YHWH's vassals, whom he had liberated from slavery in Egypt, they were forbidden from enslaving one another (cf. Jer. 34:9) or opportunistically staking their own claims to the land. The Jubilee was designed to serve two purposes: (1) to guarantee the integrity of Israelites' relationships with one another by releasing all who had been enslaved for debt and (2) to guarantee the integrity of the people's relationship to the land, restoring every plot of land to the family to which it had been assigned when the land was distributed among the tribes.[37] As with the previous heptadic

---

34. Exodus 23:11 uses the corresponding verb for releasing the land from the control of human hands.

35. Deuteronomy 31:10 associates "the time of the year of the release" with the Festival of Booths (cf. 16:13–16; Lev. 23:34–44).

36. The name "Jubilee" derives from Hebrew yôbēl, "ram," whose horn the priests would blow to signal special events (Lev. 25:9–10; cf. Exod. 19:13).

37. This principle was explicitly violated by Ahab and Jezebel's seizure of Naboth's vineyard (1 Kings 21).

institutions, we do not know if this ordinance was ever observed in Israel, though Isaiah 61 looks forward to the future realization of its ideals.[38]

The Drama of Israel's Pentateuchal Annual Festivals

The Festival of Trumpets

The first day of the seventh month was to be marked by the loud blowing of trumpets, total cessation of work, and burnt offerings involving a variety of products from flock and field (Lev. 23:23–25; Num. 29:1–6). The theological meaning of this ritual is not explained, but it reinforced the significance of the number seven. What the seventh-day Sabbath was to the workweek, the seventh month would be to the year. Indeed, this month is renowned also for its cluster of observances: Festival of Trumpets, Day of Atonement, Festival of Booths.

Since these heptadic observances related directly to Israel's administration of the land, it is not surprising that the New Testament does not reiterate these themes. However, this does not mean that the principles underlying them were forgotten. Applying Isaiah 61:1–3 to himself, Jesus claimed he had been empowered, anointed, and sent to proclaim the release of captives and to announce the ultimate Jubilee (Luke 4:17–21). Christians keep this ordinance whenever they celebrate Jesus' redemptive work, and they are true to the other heptadic ordinances when they exhibit soft hearts and open hands toward the poor with acts of charity and compassion.

The Annual Pilgrim Festivals

Israel's annual festivals were the foci of their national economic and religious life. Some were tied closely to the agricultural year, while others were linked to Israel's historical experience of redemption. Although participation in the three annual pilgrimage festivals (Passover and Unleavened Bread, Weeks/Shavuoth, and Booths/Sukkoth) was required of all males (Exod. 23:15–16; 34:18–22; Deut. 16:16), Moses appealed to heads of households to make worship at the central sanctuary family affairs by bringing their entire households as well as aliens and Levites in their towns (Deut. 12:12, 18; 14:29; 26:11). None were excluded from participating in the drama of worship and celebrating God's saving grace.

The First Testament refers to Israel's annual festivals with several words. The expression ḥag, "festival, procession, pilgrimage," reflects the national

---

38. Since the land lay fallow in the fiftieth year as well as the forty-ninth (Lev. 25:11–12), in effect creating a two-year sabbatical, it intensified the test of Israel's faith. Could they trust YHWH for sustenance for two consecutive years without gathering crops?

significance of the three major festivals. By making the journey to the central sanctuary, to celebrate in the presence of YHWH, all Israelites were drawn into YHWH's great drama of redemption. The term *mô'ēd* (from *yā'ad*, "to appoint, designate") views these events as appointments with God,[39] that is, as "set times of corporate and communal cultic observance."[40] Concentrated in the first and seventh months (fig. 11.2), the pilgrimages/festivals tended to involve communal meals eaten either in the presence of YHWH at the central sanctuary (Deut. 12:7) or in people's homes.

The celebrations served several purposes. First, they served a dramatic purpose, breaking the routine of everyday life and focusing worshipers' attention on the divine and supernatural dimensions of life. Through the festivals, Israelites as a people identified with and participated in YHWH's drama of redemption and commemorated his providential care. Second, Israel's festivals served a didactic purpose, provoking curiosity in the young and uninitiated and providing opportunity to pass the memories of YHWH's gracious actions from generation to generation (Deut. 6:20–25). Third, the festivals served covenantal objectives. Through hearing the Torah at the Festival of Booths (*sukkôt*, Deut. 31:9–13) and through song (Deut. 31–32), the people were instructed in the dimensions of covenant relationship and challenged to recommit to YHWH and to one another. Fourth, the festivals served a social function, providing Israelites with occasions to reinforce their sense of community and deepen their collective relationship with YHWH through shared celebrations.

Passover and Unleavened Bread

We discussed the Passover briefly in the context of the ordinances, but the festival's place within the cultic calendar calls for a few additional comments. Unlike the Babylonians, for whom New Year's Day was the high point of the religious year, the Israelites apparently had no New Year celebration.[41] Exodus 12:2 notes that Israel's calendar and their national history commenced the month they left Egypt, and this month (Abib/Nisan) would mark the beginning of their New Year.[42] The location of the Passover on the fourteenth day

39. See Gen. 17:21; Exod. 9:5; Jer. 8:7. The word was also used of ordinary appointments: Judg. 20:38; 1 Sam. 20:35.

40. As in Lev. 23:2, 4, 44; Isa. 1:14; Ezek. 36:38.

41. This is disputed by scholars. See Daniel I. Block, "New Year," *International Standard Bible Encyclopedia* [*ISBE*], ed. G. W. Bromiley et al., rev. ed. (Grand Rapids: Eerdmans, 1979–88), 3:529–32.

42. In preexilic times the first month of the year was identified as Abib (Exod. 13:4; 23:15; 34:18; Deut. 16:1), but under the influence of the Babylonian calendar, after the exile the month was known as Nisan (Neh. 2:1; Esther 3:7).

of the first month may reflect a deliberate polemic against pagan New Year festivals—in effect an anti–New Year festival. The term *pesaḥ*, "Passover," applies strictly to the fourteenth day of Nisan, but it was so closely tied to the Festival of Unleavened Bread during the following week that "Passover" often covered the entire eight days of celebration.

Although Exodus 12:1–13 involves instructions for a onetime event in Egypt, in Exodus 12:14 YHWH prescribes the Passover as a future annual memorial event at the head of an eight-day festival. Repeating the actions of the first Passover, every year the blood of the lamb was to be brushed on the doorposts (vv. 21–27, 43–50). This curious ritual would provoke questions by children or outsiders concerning its meaning, thereby creating opportunities for adults to invite the entire household into the drama of the original event. The celebration was open to all, even non-Israelites, provided they had identified with Israel and with Israel's God by circumcision.

The Festival of Unleavened Bread (*maṣṣôt*) would begin at sunset the day after Passover (Abib 15) and last for seven days (until Abib 21; Exod. 12:14–20; 13:5–10). On the first day, family members were to remove every bit of leaven from the house, and for seven days thereafter no pastries were to contain yeast. Although 12:15–20 does not explain the significance of the *maṣṣôt*, in the following narrative (vv. 31–36) it is clear that the absence of leaven memorialized the haste with which the Israelites left Egypt: there was no time for the dough to rise. So long as Israel was en route to the promised land, with the tabernacle in the midst of the community, the Passover was celebrated in people's homes. However, once the people had settled in their territories, they were to make annual pilgrimages to the central sanctuary (Deut. 16:1–6)—though the festival apparently would not be observed inside the sanctuary.

The First Testament suggests that this festival was rarely observed. According to Numbers 9:1–14, the Israelites observed it as prescribed exactly one year after they had left Egypt, and Joshua 5:10–11 describes the first Passover in the promised land. Providentially, Israel entered the land with just enough time to circumcise all the males and let them heal by the fourteenth of Abib, which suggests that the festival had been neglected during the desert wanderings. According to 2 Chronicles 8:12–13, Solomon sponsored the celebration of all Israel's festivals after he had dedicated the temple. Second Chronicles 30:1–27 observes that Hezekiah led the people in celebrating the Passover in Jerusalem as a part of his efforts at religious renewal. But the Passover was neglected again until the time of Josiah (2 Kings 23:21–23; 2 Chron. 35:1–19). The intensity and enthusiasm of the Passover celebration that he sponsored was unprecedented in the history of the monarchy. Sadly, this would be the last time the Israelites would observe the festival until after the return from exile and the reconstruction of the temple (Ezra 6:19–22).

The Festival of Weeks/Harvest/Firstfruits

Because the Festival of Weeks (Hebrew *šābu'ōt*, "sevens")[43] was celebrated on the fiftieth day following the Passover, in later times it was called Pentecost (Acts 2:1; 20:16). Since it coincided with the first harvest of spring grain (Exod. 34:22), it was also known as the Festival of the Harvest and the Firstfruits of Labor (Exod. 23:16; cf. Num. 28:26), at which worshipers would offer the firstfruits of their crops as thanksgiving offerings in proportion to YHWH's blessing (Deut. 16:9–12) and as acknowledgment that YHWH owns it all. This celebration was open to the entire family, including children and servants, as well as economically marginalized neighbors, and memorialized Israel's past experience as marginalized slaves in Egypt.

In Deuteronomy 26:1–11 Moses prescribed a dramatic ritual to be performed by worshipers at the festival. As the worshiper presented his basket of produce to the priest, he was to declare, "Today I declare to YHWH your God that I have come into the land that YHWH swore to our ancestors to give us" (v. 3). As the priest accepted the basket and deposited it before the altar, the worshiper was to recite the beautiful creed-like statement recorded in verses 5–10. The recitation of this creed in the context of a harvest ritual raised Israel's faith above the fertility rituals of their neighbors, as they not only celebrated the annual drama of seedtime and harvest but also linked this to YHWH's redemption of the nation. This was dramatic worship at its finest. After prostrating himself before YHWH, the worshiper could rise and, together with his family, the Levite, and the aliens who lived in his village, celebrate with great joy the lavish goodness of God.

The Day of Atonement

Celebrated on the tenth day of the seventh month (Tishri), *yôm kippûr* was the holiest and most solemn day of the year. On this day all work was to cease, and the people were to observe a strict fast. Leviticus 16 spells out the rituals of the Day of Atonement in detail. These involve the high priest's making atonement for himself and his household with a sacrificed bull, followed by a goat sacrificed for the sins of the people. In addition, the priest confesses over a second goat all the sins of the people and then releases it into the desert.

The Day of Atonement served two purposes: to cleanse the priesthood and the sanctuary so that YHWH would accept the rituals performed during the rest of the year, and to atone for the sins of the people. Presumably, as the priests presented the people's sin and guilt offerings during the year, the people were

43. See Exod. 34:22; Num. 28:26; Deut. 16:9–12; 2 Chron. 8:13.

cleansed, but the contamination remained on the altar and in the sanctuary. Although the Day of Atonement was a supremely sober observance, it was an extraordinarily gracious provision for dealing with the problem of sin. So long as the sanctuary was contaminated by the sins of the people, God's wrath hung over them. However, once a year the entire sanctuary could be flushed of the contamination, which would be sent into the desert, never to be held against the people again.

Since AD 70 no sacrifices have been presented on Yom Kippur, but Jews still mark the day with intense solemnity, fasting, and total abstinence from labor. The observance begins with the blast of the shofar, calling the people to worship in the synagogue. In the service "all vows" are chanted, as the congregation implores God to forgive them for the sins of the past year and the vows they have broken. The services continue the next day from sunrise to sunset, when one more blast of the shofar ends the Day of Atonement.

The Festival of Booths/Tabernacles

While Exodus 23:16b and 34:22b identify this weeklong festival (Lev. 23:33–36; Deut. 16:13–15) as "the Festival of Ingathering" (*ḥag hā'āsîp*), the designation "Festival of Booths" (*ḥag sukkôt*) comes from Leviticus 23:34.[44] Exodus 23:16 times this festival at the end of the agricultural cycle, though technically it was not a harvest festival.[45] Linked to processing and storage of the foodstuffs, Booths was the happiest of all the festivals (Deut. 16:13–15).[46] The designation "Booths/Tabernacles" derives from the dramatic practice of worshipers' living in shelters made of palm branches for the duration of the week, recalling the palm shelters in which the Israelites lived when YHWH rescued them from Egypt (Lev. 23:39–44).[47] This festival involved a distinctive pattern of offerings at the sanctuary. These included constant amounts of grain offerings and male lamb and goat sacrifices, but bulls were sacrificed in diminishing numbers—thirteen on the first day, and one fewer each day until

44. Instead of referring to the festival by name, Num. 29:12–39 speaks generally of "a sacred proclamation" (*miqrā'-qōdeš*, v. 12), a "mandatory assembly" (*'ăṣeret*, v. 35), and includes it in the sacred appointments (*mô'ădîm*, v. 39).

45. The term "ingathering" refers not to the actual harvest but to the collection of processed grain and unfermented grape juice and their storage in granaries and vats, to be available through the winter months.

46. See further Jeffrey H. Tigay, *Deuteronomy*, JPS Torah Commentary (Philadelphia: Jewish Publication Society, 1996), 157–58.

47. Structurally this Festival of Booths mirrors Passover and Unleavened Bread in the first month. Both commemorate Israel's departure from Egypt, and both last for eight days, though the pattern of 1 + 7 of the spring festival is reversed as 7 + 1, an extra specially holy day of sacrifices being attached to the end.

the seventh day, when seven would be offered. On the climactic eighth day the offering consisted of one ram, one male goat, and seven male lambs. In Deuteronomy 31:9–13 Moses supplements these sacrificial rituals with the ritual reading of the entire Torah (his addresses in Deuteronomy) every seventh year.

We read of this festival as being observed in the days of Solomon (2 Chron. 8:13), Hezekiah (31:3), and after the exile (Ezra 3:4; Zech. 14:16–19). By the time of Christ "the great day of the feast" (that is, the eighth day) included a custom of ritual water-pouring, perhaps in recognition of rain as a gift of God (cf. Zech. 14:17).

Israel's Festivals Added Later

All the festivals prescribed in the Pentateuch fall in the first seven months of the year (the growing season). The five-month gap in the ritual calendar was broken up by adding several festivals rooted in Israel's postexilic experience.

Rosh Hashanah

As noted earlier, the First Testament religious calendar did not include a New Year festival. Since the so-called Gezer Calendar,[48] dated to the early monarchy, begins the agricultural cycle in the autumn, and Jews later celebrated Rosh Hashanah on Tishri 1, it appears that the Israelites had two systems of reckoning time: the cultic calendar began with Nisan (in the spring), and the agricultural calendar began with Tishri (in the fall). The phrase *rō'š haššānâ*, literally, "head of the year," occurs only in Ezekiel 40:1, where it represents the traditional springtime New Year, though without any hint of a festival. The origins of the autumnal New Year as recognized by Jews today are unknown, but by the time the festival had become a significant event, the position of the New Year had shifted 180 degrees and become an autumnal celebration.

Purim

The name derives from the term *pûr*, a loanword from Assyrian *pūru(m)*, "a small stone, a pebble used in casting lots" (Esther 3:7; 9:24–26). Located in the twelfth month (Adar 15; late winter), this festival commemorates Esther's work in annulling Haman's diabolical plot to get rid of the Jews. Second

---

48. J. B. Pritchard, ed., *Ancient Near Eastern Texts Relating to the Old Testament*, 3rd ed. (Princeton: Princeton University Press, 1969), 320.

Maccabees 15:36, which concerns Judas Maccabaeus's defeat of Nicanor in 161 BC, recounts the earliest known observance of Purim.

Hanukkah (Festival of Lights)

Beginning on Kislev 25 (late fall), the ninth month of the religious calendar, this festival runs for eight days. The observance commemorates the victory of Judas Maccabaeus over Antiochus Epiphanes in 164 BC, specifically the rededication of the temple after Antiochus's desecration of the building. This is probably the feast referred to in John 10:22.

Summary of First Testament Festivals

Our survey of Israelite festivals suggests that drama played an important role in Israelite worship and served several purposes. First, drama served the theological purpose of instilling in worshipers a high view of God, who had revealed himself through historical events and through the proclaimed word. Second, for children and newcomers to the faith, it served the didactic purpose of instruction in the history of Israel's pilgrimage with God. Third, drama served a communal purpose, developing in all Israelites a corporate sense of identity based upon shared awareness of themselves as the redeemed people of YHWH. Finally, it served a social and ethical purpose, providing opportunities to involve the marginalized in the mainstream of Israelite faith and life and express compassion to those in need. True worship cries for an ethical outlet. Unfortunately, the history of Israelite worship is characterized by a pervasive tendency to empty celebrations of their theological meaning and continue the forms of the celebrations long after hearts have turned from YHWH. This was the false and empty worship denounced by prophet after prophet.[49]

The Drama of Worship in the New Testament

The New Testament has relatively little to say about seasons and festivals of corporate celebration. The Gospels note Jesus' presence in Jerusalem at festival time—Passover,[50] the Festival of Booths (John 7:2–37), and Hanukkah (John 10:22); Hebrews remembers Moses' celebration of the original Passover

49. See, e.g., Isa. 1; Jer. 7:21–22; Ezek. 20:19–26; Amos 5:21–6:7.
50. See Matt. 26:1–19; Mark 14:1–16; Luke 2:41–42; 22:1–13; John 2:23; 6:4; 11:55–56; 12:20; 13:1, 29.

as evidence of faith (Heb. 11:28); and Paul identifies Jesus Christ as "our Passover" (1 Cor. 5:7 HCSB).

Paul had little to say about Christian observances.[51] His comments in Romans 14:5–6 are vague: "Let everyone be convinced in his own mind" relates as much to feasting and fasting as to Jewish holidays. In Galatians 4:8–10 he suggests that for gentiles to observe "days, months, seasons, and years" is tantamount to returning to slavery and being enfeebled by weak elements. While some equate these "elemental things" (*stoicheia*) with Jewish festivals, the elements probably refer to earth, air, fire, and water, or to the heavenly bodies of astrology. Paul is not talking about First Testament observances but about pagan rituals that stand in opposition to commitment to Christ. The issues differ in Colossians 2:16, which concerns regulations about food and drink as well as Jewish festivals, new moon observances, and sabbaths. Paul recognizes that these are shadows of the reality that appears in Christ, but he does not declare them mutually exclusive. Nor does he denounce the festivals as "elements" of the cosmos. Paul appears to be indifferent to whether people observe these customs.

The Drama of the Church's Worship in Our Time

With one voice, New Testament writers assert that the sacrifice of Christ renders obsolete any and all First Testament sacrificial rituals; thus they imply the end of cultic observances associated with the tabernacle and the temple. But does this mean that Christians should avoid the Jewish cultic calendar entirely? How should believers in Jesus relate to the sabbaths and festivals of the First Testament? Three factors affect the answer to these questions.

First, whereas most of Israel's festivals were tied to their cultic system and hence ended with Christ, the Passover was neither associated with tabernacle/temple worship nor finished with Christ. Rather, as we observed in chapter 6, Jesus transformed the Israelite Passover into the Lord's Supper. Each time we eat and drink at the Lord's Table, we participate in the drama of redemption, memorializing and experiencing the grace of Christ's sacrifice.

Second, recognizing that the seventh-day Sabbath was grounded in creation and disconnected from sanctuary worship, and in the absence of explicit New Testament termination of the institution, we assume that it continues. However, recognizing the fundamental shift in kingdom realities that has occurred with the passion and resurrection of Christ, we customarily

---

51. See D. R. DeLacy, "Holy Days," in *Dictionary of Paul and His Letters*, ed. G. F. Hawthorne, R. P. Martin, and D. G. Reid (Downers Grove, IL: InterVarsity, 1993), 404.

observe the first rather than the last day of the week as "the Lord's day." This was the day of Jesus' resurrection, which inaugurated a new era and a new spiritual race.

Third, in reflecting on the role of a liturgical calendar for Christians, we do well to relate the functions of Christian observances to functions of festivals in Israel. Through festivals we too may (a) dramatize and actualize the saving work of Christ in our lives; (b) keep alive the memory of God's creative and saving acts and provide opportunities for instructing the uninitiated; (c) strengthen relationships between worshiper and God and between worshiper and the community of faith; and (d) rejoice in the providential care of God and share his bounty through acts of charity to the poor and oppressed.

So how might we apply all we have discussed in the context of the local church? First, congregations should treat the festivals of the church year as opportunities for celebration rather than obligations to observe. Like Israel in Deuteronomy 12, we need to take great joy in celebrating the significant moments in the birth of the church: the incarnation, crucifixion, resurrection, and ascension of Jesus, as well as his outpouring of the Holy Spirit at Pentecost.

Second, as in ancient Israel, mere attendance at and participation in cultic festivals has no merit in the eyes of God if one's heart is not submissive to him and one's life does not demonstrate commitment to his will. Hypocritical celebration is worse than no celebration at all.

Third, worshipers should major on the majors and let the minors be minor. The established church has a long tradition of cluttering up the calendar with observances[52] that have no warrant in Scripture and detract from the foundational observances of Advent, Holy Week, Ascension, Pentecost, and the seventh-day Sabbath. By observing the traditional holy days of the church, universal evangelical Christians identify with the rest of Christendom. But even then these days should be kept in proper proportion. While the Scriptures offer no direct support for Lenten asceticism, the Eastern church's focus on the passion and resurrection of Christ is certainly much healthier than the sentimental and garish Western observance of Christmas, or the Western desecration of Easter with images of bunnies and chocolate eggs. The heart of the gospel is at stake. Given the role of individual and corporate thanksgiving in the Scriptures, annual Thanksgiving services that go beyond turkey and romantic images of the Pilgrim Fathers would certainly be worthy additions to the liturgical calendar.

---

52. See, e.g., the "Churchman's Ordo Kalendar," published by the Episcopal Bookstore and accessible at www.episcopalnet.org/Kalendars/2012/Jan12.html, which clutters the calendar with days dedicated to a host of "saints"—not only detracting from the essential Christian observances, but also creating the impression of a special category of saintly people.

Fourth, although we do not follow the Jewish liturgical calendar and the New Testament offers little guidance in normative patterns of corporate cultic celebration, the theology and principles underlying First Testament festivals have much to teach us. As we plan worship services for the year, we should recognize the potential for drawing worshipers into the divine drama of redemption. We should also capitalize on the didactic force of worship by instructing people in the forms, functions, and theology of First Testament worship, and structuring our own calendars around the pillar events on which the church was founded.

Fifth, individual congregations, churches within a community, and denominations would do well to set aside special days and events to commemorate God's grace toward these local expressions of the body of Christ. In so doing, every generation is invited to become a part of the congregation's story and to participate in the drama of its worship. However, we must guard against letting such celebrations degenerate into commemoration of human achievements or sanitizing our history the way the Israelites tended to sanitize theirs. The Lord's view of our past may be quite different from our own.[53]

Sixth, we need to establish liturgies that focus on the specific work of Christ on our behalf rather than vain repetitions and empty generalizations that say little and leave the unregenerate smug in their sin. This matter deserves more attention than we can give here, but evangelical churches must give more attention to making special occasions in the lives of their members deeply worshipful experiences. Such celebrations might revolve around the seasons of life: birthdays, conversions, baptisms, weddings, and anniversaries; the ordination of ministers, elders, and deacons; the commissioning of teachers, evangelists, and missionaries; lamentation services when a member must be disciplined; and celebrations when wayward members return to Christ.[54] May the Lord open our eyes to the countless reasons he has given us to celebrate, and open our ears to his promptings to lament. May the Holy Spirit of God energize us to participate in these dramatic moments to the praise and glory of God the Father and Jesus Christ his Son.

53. Cf. Ezekiel's revisionist writing of Israel's history with God's point of view in Ezek. 16; 20; and 23.

54. We need not mark such events as annual observances and certainly should not canonize them for other congregations.

12

The Design and Theology of Sacred Space

True worship involves reverential human acts of submission and homage before the divine Sovereign in response to his gracious revelation of himself and in accord with his will.

In John 4:21–24 Jesus tells the Samaritan woman that the day is coming when the significance of the place of worship will be minimized; people will worship the Father neither on Mount Gerizim nor in Jerusalem, but in spirit and in truth. He makes it sound as if "spirit" and "truth" are places that will substitute for "on this mountain" and "in Jerusalem"—as if spiritual geography will eclipse physical geography. But around the world Christians still worship in places they identify as "sanctuaries" or "houses of God." Do we betray Jesus' vision by localizing worship? How should we think about the spaces where we gather for our audiences with God? To answer this question, we must ask how the Scriptures think about the places where God's people worshiped.

The Creation of the World as Sacred Space

The Torah opens with a grand celebration of God's creation (Gen. 1–3). Cast in elegant catechetical prose, Genesis 1:1–2:4a exhibits a liturgical flavor.

The repetition and formulaic structure celebrate the goodness and order that pervades all of God's creation and ensure that this text is easily committed to memory. With the triumphant assessment "Look! It is very good!" (1:31), God completed his workweek. Having ceased his creative activity, God marked the moment by blessing the seventh day and consecrating it.

Based on priestly elements and links with the instructions for the tabernacle's construction (Exod. 25–31), many argue that God created the cosmos, and even the garden of Eden, as a temple.[1] However, this interpretation is doubtful on three counts.[2] First, all the supposedly priestly elements are capable of different interpretations. Second, while the instructions concerning the tabernacle suggest that the structure was designed as a microcosm of creation, this does not mean creation is a macrocosm of the tabernacle. Finally, the interpretation is precluded by the function of sanctuaries in the Bible and the ancient Near East. Temples were constructed as residences for deity. Although God walked about in the garden, he did not live there; nor did he create the world so he could have a home.

The idea of the cosmos as sacred space is recognized in Numbers 14:21, where YHWH begins a warning with an oath: "By my life, and as surely as the glory of YHWH will fill the whole earth . . ."; and in Isaiah 6:3, where the seraphim declare, "Holy! Holy! Holy! The fullness of the whole earth is his glory!" Also, in Psalm 72:19 the psalmist declares, "Blessed be his glorious name forever; may his glory fill the whole earth" (NRSV).[3] The creation of the cosmos as sacred space underlies the hope of ultimate universal worship of YHWH,[4] but the earth is never portrayed as the temple of God—that is, as his residence. He dwells in and reigns from his glorious palace in the heavens.

In Genesis 2–3 we begin to see gradations of sanctity in creation (fig. 12.1). The garden was sacred space because YHWH made it, owned it, and placed his image (humankind) there, but this was not a temple garden functioning as his home. Rather, Eden is portrayed as a royal park, the special preserve of

1. See Gordon J. Wenham, "Sanctuary Symbolism in the Garden of Eden Story," in *I Studied Inscriptions before the Flood*, ed. R. S. Hess and D. T. Tsumura, Sources for Biblical and Theological Study 4 (Winona Lake, IN: Eisenbrauns, 1994), 399–404; Greg Beale, *A New Testament Biblical Theology: The Unfolding of the Old Testament in the New* (Grand Rapids: Baker Academic, 2011), 617–22; Beale, *The Temple and the Church's Mission: A Biblical Theology of the Dwelling Place of God*, New Studies in Biblical Theology 17 (Downers Grove, IL: InterVarsity, 2004), 66–75.

2. For fuller discussion and bibliography, see Daniel I. Block, "Eden: A Temple? A Reassessment of the Biblical Evidence," in *From Creation to New Creation: Biblical Theology and Exegesis*, edited by D. M. Gurtner and B. L. Gladd (Peabody, MA: Hendrickson, 2013), 3–32.

3. Cf. Hab. 2:14, "The earth will be filled with the knowledge of the glory of YHWH, as the waters cover the sea."

4. As in Pss. 22:27; 86:8–10; 93:1–5; 95:1–5; 96:1–11; 97:1–12; 98:1–9; Isa. 11:9; Zech. 14:9.

the divine King, with humans as its primary occupants. Adam is the governor of this park, assigned with the task of "serving" and "guarding" the garden.[5] This garden is sacred, but it is not God's house, and there is no hint here of cultic service. It is the dwelling of his creatures, humans and others. By eating from the tree of the knowledge of good and evil, the first humans tried to make Eden into a temple and assume the role of deity. For this rebellion they were expelled to a world governed by tooth and claw.

FIGURE 12.1
Edenic Gradations of Sacred Space

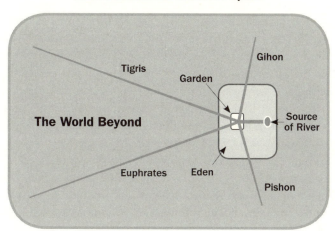

Sacred Space in the Patriarchal Narratives

In the patriarchal narratives God reserved the land of Canaan as an eternal homeland for his chosen people. However, allusions to this land as sacred space are scarce. Abraham built altars to mark a series of locations where YHWH encountered him, but their function is not clear.[6] The narrator identifies the sites where YHWH appeared to Abraham (Gen. 12:6–7) and where Abraham called on the name of YHWH (12:8; 13:4; 21:33; 26:25; cf. 4:26),[7] but only 22:9

5. On the significance of these expressions, see Daniel I. Block, "To Serve and to Keep: Toward a Biblical Understanding of Humanity's Responsibility in the Face of the Biodiversity Crisis," in *Keeping God's Earth: The Global Environment in Biblical Perspective,* ed. D. I. Block and N. J. Toly (Downers Grove, IL: InterVarsity, 2010), 126–32.

6. The oak of Moreh at Shechem (Gen. 12:7); Bethel (12:8; cf. 13:3); Hebron (13:18); and Moriah (22:9).

7. Gordon J. Wenham (*Genesis 1–15,* Word Biblical Commentary 1 [Waco: Word, 1987], 116) interprets this as an umbrella term for worship, involving most obviously sacrifice and prayer. Allan Ross ("שֵׁם," in *New International Dictionary of Old Testament Theology and Exegesis*

associates an altar with sacrifice. With hindsight we recognize premonitions of the future Jerusalem in the story of Abraham's paying his tithe to Melchizedek, king of Salem and priest of El Elyon (Gen. 14:18–20). The supreme test of Abraham's faith occurred on Mount Moriah (Gen. 22:1–19). This mountain would become extremely significant in Israel's spiritual geography; it was the place that YHWH would choose to establish his name and where Solomon would build the temple (2 Chron. 3:1).[8]

Both Isaac and Jacob continued Abraham's practice of building altars where they encountered God,[9] but Bethel was especially significant for Jacob. While running from his brother and apparently from the presence of God, he lay down to sleep at Bethel (Gen. 28:10–22). In a dream he saw YHWH and his heavenly host and heard the renewal of the Abrahamic promise and the guarantee of divine presence wherever he went. Jacob recognized the sanctity of this place by (1) verbally declaring, "YHWH is in this place"; (2) naming this place Beth-El, "the house of God," and viewing it as the gateway to heaven (v. 17); (3) erecting a pillar and through ceremonial anointing marking this as a sacred spot (v. 18); (4) changing the name of the nearby Canaanite town from Luz to Bethel (v. 19); (5) vowing to acknowledge YHWH as his God if he would take care of him and bring him back to this land (vv. 20–21); (6) declaring the pillar to be God's house (v. 22a); and (7) promising to give his tithe to God. The events of that night transformed an ordinary place where Jacob simply intended to spend the night into a site recognized as sacred throughout Israel's history.[10]

Mount Sinai as Sacred Space

No encounter with God in the First Testament matched what transpired on Mount Sinai (Exod. 19–24). Moses was introduced to the sanctity of this place while herding his father-in-law's sheep (3:1–6). He heard a voice from a burning bush commanding him to stand back and remove his shoes, for the place where he was standing was holy ground. YHWH told Moses this would

---

[NIDOTTE], ed. W. A. VanGemeren [Grand Rapids: Eerdmans, 1997], 4:148) suggests that he made proclamation of YHWH by name, which may imply proclaiming what YHWH is like (cf. Exod. 34:5–7, where the same construction occurs: *wayyiqrāʾ bĕšēm YHWH*).

8. Elsewhere the expression "mountain of God" is used of Eden (Ezek. 28:14, 16) and Sinai (Exod. 3:1; 4:27; 18:5; 24:13; 1 Kings 19:8); cf. Sinai as "mountain of YHWH" in Num. 10:33, though elsewhere this is a favorite expression for Jerusalem/Zion (Isa. 2:3; 30:29; Mic. 4:2; Zech. 8:3).

9. Isaac at Beersheba (Gen. 26:25); Jacob at Shechem (33:20) and Bethel (35:1, 3, 7).

10. See, e.g., Judg. 20:18, 26; 21:2; 1 Sam. 10:3; 1 Kings 12:29–33; 13:32; 2 Kings 10:29; 23:15–19; Amos 3:14; 7:10.

not be the last time YHWH would meet him here; when Moses had led the Israelites out of Egypt, they would "serve" God at this mountain (v. 12; cf. 4:23; 7:16; 8:1; 10:25–26). YHWH kept his word by bringing the newly freed Israelites to this "mountain of God" (*har hāʾĕlōhîm*) three months after they had left Egypt (19:1).[11]

The Sinai narratives illustrate the sanctity of space on earth occupied by the holy God. The ascending intensity of holiness on Mount Sinai is clearly reflected in the roles the participants played in the covenant-ratifying procedures (Exod. 19–24; fig. 12.2). As noted earlier, the Israelites could approach the mountain only by invitation from YHWH, only after they had consecrated themselves and erected a barrier around the mountain, and only at the signal of the trumpet blast. At the next level of sanctity, the elders, who represented the people, participated in a meal hosted by the heavenly King himself (24:9–11). At the third level, Moses entered the presence of God at the top of the mountain to receive the covenant document from him (vv. 12–18).

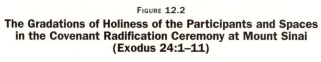

FIGURE 12.2
The Gradations of Holiness of the Participants and Spaces in the Covenant Radification Ceremony at Mount Sinai (Exodus 24:1–11)

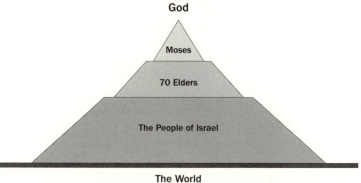

Although this event was remarkable,[12] YHWH never intended for Sinai to be his permanent earthly residence; that privilege was reserved for Zion/Jerusalem. But for a dramatic moment, Sinai functioned as sacred space, where heavenly perfection and human imperfection met. Mount Sinai played no further role

11. See Exod. 3:1; 4:27; 18:5; 24:13; 1 Kings 19:8.

12. Reflecting on this event forty years later, Moses recognized how extraordinary it was: "Has any people heard the voice of a god speaking out of a fire, as you have, and survived? . . . From the heavens He let you hear His voice to discipline you; on earth He let you see His great fire; and from amidst that fire you heard His words" (Deut. 4:33, 36 NJPS).

in Israel's history until Elijah returned five hundred years later for a personal encounter with the Creator of heaven and earth (1 Kings 19:9–14).

The Tabernacle as Sacred Space

While still at Sinai, at YHWH's command the Israelites built a structure that would ensure his presence in their midst as they journeyed to the promised land (Exod. 25–31; 35–40). The Hebrew designations for the tabernacle reflect its functions: it was the "house of YHWH" (*bêt yhwh*, Exod. 34:26), his "big house" (*hêkāl*; 1 Sam. 1:9; 3:3), his "dwelling place" (*miškān*), and his "sanctuary" (*miqdāš*, Exod. 25:8–9). The last expression reflects YHWH's transcendent holiness and identifies the tabernacle compound as sacred space. Like Mount Sinai itself, the tabernacle was rendered holy by YHWH's presence, symbolized by the "glory" (*kābôd*). The tabernacle was also called the "tent of appointment" (*'ōhel mô'ēd*), a term that originally identified a tent pitched outside the camp where Moses would receive instructions from YHWH (Exod. 33:7–10). Applied to the tabernacle, this expression highlighted YHWH's desire to meet with his people.

The Divine Nature of the Tabernacle

Since ancient Near Easterners generally believed that the gods personally designed their residences, determined where those residences should be built, and appointed those who would construct them, it is not surprising that the Scriptures present the tabernacle as a divine work from start to finish. YHWH revealed the plan to Moses on the mountain (Exod. 25–31).[13] In keeping with his divine majesty, YHWH prescribed that the most valuable materials be used in its construction and service (25:3–7). YHWH inspired the people to contribute to the project (25:2), appointed people to design and construct the tabernacle (31:2, 6; 35:30, 34), and endowed the craftsmen and workers with special gifts to perform their tasks (31:3–11; 35:31–35). Finally, YHWH determined the date for the initial erection of the tabernacle (40:2). This was indeed a sacred structure, sanctioned, designed, and legitimized by the One who would reside in it.

The Design of the Tabernacle

We have already suggested that the design of the tabernacle, its furnishings, and its rituals were based on the celestial reality that Moses saw on Mount

13. See Exod. 25:9, 40; 26:30; Num. 8:4; Acts 7:44; Heb. 8:5.

Figure 12.3. Relationship of heavenly and earthly residences of God (Concept by John H. Walton, drawing by Alva Steffler. Used with permission.)

Sinai. The correspondence is captured in a reconstruction of cosmic realities (fig. 12.3). Many have recognized links between the instructions concerning the construction of the tabernacle (Exod. 25–31) and Genesis 1. The instructions for the tabernacle consist of seven divine speeches, each introduced with "And YHWH spoke/said to Moses,"[14] which correspond to the six days of creation, also marked by divine speech: "And God said." Six of these speeches deal with creative activity, and the seventh deals with the gift of the Sabbath, which is explicitly grounded in creation (31:12–17). Like the creation account, this account ends with a reference to YHWH "finishing" (kālâ) his instructions for the new creation (31:18). The seven lights of the menorah (candlestick, 25:31–40) recall the seven days of creation. Leviticus 19:30 and 26:2 explicitly link the tabernacle with the Sabbath: "You shall keep my Sabbaths and revere my sanctuary; I am YHWH." The erection of the tabernacle on New Year's Day (Exod. 40:2, 17; cf. 9:31, springtime) signaled a new creation and the beginning of a new era in cosmic history. The symmetry and proportion of the tabernacle reflect the symmetry and order built into the universe.[15]

14. As in Exod. 25:1; 30:11, 17, 22, 34; 31:1, 12.

15. We may also hear verbal allusions to Genesis in the account of the construction of the tabernacle. Cf. Exod. 39:32 and Gen. 2:1; Exod. 39:43 and Gen. 1:31; Exod. 40:33 and Gen. 2:2.

The tabernacle also derives much of its conceptual vocabulary from the Eden narrative (Gen. 2–3): *kĕrubîm* guarding the way to the tree of life (Gen. 3:24; cf. Exod. 25:18–22; 26:31), themselves being reflected in the menorah; the charge to Adam "to serve and to keep" the garden (Gen. 2:15), echoed in the assignment of the Levitical priests (Num. 3:7–8; 8:26; 18:5–6); and the entrance on the east side (Gen. 3:24; cf. Ezek. 40:6). These features are extremely significant for grasping the function of the tabernacle in Israelite thinking. In its design as a microcosm of the heavenly residence of God, the sanctuary provided an earthly dwelling for YHWH in the midst of a fallen people, and its rituals provided a means whereby covenant relationship between a sinful people and a holy God could be maintained. In its design as a microcosm of Eden, the tabernacle addressed both the alienation of humanity from the divine Suzerain and the alienation of creation from God and humanity in general. The tabernacle symbolized YHWH's gracious determination to lift the effects of the curse from his people; it functioned as the place from which his blessing and rule could radiate (Ps. 50:2–4).

Like most temples in the ancient Near East, the tabernacle was a rectangle, oriented on an east-west axis, with the entrance on the east side and the holy of holies on the west (fig. 12.4). The sanctuary complex consisted of four major areas: an outer court, fifty cubits wide and one hundred cubits long; the tabernacle itself, ten cubits wide and thirty cubits long (Exod. 27); the front room of the tabernacle, the holy place (*haqqōdeš*), containing the menorah, the table with the bread of the Presence, and the altar of incense; and the back room, the holy of holies (*qōdeš haqqŏdāšîm*, 26:31–35), holding the ark of the covenant, which served as YHWH's throne.[16]

The proportions of the compound are striking. It was divided into two equal squares, fifty cubits by fifty cubits. The altar, symbolizing the worshipers' reaching out to God and God's gracious condescension, was the focal point of the front square, while the ark of the covenant, symbolizing YHWH's commitment to his people, was the focal point of the rear square. The tabernacle proper was also divided into two parts, exhibiting a two-to-one ratio. The holy place was a perfectly proportioned rectangle, ten cubits wide and twenty cubits long. The holy of holies was square, ten cubits by ten cubits.[17] The sizes of the

16. First Sam. 4:4 identifies YHWH as "YHWH of Hosts, who sits [enthroned] above the cherubim."

17. The perfect proportioning extended to the furnishings. The altar of burnt offering was three cubits high, but its horizontal dimensions were square, each side being five cubits (Exod. 27:1–8); the altar of incense was one cubit long by one cubit wide by two cubits high (30:1–10); the table with the bread of the Presence was two cubits long by one cubit wide by one-and-a-half cubits high (25:23–30); the menorah consisted of a central stem with seven lights (25:31–40); the ark of the covenant was a rectangular box two and a half cubits long, one and a half cubits wide, and one and a half cubits high (25:10–22). Dimensions are lacking only for the laver (30:17–21).

FIGURE 12.4
The Ground Plan of the Tabernacle

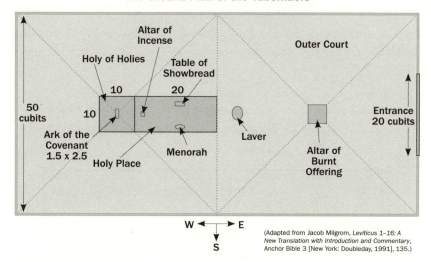

W ◄——► E
S

(Adapted from Jacob Milgrom, *Leviticus 1–16: A New Translation with Introduction and Commentary,* Anchor Bible 3 [New York: Doubleday, 1991], 135.)

entrances to the compound reflected the increasing sanctity of the areas they guarded: the gate of the outer court, twenty cubits; the gate of the tabernacle proper, ten cubits; the gate to the holy of holies, lacking. This proportional perfection reflects both the divine order of the universe and the perfections of YHWH's heavenly dwelling.

The materials used to construct the tabernacle served both utilitarian and aesthetic functions.[18] Like Aaron's garments (Exod. 28:2, 40), everything about this place proclaimed the glory and magnificence of the One enthroned above the cherubim. At the same time, the tabernacle was designed so it could be easily dismantled, transported, and reassembled at the next campsite. This was a spectacularly crafted, portable palace, so designed that the Israelites' encounter with YHWH at Mount Sinai could be experienced repeatedly hereafter. YHWH was no absentee Sovereign: he was the holy God who delighted to dwell among his people.

18. The outside covering of cloth from goats' hair protected the entire building from heat and dust (36:14–18). Two curtains covered the tabernacle proper, the upper curtain made of goatskin leather and the lower curtain of rams' skins dyed red (36:19). Bronze pillars decorated with silver supported the outer curtains (27:9–19), which were made of fine twisted linen, dyed royal blue-purple and red-purple (36:8–14). The walls for the tabernacle proper consisted of acacia wood panels set in sockets of silver (36:20–30). A veil of fine royal blue-purple and red-purple, skillfully decorated with cherubim, closed off the holy of holies. This veil was supported by pillars of acacia wood overlaid with gold and set in sockets of silver (36:35–38). The ark of the covenant was made of acacia wood and completely overlaid with gold, finely decorated with gold molding, and covered by a special covering molded from a single piece of gold (37:1–9).

The Temple as Sacred Space

Although the temple in Jerusalem was built as a permanent structure, we know less about its design than we do about the tabernacle's. Many of the temple's features mirror those of the tabernacle, though on a much grander scale (fig. 12.5).

FIGURE 12.5

A Comparison of the Ground Plans of the Tabernacle and Temple

——Outline of the Tabernacle   − − − Outline of the Temple

Courtyard and Building

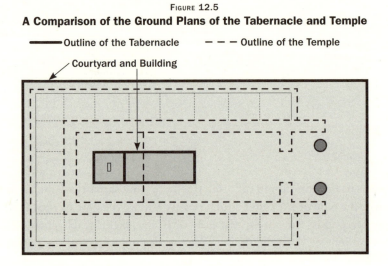

The Divine Nature of the Temple

Like the tabernacle, the temple in Jerusalem was a divine project. Fulfilling the words of Moses (e.g., Deut. 12:5; 16:16), YHWH chose the place where the temple was to be constructed (Ps. 132:13–16), then inspired David to make arrangements for its construction and worship. Although David did not see the temple built in his lifetime, he received its blueprint directly from the hand of God (1 Chron. 28:11–19); gathered a major portion of the resources needed to build it (22:14); assembled, commissioned, and blessed the craftsmen for the project (22:15–16); organized the temple personnel, including the supervisors, gatekeepers, musicians, priests, and temple treasurers (1 Chron. 23–26); and dedicated the temple furniture and vessels to YHWH (1 Kings 7:51). David's role in the temple project paralleled that of Moses in connection with the tabernacle (table 12.1).[19]

19. For this reason, if we must identify the temple with a human being, it should be called David's rather than Solomon's temple. Solomon was to this project what Bezalel was to the construction of the tabernacle.

Table 12.1. Comparing the Tabernacle and Temple Projects

Feature	The Tabernacle	The Temple
Place of construction	At Sinai Exod. 25–40	In Jerusalem-Zion 2 Sam. 6:1–7:1; 1 Chron. 21:18–22:1; Pss. 48; 78:65–72; 87:1–3; 132:10–18
Purpose	Portable residence for YHWH Exod. 25:8	Permanent residence for YHWH 2 Sam. 7:2; 1 Kings 6:12–13; 8; Ps. 132:10–18
Origin of design	Based on a replica (*tabnît*) revealed visually Exod. 25:9, 40; 26:30	Based on a replica (*tabnît*) revealed in writing 1 Chron. 28:11–19
Recipient of the revelation	Moses Exod. 25–31	David 2 Sam. 7:13; 1 Chron. 17:12; 28:11–19
Executor of the project	Bezalel, endowed with wisdom and special gifts, and Oholiab Exod. 31:1–6a; 35:30–36:1a	Solomon, endowed with wisdom, and Hiram of Tyre 1 Kings 5:12 [26]; 7:13–50
Auxiliary workers	Other gifted artisans Exod. 31:6b; 36:1b	Skillful men recruited by David, laborers conscripted by David and Solomon 1 Chron. 22:2, 15; 1 Kings 5:13–18 [27–32]
Source of the materials	Freewill gifts of people whose spirits moved them Exod. 25:2–7; 35:5–6	David's freewill offerings 1 Chron. 22:14
Organizer of personnel	Moses Exod. 28–30; Lev. 8–10; Num. 3–4; 6:22–27; 18:1–32	David 1 Chron. 23–26
Sign of divine approval	Descent of the cloud and fire after erection of the outer court Exod. 40:31–38	Descent of cloud after the ark was placed in the holy of holies 1 Kings 8:6–12 = 2 Chron. 5:7–14
Orientation of the building	Eastward Exod. 27:13; 38:13	Eastward Ezek. 8:16
Components of the building	Holy of holies (*qōdeš haqqŏdāšîm*) Exod. 26:33–34	Holy of holies (*qōdeš haqqŏdāšîm*) 1 Kings 6:16; 7:50; 8:6; 1 Chron. 6:49; 2 Chron. 3:8, 10; 4:22; 5:7 Inner sanctum (*dĕbîr*) 1 Kings 6:5, 16, 19, 23, 31; 8:6, 8; Ps. 28:2
	Holy place (*qōdeš*) Exod. 26:33; 28:29, 35, 43	Holy place (*qōdeš*) 1 Kings 8:8, 10; 2 Chron. 29:5, 7; 35:5
	Court Exod. 27:9–19	Court 1 Kings 6:36; 8:64; Ezek. 8:1–13

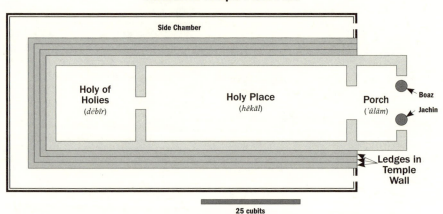

FIGURE 12.6
Jerusalem Temple Floor Plan

YHWH appointed the supervisor for the actual construction of the temple (2 Sam. 7:13 = 1 Chron. 17:12; 28:5–10). Just as Bezalel was the executor of the sanctuary revealed to Moses, so Solomon was the executor of the Davidic idea and plan that YHWH had revealed to him.[20] Like Bezalel, Solomon engaged others (especially his ally King Hiram of Tyre, 1 Kings 5:1–12) both for help in acquiring raw materials and in involving a master craftsman, another Hiram (son of a Jewish mother, 1 Kings 7:13–50). Nevertheless, apparently not all of Solomon's policies were commendable. First Kings 5:13–18 [27–32] notes that Solomon conscripted thirty thousand forced laborers to assist in the project.[21]

YHWH also designed the temple and all its ornamentation and furniture and revealed it to David in writing (1 Chron. 28:9–19). Since tabernacle and temple served the same purpose and came from the same source, their similarities in design are not surprising (fig. 12.5). Both structures were rectangular in shape, oriented on an east-west axis, with the entrance on the east side and the holy of holies on the west. Both consisted of two main rooms: the holy of holies, which housed the ark of the covenant; and the larger front room, the holy place, also called *hêkāl*, "temple/sanctuary" (1 Kings 6:3, 5). Both were located within in a larger court, with an altar for sacrifices and a laver for ritual cleansing in front. Both rooms were lavishly decorated with gold and silver, and colors and figures associated with royalty, befitting the divine King who resided within. And both were decorated with motifs from the Eden narrative.

20. See 1 Kings 5:12 [5:26]; 6:14; cf. Exod. 31:1–6; 35:30–35.
21. On the basis of 1 Kings 9:15–23, some argue that these were Canaanites living in Israel, rather than Israelites.

The differences between tabernacle and temple were determined by the former being a portable residence and the latter being YHWH's permanent dwelling place on Zion. Both were publicly authenticated as true places of worship by the Glory that occupied the respective structures, symbolizing YHWH's residence on his throne in the holy of holies (Exod. 40:33–38; 1 Kings 8:9–11).

The Physical Features of the Temple

The narratives of 1 and 2 Kings seem to identify three courtyards in the temple: a "great court," encompassing the royal buildings at a level lower than the temple (1 Kings 7:12); a "middle court," which included Solomon's palace south of the Temple Mount (2 Kings 20:4); and a paved "inner court," surrounding the temple (1 Kings 6:36; 2 Chron. 7:3).[22] Approaching the temple, a worshiper would have been struck by the sight of two freestanding bronze columns eighteen cubits high (1 Kings 7:15–21). If these represented the pillars on which YHWH founded the earth, they reinforce the notion that the temple was a microcosm of the world itself and symbolize the stability that came with YHWH's reign. Perhaps they replaced the bovine or leonine figures that often guarded the entryways of pagan temples (cf. Ezek. 8:3, 5).

As figure 12.5 suggests, the temple building would have covered almost the entire courtyard of the tabernacle. Retaining the two-to-one proportions of the rooms within the tabernacle itself, the temple proper was a perfectly proportioned rectangle, twenty cubits wide and sixty cubits long. Priests entered the temple through a vestibule twenty cubits wide by ten cubits deep. The holy place was a great hall twenty cubits wide by forty cubits deep. Behind it was the holy of holies, designed as a cube twenty cubits wide by twenty cubits deep by twenty cubits high (1 Kings 6:20). This room was dominated by the ark of the covenant, above which YHWH sat enthroned; the ark housed two written copies of the Decalogue. Two gigantic cherubim made of olive wood and plated with gold guarded the ark, each ten cubits high and having wingspans of ten cubits (2 Kings 6:23–28). The south, west, and north walls of the main structure were buttressed by three-story structures, apparently used to house temple personnel and store temple furniture and utensils (1 Kings 6:5–10).

The Theological Significance of the Temple

The temple in Jerusalem was a remarkable achievement. Although built at tremendous cost, its magnificence matched that of any known temple structure

---

22. Like the tabernacle, the temple built by Solomon had no discriminatory courts either for gentiles or women.

in the ancient Near East at this time, and it became a symbol of a nation come of age. While the faithful continued to express homage and submission to YHWH in their homes and villages, Jerusalem quickly became the focal point of the national religion. Even after the northern ten tribes separated from the Davidic monarchy after the death of Solomon, the prophets insisted the Jerusalem temple was the only legitimate place for Israelites to worship.

For worshipers this building symbolized YHWH's presence on earth. As such, it was both the object of his special affection (1 Kings 8:29; Ps. 132:13–18) and the reflection of his transcendent glory (1 Kings 8:12–13). As Solomon recognized (8:27), though the earth itself could not house God, the temple symbolized his presence among his people and his accessibility through prayer. No matter where YHWH's people found themselves, if they would turn toward this place and seek his face, he would hear them (8:28–30). Like Mount Sinai centuries earlier, the temple represented the focal point of holiness. As God's creation, the earth itself was recognized as sacred space, and the land of Israel was deemed a holy land (Zech. 2:12 [16]). But the temple, and the holy of holies in particular, represented the holiest place on earth (fig. 12.7).

FIGURE 12.7
Territorial Gradations of Holiness

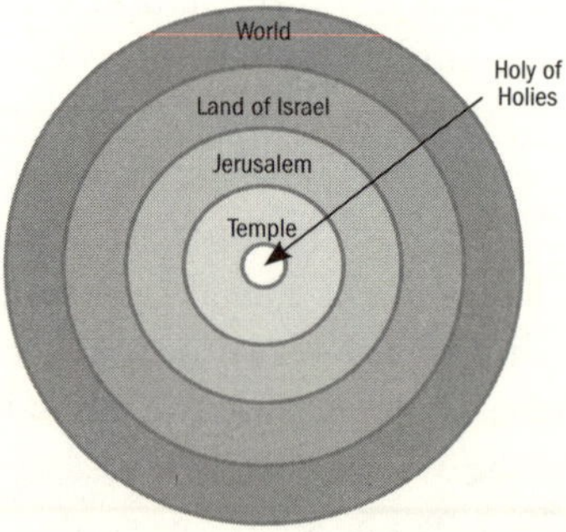

Although the temple was an earthly replica of YHWH's true heavenly residence, it also functioned as a microcosm of the cosmos, perfectly proportioned and designed with cosmic and Edenic features.[23] Not only did it

23. Several features link its design with creation: (a) it took seven years to build (1 Kings 6:37–38), corresponding to the seven days of creation; (b) the pillars Jachin and Boaz seem to symbolize the pillars on which the earth was founded (Job 9:6; 26:5–14; Ps. 75:3); (c) the decorative carvings of cherubim, palm trees, and open flowers recall the garden of Eden (1 Kings 6:29, 32, 35); (d) the ten massive lavers, each holding more than 240 gallons and set on elaborate stands (1 Kings 7:27–39), recall the primordial waters of těhôm, "the great deep."

symbolize the divine ideal for the earth but it also represented the source of Israel's and ultimately the world's re-creation as the divine Resident lifts the curse and causes his blessing and rule (the delights of Eden) to radiate forth (Ps. 50:2–4).

The temple also symbolized YHWH's covenant faithfulness. He had promised that he would choose a place for his name to be established. As such, the temple symbolized his claim to Israel, eclipsing the names of the gods that had previously claimed this land. Given the tight link between Zion and David, the temple symbolized YHWH's eternal covenant with David and with Israel, so much so that by the sixth century BC the people interpreted it as a sign of YHWH's unconditional and irrevocable commitment to them—even when they rejected the obligations of covenant relationship (Jer. 7:4, 8).

Finally, the temple and its prescribed worship provided a means whereby Israelites could maintain open communication with their God. Through sacrifice and the intermediary work of the priests, their sins could be removed; through their festivals, they could express their gratitude to God. As Solomon recognized in his dedicatory prayer (1 Kings 8:46–53), the temple also symbolized YHWH's invitation for the people to address him in prayer. Indeed, this symbol proved so strong that even after it had been destroyed, Daniel turned to Jerusalem three times a day to pray for the restoration of Israel (Dan. 6:10; cf. 9:1–19). Although the Glory represented YHWH in the temple, this did not mean that he was boxed inside the building or that he was inaccessible apart from it. On the contrary, YHWH's frequent promises of personal presence with his people (e.g., Deut. 7:21; Josh. 22:31; Ruth 2:4; 1 Sam. 17:37) assured them that where they were, there he was.

The End of the Temple

The glory of the Solomonic era was short-lived. In 931 BC the northern tribes declared their independence and established sanctuaries at Bethel and Dan to rival Jerusalem and give the northern kingdom an independent religious identity. For their rebellion against YHWH, the northern kingdom fell to the Assyrians in the eighth century BC. By 586 BC, because of Judah's rebellion, YHWH had written them off too. After the Judeans desecrated the temple with a host of evils, the glory of YHWH finally left, reducing this sacred shrine to a mere box and inviting Nebuchadnezzar to come and raze it (see especially Ezek. 8–11). Although the Judeans believed that YHWH would defend his own residence against pagan foreigners, he did not. Nebuchadnezzar's forces reduced the magnificent building to rubble and took the gold and silver that lined its halls to Babylon.

Ezekiel's Vision of the Restored Temple

But the hope represented by the temple did not die. Although the people's crimes had desecrated the land (Ezek. 36:17), the city of Jerusalem, and the temple itself (chaps. 8–9), causing YHWH to abandon his dwelling and his people, the story would not end there. The book of Ezekiel concludes with a magnificent vision of another temple, restored to perfection, housing the divine Glory once more (Ezek. 43:1–12). While interpreters debate over how to understand Ezekiel 40–48, particularly whether these chapters provide a blueprint for an eschatological temple, many features of this vision suggest that it is the glorious theological statement of a people, land, and Deity finally enjoying healthy covenant relationship. Using the language of sacred space, temple, and ritual, Ezekiel describes that new spiritual reality.[24]

To Ezekiel's audience, the disillusioned exiles, this temple vision announced the renewal of God's covenant, his reunion of the people with their homeland, and his residence in their midst as a sign that now finally all is well. To those who despaired of finding acceptance with YHWH again, the envisioned design of the temple offered hope. Although they were stuck in a pagan land, Ezekiel's vision declared that communion with YHWH would be restored, and one day their acts of submission and homage would be accepted.

This vision proclaimed that YHWH was still the divine King of Israel. His kingship may have been thrown into question by his departure from the temple, but the return of the divine *kābôd* (Glory) envisioned in 43:1–9 established the sacred precinct as "the place of my throne and the place of the soles of my feet, where I will dwell in the midst of the descendants of Israel forever" (v. 7). This message is reinforced by the name given to "the City" in the final declaration of the book: *YHWH šammâ*, "YHWH is There" (48:35).

To a people exiled because they had failed to distinguish between holy and profane (cf. 44:23) and had flagrantly violated sacred space, this vision also proclaimed the holiness of God and all that he touches. When YHWH would enter this city, it would become holy ground, and from this mountain his holiness would emanate throughout the land. In addition, to a people exiled largely because their leaders had led them astray, Ezekiel's vision declared an end to the old abuses. No kings would encroach on sacred space again, dragging in their pagan images, as Manasseh had done (2 Kings

24. For further discussion on how to interpret these chapters, see Daniel I. Block, *Ezekiel, Chapters 25–48*, New International Commentary on the Old Testament (Grand Rapids: Eerdmans, 1998), 494–506; Block, *Beyond the River Chebar: Studies in Kingship and Eschatology in the Book of Ezekiel* (Eugene, OR: Cascade Books, 2013), 158–64.

21:1–9). Indeed, even "the prince," who represents a humbled royal house,[25] was transformed. He was allotted special land on either side of the sacred reserve in the heart of Israel, presumably to pasture livestock that the people bring for sacrifices, but he would have no throne, no palace, and no capital city. With twelve gates named after the tribes of Israel, the city that appears in chapter 48 would not be the king's city or "the City of David." Rather, it will be the city of the people among whom YHWH the divine King resides: hence the name *šammâ!*[26]

Finally, to exiles in a foreign land, this vision affirms that *they* are still YHWH's people. The mountain is not portrayed as the cosmic mountain, to which the nations come; instead, the city and the altar address YHWH's relationship to his chosen people in particular. To be sure, non-Israelites are to be treated like native Israelites when the property is distributed (47:22–23), but the text assumes that each of these families will be integrated into one of the twelve tribes. Like the rest of the book, the territorial rhetoric of the vision concerns primarily—if not exclusively—Israel.

The Second Temple

We know little of the temple built by those who returned from exile in 538 BC and the decades following.[27] While the narratives stress the divine origin of this temple, especially with YHWH's appointment of Cyrus to build him a house in Jerusalem (2 Chron. 36:22–23; Ezra 1:1–4), little is said about YHWH's involvement in the project. This temple was much smaller than the original temple and vastly inferior to it, and Ezekiel's prediction of the return of the glory of YHWH (Ezek. 43:1–10) never materialized, leading to widespread cynicism and despondency in Jerusalem (Ezra 3:10; 4:24; Hag. 2:1–9; Zech. 4:10). While some who witnessed the laying of the foundation celebrated with great joy, priests, Levites, and older people who remembered the glory of the first temple wept (Ezra 3:10–13). The project ground to a halt (4:24) and was not resumed until 520 BC. Inspired by Haggai and Zechariah (Ezra 5:1–5), the building was completed in 515 BC.

25. The epithet *hannāśîʾ*, "the prince," is used of Davidic rulers in Ezek. 34:23–24 and 37:24–25.
26. For further discussion of the *nāśîʾ*'s role, see Daniel I. Block, "Bringing Back David: Ezekiel's Messianic Hope," in *The Lord's Anointed: Interpretation of Old Testament Messianic Texts*, ed. P. E. Satterthwaite et al. (Grand Rapids: Baker, 1995), 167–88.
27. For a full discussion of the design of the second temple, see Leen Ritmeyer, *The Quest: Revealing the Temple Mount in Jerusalem* (Jerusalem: Carta, 2006), 317–25; Ritmeyer, *Beyond the River Chebar*, 74–94.

According to Hecataeus,[28] the temple area measured about 500 feet by 150 feet, but the dimensions of the building itself are unknown. First Maccabees 1:21–22 and 4:49–51 suggest that the holy place contained one golden lampstand (cf. Solomon's plurality, in 1 Kings 7:48–50), a table for the bread of the Presence, a gold altar of incense, and sacred vessels. A veil divided the holy place from the holy of holies, but lacking both ark and the divine Glory, this room was empty. Even so, the people celebrated the completion of the temple with great fanfare, involving hundreds of sacrifices and the Passover meal (Ezra 6:13–22).

While this temple signified the return of YHWH's favor to his people, it also served as a test of their faith (Hag. 1:5–11; 2:15–19; Mal. 3:10–12) and became a symbol of the new community's spiritual lethargy, as distinctions between the holy and the profane were neglected once more (Ezra 9:1–2; Neh. 9:2). In the fifth century BC the people grew increasingly cynical of their status as the people of YHWH (Mal. 1:1–2:9). By the second century BC the priesthood was being sold to the highest bidder as Hellenistic candidates vied for the favor of Antiochus IV Epiphanes. The history of this temple sank to its low point in 167 BC, when Antiochus's forces slaughtered most males in Jerusalem and enslaved the women and children. They destroyed the city walls, abolished all Jewish rites, and rededicated the temple to the Olympian Zeus. On Kislev 15 (December 6) Antiochus committed "the abomination of desolation" (Dan. 11:31; 12:11; 1 Macc. 1:54; Mark 13:14) in the temple. Three years later Judas Maccabeus recovered control of the building. He repaired and purified it, an event celebrated to this day in the Jewish Feast of Hanukkah.

Herod's Temple

The Scriptures show little interest in the construction or design of the temple that stood in Jerusalem during the New Testament period.[29] Nevertheless, this temple was an elaborate project undertaken by the Idumean king Herod the Great (40–4 BC), not to glorify God, but to pacify his Jewish subjects.[30] Although it failed in this respect, the temple was an engineering wonder. Herod doubled the original area of the Temple Mount by lowering the northwest corner of Mount Moriah and using the materials removed to build up the southern slope.[31]

28. As cited by Josephus, *Against Apion* 1.22.
29. In John 2:20 Jewish leaders note that it took forty-six years to build.
30. To declare his loyalty to the emperor, Herod also built a temple to the goddess Roma in coastal Caesarea.
31. For a full discussion of the construction and design of Herod's temple, see Ritmeyer, *Quest*, 339–400.

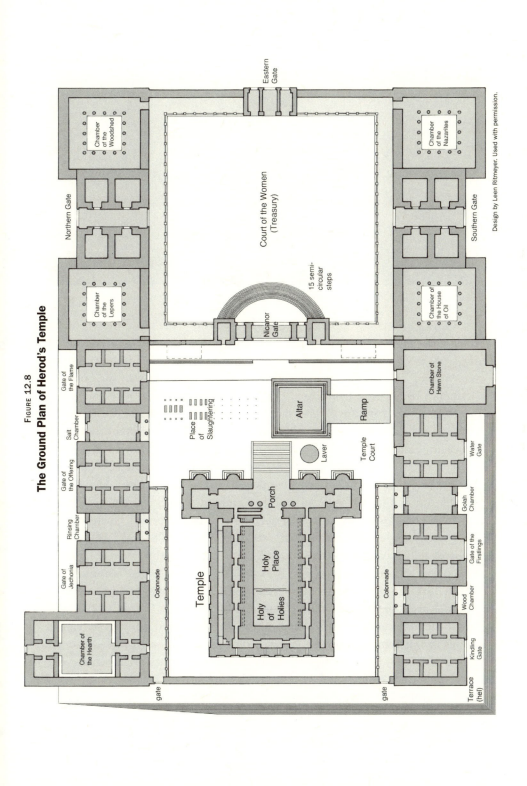

FIGURE 12.8
The Ground Plan of Herod's Temple

Chamber of the Woodshed

Northern Gate

Chamber of the Lepers

Gate of the Flame

Salt Chamber

Gate of the Offering

Rinsing Chamber

Gate of Jechonia

Colonnade

Chamber of the Hearth

gate

Temple

Holy of Holies

Holy Place

Porch

Place of Slaughtering

Altar

Ramp

Laver

Temple Court

Colonnade

gate

Terrace (hel)

Kindling Gate

Wood Chamber

Gate of the Firstlings

Golah Chamber

Water Gate

Chamber of Hewn Stone

Court of the Women (Treasury)

15 semi-circular steps

Nicanor Gate

Eastern Gate

Chamber of the Nazarites

Southern Gate

Chamber of the House of Oil

Design by Leen Ritmeyer. Used with permission.

Figure 12.9. The Dome of the Rock on the Temple Mount (Photograph by J. Marr Miller. Used with permission.)

Apart from its extravagant size and decoration, the basic design of the temple itself shared with previous versions the three-part structure involving the front porch, the holy place, and the holy of holies (see Josephus, *Jewish Antiquities* 15.11). The most striking modifications involved the complex system of courtyards. Inside the Nicanor Gate was a sixteen-foot-wide court of the Israelites, running the width of the temple area (*Middot* 2.6), accessible only to purified Israelite men (see Luke 18:10; Acts 3:1). In front of the temple was a large square court, each side measuring 135 cubits, known as the Court of Women (Mishnah, *Middot* 2.3–5), not because it was restricted to women, but because this was as far as women could go.[32] This area was deemed less sacred than the Court of Israel and the Court of the Priests, but it provided space for great festivities, especially during the Feast of Booths. Thirteen offering chests were located in this court (see Mark 12:41; John 8:20). Beyond the walls of these courts was the Court of the Gentiles. In the porticoes around the court, teachers would address the crowds or engage in discussions (Mark 11:27; 12:35). Since animals needed for sacrifice were bought and sold here, this was also the place of Jesus' cleansing of the temple.[33]

At the very moment Jesus died on the cross, the veil before the holy of holies in this temple was torn in two from top to bottom (Matt. 27:50–53; Mark 15:37–38; Luke 23:44–46). The death of Jesus was an epochal event, marking the end of foreshadowing sacrificial liturgies and of the temple as the man-made replica of the temple in heaven. As High Priest of the "good things

32. Ibid., 349.
33. Matt. 21:12–17, 23–27; Mark 11:15–19, 27–33; Luke 19:45–48; 20:1–8; John 2:13–16.

that have come" (Heb. 9:11), Jesus Christ entered the heavenly holy of holies, presenting his own blood to God for the forgiveness of sins (vv. 12–14). The torn veil signaled the termination of the old system of covenant maintenance, but it also exposed Herod's temple for the sham that it was. In this temple, God met with those who worshiped him in spirit and in truth,[34] but this had less to do with the temple itself than with God's commitment to meeting his people at the place he had established for his name.

In AD 70, under Titus, Roman legions destroyed much of Jerusalem and razed the temple, the symbol of Jewish nationalism. However, the ultimate insult occurred in AD 135, when Hadrian answered a revolt led by Bar Kokhba, devastated what was left of Jerusalem, and reestablished it as a pagan city named Aelia Capitolina. Today the Dome of the Rock, Islam's third holiest shrine, occupies the Temple Mount, commemorating Muhammad's supposed ascent to heaven.

Sacred Space in the New Testament

Although Jews treasured the temple throughout the New Testament era, Jesus and his followers expressed several different perspectives on the place. First, they continued to worship in the temple. Luke highlights the role of the temple and its staff in his infancy narratives (1:8–23; 2:22–38, 46–50). Temple personnel as a whole seem to have been corrupt, but with expectant faith Zechariah, Simeon, Anna, Mary, and Joseph represented the best of "temple piety." The Gospel of John notes Jesus' attendance at festivals in Jerusalem (John 2:13; 5:1; 7:10, 14; 10:22–23), and despite the dubious origins of "Herod's temple," Jesus speaks of it as God's dwelling (Matt. 23:21). The temple figures prominently in Acts as a place of Christian corporate worship (2:43–47) and prayer (3:1–10), teaching and proclaiming the resurrection of Jesus (4:1–2; 5:17–25, 42), purification rituals and sacrifices for Jewish Christian converts (21:26), personal prayer (22:17), and to deposit alms (24:18).

Second, Jesus and his followers criticized the abuses of temple worship. Driven by "passion" for YHWH's house (John 2:17; cf. Ps. 69:9 [10]), Jesus expelled merchants who desecrated its space and transformed his Father's house into a money market.[35] In Acts 7:46–50 Stephen seems ambiguous about the temple itself,[36] but his primary issue is the theology that developed from

---

34. Note the angelic visitation of Zechariah in the temple (Luke 1:8–23) and the prophetic utterances of godly Simeon and Anna when Jesus was presented in the temple (2:22–38).

35. See Matt. 21:12–16; Mark 11:15–18; Luke 19:45–47; John 2:13–16 (alluding to Zech. 14:21).

36. Many commentators interpret Stephen's comments on Solomon as criticism for having built the temple. However, this would be a direct contradiction of the narrative in 2 Samuel–1 Kings,

its existence. The people's rebellion arose from the conviction that with the temple's construction, they had God in a box and could control him. They had forgotten that God actually resides in heaven, a point Solomon had emphasized in his dedicatory prayer in 1 Kings 8. It was not the temple—as opposed to the tabernacle—that underlay their history of rebellion and their persistent resistance of the Holy Spirit; rather it was this perversion in theology.

Third, the New Testament speaks of Jesus as personally replacing the temple. In Mark 14:58 Jewish leaders accuse him of threatening to destroy the temple and construct a replacement made without human hands. John 2:19 confirms that Jesus said this, though the evangelist interprets this as a figure of speech (vv. 21–22). Even so, the statement suggests that Jesus is about to replace the current system of worship with something new. In John 4:20–24 he tells the Samaritan woman that in the future both Gerizim and Jerusalem will lose their privileged status as places of worship, as the Father seeks those who will worship him in spirit and in truth. The issue here is not the superiority of spiritual (internal) worship over material (external) worship—true worship in ancient Israel was both in spirit and in truth[37]—but the inauguration of a new order. With Jesus' appearance the old order involving replicas of heavenly realities is replaced by direct worship of God through his Son (cf. John 1:51).

The replacement theme continues in Paul, though with a different emphasis. On the one hand, the apostle declares that because individual believers are temples of God, indwelt by the Holy Spirit (1 Cor. 6:19–20), they must maintain the sanctity of their bodies by avoiding relationships with unholy persons and practicing immorality. Just as introducing dead idols into the temple of the living God had defiled the physical temple, so also union with representatives of the kingdom of darkness defiles citizens of the kingdom of light. Such contamination prevents believers from glorifying God in their bodies.

On the other hand, Paul treats the Christian community as the temple of God. Indwelt by the Spirit of God (1 Cor. 2:12; 3:16–17), the corporate body is rendered into sacred space. Therefore God will destroy those who jeopardize the integrity of this temple through divisive and self-serving behavior (the context of 1 Cor. 1:10–3:23). Paul reiterates this point in 2 Corinthians, declaring the incompatibility of righteousness and lawlessness, light and darkness, Christ and Belial, believers and unbelievers, the temple of God and idols (2 Cor. 6:14–16a). Because believers are "the temple of the living God," Paul applies

---

which presents the temple as YHWH's project from the beginning, and anticipated centuries earlier in Deuteronomy. See above, under the heading "The Temple as Sacred Space."

37. For full discussion, see Daniel I. Block, "'In Spirit and in Truth': The Mosaic Vision of Worship," in *The Gospel according to Moses: Theological and Ethical Reflections on the Book of Deuteronomy* (Eugene, OR: Wipf & Stock, 2012), 288.

to the community of believers the ancient covenant formula (v. 16b): "I will reside in them,[38] and I will walk among them,[39] and I will be their God,[40] and they shall be my people."[41] This is temple theology at its highest.

In Ephesians 2:11–22 Paul reiterates that Christians are God's house, Christ Jesus being the cornerstone through whom the whole building coheres and in whom believers are built together into a dwelling of God (vv. 19–20). Alluding to the barriers in Herod's temple that excluded women and gentiles from many worship activities, he emphasizes that by the blood of Christ old dividing walls are demolished so that strangers and aliens may be fellow citizens with the saints, enjoying equal access in the Spirit to the Father through Christ (vv. 11–19).[42]

First Peter 2:4–10 declares that by coming to Christ the living stone, believers are built up as a spiritual house for a holy priesthood, to offer spiritual sacrifices acceptable to God through Jesus Christ. Just as tabernacle and temple proclaimed the glory of God in the old order, now as a royal priesthood and holy nation, believers collectively proclaim the excellencies of him who has called them out of darkness into light.[43]

To summarize, in the new order, what the physical temple was to Israel, the church as a spiritual community has become to the world: the holy residence of God indwelt by his Spirit. This does not mean that in the old order believers could not have been considered temples of God, since the same Holy Spirit indwelt them (Ezek. 36:16–38), and God was present wherever his people were found.[44] However, these notions are not developed in the First Testament, presumably because the physical temple minimized the need to declare them explicitly. However, with the coming of Christ, the divine Glory resides among us in incarnate form (John 1:14), ending the need for a temple as the embodiment of divine Glory and the center of cultic performances to maintain relationship with God.

The Apocalypse invites us to gaze beyond terrestrial realities into the heavenly temple.[45] The description of the heavenly temple returns to familiar First

38. See Exod. 29:45–46; Num. 35:34; Ezek. 43:7; Zech. 8:3.

39. See Lev. 26:12; Deut. 23:14 [15]. In Gen. 3:8 God walks about in the garden of Eden.

40. This part of the formula is first declared to Abraham in Gen. 17:7; cf. Exod. 6:7.

41. The combination of phrases occurs often, some examples are Lev. 26:12; Jer. 7:23; 31:33; Ezek. 37:27.

42. This would not have been an issue in the First Testament. Deuteronomy invites all to come to the presence of YHWH: men, women, children, and aliens in their towns (12:12, 18; 16:11, 14).

43. In Matt. 16:18 Jesus uses temple language when he speaks of "building his church" on this rock.

44. See further Daniel I. Block, "The View from the Top: The Holy Spirit in the Prophets," in *Presence, Power and Promise: The Role of the Holy Spirit in the Old Testament*, ed. David G. Firth and Paul D. Wegner (Downers Grove, IL: InterVarsity, 2011), 191–201.

45. The key texts are Rev. 3:12; 7:10–17; 11:1–19; 14:15, 17; 15:5–8; 16:1, 17; 21:1–22:5.

Testament patterns, with an increasing intensity of holiness as one moves from the outside inward. Revelation 3:12 calls the "city of God" the new Jerusalem, which "comes down from heaven." Elsewhere it is characterized as a "holy city" and "the beloved city" (20:9). Chapter 21 contains the most detailed picture of the holy city. Here it is situated within the new heaven and the new earth. The new city is prepared as a bride for her husband and becomes the residence of God. Echoing First Testament formulas, God dwells among human beings, establishing forever the ancient covenant summarized in the formula "See, the dwelling of God is with human beings; he will dwell with them; they will be his peoples, and God himself will be with them" (21:3).

Mixing a series of metaphors, Revelation 21:9–21 describes the city, referred to as the bride of the Lamb, in all her splendor. Situated on a high mountain (cf. Ezek. 40:2), the holy city comes down from heaven, bearing the full weight of God's glory and glistening with precious jewels and crystal-clear jasper. The city is a perfect cube, each side measuring 1,200 stadia (ca. 1,500 miles), reminiscent of the holy of holies in the temple (1 Kings 6:20). The entire city is portrayed as the holiest part of the sanctuary. Its boundaries are marked by walls 144 cubits high. Each wall has three gates guarded by angels and named after the twelve tribes. However, old and new combine in walls built on foundation stones inscribed with the names of the twelve apostles. These foundation stones are decorated with every conceivable precious stone, and the streets are made of pure gold, clear as glass. As in Ezekiel's city, "YHWH is There" (Ezek. 48:30–35), the number of gates symbolizes the city's accessibility—in contrast to the gates and doorways of the tabernacle and temple, whose function was to limit access. Revelation 21:25 notes that the gates will never be closed to bar the forbidden and the unclean, for those who seek to enter will be those whose names are written in the Lamb's book of life (v. 27). These wear washed robes and have access to the tree of life (22:14). This new Jerusalem needs no temple to symbolize the presence of God, for YHWH God the Almighty and the Lamb are its temple (21:22). Nor is there any need for a symbolic glory, for the radiance of God emanates directly from the Lamb.

This picture of a new Jerusalem without a temple printed in chapters 21–22 symbolizes the final [new] earthly state of the redeemed. The preceding chapters describe the pre-consummation heavenly reality, prior to the final judgment of evil and the glorification of the righteous. This temple does not come down from heaven; it is the heavenly temple. Although the heavenly temple is never described in detail, Revelation 4–5 provides an impressive picture of the scene, described in glorious and extravagant terms, appropriate for the residence of God himself. The centerpiece of this temple is the throne on which the Lamb is seated (7:9–17). He is surrounded by angels, elders, and four living creatures, who prostrate themselves in worship before him. Those who are clothed in robes washed white by the blood of the Lamb are authorized to serve God before the throne night and day. While chapter 11 offers a full description, elsewhere we learn that angels are sent out on God's behalf from this heavenly courtroom to execute his judgment on the wicked (Rev. 14:15, 17; 15:5–8; 16:1, 17).

The Scriptures conclude with this portrayal of sacred space. Although the images are largely heavenly, this eschatological vision should inspire Christian worship today. The environment in which believers offer true worship is neither unimportant nor irrelevant. Every detail in this portrait not only declares a profound theology but also contributes to the aura of awe surrounding the divine Sovereign before whom we worship.

Sacred Space in the Christian Community

This lengthy discussion raises the critical question of the place of sacred space in Christian worship. Does the silence of the New Testament on Christian worship space mean that Christians need not think of sacred space at all? Or does it assume that some of the theology underlying First Testament institutions remains in force? If so, to what extent should First Testament conceptions govern our thinking? Contemporary answers to these questions range from Old Order Amish, who meet for worship in homes or the threshing floors of barns, to church plants that meet in gymnasiums and theaters; from simple, unadorned meetinghouses specially built for religious exercises, to ornate cathedrals like Saint Peter's Basilica in Rome or Saint Paul's Cathedral in London. The theology underlying these responses may differ from that which governed Israel's tabernacle and temple, but each solution reflects a particular theology.

Sacred Space in the Earliest Church

So long as the temple stood, the formal religious exercises of the church in Jerusalem were divided between the temple and homes (Acts 2:42–47). But away from the temple and especially when the temple was destroyed, Christians were forced to adapt. Very quickly religious exercises were associated with specific places. In Acts 16:13, 16, Luke accompanies Paul to "the place of prayer" by the riverside in Philippi, to which people would go on the Sabbath. While this seems to have been where Jews congregated, we cannot tell if it involved a building or if it was outdoors. Presumably, when congregations outgrew the spaces available in homes and were barred from public buildings, they began to meet in sheltered areas[46] and to construct "sanctuaries" for divine service. But the "house church" (*domus ecclesia*) model begun in New Testament times[47] seems to have prevailed for the first couple of centuries—which meant that congregations would rarely exceed twenty or thirty people, the number that could comfortably gather in one room.

Worship in house churches featured prayer, Scripture reading, preaching, the Eucharist, and communal dinners. By the third century congregational social structures became more complex; ordained clergy officiated in the rituals, which became increasingly formal, creating the need for space for baptisms, teaching, and other clerical duties. Simple assemblies for prayer evolved into divine liturgies performed from a dais at the eastern end of the hall.[48]

The Influence of the Jewish Synagogue

The influence of Jewish tradition and practice on the early church is evident in the design of both the Christian liturgy and the places of Christian worship. In the New Testament the term "synagogue" ("assembly," "coming together") denoted the place where Jews gathered as well as the gathering itself. While the origins of the synagogue are obscure, by New Testament times synagogues were found throughout the Roman Empire, wherever Diaspora Jews lived. After the temple was destroyed in AD 70, synagogues throughout the Roman Empire tended to be oriented so that worshipers faced not only the holy ark containing the Torah scroll but Jerusalem as well, in anticipation of the Messiah's coming and in compliance with Solomon's prayer, which invites people in the Diaspora to pray toward this place (1 Kings 8; see also Dan. 6:10).

Although no design features were prescribed, synagogues tended to follow a simple pattern (fig. 12.10). The doorway led into a vestibule. From here, stairs may have led up to a gallery, from which women could observe the proceedings below. The focal point of the room was the *bimah*, a raised platform from which someone read from the Torah scroll and which oriented worshipers toward Jerusalem when they prayed. The rabbi instructed the people from a lectern.

46. Perhaps like a cave dating to the first century AD recently discovered under St. Georgeous Church in Rihab, northern Jordan. See the report at *Rihab Center for Archaeological Studies and Research in Jordan,* http://rihabresearchcenter.blogspot.com/. However, the conclusions have not been widely accepted. Even if Christians gathered in this cave, calling a place where they met in the first century a "church" would be anachronistic: the word *ekklēsia* then referred to an assembly of people, not the place where they gathered. An early third-century "prayer chapel" recently uncovered at Megiddo is a more likely candidate for an early building used for worship. See Vassilios Tzaferis, "Inscribed 'To God Jesus Christ': Early Christian Prayer Hall Found in Megiddo Prison," *Biblical Archaeology Review* 33, no. 2 (March–April, 2007): 38–49.

47. See Mark 14:15; Luke 22:12; Acts 10:9; Rom. 16:5, 23; Col. 4:16.

48. See further Tzaferis, "Inscribed 'To God Jesus Christ,'" 48–49.

The Basic Design of a Traditional Synagogue

Often an eternal light was suspended above/in front of the ark, recalling the menorah of the tabernacle and temple. At the front, chairs could be positioned on either side of the ark for persons serving in the service, including the cantor and rabbi. The most important feature of a synagogue was the holy ark, which housed the Torah scroll. The ark was screened from public view by a curtain modeled after the veil shielding the holy of holies in the tabernacle.

Theology of Sacred Space and Church Design

Because the New Testament does not speak of structures built to serve as houses of worship, some argue that church buildings are by definition wrong. They say that God will not be restricted to one holy place. Furthermore, the temple as the residence of God has been replaced by individual believers indwelt by the Spirit of God. When Paul spoke of the church, he referred not to the building but to the people who make up the church (2 Cor. 6:14–18). And Jesus himself said that where two or three are gathered, God is there in their midst (Matt. 18:20).

However, few Christians actually follow this reasoning. Despite the absence of instructions on church buildings in the New Testament, structures built or designed for worship soon were called "the house of God" (*domus Dei*),[49] and the rituals performed in them were understood as "worship." Today most

49. F. J. Dölger, "'*Kirche' als Name für den christlichen Kultbau: Sprach und Kulturgeschichtliches zu den Bezeichnungen* Κυριακόν, οἶκος κυριακός, dominicum, basilica, basilica," *Antike und Christentum* 6 (1941): 161–95.

Christians worship in buildings specially created for this purpose. Having decided to erect a worship structure, however, tough decisions remain—decisions that are much more fundamental than financing. What is the purpose of this building? Even more basic, why does the church gather in one place? And should Christians treat the buildings and grounds where they gather as more sacred than other space? The answers to these questions will affect not only how we design the buildings but also how we act inside them.

What we call our church buildings should also affect our actions and focus inside them. For example, designating a house of worship "the house of God" should produce a theocentric design; calling it "the assembly" or "synagogue" might produce an anthropocentric design. Examining some basic forms that have been used in the past and are used today will illustrate this point (fig. 12.11).[50] Buildings erected or furbished for cultic service will reflect church leaders' theology of worship, if not the assembly's theology as a whole. Congregations that view fellowship as the primary reason for gathering may desire flexible seating arrangements. Those that emphasize instruction in the Word may highlight the pulpit. Those that gather to lift people's spirits and inspire lofty thoughts about God may give prominence to decoration and stained-glass windows.

Since the New Testament does not reveal a design for church buildings, it would be foolish and presumptuous to prescribe the worship environment for anyone, let alone a design that fits Christians around the world. How Christians design sacred space will depend upon their theology of worship, as well as on cultural propriety, materials available, and finances. But this should not prevent us from discussing values that might enter into the discussion. In the following I present my own ruminations on the matter.

First, when Christians gather for worship, they gather for an audience with God. With the psalmist (Ps. 95:1–2) we rejoice that YHWH, the great King above all gods, incarnate in Jesus Christ, has graciously invited us to an audience with himself. He delights in our presence, and if we draw near to him with undivided devotion and pure lives, he promises to draw near to us (James 4:8). According to pagan thinking, worship involves figuring out how to talk to God; for us, it involves opening our ears and hearts to hear God talking to us. By his Holy Spirit, through his Word, and through fellow believers, God may indeed speak to us anytime and anywhere, but times and places set apart for worship are necessary to draw the community of faith to focus on God. Since

50. These diagrams are adapted from Bill Beard, "Six Architectural Settings and Worship Renewal," in *The Complete Library of Christian Worship*, vol. 4, *Music and the Arts in Christian Worship, Book Two*, ed. R. E. Webber (Nashville: Star Song, 1994), 578–80.

FIGURE 12.11
Some Basic Church Floor Plans

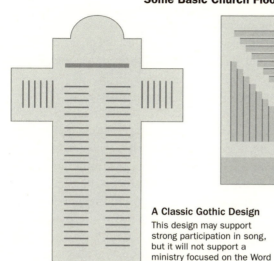

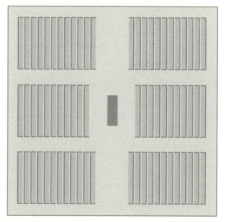

A Classic Gothic Design

This design may support strong participation in song, but it will not support a ministry focused on the Word or member participation.

Classic American Free Church Design

Radial amphitheatre keeps all near the action; good for proclaiming the Word and responsive liturgy.

Traditional Processional Design

All right for formal liturgical styles, but not helpful for developing community. Participants tend to see themselves as an audience.

Antiphonal Design

The table is central and member participation encouraged.

God is most glorified when we are receptive to his speech, sacred places of worship should be designed so that God's voice is heard and his revelation is clear.

Second, when we gather for worship, we gather for corporate acts of homage and submission. God-honoring worship takes many forms, but Hebrews 12:28 declares that acceptable worship arises from hearts filled with reverence and awe at the glory and mercy of the One we worship. However, reverent awe is not only a prerequisite for acceptable worship; but deeper reverence is also the goal and effect of true worship. Moses captured the recipe precisely: when godly worshipers hear the Torah, they will learn to fear God, which will foster obedience to his will and thereby result in life (Deut. 31:9–13; cf. 17:19–20). If the design of worship space enhances the revelation of God, it will promote reverence and awe.

Third, when we gather for worship, we gather with an eschatological vision. We acknowledge that all space is God's space, but we also recognize that it is contaminated by human rebellion. In worship we experience in microcosm what we will enjoy for all eternity, and we anticipate the day when God will make all things new. In the meantime, worship space that lifts our minds and spirits out of the mundane world to God, who resides in ineffable glory in the heavens, brings glory to him and transformation to the worshiper. It reminds us that our primary citizenship is not here in this world torn by sin and strife, but in the City whose maker and builder is God.[51] Within sacred space we are cleansed from the contamination of this world and equipped to reenter it as cleansed agents of grace, as God's polished royal treasure, declaring the praises of him who has called us out of darkness into his marvelous light (1 Pet. 2:9).

Fourth, when we gather for worship, we gather to edify and build up the body of Christ. This edification may be achieved through many means: the reading and preaching of the Word, public prayer, songs of lamentation and praise, public testimonies of God's grace, celebrating in communion, joining hands in ministries to those in need. But we waste a glorious opportunity if the design of the worship environment is purely utilitarian. Buildings referred to as "the house of God" or "the house of worship" should proclaim the excellencies of the One in whose honor they are constructed and in whose honor we gather. The second command of the Decalogue, "You shall not bear the name of YHWH your God in vain," applies not only to individual believers and to the church as a body, but also to the buildings we have consecrated for worship. Structures that bear the brand of the Lord but reflect the materialistic values or chaos of our culture shame the name of Christ. Sacred space should be as countercultural as believers' personal lives, responding to the surrounding disorder and tension with a message of hope and grace and order, expressing the lofty ideals of "the heavenlies," to which we have access through Christ (Eph. 1:1–14). Having been in this sacred place, we return to

---

51. The recently completed Church of the Transfiguration on Cape Cod presents an inspiring illustration. For a photo essay on this structure, see David Neff, "The Art of Glory," *Christianity Today* 54, no. 10 (October 2010): 34–39.

the world energized, ready to live out the gospel until every stronghold of the kingdom of darkness is torn down and the world resounds with praise and glory to God. N. T. Wright rightly declares,

> Thus the church that takes sacred space seriously (not as a retreat from the world but as a bridgehead into it) will go straight from worshiping in the sanctuary to debating in the council chamber; to discussing matters of town planning, of harmonizing and humanizing beauty in architecture, green spaces, and road traffic schemes; and to environmental work, creative and healthy farming methods, and proper use of resources. If it is true, as I have argued, that the whole world is now God's holy land, we must not rest as long as that land is spoiled and defaced. This is not an extra to the church's mission. It is central.[52]

But what will such sacred space look like? How do these considerations affect the aesthetics of church design? While Roman Catholics, Eastern Orthodox Christians, and Anglicans have paid careful attention to these matters, those in Reformed and free-church traditions have often missed the opportunity to express their worship through the design of the worship environment. Puritan and Anabaptist iconoclasts have sometimes thrown the proverbial baby out with the bathwater: practices are repudiated simply because those actions are what Catholics do, whether such observances are theologically justified and scripturally based.

I conclude this chapter with thoughts on how biblical perspectives on sacred space might aid us in designing places of worship that glorify God and inspire his people. Some of the ideas expressed obviously reflect my own idiosyncratic values and should perhaps be rejected as such; some may be mutually exclusive—we cannot have it all; still others may be impractical in particular contexts. But this is a place to start the discussion.

Orientation

Churches might be so designed that when believers gather for worship, their gaze is directed not only to the cross at the front of the building but also beyond it to Calvary, the source of our salvation, and to the Mount of Olives, the hope of our salvation (Acts 1:11). Although we do not worship in Jerusalem, by orienting worshipers toward this city we identify with God's people of the past, remember the work of Christ on the cross, and look forward to the day when Jesus will return—when the Torah will go forth from Zion, God

52. N. T. Wright, *Surprised by Hope: Rethinking Heaven, the Resurrection, and the Mission of the Church* (San Francisco: HarperOne, 2008), 265–66.

will rule over the nations, and peace will cover the earth as the waters cover the sea (Isa. 2:2–4; Mic. 4:1–5).

People in other religious traditions understand this concept. When Jews gather in synagogues on the Sabbath, they pray with faces toward Jerusalem. Five times a day Muslims kneel in prayer in their sacred spaces (on their prayer rugs), prostrating themselves before God while facing the Kaaba (ka'ba) in Mecca, Saudi Arabia. Most Gothic cathedrals of Europe were constructed with the front of the church to the east. This orientation also determined the themes for the interior decoration. Reflecting the long-standing if not Marcionite perception of a vast divide between the First and New Testaments, images from the First Testament, associated with darkness and cold, dominated the north facades, and the brighter and warmer south facade contained images from the New Testament. Anglican parish churches in England are usually oriented so the main altar is to the east and worshipers theoretically face Jerusalem.[53]

Proportion and Symmetry

In the past, houses of worship have been designed as microcosms of the cosmos, sacred worlds created in harmony with the plan of God and anticipating a new world governed by rules of beauty and order. Admittedly, people's definitions of beauty vary, but worshipers need a retreat from the busyness and chaos of everyday life—a place of rest, quiet streams, and caring nurture. The more chaotic and dingier our world becomes, the greater should be the contrast when we enter this world of grace and light. And this vision of beauty and holiness should drive us into the world with even more passion in our service for Christ.

Focus

Since the community gathered is by definition the community of the redeemed, the saving grace of Christ should be expressed throughout the building, in its design, decoration, and symbolism. The outside should be inviting but declare unequivocally that this is the meeting place of God's people. On the inside, attention should be lifted up to the Savior. The sacramental nature

53. Significantly, St. Thomas' Cathedral, the oldest English building in Mumbai (construction began in 1672), is oriented westward. Seventeenth-century Puritans in both England and New England rotated their "Meetinghouses" ninety degrees so that the door was to the south and the pulpit at the north end. This orientation served the pragmatic concern for a warmer (south) entryway, but seems also to have been driven by a determination not to be like Anglicans. On Puritan architecture in New England, see Horton Davies, *The Worship of the American Puritans* (Morgan, PA: Soli Deo Gloria Publications, 1999), 277.

FIGURE 12.12
The Cruciform Design of the Chartres Cathedral (AD 1145–1220)

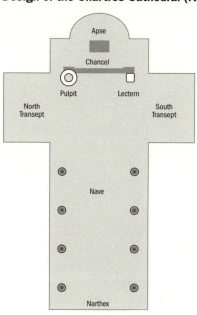

of Anglican and Roman Catholic worship is reflected in the floor plans of their churches. Traditional Gothic churches were cross-shaped, with the altar taking up the space at the east end (fig. 12.12). This form is retained in many Anglican and Catholic churches today. In Reformed churches the basic plan was and continues to be much simpler (fig. 12.13).

Many nondenominational churches have dispensed with any theological messages in their architecture. The great room is no longer a "sanctuary" but a "great hall" or an "auditorium," and the floor plan is designed with stage performances in mind. In many churches that have moved from a "traditional" to a "contemporary" style of services, a symbolic act is performed every Sunday: before the service, a large screen comes down over the stage, often hiding the cross and replacing it with pious but narcissistic words of devotion. Instead of celebrating God's love for us, we celebrate our love for God. Yet if we understand the worship event as an audience with God, and that what God has to say to us is primary and more important than what we say to him, this should be reflected in the design.

Since God speaks to his people collectively primarily through the Word, in my view the pulpit should be prominent, designed to draw the people's attention away from the messenger to the One in whose name he speaks. This

FIGURE 12.13
Church Building in the Reformed Tradition

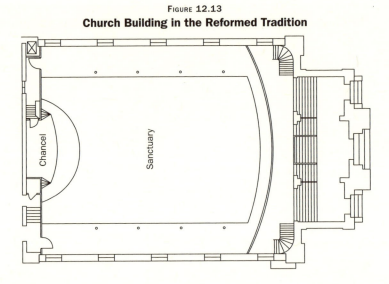

principle extends to arrangements for musical aspects of worship. The design must deflect people's attention away from the musicians to the One about whom they sing or play. Since a house of worship is not a concert hall, the best place for a choir or musical groups is on the balcony at the back. Furthermore, since worship involves reverential acts of homage and submission before God, the design of the building and its furniture should invite and enable worshipers to express such homage. Kneeling benches attached to pews seem appropriate for physical expressions of worship.

Atmosphere

Since worship involves reverential acts of homage before God, every detail of the sanctuary should evoke awe before him, rather than before the human architect or the decorators.[54] This may be reflected in the choice of materials, architectural lines, colors, visual images, and even lighting. Effects that detract from the worship of God should not be allowed to encroach on sacred space. If we must have a flag, then have flags of many nations, illustrating the transnational nature of the body of Christ; to display only an American flag borders on civil religion and is distracting and offensive especially to non-American visitors. There may be a place for celebrating the history of individual con-

54. As is the case with the Cathedral Church of Christ in Liverpool, the fifth largest cathedral in the world. The cathedral tower is 330 feet high. At the center of the building, beneath the tower, the inscription does homage to the architect, Sir Giles Gilbert Scott (see fig. 12.14).

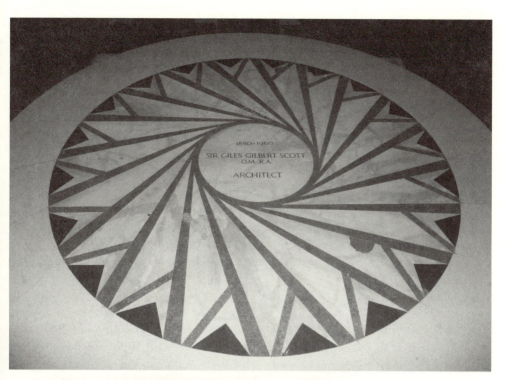

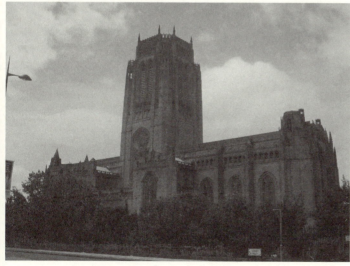

Figure 12.14. Cathedral Church of Christ in Liverpool (Cathedral: ReptOn1x/Wikimedia Commons. Mosaic: Courtesy of Bill Wootten. Used with permission.)

gregations and of the church catholic in the decoration, but commemorative images of significant people belong on the back wall or in side rooms. Finally, the front of the sanctuary should be neat, rather than cluttered with musicians' "junk," which reflects too much the chaos and noise of the world outside and detracts from true worship.

Fellowship

Worship may be primarily about God's speaking to us as individuals, but it involves God's communicating to the church community. His voice is obviously not restricted to the proclamation of the Word from the pulpit or the distribution of the elements in the Eucharist. God also speaks through other worshipers. Ephesians 5:18–20 speaks of being filled with the Spirit, *speaking to one another in psalms, hymns, and spiritual songs*. Worship space should be so designed that believers inspire one another. This is difficult to achieve in traditional seating arrangements where we see only the backs of fellow worshipers or in structures that have poor acoustics. On the other hand, U-shaped seating arrangements remind us that we do not worship as individuals, but as the body of Christ.

In short, the place of worship should inspire awe and reverence for God as we enter the building, and joy and celebration as we depart. When God's people gather in a space that has been consecrated for worship, that space bears a particular sanctity. However, ultimately the sanctity of the body of Christ should be our main concern. This body is the temple indwelt by the Spirit of God; this is the context in which and through which Christ serves.

13

Leaders in Worship

True worship involves reverential human acts of submission and homage before the divine Sovereign in response to his gracious revelation of himself and in accord with his will.

Although God's people are called individually and collectively to worship, some are charged with the particular duty of leading the assembly in corporate expressions of submission and homage. But what roles do these leaders fulfill in worship? One response has officiators doing virtually everything on behalf of the people, who watch as spectators. At best they are awed by the mystery of the worship leaders' actions; at worst they are disengaged and bored with the proceedings. The other extreme involves an egalitarian congregation that rejects the notion of leaders in worship altogether. All have an equal right to minister when the church gathers. Who is right? And what do the Scriptures have to say about this matter? In this chapter we will explore how leaders in worship are portrayed in the Scriptures, concluding with reflections on how these observations might inform our practice.

Primeval and Patriarchal Leadership in Worship

The first eleven chapters of Genesis offer little information on corporate worship. Genesis 4:1–5 portrays Cain and Abel's sacrifices as individual expressions of submission and homage. In the days of Enosh, the son of Seth, people began to address YHWH in worship (4:26), but how this was done is not stated. As his first act of homage following his rescue from the flood, on behalf of his family—and perhaps of the animals that survived with him—Noah built an altar to YHWH and offered acceptable sacrifices to him (8:20–22). In 9:8–17 the narrator emphasizes that the covenant God made with Noah covered his descendants and all living creatures on earth. Noah served as the head of the human race and the representative of creation.

From the beginning of the patriarchal narratives, it is evident that God called Abraham to a relationship with himself, not merely for the sake of the patriarch and his descendants but also that the world might be blessed through them (Gen. 12:1–3). Abraham repeatedly responded to God's grace by building altars (12:7, 8; 13:4, 18; cf. 26:25; 33:20; 35:7), but nowhere are the members of his household in the picture. He did of course lead in family worship when he circumcised all the males of his household as participants in God's covenant (17:22–27). Occasionally Abraham performed cultic service on behalf of others by interceding for them (18:22–33; 20:7, 17–18).[1] The patriarch's imposition of the oath of fidelity upon his servant in 24:7–9 was a cultic moment performed in the interests of posterity, but no one else of the household was involved. In far off Aram, Bethuel and Laban performed cultic service on Rebekah's behalf by blessing her as she left for Isaac (24:60).[2] Jacob performed cultic service on numerous occasions (28:18–22; 32:7–21; 33:20), but even his covenant with Laban at Gilead was a private affair between father-in-law and son-in-law (31:43–53). However, Jacob invited his family to the sacrificial meal to celebrate the peace (v. 54).

Genesis 35:1–15 provides the most impressive picture of corporate worship in the patriarchal narratives. As head of his household, Jacob commanded all in it to get rid of foreign gods, purify themselves for worship, and change their garments. Their idols and jewelry associated with pagan worship he took and buried near Shechem. Then he led the clan in procession to Bethel, where he built an altar and renamed the place El-Bethel, commemorating God's revelation at this place decades earlier. After Rebekah's nurse died and God had renewed the blessing and promise to Abraham, Jacob repeated the cultic actions performed in 28:18–22. This patricentric pattern of worship also occurs in the prologue to the book of Job (1:1–5).

---

1. Before his sacrifice of Isaac, Abraham interpreted the event as worship (22:5, *hištaḥāwâ*), but verse 1 specifies that this was an individual act of worship—a test of his devotion to God; Isaac was a passive "victim."

2. Other patriarchs repeated this pattern of blessing children in cultic ceremonies: Isaac, in Gen. 27:27–29, 39–40; 28:1; Jacob, in Gen. 48:8–22; 49:1–33.

Premonarchic Leadership in Israelite Worship

While Moses and Aaron effectively led the Israelites out of Egypt, the narrator provides little information on corporate worship while they traveled to Sinai. The elders of Israel figure prominently, but they led in worship only in Exodus 12:21–28, when Moses instructed them to procure lambs for the Passover sacrifice and organize the event according to the nation's families and clans. Elsewhere they represented the people when Moses produced water from a rock (17:6), in a sacrificial meal before God with Moses and Jethro (18:12), and in worship at a safe distance from YHWH on Mount Sinai (24:1, 9, 14). Exodus 19:22–24 suggests that "priests" led the Israelites in worship even before Aaron and the Levites were ordained for the role.[3] Prior to YHWH's verbal revelation at Sinai, Moses charged these professional worshipers "who approach YHWH" to consecrate themselves and warned them not to break through to YHWH (v. 22).

Moses dominates the events associated with the exodus and Israel's stay at Sinai. He began his public role by appearing before Pharaoh and announcing that the Israelites needed to make a three-day pilgrimage into the desert to worship YHWH (Exod. 5:1–3; 8:1). As worship leader he repeatedly interceded before YHWH on behalf of the people (5:22–23; 16:1–12; 17:1–7); he received revelation directly from YHWH;[4] he led the people in celebrating the Passover (12:21–28); he led them in a song of celebration after crossing the Red Sea (15:1–18); he oversaw the observance of the Sabbath (16:22–30); he established cultic traditions (16:31–34); he transcribed accounts of divine activity on the people's behalf and constructed altars as memorials (17:14–16); he restructured the administration of the community of the redeemed (18:13–27); he led in the official worship of YHWH at Mount Sinai (19:1–20:21); he relayed divine revelation to the people and produced a written record thereof (24:3–4); he presided over the covenant ratification ritual (24:4–8); and he led the representatives of the people in the covenant meal eaten in the presence of God (24:9–11). Although commonly perceived primarily as a lawgiver, prior to the establishment of the Levitical priesthood, Moses towered over the Israelite community as leader in worship. Not even David would dominate Israel's worship as Moses did.

Moses continued to sponsor and guard the cult after tabernacle worship was instituted (Exod. 32:1–34:35; Lev. 10:1–7), but at Sinai YHWH prescribed

3. Joel S. Baden suggests that Exod. 32:26–29 originally followed Exod. 17:1–7. See "The Violent Origins of the Levites: Text and Tradition," in *Levites and Priests in Biblical History and Tradition*, ed. M. A. Leuchter and J. M. Hutton, Ancient Israel and Its Literature (Atlanta: Society of Biblical Literature, 2011), 109–11. However, this view is speculative.

4. As in Exod. 6:2–9; 6:28–29; 7:1–7; 11:1–2; 12:1–20; 13:1–16; 16:1–12; 20:22–23:33.

a system of priestly orders that governed Israel's worship for more than a millennium. Other elements of Israel's social structures would come and go, but these priestly orders survived the dark days of the judges, the monarchy, the exile, and the reconstituted postexilic community.

The Role of the Levites in Israel's Worship

We hear a premonition of the Levites' future role within Israel in Jacob's "curse" of Simeon and Levi in Genesis 49:5–7: they would be dispersed throughout the nation. In the genealogy of Exodus 6:14–27 the narrator hints at their significance by tracing the lines of Jacob's three oldest sons, Reuben, Simeon, and Levi (cf. Gen. 29:31–34). According to Exodus 27:21, the Aaronide branch of Levites was destined for priestly duty, but the cultic role of the Levites as a tribe first surfaces in 32:25–29. As a reward for the Levites' standing with YHWH when the Israelites worshiped the golden calf, Moses instructed these men to "ordain themselves"[5] and prepare for a blessing that YHWH was about to bestow. Exodus 38:21 links them to the tabernacle for the first time, and Numbers 3–4 and 18:1–7 explain the roles of the respective clans in relation to the tabernacle. Leviticus 25:32–34 teases the reader with a reference to Levitical towns once they arrive in the promised land, but we do not encounter this topic again until Numbers 35 and Joshua 21.

Moses summarizes the Levites' special role and ministry in Numbers 16:9: the God of Israel separated them from the congregation of Israel and authorized them to approach him, to perform the services of YHWH's tabernacle, to stand before the congregation, and minister to them. The Levites were to support ($š\bar{e}r\bar{e}t$, "serve") the high-priestly ministry of Aaron (3:6; 18:2) by performing guard duty for him and the congregation before the tent of meeting / tabernacle (3:7; 18:1–7). Although Numbers 1:53 arranges for the Levites to camp around the tabernacle to prevent the people from encroaching on sacred space (3:10), they were not admitted to the tabernacle proper; Aaronide priests guarded the central building and the altar inside the court (18:3–7), while the Levites took care of the tabernacle: dismantling, transporting, and assembling it during the desert journeys, as well as maintaining it and its furnishings (3:7, 14–39; 18:6).

5. The idiom *millē' yād* "to fill the hand," is used elsewhere of ordaining men for priestly ministry (Exod. 28:41, 29:9, 29, 33, 35; Lev. 8:33; 16:32; 21:10; Num. 3:3; Judg. 17:5, 12; 1 Kings 13:33; 2 Chron. 13:9; 29:31) or other sacred work (1 Chron. 29:5), even of dedicating an altar (Ezek. 43:26).

Anticipating a settled life in the promised land, Moses again summarizes the duties of Levitical priests in Deuteronomy: (1) carry the ark of the covenant (10:8; 31:9);[6] (2) stand before YHWH and serve him (10:8; 18:6–7), presumably by assisting the priests; (3) bless the people in the name of YHWH (10:8; cf. 21:5), presumably pronouncing the Aaronic blessing (Num. 6:22–27); (4) adjudicate disputes within the community (Deut. 21:5);[7] and (5) serve as custodians of the Torah (Deut. 17:18; 32:9–13; 33:10).

Regarding the last duty, Moses charged future kings to copy the Torah for themselves in the presence of the Levitical priests (Deut. 17:18–20), apparently to ensure that they copied it entirely, without adding, deleting, or changing the text. The Torah in question involved Moses' speeches preserved in Deuteronomy, which he transcribed and charged them to read before all the people every seven years at the Festival of Booths (31:9–13).[8] Moses reinforced the Levitical priests' instructional role in his blessing of Levi:

> "Your Tummim and Urim belong to the one who was loyal to you,
> whom you tested at Massah;
> with whom you contended at the waters of Meribah."
> He said of his father and mother, "I am not concerned about them."
> He disregarded his brothers and ignored his own children,
> but he guarded your word and kept your covenant.
> They teach your ordinances to Jacob and your Torah to Israel.
> They offer incense before you and whole burnt offerings on your altar.
>   (Deut. 33:8–10)

But how would the Levites fulfill this instructional role? Although we tend to view Israelite worship as highly centralized, the people actually gathered at the central sanctuary only a few weeks of the year for the required festivals and perhaps the Day of Atonement. However, the religious structure seems to have been quite federal in nature, with observances related to Israel as a nation being located at the central sanctuary and everyday worship happening in homes and villages. In Numbers 35:1–8 YHWH charges the Israelites to allocate to Levites forty-eight towns and surrounding pasturelands scattered throughout the land.[9]

---

6. Numbers 4:1–5 and 10:21 specify the Kohathite branch as those who carried the ark.

7. Deuteronomy 17:8–13 suggests that the final court of appeal was the priestly judge on duty at the central sanctuary. Apparently, when normal judicial procedures were unable to establish a verdict, an oracle from YHWH would resolve the issue. See Daniel I. Block, *Deuteronomy*, NIV Application Commentary (Grand Rapids: Zondervan, 2010), 408–12.

8. While Mal. 2:1–9 provides the fullest statement of the priests' instructional function, the prophet's concern is to expose the Levites' failure to teach Torah and live by it.

9. For the fulfillment of this charge and a list of the towns, see Josh. 21:1–42 (cf. 1 Chron. 6:54–81 [39–66]). For a full discussion of the function of Levitical towns and their relationship

Although the function of Levitical towns is never explained, we may imagine that they were designed to ensure ongoing pastoral care throughout the land (Lev. 25:32–34). This would involve caring for the needy, administering cleansing rituals, presiding over local sacrifices[10] and ceremonies of blessing and cursing (cf. 27:9–14; Josh. 8:33), teaching Torah (Deut. 31:9–13; 33:8–11), and encouraging covenant fidelity by keeping alive the traditions of Israel and representing the central sanctuary in the far-flung regions of the land (fig. 13.1).

FIGURE 13.1

A Schematic Portrayal of the Location and Function of the Levitical Cities

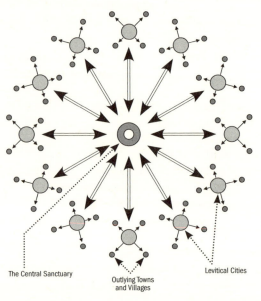

The Central Sanctuary

Outlying Towns and Villages

Levitical Cities

Despite the Levites' special spiritual role within Israel, they were economically vulnerable. Instead of receiving a grant of land in Canaan, they had YHWH as their grant (Deut. 10:9). Like the fatherless, widows, and aliens, their well-being depended on the generosity and spiritual fidelity of the Israelites.[11] Although Levitical towns are never featured in First Testament narratives,[12] the

---

to the Levitical priests, see Daniel I. Block, "'The Meeting Places of God in the Land': Another Look at the Town of the Levites," in *Current Issues in Priestly and Related Literature: The Legacy of Jacob Milgrom and Beyond*, ed. Roy Gane and Ada Taggar-Cohen, Resources for Biblical Study (Atlanta: Society of Biblical Literature, 2014), forthcoming.

10. See 1 Sam. 9:12–13; cf. 8:16–17; 9:12–24; 16:1–6.

11. Cf. Deut. 12:12, 18–19; 14:27, 29; 16:11, 14; 26:11–13.

12. This lack contributes to the skepticism among critical scholars regarding the historical reliability of these accounts. See J. R. Spencer, "Levitical Cities," in *Anchor Bible Dictionary* [*ABD*], ed. D. N. Freedman (New York: Doubleday, 1992), 4:310–11.

shiftlessness of the Levites in Judges 17–18 and 19–20 suggests that after the settlement they quickly lost their spiritual way, which undoubtedly contributed to the nation's downfall (Judg. 2:10).[13]

The Aaronic Priests

Within this federal religious structure, the central sanctuary should have symbolized the unity of the twelve tribes and inspired steadfast devotion to YHWH through celebration of the annual festivals, the Day of Atonement, and the public reading of the Torah (Deut. 31:9–13). Worship at the central sanctuary was led by the Aaronic priests, a particular branch of Levites. Aaron and his sons are introduced as priestly officials for the first time in Exodus 28:1. The attention to the details

Figure 13.2. The garments of Israel's high priest (Andreas F. Borchert/Wikimedia Commons)

of the high priest's dress in Exodus 28 (cf. chap. 39) and to Aaron's ordination in Exodus 29 (cf. Lev. 8) highlights the special status of Aaron and his descendants.

The primary responsibility of the Aaronic priest was to serve before YHWH within the tabernacle/temple. As the highest-ranking courtier in the earthly replica of the heavenly court, everything about him—his demeanor, cultic actions, and dress—was to proclaim the glory and splendor of YHWH (Exod. 28:2, 40), and in so doing, evoke awe in worshipers who observed him (cf. Ps. 132:16). Accordingly, the high priest's outer garments were made of luxury cloth in royal colors and decorated with gold trim (fig. 13.2), and his undergarments were made of special linen to minimize perspiration. In keeping with his formal dress, his official actions within the tabernacle were carefully prescribed and choreographed.

13. Ezekiel (44:15) complains that the Levitical priests in charge of the central sanctuary have defected from YHWH.

Since by definition priests mediate between deities and their subjects, the Aaronic priest served Israel especially by representing them before YHWH. This role was symbolized by the breastpiece of judgment—an ornately designed article made of dark blue-purple and red-purple linen cloth, embroidered with gold and mounted with gemstones representing the twelve tribes of Israel (Exod. 28:15–29)—and by two onyx stones worn on the priest's shoulders, each engraved with the names of six tribes (28:9–14). The priest also represented YHWH before Israel by speaking for him and blessing the people in his name (Num. 6:23–27; Deut. 10:8; 21:5). This function was symbolized by the Urim and Tummim, two objects carried within the breastpiece that were manipulated to determine the will of God (Exod. 28:30; Num. 27:21).

In addition to reflecting the splendor of YHWH, the high priest was to embody supreme holiness, a role symbolized by a gold medallion on the front of his turban engraved with "Holy [belonging] to YHWH" (*qōdeš layhwh*, Exod. 28:36). His status was highlighted by a special seven-day ordination ritual (29:1–36) and special regulations regarding the wearing of the official garments (vv. 29–30). Special laws governing priests reinforced their sanctity, such as restricting the office to physically perfect candidates, prohibiting tattoos and certain kinds of haircuts, and restricting marriage to a virgin (Lev. 21:1–22:16).

The First Testament mentions a variety of duties that high priests performed: (1) officiating in all the rituals involving the altar and maintaining the inside of the tabernacle (Num. 18:1–7); (2) sprinkling the cover of the ark with sacrificial blood on the Day of Atonement (Lev. 16); (3) officiating in purification rituals;[14] and (4) instructing the people in Torah (Jer. 18:18; Hosea 4:1–6). Jewish tradition reports that in the 410 years of the first temple, Israel had eighteen high priests, suggesting that their tenures averaged almost twenty-three years.[15] If they were ordained at age thirty, many would have served beyond the fifty-year mandatory Levitical retirement age.[16]

Evidence for degeneration in the priesthood appears early. Before the Israelites left Sinai, Aaron provided the people with the golden calf (Exod.

14. For women after childbirth (Lev. 12:1–8), those healed of skin diseases (13:1–14:32), persons defiled by bodily emissions (15:33), and houses and other inanimate objects defiled by "leprous infections" (14:33–57).

15. Babylonian Talmud, *Yoma* 18a. This contrasts with the 420 years of the second temple, which involved the service of more than three hundred high priests. Of these, the four righteous priests ministered 141 years, suggesting that 296+ priests served 279 years. Apparently few survived the year of installation.

16. Numbers 4:3, 23, 30, 35, 39, 43, and 47 specify that Levites qualified for tabernacle service at age thirty and could serve until they were fifty, but these texts do not deal specifically with Aaronic priests.

32:1–6, 21–24), and Nadab and Abihu desecrated the sanctuary with unholy fire (Lev. 10:1–7). Shortly thereafter Aaron and Miriam infuriated YHWH by revolting against Moses' leadership (Num. 12:1–15), and the Levitical sons of Korah rebelled against Moses and Aaron, accusing them of claiming special status (16:1–50). Undoubtedly priests and Levites bore major responsibility for Israel's rapid spiritual decline after the death of Joshua (Judg. 2:6–3:6). First Samuel portrays Eli as an overstuffed priest (4:18) who sat on his throne outside the tabernacle at Shiloh (1:9), and as the father of two scoundrels who desecrated the sacrifices and abused the people (2:12–26; cf. vv. 27–36).

Other Worship Leaders in the Tabernacle Period

According to the book of Deuteronomy, Moses' last official duty was to preside over an extended worship service on the plains of Moab. The bulk of the book consists of his three valedictory addresses (1:6–4:40; 5:1b–26:19; 28:1–68; 29:2 [1]–30:20), a hymn (cast as Israel's national anthem, in 32:1–43), and a closing benediction for each of the tribes (33:1–29). In his speeches and the anthem, Moses seeks to inspire the Israelites to gratitude for YHWH's grace, and to promote fear, faith, and covenant commitment (love) demonstrated in joyful obedience.

Moses' successor Joshua also presided over several corporate worship events. In keeping with Deuteronomy 17:18–20, YHWH charged him to read the Torah for himself continuously (Josh. 1:1–9); as with later kings, Joshua's primary function as leader was to embody covenant righteousness. However, as worship leader, Joshua directed Israel in holy procession across the Jordan River (2:1–17) and supervised the erection of memorials in the middle of the river (4:9) and at Gilgal (4:19–20); he also oversaw the circumcision of all males and the celebration of the Passover (5:1–12). In Joshua 6:1–27 Joshua instructed the priests concerning the ark and the procession involved in the conquest of Jericho. Later we observe him interceding on the people's behalf because of the defeat at Ai (7:6–15) and presiding over the inquisition and execution of Achan and his household (vv. 16–26). As Moses had instructed (Deut. 11:26–32; 27:1–26), Joshua built an altar to YHWH at Mount Ebal, transcribed the words of the Torah on stones, and supervised the covenant-renewal ceremony (Josh. 8:30–35). Subsequently he authorized the Gibeonites to serve the people and the altar (9:22–27); interceded before YHWH on behalf of Israel, resulting in the sun's standing still (10:12–15); and presided over the distribution of the land among the tribes (chaps. 13–14). Like Moses, he ended his ministry with a sermon, appealing for fidelity to the covenant (23:1–16) and presiding over one more covenant-renewal ceremony (24:1–28).

Samuel was destined for leadership in Israel even before he was born, and his mother dedicated him for service as a Nazirite when he was an infant (1 Sam. 1:11, 24–28). Of Ephraimite (1 Sam. 1:1) and Levitical (Kohathite, 1 Chron. 6:22–28) lineage, Samuel grew up in the tabernacle compound at Shiloh, where he served as an assistant to Eli the priest, wore the ephod, and ministered before YHWH (1 Sam. 2:18, 21, 26). Called to prophetic service as a young man, Samuel was assigned the difficult task of condemning the household of Eli and leading the people back to YHWH. The people recognized him as a true and faithful prophet (3:19–21), but he also performed many public priestly acts of worship. Prior to battle with the Philistines, he gathered the people at Mizpah and led them in fasting, prayers of repentance, and offering sacrifices before YHWH; after the victory he erected a memorial stone in YHWH's honor (7:1–9, 12). After privately anointing Saul as king at the high place of Zuph (9:1–27), he presided over the public election of Saul as king at Mizpah (10:17–27). In a kingdom-renewal ceremony he offered peace offerings and delivered a lengthy sermon, admonishing the people to be faithful to YHWH and promising to pray for the people (11:14–12:25). Later he supervised the consecration of elders, at which time he anointed David as king in Saul's place (16:1–13). While wearing many hats, Samuel saw Israel through the transition from a loose tribal confederacy to the monarchy.

Royal Leaders in First Temple Worship

In the narratives of Israel's monarchic history, priests play a remarkably minor role. For the most part the priesthood apparently proved unable or unwilling to lead spiritually. With the decline of the priesthood, God raised up prophets to call the people back to himself. Although Jeremiah and Ezekiel were of priestly lineage, prophets generally served more as critics of public and private worship in Israel than as proponents of or leaders in worship. Prophets had no enduring authority over the people; they had no subjects obliged to follow their directives and no territory over which they ruled. Lacking civil power and the means to enforce covenant renewal, all they could do was plead for authenticity and integrity in worship.[17]

Ancient Near Easterners generally recognized three primary types of kingly responsibilities: military, defending their nation against foreign threats; judicial, defending against internal injustices; spiritual, defending against divine threats. The last agenda was accomplished by providing the national deity with

17. See further Daniel I. Block, "Worship," in *Dictionary of the Old Testament: Prophets*, ed. Mark J. Boda and J. Gordon McConville (Downers Grove, IL: InterVarsity, 2012), 867–78.

an appropriate residence and sponsoring the cult of that deity. Remarkably Deuteronomy's vision of kingship is not concerned about any of these matters; instead, the king is to lead the worship of his people by embodying covenant righteousness as described in the Torah (17:14–20). However, in keeping with ancient perspectives, Hebrew historians highlight the relationships of kings to the cult. The following discussion flags the most notable contributions of kings to Israel's worship.

David

As the royal patron of worship, David exercised leadership in three primary areas. First, he provided the ark of the covenant (YHWH's throne) with a home. Having completed his conquests, with great fanfare and celebration he brought the ark to Jerusalem and placed it in a tent that he had pitched for it (2 Sam. 6:1–19).[18] All the officials in the procession, including David himself, were dressed in cultic/festive garments (vv. 14, 16, 20): they worshiped YHWH in the splendor of holiness (Ps. 96:9). Once in Jerusalem, David presided over the worship activities: burnt offerings and peace offerings (1 Chron. 16:1–2a); blessing the people in the name of YHWH (v. 2b); distributing food to everyone who had gathered from all over the country (v. 3); appointing Levites to serve before the ark by commemorating (*hizkîr*; literally, "invoking") the name of God (cf. Exod. 34:6–7); giving thanks (*hôdâ*) and praising (*hillēl*) YHWH, the God of Israel (1 Chron. 16:4–6); specifically charging Asaph and his relatives to give thanks to YHWH;[19] and arranging for the permanent care of the ark and the rituals (16:37–38), and for the proper care of the tabernacle, which was located in Gibeon at the time (vv. 39; cf. 21:29 and 1 Kings 3:4).[20]

Second, David established Jerusalem as the center for the worship of YHWH. Recognizing that he and his people enjoyed the rest promised by YHWH in Deuteronomy 12, David proposed to build a permanent place for YHWH's name (2 Sam. 7:1–2; 1 Chron. 17:1–2). Although YHWH rejected the offer and promised to build an eternal house for David, he affirmed David's impulse,

18. Thus 1 Chron. 13:1–3 reports that David consulted with his officials and invited people from throughout the land, including priests and Levites, to participate in the occasion; 1 Chron. 15:1–16:3 describes in detail his cultic scrupulosity on this occasion.

19. Presumably by reciting or singing a song that combines Pss. 96:1–13; 105:1–15; and 106:47–48; and all the people joined in (1 Chron. 16:7–36).

20. This included affirming the status of Zadok and his relatives as priests, which meant they would offer the regular offerings as required by the Torah. Grateful for YHWH's everlasting *hesed*, David assigned Heman, Jeduthun, and other Levites responsibility for leading the music at the tabernacle, while Asaph and his group led the worship before the ark in Jerusalem (1 Chron. 16:39–42). Although the ark was in Jerusalem, the tabernacle in Gibeon was still perceived as the center of the national cult, and this is where the high priest served.

declaring that David's son would build the house that David had in mind (2 Sam. 7:13; 1 Chron. 17:12). Instructed by the prophet Gad, David purchased the threshing floor of Araunah/Ornan and built an altar to YHWH there (2 Sam. 24:1–25; 1 Chron. 21:21–30). As discussed in the previous chapter, David did all he could to prepare for the temple's construction, short of actually beginning the project. First Chronicles 28 describes the ceremony in which David made a final address about the temple and publicly charged Solomon to complete the project. The Chronicler concludes with David's magnificent prayer, giving all the glory to God and pleading that YHWH would give Solomon a perfect heart to keep the Torah and build the temple (29:10–19). David's last actions represent worship at its best: with great joy he offered thousands of animals as sacrifices, and the people ate and drank in the presence of YHWH (29:20–22).

Although the narratives of 1–2 Samuel paint a picture of a king with serious character flaws, as royal patron of the national religion, David was a model worship leader, exhibiting personal humility, deep spiritual sensitivity to the will of God, a concern for the glory of God, skill in involving all the people in the worship, and joyful willingness to pass the reins over to his successor. Although Solomon would complete the temple project with special attention to visual effects, David's unique contribution to Israel's corporate worship involved the sound of worship. His innovations seem to have revolutionized Israel's corporate expressions of homage and submission. Inspired by YHWH's *ḥesed* ("steadfast love," 1 Chron. 16:41), David made music a permanent feature of worship before the ark of the covenant of God (1 Chron. 16:1–38). First Chronicles 6:31–48 and 16:39–42 suggest that his musical reforms extended to the tabernacle worship in Gibeon, apparently assigning Heman and Jeduthun leadership in the music to be played and sung there. Far from a casual approach to music and worship, the orderly organization of the musicians matched perfectly the symmetry and beauty of both tabernacle and the temple to follow.

Third, David provided a paradigm for the music by personally composing many songs that would be used in temple worship. His reputation as a young musician thrust him onto the public stage when Saul hired him to play his lyre in the court (1 Sam. 16:23; 18:10). Amos 6:5 reinforces this reputation for musical talent, suggesting that David was also renowned as an inventor of instruments. David acknowledged his lyrical gifts with the self-designation "the favored psalmist of Israel" (2 Sam. 23:1)[21] and spoke self-consciously of

21. The Hebrew *nĕ'îm zĕmirôt yiśrā'ēl* is rendered variously in the translations: "sweet psalmist of Israel" (ESV, NASB, NLT, RSV); "favorite of the songs of Israel" (NJPS); "favorite of the

divine inspiration (23:1–7). His poetic gifts are evident in his prayers (e.g., 1 Chron. 29:10–20) as well as in the lyrics of several poems/songs embedded in narratives about him.[22] The tradition of David as a lyricist is reflected in seventy-three titles in the Psalter that explicitly associate these compositions with him. Although the expression *lĕdāwid*, "of David," need not signify Davidic authorship,[23] dozens of these psalms must come from his own hand.[24] These psalms reveal a man humble and submissive before God in his personal life, but also passionate in leading his people in corporate expressions of cultic worship.

Solomon

Solomon's temple was a glorious accomplishment, massively built and lavishly adorned.[25] YHWH provided the blueprint for the building (1 Chron. 28:11, 19), but the Phoenician artists and architects that Solomon engaged ensured that its design and ornamentation were perfectly at home in the ancient Near Eastern world. Solomon built this house to declare YHWH's glory in the superlative degree: "The house that I am to build will be great, for our God is greater than all gods" (2 Chron. 2:5). In his prayer he acknowledged that although no earthly structure could house YHWH, this "exalted house" (1 Kings 8:13) symbolized YHWH's faithfulness to Israel and David, as well as his desire to dwell among his people. In living among his people, YHWH demonstrated his willingness to forgive their sin and rescue them in time of need.[26] Solomon recognized the temple's significance beyond Israel: YHWH

Strong One of Israel" (NRSV). The LXX rendered *nĕ'îm* as *euprepeis*, "beautiful." In 2 Sam. 1:23 this word is associated with *ne'ĕhābîm*, "beloved."

22. A lament over the death of Saul and Jonathan (2 Sam. 1:19–27); hymns of thanksgiving (2 Sam. 22:2–51; 1 Chron. 16:8–36); his final testimonial (2 Sam. 23:1–7).

23. The expression could mean "by David," "dedicated to David," "about David," "in David's honor," or "for the use of the Davidic kings."

24. The entire Psalter bears a pronounced royal and Davidic stamp. See Bruce K. Waltke, "Canonical Process Approach to the Psalms," in *Tradition and Testament: Essays in Honor of Charles Lee Feinberg*, ed. J. S. Feinberg and P. D. Feinberg (Chicago: Moody, 1981), 3–19; Waltke, *An Old Testament Theology: An Exegetical, Canonical, and Thematic Approach* (Grand Rapids: Zondervan, 2007), 872–74.

25. The account is organized after the pattern of temple-building accounts in the ancient world. On ancient temple construction, see Victor Hurowitz, *I Have Built You an Exalted House: Temple Building in the Bible in the Light of Mesopotamian and North-West Semitic Writings*, Journal for the Study of the Old Testament: Supplement Series 115 (Sheffield: JSOT Press, 1992), 130–322.

26. The need for justice (1 Kings 8:27–32), deliverance from enemy conquerors (vv. 33–34), rescue from economic crises (vv. 35–40), support in battle (vv. 44–45), and restoration after exile from the land (vv. 46–53).

would also aid foreigners who cried out to him. Solomon explicitly expressed the temple's missiological function in 1 Kings 8:43–44: "that all the peoples of the earth may know your name and fear you, as do your people Israel, and that they may know that this house that I have built bears the stamp of your name."[27]

Although Solomon exhibited exemplary leadership in constructing a glorious building worthy of its divine Resident, his leadership was disastrous in other respects. Despite David's charge that he read the Torah of Moses and embody covenant righteousness (1 Kings 2:2–4; cf. Deut. 17:14–20), Solomon ruled like many oriental despots, multiplying horses, women, and silver and gold for himself, and enslaving his own people for his projects (1 Kings 5:13–18). Worse still, he started Israel down the long and ultimately fatal road of court-sponsored apostasy (11:1–40). Confirming Deuteronomy 7:4 and 17:17, his foreign wives turned his heart away from YHWH to serve other gods: he built pagan cult installations for them inside Israel's boundaries (1 Kings 11:1–8). If David was the embodiment of the Mosaic royal ideals (Deut. 17:14–20), Solomon was the opposite. Living on inherited faith, he illustrated the awesome consequences of a leader's taking a wrong course in his personal and cultic life and dragging his people down with him.

Jeroboam I

As the case of Solomon demonstrates, leaders in worship do not always glorify God. After Solomon's death the kingdom of David was divided into the southern kingdom (Judah) and northern kingdom (Israel). To consolidate his political power, Jeroboam, the latter's first king, established a national cult for his kingdom, anchored by shrines at Bethel and Dan (1 Kings 12:25–33). Designed to counter the magnetism of the temple in Jerusalem and YHWH's claim to all Israel, Jeroboam's system of worship was an ingenious combination of orthodox theology and pagan forms. On the surface Jeroboam did not call for the worship of a new god. Borrowing a traditional refrain, "See your gods, O Israel, who brought you up from the land of Egypt" (v. 28), his inaugural declaration sounds perfectly orthodox. However, everything about

27. The Hebrew clause kî-šimĕkā niqrā' 'al-habbayit hazzeh translates literally as "that your name is read on this house" (1 Kings 8:43). This statement alludes to YHWH's promise in Deuteronomy to choose a place on which to establish/fix his name, a reference to inscribing foundation stones with the name of the owner of a house. The dedicatory prayer places the revelatory significance of the building in the same class as other momentous historical events: the exodus (Exod. 7:5; 14:4, 18), Israel's crossing of the Jordan (Josh. 4:21–24), David's defeat of Goliath (1 Sam. 17:46), and YHWH's miraculous victory over the Assyrians in Hezekiah's time (2 Kings 19:14–19).

this system was wrong: the plural subject, "gods"; the manufacture of images; the locations of Bethel and Dan instead of Jerusalem; non-Levites as priests; and a new religious calendar and sacrificial system disconnected from YHWH's revelation at Sinai. Whereas true worship involves acts of submission and homage in response to God's revelation of himself and in accord with his will, this was a religion devised in Jeroboam's own heart (v. 33), leadership in worship run amok.

Josiah

Dragged deep into idolatry, the doom of the kingdom of Judah seemed certain until young Josiah's ascension to the throne in ca. 641 BC. In contrast to Manasseh and his immediate predecessor, Amon, Josiah modeled the qualities required of those who lead worship. Above all, he committed his heart to doing right in the sight of God (2 Kings 22:1–2; 2 Chron. 34:1–2). YHWH acknowledged Josiah's humility and tenderness of heart (2 Kings 22:19; 2 Chron. 34:27), and the historian credited him with unmatched piety: "Before him there was no king like him, who turned to YHWH with all his heart/mind, with all his being, and with all his resources, according to the entire Torah of Moses; nor did any like him arise after him" (2 Kings 23:25). The echoes of the Shema suggest that Josiah embodied the highest level of covenant righteousness.

Against the grain of decades of apostasy, Josiah initiated religious reforms involving the destruction of pagan cult centers throughout the land of Judah, even extending these reforms into the territory of the northern kingdom, now an Assyrian province (2 Chron. 34:3–7). He sought to restore the glory of the sanctuary, and with it the reputation of YHWH, by commissioning his people to repair and refurbish it (2 Chron. 34:8–13). In the course of those repairs, the Torah scroll was found, so Josiah led the people in repentance and prayer (34:14–28), humbling himself, tearing his clothes, and weeping before YHWH. Next he read the Torah to the assembled people (34:29–30). As a result of this assembly, Josiah and the people renewed their covenant with YHWH, then celebrated the Passover with an enthusiasm that the nation had not witnessed since before the monarchy was established (35:1–19).

For all its positive qualities, this story illustrates what happens when reforms of worship are instituted from the top against the grain of popular spirituality, viz., unspirituality. Josiah himself may have been tender of heart and fully devoted to YHWH, but his reforms did not change the hearts of his subjects. Within decades of his death, Nebuchadnezzar would come as the agent of YHWH's fury and put an end to Judah's hypocritical worship. Even so, the hardness of people's hearts is no reason for leaders to give up their personal spiritual commitments or stop trying to lead God's people in righteous paths and God-honoring worship.

Leaders in Second Temple Worship

As royal patrons and sponsors of the national cult, the kings of Israel provided significant leadership in worship. But they were not worship leaders as we understand them—that is, individuals who led the people in regular worship services. The best examples of this kind of leadership derive from the postexilic period.

Ungodly Leadership in the Postexilic Community

The prophet Malachi appeared on the scene when the enthusiasm in worship and faith in God that had accompanied the dedication of the second temple had given way to despondency, religious cynicism, and even contempt for YHWH. These were third-generation believers who could parrot their theological creeds but demonstrated lack of reverence for God in every aspect of life. In Malachi 2:1–9 the prophet puts responsibility for the spiritual state of the community squarely on the priests, exposing a defect in their attitudes toward God and their office.[28] In attempting to set the Levites straight, Malachi provides the most complete statement of the priesthood's teaching ministry in the First Testament.

Malachi highlights the privilege of priestly ministry with three significant statements. First, the priests were beneficiaries of God's covenant with Levi (2:4–5),[29] a covenant driven by three goals: life, peace, and reverence. The first two function as shorthand for God's desire for Israel, which they would enjoy if they were faithful to him. The third speaks of the proper disposition toward God required of worshipers: trusting awe. Second, the priests were guardians of knowledge (v. 7). By "knowledge" (*da'at*) Malachi means the content of the gospel preserved in the Torah—YHWH's salvation, his gracious covenant with Israel, and his gift of the land—and the divinely revealed way of responding to the gospel. This revelation was a "treasure" placed in their hands for safekeeping, to be dispensed to the people, whose lives depended on it.[30] Third, the

28. For a fuller discussion of this text, see Daniel I. Block, "Reviving God's Covenant: Reflections on Malachi 2:1–9," *Reformation and Revival Journal* 3 (1995): 121–36.

29. The word "covenant" (*běrît*) is used of YHWH's arrangement with the Levites elsewhere in Jer. 33:21 and Neh. 13:29; cf. the reference to the covenant with Aaronides in Num. 25:12.

30. Cf. 2 Tim. 1:12–14, where Paul tells Timothy to guard the treasure entrusted to him.

priests were messengers of YHWH of Hosts (v. 7). The term *mal'āk* refers not to winged creatures but to a person commissioned and authorized to speak for a higher authority—in this case, the divine King.[31] Such is the privilege of all priestly ministers, leaders in worship: they are heirs of the covenant of life, peace, and reverence; guardians of the truth; and spokespersons for God.

With privilege comes responsibility. Looking back on how priests functioned historically, Malachi highlights three matters of ministry. First, in the past, priests provided true instruction with integrity. "Instruction of truth" (*tôrat 'ĕmet*, v. 6) involves more than simply defending truth against heresy; it also means declaring what is true in the spirit and with the transformative intentions for which it was originally given. Second, in the past, priests modeled true piety: their relationships with YHWH were right. The remarkably rare expression "to walk with God"[32] speaks primarily of communion with God, but here "walk" (*hālak*) refers to incarnational leadership, professional and personal conduct characterized by "peace" (*šālôm*) and "uprightness" (*mîšôr*, v. 6). Third, in the past, priests called people to repentance, which in Hebrew means to turn from sin and redirect one's allegiance toward God. Far from merely affirming people, the priests exposed the people's sin and appealed for them to repent and abandon their iniquity. In 2:8–9 Malachi describes how his contemporaries have fallen short of their high calling in these three areas. Personally, instead of embodying righteousness as YHWH ordained, the priests have turned aside from the course of truth and righteousness. Publicly, in their perversion with their instruction, they have tripped up the very people for whom they should have been agents of life and peace. Professionally, they have betrayed their calling, corrupting the covenant of the Levites.

Malachi offers a summary warning for the priests in verse 9. Because they have not kept the ways of YHWH but have adapted their instruction to satisfy the whims of the people,[33] God himself will disgrace them before the people. Because professional "honorers of YHWH" have refused to honor him, he will turn their world upside down, cursing their blessings,[34] shaming them

31. The expression may be an intentional pun on the name "Malachi," which means "my messenger." Was Malachi one of these priests?

32. Used elsewhere of Enoch (Gen. 5:22, 24) and Noah (6:9), and in a general sense, Mic. 6:8.

33. In judicial and teaching settings, the expression *nāśā' pānîm*, "to lift the face," refers to a judge's looking at the faces of the people before him and letting the identity of the person determine the verdict. Deuteronomy 10:17–18 portrays YHWH as the perfect model of impartiality.

34. Which means withdrawing the privileges and benefits that came with the priestly office (tithes, atonement money, portions of the sacrifices, special standing in the community, etc.) and replacing them with curses, such as those listed in Lev. 26 and Deut. 28.

publicly,[35] and disposing of them like rubbish at the garbage dump. Malachi's words for modern worship leaders are strong. Ministers who use their office merely for personal advantage, who adapt their ministry to the wishes of the people, instead of promoting fear of God by teaching biblical truth for their life, well-being, and transformation—such ministers are repugnant to God.

Ezra: A Model of Godly Leadership

It appears that the author of Ezra-Nehemiah intended to present Ezra as a model Levitical priest, YHWH's answer to the abuses portrayed in Malachi 2:1–9. Although the book of Ezra is named after the man, he does not appear until 7:1–10, where he is introduced as the leader of a new wave of Jews returning from exile in 458 BC. Ezra's credentials for ministry are summarized with two words in 7:11: he was a priest and a scribe. Jewish tradition suggests that Ezra served as high priest (Josephus, *Jewish Antiquities* 11.121; 1 Esdras 9:40), but even if he did not, the genealogy in Ezra 7:1–5 shows that he was a direct descendant of Aaron. Unlike the scribes in the Gospels, Ezra's role as scribe should not be interpreted negatively. In the First Testament the word usually denotes a high officer of the court, a secretary appointed to record official business.[36] As a descendant of Aaron and a man skilled in the Torah of Moses, Ezra possessed the right professional skills for his role as leader in worship.

However, the key to Ezra's ministry was found not in his professional qualifications but in his personal commitments. He was submissive to both the *hand* of God[37] and the *will* of God. The latter is expressed classically in Ezra 7:10: he determined to study, apply, and teach the Torah of YHWH and his statutes and ordinances.[38] With this commitment he complied with Artaxerxes' authorization (7:25), but more important, he fulfilled his role as Levitical priest (cf. Deut. 33:10). Ezra sought to revitalize the community spiritually by grounding the people's faith in the old revelation—the authoritative will of God preserved in the sacred writings.

35. That is, "spreading feces on their faces." Hebrew *pereš* refers to the offal removed from an animal butchered or prepared for sacrifice. See Exod. 29:14; Lev. 4:11; 8:17; 16:27; Num. 19:5.

36. He may have earned this title through service in the Persian court. Some suggest that Ezra served as High Commissioner for Jewish Affairs in the imperial cabinet of Artaxerxes. In any case, his authorization for this mission (Ezra 7:6) reflects the emperor's confidence in him.

37. Note the acknowledgment of the hand of God being *upon* him (Ezra 7:6, 9) and being good *for* all who seek him (8:22; cf. 7:28; 8:18).

38. "The Torah of YHWH" is shorthand for "the Torah of Moses that YHWH God of Israel had given" (Ezra 7:6) and refers primarily to the book of Deuteronomy. "The words of the commandments of YHWH and his statutes concerning/to Israel" (v. 11) refers to the entire body of constitutional literature, especially the revelation given at Sinai and the supplements in Numbers.

The significance of Ezra's triple commitment extends beyond the individual elements to the order in which the narrator identifies them: study, apply, and teach. *Without disciplined study*, understanding is shallow, the personal life may be skewed, and the proclamation will be vacuous. *Without application*, study is esoteric and academic, and proclamation is hypocritical and hypothetical. Unless leaders embody godliness, they lack credibility. *Without teaching*, the priestly calling is unfulfilled. Study, apply, teach—this is what Paul means by "handl[ing] accurately the word of truth" (2 Tim. 2:15).

Ezra's involvement in communal worship is presented most clearly in Nehemiah 8.[39] Here we see the public face of a man privately committed to the study, application, and teaching of Torah. For reasons unknown, the people had gathered for worship, not at the temple, but in the square in front of the Water Gate (v. 1). Hungry for the Torah, they requested Ezra to come and read it to them. By the time Ezra was finished reading, all the people were emotionally stirred and wept as a result. But Ezra, Nehemiah, and the Levites calmed them down, inviting them to celebrate, rather than mourn, at the reading of the Torah, for this was a holy day to YHWH (vv. 9–12). Trusting their leaders, the people's mourning turned to celebration.

In the course of the reading, the people encountered Deuteronomy 31:9–13. Since it was the seventh month, in keeping with Moses' instructions, the heads of households, priests, and Levites who had gathered sent a proclamation to all the towns and villages to come to Jerusalem to observe the Festival of Booths as prescribed in the ordinance (Neh. 8:18).[40] Every day throughout the seven-day festival, Ezra read from the book of the Torah of YHWH their God. Ezra the priest was indeed a messenger of YHWH Sebaoth (*ṣĕbā'ōt*, "of Hosts"): he stood in awe of YHWH's name; true instruction was found on his lips; he walked with YHWH in peace and uprightness; and through reading the Torah, he turned the people's hearts to YHWH (Mal. 2:5–7).

Worship Leadership in the New Testament

We have noted several times that the Gospels provide little information on how Christian corporate worship is to be conducted. For the most part, where leadership is concerned, New Testament models are negative (i.e., scribes, Pharisees, Sadducees, and priests). By contrast, Jesus was the model teacher,

39. For earlier discussion of this text, see chapter 7, under "The Torah in the Postexilic Community."

40. Hebrew *mišpāṭ*; see *mišpāṭîm* (plural) in Exod. 21:1; the ordinance in question is presumably in Exod. 23:16b (Festival of Ingathering/Booths) or Lev. 23:33–44, since Deut. 16:13–15 actually offers few details on how the festival is to be celebrated.

who not only taught these men concerning the kingdom of God, but also taught his disciples how to pray—an important aspect of worship (Matt. 6:5–15). The Gospels portray Jesus as working deliberately with his disciples, preparing them for leadership roles in the future.

Worship Leading in the Earliest Church

Since the book of Acts reports few worship services as we understand them, it is difficult to establish how leaders led. However, the book does offer insight into who leaders were and the roles they fulfilled. The most important catalogs of early church leaders occur in three epistolary texts. In 1 Corinthians 12:28 Paul lists apostles, prophets, teachers, miracles, healing, aid, administrations, and tongues as gifts to the church. The first three represent offices of ministry, while the last five are forms of ministry. In Ephesians 4:11 Paul lists apostles, prophets, evangelists, and pastor-teachers as God's gifts to the church, to equip saints for the work of service, thereby building up the body of Christ and bringing all believers to unity and maturity in him. In 1 Peter 5:1–5 Peter speaks of elders, who have oversight over the church and serve as its pastors. In addition, Revelation 18:20 speaks of saints and apostles and prophets.

Apostle (apostolos). Specially commissioned by Jesus Christ and empowered by the Spirit (John 20:21–23), the disciples dominate the early chapters of Acts. Acts 1:21–26 recognizes "apostleship" as a distinct office held by the Twelve. The process whereby Matthias was added to replace Judas highlights the qualifications for apostleship: candidates must have witnessed Jesus' resurrection and accompanied the other apostles from Jesus' baptism until his ascension. The ministries of the apostles were diverse: proclaiming Christ and boldly calling for repentance (2:14–40; 3:11–26; 4:8–22); baptizing new believers (2:41); leading in teaching, fellowship, breaking bread, and prayer (2:42); managing contributions from believers (4:32–37); healing the sick (3:1–10; 5:12–16; 8:4–8), raising the dead (9:36–43), and caring for the needy (6:1–7); disciplining problem members (5:1–11); organizing the ministry (6:1–6); evangelizing (8:9–13, 25, 26–40); serving as agents through whom the Holy Spirit came upon people with visible demonstrations of his presence;[41] interpreting the new realities in the light of Christ, settling theological questions, and helping believers mature in their understanding of the gospel (11:1–18; 15:1–29); and instructing and discipling new believers (11:19–26).

41. Among Diaspora Jews (Acts 2:5–21), Samaritans (8:14–24), and gentile God-fearers (10:44–48). Acts 10:35–43 speaks of those who feared God, did what is right, and received forgiveness for their sins by believing in Jesus.

Apart from "servant of Christ," "apostle" is Paul's favorite official self-designation.[42] His own apostleship was critical in the Corinthian correspondence and in Galatians.[43] Elsewhere he links apostles and prophets, recognizing them as the foundation upon which the church is being built (Eph. 2:20) and as recipients of the Spirit's revelation of the mystery of Christ (Eph. 3:4–5; cf. also 2 Pet. 3:2). In Romans 16:7 Paul characterizes Andronicus and Junia as fellow Jews, highly regarded among the apostles.[44]

Deacon (diakonos). The congregation in Jerusalem chose the first deacons at the counsel of the apostles (Acts 6:1–3). Prerequisites for the office included a good reputation and being full of the Spirit, wisdom, and faith (6:3, 5). Chosen by the congregation, deacons were formally presented to the apostles, then ordained by prayer and laying on of hands (6:6). As the title *diakonos* ("servant") suggests, their responsibilities were practical in nature: serving at tables and caring for believers, thereby freeing the apostles to pray and minister the word (6:4). Luke singles out Stephen, who was known particularly as full of the Holy Spirit, faith, grace, and power, and able to perform great wonders and signs among the people (6:5, 8).

Deacons surface twice in Paul's Letters. In Philippians 1:1 he greets all the saints in Philippi, including the overseers and deacons. In 1 Timothy 3:8–13 he provides specific counsel for Timothy on the qualifications and conduct of deacons. Although Paul names "our sister Phoebe" as a deaconess of the church at Cenchreae in Romans 16:1, and although *gynaikes* in 1 Timothy 3:11 may identify female persons in this office, these instructions suggest that most deacons were male. In any case, like all church offices, the diaconate was deemed a privileged office, bringing with it significant and spiritual rewards, but also demanding persons of integrity and godliness.

Prophet (prophētēs). Information on prophets in Acts is entirely anecdotal. Though Luke does not indicate how they were appointed or specify their roles, we may assume they were specially called by God to declare his word. Although Acts never portrays prophets involved in formal worship services, Antioch seems to have been a hotbed of prophetic activity. The church there included resident prophets and teachers, some of whom are identified by name:

---

42. As in Rom. 1:1; 11:13; 1 Cor. 1:1; 9:1–2; 15:9; 2 Cor. 1:1 (cf. 12:12); Gal. 1:1; Eph. 1:1; Col. 1:1; 1 Tim. 1:1; 2:7; 2 Tim. 1:1, 11; Titus 1:1 (cf. 1 Pet. 1:1; 2 Pet. 1:1).

43. As in 1 Cor. 4:9; 9:5; 12:28–29; 15:7, 9; 2 Cor. 11:5, 13; 12:11; Gal. 1:17, 19; see also 1 Thess. 2:7.

44. The rendering of the second name is inconsistent in early manuscripts. Although traditionally rendered in translation as masculine (Junias), the weight of textual evidence slightly favors reading the name as feminine (Junia), in which case Andronicus and Junia were probably husband and wife. For discussion, see Comfort, *New Testament Text and Translation Commentary*, 476. In either case, Paul apparently does not identify them as apostles.

Barnabas, Simeon Niger, Lucius of Cyrene, Manaen, and Saul (13:1–3). Two other prophets, Judas and Silas, encouraged and strengthened the church with their words from God (15:30–35). Some prophets, like Agabus, were able to predict the future. His prediction of a famine prepared the believers in Antioch to send support to the believers in Jerusalem (11:27–30). Through the agency of Paul and Barnabas in Cyprus, God blinded Elymas, a magician and false prophet, which led to the conversion of the proconsul (Acts 13:4–12). In Acts 21:10–14 Agabus warns Paul with a prophetic sign-act of what will happen to him if he goes to Jerusalem; he will be arrested by the Jewish leaders and handed over to gentile authorities. The incident is striking because it demonstrates Paul's determination to go despite the prophetic warning (11:28).

References to prophets occur frequently in the Epistles. As noted above, sometimes they are listed between apostles and teachers (1 Cor. 12:28–29); other times they appear along with apostles as the foundation of the church (Eph. 2:20). Although in 1 Corinthians 14:37 Paul asserts that true prophets and truly spiritual people will recognize the authority of his writings, earlier he has recognized the problems that prophets can create in the church; when they all speak at once, they create confusion. In light of 14:26–28, he seems not to be speaking of persons who hold the office of prophet, but laypersons who declare prophetic utterances in the assembly of believers. Such utterances are to be carefully assessed to ensure orderly worship (v. 33).

Elders (presbyteroi). This office derived naturally from a civil office in Jewish society involving men who, by virtue of age, maturity, and experience, were respected as authorities in the community.[45] As with the prophets, information on elders' work in Acts is anecdotal. Barnabas and Paul delivered gifts from the church at Antioch to elders of the church in Jerusalem (Acts 11:30). Apparently they appointed elders in every church in Asia Minor. After praying over them and fasting, they would commend them to the Lord, in whom they had believed (14:23). In the account of Paul and Barnabas's dispute with the church in Jerusalem, "apostles and elders" appear as a standardized pair of words, suggesting a close alignment in the theological debate.[46] According to 20:17–38, when Paul arrived in Ephesus from Miletus, he called for the elders of the church and delivered a powerful charge for them to guard themselves and the flock and to shepherd the church of God that Jesus purchased with his own blood (v. 28). He also appealed to them to help the weak with their hands as he had done and to remember the words of Jesus: "It is more blessed

45. Jewish elders appear with scribes (Acts 4:5, 8; 6:12) or priests/the high priest (4:23; 22:5; 23:14; 24:1; 25:15).
46. Acts 15:2, 4, 6, 22, 23; 16:4. "Apostles" is always first. It is clear from 15:23 that the terms are not synonymous.

to give than to receive." Back in Jerusalem, James and the elders rejoiced when Paul reported what God was doing among the gentiles. When the elders requested that Paul take some Jewish Christian converts to the temple for ritual purification and to offer sacrifices, Paul obliged (21:18–26).

In his writings Paul mentions elders only three times, all in the Pastoral Epistles. He instructed Titus to appoint elders in every city (Titus 1:5) and encouraged Timothy and all who read his letter to treat elders with double honor, especially those who were diligent in preaching and teaching (1 Tim. 5:17, 19). James encouraged the ill to call the elders to pray over them and anoint them with oil, adding that the prayer of faith would restore them (James 5:14). Peter exhorted the elders in his audience to shepherd the flock of God with eagerness and humility, being examples to them (1 Pet. 5:1–6). Reminiscent of Moses' image of servant leadership, he adds that those who shepherd this way will receive an unfading crown of glory from the Chief Shepherd.

Bishop/overseer (episcopos). References to "overseers" appear in Acts only in 20:28, where the elders are said to be made overseers by the Holy Spirit, and only four times in the Epistles. In 1 Timothy 3:1–7 and Titus 1:7 Paul offers a detailed description of qualifications for the office, emphasizing personal qualities: character, maturity, responsibility in managing the Lord's house, a good reputation outside the church, commitment to the Scriptures, and diligence in instructing and exhorting believers.

Pastors (Greek poimenes*; Latin* pastores*).* Luke never mentions pastors in Acts, and the Greek noun *poimenes* is applied to church leaders only in Ephesians 4:11, where pastor-teachers are named along with apostles, prophets, and evangelists. However, the verb *poimainō*, "to tend, to care for," occurs in two critical texts. In John 21:16 Jesus commissions Peter to "tend" Jesus' flock. First Peter 5:1–6 is especially significant for this discussion on leaders in worship. Here the apostle instructs elders how to "pastor" the flock of God.

Now as an elder myself and a witness of the sufferings of Christ, as well as one who shares in the glory to be revealed, I exhort the elders among you to tend [*poimainō*] the flock of God that is in your charge, exercising the oversight, not under compulsion but willingly, *as God would have you do it*—not for sordid gain but eagerly. Do not lord it over those in your charge, but be examples to the flock. And when the chief shepherd appears, you will win the crown of glory that never fades away. In the same way, you who are younger must accept the authority of the elders. And all of you must clothe yourselves with humility in your dealings with one another, for

> "God opposes the proud,
>   but gives grace to the humble."

Humble yourselves therefore under the mighty hand of God, so that he may exalt you in due time. (1 Pet. 5:1–6 NRSV, emphasis added)

The critical phrase *kata theon* ("as God would have you do it," v. 2) translates literally as "according to God"—that is, according to the standard by which God shepherds.

Psalm 23, a beautiful ode written by a sheep in praise of his divine Pastor (*pastor* is Latin for "shepherd"), offers a striking paradigm for human pastors. This Pastor exhibits five qualities that human pastors are to emulate: (1) He gives the sheep what they need: nourishment and rest (vv. 1–3a). (2) He leads his sheep in paths of righteousness (v. 3b). (3) He walks with his sheep through difficult valleys (v. 4). (4) He invites the sheep to eat at his table; indeed, he invites them into his house (vv. 5–6b). (5) He sends his hounds of "goodness" (*tôb*) and "loving-kindness" (*hesed*) after his sheep (v. 6a). Peter appeals for pastors for whom the interests of the flock are always paramount.

Servant of Christ/the Lord (doulos Christou). Next to "apostle of Jesus Christ," this is Paul's favorite self-designation,[47] but the title is also claimed by James (James 1:1), Peter (2 Pet. 1:1), and Jude (Jude 1), and is attributed to those who serve God and the Lamb in Revelation 22:3. The First Testament background to this expression (*'ebed yhwh*, "servant of YHWH") and Paul's ready interchanging of *doulos*, "servant," with *apostolos*, "messenger, envoy," confirms that the word does not primarily mean "slave" but serves as an honorific designation for a "specially appointed and commissioned agent" of God. Whether or not this expression denotes an office, it does describe a role that leaders in worship fulfill and the disposition with which they should fulfill it. As worship leaders their responsibility is primarily to God, not to the audience. They serve as his mouthpieces, minister with his authority, and embody his covenant righteousness. "Servants of YHWH" serve the Lord by caring for his flock (John 21:16–17) his way (1 Pet. 5:2).

From First Testament to New Testament on Worship Leadership

In reflecting on the biblical disposition toward leadership, particularly how worship leaders are to fulfill their roles, the First and New Testaments display many common features.

First, leadership offices tended to evolve over time and often exhibit an ad hoc quality, changing with circumstances. This is particularly apparent in the First Testament, which traces the history of Israel from patricentric tribal

---

47. As in Rom. 1:1; Gal. 1:10; Phil. 1:1; cf. Col. 4:12; 2 Tim. 2:24.

and clan structures, onward to the highly centralized administration of the monarchy, and then to the priest-dominated community of regathered exiles in Jerusalem. This fluidity in organization continues in the New Testament. Jesus and the apostles never prescribe precise forms of church leadership, let alone describe how to lead worship services. Jesus began by commissioning twelve disciples as apostles, who like the "envoys" (*mal'ākîm*) of the First Testament carried on his work after he ascended into heaven (Matt. 28:18–20; Acts 1:1–8). The early church ordained deacons to carry out the practical and logistical work as the church grew and as needs arose (Acts 6:1–6). Elders surface for the first time in Acts 11:30, though by the time of the Council of Jerusalem they appear repeatedly in conjunction with the apostles (15:2, 4, 6, 22–23). Paul and Barnabas appear to have appointed elders in all the churches they founded on their first journey through Asia Minor (14:23), and according to Titus 1:5, Paul directed others to do the same.

Second, people believed that leadership offices were filled by divine choice. In the First Testament this was certainly true of prophets, kings, and priests, but in the New Testament it also applied to apostles, who were personally chosen and commissioned by Christ. When early Christians commissioned people to special offices, they did so under the guidance of the Holy Spirit (Acts 13:2; 15:23–29). The same is implied in 1 Peter 5:1–5, which speaks of pastors as under the authority of the Chief Shepherd.

Third, leadership involves primarily the exercise of responsibility rather than power. The First Testament's paradigm of servant leadership is embodied by Moses, who was willing to give his life if YHWH would spare the people (Exod. 32:30–35); it is prescribed in Deuteronomy 17:14–20, which warns future kings not to use their offices for personal gain; and it is exemplified in Psalm 23, which portrays YHWH as the ideal Pastor/Shepherd. However, this paradigm was honored more in the breach than in the observance, which eventually contributed significantly to Israel's demise.

Since the members of the Sanhedrin generally opposed Jesus and his followers, it is not surprising that the New Testament consistently portrays their leadership negatively; to Jesus and the Gospel writers, they were arrogant and held the people they led in contempt (Matt. 9:10–11; Luke 7:39; 15:2). These men relished honorific titles (Matt. 23:6–12). They were self-righteous and eager to display external expressions of piety (6:5, 16), but lacking in the fundamental righteousness demanded by God (5:20; 21:23–32). They set themselves up as watchdogs of theological orthodoxy yet were ignorant of the very Scriptures and traditions they prided themselves in knowing. They were hypocritical, posing as searchers for truth, but their minds were closed to Jesus' teaching (12:38). They claimed to be scrupulous observers of the law and the traditions, but they missed the weightier issues of covenant relationship.[48] They appeared authoritative to the people but lacked authority altogether (Matt. 7:29; Mark 1:22). They claimed to guide the people in the right path but were blind (Matt. 23:16, 24) and led them astray (John 7:45–52). They claimed to be the people of God but refused to accept the message of God presented by Jesus (Matt. 21:45–46), even when the people did (Luke 7:29–30). Posing as gatekeepers to the kingdom of God, they were more interested in closing gates than in opening them to the people (Matt. 23:13–15). For these and many more reasons, Jesus and others denounced such religious leaders of the Jews as "snakes" and "a brood of vipers" (Matt. 3:7; 12:34; 23:33), an evil and adulterous generation (Matt. 12:39; 16:4), hypocrites,[49] and blind guides.[50] Their style of leadership was the antithesis of the model advocated by Jesus and the Gospel writers.

Standing in sharp contrast, Jesus was the disciples' master teacher (*rabbi*, "my great one"), and they were his "learners" (*mathētai*, "disciples"). From the beginning, Jesus aimed to prepare them for leadership roles, teaching them that their mission concerned the kingdom of God, not their own advancement. In so doing, he taught many lessons on leadership that should characterize all who lead cultic worship. First, the disciples' mission concerned the kingdom of God. They were to go to the lost sheep of Israel, preaching the gospel of the kingdom, healing the sick, casting out demons, and pouring themselves out for others (Matt. 10:5–15; cf. Luke 12:22–34). Second, Jesus taught that, unlike false shepherds (Ezek. 34:1–10; John 10:1, 8, 12–13), their roles were not to be exploited for personal advancement or filling their own pockets, but to confess Jesus before others. Since no one is above his master, they must be willing to take up their crosses and follow him (Matt. 10:24–39; 16:23–28; Luke 10:1–8). Third, the disciples' mission involved going to the ends of the earth, making disciples of all nations, baptizing them in the name of the Father and the Son and the Holy Spirit, and teaching them the ways of Christ (Matt. 28:18–20; Mark 16:15–18). Finally, they were to follow the pastoral model presented by Jesus himself, caring for the sheep and giving their lives for them if need be (Matt. 10:18; John 10:11; cf. Matt. 20:25–28).

Fourth, the primary role of leaders in the Scriptures was to embody righteousness and promote justice within the community. The personal character of candidates for ministry, as emphasized by Paul (1 Tim. 3:1–13; Titus 1:5–9) and reinforced by Peter (1 Pet. 5:1–6), accords perfectly with the royal

48. See Matt. 15:1–11; 16:11–12; 23:1–4; 23:13–26; Mark 7:1–13; Luke 11:37–54; 14:1–6.
49. As in Matt. 6:2, 5, 16; 15:7; 22:18; 23:13, 15, 23, 25, 27, 29; 24:51; Mark 7:6; Luke 12:56; 13:15.
50. See Matt. 23:16, 24; cf. vv. 19, 26; John 9:35–41.

model in Deuteronomy 17:14–20. The king was to read the Torah *for himself* to prevent his heart from being lifted up above "his brothers," and *he* was not to turn aside from the way of YHWH. According to 1 Timothy 1:3–7, false teachers not only teach strange doctrines, dangerous myths, and futile speculations, but are also personally ambitious, seeking influence even when they are ignorant about the issues they are teaching. Elsewhere Paul condemns them for using their positions for selfish advantage. To teach what people want to hear rather than what they need to hear is a particularly pernicious temptation (2 Tim. 4:3–4). By contrast, Titus 2:6–14 encourages Christians to adorn the doctrine of God with upright living. Elders who rule well and devote themselves to preaching and teaching well deserve a double honor (1 Tim. 5:17).

Fifth, in the New Testament, regardless of the person's office, leadership in worship rarely if ever involves primarily leading a worship service. Instead, it involves practical ministry: teaching, encouraging the saints, guarding the flock, caring for the needy, and so forth. As a corollary, in contrast to prevailing contemporary practice, the Scriptures never portray musicians as primary worship leaders. If anything, the New Testament calls on believers to sing to each other (Eph. 5:15–21; Col. 3:12–17). While this does not mean that musicians may not lead in worship, it does suggest that we must understand the word "worship" as much more than music, and we must stop referring to the chief musician in the church as "the worship leader."

Conclusions for Today's Worship

Finally, true worship involves reverential human acts of submission and homage before the divine Sovereign in response to his gracious revelation of himself and in accord with his will. Therefore, promoting worshipers' awe and reverence before God must be a primary goal of those who lead worship. Apart from exhortations to minister the word faithfully and to ensure that worshipers' conduct is appropriate and orderly (1 Cor. 12–14), the New Testament says little about the structure or atmosphere of true worship. However, given the overall tenor of Scripture and the appeal to offer to God "acceptable worship with reverence and awe" (Heb. 12:28), we can conclude with eight exhortations for those who lead worship.

1. Worship leaders must first offer their entire persons as a sacrifice of worship to God and maintain a purity of life worthy of acceptance with God.

2. Worship leaders must conduct themselves before God and in the company of the saints in keeping with the glory and majesty of the One they serve.

3. Worship leaders' conduct, their performance of duties, and their entire bearing as representatives of God must enhance worshipers' awe and reverence before God.

4. Worship leaders must aim above all to ensure that divine revelation is transmitted to worshipers. Whether through reading and expounding Scripture, musical performance, or other cultic acts, leaders must ensure that everything in the service contributes to the clear, unequivocal, and truthful communication of divine truth.

5. Worship leaders must make every effort to deflect attention away from themselves to God. Whether through dress or public demeanor, drawing attention to those leading worship borders on idolatry.

6. Worship leaders must promote the engagement of the congregation in worship. In communal worship, people should instruct and exhort one another, sing to one another, and intercede on behalf of one another. The role of worship leaders is to develop this kind of community and to promote the genuine participation of all believers in corporate expressions of homage and submission.

7. Worship leaders must identify with the worshipers, not only by leading them in confessing sin and praising God for his forgiveness and acceptance, but also by walking with them through the week and feeling their pains and joys.

8. Worship leaders must recognize that access to God is made possible only through the work of Christ himself. Worship must be focused on Christ rather than on the preacher or musicians and the performance or liturgy. When people assemble for worship, they gather for a meeting with God, not for a meeting with the preacher or other leaders.

Appendix A

Doxologies of the New Testament

This appendix is in two parts, "Narrated Doxologies" followed by "Declared Doxologies." The former involve modal expressions of praise to God; the latter involve references in the indicative mood to people actually giving praise to God.

1. Narrated Doxologies

Text	From ESV (modified)	Addressee	Subject (acting)	Setting	Reason/Occasion
a. Praise, praising (*ainesis, aineō, ainos*)					
Matt. 21:16	And Jesus said to them, "Yes; have you never read, 'Out of the mouth of infants and nursing babies you have prepared **praise**'?"	God (?)	God has prepared children to praise him	In the temple	Healings
Luke 2:13	And suddenly there was with the angel a multitude of the heavenly host **praising** God and saying,	God	Heavenly host	In the shepherds' field near Bethlehem	Birth of a Savior, Christ the Lord
Luke 2:20	And the shepherds returned, glorifying and **praising** God for all they had heard and seen, as it had been told them.	God	Shepherds	Returning	All they had heard and seen
Luke 18:43	And immediately he recovered his sight and followed him, glorifying God. And all the people, when they saw it, gave **praise** to God.	God	Witnesses to healing of the blind man	Nearing Jericho	Healing of the blind man
Luke 19:37	The whole multitude of his disciples began to rejoice and **praise** God with a loud voice for all the mighty works that they had seen.	God	Multitude of disciples	Nearing Jerusalem	All the miracles they had seen
Acts 2:46–47	They received their food with glad and generous hearts, **praising** God and having favor with all the people.	God	Disciples and other believers	In homes	Food [and salvation]
Acts 3:8–9	And leaping up he stood and began to walk, and entered the temple with them, walking and leaping and **praising** God. And all the people saw him walking and praising God.	God	Healed lame man	In the temple	Healing
b. Praise, blessed, bestow a blessing (*eulogia, eulogētos, eulogeō*)					
Luke 1:64	And immediately his mouth was opened and his tongue loosed, and he spoke, blessing God.	God	Zacharias	At home	Birth of John the Baptist

Text	From ESV (modified)	Addressee	Subject (acting)	Setting	Reason/Occasion
Luke 2:28–32	He took him up in his arms and **blessed** God and said, "Lord, now you are letting your servant depart in peace, according to your word; for my eyes have seen your salvation that you have prepared in the presence of all peoples, a light for revelation to the gentiles, and for glory to your people Israel."	God	Simeon	At the temple	Presentation of Jesus
Luke 24:52–53	And they worshiped him and returned to Jerusalem with great joy, and were continually in the temple **blessing** God.	God	Disciples and other believers	In the temple	Ascension of Jesus
Rom. 1:25	Because they exchanged the truth about God for a lie and worshiped and served the creature rather than the Creator, who is **blessed** forever! Amen.	Creator	Idolaters	Anywhere	Ungodly not serving God
Rom. 9:5	To them belong the patriarchs, and from their race, according to the flesh, is the Christ, who is God over all, **blessed** forever. Amen.	God	Paul	A letter	Christ from the Israelites
2 Cor. 11:31	The God and Father of the Lord Jesus, he who is **blessed** forever, knows that I am not lying.	God and Father of our Lord Jesus Christ	Paul	A letter	God's sending Jesus

c. Glory, glorify (*doxa, doxazō*)

Text	From ESV (modified)	Addressee	Subject (acting)	Setting	Reason/Occasion
Matt. 9:8 // Mark 2:12 // Luke 5:26	When the crowds saw it, they were afraid, and they **glorified** God, who had given such authority to men.	God	Crowds	In Capernaum synagogue	Healing of paralytic
Matt. 15:31	The crowd wondered, when they saw the mute speaking, the crippled healthy, the lame walking, and the blind seeing. And they **glorified the** God of Israel.	God of Israel	The crowd	On the mountain	Healing of the infirm
Luke 2:20	And the shepherds returned, **glorifying** and praising God for all they had heard and seen, as it had been told them.	God	Shepherds	Returning	For all they has heard and seen

Text	From ESV (modified)	Addressee	Subject (acting)	Setting	Reason/Occasion
Luke 5:25	And immediately he rose up before them and picked up what he had been lying on and went home, glorifying God.	God	Healed paralytic	Synagogue	Healing of paralytic
Luke 7:16	Fear seized them all, and they glorified God, saying, "A great prophet has arisen among us!" and "God has visited his people!"	God	Large multitude	Nearing Nain	Raising of dead man
Luke 13:13	And he laid his hands on her, and immediately she was made straight, and she glorified God.	God	Healed woman	In a synagogue	Healing of woman
Luke 17:15	Then one of them, when he saw that he was healed, turned back, glorifying God with a loud voice.	God	Healed Samaritan leper	Between Samaria and Galilee	Healing of ten lepers
Luke 17:18	"Was no one found to return and glorify God except this foreigner?"	God	None, except the Samaritan	Between Samaria and Galilee	Healing of ten lepers
Luke 18:43	And immediately he recovered his sight and followed him, glorifying God. And all the people, when they saw it, gave praise to God.	God	Witnesses to healing of the blind man	Nearing Jericho	Healing of blind man
Luke 23:47	Now when the centurion saw what had taken place, he glorified God, saying, "Certainly this man was innocent!"	God	Centurion	At Jesus' crucifixion	Death of Jesus
Acts 4:21	And when they had further threatened them, they let them go, finding no way to punish them, because of the people, for all were glorifying God for what had happened.	God	Disciples in Jerusalem	Before the Sanhedrin in Jerusalem	Peter and John's healing of lame man
Acts 11:18	When they heard these things they fell silent. And they glorified God, saying, "Then to the gentiles also God has granted repentance that leads to life."	God	Disciples in Jerusalem	Gathered disciples in Jerusalem	Hearing that gentiles had received the Holy Spirit
Acts 12:23	Immediately an angel of the Lord struck him down, because he did not glorify God, and he was eaten by worms and breathed his last.	God not glorified	Herod's not giving glory to God	Caesarea Maritima	Arrogance

Text	From ESV (modified)	Addressee	Subject (acting)	Setting	Reason/Occasion
Acts 21:20	And when they heard it, they **glorified** God. And they said to him, "You see, brother, how many thousands there are among the Jews of those who have believed. They are all zealous for the law."	God	Jerusalem disciples	At Jerusalem	Hearing of Paul's work among gentiles
Rom. 1:21	For although they knew God, they did not honor him as God or **glorify**, but they became futile in their thinking, and their foolish hearts were darkened.	God as God	Ungodly people's withholding honor and thanks from God	Anywhere	They knew God, yet their thinking was futile and foolish.
Rom. 4:20	No unbelief made him waver concerning the promise of God, but he grew strong in his faith as he **glorified** to God.	God	Abraham	Waiting for offspring	Grew strong in faith
2 Cor. 9:13	By their approval of this service, they will **glorify** God because of your submission that comes from your confession of the gospel of Christ, and the generosity of your contribution for them and for all others.	God	Saints in Jerusalem	Expected in Jerusalem	Because of the Corinthians' obedience to their confession of the gospel of Christ in their generosity
Gal. 1:24	And they **glorified** God because of me.	God	Believers in Judea	Judea	Paul's conversion and preaching
Rev. 11:13	And at that hour there was a great earthquake, and a tenth of the city fell. Seven thousand people were killed in the earthquake, and the rest were terrified and gave **glory** to the God of heaven.	God of heaven	Survivors of devastating earthquake	Envisioned Sodom = Jerusalem	Their survival of earthquake
Rev. 16:9	They were scorched by the fierce heat, and they cursed the name of God who had power over these plagues. They did not repent and give him **glory**.	God not glorified	Survivors of plagues	Survivors' cursing God's name and not giving him glory	Their not repenting

d. Thanks (*charis, eucharisteō*)

Text	From ESV (modified)	Addressee	Subject (acting)	Setting	Reason/Occasion
1 Tim. 1:12	I **thank** him who has given me strength, Christ Jesus our Lord, because he judged me faithful, appointing me to his service.	Christ Jesus our Lord	Paul, Timothy, and the audience	In Paul's First Letter to Timothy	Christ's giving strength to Paul

e. Cry out loudly (*legō* + "loud voice")

Text	From ESV (modified)	Subject (acting)	Addressee	Setting	Reason/Occasion
Rev. 19:1–2a	After this I heard what seemed to be the **loud voice** of a great multitude in heaven, **crying out**, "Hallelujah! Salvation and glory and power belong to our God, for his judgments are true and just."	Great multitude	Our God	In heaven	Rejoicing at God's just judgments

2. Declared Doxologies

Text	From ESV (modified)	Subject (acting)	Addressee	Setting	Reason/Occasion
a. Praise, praising (*ainesis, aineō, epainos*)					
Rom. 15:11	"**Praise** the Lord, all you gentiles, and let all the peoples extol him."	Gentiles, all peoples	YHWH	All peoples, everywhere	God's mercies (Rom. 15:9)
Eph. 1:6	To the **praise** of his glorious grace, with which he has blessed us in the Beloved.	Paul and his audience	God the Father of our Lord Jesus Christ	In his Letter to the Ephesians (and believers everywhere)	He predestined us to adoption as sons through Jesus Christ.
Phil. 1:11	Filled with the fruit of righteousness that comes through Jesus Christ, to the **glory** and praise of God.	Philippians	God	Paul, in his Letter to the Philippians	Having been filled with fruit of righteousness
Heb. 13:15	Through him then let us continually offer up a sacrifice of **praise** to God, that is, the fruit of lips that acknowledge his name.	Author and readers	God	Through Christ	Hoping for the city that is to come (v. 14)
b. Praise, blessed, bestow a blessing (*eulogia, eulogētos, eulogeō*)					
Luke 1:68	"**Blessed** be the Lord God of Israel, for he has visited and redeemed his people."	Zechariah	Lord God of Israel	At home, amid neighbors	God has visited us and brought redemption.
Luke 19:38	"**Blessed** is the King who comes in the name of the Lord! Peace in heaven and glory in the highest!"	Multitude	The King who comes in the name of the Lord	Descending Mount of Olives to Jerusalem, on Palm Sunday.	Jesus' mighty works that they had seen

Text	From ESV (modified)	Addressee	Subject (acting)	Setting	Reason/Occasion
2 Cor. 1:3	**Blessed** be the God and Father of our Lord Jesus Christ, the Father of mercies and God of all comfort.	God and Father of our Lord Jesus Christ, the Father of mercies, and the God of all comfort	Paul, Timothy, and audience	In a letter to an assembled church at Corinth	God comforts us in affliction.
Eph. 1:3	**Blessed** be the God and Father of our Lord Jesus Christ, who has blessed us in Christ with every spiritual blessing in the heavenly places.	God and Father of our Lord Jesus Christ	Paul and audience	In a letter to assembled saints at Ephesus (or anywhere)	God has blessed us with every spiritual blessing
1 Pet. 1:3	**Blessed** be the God and Father of our Lord Jesus Christ! According to his great mercy, he has caused us to be born again to a living hope through the resurrection of Jesus Christ from the dead.	God and Father of our Lord Jesus Christ	Peter and audience	In a letter to believers in rural Asia Minor	God has caused us to be born again.
Rev. 5:12	"Worthy is the Lamb who was slain, to receive power and wealth and wisdom and might and honor and **glory** and **blessing**!"	The Lamb who was slain	Myriads and myriads of angels	Around God's throne, praising the Lamb as worthy of receiving sevenfold blessing	Because by his blood the slain Lamb has ransomed saints for God from everywhere
Rev. 5:13	And I heard every creature in heaven and on earth and under the earth and in the sea, and all that is in them, saying, "To him who sits on the throne and to the Lamb be **blessing** and honor and **glory** and might forever and ever!"	The One who sits on the throne (God) and the Lamb	Every creature of heaven and of earth	John's audition of praise coming from everywhere	For redemption through the Lamb
Rev. 7:12	"Amen! **Blessing** and **glory** and wisdom and thanksgiving and honor and power and might be to our God forever and ever! Amen."	Our God	Angels, elders, and four living creatures	Around the throne of God, giving a sevenfold blessing	Because salvation belongs to our God and to the Lamb (7:10)

c. Glory, glorify *(doxa, doxazō)*

Matt. 5:16	"In the same way, let your light shine before others, so that they may see your good works and give **glory** to your Father who is in heaven."	Your Father who is in heaven	You, the audience of Jesus	Jesus' teaching in the Sermon on the Mount	Because of your good works

Text	From ESV (modified)	Addressee	Subject (acting)	Setting	Reason/Occasion
Matt. 6:13, margin	"For yours is the kingdom and the power and the **glory**, forever. Amen."	Our Father in heaven	The audience of Jesus	Jesus' teaching the Lord's Prayer, in the Sermon on the Mount	To acknowledge God's sovereignty
Luke 2:14	"**Glory** to God in the highest, and on earth peace among those with whom he is pleased!"	God in the highest	Heavenly host	In the shepherds' field near Bethlehem	Birth of a Savior, Christ the Lord
Luke 19:38	"Blessed is the King who comes in the name of the Lord! Peace in heaven and **glory** in the highest!"	The King and the highest heaven	Multitude of disciples	Descending Mount of Olives, to Jerusalem, on Palm Sunday	Jesus' mighty works that they had seen
John 9:24	So for the second time they called the man who had been blind and said to him, "Give **glory** to God. We know that this man is a sinner."	God	Man born blind, healed by Jesus	In Jerusalem: Jewish religious leaders order a healed blind man to give glory to God, not to Jesus	Healing of blind man
Rom. 11:36	For from him and through him and to him are all things. To him be **glory** forever. Amen.	God	Paul and his audience	Paul, in his Letter to the Romans	God's wonderful wisdom, knowledge, and judgments
Rom. 15:5–6	Live in such harmony . . . that together you may with one voice **glorify** the God and Father of our Lord Jesus Christ.	God and Father of our Lord Jesus Christ	Believers at Rome	Paul, in his Letter to the Romans	God gives perseverance, hope, and encouragement
Rom. 15:9	That the gentiles might **glorify** God for his mercy. As it is written, "Therefore I will praise you among the gentiles, and sing to your name."	God	Gentiles	Paul, in his Letter to the Romans	For his mercy
Rom. 16:27	To the only wise God be **glory** forevermore through Jesus Christ! Amen.	The only wise God	Paul and his audience	Paul, in Romans, giving glory through Jesus Christ	Revelation of the gospel's mystery to all nations, leading to the obedience of faith
1 Cor. 6:20	You were bought with a price. So **glorify** God in your body.	God	Believers	In your body	You have been bought with a price

Text	From ESV (modified)	Addressee	Subject (acting)	Setting	Reason/Occasion
1 Cor. 10:31	Whether you eat or drink, or whatever you do, do all to the **glory** of God.	God	Believers	In all things	Thankfulness to God and desire for others to be saved
2 Cor. 4:15	For it is all for your sake, so that as grace extends to more and more people it may increase thanksgiving, to the **glory** of God.	God	Believers	At Corinth	God's grace is spreading to more and more people
Gal. 1:5	To whom be the **glory** forever and ever. Amen.	Our God and Father	Paul and his audience	In Paul's Letter to the Galatians	God's gracious will for our salvation through Christ
Eph. 3:20–21	Now to him who is able to do far more abundantly than all that we ask or think, according to the power at work within us, to him be **glory** in the church and in Christ Jesus throughout all generations, forever and ever. Amen.	God, who is able to do far more than we can imagine	Paul and his audience	In Paul's Letter to the Ephesian believers and thus to all generations	God's wonderful work in believers, through the Spirit and Christ
Phil. 1:11	Filled with the fruit of righteousness that comes through Jesus Christ, to the **glory** and praise of God.	God	Philippians	Paul, in his Letter to the Philippians	Having been filled with fruit of righteousness
Phil. 2:11	Every tongue [should] confess that Jesus Christ is Lord, to the **glory** of God the Father.	God the Father	Everyone	Paul, in his Letter to the Philippians	Confessing Jesus Christ as Lord
1 Tim. 1:17	To the King of ages, immortal, invisible, the only God, be honor and **glory** forever and ever. Amen.	The King eternal, immortal, invisible, the only God	Paul and his audience, including Timothy	Paul in his First Letter to Timothy	For God's mercy received through Jesus Christ
Heb. 13:21	[May the God of peace] equip you with everything good that you may do his will, working in us that which is pleasing in his sight, through Jesus Christ, to whom be **glory** forever and ever. Amen.	Jesus Christ (and/ or God)	You, the audience of Hebrews	In the Letter to the Hebrews	God's working in us what is pleasing in his sight
2 Pet. 3:18	But grow in the grace and knowledge of our Lord and Savior Jesus Christ. To him be the **glory** both now and to the day of eternity. Amen.	Our Lord and Savior Jesus Christ	Peter and his audience	Peter in his Second Letter	For keeping believers secure and growing in faith

Text	From ESV (modified)	Addressee	Subject (acting)	Setting	Reason/Occasion
Jude 24–25	Now to him who is able to keep you from stumbling and to present you blameless before the presence of his **glory** with great joy, to the only God, our Savior, through Jesus Christ our Lord, be glory, majesty, dominion, and authority, before all time and now and forever. Amen.	The only God, our Savior, who is able to keep believers from falling	Jude and his audience	In the Letter of Jude, to believers	For preserving believers
Rev. 1:6	[Christ has] made us a kingdom, priests to his God and Father, to him be **glory** and dominion forever and ever. Amen.	Jesus Christ, who has redeemed us (see 1:5)	John (on Patmos) and his audience, the seven churches	John, writing to the seven churches of western Asia Minor	Salvation through Christ, making believers to be a kingdom, priests serving God
Rev. 4:11	"Worthy are you, our Lord and God, to receive **glory** and honor and power, for you created all things, and by your will they existed and were created."	The One who sits on the throne, our Lord and our God	24 elders	John's vision of the glory of God	Because God created all things
Rev. 7:12	"Amen! Blessing and **glory** and wisdom and thanksgiving and honor and power and might be to our God forever and ever! Amen."	Our God	Angels, elders, and four living creatures	Around the throne of God, giving a sevenfold blessing	Because salvation belongs to Our God and to the Lamb (7:10)
Rev. 14:7	"Fear God and give him **glory**, because the hour of his judgment has come, and worship him who made heaven and earth, the sea and the springs of water."	God	All peoples on earth	John's visions to prepare people for God's judgment	The hour of judgment has come; all need to fear God and worship the Creator
Rev. 19:1–2a	"Hallelujah! Salvation and **glory** and power belong to our God, for his judgments are true and just."	Our God	Great multitude	In heaven	Rejoicing at God's just judgments
Rev. 19:7	Let us rejoice and exult and give him the **glory**, for the marriage of the Lamb has come, and his Bride has made herself ready.	The Lord our God, the Almighty who reigns	Great multitude of God's servants	John's audition of a heavenly multitude ready to rejoice and give glory to God	The marriage supper of the Lamb has come, and the bride has made herself ready.

Text	From ESV (modified)	Addressee	Subject (acting)	Setting	Reason/Occasion
d. Thanks (*charis, eucharisteō, eucharistia*)					
Rom. 6:17	But **thanks** be to God, that you who were once slaves of sin have become obedient from the heart to the standard of teaching to which you were committed.	God	Paul and his audience	In the Letter to the Romans	Roman believers, freed from sin, now obedient to the gospel
Rom. 7:25	**Thanks** be to God through Jesus Christ our Lord! So then, I myself serve the law of God with my mind, but with my flesh I serve the law of sin.	God	Paul and his audience, including us	In the Letter to the Romans	Believers set free from sin through Jesus Christ our Lord
1 Cor. 15:57	But **thanks** be to God, who gives us the victory through our Lord Jesus Christ.	God	Paul and his audience, including us	In the Letter to the Romans	For victory God gives through our Lord Jesus Christ
2 Cor. 2:14	But **thanks** be to God, who in Christ always leads us in triumphal procession, and through us spreads the fragrance of the knowledge of him everywhere.	God	Paul and his audience	In a letter to believers at Corinth	He always leads us in his triumph in Christ.
2 Cor. 8:16	But **thanks** be to God, who put into the heart of Titus the same earnest care I have for you.	God	Paul and his audience	In a letter to believers at Corinth	He put earnestness in Titus's heart.
Eph. 1:6	To the praise of his **glorious grace**, with which he has blessed us in the Beloved.	God the Father of our Lord Jesus Christ	Paul and his audience	In his Letter to the Ephesians (and believers everywhere)	He predestined us to adoption as sons through Jesus Christ.
Rev. 7:12	"Amen! Blessing and glory and wisdom and **thanksgiving** and honor and power and might be to our God forever and ever! Amen."	Our God	Angels, elders, and four living creatures	Around the throne of God, giving a sevenfold blessing	Because salvation belongs to our God and to the Lamb (7:10)
e. Dominion (*kratos*)					
1 Tim. 6:16	Who alone has immortality, who dwells in unapproachable light, whom no one has ever seen or can see. To him be honor and eternal **dominion**.	God, the Blessed One, the only Sovereign, the King of kings and Lord of lords (6:15)	Paul, Timothy, and the audience	In Paul's First Letter to Timothy	God's honor and eternal dominion

Text	From ESV (modified)	Addressee	Subject (acting)	Setting	Reason/Occasion
1 Pet. 4:11	Whoever speaks, as one who speaks oracles of God; whoever serves, as one who serves by the strength that God supplies—in order that in everything God may be glorified through Jesus Christ. To him belong glory and **dominion** forever and ever. Amen.	Jesus Christ (and/ or God)	Peter and his audience	In a letter to believers in Asia Minor	Glory and dominion of Christ (and/ or God)
1 Pet. 5:11	To him be the **dominion** forever and ever. Amen.	God of all grace	Peter and his audience	In a letter to believers in Asia Minor	God's grace and saving help
Jude 24–25	Now to him who is able to keep you from stumbling and to present you blameless before the presence of his glory with great joy, to the only God, our Savior, through Jesus Christ our Lord, be glory, majesty, **dominion**, and authority, before all time and now and forever. Amen.	God our Savior	Jude and his audience	In a letter to believers	Through Jesus Christ our Lord, God keeps believers from falling.
Rev. 1:6	[Christ has] made us a kingdom, priests to his God and Father, to him be glory and **dominion** forever and ever. Amen.	Jesus Christ, who loves us and has redeemed us (see 1:5)	John (on Patmos) and his audience, the seven churches	In a letter to the seven churches in western Asia Minor	Salvation through Christ, making believers to be a kingdom, priests serving God
Rev. 5:13	And I heard every creature in heaven and on earth and under the earth and in the sea, and all that is in them, saying, "To him who sits on the throne and to the Lamb be blessing and honor and glory and **dominion** forever and ever!"	The One who sits on the throne (God) and the Lamb	Every creature of heaven and earth	John's audition of praise coming from everywhere	For redemption through the Lamb
f. Honor (timē, timaō)					
1 Tim. 1:17	To the King of ages, immortal, invisible, the only God, be **honor** and glory forever and ever. Amen.	The King eternal, immortal, invisible, the only God	Paul, Timothy, and the audience	In Paul's First Letter to Timothy	For God's mercy received through Jesus Christ
1 Tim. 6:16	Who alone has immortality, who dwells in unapproachable light, whom no one has ever seen or can see. To him be **honor** and eternal dominion. Amen.	God, the Blessed One, the only Sovereign, the King of kings and Lord of lords (6:15)	Paul, Timothy, and the audience	In Paul's First Letter to Timothy	God's honor and eternal dominion

Text	From ESV (modified)	Addressee	Subject (acting)	Setting	Reason/Occasion
Rev. 4:11	"Worthy are you, our Lord and God, to receive glory and **honor** and power, for you created all things, and by your will they existed and were created."	The One who sits on the throne, our Lord and our God	24 elders	John's vision of the glory of God	Because God created all things
Rev. 5:13	And I heard every creature in heaven and on earth and under the earth and in the sea, and all that is in them, saying, "To him who sits on the throne and to the Lamb be blessing and **honor** and glory and might forever and ever!"	The One who sits on the throne (God) and the Lamb	Every creature of heaven and earth	John's audition of praise coming from everywhere	For redemption through the Lamb
Rev. 7:12	"Amen! Blessing and glory and wisdom and thanksgiving and **honor** and power and might be to our God forever and ever! Amen."	Our God	Angels, elders, and four living creatures	Around the throne of God, giving a sevenfold blessing	Because salvation belongs to our God and to the Lamb (7:10)
g. Wisdom (*sophia*)					
Rev. 7:12	"Amen! Blessing and glory and **wisdom** and thanksgiving and honor and power and might be to our God forever and ever! Amen."	Our God	Angels, elders, and four living creatures	Around the throne of God, giving a sevenfold blessing	Because salvation belongs to our God and to the Lamb (7:10)
i. Power (*dynamis*)					
Matt. 6:13, margin	"For yours is the kingdom and the **power** and the glory, forever, Amen."	Our Father in heaven	The audience of Jesus	Jesus' teaching the Lord's Prayer, in the Sermon on the Mount	To acknowledge God's sovereignty
Rev. 4:11	"Worthy are you, our Lord and God, to receive glory and honor and **power**, for you created all things, and by your will they existed and were created."	The One who sits on the throne, our Lord and our God	24 elders	John's vision of the glory of God	Because God created all things
Rev. 7:12	"Amen! Blessing and glory and wisdom and thanksgiving and honor and **power** and might be to our God forever and ever! Amen."	Our God	Angels, elders, and four living creatures	Around the throne of God, giving a sevenfold blessing	Because salvation belongs to our God and to the Lamb (7:10)

Text	From ESV (modified)	Addressee	Subject (acting)	Setting	Reason/Occasion
j. Might (*ischys*)					
Rev. 5:12	"Worthy is the Lamb who was slain, to receive power and wealth and wisdom and **might** and honor and glory and blessing!"	The Lamb who was slain	Myriads and myriads of angels	Around God's throne, praising the Lamb as worthy of receiving sevenfold blessing	Because by his blood the slain Lamb has ransomed saints for God from everywhere
Rev. 7:12	"Amen! Blessing and glory and wisdom and thanksgiving and honor and power and **might** be to our God forever and ever! Amen."	Our God	Angels, elders, and four living creatures	Around the throne of God, giving a sevenfold blessing	Because salvation belongs to our God and to the Lamb (7:10)

Appendix B

Hymnic Fragments in the Pauline Epistles

1. Christological Hymns

Philippians 2:5–11*
Let the same mind be in you that was in
 Christ Jesus,
who, though he was in the form of God,
did not regard equality with God as something to be exploited,
but emptied himself,
taking the form of a slave,
being born in human likeness.
And being found in human form,
he humbled himself
and became obedient to the point of
 death—
even death on a cross.
Therefore God also highly exalted him
and gave him the name that is above every
 name,
so that at the name of Jesus every knee
 should bend,
in heaven and on earth and under the earth,
and every tongue should confess that Jesus
 Christ is Lord [i.e., YHWH],
to the glory of God the Father.

Colossians 1:15–20
He is the image of the invisible God,
the firstborn of all creation;
for in him all things in heaven and on
 earth were created,
things visible and invisible,
whether thrones or dominions or rulers or
 powers—
all things have been created through him
 and for him.
He himself is before all things,
and in him all things hold together.
He is the head of the body, the church;
he is the beginning, the firstborn from the
 dead,
so that he might come to have first place in
 everything.
For in him all the fullness of God was
 pleased to dwell,
and through him God was pleased to reconcile to himself all things,
whether on earth or in heaven,
by making peace through the blood of his
 cross.

*All readings in this appendix are adapted from NRSV.

1. Christological Hymns

1 Timothy 1:17
To the King of the ages,
immortal, invisible, the only God,
be honor and glory forever and ever. Amen.

1 Timothy 2:5–6
For there is one God;
there is also one mediator between God
    and humankind,
Christ Jesus, himself human,
who gave himself a ransom for all—
this was attested at the right time.

1 Timothy 3:16
Without any doubt, the mystery of our reli-
    gion is great:
He was revealed in flesh,
vindicated in spirit,
seen by angels,
proclaimed among gentiles,
believed in throughout the world,
taken up in glory.

1 Timothy 6:15–16
He who is the blessed and only Sovereign,
the King of kings and Lord of lords.
It is he alone who has immortality
and dwells in unapproachable light,
whom no one has ever seen or can see;
to him be honor and eternal dominion.
    Amen.

2 Timothy 1:9–10
[He] saved us
and called us with a holy calling,
not according to our works
but according to his own purpose and grace.
This grace was given to us in Christ Jesus
    before the ages began,
but it has now been revealed through the ap-
    pearing of our Savior Christ Jesus, who
    abolished death and brought life and im-
    mortality to light through the gospel.

Titus 3:4–7
God our Savior saved us,
not because of any works of righteousness
    that we had done,
but according to his mercy,
through the water of rebirth
and renewal by the Holy Spirit.
This Spirit he poured out on us richly
    through Jesus Christ our Savior,
so that, having been justified by his grace
we might become heirs according to the
    hope of eternal life.

2. Other Hymns/Confessions

Romans 11:33–36 (using Isa. 40:13–14)
O the depth of the riches and wisdom and
    knowledge of God!
How unsearchable are his judgments
and how inscrutable his ways!
"For who has known the mind of the Lord?
Or who has been his counselor?"
"Or who has given a gift to him,
to receive a gift in return?"
For from him and through him and to him
    are all things.
To him be the glory forever. Amen.

1 Corinthians 15:3–8
Christ died for our sins in accordance
    with the scriptures,
and he was buried,
and he was raised on the third day in ac-
    cordance with the scriptures,
and he appeared to Cephas, then to the
    twelve.
Then he appeared to more than five hun-
    dred brothers and sisters
at one time,
most of whom are still alive, though some
    have died.
Then he appeared to James, then to all
    the apostles.
Last of all, as to one untimely born, he
    appeared also to me.

2. Other Hymns/Confessions

Ephesians 4:4–6
There is one body and one Spirit,
just as you were called to the one hope of
    your calling,
one Lord, one faith, one baptism,
one God and Father of all,
who is above all and through all and in all.

Ephesians 5:14
Therefore it says,
"Sleeper, awake!
Rise from the dead,
and Christ will shine on you."

2 Timothy 2:11–13
The saying is sure:
If we have died with him, we will also live
    with him;
if we endure, we will also reign with him;
if we deny him, he will also deny us;
if we are faithless, he remains faithful—
for he cannot deny himself.

Hebrews 1:3 (a non-Pauline hymnic
fragment)
He is the reflection of God's glory,
the exact imprint of God's very being,
and he sustains all things by his powerful
    word.
When he had made purification for sins,
he sat down at the right hand of the Maj-
    esty on high.

Appendix C

Sunday Worship in Early Christianity

Didache 14.1–2 (ca. AD 100)

On the Lord's own day [*kata kyriakēn de kyriou*] gather together and break bread and give thanks, having first confessed your sins so that your sacrifice may be pure. But let no one who has a quarrel with a companion join you until they have been reconciled, so that your sacrifice may not be defiled. For this is the sacrifice concerning which the Lord said, "In every place and time offer me a pure sacrifice, for I am a great king, says the Lord, and my name is marvelous among the nations."[1]

Ignatius, *Epistle to the Magnesians* 9.1–2 (ca. AD 110)

If then those who had lived according to ancient practices came to the newness of hope, *no longer keeping the Sabbath but living in accordance with the Lord's day* [kata kyriakēn], *on which our life also arose through him and his death (which some deny)*, the mystery through which we came to believe, and because of which we patiently endure, in order that we may be found

1. As translated by Michael Holmes, *The Apostolic Fathers: Greek Texts and English Translations*, 3rd, rev. ed. (Grand Rapids: Baker Academic, 2007), 367. Emphasis throughout has been added.

to be disciples of Jesus Christ, our only teacher, how could we possibly live
without him, whom even the prophets, who were his disciples in the Spirit,
were expecting as their teacher? That is why the one for whom they rightly
waited raised them from the dead when he came.[2]

Epistle of Barnabas 15.1–9 (ca. AD 100)

Furthermore, concerning the Sabbath it is also written, in the Ten Words
that he spoke to Moses face to face on Mount Sinai: "And sanctify the Lord's
Sabbath, with clean hands and a clean heart." And in another place he says:
"If my children guard the Sabbath, then I will bestow my mercy upon them."
He speaks of the Sabbath at the beginning of the creation: "And God made
the works of his hands in six days, and finished on the seventh day, and
rested on it, and sanctified it." Observe, children, what "he finished in six
days" means. It means this: that in six thousand years the Lord will bring
everything to an end, for with him a day signifies a thousand years. And he
himself bears me witness when he says, "Behold, the day of the Lord will be
as a thousand years." Therefore, children, in six days—that is, in six thousand
years—everything will be brought to an end. "And he rested on the seventh
day." This means: when his son comes, he will destroy the time of the lawless
one and will judge the ungodly and will change the sun and the moon and
the stars, and then he will truly rest on the seventh day. Furthermore, he says:
"You shall sanctify it with clean hands and a clean heart." If, therefore, anyone
now is able, by being clean of heart, to sanctify the day that God sanctified,
we have been deceived in every respect. But if that is not the case, accordingly
then we will truly rest and sanctify it only when we ourselves will be able to
do so, after being justified and receiving the promise; when lawlessness no
longer exists, and all things have been made new by the Lord, then we will
be able to sanctify it, because we ourselves will have been sanctified first.
Finally, he says to them: "I cannot stand your new moons and sabbaths."
You see what he means: it is not the present Sabbaths that are acceptable to
me, but the one that I have made; *on that Sabbath, after I have set everything
at rest, I will create the beginning of an eighth day, which is the beginning
of another world. This is why we spend the eighth day in celebration, the
day on which Jesus both arose from the dead and, after appearing again,
ascended into heaven.*[3]

2. As translated by ibid., 209.
3. As translated by ibid., 427, 429.

Justin Martyr, *1 Apology* 67 (ca. AD 150)

And we afterwards continually remind each other of these things. And the wealthy among us help the needy; and we always keep together; and for all things wherewith we are supplied, we bless the Maker of all through His Son Jesus Christ, and through the Holy Ghost. *And on the day called Sunday, all who live in cities or in the country gather together to one place*, and the memoirs of the apostles or the writings of the prophets are read, as long as time permits; then, when the reader has ceased, the president verbally instructs, and exhorts to the imitation of these good things. Then we all rise together and pray, and, as we before said, when our prayer is ended, bread and wine and water are brought, and the president in like manner offers prayers and thanksgivings, according to his ability, and the people assent, saying Amen; and there is a distribution to each, and a participation of that over which thanks have been given, and to those who are absent a portion is sent by the deacons. And they who are well to do, and willing, give what each thinks fit; and what is collected is deposited with the president, who succours the orphans and widows and those who, through sickness or any other cause, are in want, and those who are in bonds and the strangers sojourning among us, and in a word takes care of all who are in need. But Sunday is the day on which we all hold our common assembly, because it is the first day on which God, having wrought a change in the darkness and matter, made the world; and Jesus Christ our Saviour on the same day rose from the dead. For He was crucified on the day before that of Saturn [Saturday]; and on the day after that of Saturn, which is the day of the Sun, having appeared to His apostles and disciples, He taught them these things, which we have submitted to you also for your consideration.[4]

---

4. As translated by Philip Schaff, *Ante-Nicene Fathers*, vol. 1, *The Apostolic Fathers with Justin Martyr and Irenaeus* (1884; reprint, Peabody, MA: Hendrickson, 1995), 185–86.

Select Bibliography

Balentine, Samuel E. *Prayer in the Hebrew Bible: The Drama of Divine-Human Dialogue*. Minneapolis: Fortress, 1993.

Bergler, Thomas E. *The Juvenilization of American Christianity*. Grand Rapids: Eerdmans, 2012.

Best, Harold M. *Unceasing Worship: Biblical Perspectives on Worship and the Arts*. Downers Grove, IL: InterVarsity, 2003.

Block, Daniel I. "Marriage and Family in Ancient Israel." In *Marriage and Family in the Biblical World*, edited by K. Campbell, 33–102. Downers Grove, IL: InterVarsity, 2003.

———. "'In Spirit and in Truth': The Mosaic Vision of Worship." In *The Gospel according to Moses: Theological and Ethical Reflections on the Book of Deuteronomy*, 272–98. Eugene, OR: Cascade, 2012.

———. "'That They May Hear': Biblical Foundations for the Oral Reading of Scripture in Worship." *Journal of Spiritual Formation and Soul Care* 5 (2012): 5–34.

———. "Worship." In *Dictionary of the Old Testament: Prophets*, edited by Mark J. Boda and J. Gordon McConville, 867–78. Downers Grove, IL: InterVarsity, 2012.

Braun, Joachim. *Music in Ancient Israel/Palestine*. Grand Rapids: Eerdmans, 2002.

Carson, D. A., ed. *Worship by the Book*. Grand Rapids: Eerdmans, 2002.

Chapell, Bryan. *Christ-Centered Worship: Letting the Gospel Shape Our Practice*. Grand Rapids: Baker Academic, 2009.

Davies, Horton. *The Worship of the American Puritans*. Morgan, PA: Soli Deo Gloria Publications, 1999.

Dawn, Marva J. *Keeping the Sabbath Wholly: Ceasing, Resting, Embracing, Feasting*. Grand Rapids: Eerdmans, 1989.

———. *Reaching Out without Dumbing Down: A Theology of the Turn-of-the-Century Church*. Grand Rapids: Eerdmans, 1995.

Frame, John. *Worship in Spirit and Truth*. Phillipsburg, NJ: P&R, 1996.

Frankforter, A. Daniel. *Stones for Bread: A Critique of Contemporary Worship*. Louisville: Westminster John Knox, 2001.

Hill, Andrew. *Enter His Courts with Praise: Old Testament Worship for the New Testament Church*. Nashville: Star Song, 1993.

Humphrey, Edith M. *Grand Entrance: Worship on Earth as in Heaven*. Grand Rapids: Brazos, 2011.

Hurtado, Larry W. *At the Origins of Christian Worship: The Context and Character of Earliest Christian Devotion*. Grand Rapids: Eerdmans, 1999.

Hustad, Donald. *True Worship: Reclaiming the Wonder and the Majesty*. Carol Stream, IL: Hope, 1998.

Lamb, John A. *The Psalms in Christian Worship*. London: Faith Press, 1962.

Lloyd-Jones, D. Martyn. *Preaching and Preachers*. Grand Rapids: Zondervan, 1971.

Longenecker, Richard N., ed. *Into God's Presence: Prayer in the New Testament*. McMaster New Testament Studies. Grand Rapids: Eerdmans, 2001.

Lucarni, Dan. *Why I Left the Contemporary Christian Music Movement: Confessions of a Former Worship Leader*. Webster, NY: Evangelical Press, 2002.

Martin, Ralph P. *Worship in the Early Church*. Grand Rapids: Eerdmans, 1975.

Meyers, Jeffrey J. *The Lord's Service: The Grace of Covenant Renewal Worship*. Moscow, ID: Canon, 2003.

Old, Hughes Oliphant. *Worship: Reformed according to Scripture*. Rev. ed. Louisville: Westminster John Knox, 2002.

Peterson, David G. *Engaging with God: A Biblical Theology of Worship*. Downers Grove, IL: InterVarsity, 1992.

Ross, Allen P. *Recalling the Hope of Glory: Biblical Worship from the Garden to the New Creation*. Grand Rapids: Kregel, 2006.

Segler, F. M. *Understanding, Preparing for, and Practicing Christian Worship*. 2nd ed., revised by R. Bradley. Nashville: Broadman & Holman, 1996.

Webber, Robert E., ed. *The Complete Library of Christian Worship*. 5 vols. Nashville: Star Song, 1994.

———. *Worship Is a Verb: Celebrating God's Mighty Deeds of Salvation*. Nashville: Star Song, 2006.

Witvliet, John D. *Worship Seeking Understanding: Windows into Christian Practice*. Grand Rapids: Baker Academic, 2003.

Wright, Christopher J. H. *Old Testament Ethics for the People of God*. Downers Grove, IL: InterVarsity, 2004.

Zahl, Paul, et al. *Exploring the Worship Spectrum: 6 Views*. Edited by Paul A. Brasden. Grand Rapids: Zondervan, 2004.

Subject Index

Scripture Index

Author Index